Warman's
ORIENTAL ANTIQUES

Other Volumes in the
Encyclopedia of Antiques and Collectibles

Harry L. Rinker, Series Editor

Warman's Americana & Collectibles, 5th Edition,
edited by Harry L. Rinker

Warman's Country Antiques & Collectibles,
by Dana N. Morykan and Harry L. Rinker

Warman's English & Continental Pottery & Porcelain, 2nd Edition,
by Susan and Al Bagdade

Warman's ORIENTAL ANTIQUES

GLORIA AND ROBERT MASCARELLI

Wallace-Homestead Book Company
Radnor, Pennsylvania

Front cover: Chinese cloisonné gilt and enamel Buddha, 12″ h., 19th century, **$1,200.00**; Chinese jadeite carving of Guanyin, 7″ h, 19th century, shown holding rosary and scroll, variegated colors, **$3,200.00**; Japanese shin hanga woodblock print of Bijin holding an umbrella in the rain, 10″ x 14″, ITO SHINSUI (1898-1972), **$2,200.00**; Chinese sang de boeuf (oxblood) water coupe, 4¾″ dia., 18th century, **$650.00**; Chinese yellow ground vase with separately potted cover, 10¾″ h., Jiaqing seal mark and period, Buddhistic metal shape, **$3,200.00**; Japanese wine ewer, Hirado, 19th century, underglaze blue "Three Friends" motif (bamboo, pine, and prunus), **$2,800.00**.

Copyright © 1992 by Gloria and Robert Mascarelli

All Rights Reserved
Published in Radnor, Pennsylvania 19089, by Wallace-Homestead, a division of Chilton Book Company

Manufactured in the United States of America

Library of Congress Cataloging-in-Publication Data
Mascarelli, Gloria.
    Warman's oriental antiques / Gloria Mascarelli, Robert Mascarelli.
        p.   cm. — (Encyclopedia of antiques and collectibles)
    ISBN 0-87069-573-8 (pbk.)
        1. Antiques—East Asia. 2. Art objects—East Asia.
    I. Mascarelli, Robert. II. Title. III. Series.
    NK1056.M37   1992
    745.1'0951—dc20   91-50680
                                                                    CIP

1 2 3 4 5 6 7 8 9 0   9 8 7 6 5 4 3 2

This book is lovingly dedicated to Gloria's uncle,
Rear Admiral Samuel B. Frankel U.S.N., Ret.,
the person responsible for setting her standards
for excellence and steadfast love;

and to Robert's parents,

Patrick and Lillian Mascarelli,
who have given him unstinting support
in the pursuit of his goals.

Contents

Board of Advisors

Acknowledgments

Special thanks go to the auction house of Butterfield and Butterfield, particularly to Cynthia Stern, director of public relations in San Francisco, who provided us with catalogs, photographs, and her good wishes. Thanks, too, to our dedicated board of advisors, who provided many or all of the listings and photographs used to illustrate their topics, and to the unknown others who assisted them by providing photos of items in their private collections. Our appreciation also goes to Phillips of London and Skinners in Massachusetts for providing back catalog issues of some of their recent auctions.

For their excellent photographic work we thank Joy Epstein and Michael Walther. Our particular gratitude goes to Anthony Cipolla, also Sharon Mandell of Serenity Photo, who helped us with our personal photographic work and developing.

We wish to thank the following people/businesses for allowing us to photograph from their collections: Russell and Janet Ieradi, Phillip and Rozalind Taylor, Dr. and Mrs. Spenser Richmond, Mary Pascal, Robert Walker, Wayne Williamson, The Gilded Swan, Jan-tiques, and any others whom we may have inadvertently omitted. We appreciate the help of other dealers who allowed us to photograph their wares. Regretfully, some photos were not used because of space limitations.

Finally, for his guidance and support, we thank Harry Rinker, the person responsible for inviting us to participate in Warman's Encyclopedia of Antiques and Collectibles Series project.

Introduction

Bob and I meet many collectors of Oriental works of art because we are antiques dealers, a job that involves traveling to and participating in some of the larger antiques shows in the country. Active involvement in the antiques world places us, at this moment in time, at our computer keyboard. This book is our attempt to provide information that will answer some of the most frequently asked questions encountered at antiques shows.

Many years ago, long before the thought of a profession in the antiques business ever crossed my mind, I was awed by the glamour and richness of a friend's apartment in Manhattan. It was furnished solely with antiques. That type of environment was a far cry from my ordinary experience. My curious question to my hostess was "What made you decide to furnish with antiques?" Her approach was very pragmatic. "Well, my dear," she said, "one day after you buy a new sofa, it is worth only a fraction of what you paid, and the same goes for all other household goods. I furnished with antiques because they are worth the same amount that I paid for them the day after my purchase, and they can only go up in value in time." Those words sent me, soon after, to the nearest bookstore to find some information about collecting antiques. My first acquisition (amazingly prophetic in nature) was *Warman's Antiques and Their Prices*. My eyes were opened to a whole new world, and my life as an antiques shopper had begun!

It is our wish that this book will open the eyes of many to the fascinating field of Oriental works of art. To those of our readers who are already collectors, we hope to add dimension to your knowledge and provide information on topics with which you may not yet be familiar. To dealers in this and other fields, we hope to provide a resource book that will be a guide for buying as well as selling. To all, we hope it will answer some of the questions that have not been addressed in previously published works on the subject. The format of the book is planned to give information that will encourage further study in the respective topics. We have provided excellent reference resources and museum lists with this future education in mind.

Since one of the prime goals of the book was to present the public with concrete information that would assist them in acquiring Oriental antiques, its needs were best served by including the expertise of some of our colleagues and also some private collectors who have amassed knowledge in certain fields. They have become the vital framework for this enterprise. Our board of advisors, listed in the first pages of this book, have readily agreed to have their names and addresses made available to the readers so that they can be directly approached for further consultation in their areas of expertise.

Those of us who have had reason to research Chinese works of art over a period of years are aware of the change from the Wade-Giles system of Chinese spelling to the new Pinyin system. The differences, as they apply to the names of dynasties and types of wares, have been explained in Appendix II. We advise all readers to familiarize themselves with these changes before reading the section on Chinese antiques, since the spellings have been used interchangeably in various articles.

Most price guides advise caution when considering the prices quoted for individual items. This book is not an exception to this rule, particularly since many of the descriptions given have been obtained from several different auction houses and, in many cases, do not reflect the 10-percent buyer's premium in their postauction published price lists. Some listings and photographs have been taken from antiques shops and shows and reflect the individual dealer's current ticketed prices. Regional influences that affect prices also should be kept in mind. Big city shop and auction prices may differ considerably from those of more rural areas on similar items. The public should also be cognizant of the fact that price information for this book has been gathered over a two-year period; there may be some current reversal of trends that will affect a change in price at the time of their reading.

At the time of this writing, the two largest international auction houses have announced a policy restricting acceptance of any Oriental merchandise with expectations of less than $5,000 for their Oriental sales, there has been a growing interest, in other domestic auction houses, of presenting Oriental specialty sales with varieties of quality offered. Thanks to the generous help of Butterfield and Butterfield of Los Angeles and San Francisco, California, we were able to present many listings and photographs reflecting realized prices of items sold at their recent auctions. We invite any auction house with Oriental sales or special Oriental sections of their decorative art sales to send us their catalogs or contact us for representation in our future editions.

As antiques dealers we encounter many people who are preoccupied with finding 'perfect' pieces for their collections. We hope to dispel the myth that imperfect antiques are without value. Please note that many of the quoted auction descriptions list damages, and yet these items do sell, often for rather high prices. Clearly, the value of a piece does not have to be grossly undermined by some minor damage if it is worthy in other aspects, particularly rarity and age. This is certainly true in the area of Chinese porcelain. Restoration, if done well, should not deter a buyer if the piece is desirable. Such items are not expected to sell without some adjustment in price, unless, of course, they are so rare that they are desirable in any condition. A reputable dealer will point out any imperfections or restorations to a client before purchase. Please be aware, however, not all auction houses note damages in their catalogs. Personal inspection is necessary most of the time.

We are aware that there are popular areas of collecting that have not been covered in this edition of the price guide, and we plan to include these in the next edition. Japanese swords and sword furniture; bronzes and dolls; Chinese fans, bronzes, jewelry, and wood carvings; Korean furniture; and Southeast Asian ceramics are some of our future concerns. We welcome our readers' participation in the choice of other topics as well as comments on the book. Our mailing address is

Robert and Gloria Mascarelli
Accent East Gallery
P.O. Box 599
Sayville, NY 11782-0599
(516) 567-7117

Organization of the Book

Warman's Oriental Antiques is organized to provide the reader with history on each category of antiques and supplement that with a variety of resources and information relevant to the category. Each category includes sections on History, References, Museums, Reproduction Alert, and Collecting Hints. Listings of representative pieces available on the market today follow and prices are included. These prices are based on values gathered from domestic and foreign (United States, Hong Kong, and continental Europe) auction houses and actual ticket prices at antiques shows and shops. The emphasis in determining prices for this book was on realized auction price results.

History: An informative survey of each category discusses leading manufacturers (both individual and company), the culture in which manfacturing took place, varieties made and now available, and stylistic progressions of the object or objects made.

References: For the reader who would like to know more about the category than is provided here, a listing of important publications is included. Author, book title, publisher, and year are provided for each title. Some of the titles listed here may be out of print or otherwise difficult to find, but many may be found through used-book dealers and book dealers who specialize in antiques and collectibles publications.

Museums: The best way to study a category in depth is to review as many documented examples as possible. Museums—both across the United State and around the world—with important or substantial collections related to a category are listed here.

Reproduction Alert: Knowledge about reproductions (many or most of which are unmarked) is critical when collecting, and some of the items covered in this book have been reproduced (and some of those extensively). The Reproduction Alert informs the reader of reproductions as well as possible fakes circulating in the antiques and collectibles market and saves the novice collector money and the advanced collector embarrassment.

Collecting Hints: Specific, helpful hints on collecting—such as variability of pricing, availability of items, and quality of available items—are featured.

Listings: Descriptive and concise, the listings provide the name or type of the item, size, and approximate date of manufacture, informative details (color, finish, carving or illustration shown, and so forth), condition, and price. Listings are generally arranged alphabetically by category and by size within subcategories. Abbreviations include b. (born), c. (century), ca. (circa), dia. (diameter), h. (height), l. (length), and w. (width).

CHINESE ANTIQUES

ARMORIAL EXPORT PORCELAIN

History: Chinese armorial export porcelain constitutes the rarest subset of painted Chinese porcelains. They were painted with armorial crests of titled nobility; with crests and decoration of clubs, organizations, and lodges; or with historical or scenic landscapes of specific places. Every one of these patterns was sent to China to be copied onto the porcelain, usually with a three-year wait. They were expensive then, costing about five times as much as ordinary porcelain. They are the most unusual surviving form of seventeenth- to nineteenth-century Oriental art. Most of the pieces produced were in the form of dinner services, as that was the style of the time. The exception to the rule was specific presentation pieces. The porcelain dinner services contained as few as 200 to as many as 1,300 pieces. But even to find one piece of the 1,300 would be difficult these days, and the prices for armorial porcelain reflect that.

Considered to be a subset of armorial porcelain are those services enameled with just initials. It is currently believed that this was done when a nontitled member of a noble family ordered a dinner service, as the title only passed to the firstborn. It occurred when the person ordering the service did not possess a title, as in the case of a merchant or ship's captain. Although many wealthy, titled Europeans came to America, where titles were frowned upon, "initials only" services were more usual than crested services. But U.S. history begins in the very late eighteenth century, and the custom of a family armorial service had begun to lose favor by then. Thus American services are not found in the same numbers as English and European services. Many preexisting services were brought from Europe to America, and because of the prominence of the family, the services are considered American. The rarest of the American services is the Order of Cincinnati service. It was ordered by George Washington and friends in the 1790s.

Throughout the history of Chinese armorial art, as chronicled by David S. Howard's *Chinese Armorial Porcelain*, the style of decoration, color palette, border color, and decoration used were changed every few years. He has used this fact to organize the datings of about 3,000 of the known British services. Yet there are thousands of services that he does not record there, particularly those of the European nobility and North and South America.

Early services were done in blue and white, followed in the late seventeenth century with Chinese Imari and famille verte services. Pink was added to the palette in about 1720 and predominated until the end of the eighteenth century, when blue and white Fitzhugh-type patterns and Rose Medallion-type patterns were used more frequently. Early services were mostly just plates and large circular dishes in various sizes. By the end of the eighteenth century, all of the silver-form and European ceramic-inspired volumetric shapes were added. This would include such varied shapes as chocolate pots, mustard and condiment pots, sugar shakers and creamers, cider and ale jugs, wine and fruit coolers, monteiths (wine-glass chillers), and deep dishes with pierced inserts. The list is long and imaginative. Each piece was carefully painted with the crest of the service, as well as all of the other designs of that service. (See: Chinese Export Porcelain; Fitzhugh Pattern Porcelain.)

References: D. S. Howard, *Chinese Armorial Porcelain*, Faber and Faber Ltd., 1974; D. S. Howard and L. Ayers, *China for the West*, Sotheby Parke Bernet, 1978. 2 vols.; A. M. Palmer, *A Winterthur Guide to Chinese Export Porcelain*, Crown Publishers, 1976; D. F. Lunsingh Scheurleer, *Chinese Export Porcelain*, Faber and Faber Ltd., 1974.

Reproduction Alert: There are a few services that have been copied, mostly by adding the armorial device to an existing antique piece. The American Order of Cincinnati service lends itself to this, as do some of the American Eagle pieces. Several of the English- and Dutch-inspired East India services were copied in Hong Kong at the turn of the century. These forgeries were intended for the tourist to find, but now are almost antiques in themselves. They just are not worth what the originals are worth. A competent dealer will be happy to assist in the verification of any of these pieces.

Collecting Hints: Chinese armorial export porcelains are hard to find. They are eagerly sought after by a select group of avid collectors who are attracted by their scarcity and are undaunted by their price. Dollar for dollar, these porcelain items are the most expensive of all the pattern export wares sent to the West.

The highest recently recorded price for a piece of Chinese armorial porcelain is $150,000 for a platter from the Oakover service with twelve armorial crests. These prices have risen dramatically in the last several years as the collecting pressure on a diminishing supply has taken its toll. Be particularly aware that restoration of armorial china was done as far back as 200 years ago, reflecting the concern for and rarity of the pieces even then.

Advisor: Clinton R. Weil, Ph.D.

Charger, 15″ dia., circa 1745, the center painted in iron-red, blue, rose and gilt with a coat-of-arms within shell scrolls and surmounted by a coronet and goose's head, within a gilt foliate scroll band at the cavetto and four foliate clusters on the brown stained rim **1,600.00**

Cup and Saucer
5″ saucer, circa 1760, unrecorded English Arms **300.00**
Qianlong, coffee cup and saucer, gilt and painted in blue, iron-red, gold, black and turquoise with a crowned quarterly coat of arms below a crest and surrounded by 8 smaller coats of arms labelled with the names of the great-grand-parents of the original owner, all within a circular medallion, the rims with foliate and cell bands picked out in gold **950.00**

Dish
Saucer dish, 13¾″ dia., Yongzheng, gilt and painted in opaque enamels in the center with a medallion enclosing an insect and edged in butterfly wings, surrounded by a shield shaped crowned coat-of-arms flanked by bird supporters and crowned initials at the cardinal points of the

deeply curved rim, with a puce and turquoise border pattern **1,400.00**
triangular, 10½″ dia., circa 1775, painted in enamels at the center with a coat-of-arms beneath a coronet and flanked by flag banners within a gilt twisted link band and rose foliate festoons below a molded rim notched at each corner **1,000.00**

Ginger jars, pair, circa 1825, SAMPSON, unidentifiable arms, now mounted as lamps **2,000.00**

Gravy boat, 8½″ l., circa 1745, the oval body based on a silver form, with molded shaped rim and spout painted and gilt with family crest flanked by quartrefoil landscape panels, the interior rim with iron-red and gilt spearhead band, twig handle **1,200.00**

Meat Dish, 9″ x 6″, circa 1760, unrecorded English arms. **750.00**

Meat platter, 17″ x 13″, circa 1760, underglaze blue with gilding, Arms of "LATHAM," English ship captain **1,975.00**

Mug, 4″, circa 1825, SAMPSON (French replacement), unidentifiable arms **135.00**

Plate
9″, Famille rose, circa 1755, Arms of "BAYLY impaling WILKINSON," restored **675.00**
pair, 9″, circa 1765, orange enamel armorial crest, famille rose border, unlisted Portuguese arms . . . **2,800.00**

Platter
12¼″, circa 1770, oval deep platter, painted in enamels at the center with an accollée coat-of-arms tied with a garland and puce ribbon within a gilt and sepia double chain band and a puce bamboo and floral border **1,200.00**
17″ l., circa 1750, octagonal form, painted at the center in white, blue, iron-red and puce with a

Plate, 9″, Qianlong period, armorial, circa 1760 famille rose, arms of Joseph Clerke, English ship captain. $850.00

Sauceboats, Pair, 8″ x 3½″, Qianlong period, circa 1765, armorial famille rose enamels, arms of Bacon impaling Garth. $2,250.00

Left, Plates, Pair 9″, Qianlong period, circa 1750, armorial, verte rose enamels, Arms of Rowsewell impaling Colthurst, $2,300.00; *right*, Soup Plate 9″, Qianlong period, circa 1760, armorial, unrecorded Portugese arms, famille rose enamel with gilded border. $900.00

coat-of-arms enclosing three stars below a crowned fish, flanked by foliate scroll devices, the cavetto with berried vine band in underglaze blue, the armorial repeated on the rim below a gilt spearhead border. **1,600.00**

Soup Tureen
11½″ l., circa 1800, oval shape, decorated with the coat-of-arms of the "Honourable East India Company," within gilt spearhead border and scattered puce floral sprigs, the domed lid with gilt foliate knop, the tureen with gilt interlaced strap handles. **2,500.00**

15″ x 8″, circa 1760, English coat of Arms, matching underplate, Famille rose enamels **7,500.00**

16″ x 8″, circa 1920, tourist trade copy of American eagle with "In God We Trust" motto, underplate **300.00**

Tea caddy, 3¼″ h., Yongzheng, circa 1730, rectangular shape, on four angular bracket feet, gilt and painted in opaque enamels on the front with a medallion with a mantled coat-of-arms below a helm and thistle crest **1,000.00**

Vegetable Dish, Covered, 12″ x 8″, circa 1798, Arms of the "Honorable East India Company" of London, Sepia enamels, House service **5,200.00**

BLANC DE CHINE PORCELAIN

History: Blanc de chine (Chinese white) porcelain originated in provincial kilns in the area of Tê-hua in Fukien Province sometime in the latter part of the Ming Dynasty. There is no recorded history of this ware being exported prior to the early seventeenth century, when it was recorded in Dutch inventories. By the late seventeenth, early eighteenth century, Europe had become the largest importer, but records indicate that it was also exported to Japan, the East Indies, and other worldwide ports. Production was managed by potter families whose output was not directly under imperial control. The lack of imperial constraints led to the creation of wares for several markets. Two were designed for the Chinese themselves: the local populace, who would come to buy figures of worship, and the scholar class, who purchased objects for writing or painting. The third market was for export and was influenced by foreign tastes.

The clay of blanc de chine was particularly fine in grain and very malleable in nature, thus inspiring the potter to create and model figures. The resulting pure white porcelain figurine production made Tê-hua famous in the West. The fineness of the grain enabled the glaze to bond in the firing so that it seemed to be integrated with the body. This gave the porcelain a glossy appearance. Both the glaze and the paste are smooth to the touch. The glazes commonly appeared as pure white, ivory, or cream colored or with a slightly pinkish cast. Production during the Kangxi period was typified by a slight pink tint glaze (seen when held to the light), while Qianlong blanc de chine is somewhat bluish white.

Figurines were produced to represent the religious deities during the Ming Dynasty. Subjects included Buddha, Kuan-ti and Kuan-yin. European subjects (Adam and Eve and figure groups of Dutchmen, and so forth) emerged in the eighteenth century. Fu dogs, mounted on pedestals, were also portrayed. Although figurine production predominated, other blanc de chine items were made as well. Boxes, brush holders, censers, teapots, cups, writing accessories, wine jars, animal-form joss stick holders, and small vases were produced. Ornamental wine cups (libation cups), made to imitate rhinoceros horn carvings, were also produced in large quantities. Many of the items that were made for export frequently assumed shapes uncharacteristic of Chinese wares, i.e. barber bowls, porridgers copied from English silver, and tankards copied from the Germans and English. Vases were produced with decorations of dragons or plum blossoms molded in relief.

Ornamentation of blanc de chine porcelain was limited to incised, impressed, molded, or applied decoration. Relief decoration is common, often applied by slip. Incised design is rarer and limited to items produced no later than the mid-eighteenth century. An Hua (hidden) decoration of finely incised patterns was sometimes used, particularly on borders. Marks are most often found on blanc de chine wares during the Ming Dynasty and Kangxi period, less often in the late eighteenth and nineteenth centuries.

References: P. J. Donnelly, *Blanc de Chine*, Fredrick A. Praeger, Inc., 1969; Daisy Lion-Goldschmidt, *Ming Porcelain*, Rizzoli International Publications, Inc., 1978; R. L. Hobson *Chinese Pottery and Porcelain*, Dover Publications Inc., 1976.

Museums: Chicago Art Institute, Chicago, Illinois; Walters Art Gallery, Baltimore, Maryland; Museum of Fine Arts, Boston, Massachusetts; Detroit Institute of Fine Arts, Detroit, Michigan; Metropolitan Museum of Art, New York, New York; Philadelphia Museum of Fine Art, Philadelphia, Pennsylvania; Seattle Art Museum, Seattle, Washington; Royal Ontario Museum, Toronto, Canada; National Museum, Copenhagen, Denmark; Ashmolean Museum, Oxford, England; British Museum, London, England; Victoria and Albert Museum, London, England; Musee Guimet, Paris, France; Rijksmuseum, Amsterdam, the Netherlands; Scottish Museum, Edinburgh, Scotland.

Reproduction Alert: Blanc de chine is still being made in Tê-hua. It is possible to come across some twentieth-century figurines at antiques shows and shops, particularly molded figures of the Buddhist diety Kuan-yin, who is most often represented holding a child in a standing or seated position. Even antiques dealers oftentimes find it very difficult to distinguish the older pieces from their nineteenth-century copies. One tip is to look for translucency when the object is held up to the light, a characteristic of early blanc de chine. Also, examine the base. Many late-seventeenth and eighteenth-century export pieces were hollow-molded. Early wares had their fine-grained porcelain bases left unglazed, whereas many more modern pieces have their bases glazed to obscure the coarser-textured porcelain that replaced the older fine-grained body.

In the nineteenth century the Japanese attempted to copy the Ming and Early Ch'ing Dynasty figures. These are harder to distinguish from the old than are their twentieth-century counterparts. The novice collector should also be aware of the fact that early Meissen, St. Cloud, Bow, and Chelsea copied Tê-hua porcelain during the Kangxi period. These European copies are more correct in glaze and porcelain quality than they are in form.

Collecting Hints: There is a problem in distinguishing the earliest blanc de chine objects (from the early seventeenth century) from those made in the eighteenth century. Original molds could have lasted many years, and both seventeenth- and eighteenth-century pieces were hand-finished. Intricate detailing is best seen in the dainty rendition of hands and fingers and the rich folding of the garments on statuettes and figurines.

The seventeenth- and eighteenth-century figures are thickly potted and feel heavy despite the fact that all of them are hollow inside. The thickness of the walls often caused cracking at the base during firing. Such cracking is not considered a defect; if found, it is an expected confirmation of age. Looking into the base reveals an inner wall that is roughly potted. The inner wall sometimes reveals the pressure marks of the potter's fingers as he pushed the soft clay into the mold.

Older figures of male deities may have air vent holes on their faces, which served as receptacles for human hair. Strands of hair were threaded through the openings in order to depict realistic mustaches and beards.

Candlestick, unusual, 7⅞″, 19th century, in the form of an altar, representing Guanyin seated padmasana on a high double-lotus throne, flanked by two small nozzles for tapers molded in the form of swirling smoke, a larger lotus-form nozzle supported by her flaming mandorla, the reverse molded with swirling clouds above the throne **450.00**

Censer
4½″ h., Kangxi period, the cylindrical sides above tripod feet **875.00**
5″ dia., 17th century, molded with a pair of lion mask handles **850.00**

Cup, leaf-shaped "trick" cup, 3½″ l., 17th/18th century, modeled as a foliate peach, inside with a standing figure of an immortal with pierced hole beneath his robe to fool the unlucky drinker **750.00**

Figure
Arhat, 9¼″ h., 19th century, boldly modelled and dressed in long robe on a swirling wave and pearl-encrusted base, holding a fly whisk in his right hand, his left hand clutching the fringe of his garment **550.00**

Figure, fu dog, 12" h., Ming Dynasty, standing on a rectangular base, front paw on a pierced ball, with a ribbon between its jaws. $825.00

Buddha, 5⅞" h., 18th century, the rotund figure well-modeled with broadly grinning face, dressed in loose robes and reclining against a cushion, supporting three young boys on his leg and arm and shoulder, each figure holding a different attribute, Buddha's left hand holding the peach of longevity, minute chips **1,400.00**

Figure of Liuhai, 12" h., impressed four character seal mark on the backside reading "Tu Qi Yu Ren" (virtue extends to all, even fishermen), $4,675.00. Courtesy of Butterfield and Butterfield.

Guanyin
4½" h., 18th century, the bodhi-sattva figure in royal ease, wearing a loosely flowing robe, her hair upswept, all under a creamy glaze, impressed pot-ter's mark (stand and fitted box) **1,500.00**
5¾" h., 18th century, well-mod-eled, the deity shown seated in a composed position, her heav-ily draped robes extending over the base, her face in a medita-tive expression, covered with a milky white glaze **1,200.00**
10" h., 19th century, modelled seated in royal ease on a double lotus-petal base, engulfed in swirling waves, wearing a loose skirt tied with a ribboned sash at the midriff below a jewelled pectoral, her hair swept behind and falling in two long plaits over her shoulders, holding prayer beads in one hand and scroll in the other **375.00**
10'h., Guanyin flanked by two at-tendants, 17th century, seated on a rockwork throne flanked by a small perched bird on one side and a tall vase on the other, draped in robes and pearls, the head slightly lowered toward the two frontally turned aco-lytes **1,800.00**
14¾", 18th century, the serene goddess well-modeled, shown standing on a dragon emerging from swirling waves, wearing

Figure, Guanyin, 13" h., late 18th/early 19th century, shown standing with bas-ket. $1,200.00

long layered robes bared at the chest to show a ruyi pendant, the face with crisply modeled features framed by pendulous ears and long hair swept into a high chignon dressed with ruyi hairpins, her left hand holding a scroll, the back with an impressed seal pu ji yu ren, pitting 15½" h., portrayed with her deer, carved wood stand, circa 1800, the loosely robed beauty holding a basket of tree peony and lingzhi, her attendant deer standing beside her on a rockwork base with a spray of lingzhi in its mouth. **1,600.00**

22⅜" h., 18th century, shown standing on a swirling cloud-form base wearing long flowing robes vigorously modeled in sweeping folds billowing out to one side, her hair in a high chignon behind a diadem applied with flowers and a small figure of Amitabha, with knotted tresses falling over her shoulders, her face with softly-contoured features, downcast eyes and serene expression, the back with an impressed four-character seal, puzhi yuren, which can be translated as "virtue extends even to fishermen," chips. **8,500.00**

Jar, globular tripod shape, 4½" h., wood cover, 17th century, modelled after an archaic bronze, supported by lion mask feet, applied with a pair of handles formed as clambering chilong and with four spaced looped lugs at the mouth, an incised band of squared spiral below masks and scrolls around the body **950.00**

Vase
6½" h., 18th century, of baluster form with wide flaring mouth . . . **875.00**

Covered jar, 5" h., 19th century, three lion mask feet, the body with incised bands, the rim with applied lappets, the reticulated cover with fantail carp surmounted by a fu-dog finial. $520.00. Courtesy of Butterfield and Butterfield.

7½" h., 18th century, of gu form, characters incised on the bulb. . . **1,100.00**
8½" h., bronze-form, Transitional, of tapered cylindrical form with short flaring neck, applied with two lion masks, each with a wide pierced grin and fierce expression, encircled with a curling mane, beneath a glaze of slight grayish-green tint. **1,200.00**

CANTON AND NANKING PATTERN BLUE AND WHITE PORCELAIN

History: During most of the Qing Dynasty Europe dominated and dictated the fashions and trends for Chinese export porcelain. Yet, it is the United States that can claim credit for continuing the demand for blue and white china well into the nineteenth century. By then Europe was promoting its own porcelain industry and at the same time looking toward Japan as a primary source of imports. Although Southeast Asia continued to import blue and white porcelain for utilitarian use, the United States, as early as the late-eighteenth century, was importing the then-faddish Nanking pattern ware (so named after its port of shipment). This popular blue and white porcelain tableware was soon followed by the even more popular Canton pattern export. Both patterns were manufactured at Ching-te-chen. The similarity between the two designs is immediately obvious. They both employ a central coastal village scene (typically a view of an arched-bridge-covered stream alongside a teahouse framed by willow and pine trees) with mountains in the distance. The tea-house window sometimes reveals

Libation cup, 5" w., early 18th century, molded with leafy branches and deer. $475.00

long layered robes bared at the chest to show a ruyi pendant, the face with crisply modeled features framed by pendulous ears and long hair swept into a high chignon dressed with ruyi hairpins, her left hand holding a scroll, the back with an impressed seal pu ji yu ren, pitting **1,800.00** the shadow of a figure. Both patterns strongly resemble the ever-fashionable blue and white willow pattern, which later became a Western adaptation of this decorative ware.

Both Canton and Nanking patterns were imported as tea sets and dinnerware. The earlier Nanking porcelain was finer in quality and the execution of its painting was consistent. Canton ware pigment color varied from a washed-out greyish blue to a strong, dark blue in the firing, and the drawing quality was unreliable as well. Other than color and aesthetic differences, the main features that separate these comparable patterns are their use of different border designs and the application of burnished gold, which is sometimes found on the rims of Nanking pattern porcelains.

The Nanking border is typically a lattice and spearhead design. A variation of the border sometimes included butterflies, flowering branches, and pomegranates much in the style of the Fitzhugh pattern. The Canton pattern has a latticework border and an inner, wavy or scalloped line edging. Both patterns were transported in the holds of the ships, which resulted in their being called ballast wares, a term now reserved for rather crude heavily potted Canton blue and white jars.

Canton dinner services were very common in post-revolutionary America and were favored by all classes of people. There is no doubt that their affordability encouraged their popularity. Dinner sets consisted of dishes of many sizes, cups and saucers, vegetable dishes (with covers), covered tureens (in several sizes), salad and fruit bowls, sugars and creamers, teapots, and so forth.

Canton wares were still being produced in China in the early twentieth century. Some of them, which should have rightly been stamped "Made in China," arrived here with paper labels years after the U.S. Stamp Act of 1894 was in effect.

The popularity of these porcelains waned toward the end of the nineteenth century, as did the general enthusiasm for all Chinese export porcelain.

References: Esten, Wahlund, and Fischell, *Blue and White China, Origins/Western Influences*, Little, Brown and Company, 1987; Duncan Macintosh, *Chinese Blue and White Porcelain*, Charles E. Tuttle Co., Inc., 1977.

Museums: Canton wares are most frequently seen at antiques shows and shops. They can also be found in collections of export porcelain on view at the following museums: Avery Brundage Collection in the San Francisco City Art Museum, San Francisco, California; Museum of the China Trade, Mystic, Connecticut; Ira Koger Museum of the City of Jacksonville, Jacksonville, Florida; Boston City Art Museum, Boston, Massachusetts; Metropolitan Museum of Art, New York, New York.

Reproduction Alert: The Chinese willow pattern has been copied with variations since the late nineteenth century by both American and European ceramic factories. Many tablewares using this motif are found with obvious transfer designs, which differ radically in appearance from the hand-painted Chinese design. The best reproductions are those being currently produced in Portugal, which reproduce the old hand-painted Canton pattern faithfully, although the body of the porcelain is quite thin when compared with old Canton wares. Fortunately, these pieces are signed with the name "Mottahedeh" on the underside, leaving no doubt of their authenticity even to the novice collector. Other recent copies of the Canton pattern seem to be coming in from the Far East. These will present more of a problem to the new collector of Canton ware. A careful comparison of the unglazed clay at the foot should show differences resulting from modern firing techniques.

Collecting Hints: Canton pattern porcelain, and to a lesser extent Nanking pattern porcelain, was imported in such large quantities in the nineteenth century that much of it still survives today. Of particular interest to the collector are pieces of unusual shape or size that were less common even in their time. Cider jugs, ewers, and stacked vegetable dishes are good examples of these rarities. Canton appears to be a more popular pattern than Nanking, perhaps because the supply is more plentiful. Most prices reflect the quality of the color; the deeper blues reflect higher price tags. Shades of Canton blue do vary. For the collector who hopes to amass a complete dinner service, it would be best to travel with a sample piece when on buying trips.

It is ironic that the ballast goods of their era, common and easily acquired, have become one of the most collectable items of our day. When compared with earlier Chinese blue and white porcelains, which were more artistically rendered and are considerably scarcer, these later blue and white pattern wares have become relatively expensive. Nevertheless, like the famille rose patterns (Rose Medallion, etc.), they are widely available, and when assembled into groupings for display or dining they remain as charming and appealing as they did in George Washington's day. They are part of our history, filled with nostalgia of the days when our country's New Englanders eagerly awaited their shiploads of precious tea; the aromatic tea cargo held balanced in the seas by the hold's treasure, the blue and white tableware from China.

NANKING PATTERN

Cider Jug
  7¾" h., early 19th century, no cover, double entwined handle terminating at molded flowers and leaves,

coastal village scene, (base rim chip)...................... 400.00

10¼″ h., with cover, early 19th century, double-twisted handle terminating in molded floral designs, foo dog finial, continuous coastal village scene with cell, trellis, and spearhead borders, (damaged) .. 375.00

Dish, 12″, circa 1830, perfect condition 595.00

Hot Water Pot (covered) 9½″ h., c.1800, pomegranate finial, loop handle with raised molded heart at top and bottom, double cell border with continuous central coastal village scene, gilt trim, (slight gilt wear) 650.00

Platter

13″ l., oval, second half of 19th century, raised rim with flat edge around a Nanking scene with patterned borders, inscribed on the reverse with the owner's name and the and dated 1759 .... 650.00

13″ x 16″, oval, early 19th century, coastal village scene with lattice and spearhead border (glaze wear) 375.00

15¾″ x 18½″, oval, early 19th century, coastal village scene with lattice and spearhead border.... 850.00

15″ x 19″, oval, well and tree platter, early 19th century, spearhead and lattice border, Ex-Kelly collection 650.00

17⅞″ x 20″, early 19th century, coastal village scene with spearhead and lattice borders, (minor glaze damage) 850.00

Punch Bowl, 11″ dia., early 19th century, coastal landscape scenes with lattice and spearhead borders, (slight glaze imperfection) 1,100.00

Sauce Tureen, with underplate, 7″ x 4″, Qianlong period, Nanking export with lake and pagodas scene .. 1,575.00

Tureen (covered), 13¾″ handle to handle, c.1800, double entwined handles and sunflower finial, spearhead and lattice borders with central coastal village scenes, (restored chips to cover)................ 550.00

Vegetable Dish, 8¼″ x 10″, early 19th century, spearhead and lattice borders with central coastal village scene.................... 200.00

Wine cooler, 9½″ tall x 8″ dia., circa 1780, unglazed rim, no mark 2,100.00

CANTON PATTERN

Bidet, 23¾″, mid 19th century, cloud border with floral exterior, coastal

Charger, 16″ dia., 19th century, typical Canton scene. $600.00

village scene interior, mid to dark blue, damaged 750.00

Butter dish (covered with strainer)

6¾″ dia., round shape with dome cover, mid to dark blue, coastal village scenes with cloud borders 2,000.00

7″ dia., round shape with domed cover, middle blue, coastal village scene with cloud borders, (nicks, glaze loss)........... 700.00

Charger, 16″ dia., 19th century, circular scene with patterned banded borders 600.00

Chop Plate, 16″ dia., mid 19th century, deep blue, central coastal village scene with cloud border, (firing imperfections) 1,300.00

Coffee Pot (covered)

7″ h., mid 19th century, double entwined handles, cloud border with coastal village scene, (cover not original)............... 600.00

8¾″ h., mid 19th century, cloud border with coastal village scene, middle blue, original cover..... 1,250.00

Covered Dishes (pair), 7½″ x 9″, 19th century, rectangular, middle blue, cut-corners and pine cone finials, coastal village scene with cloud borders, (nicks) 700.00

Ginger Jar (covered), 6½″, 19th century, grey-blue, (pitting) 200.00

Fruit basket with Underdish

7½″ x 8¾″, mid 19th century, pierced sides, village scenes with cloud border, rim chip. 950.00

8¼″ x 9¼″, mid 19th century, pierced sides, village scenes with cloud border, (basket rim roughage) ... 800.00

Ginger Jar (mounted as a lamp), jar 5¾″ h., late 19th century, grey-blue, coastal village scene with straight line border 225.00

Garden Seats, Pair, 18½" h., 19th century, hexaganol bodies, pavilion and waterways scene with cash emblems on two sides, floral sprays and raised bosses above and below, surface scratches, hairline cracks. $5,500.00. Courtesy of Butterfield and Butterfield.

Helmet Pitcher, 4¼", mid 19th century, middle blue, coastal village scene with cloud border, (rim chip) **475.00**

Mug, 4¼" h., mid 19th century, mid to dark blue, coastal village scene with cloud borders, double twist handles, (hairline on handle, glaze chips) . . . **475.00**

Platter

14¼" x 18", rectangular shape with cut corners, mid 19th century, mid to dark blue, cloud border with central coastal village scene, (glaze flaws, rim nick) **475.00**

14½" x 17½", oblong shape, deep blue, mid 19th century, coastal village scene with cloud border, (glaze wear). **650.00**

Salad Bowl

9¼" dia., mid 19th century, middle blue, wide scalloped rim, coastal village scene with cloud border **950.00**

9½" dia., mid 19th century, middle blue, wide scalloped rim, coastal village scene with cloud border **1,000.00**

Sauce Tureen (covered) and underdish, 7" handle to handle, mid 19th century, mid to dark blue, boar handles, cloud border with coastal village scene. **550.00**

Soup tureen, 14" x 9", circa 1780, Canton export scene of pagodas and buildings in a mountainous lake setting **2,100.00**

Sugar bowl (covered), 4" h., 19th century, middle blue, double twist handles to either side, pomegranate finial, coastal village scene with cloud border. **325.00**

Tazza

8" dia., mid to late 19th century,

middle blue, straight line border with central village scene **650.00**

8¼" dia., late 19th century, middle blue, coastal landscape scene with straight line border, (rim nicks) **500.00**

Tea Tile

4¾" across, octagonal, mid 19th century, mid to dark blue, coastal village scene with criss-cross border (rim roughage, wear) **550.00**

6¼", mid 19th century, mid to dark blue, octagonal shape with coastal village scene, criss cross and cloud borders, (rim nicks) . . . **900.00**

Tureen (covered), 12¾" handle to handle, early to mid 19th century, mid to dark blue, boar head handles, coastal village scenes with cloud border **1,500.00**

Water Bottle, 8¾" h., middle blue-gray, mid 19th century, coastal landscape scene **425.00**

Water Pitcher, 8½" to handle, mid 19th century, middle blue, coastal village scene with cloud border. **1,200.00**

Well and Tree Platter, 11½" x 14½", oblong, mid to deep blue, 19th century, coastal village scene with cloud border, (glaze wear) **325.00**

CELADON GLAZED WARES

History: There is so much folklore surrounding the origin of the name "celadon" that no one knows for sure how it originated. It would take several pages to elaborate on all the various theories regarding the French origin of the name. In essence, *celadon* is a French term for a particular range of green colors that were manufactured in and exported from China. From its origin as a deep olive green color applied to a stoneware body to its evolution in the eighteenth century to a thin blue-green tint applied to a porcelain body, celadon has been prized by both the Chinese and the West. The earliest green-glazed wares, (pre-Tang and Tang Dynasty) are not generally termed celadon but are known by the names proto-Yueh and Yueh wares. Yueh wares were widely exported to Egypt, India, and Persia.

This section on celadon focuses on its development since the Song Dynasty, the period during which celadon wares (as we now refer to them) flourished and were exported to Europe as well as the Far East.

Europe did not receive these green-glazed imports until the fourteenth century. The early celadon colors ranged from a bluish or greyish green to a true olive green and were used over a rather heavily potted porcelaneous stoneware body. Green-glazed pieces where thought to have magical properties and were considered to be very valuable. It was believed that the celadon glaze would reveal poison in any food that was served on it. Apparently, food poisoning was much feared during Song times and this created a real seller's market for Chinese celadon exports.

The primary early production sites were at Yaochou in Shensi and Lin-ju Hsien at Honan in the northern Song. The early southern kiln sites were located in Lung Ch'uan (Longquan) in the southwest of Chekiang Province, from which celadon products were sent to the Near East, Japan, and Central and Southeast Asia. The difference in the shade of green between the northern and southern celadons is accounted for in the difference in the fuel used in the kilns. In the north the fuel was coal while the south used wood. Northern celadons are noted for their dark, transparent olive green or olive brown color and deep pooling in the glaze. The exposed body turned a dull brown or grey color in the firing. The firing techniques and the iron in the clay in the southern celadons caused the unglazed parts of the body (footrims, applied decoration) to burn to a rich red-brown color in the firing. The very thick opaque grey-green or grey-blue glazes of the twelfth and thirteenth centuries became more transparent in the fifteenth century when higher temperatures were used for firing.

Southern Song Lung Ch'uan celadons often imitated archaic bronze forms in shape. They also produced simple bowls with carved petals on the outside. It was not until the end of the dynasty and the Mongol period that the decoration became more innovative, reflected in the increase of size and change of shape of celadon-glazed items. The Topkapi Saray Museum in Istanbul, Turkey, has more than 2,000 excellent examples of these Song, Yuan, and Ming celadon wares. There are large and heavy dishes, bowls, basins, and plates, some with incised or carved flower designs under the glaze or molded in relief under the glaze (twin fish dishes) or with relief decoration applied over the celadon glaze and fired in the biscuit (dragons, rosettes).

Another Yuan Dynasty thirteenth- and fourteenth-century celadon technique was the inclusion of black or dark brown spots on a greyish green celadon ground. This was achieved by applying concentrated iron oxide directly on the body of the ware, resulting in the finished "spotted celadon," which has become very popular in Japan. Other than this new technique, there is very little to distinguish Yuan Dynasty production from the earlier Song Lung Ch'uan products.

The early Ming Dynasty saw the establishment of additional celadon kiln sites at Ch'u Chou. The Lung Ch'uan kilns continued with their production. These early Ming examples saw a decline in quality; the celadon colors turning a yellowish

green. Also noted, was a degeneration of body and style. Mass production seemed to have taken its toll. By the end of the Ming Dynasty these kilns were mostly deserted. The remarkable glaze that had made celadon so sought after had degenerated to a thin, transparent bluish green. The market was replaced by the application of celadon glazes on a porcelain body which was then being done in Jingdezhen.

Porcelain-bodied celadons of the Qing Dynasty were typified by a thin-transparent olive or sea green shade, which was lightened by the white porcelain body beneath the glaze. It became just one of the many monochrome colors that were developed during the Qing Dynasty. Celadon had lost all the qualities that had made it so distinct during the earlier days of its production. As a monochrome, it appeared with incised decorations beneath the glaze or along with a white slip design over the glaze. Apart from use as a monochrome, celadon glazes also were used over underglaze blue and red designs. Some eighteenth-century celadon production was embellished after import by the French, who added bronze ormolu mountings to favored pieces. Celadon production continued throughout the nineteenth century.

References: Michel Beurdeley, *Chinese Trade Porcelain*, Charles E. Tuttle Co., Inc., 1969; G.M. Gompertz, *Chinese Celadon Wares*, second ed., Faber and Faber Inc., 1980; Margaret Medley, *Illustrated Catalogue of Celadon Wares*, University of London, Percival David Foundation of Chinese Art, 1977; John Alexander Pope, *Chinese Porcelains from the Ardebil Shrine*, Sotheby Parke Bernet Publications, 1981; *Special Exhibition of Cultural Relics Found Off Sinan Coast*, National Museum of Korea, 1977; Southeast Asia Ceramic Society *Chinese Celadons and Other Related Wares in Southeast Asia*, Arts Orientalis, 1979.

Museums: Museum of Fine Arts, Boston, Massachusetts; Metropolitan Museum of Art, New York, New York; Cleveland Museum of Art, Cleveland, Ohio; Freer Gallery, Washington, D.C.; Ashmolean Museum, Oxford, England; British Museum, London, England; Fitzwilliam Museum, Cambridge, England; Sir Percival David Foundation, London, England; Victoria and Albert Museum, London, England; Museum Pusat, Jakarta, Indonesia; Salar Jung Museum, Hyderabad, India; Hakone Art Museum, Hakone, Japan; Kyoto Museum, Kyoto, Japan; Tokyo National Museum, Tokyo, Japan; National Museum of Korea, Seoul, Korea; National Museum of Singapore, Singapore; Topkapi Saray Palace Museum, Istanbul, Turkey.

Reproduction Alert: During the Qing Dynasty, there were copies of earlier Song Dynasty wares excellent enough to pass as originals in their day. Such items are probably as desirable as the originals in terms of rarity today but should, of course, be purchased as eighteenth-century reproductions.

Collecting Hints: Eighteenth-century and later celadon wares have obvious differences from the earlier wares and appeal to a larger collector's market than the earlier wares. They are, as their Qing manufacturers intended, beautiful monochromes and make a worthwhile addition to any monochrome collection. They have become as scarce as any other fine Qing Dynasty porcelain, and the prices have risen accordingly. Fine signed pieces that bear the reign mark and are of the imperial kilns are priced at $5,000 and up. There are also some very nice examples from the eighteenth and nineteenth centuries that are unsigned and will cost considerably less. The market is brisk for all Qing monochromes, including celadon-glazed porcelains.

Of the early celadon wares, the northern celadons are by far the rarest. They have a distinct dark tone that differs from the southern Lung Ch'uan celadons, which have more of a range of color and quality. The southern wares have, however, a greater variety of styles and molding techniques, which are not represented in the northern types.

At this time both types of wares seemed to have lost popular favor. This may be due to the influx and availability of the earlier pottery wares of the Han and Tang dynasties, and other porcelaneous wares of the Song Dynasty, which were inaccessible until recently. There also has been a shift in collecting interest towards the later Qing Dynasty porcelains. This is but a temporary lull in the early celadon market and the prices are certain to increase in the near future, especially if the illegal exportation of early pottery from China is cut off. Since so much celadon was exported to the Far East and the West, there is still an available supply on the market.

Basin, 15⅜" dia., Ming Dynasty, longquan, the deep interior carved with a large peony blossom within a double-line border below the thick lipped rim incised with three detached scrolling vine motifs, covered overall with a lustrous sea-green glaze, save the unglazed ring on the base burnt red in the firing. . . **5,800.00**

Bowl

3" x 5" h., Yuan Dynasty, the bowl in Longquan style with deep straight sides and a high cylindrical foot, the glaze an olive green around the rim and the interior painted with a single character in black ink. **300.00**

3⅞" dia., petal-rimmed, Song Dynasty, of shallow form, the sides delicately molded into fifteen fluted petals, the interior containing raised slip decoration, showing peaches amid leafy scrolls, the petals with lappets of further scrollwork, covered with a bubble-suffused olive-green glaze, the recessed base and surrounding area left plain, minute rim chip **2,500.00**

4½" dia., lotus-form, Song Dynasty, the small bowl cleverly molded as a lotus leaf with the sides rolled up to form the rounded sides and frilled rim, the interior deftly incised simulating the veins of the lily pad, centered with a small tortoise, all beneath a thick glaze of pale green color. **1,500.00**

4½" dia., fine carved northern celadon bowl, Northern Song Dynasty, of deep form with glazed rim freely and deeply carved on the exterior with lotus beneath an olive glaze. **3,200.00**

5⅞" dia., molded lotus bowl, Song Dynasty, evenly molded on the exterior with thin lotus petals radiating from the foot and rising to the slightly everted rim, covered overall in a rich pale celadon glaze pooling to deeper tones in the flutes leaving the petal ribs almost white **1,500.00**

6" dia., shallow conical bowl, Northern celadon, Song Dynasty, with subtly rounded everted rim, covered in an even olive-green glaze pooling on the exterior of the obliquely-cut orange-fired grey biscuit foot **1,100.00**

8" dia., Song Dynasty, carved decoration, well-potted with deep flared sides, the interior crisply carved with a large leafy sprig bearing one peony blossom and serrated leaves, all with combed details beneath a bubble-suffused glaze of olive-green color, restored **3,500.00**

4½" x 12" h., Ming Dynasty, the longquan tripod bowl with rounded sides and a waisted rim, decorated with a carved lotus, scrollage and raised studs, supported on mask bracket feet, both the interior and the feet burnt-brown in the firing **475.00**

Bulb bowl

9¼" dia., Ming, tripod bulb bowl, Chekiang, late 15th/early 16th century, the bombe body incised with cloud whorls within a trellis pattern, supported on mask-

Bowl, Longquan , 9" dia., Yuan Dynasty, overall floral pattern with a keyfret border at the rim, the glaze a thick sea green hue, fine crackle. $2,000.00

molded feet, the interior center and base burnt reddish-brown. . .   **1,200.00**

11" dia., Ming, heavily potted tripod bulb bowl, 14th-15th century, on short mask and paw feet, molded on the exterior with two narrow spaced horizontal bands of small bosses, and covered in a thick glaze darkening in the interior and stopping unevenly at the orange-fired exposed biscuit at the center, short rim crack **1,400.00**

12¼" dia., Ming, narcissus bowl, Chekiang, late 15th century, the squat circular body incised with stylized floral motifs, with flattened rim, raised on three molded short feet, the interior center and base burnt reddish-brown. **1,375.00**

Candle-holder, 3" h., 17th century, with square holder raised on four curving legs **500.00**

Censer

3¾⁄₁₆" dia., tripod legs, Yuan Dynasty, circular section supported on three feet, molded around the sides with the Eight Trigrams below the flat everted rim, covered overall in a bubbly sea-green glaze, glaze chips **1,000.00**

13¾" dia., Chekiang celadon censer, Ming Dynasty, the rounded sides with trellis patternings, tripod feet (fritted) **2,400.00**

Cup Stand, 7½" dia., molded, foliate, Ming Dynasty, carved around the center with lingzhi and flowering foliate vines below a hatched band at the scalloped rim, covered overall in a pale sea-green glaze draining to darker tones in the flutes. **2,500.00**

Dish

5" dia., carved, Yuan Dynasty, decorated with bands of peony **550.00**

5½" dia., twin fish dish, longquan, Southern Song Dynasty, the cen-

ter of the interior molded with the two fish swimming idly about below the gently curving well and flat everted rim, the exterior molded as the petals of an open flower, covered all over with a fine bluish-green glaze wiped clean on the footring, the base also glazed, crack **600.00**

6½" dia., longquan, Southern Song Dynasty, The slightly rounded shallow sides rising from a well-cut foot, the exterior carved with lotus petals, the interior plain, all under a pale olive-green glaze. . .   **900.00**

6¾" dia., longquan lotus petal, Song Dynasty, the classic carved design of a full-blown flower covered in a clear glaze thickening on the outside and evenly covering the undecorated interior **600.00**

8" dia., twin fish dish, Yuan Dynasty, molded in relief in the center of the interior with two carp swimming in mutual pursuit below the flat everted rim, carved on the exterior with a continuous band of petals, all under an even green glaze, rim crack and chips repaired in gilt lacquer **700.00**

10" dia., Yuan Dynasty, the glaze of rich pea green tone, the center impressed with floral design, the sides in free flowing floral scrolls   **2,500.00**

13¾" dia., early Ming Dynasty, carved and molded barbed dish, the slightly domed center molded with a foliate spray within a carved barbed medallion, surrounded by freely carved lotus sprays in the fluted well below the everted rim, covered in a glaze of soft celadon color continuing over the ring foot, and unglazed circle on the base burnt orange in the firing, minor glaze chips to rim . .   **1,100.00**

13⅝" dia., Yuan Dynasty, longquan dragon dish, molded in the center with a writhing scaly dragon, encircled by broad freely treated leaves around the cavetto and below the wide everted rim, the exterior molded and carved with petals radiating from the footring, covered overall in a sea-green glaze, minute chips to footring, firing crack **4,000.00**

15" dia., 15th/16th century Ming, shallow, freely carved at the center with a lotus spray, the everted rim with foliate scrolls, the glaze a rich even olive green, burnt or-

Dish, 12" dia., Yuan Dynasty, with floral center, scrolling lines forming stylized leaves in the steep sided cavetto, foliate rim. $1,400.00

ange at the exposed biscuit of the base **1,400.00**

15¼" dia., Ming Dynasty, longquan, well carved in the center with a large camellia encircled by a double line border below scrolling lotus in the well and detached classic scroll on the everted rim, the exterior with further lotus scroll, all under a good bluish olivegreen glaze except for an unglazed circle on the base burnt orange in the firing **2,500.00**

15¼" dia., Yuan Dynasty, with incised lotus in the center and incised border **2,600.00**

17" dia., 15th/16th century, large and deep, the interior lightly carved with a pair of phoenix within a border of writhing dragons, the crackled glaze an olive tone, the base burnt orange at the expored biscuit **1,500.00**

19" dia., Ming Dynasty, large longquan, impressed in the center with a trellis pattern enclosed by a quatrefoil within a freely carved lotus meander in the wide well, repeated on the underside, all beneath an olive-green glaze, unglazed ring on the base **3,000.00**

12" x 19½" h., saucer dish, Ming Dynasty, longquan, shallow with an everted rim and carved with a central peony within a trellis cloud border, the rim with a simple comb swirl, the glaze a pale tone bleeding to white on the rim, the foot with a brown wash and a character written in ink **600.00**

Garden seat, 17" h., barrel-form, Ming Dynasty, molded with four lion-mask and ring mock handles, the top carved with floral motifs . . . **2,500.00**

Jardiniere

16" h., Qianlong period, the rounded sides carved with a band of archaic decoration, formal borders above and below **3,800.00**

21" dia. x 26¼" h., with gilt lacquer stand, Ming Dynasty, the rounded sides below the everted rim and molded with two rows of lotus blossoms among leafy scrolls above a band of ruyi heads, the sea green glaze stopping short on the pierced base to reveal the biscuit burnt reddish-brown in the firing, the fitted lacquered wood stand raised on high sides, gilt painted with bats amid clouds, and on eight low feet **9,000.00**

Oil lamp, 3¼" h., Song Dynasty, longquan, the receptacle set within a hollow molded lotus bulb, the sides molded with overlapping leaves raised on a flanged stem molded with petal flutes, all beneath a thick and bubble-suffused glaze of pale bluish-green, the unglazed base burnt bright red in the firing **4,500.00**

Stem cup, 3½" dia., Yuan Dynasty, longquan, the rounded sides below and everted rim, supported on a high slender foot, covered in an even olive-green glaze stopping above the oxidized exposed footring **800.00**

Vase

6⅛" h., arrow vase, Song Dynasty,

Shrine, 10" h., Ming Dynasty 15th century, featuring an unglazed biscuit Guanyin seated within a celadon glazed grotto. $1,400.00

Plate, 14″ dia., Ming Dynasty, with incised central floral design, ribbed cavetto terminating in a dished rim. $1,300.00

longquan, the globular body below a tall cylindrical neck attached with two tubular handles, covered all over in a glaze of deep olive-green tone stopping short of the footrim to reveal the gray stoneware burnt a deep orange   5,000.00

12″ h., 13th Century, the trumpet form upper portion sitting on small squat body, small repair at rim 1,200.00

12½″ h., Song/Ming Dynasty, Yen-Yen shape, molded, applied around the bulbous body with scrolling peony blossoms and foliage above a band of stiff upright leaves, the neck with tree upright foliate sprays below molded concentric rings at the lip, all under a sea-green glaze 7,000.00

13″ h., Ming, Chekiang celadon, 15th/16th century, ovoid shape,

Vase, 14½″ h., Ming Dynasty, ovoid body, carved with blossoming peony, thick crackle glaze. $1,430.00

decorated with a combed diaper pattern enclosing cloud scrolls, above a lappet border and below a cloud band at the short neck . . .   1,800.00

13½″ h., Ming, Chekiang celadon, 15th/16th century, shouldered ovoid form, carved with quatrefoil panels of peony sprays below a foliate band at the short neck, under a crackled olive green glaze   2,200.00

Vessel (tripod), 10″ dia., 15th century Ming, the heavily potted ribbed cylindrical body raised on three stout legs, lightly carved with a band of foliage (the base with firing cracks and pierced), wooden cover and stand 1,200.00

CHINESE CLOISONNÉ AND OTHER ENAMELS

History: The art of enameling on metal with fused multicolored glass did not begin in China until the early Ming Dynasty. The precedent was set however, in the Shang Dynasty when colored inlays of malachite and turquoise were set in grooves that were molded in bronze items. The Chinese, the renowned inventors of porcelain and the most admired artists of the ceramic field, were not the first culture to have developed the art of enameling on metal.

The foundations of cloisonné and other enameling can be found in Mycenaean Greece in the thirteenth century B.C., in southern Russia of the pre-Christian era, in Celtic work at the beginning of the Christian era, in the Byzantines from the fifth to sixth centuries onward, and in European champlevé and cloisonné enamels (Germany, France, Spain, and England) by the end of the eleventh century. Painted enameling techniques (which later set the precedent for the Peking and Canton enamels) were well established in Limoges and southern Germany in the seventeenth century.

Although the Chinese had the ability to develop similar techniques, there is no doubt that preoccupation with their ceramic arts took precedence over the development of early glass experimentation. The production of Fa Hua porcelain ware is an example of a type of cloisonné in which the cloisons are threads of clay into which different colors of ceramic glazes were applied. Fa Hua porcelains were produced during the early Ming Dynasty.

The first glass developed in China was used to imitate precious stones. Although we can only guess about its introduction to China, it can be supposed that exposure to cloisonné and other enamel techniques came from China's contacts with the Near East and West through trade. When the art of cloisonné became established during the Ming Dynasty (fifteenth century), it was regarded by the clergy and scholarly class as being gaudy, frivolous, and suited to women because of its bold application of color and gilding. It was also named "wares from the devil's lands." The present accepted Chinese term for cloisonné is Jingtai lan, meaning "the blue of the Jingtai era." It was during this period (1450–1456) that the art of cloisonné enameling first flourished and the name has become synonymous with cloisonné in general. The reference to "blue" stems from the original cloisonné palette of the period, which used turquoise blue as the background color, (the most distinguishing color of Chinese cloisonné production, which sets it apart from all Japanese copies before 1900). This blue was used along with a cobalt blue, dull red, dark green, yellow, and white to complete the early Ming color scheme. The cobalt blue was of a fine violet blue color, a shade that for some reason was discontinued in the sixteenth century. Violet blue did not appear again until the seventeenth century in cloisonné decorated metals, although it was widely used in porcelain production throughout the Ming Dynasty. A Ming pink color was created by the phenomenon of red and white pigment fusing together during firing, a color-combining technique of the late fifteenth century. In the sixteenth century, new colors were added in mixed combinations, up to three different pastes for one color were used within a cell.

Ming cloisonné was first produced on a cast bronze body using bronze wire. In the sixteenth century, the body material was changed to sheet copper, which was cut, shaped, and soldered to form a base for the enamels. The use of bronze for fittings and wires continued, however. The earliest designs used no spirals and scrolls to fill the empty spaces. Sixteenth-century motifs depended on stylized lotus scrolls as backgrounds, dragons and other animals from mythology as topics, and stiff leaf and wave patterns as borders.

The cloisonné technique developed during this time, which still is used, consists of many procedures that can be outlined as follows: (1) The *cloison* wire (french term meaning "walls that form the cell") is attached to the metal body by solder (Ming Dynasty) or other means (adhesive in the Qing Dynasty) in the pattern of a design that has been outlined on the object; (2) The cells that are formed by the placed wires are filled with a glass paste, consisting of powdered enamels mixed with water, by means of a brush or spatula; (3) The item is fired until the paste melts and fuses; (4) The object is removed and cooled; (5) The cells are filled again to compensate for shrinkage resulting from the first firing; a process that is repeated until the cooled enamel attains a grade slightly higher than the cloisons; (6) The enamel is ground down to the level of the cloi-

sons; (7) The enamel is polished (a characteristic of Japanese cloisonné, rarely used on early and most later Chinese products); (8) The exposed metal, cloisons included, is gilded (a Chinese technique not often found on Japanese cloisonné).

During the Transitional period of Chinese art history, (1621 until the establishment of the Qing Emperor Kangxi), cloisonné manufacture underwent some changes. The necessity of economic pressures due to a lack of imperial support of the arts lead to the replacement of bronze wire with copper wire. As all exposed metal was gilded, the change from bronze to copper was not at all obvious. The copper wire was pulled through drawplates, which resulted in a speedier more economic method of production and gave the added benefit of not having the wires split during firing.

The discontinuance of the use of solder to attach the cloisons to the body resulted in a more refined appearance, since solder sometimes bubbled up to the surface during firing and caused discoloration of the enamel. Solder was replaced by temporary glue, which was burned away in the firing. New colors were added to the limited range of Ming Dynasty colors. Controlled firing conditions eliminated much of the bubbling of the paste during the firing process and resulted in a surface that had less pitting.

Large vases and altar pieces were created for Buddhist temples during the seventeenth century. More complex color combinations were achieved, using up to four different colors in a single cell. By the end of the Kangxi period, the foreign color pink was established and replaced the Ming pink, which was used prior to the eighteenth century. Imperial control of cloisonné production was undertaken, and colors became standardized. Emperor Yongzheng continued his father's practice of giving gifts of large cloisonné vessels to Buddhist temples. A massive pair of cloisonné fu dogs measuring 7'9½" and dating from the late seventeenth to the early eighteenth century is now resident in the Philadelphia Museum of Art; they represent the large Qing pieces that were created for Buddhist temples.

The use of the foreign opaque color rose pink became well established at this time. Although these were definite improvements in the evolution of cloisonné methods, some items continued to be made in the Ming style—a practice that continued throughout the Qing Dynasty. Many of these items were signed with Ming marks as a commemoration of earlier times, creating a great deal of difficulty for collectors of cloisonné both in the Qing period and the present. From the time of Emperor Kangxi, the Qing emperors supported the production of cloisonné, which was made for both the palace and the temples. The Qinglong Emperor was a noted supporter of the arts and ordered the creation of cloisonné vases in the old Ming style. New colors that joined the cloisonné palette during his reign were yellowish green, dark turquoise green, purple, and shades of lilac.

Human and animal figures were added to cloisonné production during the later part of the Qianlong period. Some figures of animals and birds had been produced in the sixteenth and seventeenth centuries but the eighteenth century added many others such as elephants, buffalos, and rams. Quails, ducks, and cranes were the most popular, however. Sometimes champlevé techniques were included with cloisonné techniques, although the vast amount of champlevé production, as we recognize it, belongs to the Japanese. (See: Japanese Cloisonné and Champlevé.) The motifs and the patterns became busier and more preoccupied with naturalistic themes. The later years of the Qing Dynasty (after the middle of the reign of Emperor Qianlong), showed degeneration of quality in all the art forms, including cloisonné.

Repoussé techniques were widely used in the eighteenth century. In this technique, the design is formed in relief by being pressed or hammered from the back. The glass enamels were not ground to an even surface but left instead in their natural state after firing. Since the glass enamel does not have cloisons to hold it in place, this type of enamel is subject to chipping away and is often found in disrepair. This enamel technique was also used on silver-bodied repoussé in the nineteenth century.

Another relief technique involved appling silver or gold foil in certain areas of the design under a transparent glaze and was used in China for a short period in the early nineteenth century. Openwork cloisonné, which features a plain gilded background with a circumscribed area of cells that are filled in the cloisonné technique, also appeared in the nineteenth century, sometimes with twisted wire used as cloisons. Enamelless cloisonné features exposed wires without enamel as the surface decoration. This type is sometimes found with with semiprecious jewels in the cells. When enamelless cloisonné is found with wires that have been twisted or intertwined it is called filagree.

The fine Qing cloisonné products that were often produced in archaic bronze forms were replaced at the turn of the twentieth century by export novelties such as napkin rings, matchboxes, tea jars, ashtrays, small vases, etc. These poorly executed and mass-produced items were made with thin copper bodies and pitted enamels. The pitting was compensated for by the application of colored wax to hide the defects.

PEKING AND CANTON ENAMELS

Peking enamels were the first examples of an art introduced to China from France in the beginning of the eighteenth century. It was during the fifteenth century that the Limoges factory first dispensed with cloisonnés and developed a way to cover a copper body with a continuous layer of enamel. Experimentation led to perfection of this technique in the seventeenth century. The first Chinese manufacture of enamel work of this type was done in the imperial and private factories at Peking. Western themes were often incorporated into the fine, brush-applied painting over enamel. The common Chinese term for these wares was "foreign porcelain." Peking enamels featured the inclusion of the foreign color rose pink (an early eighteenth-century color derived from colloidal gold). Rose pink was quickly adapted by the porcelain painters of Jingdezhen, leading the way for the development of the famille rose export porcelains. During the Yongzheng period, beautifully painted enamels with vignettes of flowers and fauna appeared. In the Qianlong period, Western figures appeared in cartouches surrounded by flowers and brocade patterns. The practice of painting on enamel soon shifted to Canton, where wares in this style were produced for the export trade.

Canton and Peking enamels were first covered with an opaque white base over which fine hand-painted designs in polychrome color were applied. Sometimes a second color of enamel was painted over the white to provide a different base color to be hand-painted. The decoration of these enamels was executed in a manner that earlier had only been applied to porcelain. (See: Japanese Cloisonné and Champlevé.)

References: W. F. Alexander, *Cloisonné and Related Arts*, Wallace-Homestead Book Co., 1972; W. F. Alexander and Donald K. Gerber, *Cloisonné Extrordinaire*, Wallace-Homestead Book Co., 1977; Helmut Brinker and Albert Lutz, *Chinese Cloisonné—The Pierre Uldry Collection*, Asia Society Galleries, in association with Bamboo Publishing, 1989; Arthur and Grace Chu, *Oriental Cloisonné and Other Enamels*, Crown Publishers Inc., 1975; Sir Harry Garner, *Chinese and Japanese Cloisonné Enamels*, Faber and Faber Inc., 1962; National Palace Museum, *Masterpieces of Chinese Enamel ware in the National Palace Museum*, National Palace Museum publication, 1971.

Museums: Asian Art Museum of San Francisco, San Francisco, California; Art Institute of Chicago, Chicago, Illinois; Walter Art Gallery, Baltimore, Maryland; Museum of China Trade, Milton, Massachusetts; Detroit Institute of Arts, Detroit Michigan; Brooklyn Museum, Brooklyn, New York; Metropolitan Museum of Art, New York, New York; Cleveland Museum of Art, Cleveland Ohio; University Museum, Philadelphia, Pennsylvania; Philadelphia Museum of Art, Philadelphia, Pennsylvania; Virginia Museum of

Fine Arts, Richmond, Virginia; Freer Gallery of Art, Washington, D.C.; Seattle Art Museum, Seattle, Washington; Palace Museum, Beijing, China; British Museum, London, England; Victoria and Albert Museum, London, England; National Palace Museum, Taipei, Taiwan.

Reproduction Alert: The distinguishing factors of Early Ming as opposed to later cloisonné products are bronze wire and fittings as opposed to the use of copper in the mid-seventeenth century; evidence of split wires under magnification, which are rare after the mid-seventeenth century; uncomplicated backgrounds without scrolls and spirals, which made their first appearance in the sixteenth century; a simple color palette made of coarsely mixed colors as opposed to fine color production in the late sixteenth and early seventeenth centuries; no use of the color rose pink, although a Ming pink appeared at the end of the fifteenth century; evidence of solder-applied cloisons as opposed to solderless methods introduced in the Qing Dynasty.

Ming marks were widely used during the Qing Dynasty and are really useless as a means of identification. Qianlong marks when they appear are usually more reliable when they are found cast in the base.

Modern cloisonné is being produced in both mainland China and Taiwan. The products of the People's Republic of China are finely executed and are produced in both archaic forms and naturalistic themes. Some are difficult to distinguish from the products of the early 1800s. The Millefleur (Thousand Flower) pattern which appears in brown-orange, yellow, green, and red tones is a product of this market, as are copies of human and animal figures that first appeared in the eighteenth century. Cloisonné clocks also have been imported in recent years. Large vases and dishes depicting horses, flowers, pavilions, and other naturalistic subjects have been exported since the 1970s. This new cloisonné is quite expensive, but the high price tag is a warranted reflection of the detailed work that is involved in its production.

Taiwan manufactures jewelry, small vases and plates, ginger jars, pictures, and so forth. They have not reproduced cloisonné in the old style, and their borders are entirely different than those produced in the People's Republic of China. The factories have only been in production since 1972. The quality of work is not exceptional. Recently, collectors have seen some new silvered eggs decorated in twisted-wire open cloisonné, some sections of which were filled with enamel and others were left open. Another variety used only open wire work with no enamels. The price was $35.00 for either kind.

New Canton enamel is being exported from China. Large vases are typical. The on-enamel painting is not as fine or as detailed as the originals, and the colors used are brighter.

Collecting Hints: The majority of Ming and Early Qing Dynasty cloisonné is to be found only in museum collections, though a great quantity of later Qing and modern cloisonné is being sold in the collector's market. The modern examples are oftentimes more beautifully and expertly crafted than their earlier counterparts. Later cloisonné is dazzling, but when purchased, it should be judged by its workmanship before being added to any collection. Criteria for collecting should include the amount and complexity of the wire work, the artistic work of the enamel, and the quality of gilding and finishing techniques.

According to authors Arthur and Grace Chu, Canton enamel prices should be keyed to cloisonné prices as worth one-quarter to one-third less. If the work is exeptional, they are to be valued at an equal level.

CHINESE CLOISONNÉ

Altar garniture

12¼'' h., 19th century, three pieces, the three dishes supported by cylindrical stems raised on bell-shaped bases, enameled in yellow, blue, red, and green with floral medallions interspersed with double happiness symbols and Buddhistic symbols on a turquoise ground, the center dish with petal rim **2,400.00**

three-piece, candlesticks 9⅝'' h., censer 13½'' h., 18th century, the globular censer set on three gilt-bronze-incised cabriole legs issuing from curly-maned-monster masks, decorated around the sides with lotus-blossoming-foliate vines, reserved on a turquoise ground, with two pierced S-scroll handles with matching decoration, surmounted by a reticulated and knopped gilt cover with shou

Garden Seats, 19'' h., barrel form with two cut-out handles at the sides. $1,430.00. Courtesy of Butterfield and Butterfield.

character, dragons and flowering foliate scrollwork; with two candlestick holders, each with bell-shaped base supporting a taper and smaller drip pan, decorated overall with flowering lotus vines reserved on a turquoise ground   **2,500.00**

Bowl, 10¼" dia., 19th century, Ming-style, decorated to the exterior with leaping horses above foaming waves, the interior similarly decorated with horses around a central roundel of a carp leaping from waves, all on a turquoise ground. . .   **350.00**

Box and cover

pair, domed, 4½" dia., 19th century, decorated with roundels of butterflies among flowers on red grounds, within bands of flowerhead roundels and cloud scrolls on a white ground above bands of lappets **275.00**

8" dia., 19th century, peach form, the raised design of peaches, flowers, leaves, and bats on a turquoise geometric ground, the interior decorated with bats amid clouds on a french blue background, wood stands **900.00**

Candlesticks (altar), 11" h., Ming Dynasty, pair, with cylindrical shafts with large drip pans and flaring base, decorated with scrolling peony design on a sky blue ground, now mounted as lamps **1,500.00**

Censer

5¼" h., Ming Dynasty, the spherical vessel on three elephant-head supports and with pair of qilin handles. **1,400.00**

19½" h., with cover, late Qianlong, the globular body with pair of flange handles and on tripod supports terminating in animal masks, the domed cover with dragon finial **3,000.00**

Dish, 16¾" dia., 19th century, set on three raised gilt bronze feet modeled as elephant heads, shallow form bowl with wide everted lip, turquoise ground, decorated with carp and a dragon rising from green waves, with phoenix birds flying around the rim over the waves, the exterior with a scrolling lotus meander interspersed with chilong, the rim with similar decoration and chilong reserves, the base with prunus flowers on a blue "cracked ice" ground **2,100.00**

Figure

Cranes, 54" h., late 19th/early 20th century, pair, each spreading their wings to fly, standing with one leg slightly ahead of the other, the body covered with a vividly colored pattern of birds, dragons, and flame-like scrolls on a turquoise ground, the detachable back feathers and wings covered in red, green, blue, and greyish-pink, the gilt beak holding a gilt-metal pricket candlestick, wood stand **6,500.00**

Deity, 9¼" h., late 19th century, the bearded figure wearing high official's hat, cast with three character mark **625.00**

Elephant form vessels, 7½" h., 20th century, each formed as an elephant seated on its hind legs, the lid cast as the head with trunk and tusks upraised, with a second interior dome-shaped lid, decorated with abstract birds and floral sprigs on a turquoise ground, chips **800.00**

Elephants, 11¾", 19th century, pair, white bodies with gilt details, tusks, ears and trappings, each wearing an elaborate saddle blanket and carrying a vase **2,000.00**

Fu lions on stands, 14½" h., pair, each beast seated and scratching his ear with his hind leg, decorated with stylized kui dragons and foliate scrolls on a blue ground, the curved tail ending in a gilt tuft, the separate square stand covered with drapery, and decorated with scrolling peony blossoms around a central green medallion **2,500.00**

Roosters, 16¼" h., 20th century, each standing upright on a circular pedestal decorated with butterflies and blossoms, with tail feathers, wings and comb all depicted in colorful enamels, the body decorated with scrolling tendrils on a turquoise ground **450.00**

Sheep, 44" h., late 19th/early 20th century, pair, each animal standing foursquare, its head slightly turned, the bodies with overall stylized bird and floral motifs on a cream ground, the legs and faces with floral motifs on a blue ground, the rectangular bases with shaped aprons conforming in decoration. **15,000.00**

Garden seats, 19" h., 20th century, barrel form, each decorated with four flori-form reserves filled with blossoms of peony, lotus, chrysanthemum and other flowers, all on a white keyfret ground, the base and top rim banded with plum blossoms, the top decorated en suite, the sides fitted with two cut out handles **1,500.00**

Incense burner

22½″ h., Qianlong, the bulbous body with flange handles, and tripod supports terminating in animal masks, the domed cover decorated with lotus and birds on a sky blue ground, wood stand . . .   **7,000.00**

38½″ h., Qianlong, pagoda-form, the tubular shaft pierced with clouds and encircled by a gilt dragon, pagoda roof top and hexagonal base **7,500.00**

Jar (with cover), 6″ h., 19th century, of barrel form and decorated in multicolored enamels with a continuous band of flowers amid scrolling leafy tendrils flanked by "butterfly"-shaped garland bands to the top and bottom, the slightly curved circular lid with similar design and surmounted by a large knob, surface wear **250.00**

Jardiniere, 15″ l., of canted rectangular form, each slightly rounded side with a turquoise panel of fu dogs playing with brocade balls, reserved on a blue lotus scroll ground repeated on the everted rim, raised on four ruyi-form feet, base with prunusa flowers on a "cracked ice" ground **1,400.00**

Mantel clock, 15½″ h., late 19th century, the circular clock suspended from a frame composed of two cylindrical columns joined by a molded gilt metal pediment, the base composed of two gilt metal fu lions seated on plinths, the whole enameled in yellow, dark blue, red, white and green with stylized flowers on a turquoise ground **2,000.00**

Pilgrim flasks, 14¼″ h., pair, bearing Jiaqing four-character mark but later, each decorated with a circular medallion containing peony issuing from rockwork, reserved on a diapered blue ground with stylized shou medallion, the neck with stylized bat and leaf blades flanked by gilt dragon-form handles **1,800.00**

Scholar's set, 10⅜″, 19th century, censer on three elephant-head supports, the pierced cover with elephant finial, a beaker-form vase and a covered spherical box, each on a recumbent elephant base, and a pair of bronze chopsticks **1,500.00**

Table screen, 19¾″ h., on carved and reticulated wooden stand, rectangu-

lar, the front decorated with a depiction of flowering leafy sprigs dominated by a large peony blossom on a patterned turquoise blue ground, the reverse with an allover pattern of cloud scroll in muted blue, the carved hardwood stand with foliate pattern openwork motifs   **1,250.00**

Tea pot, 9¾″ l., late 19th century, of compressed ovoid body fashioned as a "Buddha's hand citron" with the converging fingers forming the spout opposed by a gilt curving stalk form handle, decorated in bright polychrome enamels with butterflies and further fruiting vines on a bright yellow ground the inset circular lid decorated en suite and with a gilt melon shaped finial **675.00**

Vase

8″ h., pair, decorated with butterflies among flower sprays and lotus on turquoise T-pattern grounds   **250.00**

13½″ h., pair, rouleau form, decorated with butterflies among flowers issuing from rockwork on a white T-pattern ground **375.00**

15⅝″, Qianlong, gu-form, decorated with stylized lotus on a pale blue ground **2,500.00**

16″ h., 18th/19th century, gu-form, the central bulbous section decorated with lotus blossoms and leafy scrolls between a prunus-blossom-incised gilt band and key-fret borders, the tall flaring neck and spreading base with green-ground, tall leaves reserved on a scroll- and lotus-blossom decorated turquoise ground interspersed with Buddhist em-

Tray, 6⅛″ x 8½″ l., circa 1900, decorated in a dense floral and butterfly pattern on the front, the reverse with bats, executed in polychrome colors on a black ground color. $650.00

Back view of tray on previous page.

blems, the gilt rim with key-fret
pattern, pitting, casting flaw **1,000.00**
17⅞″ h., pair, stick neck shape, each
of faceted low-slung ovoid shape
resting on a waisted pedestal foot
and tapering to a tall neck flaring
toward the mouth, each of the
vertical bands decorated in multicolored enamels with auspicious
emblems amid cloud scrolls on a
turquoise-blue ground, the base
with apocryphal *Xuande mark*,
wear. **1,600.00**
18⅜″ h., circa 1900, rouleau
form, each with two panels of peony or chrysanthemum, green,
red, yellow and aubergine on a
white ground, along with two
smaller panels decorated in like
manner, all on a turquoise
"cracked ice" ground with prunus
flowers and butterflies, the neck
with phoenix among cloud scrolls **1,440.00**

**Vases, Pair, hu (archaic) form, decorated
with animals in a landscape setting, the
base with galloping horses, the corners
cast with flanges and the rims with keyfret
band. $1,430.00. Courtesy of Butterfield
and Butterfield.**

23⅞″ h., 17th century, yen-yen
form, set on a splayed foot, the
baluster body decorated with
flowering lotus foliate scroll on a
bluish-turquoise ground, the
trumpet neck decorated with stiff
leaves enclosing stylized dragons
reserved on a bluish-turquoise
ground with flowering lotus
scroll, divided by four flanges extending from the base to the rim,
the foot and mouth all bound with
copper bands, the gilt underside
with a two-character Jing Tai mark
within double ring borders, losses
to enamel, casting flaw. **1,700.00**

CANTON AND PEKING ENAMELS

Bowl(s)
pair, with covers, 4″ dia., Jiaqing/
Daoguang Period, each of inverted bell form with a dished rim
and resting on a tall ring foot, the
interior delicately painted in
"famille rose" polychrome enamels with fruiting and flowering
sprigs below a keyfret band, a foliate-patterned band encircling the
foot and the circular knob of the
domed cover decorated en suite,
(wear). **750.00**
4½″, late 18th century, decorated on
the exterior with a blue dragon
amidst pink and green foliate
scrolls on a yellow ground, the
interior painted on floral motif
with famille rose enamels on a
white ground. **350.00**
16″ dia., 18th century, shallow
form, painted in famille rose enamels, showing western figures in
a landscape setting, with flower
sprays reserved on a black and
green foliate ground, in the shallow well and on a black and turquoise ground on the barbed rim **2,200.00**
Box and cover, 4⅜″, early 18th century, the cover showing two
pheasants seated on a rocky
mount with peony and magnolia
blossoms within a hexagonal
lobed reserve on a white enamel
ground, the sides with butterflies
and foliate scrolls in famille rose
enamels and black, some restora-
tion and cracks **1,000.00**
Dish(es)
3¼″, square, 19th century, canted
shallow form, on four bracket
feet, the interior painted with a
European lady breast feeding an

infant with the father seated nearby, famille rose enamels , blue scrolled border, damamges 10½″ dia., 20th century, eight lobed shallow form, painted in the center with a scene of songbirds in peony and prunus branches, encircled by baroque-style scrolling leaves and flowers, the well covered in a grayish blue, thelobed lipaa with a metal rim, chip. **225.00**

Lamps, pair, Canton enamel, 21⅛″ h. without rod, 19th century, each of square stepped gu form decorated overall with foliate and flowering scrolls, punctuated by bands of upright stiff leaves and lappets, each of the upper center sections with a front-facing gilt-decorated dragon, all reserved on a pale yellow ground, losses to enamel, mounted for electricity. **1,500.00**

Plates

4¾″ dia., pair, Peking enamel, Qianlong, made for the European market, each painted with two figures in European dress seated under a tree, yellow diaper borders with floral reserves **1,000.00**

11″ dia., late 18th /early 19th century, each interior well painted in colored enamels with a mirror image of butterfly and multicolored blossoming peonies plants and bamboo on a white ground, all encircled on the cavetto by a band with shaped floral reserved on a diaper patterned ground the wide rim with further flowering peony sprigs and a narrow blue rim band, the exterior enameled a bright yellow extended over the base painted with a peony, chop, fine cracks, wear **1,900.00**

Tray, 10″ l., 18th century, rectangular, set on four shaped feet, painted in the famille rose palette on white background, showing scholars and attendants in a garden setting, cracks, restored, chips **1,100.00**

Vase(s)

4″, (miniature), pair, Peking enamel, Qianlong mark and period, of tapered square form, painted with panels of European figures   **1,500.00**

37¾″ h., Canton enamel, gu-form, of quadrangular section, each side with panels enclosing figural scenes reserved on a floral scroll-decorated blue ground, supported on a steeped tiered base, damage to enamel, losses, dents **1,500.00**

CHAMPLEVÉ ENAMELS

Censer, 18¼″ h., late 19th/early 20th century, of ovoid form flanked by two abstract phoenix-form handles and raised on three legs supported by a circular base, attached to a wooden stand, decorated in enamels with figures in a garden setting and applied glass bosses at the shoulder, the dome lid surmounted with a fu-dog finial wear, losses . . .   **600.00**

11½″ h., pair, gilt, 18th century, each of lobed gu form, with flared neck and base encircled by tall enamel lappets, between recessed floral bands, the cental bulb decorated with lotus scroll repeated below the lipped key-fret rim, the exterior covered in gilt, casting flaw **3,500.00**

Vases, pair, 14″ h., 19th century, each of low slug ovoid shape resting on a waisted pedestal base and surmounted by a tall neck with a central bulge applied with a pair of large animal mask handles below the flared rim, the sides and neck with bands of archaic bird-form, *taotieh*, and foliate designs accented in colored enamels on a *leiwen* ground, the base with four-character studio mark, wear **950.00**

CHINESE EXPORT PORCELAIN

History: The initial usage for Chinese ceramics by the well-to-do in any culture was for food service. The quality that makes Chinese porcelain so desirable is its nonporous surface. In addition, as a byproduct of its chemical nature, it is resonant and translucent. Sanitary conditions in earlier times were not what they are today. No one knew what caused disease or why people got sick after eating from wooden or pottery dishes. Chinese porcelain was different from the local ceramic product made in other countries until the eighteenth century. Food left on the surface of Chinese porcelain long enough to decay could not seep into the body of the dish. On European ceramics, powerful bacteria from remaining food lay in wait to sicken or kill the next user. Chinese porcelain dishes had a magical property about them; the people who ate from them did not get sick.

Europe first came into contact with Chinese ceramics during the Crusades in the Middle East, beginning in the eleventh century. The Europeans found that the Ottoman Empire had been importing Chinese Sung Dynasty celadons since the ninth century. The ceramics had traveled overland via the silk route. The magical property that protected the user from sickness was a powerful sales tool.

Ceramics, silk, and spices were the goals of the European trader. Historically, the trade had to wait until navigational instruments were developed that would ensure that the traders would return with their desired cargo. Building ships and outfitting them for years at sea was expensive. The kings of the European nations already had naval vessels, eager captains, and an intense desire for additional income. The value of the early cargoes was so great that one successful voyage could make the captain well-to-do for life. The first traders to venture all the way to China were the Portuguese, who arrived in Canton in 1517. They controlled the sea-lanes throughout the first half of the sixteenth century and established themselves at Macao in 1557. During the latter half of the sixteenth century, they were allowed trading voyages to Canton twice a year.

The Dutch East India Company was founded in 1602. During the first part of the seventeenth century, it took control of the trading routes from the Portuguese. This early trade was in the blue and white wares of the Ming Dynasty (1368–1644). The English East India Company was set up in 1599 and traded to the Indian markets in the seventeenth century. By the eighteenth century all of the seagoing nations of Europe were trading with China. America did not become part of this trade until the nineteenth century—very late in the game.

Up until the nineteenth century the Chinese merchants dumped the unsold porcelain from their warehouses on the unsuspecting European foreign merchants, making a handsome profit in the transaction. Some of the pieces from these storehouses had been made at Ching-te-chen (Jingdezhen) and bore the nien ho (reign mark) of the Chinese emperors in whose reign that style of ware originated. It was in this manner that some pieces of porcelain with Chinese marks found their way to Europe. Beginning in the 1680s the European traders asked the Chinese to make special wares just for their markets. None of these pieces bear the Chinese nien ho or reign marks, as these were intended for the use of "heathens" and marking them would be demeaning to the emperor.

European merchants brought bookplates, engravings, pieces of pewter and silver, and drawn designs to their Chinese counterparts and asked that these designs be produced in porcelain. Many of the preexisting Chinese shapes and sizes remained the same, but the decorations were distinctly European. The Chinese artist was limited only by his ability to copy sometimes very complex designs into the Chinese porcelain medium. Some of the European influenced shapes include

tureens, mugs, covered bouillon cups, salts, sauceboats, and candlesticks to name a few.

There was also a demand in Europe during the late seventeenth and eighteenth centuries for purely decorative Chinese porcelain. The wealthy had porcelain rooms lined with niches on the walls to display vast quantities of small blue and white ceramics. Some of the pieces were enhanced in Europe with additions of enamels in the local styles or with fine gold doré bronze mounts. Some of the pieces were enhanced with silver additions, a style learned from the Near East and going as far back as the fourteenth century.

Beginning in the early eighteenth century, Europeans began to duplicate some of the properties of Chinese porcelain, notably at Meissen in Germany, Limoges in France, and at various places in England. What they found was that the addition of chemically treated animal bone to the clays found in Europe would approximate the appearance of Chinese ceramics. Hence the rise of the name "bone china," but the Chinese wares were still superior and the trade continued. By the early nineteenth century the quality of the wares produced in China was rapidly decreasing. Political upheaval in China, the secrecy with which the formulas for Chinese porcelain were kept, and the failure of artisans to pass on their knowledge all contributed to the decline of the China trade.

CHINESE EXPORT BLUE AND WHITE WARES

Blue and white wares owe their coloration to cobalt, which is sandwiched between the body of the ware and the glaze. It cannot fade or change throughout the life of the porcelain. The translucency comes from the chemical nature of magnesium aluminosilicate. Porcelain was fired at about $1,300°C$ in updraft charcoal-fired kilns. Being of very similar chemical composition, the body and the glaze fuse and trap the color layer immutably between them. Thus, light can pass completely through the ware.

The European china trade has to be correlated to Chinese political history. The Ming Dynasty ended in 1644, and with it the major city of porcelain manufacture, Ching-te-chen, was sacked and burned, severely diminishing their participation in th export market. During the transitional period between the Ming and Qing Dynasties, European traders bought whatever was available, including blanc-de-chine (white-only wares). For the thirty years until Qing Dynasty Emperor Kangxi ascended the throne, the Japanese predominated the export ceramic market. Kangxi was the first patron of the ceramics arts of the Qing Dynasty and rebuilt Ching-te-chen in the early 1680s. This begins the finest period of Chinese blue and white porcelain, which lasted until about 1800. The wares were beautifully and symmetrically potted, precisely drawn in their decoration, and finely finished with a keen eye for detail. The cobalt blue used was different from that of the Ming Dynasty, and was from different sources and more finely ground and mixed. Some of the pieces tended to be a purplish blue because the color saturation was so intense. The export trade continued through the reigns of Chinese emperors Yongzheng (1723–1735), Qianlong (1736–1795), Jiaqing (1796–1820), and Daoguang (1821–1850). By 1840 the predominant blue and white ceramics coming from China were called Canton ware or ballast ware. They were, like the early Ming Dynasty wares, coarse, poorly painted, and roughly finished, but they were cheap enough to warrant their continued transportation and sale.

CHINESE EXPORT PORCELAIN WITH COLORED DECORATION

Two types of colored or polychrome porcelain were exported: those made for the Chinese market (and later exported), and those made to order for foreign merchants. The shape and decoration subjects of the first is distinctly Chinese, while the second, Western-style wares show transcultural influences in shape and decoration.

Coloration can be divided into two major classes, with some pieces featuring multiple methods of decoration. These classes include color under the glaze based on specific metallic oxides that under the influence of the kiln develop certain ranges of color, and enamels painted over the exterior glaze surface. Colors used under the glaze are fired once at the same time the body of the porcelain ware is fired. Enamels are applied on the fired body and then secondarily fired at much lower temperatures to set or fuse the enamels to the exterior glaze. Occasionally, different enamels require multiple firings. Gilding was added with a third or final firing at still lower temperatures.

The underglaze metallic pigments and their colors used included iron orange, manganese purple, magnesium purple-red, antimony yellow, chromium yellow, and copper green to pink. These were used alone or in addition to cobalt blue or in combination with other underglaze and overglaze colors. When used alone, the resulting ware is called monochrome or single color. When multiple colors are used the ware is termed polychrome.

The enamel colors were developed during the sixteenth and seventeenth centuries. The early Ming Dynasty enamels include brown, green, aubergine (eggplant purple), yellow, and red-orange. These were used until the early eighteenth century, when foreign merchants and missionaries introduced two new colors that changed

Chinese porcelain forever. The new colors were based on arsenic of lead to produce a white enamel and cassius of gold to produce pink. Shading was achieved by mixing white with pink and adding a gum base. The pink is known in Chinese only as "foreign color." After its introduction to China about 1715, it became the predominant and preferred enamel.

The enamels were used in specific combinations of colors referred to as "palettes." They were named in French by Jacquemart, a Jesuit priest at the court of Kangxi. For convenience the names are used around the world. The palettes are called famille (family) verte, noire, jaune, and rose. The verte palette is composed of green, yellow, aubergine, orange, and blue. This was the predominant enamel palette until 1720, but it also was used throughout the eighteenth century. The noire palette normally used the verte palette with a black background, but by the mid-eighteenth century famille rose was occasionally used. The jaune palette used famille rose colors with a yellow background. The famille rose, or rose famille palette added shadings of pink to the verte palette, and pink predominated over green. Gradations of color, translucency, and juxtapositions of color are used as dating tools, as these changed periodically and were well recorded.

As with the blue and white, foreign merchants supplied European designs to be produced in porcelain and painted in the enamel colors. Uniquely, since Chinese painted art was not adept at conveying depth, Western subjects took on a decidedly Oriental flavor. This was so well accepted by the European community that when European artists painted ceramics with Oriental motifs in the eighteenth and nineteenth centuries, they attempted to copy this flat style. The result was distinctly European and non-Oriental. Certain designs and combinations of motifs met with greater success in one country of Europe than another. Thus, there are legitimate references to pieces being made for a given "market," be it French, Dutch, English, or other.

One of the curious results of European-influenced designs is the type of ware painted en grisaille. On these pieces black enamel was used to approximate the black ink from steel engravings on paper, which were presented to the Chinese artists to render on porcelain. There were a large number of Christian religious themes interpreted in this style, which are referred to as "Jesuit" china. When colored lithographs were sent to China, the artists used colors closely approximating their samples. Finally, the name Lowestoft china was a misnomer or error arising from some English authors assuming that blank pieces were sent to England for enameling. With the exception of the Dutch "clobbered" pieces, the vast majority were completely finished in China. (See Canton and Nanking Pattern Blue and White Porcelain; Armorial Export Porcelain; Chinese Imari;

Fitzhugh Pattern Porcelain; Famille Rose and Rose Pattern Porcelain; Qing Dynasty Porcelain.)

References: John Ayers, *China for the West*, 2 vols., Sotheby Parke Bernet, 1978; M. Beurdeley, *A Connoisseur's Guide to Chinese Ceramics*, Harper and Row, 1974; E. Gordon, *Chinese Export Porcelain*, Main Street Press, 1984; S. Jenyns, *Later Chinese Porcelain*, Faber and Faber Ltd., 1977; C. J. A. Jorg, *The Geldermalsen, History and Porcelain*, Kemper Publishers, 1986; A. M. Palmer, *A Winterthur Guide to Chinese Export Porcelain*, Crown Publishers, 1976; D. F. Lunsingh Scheurleer, *Chinese Export Porcelain*, Faber and Faber Ltd., 1974; H. A. Van Oort, *Chinese Porcelain of the Nineteenth and Twentieth Century*, Uitgeversmaatcshappij De Tijdstroom B. V., 1977; S. T. Yao and J. Martin, *Chinese Blue and White Ceramics*, Arts Orientalis, 1978.

Museums: Avery Brundage Collection in the San Francisco City Art Museum, San Francisco, California; Museum of the China Trade, Mystic, Connecticut; Ira Koger Museum of the City of Jacksonville, Jacksonville, Florida; Boston City Art Museum, Boston, Massachusetts; Metropolitan Museum of Art, New York, New York; Victoria and Albert Museum, London, England; British Museum, London, England; The Brighton Pavillion, Brighton, England; Ashmolean Museum, Oxford, England; The Louvre, Paris, France; Eumorfopoulos Collection in the Benaki Museum, Athens, Greece; Rijksmuseum, Amsterdam, the Netherlands; Friesland Museum and the Princesshof Museum, Leeuwarden, the Netherlands; Topkapi Saray Palace Museum, Istanbul, Turkey.

Reproduction Alert: America has been flooded with modern Chinese ceramics for the last twenty years. These are *not* reproductions. They look totally different from the antiques. Modern Chinese ceramic is *not* porcelain, it is stoneware. As such, it is not translucent, and light will not pass through it. The modern ceramics are covered in a white glaze to approximate the original color of the body of the earlier wares, which is translucent. In other words, the chemical nature of the body and the glaze of modern Chinese wares is completely different. Finally, the vast majority of the modern blue and white wares have been transfer-printed. In this process the coloration is first applied to a paper design mask by a machine. This mask is then applied to the body of the raw ceramic, and with rubbing the color is transferred. Transfer prints do not show even application of the color because of uneven pressure during transfer. Brushstrokes (color heavier at the edges of a line than in the middle) cannot be duplicated by transfer printing. All antique wares before 1840 were hand-painted. Occasionally, the transfer even wrinkles upon application,

causing smearing of the design and loss of detail in the resulting overlap areas. True antique Chinese blue and white shows none of these traits.

There have been a few attempts to reproduce famille rose. In Hong Kong in the early twentieth century, certain highly desirable designs, notably those featuring the American eagle, were made for the tourist trade. There can be no confusion between eighteenth-century wares and modern Chinese enameling. The latter is exceptionally poor.

Collecting Hints: Prices for blue and white export wares are not as high as those paid for their polychrome enamel and armorial counterparts. This is due, no doubt, to the greater availability of blue and white export wares on the market. The Kangxi period export blue and white porcelain, however, is an exception. Because of its superb porcelain quality and color, it is the most expensive of all the blue and white export wares.

The eighteenth- and nineteenth-century famille rose export ware is gradually disappearing from the market. The rarest of these wares, made during the Yongzheng period, were the ruby back plates and bowls that sell in the $5,000 to $10,000 range. Famille rose export wares, for the purpose of our definition, are not to be confused with the famille rose "pattern" wares of the eighteenth, nineteenth and twentieth centuries, which are treated in their own category elsewhere in this volume.

Advisor: Clinton R. Weil, Ph.D.

BLUE AND WHITE DECORATION

Basin, 19½″ x 5″ h., Wanli period, circa 1590, bird in rock garden, flared rim, perfect condition **12,000.00**

Bowl
5″ dia., pale blue monochrome glaze, Kangxi mark on white base, and of the period, carved floral design. **695.00**

8½″ dia., Kangxi period, flared rim, scholars in a garden setting, scholar's symbol mark on base . . **2,300.00**

Barber's bowl, 12″ x 9″, Qialong period, helmet shaped with original cutout for neck **1,875.00**

10¾″ dia., late 18th century, famille rose palette, exterior with central gilt band in diaper design, leafy fruits and flowers entwined within band, interior with scroll and bell flower borders, central floral spray **800.00**

13¾″ dia., "Masonic", 18th century, blue enamel with star border, enamel decorated armorial crests and Masonic emblems to exterior, interior with blue enamel spray to center, (restored) **1,900.00**

7", Daoguang mark and period, circa 1835, Exterior enhanced with famille rose enamels **1,100.00**

10", Qianlong period, Dutch decorated with enamels over Nanking style scene. **1,495.00**

Brushpot

5" x 2½" dia., circa 1840, scholar and boy design, furniture for the scholar's desk **125.00**

11", circa 1830, One hundred antiques pattern and pierced with six cutouts **395.00**

Charger

14", circa 1760, extensive floral decoration with gold enhancements **1,650.00**

15", Kangxi period, finely drawn Mandarin figures in a courtyard **2,075.00**

16", circa 1730, vases and leaves decoration, finely drawn **2,250.00**

Cups, pair, for wine, 1½" tall and dia., Kangxi mark and period, scholar's symbol design. **400.00**

Cups and Saucers, 5" saucers, Kangxi period, circa 1700, Set of four, For the Dutch market, hand formed in wooden molds in foliated and raised panels **1,400.00**

Dish

covered, 6", Kangxi period, An "Equelle" based on a French silver design **3,500.00**

Saucer, 8", Wanli period, floral design with "heaped and piled" cobalt, circa 1600, perfect condition **5,800.00**

saucer shape, 8", heavily potted, inscribed in underglaze blue in arabic language, shao border. **495.00**

Dish, 8", Kangxi period, Dutch market design of ladies sewing, restorations **750.00**

Ewer, 8½" tall, balaster shape with spout, original lid, period of Qianlong, circa 1790 . . . . **1,400.00**

Ginger Jar

8", Kangxi period, Kyrins and fantastic animals, wood lid **1,850.00**

8½", Qianlong period, "Three Friends" decoration of Pine, Prunus, and Bamboo. **1,550.00**

Jug, for Milk, with cover, 5", circa 1760, Floral decoration and European inspired handle **795.00**

Planter, 10" x 8" h., circa 1800, Eight immortals decoration, original drainage hole **1,475.00**

Plate

7½" dia., Kangxi period, flower bas-

Ginger Jar, 9" x 9½", Kangxi period, blue and white, unmarked, carved with ribbed design, dragon and phoenix cartouches. $4,375.00.

ket design, Bronze form "TING" mark on base, perfect condition **900.00**

9" dia., Qianlong export, landscape scene **195.00**

11", Kangxi period, circa 1700, shell mark, hand molded in wooden form with raised panels called "petal foliate," very popular in the Dutch market **1,250.00**

Plates, pair, 10", Yongzheng period, circa 1730, Underglaze blue chrysanthemum mark, For the French market, Part of non-Armorial dinner service for a Scottish family **1,800.00**

Platter,

14" dia., 3½" raised dome center panel, Kangxi period, circa 1700, design of figures in a garden setting. **1,800.00**

13¼" x 16", for meat, with strainer insert, 18th century, octagonal shape with cell and floral border and central coastal landscape scene in the Nanking style, minor restoration of rim chips **1,300.00**

14" across, with "well and tree", circa 1790, based on silver de-

Mugs, 6½" x 5½", Qianlong period, circa 1745, blue and white, export ale mugs for English market, based on pewter shapes. $1,900.00

Soup Tureen, 14" x 9", Qianlong period, circa 1765, blue and white, raised applied porcelain eagles with carved rose finial. $5,200.00.

sign, Nanking export design, perfect condition **900.00**
Punch Bowl, 12½", circa 1750, Underglaze blue borders inside and out, with famille rose enamels. **3,500.00**
Sauce Tureen, with underplate, 7" x 4", Qianlong period, Nanking export with lake and pagodas scene . .   **1,575.00**
Soup plate
9", Qianlong period, Floral decoration.   **235.00**

Soup Tureen, 12" x 6" x 7" h., Yongzheng period, blue and white, underglaze blue flower mark, French market bombé shape based on a silver form. $3,400.00

Punch Bowl, 12½", Qianlong period, circa 1750, blue and white, underglaze blue borders inside and out, with famille rose enamels. $3,400.00

Vases, Pair, 10¾" x 5½", Kangxi period porcelain, 18th century mounts, blue and white, Chinese Imari pattern, with French doré bronze mounts. $10,500.00.

9", Kangxi period, circa 1720, Figures in a Garden scene **495.00**
Soup Tureen, oval, 19½" x 12¾", with cover, mid 18th Century, lotus decorated finial with central coastal village scene on cover and sides of tureen, lattice borders with octagonal shaped drip rim and ochre enamel trim, minor glaze nicks **2,100.00**
Vase
8" h., "Meiping" shape, double circle mark, period of Yongzheng, circa 1730, design of peaches, pomegranate, and citron, on original wood base **4,800.00**
9" h., Ming dynasty style of floral decoration, period of Daoquang, circa 1830. . . . .   **825.00**
14½" h., Kangxi period, flower mark, Beaker shape vase with "carved petal foliate" design. . . .   **4,900.00**
17", Qianlong period, with cover, carved "Chicken Skin" with raised cartouches **7,800.00**
Vases, pair, 15" tall, period of Daoquang, circa 1840, floral designs, "JU-I" scepter handles on both sides **2,100.00**
Vegetable dish, covered, 10" x 7", 18th century, Fine Canton export from a dinner service **1,195.00**

COLOR DECORATION

Bowl, 8", circa 1770, Famille rose and Chinese Imari, restored hairline . . .   **395.00**
Ginger Jar, 9" x 8", circa 1800, "Cafe-au-lait" ground with famille verte cartouche reserves, original cover   **1,950.00**

Bowl, 6" dia., Qianlong period, circa 1760, famille rose enamel, Dutch decorated bowl with portraits of Willliam Friso and wife. $2,500.00

Cup Stand, 9" x 3½", Qianlong period, 1750, footed, famille rose, fan-shaped French market *trembleuse* $4,700.00

Mug
  5" x 4", circa 1770, Famille rose cartouches with raised blue and white floral design **1,150.00**
  6" x 6", circa 1745, Famille rose with gilded "Y" diaper border for French market **1,900.00**
Plate
  8.5", circa 1740, Famille noire enamels with bright orange rooster **1,950.00**

8.5", circa 1755, Famille rose enamels of brown bird in naturalistic setting **795.00**
9", circa 1740, Orange enameled design border, Famille rose interior **1,575.00**
9", circa 1770, Famille rose enamels of vase with flowers **675.00**
9", circa 1740, Famille rose enameled scene, White enamel "Pate-sur-pate" border **850.00**
Platter, 12.5", circa 1745, Famille rose enamels, with Western theme, "Meissen" inspired design **2,650.00**
Platters, European Subject, pair, 15", delivered in 1743, Made for an officer of English "East India Company", ...**12,500.00**
Saucer Dish, 9", circa 1730, rose verte, Central peacock with floral festoons, semi-eggshell body **1,575.00**
Soup plate, 8", Kangxi, circa 1710, Famille verte enamel border, underglaze blue central design **975.00**
Soup plates, pair, 9", circa 1760, Famille rose floral festoons for the French Market **900.00**
Table screen, Rosewood frame and stand, 30" h. x 16" w., Circa 1795, Famille rose enamels with artist's colophon **4,500.00**
Tea Service, four pieces, 8" waste dish, circa 1750, painted in the "En Grisaille" manner with European figures, comprising Teapot, Sugar, Creamer, and waste dish **3,675.00**
Vase
  Export, 10", circa 1730s, "Hu" form, monochrome underglaze pale blue ground, Famille rose peony flowers **3,000.00**
  11", circa 1770, Famille rose enamels in Mandarin scene on bea-

Left to right: Plate, 9", Qianlong period, Circa 1750, *en grisaille* decoration, seamstress design based on English steel engraving, $450.00; Plate, 8¾", Qianlong period, circa 1740, famille rose and gilding, palace ware plate from one of twelve services for Emperor Qianlong, $1,700.00; Platter, 14½", Qianlong period, circa 1765, famille rose, with brown enamels and pink peonies, $2,300.00.

Vases, 10¾", Qianlong period, Circa 1760, famille verte, quatrefoil lobed vases with kylins, dragon handles. $3,400.00

ker shape, underglaze blue floral
ground **1,800.00**
15", circa 1735, Famille noire
enamel ground, Floral design in
Famille verte palette, Archaic
bronze beaker shape **5,600.00**
Vases, pair, 9", circa 1750, Famille
rose enamels of Floral motif, 19th
century French Ormolu mounts at
base and top **4,200.00**

CHINESE EXPORT SILVER

History: Precious metalwork for the export market during the China trade period from 1785 to 1885 is commonly referred to as "Chinese export silver." It is one of the most recently recognized groups of objects of the China trade. Because many pieces are Western style and bear pseudohallmarks, it was not until the early 1960s that the existence of silver trade pieces was generally acknowledged.

There is ongoing controversy over which pieces can be classified as Chinese export silver. The controversy stems from several sources, complicated by the fact that Westerners were creating silver pieces in "chinoiserie" styles, and Chinese silversmiths created pieces in traditional Western styles. Scholars have discovered that many pieces were not exported but were created in Western style for Westerners who lived in China. Gold objects, especially jewelry made for the export market, have also been identified from this period. Objects classified as Chinese export silver are not necessarily silver, may have been made for use in China, and may not look Chinese! The following guideline for classifying Chinese export silver is suggested in Kernan's *The Chait Collection of Chinese Export Silver*, "gold or silver

wrought in China by native craftsmen using their own traditional techniques, more or less according to non-Chinese specifications, for export, for foreign residents, and at least primarily for non-Chinese use."

Objects belonging to this classification are commonly identified by a combination of ideograms with the maker's initials in English or Chinese, a shop name, and a quality stamp. The 85, 88, and 90 quality stamps are the most prevalent and probably reflect the percent of silver. The shop name, usually present as a Chinese ideogram, was the name of a group of silversmiths working together under one shop name. Fu Chi, Hsieh Ch'eng, and Kuang-yaun are examples of such shops. English letters were used as the marks for some individual silversmiths such as Cumshing (CS) and Cutshing (CUT or CU) and for famous retail shops such as Wang Hing and Tuck Chang and Company. Some well-known silversmiths like Pao yin, the rarest and earliest identified hallmark, used Chinese characters for their mark. Not all of the silversmiths marked their pieces, especially during the early China trade period. The pseudohallmarks are typically English, regardless of the intended destination of the piece.

The China trade periods are as follows: early China trade (before 1785), China trade (1785–1840), late China trade (1840–1885) and post-China trade (after 1885). The early, late, and post-China trade periods feature Chinese-style decorations and motifs, while the China trade materials are typically of Western design and patterns. The creation of porcelain for the export market follows a similar pattern. Westerners were quick to recognize the quality and economy of Chinese pieces. Early references to the manufacture of silver in Canton mention articles of silver with English cyphers and coats of arms on them. The engravers had books of heraldry, which they consulted and copied with great exactness. Western-style articles from the China trade period include urn-shaped teapots, sugar bowls, and tapered cylindrical mugs. True Chinese-style pieces were the most popular during the China trade period. Following them were the rococo revival pieces, typified by exaggerated shapes and florid ornamentation. The transition from the China trade period to the late China trade period produced many objects that were of mixed Western and Chinese styles. Mixed-style pieces initially appear to be Western. After closer observation, a bent twig handle or dragon feet reveal the Chinese origin. Salvers often showed elements of the mixed style.

Theories about the return to Chinese styles during the late and post-China trade periods include a resurgence of national pride during difficult times for China. Fortunately for the growing number of people who are developing an appreciation for Chinese export silver, there are many fine examples from each period, and as we continue to study we may find even more.

References: *Connoisseur Magazine*, selected articles on silver, November 1965 and July 1972; Carl L. Crossman, *The China Trade Export Paintings, Furniture, Silver and Other Objects*, Pyne Press, 1972; Neville John Irons, *Silver and Carving of the Old China Trade*, Hong Kong, 1983; Soame Jenyns and Margaret Jourdain, *Chinese Export Art of the 18th Century*, Spring Books, 1967; Kernan, *The Chait Collection of Chinese Export Silver*, The Ralph M. Chait Galleries, Inc., New York, 1985; Kernan and Wilkes Forbes, *Chinese Export Silver 1785 to 1885*, Museum of American China Trade, 1975.

Museums: Yale University Museum, New Haven, Connecticut; Museum of the American China Trade, Milton, Massachusetts; Peabody Musem, Salem, Massachusetts; Victoria and Albert Museum, London, England.

Advisors: Paul and Diane Haig

Bowls
  six pierced with glass liners, $4\frac{7}{8}''$ dia., circa 1900 with repoussé decorations of birds and prunus **1,650.00**
  eight pierced, $5\frac{1}{8}''$ dia., circa 1900, each with repoussé decoration of chrysanthemum blooms **3,300.00**
Candle Sticks, four George III style, stamped Zu Wen, Beijing Wu Hua, $13\frac{1}{4}''$ h., circa 1900 . . . . **10,000.00**
Ewer & Basin, ewer $14\frac{1}{4}''$ h., basin 20'' dia., circa 1860, repoussé warrior scene, both marked "GW" **6,600.00**
Goblet, $8\frac{1}{2}''$, 19th Century, chased and embossed on exterior with groups of figures in a palace garden, sup-

Box, circa 1900, stamped WH 90, Wang Hing $250.00

ported by a column in the form of a fish tailed dragon, Stamped "LC" probably Leeching. **1,430.00**
Entreé dish (covered) and serving bowl, entreé dish 8'' dia., 19th century, round with beaded rim and domed cover, impressed character marks and pseudo hallmarks **2,700.00**
Jar, small engraved, 3'' h., 19th century, bulbous body with flared neck, engraved floral pattern, marked "SS" possibly Sunshing **1,200.00**
Mug
  4'' h., 19th century, cylindrical with scrolled handle, chased with scrolling foliage on a stippled ground **450.00**
  $4\frac{1}{2}''$ h., conical form, relief decoration of faceless warriors in clouds, on waves and by a pavilion, applied with a loop handle in the form of a dragon. **475.00**

Left to right: Card Case, $4\frac{1}{8}''$ h. x $2\frac{3}{4}''$ l., circa 1865, stamped KHC, Khe Cheong. $950.00. Collection of Dr. and Mrs. Daoust; Card Case, 4'' h. x $2\frac{5}{8}''$ l., circa 1870-1875, stamped WH 90, Wang Hing. $700.00. Collection of Dr. & Mrs. Daoust

Mug, 3¾" h., circa 1860, tree twig handle, Sun Shing, $650.00. Collection of Dr. and Mrs. Daoust.

Salt Salvers, 4⅞" l., circa 1820, rectangular form, rim applied with bands of straight gadroons leading to shell and acanthus-leaf handles, raised on shell feet, four stamps: "W" and psuedo hallmarks, probably Wongshing **3,000.00**

Tea Service

three pieces, 5" h., circa 1860-1880, teapot, sugar and creamer embossed with panels of domestic scenes, flowers and dragons, total weight 31 oz. **2,475.00**

five pieces, kettle on stand 14½" h., circa 1900, marked "C.J. Sterling", comprising a creamer, sugar, teapot, tongs and hot water kettle and stand, each piece with a hammered surface embossed with bamboo in original fitted wooden boxes, total weight 78 oz. **2,475.00**

five pieces, teapot 4½" h., circa 1890, marked "He Chang, MT and Leunwo Zhao Ji, Shanghai" comprising a teapot, sugar, creamer, and sugar tongs, each of compressed globular lobed form with repoussé and incised decoration of various flowers, figures and dragons, all on a matte ground, minor dents, teapot cover unhinged, total weight 29 oz. . . . **1,650.00**

Toiletry Set, three brushes, a shoe horn, a mirror frame, and a covered soap dish with Chinese courtyard scenes, possibly Gem Wo, marked with "GW" and HeChand in Chinese characters **4,600.00**

Tray, footed, 19th century, Tuck Chang and Co., round form, reticulated rim, engraved decoration, the center with a monogram, approx. 55 oz. **2,400.00**

CHINESE FURNITURE

History: Early examples of Chinese furniture prior to the third century B.C. have survived. Abundant evidence from the Han Dynasty (202 B.C.–220 A.D.) such as picture tiles, wall paintings, stone engravings, and frescoes from tomb chambers give a vivid picture of life, including the use of furniture. Because of cold climate, houses in north China were heated by flues that ran under the elevated, brick-lined floors. The floor was covered by mats and people lived close to the floor, as they still do in northern China, as well as in Korea and Japan where Chinese traditions prevailed. People slept on futons spread over the floor or on low platform beds. Furniture was low; it included couches and tables, stools and benches, armrests and other small items.

Controversy prevails over whether the chair was introduced to China by the Chinese themselves as an independent invention; through India, by Buddhist missionaries via the Silk Road at the beginning of the Christian era, or earlier by northern nomads, because Han records refer to the *hu ch'unag* or barbarian (non-Chinese) bed, which was probably a folding stool or platform. Until the end of the first millennium, chairs were reserved for Buddhist clerics or important people. Ennin, a Japanese priest who kept a diary of his stay in China during the mid-eighth century, noted that the minister of state and the military inspector, together with senior secretaries, deputy secretaries and administrative officers of the prefecture, all were seated on chairs drinking tea. People generally sat on chairs cross-legged, in the same way they sat on mats, rather than with legs pendent as we do now. Gradually, chairs and associated furniture were adopted by the ordinary people.

After about 1000 A.D. chairs became widely used. As a result of this changed mode of living, existing furniture was modified and new styles were introduced. High tables and stands of all sorts, desks for writing, tall cupboards, and altar coffers came into use. Post-tenth-century literary descriptions, paintings, and tomb furnishings are useful for tracing the evolution of fashions and styles in furniture.

Some furniture has survived from the Ming dynasty (1368–1644), and much more from the Ch'ing (1644–1916). It belongs to two main groups—lacquered wood and hardwood. Lacquered furniture tended to be ornate and was mainly used in temples and palaces. Lacquer was applied in layers (sometimes of different colors, e.g., red, green, and yellow) to a core, then designs were carved into the lacquer to varying depths. When there were multicolored layers of lacquer, a many-colored picture emerged. Ming craftsmen applied the technique of lacquer carving (hitherto used for decorating small items such as boxes and trays) to furniture. Carved lacquer thrones, tables, and cupboards in the palaces of Peking and in museums are *tours de force* of craftsmanship.

Lacquer can be worked in several other ways. Some furniture is decorated by means of incised and colored lacquer; that is, after a design is incised into a lacquer surface, the incision marks are then filled with gilt or colored paints to produce a picture or design. Others were first given a lacquer coating and then inlaid with mother-of-pearl, precious and semiprecious stones, coral, ivory, or exotic woods. Still others were first painted with dark lacquer and then decorated in gilt and polychrome colors. Finally, a woodem surface that was covered with fine layers of mud and grass fiber could be outlined into a picture; within these outlines, the mud and grass surface would be shallowly carved and hollowed out and then painted. Furniture and especially folding screens so decorated were very popular both in China and the West. Large quantities were imported to Europe by the British East India Company, where they were called "Coromandel" lacquer (from the Indian port where the pieces from China were transshipped).

Fine furniture for well-to-do people was made of hardwood, some indigenously grown, others imported from Japan and Southeast Asia. Most of the prized hardwoods belong to the Leguminosae (rosewood) family and go by such popular Chinese names as *huang-hua-li*, *hung-mu*, and *tzu-t'an*. They tended to be made in simple design to emphasize perfect proportion and the beauty of the wood grain and texture. Chinese cabinetry was also distinguished for fine joinery techniques. As Robert Ellsworth (*Chinese Furniture*, p. 58) noted; "Chinese joinery represents the most elaborate development of the miter, mortise and tenon join ever conceived. Though simple in its general effect, this join is complex and is usually coupled with a floating tongue-and-groove panel, creating a superlative combination of structure and surface. If the floating panel needs further support, a dovetail, transverse brace is added." Glue is seldom used; nails and screws never. Thus an expert cabinetmaker can knock down and reassemble any piece with ease.

Scholars prized eccentric accent pieces such as tables and chairs made from gnarled tree roots, sometimes further carved to heighten the rustic and unusual effect. Likewise, burlwood is prized when made into accent pieces or used as inlay. In addition, porcelain garden stools and stands were popular decorative pieces in gardens and terraces. Porcelain, cloisonné, enamel, and marble plaques were also inlaid in wooden frames to embellish and decorate tabletops, folding screens, and chairs. The seating surface of chairs were of either wood or covered with woven mat.

Loose cushions and seats covers were added for comfort and decoration. Upholstered chairs with innersprings were unknown in China. Mounts such as lockplates, hinges, handles, hooks, and pulls were made from metal, sometimes silver or bronze, but commonly white or yellow brass; they were plain or embellished with incising.

Less costly furniture was made from a variety of softwoods such as elm, ash, and pine. Bamboo was also widely used for furniture, ranging from very inexpensive pieces for daily use by poor people to fine artistic pieces from decorative bamboos with exotic patterns.

Finally, most of the materials mentioned above were also used by cabinetmakers to manufacture household items such as lamp or candle stands, washing stands, ice chests, clothes chests, document and seal chests, mirror frames, toiletry cases, scroll cases, and brushpots. Craftsmen often lavished special attention on the small pieces used by ladies in their toilet and gentlemen in their study.

References: Michel Beurdeley, *Chinese Furniture*, translated from the French by Katherine Watson, Kodansha International, 1979; Gustave Ecke *Chinese Domestic Furniture*, Charles E. Tuttle Co., Inc., 1962; Robert H. Ellsworth, *Chinese Furniture: Hardwood Examples of the Ming and Early Ch'ing Dynasties*, Random House, Inc., n.d.; Charles P. Fitzgerald, *Barbarian Beds: The Origin of the Chair in China*, The Crescent Press, 1965; R. Soame Jenyns and William Watson, *Chinese Art II: Silver, Later Bronzes, Cloisonné, Canton Enamel, Lacquer, Furniture, Wood*, Rizzoli International Publishers, Inc., 1966; George N. Kate, *Chinese Household Furniture*, Dover Publications, Inc., 1948; Shixiang Wang, translated by Wang Shinxiang, Lark E. Mason, Jr., and others, *Connoissuership of Chinese Furniture—Ming and Early Qing Dynasties*, 2 vols., Art Media Resources, Ltd., 1990.

Museums: Honolulu Academy of Art, Honolulu, Hawaii; Metropolitan Museum of Art, New York, New York; Royal Ontario Museum, Toronto, Canada; Victoria and Albert Museum, London, England; National Historical Museum, Taipei, Taiwan.

Collecting Hints: Chinese furniture was made by anonymous craftsmen and was never signed. Moreover, many of the main furniture forms and workmanship did not change in style for several hundred years. It is thus impossible to be precise in the dating of any given piece, and one should be very suspicious of any claims of exact age and attribution.

The collector should first of all consult books on Chinese furniture and be acquainted with the types of wood commonly available and shapes and styles. Veneer was never used in Chinese furniture. Although the classical styles developed during the Ming Dynasty persisted, subtle changes occurred. This is especially true of furniture made during the latter part of the nineteenth century, when taste favored the ornate and heavily carved pieces.

A practiced eye will be able to pick out the older pieces because they are made with large planks of wood not available in later times, they have a richness of patina that only time can impart, they have sure proportions, and they possess integrity of decoration. The inside and under surfaces of old pieces are also generally protected with a layer of light-colored lacquer. Also look for wear, especially on the feet; old pieces should have wear. Look for altered and reduced pieces as well. Caned seats were fragile and most frequently replaced, sometimes with hard wooden seats. Pieces were altered, sometimes to make a common form rare, to give an impractical piece a modern usefulness, or to suit modern tastes. For example, chairs were reduced in height so that thick padded cushions could be added to make them more comfortable by modern standards. Many tables and desks were also shortened to accommodate Western preference. Damaged pieces were sometimes salvaged and altered, for example, a damaged large piece could be cut down.

Finally, Chinese furniture makers are still making traditional-style furniture by traditional methods. Such pieces are often well made and have intrinsic merit but are, nevertheless, reproductions. Traditional designs are also adapted and modified for modern use that were unknown in China, such as extension dining tables and glass-fronted curio cabinets.

Advisor: Jiu-Hwa Upshur, PhD

INLAID FURNITURE

Cabinet, rare hardstone mounted black lacquer, 79½" h. x 50½" l. x 25" w, 17th/18th century, the doors and shaped apron decorated with flowers and vessels set in hardstones, the sides, drawers, and interior surfaces decorated with flowers and bamboo painted in gilt, yellow brass mountings **8,000.00**

screen, six-fold hardwood mounted famille verte porcelain screens, 72½" h. x 93" w., 19th century, each panel with five shaped porcelain plaques painted with birds and flowers **5,500.00**

Table, circular, occasional, 19th century, with a grey marble inset top above pierced and carved apron, frieze and stretchers, with eight matching carved and marble inset stools **4,500.00**

Cabinet, 53½" h., x 39½" l. x 19¾" w., black lacquer and gilt decorated, the doors open to reveal a sliding stand and a shaped cut-out to the back panel, above a row of small double doors, the exterior decorated in gilt with phoenix and officials. $1,550.00. Courtesy of Butterfield and Butterfield.

tables, pair, square, 32" h., late 19th century, mother-of-pearl, the tops inset with shaped marble panels, the sides with carved and pierced aprons and single shelves **950.00**

table screen, hardwood, 18⅞" h. x

Table screen, 17¾" h., 18½" w., 19th century, marble inlaid, the Tali marble with a natural landscape scene, set in a frame above a stand with carved scrolling ends. $650.00. Courtesy of Professor Jiu Hwa Upshur.

Screen, each panel 72" h. x 15¾" w., early 19th century, four panels, the black lacquer delicately applied with ivory, mother-of-pearl, wood, agate, and other hardstones to depict a continuous scene of immortals riding fabulous beasts and others amid trees and in a pavilion, the reverse painted with birds and trees in gilt, set on brass-covered straight feet. $8,200.00.

Display cabinet, 50½" h. x 36½" l. x 14" w., hardwood, decorated with ivory overlay on sliding doors, simulated bamboo frame. $1,500.00. Courtesy of Butterfield and Butterfield.

18" w., 19th century, with a figured marble plaque set in a wood frame and stand 500.00

LACQUER FURNITURE

Armchair, black and gilt lacquered, 18/19th century, with key pattern fretwork back splats and arm supports, centered by two carved wood panels, the solid seat with simple apron molded square legs joined by stretchers, decorated all over in gilt with flower sprays, and roundels. . .   3,200.00

Armchairs with removable seats, set of six, carved cinnabar, 18th/19th century, each with a circular medallion set in the back panel, slightly downswept arms, the legs joined by stretchers, carved with landscape scenes, scrolls, flowers and plants   4,600.00

Benches, pair, 39½" l. x 17½" h., 18th century, each with a rectangular panel top above an apron carved with scrolls, set on four fluted supports joined by end stretchers, carved overall with red lacquer. . . .   2,500.00

Clothes rack, red lacquer, 77" h. x 71" w., 19th century, the upper cross bar with dragon-head tips, above central cross support carved with dragon panels, on a tresel base   1,250.00

Screen, Coromandel, eight-fold, 78" h. x 72" w., 19th century, each panel depicting elegant figures in a garden setting, the reverse painted with exotic birds and plants 6,000.00

Stand, red lacquer, 34¾" h., 18th century, the top, sides, apron, and legs all delicately and elaborately carved with flowers, key-patterns, Buddhist emblems and dragons, on cabriole legs, ... 17,999.00

SCHOLAR'S DESK ITEMS (WOOD)

Brushpot

5¾" h., cylindrical form, 18th century, bamboo, well carved and pierced with a scene of scholars gathered amid a landscape of trees, rocks and bridge, the material of a rich dark red color 1,800.00

cylindrical form, 11" h., 18th century, huang-hua-li, carved to resemble a gnarled trunk, the wood of reddish brown color 900.00

Carving

Bamboo carving of a mountain, 12½'' h., 18th/19th century, deeply pierced and carved throughout with figures, pavillions, rivers, trees and bridges set amid rocky mountain ledges, stained reddish-brown **5,000.00**

Rootwood carving of an ascetic, 7½'' h., 18th century, the natural form embelished to represent a bearded, stooped man, wrapped in a cloak fashioned from the outer layer of the wood, the wood of reddish to dark brown tones . . **2,400.00**

WOODEN FURNITURE

Altar coffer

Huanghuali, 68½'' l. x 19½'' w. x 33½'' h., 17th century, the front with three small drawers above a pair of cupboards, with incised white brass mounts. **22,000.00**

Hongmu, burlwood inset, 40'' h., 76'' l., 19th century, the framed rectangular top continuing to upward turned ends, the front with a pair of drawers over two cupboard doors, deeply carved in high relief with dragons amid swirling clouds, the stiles continuing down to form feet **2,800.00**

Altar table

Carved hardwood, 32¾'' h. x 48'' l., late 19th/early 20th century, the long rectangular top supported on four carved legs terminating in scroll feet and joined by an apron

Altar Table, 38'' h. x 81½'' l. x 19¾'' w., rosewood, the rectangular top set above a pierced apron of tubular squared scrolls joined to four rectangular supports. $1,350.00. Courtesy Butterfield and Butterfield.

carved in low relief with dragon-ended squared scrolls. **1,500.00**

Hongmu, 33'' h. x 44'' l., the panel inset with downward scroll ends pierced with cloud bands centering a pierced frieze on trestle-form supports headed by flower heads and horsetails **1,400.00**

Hardwood, 33'' h. x 82'' l., the rectangular top above a freize carved with flowers and vines and rectangular legs **850.00**

Armchair

Pair, 18/19th century, elmwood horseshoe back each with U-shaped crestrail, paneled splat and wood panel seat, the feet joined by stretchers **2,000.00**

Pair, carved hongmu, 40'' h., 19th century, with serpentine crest rail over a panel carved with mask device and flanking scrolls, the rectangular seat on straight legs ending in inward curved toes . . . **1,500.00**

Bed, elmwood, 32'' h. x 80'' l. x 39'' w., 18th century, lowback, the rear and side panels carved in high relief with scrolling dragons within beaded framework, the bed surface in cane work, set on straight legs with hoof feet **3,500.00**

Cabinet

Hongmu, low cabinet, 24'' h. x 55'' l., the rectangular superstructure centering a pair of openwork doors and two short drawers, with cupboard doors flanking, above a rectangular stand with short inward curves. **800.00**

softwood, 33'' h. x 27'' l. x 16'' w., 19th century, with a pair of drawers above the doors, standing on straight feet **700.00**

Hungmu, 62'' l. x 14¼'' w. x 14¼'' h., 19th century, low with three drawers set between two wood panels, set above a carved freize, the four rectangular legs over hoof feet **1,000.00**

Cabinet and Hat chest (Gui), large, Huanghuali, 101½'' h. x 50¼'' l. x 25¼'' w., 17th century, in two sections, each of rectangular outline, the hat chest with a pair of hinged doors with an open interior resting atop the cabinet which has a pair of hinged doors opening to an interior with a single shelf containing a pair of short drawers, on a bracket feet joined by flange brackets, the surface with both veneered and solid panels, much early black and red lacquer and undercoat remaining, the interior now stained **10,000.00**

Chairs

Pair of armchairs, gilt-decorated, Hongmu, 19th century, each with a pierced angular scroll, the backrest and arms decorated with gilt flowers, bats and scrolls, with a solid-panel seat on rectangular legs ending at block toes **2,800.00**

Pair of Hongmu carved corner chairs, 19th century, each with a carved frame of simulated bamboo, the back carved and pierced with prunus, the solid seat on legs of circular section joined by a stretcher **1,800.00**

Pair of elm side chairs, 18th/19th century, each with a low back and rectangular splat, with a hard cane seat on rounded beaded legs **1,400.00**

Pair of elmwood yokeback armchairs, 18th century, each with vigorously scrolled crests, S-scrolled rectangular splats and scrolling arms above a paneled seat, the rounded legs framed by a scrolling apron and long flange brackets **2,600.00**

Pair, hungmu, late 19th century, each side chair with a pierced splat and elaborately carved frame above solid seat on supports joined by stretchers **1,200.00**

Pair of huanghuali low yokeback side chairs, 17th/18th century, each shaped top rail above an S-curved splat, the rectangular seat

Arm Chairs, Pair, 38" h., 18th/19th century, in chi-chih mu, backrests and arms of angular fretwork and splats inset with panels of intricate landscape scenes carved from hongmu, the seats of woven cane, most of the wooden surface decorated in colored painted lacquer. $5,800.00.

Chairs, Pair, 35" h., 19th century, hardwood, horseshoe shaped, each with elegant slender curved back. solid splat on shaped supports above an apron, and on square supports joined by stretchers. $2,000.00.

with inset cane panel on circular legs joined by plain stretchers . . . **6,000.00**

Cosmetic box, huanghuali, brass mounted, 10¼" h. x 10¾" w., 18th century, the square hinged top opens to a shallow compartment, above a pair of doors that open to four drawers, above a flush base . . . **1,200.00**

Desk

Carved Hongmu, 32" h., the rectangular paneled top supported on four straight legs terminating in hoof feet, a row of three drawers carved with shou characters and archaic scrolls above two similarly carved drawers flanking the knee-hole **1,500.00**

Hongmu, 48" w. x 33" h., 19th century, with four drawers with yellow brass mountings, the rectangular legs joined by a fretwork shelf stretcher carved in a cracked-ice pattern **1,500,00**

hongmu pedestal

32" h. x 15½" l., late 19th/early 20th century, the framed top with three brass mounted frieze drawers supported on two pedestals each with two drawers over latticework shelves **1,600.00**

33½" h., the top 24½" w. x 55" l., 19th century, the rectangular top above a row of three metal-fitted drawers and supported on a pair of pedestals, each with two drawers and an open shelf **2,500.00**

Display cabinet

Hongmu, 55" h. x 36" l., 20" w., rectangular with a pair of glazed doors enclosing an arrangement of shelves **1,200.00**

Two sections, carved hardwood,

Scroll Pot, 8½" h. x 12½" d., 18th/19th century, of irregular shape, the reticulated sides formed by the knots of the ancient tree root, the wood of dark reddish brown. $1,500.00.

Vitrine, 72½" h. x 35¾" l. x 15" w., rosewood, pierced pediment of fruit vines over a central glass-panel door with conforming canted sides, the framework carved as banboo and raised on four curved supports. $950.00. Courtesy of Butterfield and Butterfield.

85" h. x 38½" w., 19th century, the cornice carved and pierced with dragons confronting pearls, the glazed doors enclosing asymmetrical interior shelves, the whole carved in relief with flowers...................... **1,650.00**

Display Cabinets, burlwalnut, 90" h. x 40" l., 19th century ... **4,200.00**

Garden seats, pair, barrel shaped, 20½" h., 19th century, hardwood with circular marble top above pierced sides, standing on four shaped feet................. **1,900.00**

Lamps (hanging), pair, hongmu, 29" h., 19th century, each of hexagonal form, carved in pierced relief with dragon heads and fretwork panels of flowers, enclosing glass panels **900.00**

Marble-Inset Stands
Pair, 33" h. x 16" w., 19th century, each carved in relief with flowers, birds and vines, on five cabriole legs joined by a shaped stretcher   **900.00**
Pair, 33" h. and 20" h., late 19th century, raised on five legs joined by a spiral pentagonal stretcher, the apron, legs and rim carved

with prunus blossoms, the top inset with marble; together with a five-legged small stand, the apron carved with foliage, the knees with phoenix heads, the top inset with a conforming marble panel, cracked.................. **1,600.00**

Seal chest, huanghuali, 15½" h. x 14½" l. x 10¾" w., 17th century, the flat hinged cover opening to an interior with a removable tray and four differing short drawers, on an outset base, retaining most of the original brass mounts, the central hexagonal lobed escutcheon decorated with rockwork and flowering lotus vines, the lower plate with similar decoration and twin-fish pulls, each hinge with lotus blossoms, the chest with several well-figured panels....... **2,000.00**

Stool
hardwood, 16½" h., 19th century,

Traveling Box, Cover and Stand, 9½" h. x 13¾" l. x 7¼" w., 19th century, hongmu the entire external surface intricately carved with inscribed cash cartouches, surrounded by geometric patterns, the three deep trays, a shallow top tray and the cover fitting into a stand with inverted U-handle attached with shaped brackets and locked by a long brass pin, brass mounts. $800.00.

Stools, pair, 20½″ h., barrel form, 18th/ 19th century, hongmu, brocade, the circular top set with burlwood, supported on five curved legs each pierced with an aperture, the plain apron below the boss embellished seat, and repeated above the ring base supported on five trefoil pad feet. $2,500.00.

with solid panels forming the legs, the front with fret spandrels	375.00
Stools, square, pair, hongmu, 19½″ square, 19½″ h., 17th century, the seats in woven matting, the straight legs joined by stretchers below waisted aprons	3,500.00
Side tables, pair, hongmu, semi-circular 33″ h. x 45″ l., 19th century, the paneled top on four cabriole legs supported on hoof feet and joined by an apron carved in low relief with lingzhi fungus stands	2,400.00

CHINESE IMARI

History: Chinese Imari porcelain was first produced in Ching-te chen (Jingdezhen) in an effort to wean away this important export market from Japan, which was doing a brisk trading business with the Dutch East India Company. China copied the Kakiemon style as well as Imari decoration. Their production included barber bowls, cups and saucers, teapots, covered bowls, dinner services (which sometimes included family crests), and other porcelains of Western form.

We have records that Imari armorial export porcelain was already established sometime in the very early eighteenth century. The first Chinese Imari dinner service produced with a coat of arms was created in 1705 for export to England. Factory notes written during the reign of Emperor Yongzhen (1723–1735) indicate that copies of Japanese Imari wares were in production at that time.

The trade between the Dutch East India Company and Jingdezhen was very brisk toward the end of the eighteenth century. The Chinese seized this opportunity to grab the entire Imari market away from Japan. They produced copies of the "old" Imari wares (decorated with underglaze blue and overglaze iron red and gold) that rivaled Japan's and were able to export them at much lower prices. They were so successful in capturing this market that the Dutch East India Company did not renew their contract with Japan at the close of the eighteenth century.

Japan later renewed its trade in Imari with the West in the latter half of the nineteenth century. When several Imari designers presented their outstanding wares at international exhibitions, the world once again turned to Japan for the export of these colorful porcelains. The late nineteenth and early twentieth centuries saw Japanese Imari exported in massive quantities. By then, Chinese Imari had fallen into disfavor as a profitable export ware and had been replaced by Famille Rose pattern ware (heavily exported to Europe) and the Nanking and Canton blue and white patterns (heavily exported to America). (See: Japanese Imari; Kakiemon.)

References: Warren Cox, *Pottery and Porcelain*, 2 vols., Crown Publishers, 1970; D. F. Lunsingh Scheurleer, *Chinese Export Porcelain (Chine de Commande)*, Pitman Publishing, 1974.

Museums: San Francisco City Art Museum, San Francisco, California; Boston City Art Museum, Boston, Massachusetts; Museum of Fine Arts, Boston, Massachusetts; Brooklyn Museum, Brooklyn, New York; Metropolitan Museum of Art, New York, New York; Seattle Museum of Art, Seattle, Washington; British Museum, London, England; Victoria and Albert Museum, London, England; Tetar van Elven Museum, Delft, the Netherlands; Rijksmuseum, Amsterdam, the Netherlands; Topkapi Saray Palace Museum, Istanbul, Turkey.

Reproduction Alert: Imari reproductions abound (see Japanese Imari), but there do not seem to be any reproductions that single out Chinese Imari per se.

Collecting Hints: The differences between Chinese and Japanese Imari are not immediately obvious to the eye. Close examination, however, will reveal deviations in the porcelain body, glaze, and enamel colors. The Chinese porcelain body is thinner, lighter, and whiter than its Japanese counterpart. The clay is denser and smoother, the Japanese ware having a somewhat "sandy" texture. The Chinese glaze has a greenish tone while the Japanese glaze is greyish. The red enamel is significantly different; the Chinese red is a thinly applied coral tone, the Japanese is a heavy, opaque "Indian" red. Color differences apply in the use of yellow and green as well; the Chinese yellow appears darker than the Japanese, and their green is more pure than the somewhat bluish green of Japan.

If one discovers the presence of spur marks on the base of a piece, there is no need to examine it any further. The Chinese never used spurs in their Imari production. Spurs, which supported the porcelain in the kiln while it was being fired, are atypical of Chinese ceramic production in general.

Chinese Imari does not dominate the Imari collecting field; the Japanese products are in much greater supply. Chinese Imari ware was produced primarily in the eighteenth century and does not have the range of design motifs that seems to attract a wide range of collectors. Imari is of particular interest to the collector of Chinese porcelains as an example of eighteenth-century ceramics; to collectors of armorial porcelain (when monogrammed); to the Dutch, who are ardent collectors of all Imari wares; and to the Japanese, who in recent years have shown a strong interest in collecting the export wares of China.

Bowl, 10¼″ dia., 18th century, the deep bowl tapering to a high foot ring, decorated in underglaze blue, gilt and shades of red enamel with a bird perched on rockwork issuing lush flowering peonies bordered by a garden gate, the interior rim with a narrow band of floral reserves on a diaper-patterned ground, hairline crack, surface wear **305.00**

Dish
9″ dia., Kangxi, painted in underglaze blue, iron-red and gilding with a basket of flowers in the center, the well and the rim with panels enclosing birds, a Buddhist

Plate, 9″ dia., 18th century, the floral motif painted with underglaze blue, red, green, and gilt enamels. $400.00.

lion and flowers separated with other floral sprays. **1,200.00**
10¾″ dia., (pair), 18th century, the interiors painted with a figure in a willow overlooking a lady in a courtyard setting, encircled by a prunus-blossom-decorated iron-red "cracked ice" band around the cavetto, below shaped panels enclosing boys at play reserved on a floral diaper band on the everted rim, underglaze firing cracks, chips, glaze gaps **1,100.00**
12″, Kangxi period, deep, round dish decorated on front and back **1,950.00**
Punch bowl, 16″ dia., 18th century, interior design of flowers overflowing a jardiniere, decorated in underglaze blue, red and gilt enamels, the exterior of the bowl left unglazed and undecorated. **1,100.00**

Plate, 9″ dia., 18th century, decorated with floral medallion encircled at the cavetto by a diaper pattern band with reserves of carp. $350.00. Courtesy of Butterfield and Butterfield.

Rose Water Sprinkler, 8¼″ h., 18th century, lobed shaped, decorated in underglaze blue and red enamels with small reserves of a single blossom, a bronze sheath at the lip rim, chip at the lip under sheath. $850.00.

Saucer dish., 11″ dia., c. 1700, decorated in underglaze blue, iron-red and gilding with a central medallion enclosing flowers encircled by leaf shaped panels with flowers, chip . .   **1,400.00**

Tankard, 6⅜″ h., 18th century, decorated with a flower filled basket and other floral sprigs in underglaze blue, iron-red and gilt **875.00**

Teapot and cover, 8″ h., Kangxi, decorated in underglaze blue, iron-red, and gilding with a continuous scene of boys on a terrace and ladies in a pavilion, fritting **1,600.00**

CINNABAR

History: Cinnabar is a term applied to the Chinese art form of carved lacquer. The raw lacquer was obtained from the resinous sap of the "lacquer" tree and went through several treatments, including its combination with native ground cinnabar for coloration, before it was suitable to be applied to its foundation. All colors, when carved, are classified under the general term cinnabar, although technically the term should be used exclusively for the red carved wares (T'i Hung). The lacquer was applied layer by layer upon a wood or metal base. As many as 200 layers may have been applied to form a base thick enough to carve. The application was accomplished by brush or spatula. The most frequently encountered and preferred color is a deep red, although other colors were used. The variety of colors employed the use of natural or chemical ingredients mixed with the lac to achieve the desired shade. Another type of "false" cinnabar (Tui Hung) was made by applying a putty, over which a thin layer of cinnabar lacquer was applied.

Carved red lacquer became popular during the Yuan Dynasty, but the cinnabar coating was too thin and did not hold up well. Written records of the Ming Dynasty support the fact that good cinnabar lacquer was being produced during the reigns of Yonglo and Xuante. Red and black cinnabar also was being produced at this time. Carved marbleized lacquer consisting of red, black, and yellow also were produced, although the date of their origin is somewhat obscure; some scholars date it back as far as the Tang Dynasty. Marbleized lacquer sometimes appears with the addition of the color green and various shades of red. Oftentimes the rims of cinnabar objects were protected by a sheath of metal.

Although the art of lacquering declined during the troubled times of the late Ming Dynasty, the art was revived by the eighteenth century Qing emperors. By this time the gouge as a tool had begun to replace the knife for cutting details in cinnabar, resulting in a speedy method of carving and allowing for more intricate patterns. Diaper pattern backgrounds began to become popular. It was not unusual to find signatures, dates, and poems executed in carved calligraphy. The centers for carved lacquer were at Peking and Soochow. Curiously, no signed or dated pieces have been found to suggest the imperial patronage of the first two Qing emperors. The art is said to have reached its zenith during the reign of Emperor Qianlong, who ordered cinnabar furniture as well as small items to decorate the palace. He had a series of pictures carved with brown lacquer applied over the red cinnabar. They were carved while the brown crust was still warm, resulting in a variety of color in the completed work. Tables, screens, chairs, couches, and other furniture as well as small cinnabar objects were produced for the Qianlong court. Occasionally, hard stones and precious metals were inlaid in the carvings.

Qianlong porcelain and cinnabar production both deteriorated in quality in the later years of his reign.

References: Stephen W. Bushell, *Chinese Art*, Rare Reprints Inc., 1977; Sir Harry Garner, *Chinese Lacquer*, Faber and Faber, Inc. 1979; —, *Masterpieces of Chinese Carved Lacquer Ware in the National Palace Museum*, Taipai, 1971.

Museums: Honolulu Academy of Arts, Honolulu, Hawaii; Nelson Gallery of Art, Kansas City, Kansas; Museum of Fine Arts, Boston, Massachusetts; Freer Gallery of Art, Washington, D.C.; Seattle Art Museum, Seattle, Washington; Palace Museum, Beijing, China; Museum of Denmark, Copenhagen, Denmark; British Museum, London, England; Victoria and Albert Museum, London, England; Royal Scottish Museum, Edinburgh, Scotland; Museum of Far Eastern Antiquities, Stockholm, Sweden; National Palace Museum, Taipai, Taiwan.

Reproduction Alert: A type of "molded" cinnabar (not hand-carved) appeared during the late eighteenth century. Such items are often signed with the Ming marks of Chenghua and Zhendge, which were not used on cinnabar during the Ming Dynasty. Molded items, when closely inspected, will not show any evidence of knife cuts. True hand-carved cinnabar from the eighteenth century should reveal excellent carving with fine, rounded and smooth edges on the design. Rough edges are typical of later production. This feature, along with the presence of a bright red color, indicate late-nineteenth- to twentieth-century attribution.

Collecting Hints: Since early cinnabar was manufactured for imperial use, much of it has been well cared for and has survived. Excellent museum displays are available. The British Museum has an outstanding collection on view.

Collecting Chinese cinnabar has never been very popular. Since supplies of good old carved pieces are scarce, it is not an item frequently seen in the antiques market. Well-carved, genuine items from the eighteenth century are still to be found, however, as "sleepers" in the antiques marketplace. It should also be mentioned that cinnabar was also carved as gems to be set in jewelry. The surrounding metal was often a low-grade silver or silver plate. Pendant ornaments and bracelets using this combination, dating to the first half of this century, are still readily available.

Bowl, 5" dia., signed "Qianlong" on
   base, heavily carved with scenes of
   children playing in a garden, chips   **400.00**
Box and cover
   6½" dia., late 18th century, shallow,
   carved in crisp relief on finely cut
   brocade patterned ground with
   panels of flowering branches to
   the sides and a figure by a palace
   in a river landscape to the center
   of the cover **800.00**
   8" l., early 20th century, stamped
   "China" on base, rectangular, the
   lid carved with human figures on
   diaper pattern, floral reserves on
   diaper pattern on the body **150.00**
   11½" dia., 18th/19th century, flower
   shaped, the cover carved with a
   panel enclosing two Immortals
   and an attendant in a mountainous landscape within a border of
   peaches, flowers and bats, the
   sides and box decorated with
   swirling waves, splits, chips, res-
   torations **2,750.00**
   12" w. x 9" x 3½" h., early 20th
   century, rectangular, carved with
   flowering peony sprays, the cover
   inset with a serpentine plaque
   carved with a basket of flowers,
   the interior and base black-lac-
   quered **390.00**
   12" dia., 6½" h., 19th century, com-
   pressed globular form, deeply
   carved to the top with a scene of
   gentlemen in a garden engaged in
   leisurely pursuits, a pavilion to the
   left, rocky outcroppings and trees
   scattered throughout, the sides
   and base decorated with roundels
   depicting scenes of children in
   landscape settings on a ground of
   peonies and foliate meander, the
   raised foot with keyfret pattern below a band of stylized lotus lap-
   pets, wear, minor chipping **1,400.00**

   12¾" dia., 16th century Ming,
   incised six-character mark of
   Xuande on the base of octagonal
   foliate section, carved in the center with officials, attendants, boys
   and equestrian figures in a garden
   setting all reserved on various flo-
   ret-diaper ground within a slightly
   concave band following the shape
   of the rim, the frieze of flower
   blooms, the underside similarly
   decorated above the narrow foot
   decorated with a band of key-fret,
   the base and footrim lacquered in
   black, splits, minor losses **17,600**
   15¾" dia., 18th century, lobed body,
   carved with eight floral panels and
   a pavilion scene on the cover . . .   **3,500.00**
   18" dia., fluted, 19th century, the
   cover carved with nine romping fu
   lions amid ribbon-tied florets and
   shou medallions, the fluted sides
   with the bajixiang amid flowers,
   the box with fruiting sprigs **800.00**
Dish
   8½" dia., barbed rim, Qianlong,
   marked with a six character mark
   on a brass plaque set in the base,
   high relief carving of children
   playing in a fenced garden **950.00**
   8½" dia., late 18th/early 19th cen-
   tury, foliate brass rim, scene of
   figures in pavilion on a diaper
   ground, the reverse an all over di-
   aper pattern **375.00**
   Pair, 9¾" dia., each well carved in
   relief through cinnabar to the dark
   brown ground with a phoenix
   standing on a rock with outstretched wings, surrounded by
   leafy peony flower sprays beneath
   a ruyi-cloud encircled sun, the reverse encircled by a floral frieze
   above the slightly tapering foot . .   **875.00**
Figural box, Ram form, 8" h. x
   10¾" l., late 19th century, the head
   with long curved horns and bared
   teeth, the exterior carved with a formal design of stylized confronted
   dragons and taotieh masks **850.00**
Game box, 11⅞" x 13¼" x 4⅝", gilt
   decorated black lacquer, late 18th/
   early 19th century, of octagonal
   form, fitted with six covered boxes
   and twelve trays, the exterior decorated with figural scenes with floral
   and fruit borders raised detailing in
   crimson color, the inner sections all
   painted with garden scenes and fig-
   ures, rim chips **1,200.00**
Panel, 24" x 36", turn of the century,
   carved in high relief with a scene of

two scholars under a pine tree along with a dragon, wide border of key frets, the back lacquered black with two vertical supports **2,500.00**

Ruyi Sceptre, 16" l., 19th century, the terminal carved in low relief with dignitary attended by two boys bearing a peach and lingzhi fungus, the center with bats hovering about a peach cluster, the shaft with eight precious symbols, ending in a circular medallion decorated with double fish and silk tassel, restored **1,200.00**

Screen, with stand, 36⅝" h. x 26¾" w., 18th/19th century, rectangular, set in H shaped base, carved with elaborate figures among pine and willow trees overlooking boating figures on a river, the reverse in plain black lacquer, chips, splits, some black lacquer flaking **3,025.00**

Tea caddy, 6" h., 19th century, cylindrical form., showing deeply carved figures with mountains in the background **275.00**

Vase
9" h., turn of the century, stamped "China," flattened rectangular form with high shoulders, short neck and flared rim, both sides carved with figures seated on rockwork near a stream, mountains in the distance **200.00**

12" h., turn of the century, baluster form, decorated with a continuous scene of figures in a landscape, between wide lotus meander bands, the neck with floral reserves **440.00**

Vase, 15" h., hu form, pear shaped, shown with paired flanges below the everted rim, deeply carved with taotieh masks. $475.00. Courtesy of Butterfield and Butterfield.

20" h., 19th century, black and red, baluster form, decorated with birds, flowering peony, lotus and rocks in a black lacquer against red lacquer trellis ground, chips   **1,500.00**

FAMILLE ROSE AND ROSE PATTERN PORCELAIN

History: Famille rose is the French term for the opaque rose-pink color on Chinese porcelain. It is really not a name for a type of ware but instead describes a group of wares that employs a system of decoration using the color pink. Under this term, the amount of pink used in the decoration is not a criteria as long as it was created using the salts of gold. This special opaque pink color was achieved by the use of chloride of gold, which had previously only been used for decoration in Europe. When first adopted by the Chinese in the early eighteenth century, it was known in China as Tang Ts'ai, "foreign color." The first use of gold-derived famille rose pink is said to have begun in Peking, where it was used in the enamel-decorated copper pieces known today as Canton enamel. The use of this color quickly spread to use on porcelain.

A plate in the British Museum bearing the date 1721 proves that pink was incorporated into the Chinese palette during the Kangxi period. There are few examples of this dating, however, while there are many examples of pink polychrome decoration during the reign of Yongzheng and throughout the remainder of the eighteenth century.

The first motifs were usually floral, along with scenes of figures or poultry which sometimes appear in reserves placed centrally or evenly spaced around the borders. The border decoration appeared with finely executed diaper designs or linear patterns. Thinly potted "eggshell" plates with "ruby backs" (rose enamel on the back) first appeared during the Yongzheng period. Rose colors were used as decoration on vases, bowls, and dishes. Most experts agree that the very best of the early famille rose-painted decoration appears on eggshell-decorated porcelains of the early eighteenth century. Armorial designs using pink were also exported during this period. Emperor Qianlong took special interest in the Ku Yueh Hsuan rose-decorated wares at the early period of his reign. His poems are sometimes seen written in calligraphy on these rose decorated wares of the early period.

Pink was used along with opaque blue, yellow, purple, green, red, and black to form the famille rose palette of colors. It was favored by the court, and some of the most beautiful and delicate porcelains were produced during the early Qianlong period. In contrast to these subtle pieces, which were created to please the Chinese senses, European orders for porcelains decorated in rose pink tended to be excessively decorated.

Mass-produced pattern ware, created for export, became popular in the late eighteenth century with the introduction of the Rose Mandarin pattern. The pattern, named for a robed mandarin who is always depicted in the design, contains panels of ladies, children, and mandarins in garden settings. The panels are separated by elaborate mosaic borders of flowers, birds, and butterflies painted in polychrome enamels. The ladies always appear with gilt decoration in their hair. The pattern was manufactured to meet Western tastes, hence the cups appear with handles and the dinner plates are flat. The pattern appears on vases, bowls, and candlesticks as well. The Rose Mandarin pattern continued in popularity until about 1840, by which time other similar patterns had captured the European audience.

Very similar to the Mandarin design was the Rose Medallion pattern, which dates from the latter part of Jiaqing's reign (1796–1820). The pattern is arranged with alternating reserves of flowers, birds, and/or butterflies along with reserves of Chinese figures. The reserves are usually four in number and are evenly spaced around a center medallion. The areas between the panels are generally filled with rose-pink peonies and green foliage (early pieces can contain a gold ground color as well as gilt decoration in the womens' hairdos). The vast majority of nineteenth-century porcelain production was executed in Ching-te-chen, but the decoration was applied in Canton. Production of dinner sets with 144 pieces has been recorded; these sets often have additional ornamental and serving items.

Another popular pattern ware of the early nineteenth century was called Rose Canton. It is similar to Rose Medallion except for the subject matter in the medallions which, in this case, is flowers rather than people. Other Canton designs include people, but the medallion portions are absent. Various other pattern names that fall into the category of Rose Canton are Black Butterfly, Butterfly and Cabbage, Millefleur, Rooster, and Rose and Long Life, among others. In the most general sense, we can consider all rose-pink-decorated enamels that do not fall into the definition of Rose Medallion or Rose Mandarin as Rose Canton. (See: Armorial Export Porcelain; Chinese Export Porcelain; Cloisonné and Canton Enamels; Qing Dynasty Porcelain.)

References: Michel Beurdeley, *Chinese Trade Porcelain*, Charles E. Tuttle Co., Inc., 1969; Rose Kerr, *Chinese Ceramics Porcelain of the Qing Dynasty 1644–1911*; Margaret Medley, *The Chinese Potter*, Phaidon Press Ltd., 1976; D. F. Lunsingh Scheurleer, *Chinese Export Porcelain: Chine de Commande*, Pitman Publishing Co., 1974; George C. Williamson, *The Book of Famille Rose*, Charles E. Tuttle Co., 1985.

Museums: Most major museums that have permanent collections of Qing porcelain will have examples of early famille rose-decorated wares. Boston Museum of Fine Arts, Boston, Massachusetts; Metropolitan Museum of Art, New York, New York; Seattle Art Museum, Seattle, Washington; Smithsonian Institute, Washington, D.C.; British Museum, London, England; Sir Percival David Foundation, London, England; Victoria and Albert Museum, London, England; Grandidier Collection, Paris, France; The Louvre, Paris, France; Johanneum Museum, Dresden, Germany; Museum fur Kunsthandwerk, Frankfurt, Germany; National Museum, Singapore.

Reproduction Alert: Famille rose eggshell porcelains continue to be made in this century, as are the pattern ware designs. One must look for translucency and frequently found iridescence of color in the older famille rose pieces. Newer pieces do not show this iridescence, and the colors often are muddy. The modern pink shade also differs from the early sharp rose-pink, tending to a reddish or wine-colored pink with a dull appearance. Some very finely executed eggshell porcelains were made during the reign of Daoguang in the nineteenth century and signed with a Kangxi mark. Other notably fine work was produced by the Jiangxi Porcelain Company in the 1920s and 1930s. Do not be fooled by the eggshell or semi-eggshell porcelains that are appearing in vases on todays' market. The application of a black border, sloppily executed, and a rough paste footing do not compare with the delicate work and smooth paste of eighteenth-century derivation. Many of these recent pieces appear with an orange-colored Qianlong seal mark stamped on their bases. When they appear in red, original Qianlong marks are usually from late in his reign. However, they always were hand-painted in a true iron red.

If you encounter an eggshell teacup with a handle, you can be sure that it is not original since original Qianlong teacups never had handles. Handles did not appear on eggshell teacups in Europe until the end of the eighteenth century. Handles did appear, however, on Kangxi period export coffee cups which were modeled with sturdier porcelain bodies. These were usually decorated in the famille verte palette.

Famille rose pieces have been abundantly copied by Samson in France. While most Samson pieces are signed, others are not and have to be examined closely to differentiate them from true famille rose. The iridescent glazes of early Qing pieces is absent. Also absent are the small black firing dots often found on original pieces. Examination of the base of newer pieces reveals an unglazed pure white rim as opposed to signs of iron oxidation from the firing. In addition, the base frequently has spur marks. Japanese copies were also made, but these show spur marks on the base, which are never found on original pieces.

Late-nineteenth-century and twentieth-century copies of rose-patterned porcelain abound. Aside from obvious color differences and meticulous attention to details, the older Rose Mandarin and Rose Medallion porcelains are not always perfectly symmetrical. They have an altogether different foot rim than their modern copies; their undersides taper to a sharp unglazed edge which is often burnt slightly orange in the kiln. Late pieces are more perfect in shape and reveal modern raised footrims that show no oxidation from kiln-firing procedures. The Rose Medallion pattern is the most frequently reproduced and can be found in the shops of any Chinatown in the United States.

Collecting Hints: Unless a piece of famille rose porcelain is specifically dated, it is difficult to determine whether it can be attributed to either the Yongzheng or early Qianlong period. Both periods employed the same type of decoration. In general it is recognized that the earliest items possess a pink that is lighter in shade and more transparent in quality, whereas the pink of Qianlong is usually brighter.

There is a definite line between the early famille rose created for the "Chinese taste" and the later mass-produced pattern ware export pieces for the European market. This difference in style and taste is reflected in two different kinds of interest among collectors. The collector of early eighteenth-century famille rose is rarely interested in pattern ware and the collector of pattern ware is seldom interested in famille rose. There is no value judgment implied in this separation; it is merely a matter of inclination. After all, "a rose by any other name would smell as sweet." Puns aside, the area of famille rose covers a wide range of attraction to collectors. There are purists who wish to own only the finest eighteenth-century mark and period pieces. There are those who are interested in amassing dinner or dessert sets in one of the popular patterns. There are collectors who are only attracted to eggshell porcelain, as well as collectors who will buy a single figural piece of rose-enameled porcelain for the decorative value it may have in a particular spot in their home. All areas of investment are wise, since famille rose-colored porcelains have a secure track record of keeping pace with inflation.

FAMILLE ROSE

Bowl, 10½" dia., late 18th century export, the sides decorated with two panels depicting court gentlemen at leisure in a garden divided by

smaller scrolled cartouches of flower clusters reserved on a gilt-foliate ground, the interior rim with gilt spearhead border and floral spray at the center **1,200.00**
Brush rest, 4⅜" l., wood stand, 18th century, reticulated, modelled as three furry-tailed squirrels painted in coral red and black and frolicking on pierced rockwork with famille rose flowerheads **850.00**
Dish
  7¼" d., saucer dish, Yongzheng mark in underglaze blue within a double circle and of the period, the interior painted in soft-toned enamels with a bird perched on a branch of iron-red leaves, emblematic of autumn, opposite a branch of blossoming tree peony and asters, cracked **3,000.00**
  7¾" dia., Yongzheng mark and of the period, decorated in gilt and characteristic colors with a lady and her attendant seated among an arrangement of traditional furniture **5,000.00**
  10" dia., Qianlong sealmark and late in the period, Celadon-ground circular dish, painted with two quail among flowers and rockwork **350.00**
  13⅛" dia., Qianlong, deep dish, enameled and gilt on the interior with lush sprays of leafy peony growing from rockwork, the design extending to the flaring rim **2,200.00**
Garden seat, 9⅜" h., Yongzheng, barrel-shaped, well painted around the middle with a butterfly and insects hovering above rocks and sprigs of various blossoms, between four foliate panels reserved on a chrysanthe-

Dish, 10¼" dia., Yongzheng period, the flowering branch set on a white background incised with fine scrolling lines. $2,600.00

Garniture Set, censer 17¼" h., vases 17" h., 19th century, decorated on a turquoise ground with densely scrolling lotus sprays, with horizontal bands of key pattern executed in polychromes. $2,400.00. Courtesy of Butterfield and Butterfield.

mum and scroll-decorated turquoise band below and stems of multi-colored lotus scroll reserved on the cloud collar above, the top with a pierced yellow cash medallion **1,200.00**

Loving cups, pair, 11¼" h., Qianlong, circa 1780, rare, covered, each deep cup on a high spreading foot molded with petal bands, the sides with foliate molded strap handles, enamelled in colors and gilt with a green medallion and floral clusters, the domed cover with a gilt branch form finial, restoration and damages   **1,500.00**

Plates, 9" dia., set of twelve, Qianlong, each painted at the center with a pink floral cluster and smaller sprigs within an iron-red barbed medallion, the borders with further floral sprays and shaped edges **1,650.00**

Platter, 16⅞" l., octagonal, Qianlong, painted and gilt with flowering peony and a foliate turnip within an iron-red diaper border reserved with

rectangular panels enclosing further floral foliage and fruit all within a molded band at the rim, some rubbing **1,500.00**

Vase

7½" h., Qianlong, gu-shaped beaker vase, gilt and painted in colored enamels with beaker vases before elaborate peony-laden censers beneath ruyi-shaped lappets, all between narrow bands of puce diaper pattern at the rim. **575.00**

9" h., pair, Qianlong iron-red seal marks, triple-gourd bottle shape, painted in opaque and translucent enamels against a lemon-yellow ground with branches of leafy lotus on the broad baluster lower bodies and around the pear-shaped necks, with lappet bands at the mouths and bases reserved against turquoise, and further lotus on the knopped central sections against further greenish-blue   **1,600.00**

14¼" h., pair, Qianlong, export covered pear-shaped vases, each of flattened lobed form applied with gilt chilong handles, painted on each side with an iron-red floral basket and a pair of birds within borders of applied berried foliage and nestling squirrels, the conforming shaped domed lids with iron-red landscape vignettes and further applied leafy tendrils and surmounted by a buddhistic lion   **6,000.00**

15", Qianlong mark and period, delicately painted with pheasants among flowering peonies and apple blossoms issuing from rockwork **15,000.00**

LATER QING PERIOD—
FAMILLE ROSE STYLE

Bowl

5" dia., pair, Guangxu, yellow ground, each decorated on the sides with four roundels enclosing iron-red characters and bats within a ruyi band all reserved on a diaper fretwork ground between further ruyi head borders, the interior with foliate gourd meander on a coral ground below gilt ruyi band **800.00**

10" w., ogee bowl and cover, Guangxu six-character mark in iron-red and of the period, the cover and bowl similarly decorated with three peony sprays . . .   **800.00**

Vase, 12" h., Beaker form, Qianlong seal mark in iron red. $4,500.00

Dishes, 7⅛'' dia., six-character Guangxu mark in under glaze blue and of the period, pair, shallow, each enameled and painted in iron-red with a confronting scale-bodied dragon and long-plumed phoenix amidst a flaming pearl and cloud scrolls, the exterior with floral scroll clusters **1,200.00**

Porcelain plaque
10¾'' x 15'', rectangular, enamelled with a scene of court dignitaries and children preparing a feast in a garden **750.00**
22¾'' h., 19th century, painted in delicate enamels with a blooming peony growing from rocks, two small birds in its branches, in a hardwood frame **800.00**

Vase
6½'' h., pair, Guangxu six-character marks in iron-red, baluster form, celadon-ground, painted in iron-red and opaque enamels on the sides in mirror image with panels of flowering prunus and tree peony, each outlined in gilt and red line borders and reserved on a floral molded ground **900.00**
13½'' h., Yongzheng four-character mark in enamel blue but later 19th/early 20th century, pear shaped two-handled vase, decorated with two circular panels depicting children, reserved on a pink ground, pierced handles . . .   **800.00**
15½'' h., 19th century, pear-shaped, with bronzed elephant-head handles, painted in pale enamels with birds among flowering branches and hanging leaves beside inscriptions **800.00**

ROSE MANDARIN PATTERN

Bowl, 10⅝'' dia., circa 1785, export Mandarin palette, the exterior painted with scrolled panels of court

Basin, 15¾'' dia. early 19th century. $1,800.00

Platter, 12'' x 17'', circa 1820, deep well. $1,250.00

figures relaxing on a terrace between smaller similar panels, reserved on a gilt and iron-red and fretted ground, the interiors with a medallion enclosing three figures on a terrace below a scale-diaper and floral panelled border. **850.00**
Cream jug with cover, 5½'' h., late 18th century, cell border with diaper background and central figural courtyard scene (chipped and repaired) **225.00**

Vase(s)
7¼'' h., pair, ovoid shape, late 18th century, each painted in the Mandarin palette with underglaze blue foliate bordered panels enclosing scenes of court figures at leisure in a landscape, reserved on an iron-red and gilt floral ground. **1,200.00**
9¾'' h., pair, square baluster vases, circa 1780, export Mandarin palette, each painted in famille rose enamels with panels of figures in courtyards within underglaze blue foliate borders, gilt highlights, chi-long-form handles **3,000.00**
12½'' h., pair, late 18th century, each with foo lion finals and dragon handles, ''chicken skin'' background on white ground and panels of raised molded figural scenes decorated in enamel colors **4,000.00**

ROSE MEDALLION PATTERN

Bowl
4½'' dia., late 19th century. **110.00**
7'' dia., late 19th century. **225.00**
8'' dia., circa 1840. . . . .   **850.00**
Candlesticks
7½'' h., late 19th century, alternating panels of floral and figural sub-

Basket and Underplate, reticulated, underplate 8″ w. $675.00

jects in typical palette, one rim
damaged. **500.00**
9¼″ h., c.1900, alternating floral
and figural panels, marked China **900.00**
Creamer, 3⅜″ h., late 19th century,
helmet shape **195.00**
Cup and Saucer, (coffee), late 19th
century, ... **65.00**
Lamps (mounted vases), 10½″ h.,
c.1860, on raised wood bases and
decorated in elongated alternating
panels of floral designs and figural
court scenes, typical enamel colors **800.00**
Plate
6″ dia., late 19th century. **65.00**
9½″ dia., late 19th century. **85.00**
Platter, Fruit, 11″ x 14¾″, mid 19th
century, shaped rim, alternating figural and floral panels, (rim chips, gilt
wear) **600.00**
12″ x 17″, late 19th century, some
wear. **675.00**
14¾″ x 18½″, mid 19th century, oval
typical enamel palette, alternating
floral and figural panels, mahog-
any custom wood stand **1,300.00**
Punch bowl
12″ dia., late 19th century. **650.00**
15¾″ dia., late 19th century. **1,300.00**
Shrimp Dish, 10¼″ l., mid 19th cen-
tury, alternating floral and figural
panels, shaped rim, (rim nicks) **550.00**
Umbrella stand, 24½″ h., late 19th
century, ribbed body, typical
enamel palette in alternating floral
and figural panels **850.00**
Vase
10″ h., bottle form, late 19th cen-
tury. **375.00**
14″ h. mid 19th century, bulbous
shape, dragons with central sun
molded in relief at neck, scalloped rim, alternating figural and
floral panels, blue bar and butter-
fly trim, (slight gilt wear to relief) **850.00**
15″ h., mid 19th century, wired as a
lamp and on a carved wood
stand, the vase with alternating

Baluster vases, 17¼″ h., 19th century, figural reserves on a gilt ground, fu dog handles. $2,200.00. Courtesy of Butterfield and Butterfield.

floral and figural panels in typical
palette (minor damages) **950.00**
16″ h., late 19th century, bottle
form. **750.00**
17½″ h., late 19th century, raised
molded double foo dog handles
and double lizards in gilt, alternating figural and floral panels in typ-
ical palette **1,200.00**
Vegetable Dish (covered)
9½″ x 11¾″, late 19th century,
shaped oval body with alternating
figural and floral panels, acorn
finial, (rim flake) **450.00**
11¾″ l., 19th century, oval with foli-
ate rim, the knopped and slightly
domed lid typically painted and
gilt, the interior decorated simi-
larly **600.00**

ROSE CANTON

Basin, 14¾″ dia., late 19th century, the
well enamelled in colors and gilt
with a central bird and blossom
roundel enclosed by fan, rectangular and oval panels of fruits, flowers
and dignitaries beside pavilions, reserved on a green and gilt millefiori
ground, the exterior plain, base
glaze cracks **850.00**
Bowl, 16″ dia., late 19th century,
painted with panels of figures on terraces and birds and butterflies
among flowers on a green scroll gold
ground **950.00**
Garden seats, 19½″ h., pair, hexago-
nal, each colorfully enamelled with
panels depicting a scene of court officials and attendants observing two

Dish, 10½" dia., late 19th century Mille-fleur pattern. $195.00

entertainers dressed in military costume in a garden pavilion, within key fret borders reserved on a fruit and foliate ground enriched with butterflies and Daoist emblems, the top and sides pierced with "cash" motifs..................... 3,800.00

Jardinieres (pair), 6¾", hexagonal shape, c.1830, continuous panels of decorations of courtyard scenes in typical rose canton palette, floral borders, (chips, one underdish missing) 1,300.00

Platter, 13¾" x 17", early 19th century, birds and floral border, central figural courtyard scene 1,300.00

Punch bowl, 15½" dia., 19th century, decorated in famille rose enamels with panels of butterflies amongst flowering foliage, around the rim bands of alternating floral and bird motifs, gilt embellished bands of dense greenery with shou characters and auspicious symbols 1,400.00

Umbrella stand, 25", 19th century, decorated in the Rose Medallion pattern with alternating panels of figures and boats in seascapes and ex-

Dish, 8½" dia., 19th century, Black Butterfly pattern. $150.00

otic birds and butterflies amongst flowers and ripened boughs of fruit, reserved on a pale green and gilt foliate ground with ornate floral borders 950.00

Vase(s)

13" h., 19th century, Celadon-ground gu-form vase with a bulbous central section and flaring neck and foot, enamelled all over with floral and fruiting boughs, butterflies and birds, between gilt enriched scrolling foliate bands   850.00

15¾", butterfly pattern, Guangxu seal mark and period, the ovoid body and the long waisted neck decorated overall with scattered butterflies, the shoulders with a band of shou characters amongst flower scrolls, a ruyi head band below the rim and a row of petals encircling the raised foot, incised seal mark on base........... 2,200.00

25" h., pair, late 19th/early 20th century, oviform with cylindrical necks and spreading feet, applied with dragon handles, iron red lingzhi and iron red dragons at the shoulders, painted with rectangular panels of dignitaries at court and ladies on terraces on grounds of birds among fruit and flower spray 1,700.00

34" (pair), 19th century, large palace vases, the pyriform vessels decorated with pate-sur-pate figural reserves on a fruit and floral painted pale celadon ground. ... 5,500

40½", 19th century, palace vase, ovoid with flaring foot and freestanding scalloped collar, painted in brilliant colors with figural reserves on a celadon ground decorated with the One Hundred Antiques, gilt dragon handles 4,800.00

FITZHUGH PATTERN PORCELAIN

History: The Fitzhugh pattern on Chinese export porcelain was a contemporary of the production of Nanking blue and white wares. Trading began during the reign of Qianlong in the late eighteenth century. The Fitzhugh design was inspired by a Welsh gentleman of that name who first ordered a service for export from China. His family had been involved in the China trade for three generations. During the years of his participation in the English factory (or hong), he sent back numerous services of dinnerware in his family's design.

The central motif of typical Fitzhugh-decorated porcelain consists of four different floral groups which denote the Chinese arts. The groups are arranged in a circular pattern. The Fitzhugh border decoration consists of trellis work interrupted by four cut pomegranates and flying butterflies. Flowering branches connected by a Greek fret pattern complete the pattern, although meander borders with diaper patterns are known to exist. The decoration was accomplished in the private kilns of Ching-te-chen. Although the Nanking pattern was produced solely in the blue and white palette, Fitzhugh porcelains sometimes departed from this color scheme and also included brown, orange, red, green, and other enamel colors. However, blue decoration is by far the most common color. American merchants became aware of the pattern on their trips to Canton in the 1780s and orders were placed for shipment to America. The pattern was exported to both England and the United States, but it became associated primarily with America because of its extensive popularity. Fitzhugh border-patterned dinner services also were exported to the Netherlands but were not greeted with as much enthusiasm there.

Fitzhugh differed from Nanking ware, which had a definite integral pattern, by sometimes having its border design separated from its usual central motif and incorporated, instead, with an armorial or other central design. Fitzhugh bordered "blanks" were ordered from Ching-te-chen by merchants to be further decorated with central designs executed in overglaze enamels. This later decoration took place in the port city of Canton. The renowned dinner service made for the Society of Cincinnati in the late 1800s carried a blue Fitzhugh border. It is recorded that George Washington bought one of the early Cincinnati insignia dinner services in the summer of 1786. The set was sold to him for the sum of $150.00 and contained 302 pieces of Fitzhugh-bordered porcelain. Other central themes receiving Canton decoration were the American eagle and personal symbols that were ordered specifically for individuals.

The popularity of the ware waned in the early nineteenth century when the tastes of the American public shifted to the production of domestic porcelain.

References: Rosalind Fischell, *Blue and White China: Origins/Western Influences*, Little, Brown and Company, 1987; Duncan Macintosh, *Chinese Blue and White Porcelain*, Charles E. Tuttle Co., Inc., 1977. D. F. Lunsingh Scheurleer, *Chinese Export Porcelain: Chine de Commande*, Pitman Publishing Company, 1974.

Museums: Museum of Fine Arts, Boston, Massachusetts; Metropolitan Museum of Art, New York, New York; Philadelphia Museum of Art, Philadelphia, Pennsylvania; Mottahedeh Collection of the Virginia Museum of Fine Arts, Richmond, Virginia.

Collecting Hints: Fitzhugh patterned porcelains are of interest to collectors of armorial porcelain as well as to those who collect export wares. As they tend to be expensive, the market is limited to those who can afford a large investment. The most expensive pieces are those that appear in colors other than the familiar blue and white combination. Orange and green decoration are next up the line in prices. Other colors are considered rare and command the most money.

Brush Box (covered), blue, rectangular, $3\frac{3}{4}$'' x 7'', early 19th century, central medallion surrounded by four floral panels, lattice and spearhead border, trimmed in Rose Canton enamel butterflies, bugs and flowers and with gilt highlighting throughout **750.00**

Pitcher, $8\frac{1}{4}$'' h., circa 1800, Fitzhugh type, the center with a monogram on a shield surrounded by Latin words and a praying angel with ribbons in famille rose enamels, the border of typical Fitzhugh design in blue **1,400.00**

Plate, 9'', early 20th century, orange border with American eagle in the center. **375.00**

Plates, 9'' dia., blue and white. $1,100.00.

Basket (oval) and stand, orange, $7\frac{1}{2}$'' and $9\frac{1}{4}$'', circa 1820, reticulated, painted in shades of orange with gilding. $1,300.00

Platter
16" l., oval (with strainer), orange,
circa 1810, the strainer pierced
with central opening with gilded
edges and three rows of small
holes, typical decoration **1,500.00**
13" x 16", oval, blue, early 19th
century, central medallion surrounded by four floral panels, lattice and spearhead borders **750.00**
18¾" l., oval, brown, circa 1800,
finely enamelled in shades of
brown in typical pattern, with gilt
at the rim. **2,800.00**
Sauce tureen, 7⅞" l., orange, late 18th/
early 19th century, interlaced strap
handles, flower formed knop on lid **900.00**
Soup plate, 10" dia., early 19th century, green color, typical decora-
tion, regilded rim. **425.00**
Soup tureen
14" l., early 19th century, blue and
white, the bombé body with interlaced strap handles and foliate
knopped domed lid, painted underglaze with typical four floral
clusters within a diaper border . . **2,200.00**
With cover and platter, 14" and
16" l., early 19th century, orange
color, typically decorated, some
chips, some restoration of handles **5,250.00**
Teabowl and Saucer, saucer 5⅜" dia.,
circa 1790, the bowl with an ogee
rim, both decorated with a Fitzhugh
and cell pattern bands below the
rim, with a family crest decorated in
colors and gilt **2,800.00**
Vegetable dish, covered, 12" l., circa
1810, blue color **1,750.00**
Warming dish
Fitzhugh type, 10¼" l., 19th century, brown and gilt decoration
with lady musicians and noble-
men, interspersed with vases
holding flowers and peacock
feathers around the central indis-
tinct gilt monogram and below a
band of cornucopias and precious
things along the rim, damages . . . **375.00**
11¾" l., blue, typical pattern, with
two open tabs at the sides for hot
water **2,200.00**

HAN DYNASTY CERAMICS

History: The Han Dynasty spanned the years
from 206 B.C. to 221 A.D. This period saw the first
Chinese contacts with the Hellenistic world and
the introduction of Buddhism, which accounts for
the Persian shapes that are found on early Han
pottery vessels.

Prior to this time it had been Chinese custom to
bury the living with the dead. Servants and animals were sacrificed so they could accompany
the corpse into the life hereafter. The ceramic
industry grew during the Han Dynasty largely because this practice was replaced by burying the
dead with pottery funerary objects.

Two basic types of ceramic wares were produced. *High-fired* porcelaneous glazed wares
were made, with centers for their production located in Chekiang in the north, Ch'ang-sha in the
south central region, and Kuangtung in the south.
High-fired wares were used for large wheel-
thrown vases, granary urns, hill jar censers, and
wine jars. These items are found with molded
decorations in the form of encircling bands. The
motifs used were animals (both real and imag-
ined), birds, and people.

Low-fired lead glazes were used on red earthenware bodies during this period, apparently exclusively for mortuary purposes. They were
produced largely in the areas of Ch'ang-an and
Lo-yang.

Anything that was deemed useful in everyday
life would accompany the dead in the form of
pottery mortuary items. The ming-ch'i figures
produced for inclusion in the tombs depicted
warriors, female dancers, court officials and
others. Also included were animal figures of
household pets and farm animals along with
imaginary animals, which were used as talismans
against evil. Common household objects such as
cooking utensils and writing implements, along
with effigies of houses and barns, were also depicted in the mortuary pottery. Tomb figures were
either left unglazed, or were painted or glazed in
a typical green or brown glaze (which takes on an
iridescent sheen derived from the degradation of
the glaze due to burial). A fine crackle in the glaze
is also typical of these wares.

It was during the construction of the railway
from Lo-yang to Kai-feng at the end of the Qing
Dynasty that many tomb objects of ancient pottery were unearthed and serious studies of mortuary figures became the preoccupation of ceramic
scholars.

References: Cecile and Michel Beurdeley, *A
Connoisseur's Guide to Chinese Ceramics*, Har-
per and Row, n. d.; Stephen W. Bushell, *Chinese
Art*, Rare Reprints Inc., 1977; Warren E. Cox,
Pottery and Porcelain, Crown Publishers Inc.,
1970; Seizo Hayashiya and Gakuji Hasebe, *Chi-
nese Ceramics*, Charles E. Tuttle Co., Inc., 1966;
R. L. Hobson, *Chinese Pottery and Porcelain*,
Dover Publications, 1976; Fujio Koyama and
John Figgess, *Two Thousand Years of Oriental Ce-
ramics*, Harry N. Abrams, Inc.; Margaret Medley,
The Chinese Potter, Charles Scribner's Sons,
1976.

Museums: Art Institute of Chicago, Chicago, Illinois; Nelson Gallery of Art, Kansas City, Kansas; Boston Museum of Art, Boston, Massachusetts; Metropolitan Museum of Art, New York, New York; Cleveland Museum of Art; Cleveland, Ohio; Freer Gallery of Art, Washington, D.C.; Seattle Art Museum, Seattle, Washington; British Museum, London, England; Victoria and Albert Museum, London, England; National Museum, Tokyo, Japan; National Museum of History, Taipei, Taiwan.

Reproduction Alert: See notes on thermoluminesent testing in section on Tang Dynasty Ceramics.

Collecting Hints: Though frequently referred to as "proto porcelain" in some of the old literature, the hard-glazed wares of the Han Dynasty were in reality nothing more than a high-fired stoneware, sometimes referred to as porcelaneous ware in the literature. Their greyish clay bodies often burned reddish brown in the firing due to the high percentage of iron content in the clay.

The prices of Han Dynasty items have fallen considerably in recent years. The large amount of wares on the market due to the plundering of tombs and consequent illegal exportation of mortuary items has driven prices downward. (See Collecting Hints in Tang Dynasty Ceramics).

Bowl, 1½" x 5", green glazed pottery, round with a ribbed motif and an everted rim, of dark green iridescent glaze, the foot unglazed **300.00**

Censer with cover, 8" h., grey pottery, the conical hill form cover, modelled with a series of craggy hillocks rising to a peak, a human figure below the crags clutching the tail of a dragon pursuing a tiger, pig and dog around the hill, extensive traces of the red, orange, blue, white and black pigments **1,400.00**

Censer, 5½" h. x 8¼" dia., cylindrical form, resting on three small feet, covered all over with an iridescent green lead glaze. $800.00

Figure
Boar, 2½" x 4", grey pottery, standing with head bowed, surface bearing earth traces **450.00**
Buffalo, 6¼" l., glazed pottery, the stocky beast standing foursquare on knife-pared feet, the head with rudimentary eyes, pointed horns and ears, the body with deftly incised hair marking, all covered with an olive-brown glaze **1,200.00**
Dog, 6" h., grey pottery, seated on haunches, its head raised, mouth slightly open, ears pricked back, tail curled forward in a loop, and forepaws touching his backpaws, traces of pigment on the collar and other details **600.00**
Duck
5" x 5", grey pottery, standing upon cylindrical legs on broad platen style feet, the head with stud eyes and a broad beak, the feathers detailed in simple grooves **700.00**

Left, Geese, pair, 7" and 8" l., each with abstract body and stylized feet, each with traces of red and white pigment, traces of earth adhering, restorations. $2,750.00; *right*, Horse, 13⅝" h., 14½" l., rare, grey pottery, traces of red pigment and earth adhering, restorations. $14,300.00. Both courtesy of Butterfield and Butterfield.

$5\frac{3}{8}''$ h., grey pottery, modelled in a lively stance as if waddling, its plumage painted in white and yellow, its beak and feet with white details on a yellow ground 300.00

Hen, $5\frac{1}{2}'' \times 4\frac{1}{2}''$, grey pottery, standing with feathers simulated by wide grooves. 400.00

Kneeling, $6\frac{3}{4}''$ h., the robe in ochre, the hands and face with traces of black and white paint 800.00

Musician, $5\frac{3}{4}''$ h., grey pottery, shown kneeling with knees tucked under, the head slightly bent forward and wearing a cap with a flat top, dressed in flowing robes, the slender arms outstretched as if to hold instrument, traces of pigment, arm reattached 2,000.00

Official, $9\frac{1}{4}''$ h., grey pottery, standing with knees slightly bent, and weight forward, his arms outstretched and fists clenched, wearing full length robe with double collar and sleeves, belted low at the waist, fine featured with small hat above black hair 2,200.00

Owl, $5\frac{3}{4}''$ h., grey pottery, shown with bulging eyes and beaks, painted in red with scale-like feathers front and back 850.00

Ox, $7'' \times 3\frac{1}{2}''$, red pottery, in recumbent pose, lower body has a tan colored glaze, the upper body is left unglazed 350.00

Ram, $3'' \times 5\frac{1}{2}''$, grey pottery, recumbent with curled horns and head held high, surface with traces of earth sediment. 300.00

Rooster
$4\frac{1}{2}'' \times 5\frac{1}{2}''$, grey pottery, head up and looking down, the wing and tail feathers are simulated by strong grooving in white gesso on a grey background. . . 400.00

$8\frac{3}{8}''$ h., shown in an alert stance, its head looking forward topped with cockscomb and wattles, its fan-shaped tail raised, traces of red, brown and green pigment highlighting its plumage 1,300.00

Tiger, $9\frac{1}{2}''$, grey pottery, modelled in a slightly curled recumbent position, the animal with rear legs tucked under and its head resting between its forepaws, painted in red and black with a series of stripes, its eyes dotted. 2,200.00

Granary Jar
$17\frac{1}{2}'' \times 7''$, rare pair of grey pottery granary jars of tall cylindrical form, the bodies showing simple incised bands, a single pouring hole on each, both painted with characters in a white gesso, along with bowl-shaped covers 2,500.00

$9\frac{1}{2}'' \times 7\frac{1}{2}''$, the tapered cylindrical body of grey pottery with faintly incised bands, the roof sloped and tiled extending toward a small rimmed mouth, the feet formed as kneeling figures 1,300.00

Incense burner, with cover, 13'' h., red pottery, the shallow dish with rounded sides supported on a cylindrical stem attached to a shallow underplate and with two separately molded covers, the first with a

Human, $11\frac{1}{4}''$ h., shown holding a child, covered in an iridescent green lead glaze. $725.00. Courtesy of Butterfield and Butterfield.

Granary Jar, 10'' h., resting on three small feet, flaring slightly to the top, applied with a circular sloping roof, covered overall with a green iridescent lead glaze. $800.00

pierced conical lower section supporting a smaller dish, itself with a small pierced conical cover surmounted by a bird finial, each cover pierced with four triangular apertures, articulated with upright petal forms traces of white pigment **2,800.00**

Jar

3½" x 4", grey pottery, the globular body with a waist, short neck with everted rim **250.00**

5", Western Han, grey stoneware, a squat baluster formed jar with a wasted neck supporting a grooved rim **300.00**

5½" x 2½", Eastern Han, grey pottery, the baluster body painted with traces of dragons, the wasted neck with a chevron motif **125.00**

7" x 5", Western Han, brown glazed pottery, the baluster body with two bands of incised double rings, the wasted neck supports a ribbed mouth, tan/brown glaze   **500.00**

12" h., glazed stoneware storage jar, the "proto-porcelain" vessel with its shoulder horizontally ribbed and applied with two strap handles molded with a mask between a ribbed, striated band below and striated projections above, and with a double coiled appliqué on the body above, all under a dark olive-green kiln gloss ending in an irregular line at midbody and falling in tears on one side over the lower body burnt orange in the firing, some chips . . .   **4,000.00**

12⅝" h., green-glazed red pottery jar, of ovoid form, with a single grooved band around the shoulder, covered in a crackled glaze of deep leaf-green color slightly iridescent and pooling in drops on the rim **3,400.00**

14¾" h., green glazed hu, molded with a band of animals divided by two fixed ring monster mask handles, covered all over in a dark spinach-green glaze stopping short of the base, restored rim . . .   **1,400.00**

16½" h., green-glazed pottery, of hu form, with taotieh masks and fixed ring handles at the shoulder, under a deep rich glaze collecting in droplets on the lip and pooling on the interior of the wide galleried mouth, the dark green glaze with areas of silvery iridescence, rim chips **3,500.00**

19½" h., painted pottery, hu form, the body applied with a pair of

molded monster form mask handles at the widest part and painted in white and red with bands of scrolls surmounted by court figures, the domed cover with traces of slip and polychrome, restored   **1,500.00**

Pottery model

House, 5", a single story house of grey pottery with ridged roof and open door **1,000.00**

Pig pen, 8½" h., the semi-circular fence enclosing a hog, one side with a ramp leading to a roofed structure, green glaze shading from leaf green to spinach **1,500.00**

Stove, 11" x 7", crafted in a plain rectangular form with a single fire opening, the top with four pot apertures **800.00**

Watchtower, 26", three stories high, birds perched on the upper two roofs, wide tiled eaves, large patches of silvery iridescence on pale spinach green glaze, old repairs **6,500.00**

Stand, 14" l., green glaze, conical form molded in low relief with a continuous band of mythical animals and birds, the flat top with a stepped back ring around the small cavity for attachment, the green glaze now flaked, restorations **2,000.00**

Vase

5" x 3", green glazed hu style, incised ring around sloping shoulder, the softly curved neck supports a grooved mouth, dark green glaze with olive tones **600.00**

5" x 4", grey pottery, Eastern Han, the squat baluster body with traces of painting in red and

Vase, 14¾" h., hu form, molded at each side with animal mask ring handles, covered with a brilliant deep green glaze streaking to a silvery irridescence. $1,980.00. Courtesy of Butterfield and Butterfield.

white, the wasted neck supports a
trumpet mouth. **400.00**
12" x 8", brown glazed pottery hu,
Western Han, the baluster body
with two bands of raised triple
rings, the wasted neck with a
trumpet mouth. **1,000**
12" x 10", grey pottery hu, Western
Han, the baluster body decorated
with a wide band motif of various
animals upon a scrolled ground,
two mock handles shaped as
rings, the wasted neck with a
broad vertical collar which is
grooved at the base, the body ta-
pering to a straight-sided foot . . .   **1,500.00**
18" x 12", green glazed hu, West-
ern Han, the baluster body of
squat form with a wide wasted
neck, a deep collar around the
rim, the shoulder with a band of
triple ribbing glaze over dark
green **2,000.00**
Water dropper, 1½" x 4½", black pot-
tery, in the form of a reclining rat, its
head resting upon its front paws, the
surface with traces of pigment. **350.00**

IVORY

History: While ivory is generally understood to
be the tusks of the elephant, Oriental "ivory"
carvings have been made from the teeth of other
animals, including the walrus, hippopotamus,
sperm whale, narwhal, and wild boar. Carvings
were also made from the seeds of fruit-bearing
trees, the most ivorylike of which is the Toko nut.
The four kinds of elephant tusks used were African (which is considered to have the best color
and quality), Asian (which tends to yellow in a
few years), Indian (which is very white and less
hard than the preceding two), and mammoth
(which, since the species has been extinct for
more than twenty thousand years, is fossilized,
dark yellow, and heavily crazed). Elephant ivory
cut in cross section exhibits growth rings discern-
able as alternating light and dark bands.

While the Chinese also carved animal bone,
most of these carvings are small and poorly done
and most probably were accomplished for the
tourist trade. A magnifying glass will determine if
the porosities which originally contained bone
cells (the Haversian system) is present, signifying
bone. Elephant tusks are entirely dentine and
enamel, with no embedded cells. One-third of
the elephant's tusk is imbedded in the jaw, which,
since it contains the tooth pulp, is hollow when
removed and dried. While this section of the tusk
is the largest in diameter, the best carvings were

done from the two-thirds that were solid throughout. The average tusk of the African elephant is
about six feet long and weighs approximately
seventy-five pounds, with both males and females
possessing tusks. The Asian elephant is a smaller
species, and the tusks are correspondingly
smaller, averaging five feet and about thirty-five
pounds. At the extreme, a weight of 188 lbs. has
been recorded for a single tusk.

The Chinese preferred to work African ivory,
but it is hard to ascertain the origin of ancient
ivory since yellowing and crazing occur in all
types over long periods. The Chinese began working in ivory over 4,000 years ago, and with other
ivorylike materials already noted for over 1,300
years. Archaic ivories that have survived are
noted to be small adornments to the dress. It is not
until the Ming Dynasty (1368–1644) that large
works were produced for temples, homes, and
palaces. These were usually left in their natural
state and color to mellow with age. During the
reign of the Qing emperor Kangxi, workshops
were set up on the grounds of the palace at Peking
which survived until the 1860s. The early years of
the Qing Dynasty produced the finest ivory carvings, many of which were embellished with color
tinting.

The subject matter of Chinese carvings was
quite limited, usually including gods, goddesses,
figures, flower baskets, dragons, and the curious
concentric balls. These, by the way, are carved
from the center out and have up to twenty-seven
layers. The calligrapher's and artist's wrist rest is
perhaps the most prized of the Chinese ivory
forms.

The twentieth century has seen an explosion in
the ivory trade, so that most countries now have a
ban on the transportation of carvings across their
borders in hopes of reducing the trade and saving
the remaining elephant herds. Nevertheless, the
quality of the Chinese carvings of this century is
excellent, with most of the work still being done
in the old ways with hand tools.

The novice collector may find it difficult to
distinguish between Chinese and Japanese ivory
carvings. It should be noted that the Japanese
carvings are more fanciful and tend to be smaller
and more intricate. They depict scenes from history and everyday life, workers and their tools,
and mythological creatures and beings. They are
commonly carved with extreme miniature detail
and finished with a variety of surfacing techniques unknown to Chinese carving. The larger
carvings are termed "Okimono," meaning literally "a piece to look at," and the smallest of the
carvings ("netsuke") are unique to Japanese culture. (See: Okimono and Netsuke in the Japanese
section of this book.)

References: Stephen W. Bushell, *Chinese Art*,
Rare Reprints, Inc., 1977; Soame Jenyns, *Chinese
Art III*, Rizzoli International, 1965, 1981; Charles

P. Woodhouse, *Ivories, A History and Guide*, Van Nostrand Reinhold, 1976.

Museums: Any of the museums listed in this book will have a small collection of ivories. The two major London collections are at the Victoria and Albert Museum and the British Museum. In this country, a significant collection of both Chinese and Japanese carvings is at the Cummer Gallery of Art in Jacksonville, Florida. Also see the Leitner Museum in nearby St. Augustine, Florida.

Reproduction Alert: Cream-colored plastic has been molded since the mid-1940s to approximate the appearance of ivory. Since ivory does not burn except by prolonged exposure to extremely high temperature, a pin heated to red-hot heat will penetrate plastic but not genuine ivory or bone. Other fakes are made of wax and painted plaster. Be sure to do the hot-pin test on each piece. If the seller will not allow this test, then do not buy the piece.

Any of the twentieth-century ivory carvings are good pieces of art, but should be purchased at lower prices than antique ivory. Twentieth-century Chinese carvings have been known to be artificially stained with tannic acid to a dark brown coloration, but this looks nothing like the deep yellow of true aged ivory. Ivory more than 200 years old tends to develop deep age cracks normally, but forgers will bake ivory in hot ashes to give this appearance. True mammoth or mastodon ivory is fossilized with minerals and is correctly no longer just "ivory."

Collecting Hints: As the availability of ivory has been reduced, the value of recent carvings, which were never cheap, has grown enormously. The best of the Chinese carvings are solid throughout with much openwork. What the viewer does not see is the large quantity of valuable material that has been carved away. Thus a straight figure is of more value than one which follows the original curve of the tusk.

Buy the best pieces that you can afford. Larger, more impressive pieces command a higher price, but with the government-enforced reduction of supply, these pieces will increase in price faster than smaller pieces. Cull out of your collection the smaller, earlier acquisitions by trading them as partial payment for new purchases, if necessary. A more modern, better-carved piece of unusual subject and quality is certainly preferable to a lesser piece of greater age.

Advisor: Clinton R. Weil

Brush Pot, 6¼" h., 19th century, the cylindrical pot carved with a continuous scene of sages in a rocky garden under a pine tree with a pavilion in the background **700.00**
Candle holders, 6" h., in the form of Fu lions **700.00**

Censer; with four jade rings, on wood stand, 15" h. **2,400.00**
Figure
Buddha, on wooden plinth, 12" h., 19th century, ...   **1,200.00**
Buddhist Figure on a Tiger, 3¾" h., the figure riding upon the back of a tiger holding the tiger's tail in his left hand, in the other he holds a peach **350.00**
Buddhistic lions, 7" h., each set on a double lotus base **850.00**
Dignitary, 7½", shown standing in carved dragon robes, polychrome enamels applied **550.00**
Doctor's lady
4" h., on wood bed **175.00**
7" h., on wood bed **450.00**
12" h., on ivory bed **1,300.00**
Emperor and Empress
Pair, 7", seated on thrones **995.00**
Pair, 15", seated on thrones **2,500.00**
Pair, 24" h., seated on dragon and phoenix thrones **4,500.00**
Figures, pair, 5¼" h., Circa 1900, each standing in a theatrical pose wearing Tibetan Buddhist costumes decorated in polychrome enamels, the lively figures well carved with animated faces, each with heads attached to springs . . .   **1,200.00**
Gautama Buddha, 8¼" h., the reverent figure stands wearing simply

Dieties, Pair, 22" h., holding woven flower filled baskets, standing on high pedestals with reserves depicting auspicious emblems. $5,225.00. Courtesy Butterfield and Butterfield.

draped robes and holding a patra (begging bowl) in his left hand, his eyes shut in meditation, a slight smile on his lips, his hair carved with tight curls and crowned, stained for effect 600.00

General, standing with sword, 18" h. 1,600.00

Guanyin
   8¾" h., Ming Period, the tall slender figure standing with her arms across her chest, holding a leaf and a rosary in her hands, good patina 950.00
   Head only, 11" h., the serene face crowned by an elaborately carved and pierced headdress depicting the eighteen lohans floating among clouds, with her hair knotted in the back and ears suspending earrings, supported by a wooden base carved as a neck and shoulders   550.00
   12" h., standing 950.00
   30" h., standing 4,500.00

Horseman
   6¼" h., the modern figure with his hand raised as if in greeting, dressed in a fur-trimmed Manchurian style coat and cap seated on a sturdy, prancing horse standing on a rocky platform 125.00
   8" h., 19th century, shown mounted on horse. 900.00

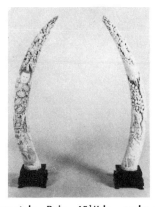

Immortals, Pair, 45½" h., male and female, Shou Lao accompanied by his deer holding a peach branch, the female with a phoenix and holding a branch of blossoming peonies, both carved with numerous other immortals and sages. $7,150.00. Courtesy of Butterfield and Butterfield.

Horses, pair, 4⅞" l., early 20th century, shown in prancing posture, the saddles ornamented with inlays of coral and turquoise, finely executed. 475.00

Hotai, the happy God, on ivory plinth, 14" h. 2,600.00

Immortal, 13" h., shown standing leaning on a cane holding a basket 750.00

Maiden
   11" h., the maiden intricately carved, a slight smile on her face, and hair elaborately dressed, wearing flowing robes, her ribbons as if fluttering in the wind, holding a large bouquet of lotus blossoms and daisies as she stands on frothy waves, a heron at her feet, flanked by large lotus blossoms and a small child 900.00
   11¼" h., polychrome, the slender figure standing in long flowing robes knotted at the waist, her hair piled high upon her head, a basket of flowers tied with a cord slung over her shoulder, the long cord extending down to her knees 900.00

Official, 7¼" h., the standing figure dressed in an official's hat and a flowing robe carved to the front with a square badge, holding a wine cup in one hand while grasping his belt with the other . .   400.00

Philosopher, 6¾" h., the official holding in one hand a fly whisk and in the other a staff, incised and stained for effect 125.00

Wise man, Mastadon carving, 6", cracks, some losses 875.00

Figure Groups
   Bears on a "hill" carving, 22" h. . . .   3,500.00
   Clam shell
      Village carved inside, 4" 300.00
      Village carved inside, 6" 750.00
   Elephant bridge, 14" l., with seven elephants 1,200.00
   Group of Nine Ivory Carved Elephants, various sizes, of graduated size, each elephant realistically depicted in a different action pose, intricately incised detailing   1,500.00
   Immortals Seated at a Banquet Table, 10½" h., each carved similarly, two seated at the front and two standing behind the table holding their attribute, a plate of peaches and a teapot on the table, all supported by a stepped shaped plinth 2,750.00

Ball, 19⅛″ h., ivory, on stand, exceptional quality, the exterior ball carved and pierced with dragons, the interior balls with geometric patterns, the pedestal carved and undercut by three celestial female musicians on cloud scrolls. $4,900.00. Courtesy of Butterfield and Butterfield.

Lotus blossoms and fronds, c. 1900,
13″ h. 2,800.00
Monk and a Female Immortal,
8¼″ h., the bald headed monk
standing in loosely draped robes
holding a bell in one hand and a
striker in the other, the immortal
standing in flowing robes tied at
the waist holding a musical instrument in her hands, her hair knot-
ted in a high chignon 300.00
Phoenix and stork, 16″ h. 2,100.00
Soldiers on horseback on "hill"
carving, 14″ h. 2,100.00
Three star Gods of happiness, 20″ x
7″ each. 6,000.00
Wise man with tiger at his feet,
solid, 14″ h. 3,800.00
Mystery ball
10 layer, on ivory stand 295.00
14 layer, on ivory stand 495.00
18 layer, on ivory stand with 8 balls 1,195.00
22 layer, on ivory stand with 10
balls and three horses, large ball
carved with dragons on exterior 3,200.00
Puzzle Ball, 14″ h., the puzzle-ball
carved with various pavilion scenes
is supported by an ivory shaft carved
below the ball with a group of deities at the foliate base under a pine
tree, and surmounted by a daisy
issuing a figure of Ho Hsien-Ku
holding a lotus blossom and a small
boy at the top of the shaft 550.00

Hollow Tusks, Pair, 21½″ h., carved with cranes and phoenix among twisting pines and peony blossoms, the eyes inset with turquoise and coral beads, traces of pigment. $1,320.00. Courtesy of Butterfield and Butterfield.

Table screen, on ivory stand, 19th c.,
with tinting 1,200.00
Tusk, carved, 31″ h., carved all over
with figures in a mountain setting . . 2,500.00
Wine vessel, 6″, on wood stand 300.00

JADE AND HARDSTONE CARVINGS

History: Jade and china have always fascinated the Sinologist—for good reason! The Chinese have used and been fascinated with jade since early Neolithic times. However, jade is not just one stone, which has led to widespread confusion among Western buyers. Jade can be conveniently subdivided into nephrite jade and jadeite. A third division, chloromelanite, is seldom found.

It should be noted that unlike many of the hardstones that were carved in China, neither of the jades came from traditional China proper. The first, nephrite, came from the western Kunlun mountains and the rivers of Khotan (in modern Sinkiang Province). The second, jadeite, found in northern Burma, was probably only introduced to the Chinese in the eighteenth century. It follows, therefore, that it was nephrite that the Chinese historically endowed with almost every positive spiritual value. In Taiwan, Singapore, Hong Kong, and wherever Chinese reside today, nephrite still evokes special attributes. When it comes to jewelry, however, most prefer jadeite, which is considered a gemstone with no equal. It is at its best when it is translucent, large, and deep in color like the best of emeralds. The increased focus of the Chinese community on jadeite for jewelry has also elevated the desirability of other jadeite carvings. However, to the true collector of Chinese jade, East or West, it is not jadeite from Burma but traditional nephrite jades from the riverbeds and mountains of the remote western regions of Khotan that are prized.

In the historical search for the best nephrite boulders, it was believed that only half-naked women should be allowed to probe the cold waters of the western mountain region in the belief that the *yang* (maleness) of nephrite would be attracted to their *yin* (femaleness). In the milieu of Confucian China, the best nephrites (usually a pure soft white with very even color and few if any impurities in the stone) were offered to the emperor, who used them in ancient rituals. Onto such early auspicious beliefs were heaped the beliefs and superstitions of a period nineteen to twenty times longer than the history of the United States. Rapid accumulation of erroneous beliefs quickly led Chinese rulers of subsequent periods to endow this stone with immortal powers, going so far as to proclaim it to be a link between heaven and earth. Confucian virtues, nephrite jade, and the ideal man were now linked together. Nephrite subsequently played an integral and central role at the governmental level. The physical evidence of Neolithic and other historical sites has been prolific and rewarding in substantiating such former beliefs. The "stone of heaven," as nephrite jade came to be called, was sought after by all. Wars were fought for specific splendid pieces of carved nephrite. It was treasured above all material items—even gold, silver, and money—for it was believed to endow the owner with both security and power. In sum, the history of China cannot be separated from its traditional association with nephrite jade. Today, a good carved piece of pure white nephrite or Ming yellow is still actively sought after, as much for its intrinsic beauty as its association with the history, rituals, and religion of China which it mirrors. Chinese jade carving not only reflected all Chinese beliefs and values of the day, but it also revealed the idiosyncrasies that are inherent to all historical periods.

In this author's collection, for example, is a three-inch-long Song Dynasty (960–1279 A.D.) black and white nephrite carving of a horse. The horse is reclining and the pebble from which it was carved had been altered very little, but a great deal of study had clearly preceded the carving. The black and white stone was carved so that the mane and the eyes of the horse were in black and the rest in white. Even more striking was the artist's simple and crudely carved Chinese characters on the back of the horse indicating that he had "sweat a bucket of blood." To any collector or student of Chinese culture, need there be any greater reward than direct communication from

three Chinese characters carved more than 1,000 years ago?

From small ritual carvings and carvings of animals and pendants executed with bamboo and sand (often mixed with the sand of crushed hardstones that could be used as an abrasive), technical advances eventually allowed much large carvings. These technical advances were quite simple but very important: first, the treadle wheel was introduced, and then, diamond-tipped carving tools were developed. Diamonds, rated a 15 on the revised and expanded Mohs' scale of hardness, easily carved the softer 6 of nephrite. Diamond carving combined with modern mining techniques, which allowed huge boulders of jade to be mined from the mountains of Khotan, resulted in extremely large carvings. The huge carving in the Imperial Palace Museum in Beijing is a testimonial to these new so-called modern processes.

To further enhance one's understanding of Chinese jade, it must be clear that the Chinese term in ancient times for both jade and hardstones was *yu.* (Some unscrupulous dealers still use this to trick an unwitting public.) Although *Yu* quickly took on a clearer meaning in Chinese to distinguish it from other stones, it was not until the introduction of jadeite around the eighteenth century that it was necessary to distinguish *linguistically* between nephrite and jadeite. Nephrite came to be called the "real or true jade," whereas jadeite was originally referred to as "hard jade" (many Chinese were not convinced it was jade at all). In addition, the collector has probably struggled through the dozens of Chinese names for nephrites, jadeites, and hardstones. I recommend Mark Chou's *Dictionary of Jade Nomenclature.* Please note that Chinese terminology is very graphic and very accurate. For example, *yu du bai* translates as "fish-belly white," or fish-belly white nephrite jade. Indeed, if one looks closely at an ancient burial jade, it often has calcification and looks like the white to be found on the belly of a Chinese fish. Furthermore, the often-misused term "mutton fat" cannot be bright white by definition—one need only to imagine the real color of congealed sheep fat, which has a very slight yellowish cast. Such off-white colors, in fact, are due to impurities in the stone (the same is true of jadeite). The most common impurity is iron, which provides the browns to the reds (tomato red is very rare, whereas brown is common).

Hardstones were traditionally treated in much the same manner as jades. Regardless of material, hardstones are carved to emphasize the best in the natural stone. An imperfection or cleavage, for example, might end up being a crevice in a mountain landscape. A spot of unusual color might be a butterfly on a rock or even a monkey. The most common hardstone is the mineral silicon dioxide, which is very plentiful. Its common name is quartz. Under this rubric of quartz can be itemized amethyst, rock crystal, smoky quartz, Tiger's eye, rose quartz, cat's-eye, hair crystal, agate (and chalcedony), carnelian, and citrine. This list is not comprehensive, but each and every one of these minerals is harder than jade. It follows, therefore, that very few hardstones were carved until the relatively recent introduction of modern methods. Those which were carved earlier were carved using the same slow and painstaking methods characteristic of jade carving. Judge them the same way that you would a jade carving. Other stones worth mentioning are lapis lazuli (with sodalite as its imitation) and turquoise. The latter two have a long history of use in both China and Tibet.

To some extent, fossils—particularly coral but also amber, jet, mother-of-pearl, and even mammoth tooth—were used.

The hardstone most often found as a jade substitute is bowenite, a hard variety of serpentine. Another nephrite substitute is steatite. Both bowenite and steatite were used continuously for a long time as substitutes. Further jade confusion is compounded by amazonite, aventurine, chrysophrase, agalmatolite, californite, some marbles, and even williamsite. For the jade collector, attention to these hardstones is imperative.

References: There is no single source that one could call comprehensive, yet the exhibition by the Asia House Gallery in New York in 1980 was very good and was accompanied by a book written by James C. Y. Watt entitled *Chinese Jades from Han to Ch'ing*, Asia Society, 1980. As previously mentioned, to sort out terms, use Mark Chou's *Dictionary of Jade Nomenclature*, New Island Printers, 1987. A standard book on materials, methods of jade carvings, and historical periods not to be ignored is S. Howard Hansford's *Chinese Jade Carvings*, Lund Humphries and Co., 1950. For archaic jades, Berthold Laufer's *Jade*, Dover Publications, 1974; and Max Loehr's *Ancient Chinese Jades*, Fogg Art Museum, Harvard University, 1975; are invaluable. For later Ming and Ching jades, J. J. Schedel's *The Splender of Jade*, E. P. Dutton & Co., 1974; and The National Palace Museum's *Masterworks of Chinese Jade*, Taipei, Taiwan, 1969 (and its supplement in 1973) are useful. In the bibliographical sections of these books are many, many other reference materials that the collector can pursue.

Museums: The jades of the Avery Brundage Collection in the Asian Art Museum of San Francisco (M. H. de Young Museum), San Francisco, California; The R. Norris Shreve Collection in the Field Museum of History, Chicago, Illinois; Indianapolis Museum of Art, Indianapolis, Indiana; the Grenville L. Winthrop Collection in the Fogg Art Museum at Harvard University, Boston, Massachusetts; the Fuller Collection in the Seattle Art Museum, Seattle, Washington; the Arthur M. Sackler Collection in the Smithsonian Center for Asian Art, Washington, D.C.; Royal Ontario Museum, Ontario, Canada; British Museum, London, England; Imperial Palace, Beijing, China; National Palace Museum collection in Taipei, Taiwan.

Most major museums display some jades, but do not overlook college and university museums such as the Minnesota Museum of Art; the University Museum in Philadelphia; Smith College Museum of Art, and others.

Reproduction Alert: With today's high rpm motors and sophisticated diamond points, a forger can rapidly carve a piece that the novice would assume to be older. Indeed, there is an ingrained Chinese tradition of copying earlier pieces to learn the craft of carving. That tradition literally has gone on for centuries. Thus it is imperative that the collector read and reread Hansford's *Chinese Jade Carvings* to fully understand what was possible during any single historical period. Recently, in an outdoor market in Hong Kong, I was offered a white nephrite seventeenth-century signed plaque done by Lu Tzu-kang (Lu Zigang), perhaps the most famous carver of all. The plaque was fairly pure in stone, was very well carved, and would deceive most people. The price—very inexpensive—was the first tip-off to its new date. The second was that the stone, under close examination, had too many flaws. The final and definitive point was that it had been carved with modern tools. There is little substitute for reading and hands-on experience. After finding time for those two activities, seek out a reliable dealer who knows jade and will work with you closely. If looking for jadeites for jewelry, be very careful. Many of the hardstones previously mentioned are inexpensive substitutes for expensive jadeites. Imperial jadeite cabs (cabochons) for rings have reached such astronomical prices that doublets and triplets are not uncommon. Other common phenomena are translucent, light-hued jadeite cabs dyed to rich emerald colors.

One last point: Be able to distinguish dark green jades from the Lake Baikal region north of China in the Soviet Union from "Taiwan jade," which at its best is a low-grade nephrite that is found, like British Columbian jade, in vast quantities. Siberian jade has been carved for centuries in China and is highly valued.

Collecting Hints: Nephrite jades are highly undervalued at the present moment. The Chinese shift to jadeite and the availability of nephrite jades from mainland China since 1972 has created a buyer's market. In my opinion, this has created an ideal climate in which to put together a great collection of nephrites. The recent dip in prices will also likely be temporary as the economies of Asia rebound, particularly Taiwan's.

More specific hints follow:

Collect beautifully colored pieces. If nephrites,

look for clean stones and soft, but rich white colors, but do not overlook yellows or mixed colors. If jadeite, look for translucency and color. A rich emerald green or a streak of the same in a rich white is always desirable.

If collecting ancient jades, always verify your purchase with an expert and be sure to get a receipt stating the stone is nephrite and of the period stated, and, if incorrect, that a full refund would be given.

Carry a small knife with you for doing a scratch test. On Mohs' revised and expanded scale of hardness, 1 is talc, 15 is a diamond. This test is not foolproof, but it will eliminate the majority of substitute stones, for both nephrites and jadeites are harder than steel. Simply put, a careful attempt to scratch jade will leave a silver line (the steel of the blade), whereas, most imitation jades will scratch and leave a small powder line. In addition, a small penlight will allow you to look through the jade and a ten-power jeweler's loupe will allow you to look at the stone's structure. A word of caution: *Be careful to do the scratch test only after getting permission, and do it in an area so as not to damage a piece if it is in fact not jade.* The exception to the hardness rule is the fact that calcified areas of ancient burial jades *will* scratch. In fact, the reproductions of these ancient pieces are often artificially fired to create the ''chicken-bone white'' look highly sought after by collectors.

Familiarize yourself with jade substitutes such as bowenite (so-called Soochow jade), Australian jade (green chalcedony), and other hardstones often sold as jade. One of the most common is green quartz.

Do not reject a piece because it is not jade. The Chinese value other carvings very highly, and many of them are quite early. A Ming Dynasty or seventeenth-century soapstone of only four inches in height can be worth as much as a good nephrite piece.

After some study one can distinguish nephrite from jadeite with ease. Nephrite, for example, because of its internal structure, takes a dull, waxy polish. Jadeite, due to its greater hardness (better than 8 on Mohs' scale) and internal structure, takes a higher polish. The latter is the primary reason why jadeite is valued as a gemstone.

Recognize that the thousands of years of appreciating nephrite has led to almost countless incorrect beliefs and superstitions about the stone's properties. Within the study of rocks (petrology), nephrite is merely an inorganic mineral. Yet those endless beliefs in its special properties guarantee that it will be collected and valued for at least another millennia. It is these latter beliefs that elevate jades from a semiprecious stone to precious in the eyes of the Chinese.

Collector's Club: *The Bulletin of the Friends of Jade* is published three to four times a year and highlights articles written by members. As such, it is a form of collector's club, and if one lives in England or is willing to travel there he or she can meet with other collectors. Their address:

Friends of Jade
P. O. Box 135
Wallington
Surrey, England

Advisors: Stewart and Barbara Hilbert

JADE

Archaic
Disk, $2\frac{1}{2}''$, Bi, Warring States, calcified white jade, the sides crisply carved with raised grain-pattern in rows further incised with C-scrolls, all within a pair of inward slanting borders at the outer and inner rim, the stone of translucent tone with shallow calcification to the surface. **4,100.00**
Grain-Pattern Disk, $2\frac{1}{2}''$ dia., Bi, Han Dynasty, carved to the side with raised study design within narrow raised borders, the stone of light even honey tone with areas of brown inclusions, box **3,650.00**
Dragon plaque
$1\frac{3}{4}''$, the thin plaque reticulated to the outline of a coiled dragon, one side incised with spiral and curls detailing the head and legs, the stone of light brown tone (restruck) **1,900.00**
$3\frac{5}{8}''$, Hongshan, green semi-translucent jade, Neolithic period, 4th millennium B.C., the fine plaque carved with a stylized dragon, the bifurcated tail curving over the back and two claws extending beneath the body, the center of the body with a shallow continuous groove, a hole pierced through the lower center (chipped) fitted box **17,600.00**
$5\frac{1}{4}''$ dia., Warring States, carved as a coiling S-shaped dragon with clawed feet and tail delineated with parallel striation, the body with spiraled comma-shaped whorls, and original green surface largely calcified to a creamy color, old minor edge chips **8,050.00**
Kneeling figure, 2'' h., Tang Dynasty, white jade, carved possibly as a Middle-Eastern servant wearing a triangular hat somewhat resembling a fez, his right hand on

Feline, 3″ l., probably Tang Dynasty, nephrite yellow jade, with mottling, head resting on forepaws, tail curved back. $3,500.00

top and his left at his protuberant waist, wearing a tunic and pantaloons falling to his feet, vertically pierced for suspension **11,000.00**

Libation cup, 5⅛″ h., Song dynasty, well carved standing on a small flared oval foot embellished with twin flanges, a triple band of archaistic spiral work, the scroll handle with a taotieh mask tab, the stone of pale green with extensive brown inclusions. **5,800.00**

Plectrum, 1⅜″ h., Die, Western Zhou Dynasty, flattened shield-shaped, carved from a stone of pale celadon tone with small russet and white inclusions, the front incised with the stylized design of an animal head, the reverse and underside pierced for attachment   **880.00**

Sword slide, 2¼″, Eastern Zhou Dynasty, celadon jade, rectangular, carved to the top with a dragon in low relief, the stone of light greenish tone with age incrustation . . .   **1,450.00**

Tiger plaque, 1¾″, Western Zhou Dynasty, Creamy-brown jade carved on one side with a humanoid face above scrolls representing the head of a tiger, the top

Ryton cup, 4½″ h., probably Song Dynasty, nephrite jade, with kylin on handle, stylized banded motif. $15,000.00

Pendant, 2½″ h., Han Dynasty, 200 B.C.-220 A.D., nephrite jade, black and white color, Yuan Weng-Chung was an ancient Chinese hero and this type of pendant is a stylized depiction of him, central perforation. $1,500.00

with white calcification, (old damage to base). **1,450.00**

Archer's ring
 Celadon and russet jade, relief qilong dragon **275.00**
 Greenish-yellow jade **120.00**
 Lavender and green jadeite **600.00**
 Jadeite, 1⅛″ dia., of characteristic cylindrical form with rounded rim at one end, the stone of semi-translucent apple green color shading to a paler tone on one side **8,800.00**

Bead, 1½″, Shang dynasty, brown and white, of rounded triangular shape, the center double-pierced for attachment, the originally pale light celadon jade with burial incrustation of bright reddish-brown tone **1,200.00**

Belt-hook, 3½″ l., Song Dynasty, the stone of very white tone, carved with a phoenix-head terminal, the shaft as a dragon with scaly body, horned head and bushy tasseled tail, the underside with lightly-incised scroll-pattern, box **6,600.00**

Bowl
 3½″ dia., covered bowl, Imperial green jade, Qianlong mark and period, well carved with steep rounded sides and everted rim, supported on a flared hollow foot, the domed cover set with a ring knop, incised in the center with the mark Qianlong yuyong, "for imperial use, Qianlong period," the stone of opaque moss-green color. **7,600.00**

 5¼″, Imperial jadeite, Jiaqing mark and period, the bright stone of apple-green color suffused with paler tones and flecked with emerald, with rounded sides rising to an everted rim and supported on a neatly finished square-cut footrim, the underside of the base incised with a four character Jiaqing mark, and with a further imperial mark Xianfeng yuyong "for imperial use of the Xianfeng (emperor)" incised in a line around the lowest part of the body above the footrim. **46,700.00**

Box and cover

3⅛", Qianlong, melon-shaped, semi-translucent pale greenish tone, well carved in the form of a butterfly resting on a large segmented melon fruit, and another pierced white jade box and cover **2,900.00**

6", chrysanthemum-shaped, Qianlong, white jade, the cover of shallow domed form carved in low relief with four tiers of radiating petals, the base carved with a continuous band of petals rising to the rim, the stone of even very pale greenish white color. . . **52,800.00**

5½" dia., circular, Ming Dynasty, white jade, of compressed form supported on a low nearly finished ring foot, the cover finely reticulated in varied relief with a circular panel enclosing a crested bird, the sides of the cover and base with pairs of archaistic S-shaped dragons within incised borders, the stone of pale grey-green color with some inclusions. **20,000.00**

Brush washer

5⅝" h., double-gourd shape, 18th

century, white jade, thinly carved with curled edges, the base formed from leaves and stalks extending around the sides. **4,400.00**

8½" dia., 19th century, nephrite, shallow oval basin with wide inverted rim and carved to the interior with a large "sacred jewel," its stylized flames extending out over the curved exterior and guarded by a large figure of a writhing dragon and qilong, the pale olive green matrix with black inclusions and russet fissure incorporated into the design **770.00**

9½", carved in the form of a large furled lotus leaf, the interior with a frog and dragonfly, all carved in high relief, the stone of apple green color with a russet highlight on one side **16,000.00**

Figure

Birds, pair, 7⅜" h., jadeite, each perched on a gnarled branch flowing from a bent tree trunk, the tail feathers falling toward the base, the stone of pale yellowing-white shaded to russet accentuating the combs and grey-green on the body. **4,700.00**

Boy immortal, 2⅝" h., Qianlong, white jade, well carved figure wearing baggy trousers and a long jacket, one hand holding a ruyi scepter, head bald except for two tufts of hair **4,400.00**

Cockerel, 3⅜" h., Qianlong, standing beside a plantain with the head turned over its shoulder, the plumage finely incised, the stone of very pale green color, with

Boulder, 6" h., 17th/18th century, nephrite jade, white with natural russet skin carved in serrated style, Shoulao and acolyte in cave with fir tree carved out of interior, later stand. $12,000.00

Female Figures, pair, 13" h., 19th/20th century, jadeite, translucent light green color, the mei rens (beautiful women) shown holding baskets of flowers, their chignons finely carved. $18,000.00

some russet inclusion and
speckling **5,800.00**
Crane, 2½″ h., 19th century, neph-
rite, the recumbent bird with head
turned backwards with a peach-
laden branch grasped in its long
beak, the stone a mottled grey-
white color with occasional inclu-
sions.   **330.00**
Equestrienne group, 8¼″ h., jadeite,
carved with long robed Meiren,
with celestial scarves billowing
about her shoulders, seated on a
prancing horse held by an attendant, opposite a female attendant
sheltering her with a fan, all supported on a pierced rockwork
base with leafy lingzhi, the stone
of light green suffused with apple
and olive in places, one side with
russet inclusion, large chip to
fan **10,250.00**
Goose, 2⅛″ h., Qianlong, white
jade, of flattened ovoid section, its
head turned back, leafy pond
weeds trailing from its beak above
the incised wings, the whitish
stone with russet speckling **2,200.00**
Guanyin, 14¾″ h., jadeite, carved
standing wearing long robes
splaying toward the base, holding
a flowering lotus sprig in one
hand, and a lingzhi in the other, a
crane perched in front, the stone
of muted green broadly suffused
with apple and deeper tones **61,600.00**
Horse, 2¾″ h., carved in a recum-
bent position with the maned
head turned back over its shoulder, the tail curled under the hind-
quarters, the stone of pale green
color with some light brown
suffusion. **6,100.00**
Meiren
9″ h., 19th century, nephrite,
standing in long flowing robes
with scarf, her hand with a
large basket of flowers, a youth
standing with a peony sprig, the
pale green matrix mottled with
white and occasional brown
flecks **1,320.00**
10″ h., lavender and apple green
jadeite, the female figure shown
holding a lotus blossom **7,500.00**
10⅜″ h., white jade, carved stand-
ing on a double lotus base,
wearing long robes tied at the
waist and holding a sprig of
lingzhi in one hand, her face
with smiling features below her

hair piled into a high coiled
chignon, the stone of even
white color lightly suffused with
very pale russet on top. **13,200.00**
Pig, 4¼″, Han dynasty, celadon and
russet jade, recumbent position,
carved form is a slender tube with
a large snout, legs tucked at the
sides, and stumpy tail **4,700.00**
Girdle hook, 5″ h., white jade, with
dragon and young **350.00**
Pendant
2″ h., white jade, in the form of a
child with a jui fungus and a
gourd vase. **300.00**
2½″ h., pear-shaped, white jade
carved in high relief with dragons
on one face, a figure of a goat
opposite **250.00**
2½″, 18th century, white jade,
carved on one side with a bat
swooping above a boy carrying a
large peach, the reverse with a bi
suspended by a ribbon, flanked by
long tassels and with scrolling
lingzhi above, the stone of even
white color, with a cylindrical
jadeite bead secured by a gold
pendant mounting **4,400.00**
Ruyi scepter
Miniature, 7″ l., Qianlong/Jiaqing,
white jade, the undulating shaft
carved in the form of a gnarled
stem with lingzhi heads, the stone
of an even pale green color **5,000.00**
14¼″ l., Qianlong, white jade, the
undulating shaft well carved in
low relief with two figures standing in a rocky gorge, the ruyi
shaped head carved with two figures on a balcony, the stone of
even pale celadon color, with
areas stained to simulate russet in-
clusions **4,100.00**
Table-screen, 8½″ h., Qianlong, cela-
don jade, finely carved with an extensive landscape scene, with an old
man standing outside the gate of his
house, mounted in a carved wooden
frame **5,500.00**
Vase
3¼″ h., white jade, early 19th century, well carved in the archaic
bronze zun form with globular
body standing on a hollow
splayed foot, with a widely flared
mouth, the stone of a semi-trans-
lucent greenish white color **8,800.00**
4⅜″ h., pair, jadeite, translucent apple-green color, gu shaped, each
carved with taotieh masks, be-

tween blades rising to the keyfret-bordered neck and further archaistic decoration. **10,000.00**

6⅞'' h., yellow jade, gu-form, of flattened well hollowed quatrefoil section rising to the lipped rim and splayed toward the base, the smooth stone of semi-translucent greenish-yellow tone suffused with broad stripes of soft brown . . **10,250.00**

With cover, 8⅜'' h., pale-green, jadeite, baluster form, thickly carved with an archaistic taotieh band around the middle, the waisted neck encircled by four loop mask handles and loose rings, the domed cover with archaistic carving and a flower knop, the stone of mottled pale green with slightly darker areas . . **13,200.00**

9⅜'' h., white jade, carved, of flattened shouldered form standing on a hollow splayed foot and rising to the angled shoulders supporting the waisted neck flanked by two lion head loop handles suspending rings, the cover with a lion holding a lingzhi bough in its mouth, flanked to one side by a crane standing on a rock holding a further lingzhi, the stone of even white color **38,000.00**

Vessel and cover, crane-shaped, 9¼'' h., white jade, the top of the body forming the cover, with the long neck turned back grasping a stem of lingzhi, standing amid pierced leafy lingzhi stems growing from pierced rockwork, a smaller crane at the side, the stone of pale greenish white, the cover cracked and repaired **7,300.00**

OTHER CARVINGS

Agate

Carving, mythical toad, 2½'' h., the recumbent three-legged amphibian carved with bulging eyes and raised spine issuing scrolling clouds from its mouth, the grayish-white stone suffused with amber-colored inclusions **250.00**

Vase and cover, 5'' h., 19th century, of flattened ovoid form, encircled by carved and pierced flowering vines picked out of the russet skin, the lid carved with a scrolling vine finial. **330.00**

Amethyst

Covered urn, 9½'' h., bulbous body supported on three lion-mask and

Pendant, 3'', 18th century, carnelian agate, squirrel on scrolling grapes, variegated color. $900.00

paw feet and carved with opposing ferocious lion-head handles spewing scrolling flames from their jaws, supporting loose rings, the domed lid carved with three loose rings and surmounted by a writhing dragon **825.00**

Figure, happy Buddha, 6'' h., holding an amethyst ball in his upraised hand **500.00**

Carnelian agate

Archer's ring, rich red bands of color **150.00**

Vase, 5'' h., carved in the form of a narrow hollow trunk of a peach tree entwined with a smaller fruiting branch, all in a bright tomato red stone streaked with white . . . **5,500.00**

Coral, red, figure group, 5'' h., depicting two immortals **1,300.00**

Lapis Lazuli

Carved boulder, 10'' h., 19th century, carved and undercut to the front with a Chinese sage seated in a recessed alcove bordered by a youthful attendant holding a ruyi-headed staff, the dark blue matrix with white inclusions, (color enhanced) **3,025.00**

Covered vase, 6⅝'' h., with shoul-

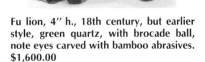

Fu lion, 4'' h., 18th century, but earlier style, green quartz, with brocade ball, note eyes carved with bamboo abrasives. $1,600.00

dered body encircled to a taotieh band in low relief, above pendent cicada blades, the shoulders set with large mythical animal mask and loop handles, the domed cover carved with a Buddhist lion, the stone of good bright color with some white rivering 7,300.00

Marble, censer, 6" l., 18th century, carved, gently sloping bowl supported on a short ring foot and bracketed by a pair of large handles fashioned as qilong head issuing scrolling flutes of water, the opaque white stone matrix with occasional black inclusions 825.00

Opal, figure group, two Meiren, 5¼" h., one holding a lute, the other kneeling at her side 2,200.00

Rock crystal

Carving of Buddha, 9" h., standing figure carved with downcast eyes, pendant lobes, and a topknot and dressed in flowing robes holding a sprig of lingzhi, (drilled for stand) 660.00

Seated Buddha, 9" h., shown seated vajrasana with hands held in the dhyana mudra, the serene face with downcast eyes and framed with a high chignon, resting on a double lotus pedestal . . . 1,210.00

Teapot and cover, 4" h., of compressed globular form and lobed oval section, the short curved spout opposite the loop handle, the cover rising to the oval knop 3,600.00

Vase and cover, 8½" h., bronze form standing on a stepped hollow foot, well carved, on one side a pair of bifid-tailed qilong and on the other a phoenix in flight above a peony tree, the angled shoulders with ruyi handles and loose rings, the cover with a lappet band, the crystal clear with minor natural fissures 5,100.00

Smoky Quartz, carving of Guanyin, 6¼" h., slender standing figure dressed in flowing robes, her hands held to the front clutching a rosary, with a rock pedestal to her side supporting a book. 700.00

Soapstone, carving of a nude, 13¼" h., 18th century, the standing figure with arms raised above her head entwined in a scarf flowing down her body, pale olive-green stone with occasional russet mottling, restoration on one arm, scarf 1,600.00

Turquoise, figure of Meiren, 5" h., holding a dish of fruit and a fan 990.00

MING DYNASTY CERAMICS

See Appendix I for table of Ming emperors.

History: The Ming Dynasty encouraged the rise and cultivation of the art of porcelain manufacture with the creation of the imperial factory at Ching-te-chen during the early reign of Emperor Hongwu. Since the factory kept records of its porcelain production for the royal family, we now have a well-documented source of information for the types of wares that were created throughout its years of production. The records reveal that the imperial factory was producing fine eggshell ("bodyless") white porcelain, blue and white ware, and gilt-decorated porcelain during the reign of Emperor Yonglo. While some celadon wares of very fine quality were made at the kilns, most of the pottery, celadon, and inferior porcelain production was relegated to the provinces of China, leaving the growing kiln sites at Ching-te-chen to fulfill their emperor's desire: the creation of beauty and art in porcelain form.

The ceramics made during the reigns of Xuante, Chenghua, Jiajing and Wanli are greatly valued for their innovative techniques and beauty. When signed with the nien ho of the reigning emperor, they are aesthetically priceless and command large sums of money in the antiques marketplace.

Although some notable porcelain was produced during the reigns of the early Ming emperors, it was not until the peaceful and prosperous reign of Xuante that the Chinese reached what they often consider to be the peak of their porcelain perfection. The emperor encouraged the porcelain production of his kilns and several new techniques and designs were created. Underglaze copper red decoration, which first appeared in the fourteenth century, was incorporated on the now-famous "stem" cups and bowls of this period. The technique was achieved by painting copper oxide on the biscuit porcelain, which was subsequently covered with a transparent glaze. While early firing conditions often turned the underglaze red to a greyish color, it appeared as a brilliant copper red during the Xuante period. The favored designs of these items were fish, pomegranates, and dragons in a white field that had the appearance of "congealed fat." Underglaze red in combination with underglaze blue and copper red monochromes were also produced.

The Chenghua period saw the emergence of the tou-ts'ai (doucai) enamel technique that used a distinctive style of underglaze blue decoration subsequently refired with overglaze enamels. The technique consisted of painting an outline and details of a design on the unfired body of a porcelain piece. The object was then glazed and fired. After cooling, transparent overglaze washes of yellow, green, aubergine, turquoise, and red were applied within the boundaries of the outline designs of the underglaze blue. The porcelain was then refired. Tou-ts'ai enameling often was used to decorate the famous "chicken cups" of this era, which are sometimes offered for sale at some of the larger auction houses. Blue and white wares were produced prolifically during this time.

Wu-ts'ai enamels (five-color ware) were introduced during the reign of Jiajing. This technique used overglaze enamels of green, aubergine, yellow, and red (outlined in red or black) on a white glazed body. The art of this technique reached its perfection during the reign of Wanli and continued to be popular well into the Qing Dynasty. "Kinrande" (the Japanese term for gold brocade), a sixteenth-century Ming novelty which featured gold tracery designs on a red or green-glazed body, was also popular at this time. It sometimes appeared with incised and cutout decoration.

Polychrome decoration (using enamel colors which are refined at a lower temperature over a previously high-fired glaze, became firmly established in the Wanli period. Tou-ts'ai and wu-ts'ai glazes continued in popularity. A combination of aubergine, green, and yellow were used to create a three-color san-ts'ai glaze. Overglaze iron red techniques, which were far less costly than underglaze red and far easier to apply, were freely employed. The most sought-after export was the blue and white glazed Kraak porcelain, so named by the Dutch after their capture of the Portuguese ships (caraques) in 1602. Kraak ware consisted mostly of deep dishes but also included decoration on water bottles, vases, bowls, and ewers. The lightweight porcelain shows small glaze pittings and has a ringing tone when struck. The blue and white decoration is distinctive in its dense overall design. A typical deep dish has a broad rim decorated with alternating broad and narrow panels which frame a central medallion that is decorated in designs including insects, animals, figures, or flower-filled vases. The rim panels are decorated with alternating birds, fruits, and emblems separated by narrow panels of ribbon or geometric designs. The production of these blue and white ceramics continued throughout the Transitional period (1620–1683).

While the imperial factories at Ching-te-chen concentrated on the refinement of porcelain techniques, interesting developments in ceramics were taking place in other areas of China. One of the more fascinating techniques was the creation of Fa Hua ware. It featured a sturdy pottery body which was decorated with a design executed in applied slip (clay). Polychrome enamel colors, often in the san-ts'ai palette—yellow, green, and deep purple or aubergine—were applied between the clay partitions which divided the colors in the design. Deep cobalt blue or bright turquoise often was used as background color.

In Fukien Province, Swatow ware was being produced and exported to Southeast Asia, Indonesia, and Japan. The coarse grey porcelain body is often seen with kiln grit adhering to the base. The ceramics were decorated mostly with inferior blue pigment but can also be found with incised or slip decoration. Polychrome versions of this ware featured red, turquoise, green, and black colors.

The sixteenth-century Tê-hua kilns were producing a fine white porcelain ware which was later named blanc de chine by the French. The potters specialized in modeling figures because the clay was very plastic in nature.

Kiangnan Ting wares were produced in an area north of Kuan-tung. The pottery bodies were covered with a thick, creamy, buff-colored glaze which was finely crackled and stained, giving the surface an appearance somewhat like the skin of an ostrich egg. Sometimes relief decoration was applied.

Another characteristic of Kiangnan Ting wares is its tear streaks (heavy, runny coagulations in the glaze).

Of all the ceramic products created during the Ming Dynasty, the most notable were the blue and white decorated porcelains which are so eagerly sought after today. Their production began in the fourteenth century. The quality of the early blue pigments was so poor that the color could vary from a dull grey to ultramarine or purple. Early decorations consisted of brushstrokes very freely drawn in bold splashes which had a "heaped and piled" effect. Black dots frequently appeared at the edges of outlines. This was caused by the glaze sinking deeply into the clay, thereby causing thick black concentrations of blue glaze pigment. The "orange peel" textured surface of these early blue and white wares is a clue to their age, as is the tone of the greenish blue glaze. A demand for finer blue pigments was answered by Persia in the form of a rich pigment named "Mohammedan" blue. In the fifteenth century the technique for painting blue decorations on white porcelain was changed from broad strokes to the use of fine outlines which were filled in with diluted pigment in the form of washes. The heaped and piled effect disappeared by the end of the century. The sixteenth century output of blue and white wares was greatly expanded to meet the needs of the export trade. The reign of Zhengde saw the appearance of Mohammedan wares bearing Arabic inscriptions. The Jiajing years were famous for the quality of the dark, brilliant purplish blue on their wares. The Wanli blue followed in this tradition but also introduced decoration in a new "silvery" blue. Kraak porcelain exports remained strong from the end of the Wanli reign through the Transitional period, leading to the establishment of the Qing Dynasty. (Also see Blanc de Chine; Celadon; Monochromes; Shiwan Ware; Yi-hsing.)

References: John Ayers, *Chinese Ceramics: The Koger Collection* Sotheby's Publications, 1985; Stephen W. Bushell, *Chinese Art*, Rare Reprints, Inc., 1977; R. L.Hobson, *Chinese Pottery and Porcelain*, Dover Publications, Inc., 1976; —, *The Wares of the Ming Dynasty*, Charles E. Tuttle Co., Inc., 1962; Daisy Lion-Goldschmidt, *Ming Porcelain*, Rizzoli International Publications, Inc., 1978; Margaret Medley, *Ming Polychrome Wares*, University of London, Percival David Foundation of Chinese Art, 1978; —, *Underglaze Blue and Copper Red Decorated Porcelains*, University of London, Percival David Foundation of Chinese Art, 1976; John Alexander Pope, *Chinese Porcelains from the Ardebil Shrine*, Sotheby Parke Bernet Publications, 1981.

Museums: Asian Art Museum, San Francisco, California; Chicago Art Institute, Chicago, Illinois; Indianapolis Museum of Art, Indianapolis, Indiana; Nelson Gallery of Art, Kansas City, Kansas; Boston Museum of Fine Arts, Boston, Massachusetts; Museum of the University of Michigan, Ann Arbor, Michigan; Detroit Institute of Arts, Detroit, Michigan; Saint Louis Art Museum, Saint Louis, Missouri; Metropolitan Museum of Art, New York, New York; Cleveland Museum of Art, Cleveland, Ohio; Philadelphia Museum of Art, Philadelphia, Pennsylvania; Victoria and Albert Museum, London, England; British Museum, London, England; Sir Percival David Museum, London, England; Ashmolean Museum, Oxford, England; Musée Guimet, Paris, France; Djakarta Pusat Museum, Djakarta, Indonesia; Archaeological Museum, Teheran, Iran; Gemeentemuseum, The Hague, the Netherlands; National Palace Museum, Stockholm, Sweden; Topkapi Saray Palace Museum, Istanbul, Turkey.

Reproduction Alert: Ming porcelains were widely reproduced during the Qing Dynasty, but such reproduction was not intended to be fraudulent. It was part of the art of porcelain manufacturing to give homage to or show respect for a particularly well-made item by signing it with the mark of an earlier emperor. Sometimes this mark of respect was put on items that did not even resemble the wares that were produced during the emperor's lifetime. Thus it is not unusual to find Qing porcelain signed with Ming marks. Learning to evaluate the true origin of a signed piece is a task for the experienced collector. This requires a fair amount of study and hands-on learning. Basically there are five things we look for in evaluating the age of any piece: (1) the type of paste that was fired. Check to see if it is smooth or rough or whether or not it shows iron oxide (rusty spots or firing rings) on the unglazed por-

tions of the base; (2) The glaze quality. Look for pitting in the glaze. If there are bubbles, examine their characteristics; (3) The glaze colors used should be appropriate to a period that agrees with the mark; (4) Size and shape factors need to agree with what we know about items produced during the period; (5) Motif should be consistent with the period of the mark and typically found on items of that reigning emperor.

Collecting Hints: Ceramic production during the Ming Dynasty was widely diversified. Rough provincial pottery was prolifically produced and is still available in abundance. Because of the relative ease in acquiring such pieces, the prices are generally in the $150.00 to $300.00 range. This includes provincial pottery, semiporcelain, and porcelain wares. This fact may come as a surprise to those who have attached a mystique to the name Ming, but the fact is that many items from this great dynasty are affordable and easily accessible to the collector. The provincal blue and white items in particular fall into this category. Porcelains produced for export or made for the imperial household fetch a higher price. Most prized items from this dynasty are those imperial wares that are signed with the nien ho of the reigning emperor.

Ming blue and white ware is as popular today as it was when it first received European acclaim in the sixteenth century. An easy way to date the early blue and white porcelain is to look for the heaped and piled effect and the blue pigment turning to black in the firing. This was the result of using inferior pigment, a condition which was corrected later by importing blue pigment from Persia. It is also important to know that the formal pattern designs were developed for the expanding European market.

It should be noted that the opaque enamel color pink was introduced in the Qing Dynasty and is never found on Ming porcelains.

Bowl
2" h. x 5½" dia., blue and white, Wanli Period, the bowl is rounded with a short foot rim and a painted shou character within a double ring.   **500.00**
4⅜" dia., blue and white, Wanli mark and period, decorated on the interior with five interlinking ruyi heads forming a florallike medallion within double line borders repeated on the rim, the exterior with three full lotus blossoms borne on continuous leafy vines divided by three playful fu lions below lotus buds, above a band of lappets encircling the base, the underside with six-character mark, restored rim chip **3,000.00**

$4\frac{7}{8}''$ dia., wucai decoration, shallow bowl, Wanli Six-character mark within a double circle and of the period, the exterior painted in deep underglaze blue with a continuous band of joined lotus scroll filled out with iron-red petals and green and yellow enameled leaves, between double-line borders, with countersunk base and unglazed footrim burnt pale orange in the firing, wide crazing to glaze **3,800.00**

$5\frac{5}{8}''$ dia., blue and white, Wanli mark and period, thinly potted, the deep sides rising to the everted rim, painted on the exterior with the four characters, "Wanli Nian Hao", each character above a large lingzhi head amid smaller lingzhi divided by cloud motifs, all between double line borders, glaze frits to rim **900.00**

Bulb bowl

$9\frac{5}{8}''$ dia., blue and white, 16th/17th Century, of compressed bombé form supported on three short feet, painted around the sides with various upright aquatic plant sprays interspersed with various fish swimming in different attitudes amid aquatic plants, all below double-line borders and a continuous flowering lotus foliate vine scroll encircling the waisted neck, the everted rim decorated with a floret diaper band, crack **2,000.00**

15" dia., blue and white, late 15th/ Early 16th Century, shallow bowl, the interior boldly painted with large lotus blossoms and spiky leaves borne on a continuous pen-

cilled scrolling stem below a double-line border, repeated on the exterior between a band of classic scroll above and lappets below, the underglaze blue of purplish tone **2,600.00**

Box and cover, $2\frac{1}{4}''$ across, enamelled, late Ming Dynasty, of square form with indented corners, the cover decorated with a horse prancing amid iron-red flames, with flames on the sides of the cover and box **550.00**

Brush holder, $4\frac{1}{2}''$ dia., blue and white, circa 1500, drum-shaped, pierced on the top with five circular apertures and a single oval aperture and molded with a narrow band at the top and bottom of the sides, painted in pale underglaze blue with a continuous band of meandering peony between key pattern borders, minor cracks **1,300.00**

Censer with cover, $11\frac{1}{4}''$ h., cobalt blue glazed, the rounded body resting on three lion mask feet and surmounted by a short thick neck and rolled rim, covered overall in a rich blue glaze, with streaks of turquoise showing through, the interior glazed turquoise, fitted with a carved and reticulated rosewood lid, kiln flaws **880.00**

Dish

$4\frac{3}{4}''$ dia., blue and white, shallow dish, Wanli Six-character mark within a double circle and of the period, with thinly potted shallow sides raised on a ring foot, boldly painted on the interior with a lively dragon leaping after a "flaming pearl" above a cloud scroll, and on the exterior with continuous foliate scroll, all within dou-

Bowl, blue and white, with stylized floral design executed in an inky blue on the interior, floral medallions on the exterior, the rim encased in a copper sheath. $950.00

Dish, 5" dia., blue and white, the sketchy loose drawing executed in dark blue sinking to black in the firing. $175.00

ble-line borders, minute rim glaze chips **2,800.00**

5¾" dia., wucai decoration, signed Tianqi, small circular, late Ming, wood box, underglaze blue "Fu" character mark, painted below the rim in the center with a bearded sage seated on a fenced bank beside a lotus pond, minor rim nicks **800.00**

5⅝" dia., saucer dish, blue and white, Wanli mark in underglaze blue and of the period, the interior painted in the center with the immortal Huan-tan riding a fantastic animal into battle against the Five Poisons (Wudu, consisting of a serpent, scorpion, centipede, salamander and a three-legged toad), below sprigs and flowers in the well, the Wudu repeated in larger scale on the exterior, restored **500.00**

6½" dia., circa 1500, blue and white, circular warming dish *Zhuguo*, solidly potted and constructed with double walls, painted in shades of underglaze blue on the concave top with five various fish swimming amid water weeds and below double lines at the rim, the sloping sides with a broad band of scrolling lotus between similar bands, pierced on the base with a circular aperture for the filling of hot water **1,800.00**

7½", doucai decoration, late Ming, square dish, with a flat rim, raised on four bracket feet, central scene depicting a figure in an ox-drawn cart beneath a tree and moun-

Dish, 5½" dia., the center with four radiating panels of pomegranate forms surrounding a center medallion of stylized floral design, the border with alternating panels of stylized and sketchily draw floral design. $475.00

tains, the well with floral panels and rim with geometric pattern, in underglaze blue with red, green and yellow overglaze enamels. **2,600.00**

15" dia., blue and white, Kraak porcelain, Wanli period, barbed edge, center medallion of birds near a lake, the wide border design of alternating panels of florals and fruits **1,500.00**

16¾" dia., blue and white, Wanli, decorated on the interior with a central stylized (shou) character in a medallion surrounded by a foliate scroll issuing from a (ruyi) head below the cavetto painted with the Three Friends motif and a pomegranate tree, all with trunks in stylized (shou) character form, the everted rim decorated with continuous scroll pattern, the exterior with prunus stems and chrysanthemum blossoms, rim chip, kiln grit **2,800.00**

Figure

Aborigine, 12½" h., molded in subservient posture, bent from the waist and with his head held to one side, the yellow glazed figure clothed in a green glazed sarong, green glaze to his bangles and hair, shown with a fierce expression, damages, losses and wear **660.00**

Elephant, 5⅛" h., Cizhou, shown standing on a footed rectangular base, the back surmounted by a flaring receptacle pierced to the interior, the head, trappings and vessel with details painted in shades of iron oxide, with restorations, damages and wear **220.00**

Female, 12⅝" h., early 17th Century, fahua glazed biscuit, seated with her hand resting on her raised right knee, wearing long beaded necklaces hanging to her waist and dressed in long flowing robes, with a chignon centered with a diadem, the figure supported on a pierced rectangular pedestal base molded on four sides with lion masks, chips, restored **1,500.00**

Fu dogs, 18½" h., pair, each raised on a rectangular galleried plinth covered with a diaper patterned brocade panel supporting each figure, with one front paw resting on appropriate ball or cub, glazed in chestnut and aubergine glazes on a turquoise body and base . . . **3,300.00**

Guandi, 10½" h., the serene figure

Chenwu, 7" h., Cizhou shown seated on his throne, covered with a white slip and decorated in brown pigment. $725.00. Courtesy of Butterfield and Butterfield.

Attendants, 10½" h., each wearing a high hat, one on a rectangular base, the other on a raised circular base, both with clothing glazed in yellow and green, glaze missing, wear. $800.00 each

seated on a large dias framed by a high-backed throne, gazing ahead with a meditative expression, the characteristic tortoise and attendants below, the figures glazed chestnut, turquoise and aubergine, minor restoration **880.00**

Guanyin, 18" h., late Ming, Wanli, blue and white, modelled with arms at the waist and right hand raised, the head bent slightly forward, wearing longsleeved full-length gown secured by a broad band at the waist and partially open at the chest, hair gathered in a rounded top-knot, the garment in underglaze bluish-black cobalt with five-clawed dragons chasing flaming pearls amid fire scrolls, jewelled pendant tassels and borders composed of flowerhead medallions reserved against a diaper ground, some restoration **3,500.00**

Guardian attendant, 17½" h., the robust figure posed on rock-form dias, wearing a long robe belted at the chest and below his plump belly, the bearded figure carrying a scroll in his left hand and gazing surreptitiously to the left, his solid features framed by a tall peaked cap, his body picked out in ochre, blue and green lead glazes, restorations **935.00**

Mounted rider, 11¾" h., the equestrian wearing a high conical hat and celadon glazed jacket over sandy yellow glazed trousers, seated on an elaborate saddle of a majestic steed, the trappings sup-

porting a drum to one side and a decorative ornament to the front, the animals head well modeled with deep set eyes, flaring nostrils and well defined jaw (glaze degraded, restorations, later base, wear) **1,100.00**

Officials, pair, 19½" h., each standing in long green-glazed flowing robes on a high stepped hexagonal base pierced to the center, one hand clenched in a fist and resting on his chest, the other to his side and hidden by the oversized sleeve, each plump face with well-defined features and surmounted by a tall conical black cap, traces of original pigment, restorations, minor loss to the glaze, retouched, wear. **5,500.00**

Figure group, 8¾" h., late Ming, 16th/17th Century, turquoise, pale Aubergine and yellow-glazed formed as an arched arbor with a seated meditative figure in long flowing robes before a small turtle and snake above a ruyi-head and lotus molded register and two acolytes, a lotus pod and leaf rising from molded waves forming the base, the arched surround with flowerhead and ribboned tendrils, the base and cylindrical reverse unglazed, minor chips **1,000.00**

Jar

8¾" w., Wanli Six-character mark and of the period, blue and white, squat baluster form, unusually painted with a partially finished scene of flying cranes for the later application of overglaze enamels,

the lappets and decoration therefore cursory, some minor restora-
tion to chips, small cracks **1,300.00**
13″ x 9″, Wanli Period, blue and
white, baluster form, with a
painted symbolic dragon and
phoenix guarding a flaming pearl,
around the foot are coral rocks
and waves, the short neck has vertical palmettes and chevron bor-
ders, the flat base is unglazed . . . **1,600.00**
19″ h., 17th Century, blue and
white, baluster form, painted
around the body with a wide band
of small insects amid various leafy
flowering branches including
prunus and peony issuing from
rockwork, with pendant lotus-
decorated lappets at the base and
circular medallions enclosing floral sprays reserved on a pencil-
line-infilled blue-ground band at
the shoulder, the domed cover
similarly decorated with a metal
and hardstone knop, glaze chips,
chips, knop later **3,800.00**
Pillow, 13½″ l., molded in the form of
a recumbent boy with upheld head,
his hands crossed over his chest
grasping the shoulder, wearing a tasseled cap picked out in green, covered overall in a rich crackled ochre
glaze **1,000.00**
Tileworks
Roof tile
6⅝″ l., x 8¾″ h., with arched base,
supporting a lion seated on its
hind legs and molded with a
curly mane and upraised tail,
covered overall with a bright,
amber glaze, chips **550.00**
10¼″ h., modeled as a leaping
Buddhist lion above scrolls, the
body glazed with aubergine,
turquoise and cobalt, right rear
foot missing, repairs **1,100.00**
11″ x 4″ h., in the form of a dol-
phin leaping over waves, the
yellow glaze with slight de-
grading **500.00**
Ridgetile
13″ h., equestrian figure, depicting a helmeted official wearing
loose green robes over armor,
his body turned to one side,
seated astride an amber pony,
now mounted on a wood stand,
chips, glaze chips **1,000.00**
15⅜″ h., x 12″ w., Bodhisattva,
inset with a green-glazed
arched alcove, the figure seated
in dhyana mudra on a lotus-

Figure of Official, 13″ h., shown wearing blue robes and seated before a turquoise glazed triptych screen, his head, shoulders, feet and hands left in the biscuit. $1,450.00

petal plinth and throne, grasping a jar and wearing an elaborate diadem, glazed overall in
golden yellow, the reverse
unglazed, chips **650.00**
Vase
4⅜″ h., late Ming Dynasty, blue and
white, pear-shaped, the bulbous
lower body freely painted with
two foliate sprays below a border
of overlapping leaf tips, with insects evenly spaced below a me-
dian rib on the neck and leaf tips
in a band above, all within single
and double-line borders **200.00**
6½″ h., late Ming Dynasty, painted
Cizhou, bottle form, the drum-
form body surmounted by a gently

"Kraak" charger, 19⅞″ dia., Wanli period, painted in deep underglaze blue with a scene of water birds in the center, the rim painted with alternating panels of flowers, fruit and "precious objects" separated by diaper panels. $3,000.00

canted shoulder below the small cylindrical neck covered all over with a grayish glaze freely painted in brown with a continuous band of flowering foliage scrolls repeated around the shoulder **800.00**

7¾" h., Jiajing, blue and white, oviform, the sides decorated with horses galloping above a (lishui) band encircling the foot, below beaded chains and tassels interspersed with florettes pendant from a band of evenly spaced demi-florettes at the base of the short cylindrical neck encircled by upright leaf tips, all within blue line borders, glaze gap on mouth rim **900.00**

8⅜" h., Cizhou polychrome, meiping form, the heavily potted sides rising from a wide raised foot and surmounted by a flaring neck with everted lip, the banded decoration consisting of a cursory classic scroll around the foot, two hexagonal panels with herons in lotus ponds bordered by lappet-like fillers on the body, a quatrefoil panel enclosing florettes around the shoulder, a petal panel beneath the neck, freely painted with underglaze turquoise, aubergine and amber tones **1,200.00**

9⅞" h., 16th Century, blue and white, meiping shape, the baluster-shaped body painted with a central band enclosing flowers among rocks divided by hovering insects, below a cloud-collar border filled with lotus, the tapered splayed foot encircled by tall lappets **800.00**

9⅞" h., Wanli, blue and white, bottle-form, set on a splayed foot and painted around the body with two writhing dragons chasing "flaming pearls" amid scrolls between sketchy waves and flowering sprigs, all below the long slender neck decorated with dangling scrollwork and stiff upright leaves, the underside with pencilled flower blossoms, cracks **1,000.00**

10" h., Cizhou turquoise-glazed, meiping shape, of characteristic form, with short trumpet-shaped neck, flanged foot and recessed flat base, covered in a white slip and painted in underglaze black iron pigment with a central band of three panels enclosing a seated male figure, a crane and a hare

5" h., Fa Hua vessel, of slightly waisted form, decorated with turquoise and aubergine glazes, the interior with a green glaze. $1,200.00

respectively, between stylized flowerheads above the foot and a band of chrysanthemums and peony around the shoulder, all under a greenish-blue glaze pooling at one side, mouth with minor chips **1,300.00**

11¾" h., Wanli, blue and white, double-gourd shape, the lower body molded with interlocking petal lappets alternating with painted floral sprays, including peony and chrysanthemum, above floral and leaf medallions and beribboned symbols and similar floral and leaf medallions below the upper bulb, decorated with floral panels interspersed with antiques, the neck with pendant lotus motifs, underglaze firing crack, restored rim chip. **1,000.00**

12⅜" h., similar pair, fahua decoration, each of rectangular ovoid form with a high shoulder contour, surmounted by a tall flaring neck molded with raised horizontal bands and flanked by a pair of large animal-mask handles, the sides with raised floral sprigs, colored in yellow and turquoise enamels on a deep blue ground, set on a high square base with rounded edges (surface wear, extensive restorations **1,650.00**

Wine cup, 2¼" dia., Tianqi Four-character mark, blue and white, wood box, and of the period, the exterior boldly painted with the characters reading "Buddha" **700.00**

MONOCHROME GLAZES

History: The production of copper red as a single-glaze technique was perfected in the fifteenth century, although it had been used in underglaze decoration at Ching-te-chen in the fourteenth century. It was during the fifteenth century that the potters discovered that firing copper oxide in a reduction furnace resulted in vibrant red color. This color, which we now call sang de boeuf, (oxblood) was subject to a variety of changes due to kiln conditions, resulting in color variations ranging from cherry red to deep blood red to dull pinkish brown. Because color results were so unstable, the use of this pigment was forbidden by the court by the early sixteenth century. The same color was revived, however, during the Kangxi period. By this time the clay had also changed and the firing in the reduction kiln was more stable. Variations of the copper oxide red monochrome glazes have been named to isolate certain shades: lang yao, a bright cherry to deep blood red; sang de pigeon, (pigeon's blood); sang de poulet, (chicken's blood); and the dull, deep pink-brown dubbed mule's liver.

Copper oxide, when fired in an oxidizing kiln atmosphere, also produces various shades of green. The combination of firing copper oxide in a reduced atmosphere and reoxidizing it during the last stage of firing was experimented with during the Kangxi period and resulted in the development of a variant glaze color that we now call peach bloom. Peach bloom glazes vary in color from a pale red to a liver pink shade and often contain spotting of olive green. Peach bloom porcelains may also appear with incised decorations, which are faintly visible under the glaze.

An orange-red glaze was substituted for copper oxide during the years that copper red monochromes were forbidden. Iron red was employed as an overglaze color and as such was subject to damage. Ordinary handling could scratch the surface. The use of this glaze as a monochrome was not successful. It is sometimes called coral red.

The employment of cobalt blue as a monochrome did not become popular until the sixteenth century. In the Wanli period, this brilliant blue glaze sometimes appeared on objects with incised decorations. Another application of cobalt blue was the technique of spraying the powdered pigment through a bamboo tube onto the unglazed porcelain. Transparent glaze was then applied over the pigment and a mottled blue/powder blue "soufflé" effect was achieved. Powder blue was developed in the late seventeenth to early eighteenth century in the imperial kiln at Ching-te-chen. (Powder blue is frequently found with gold tracery designs painted over the glaze.) The claire de lune pale blue glaze was also created about the same time. The color was achieved by using a very small quantity of cobalt blue in the glaze.

Aubergine, which is considered a purple (eggplant) shade, often appears almost brown after firing. It appeared as a background color during the Ming Dynasty, when it was frequently used as the foundation color for Fa Hua wares. It appeared as a monochrome of lackluster distinction during the seventeenth and eighteenth centuries. In the nineteenth century a beautiful, strong purple glaze was achieved.

Mirror black is a lustrous black glaze which originated during the Kangxi period. It was created by using a combination of golden brown and cobalt ferrous ore of manganese. The decoration was almost always monochrome but occasionally was decorated with gold tracery designs. The black color reflected a soft brown tone and faded to brown at the rim, where the gaze naturally thinned.

Iron rust monochrome glaze, featuring metallic specks on a deep red-brown glaze, was also invented in the Kangxi period. The teadust glaze was developed in the first half of the eighteenth century. To achieve this color, the porcelain was first glazed with a yellow-brown oxide which was followed by a fine, blown-on spray of green lead silicate. This combination achieved a color that is akin to that of tea leaves.

Monochrome yellow glazes were developed in the fifteenth century as overglaze colors and produced a pure and even tone. By the sixteenth century, yellow was being applied directly to the biscuit as an underglaze, which resulted in a less uniform but richer color. Another sixteenth-century technique that lasted through the Kangxi period was the use of a very thin, neutral "dry" glaze underneath a translucent yellow glaze. Antimoniate of iron, which created the yellow glazes, was mixed with tin oxide in the Yongzheng period to produce a bright, opaque lemon yellow glaze. Also developed during the Qing Dynasty was a particular shade called Imperial yellow that was set aside for the use of the royal family.

Green-glazed wares were among the first to be produced in China, and we can trace their history back to the early Yueh celadon. During the latter Ming Dynasty, a green lead silicate glaze was used over white porcelain finished with a transparent high-fired glaze. The Kangxi period saw the use of the same color over a greyish crackle glaze. Apple green appeared in the eighteenth century during the Yongzheng period. An opaque green glaze of a lime shade was also developed at this time.

Translucent turquoise glazes, which first appeared in the fifteenth century, were perfected during the Qing Dynasty. The glaze was finely crackled and tended to run; the "pooling" of the glaze thus enhanced any incised decoration. The eighteenth century saw the innovation of the opaque turquoise glaze.

Robin's egg glaze, although not technically a single glaze due to its speckling of copper red or dark blue, is nonetheless considered to be a monochrome. It is likely to have been one of the innovations conceived at the imperial factory at Ching-te-chen, and was very popular during the reign of Qinglong.

Café au lait glazes were also produced during this period, but appear most often with reserves of famille rose colors rather than as a monochrome ware.

The development of a monochrome glaze that was not native to Chinese taste but was copied from Europe instead was rose pink. This color, which was derived from colloidal gold, was used as a monochrome glaze on thinly potted eggshell porcelains of the early eighteenth century. (See Blanc de Chine; Celadon; Qing Dynasty; Song Dynasty; Yuan Dynasty.)

References: John Ayers, *Chinese Ceramics: The Koger Collection*, Sotheby's Publications, 1985; Rose Kerr *Chinese Ceramics: Porcelain of the Qing Dynasty 1644–1911* Victoria and Albert Museum, 1986; Margaret Medley, *Ming and Ching Monochromes*, University of London, Percival David Foundation of Chinese Art, 1973.

Museums: Most museums that house collections of Chinese porcelain will have some examples of monochrome glazes. Significant collections are housed at the University of London, Sir Percival David Foundation of Chinese Art, London, England; The Victoria and Albert Museum, London, England; the Metropolitan Museum of Art, New York, New York; the Art Gallery, Chinese University of Hong Kong, Hong Kong.

Reproduction Alert: Mirror black, sang de boeuf, and turquoise monochromes, in particular, are still being made in large quantities. Many small peach bloom items, particularly those for the scholar's desk were produced well into the nineteenth century and may be found marked with eighteenth-century commemorative marks.

Collecting Hints: This section has dealt with monochrome glazes used during the Ming Dynasty through the nineteenth century. Earlier monochromes are referred to under their respective dynasties.

Monochrome wares have always been of interest to the collector and are highly collectible today. Many colors were produced at the order of the imperial court to be used seasonally, much in the same fashion that we would change window treatments with the seasons today.

On items with gold tracery designs (mirror black, powder blue, coral red, and some green), signs of wear on the gold is to be expected. Newer, nineteenth century examples of mirror black do not reveal a fading to brown at the rim.

Many monochromes continued in production throughout the nineteenth and into the twentieth century. A footrim that is rough to the touch would be one indication of nineteenth- rather than eighteenth-century production.

Bowl, 6⅜″ dia., Kangxi mark and period, yellow glaze of egg yolk color, repaired rim chips. $1,500.00. Courtesy of Butterfield and Butterfield.

Bowl
   5″ dia., café-au-lait-glaze, Qianlong seal mark and of the period, with deep rounded flaring sides, covered in a rich café-au-lait glaze paling at the rim and stopping neatly above the foot **3,000.00**
   6″ dia., pair, peachbloom, Kangxi mark and period, each with deep rounded sides rising to a lipped rim, covered both inside and out with a soft reddish-brown glaze shaded to olive-green, one bowl with small rim chip **3,800.00**
   6″ dia., sang de boeuf, Qianlong seal mark and of the period, on spreading foot with white glazed interior **1,200.00**
   6¼″ dia., pair, liver-red glazed, Guangxu six character mark in under glaze blue and of the period, each resting on a low footrim and with rounded sides rising to a slightly flaring rim, covered overall in a mottled, dark red glaze. . .   **1,500.00**
   7¼″ dia., Imperial yellow-glazed bowl, Kangxi mark and period, with well-potted deep rounded sides rising to an everted rim cov-

Bowls, Pair, 4¾″ dia., 18th century, apple green glaze, covered in and out with a bubbled green glaze suffused with russet cracks, the rim and foot applied with a coffee colored glaze. $2,475.00. Courtesy of Butterfield and Butterfield.

ered with a rich yellow glaze, the base glazed in white, rim cracks 10¼″ dia., tripod bowl, deep soufflé blue-glazed, late Kangxi, of deep concave begging form on three knob feet, the exterior under a deep even glaze, the interior basically white . . . . **850.00** **1,200.00**

Censer (two-handled), 5¼″ w., mirror-black glaze, pierced wood cover, 19th century, on three tall mask and paw feet, gilt with dragons pursuing flaming pearls below a band of key-pattern **175.00**

Dish

5½″ dia., celadon foliate dish, Kangxi mark and period, the well-potted dish with fluted foliate sides covered with a pale green glaze, stopping short of the base with the underglaze-blue mark on the countersunk central area, the rim slightly reduced and gilt, the interior gilded with lotus scrolls, all decoration added later **2,500.00**

5⅞″ dia., aubergine glazed, incised decoration, encircled Yongzheng six-character mark and of the period, the rounded flaring sides incised to the exterior with an arching pomegranate scroll, all under a pale aubergine glaze stopping neatly above the foot. . . **3,800.00**

7″ dia., Imperial yellow, Ming Dynasty, encircled Hongzhi six-character mark and of the period, the rounded sides rising to the flaring rim, covered in a delicate mottled yellow glaze stopping at the footring, extremely fine **25,000.00**

7¼″ dia., café-au-lait-glazed chrysanthemum dish, rare, Qianlong

Censer, 5½″ h., Yongzheng mark and period, celadon, lobed, covered in a pale sea green glaze. $3,300.00. Courtesy of Butterfield and Butterfield.

Dish, 9″ dia., 18th century, mule's liver glaze. $750.00

seal mark and of the period, the finely molded sides and interior all under an even rich café-au-lait glaze **3,500.00**

8¼″ dia., liver-red-glaze, pair, encircled Yongzheng six-character marks and of the period, each with shallow rounded sides rising to a slightly flaring rim, covered in a deep liver-red glaze paling at the rim **6,000.00**

Saucer dish

5¼″ dia., blue-glazed, Qianlong mark and period, of shallow form, covered inside and out with a deep blue glaze, draining to reveal the white ware on the rim, the white-glazed base centering a six-character Zhuanshu mark **1,000.00**

5½″ dia., apple-green-glaze, Qianlong seal-mark and of the period, the well-potted sides and interior all under a slightly iridescent rich apple-green glaze, rim frit restored **3,600.00**

6½″ dia., pair, blue-glazed, Qianlong seal mark and period, of shallow circular shape, each covered in a rich blue glaze thinning to a greenish tone toward the rim edged in white, the base glazed pale blue **1,400.00**

Ewer, 6″ h., coral-glaze, 18th century, of pear-shaped form, with a long upturned spout, the curved handle and detachable cover each with small loop attached by a silver chain, covered overall with an even coral glaze, the base and interior glazed white **2,200.00**

Figures, Fu Lions, pair, turquoise-glazed $9\frac{1}{4}''$ h., 19th century, each beast modelled seated on its haunches, wearing a collar of bells and tassels, the female with a playful pup, the male with his paw resting on a pierced ball, on rectangular plinths, wood box 475.00

Jar
$3\frac{1}{4}''$ d., langyao glaze, 19th century, of stylized apple form, the rounded sides rising to a steeply incurved mouth, covered in a glaze of deep red color mottled with darker areas and falling thickly to the unglazed foot, the interior and base glazed white with a fine russet crackle. 350.00

$4\frac{1}{2}''$ h., apple-green-glaze, Kangxi, of ovoid form, covered on the exterior with a translucent green glaze over a crackled pale blue glaze, the interior and base left in pale blue. 750.00

9'' h., green-glaze, 19th century, of baluster form, covered in a thin glaze of bright apple green, the interior and base glazed white, the base with Kangxi mark 550.00

Moon flask, $9\frac{1}{2}''$ h., iron-rust-glaze, Qianlong, the flattened circular body supporting a cylindrical neck with lobed double strap handles, all on an oval foot, the deep rust glaze mottled with purple an dbrown flecks over all, draining to a muddy brown tone at the rim and handles 1,800.00

Stemcup, $4\frac{1}{2}''$ h., copper red glaze, 18th century, the widely flared bowl supported on a tall, stout cylindrical foot slightly splayed at the base, covered in a bubble-suffused glaze of very deep copper-red, the rim and interior of foot glazed white 1,400.00

Vase
$3\frac{1}{2}''$ h., Robin's egg glaze, 18th/19th century, trilobed double gourd form, the miniature vase with three circular openings molded with a tied ribbon at the waisted body, the glaze a speckled lavender blue 700.00

$5\frac{1}{4}''$ h., iron-rust-glaze, 19th century, of ovoid form, covered in a glaze of reddish-brown color, suffused with iridescent flecks, falling evenly to the unglazed footrim 200.00

$5\frac{1}{2}''$ h., Celadon vase, Kangxi, of ovoid form with flared neck and base, incised with three carp on the shoulder, covered overall with a pale celadon glaze, four-character Chenghua mark in underglaze-blue on the base. 750.00

$6\frac{1}{2}''$ h., Ru-type Gu-form vase, Yongzheng mark and period, covered overall with an even pale lavender glaze draining at the flared rim to reveal the white ware underneath, four-character mark in underglaze-blue on the base. . . . 2,500.00

$7\frac{1}{2}''$ h., greenish teadust-glaze, 18th/19th century, two-handled oviform, with tall flared neck 750.00

$8\frac{1}{2}''$ h., apple Green-glaze, bottleform, 18th century, of compressed globular form with elongated cylindrical neck, covered with an apple-green glaze suffused with brown-stained crackle, the rim, interior and base with a white crackle glaze 950.00

9'' h., iron-rust-glaze, pottery vase, 19th century, the ovoid body with slightly splayed base, the cylindrical neck tapering in from the shoulder and rising to the flared rim, covered in a ruddy brown

Ginger Jar, $4\frac{5}{8}''$ h., Kangxi period, mirror black, wooden cover. $700.00

Vase, $8\frac{1}{2}''$ h., 18th century, iron rust glaze. $1,200.00

glaze sprinkled with iridescent flecks at the shoulder **275.00**

9¼″ h., light blue-glazed (pair), 19th century, pear-shaped, Yongzheng seal mark underglaze, each body flanked by scroll handles at the neck and raised on flaring ring foot. **650.00**

9¾″ h., Coral-red-glaze, rouleau shape, 19th century, of cylindrical form with short neck and rounded galleried rim, resting on a slightly flared foot, the coral glaze with areas of darker mottling, the interior and base glazed white, chips **550.00**

11¼″ h., copper red glaze, Qianlong seal mark and period, bottle vase, of well-rounded pear shape body, surmounted by a tall cylindrical neck, covered with a rich blue glaze, the interior and rim glazed white, damage. **1,600.00**

12″ h., oxblood glaze, 18th century, pear-form, covered in rich even burgundy glaze **1,200.00**

12‴, copper red glaze, pear shaped vase, 18th century, with trumpet neck rising to a flared rim and raised on a high ring foot, the exterior covered in a deep red glaze, the rim, interior and base glazed in white. **1,000.00**

12¾″ h., teadust-glaze, Jiaqing seal mark and period, of compressed pear shape surmounted by a tall almost cylindrical neck, covered with a finely mottled olive-green glaze, the unglazed footrim covered with a dark brown slip,

incised six-character seal mark, glaze chips on seal mark **2,800.00**

13″ h., cracked yellow-glaze, 18th century, lobed octofoil slender baluster form **600.00**

13¼″ h., copper red glaze, 19th century, bottle-form, of ovoid form, the cylindrical neck with widely flaring rim, supported on a slightly splayed foot, covered in a rich even copper red glaze, the interior and base glazed white, apocryphal Qianlong mark **575.00**

14″ h., teadust glaze, square baluster shape, 19th century, the shoulders molded with mask and stationary ring handles, covered in a deep speckled green glaze, wood stand **1,200.00**

15″ h., Sang-de-boeuf glazed, 19th century, double gourd vase, the glaze turning from pale purple at the top to a deep rich red at the bottom, with wood stand **800.00**

15¼″ h., green glaze, bottle-form vase, 19th century, of compressed globular form with elongated cylindrical neck, covered in an apple-green glaze with brown-stained crackle falling thickly and unevenly at the short foot, the interior and base covered in a grayish-white crackle glaze. **850.00**

15¼″ h., mirror black-glaze, slender baluster form 19th century, with flared neck **450.00**

15½″ h., powder-blue, Kangxi, with pear-shaped body surmounted by a tall cylindrical neck, covered with a rich blue-soufflé glaze, the

Vase, 14″ h., 19th century, teadust glaze, the brownish green glaze later decorated in famille rose enamels. $975.00

Vase, 18¼″ h., 18th century, blue soufflé glaze. $1,500.00. Courtesy of Butterfield and Butterfield.

Vase, 7¾″ h., clair de lune glaze, Yong-zheng mark and period, molded with rope decoration, covered in a rich pale blue glaze. $1,800.00. Courtesy of Butterfield and Butterfield.

interior glazed in white, four-character Chenghua mark. **1,800.00**
16¾″ h., teadust-glaze, Yongzheng, pear-shaped, evenly speckled green teadust glaze molded with two ribs above the tall foot and at the shoulder, the long neck with a single rib below the flaring rim . . **3,800.00**
17″, mirror-black, bottle form, Kangxi, with almost spherical body rising to a tall cylindrical neck, with traces of gilt-painted lotus medallions and floral scrolls, the interior and base glazed in white **1,800.00**
20½″ h., blue glaze, 19th century, octagonal bottle-form, the globular body resting on a slightly flared foot and supporting a tapering neck, the blue glaze slightly bubbled **800.00**
Waterdropper, 4″ l., peach bloom, 19th century, unusual peach-form, the thinly potted fruit with a hollow leafy stem serving as the spout, an irregular hole left in the top, surmounted by a small worm, covered with a pale peach bloom glaze turning to green at the tip, the opposite end left white **575.00**

PAINTINGS

History: Painting has been considered the highest art form in China during the past 2,000 years. The pictogram that means "to paint" shows a hand holding a marker and drawing the four boundaries of a field. The painter's main tools are the brush, ink and colors, paper, and silk fabrics.

Since paper was not invented until about the beginning of the Christian era, the earliest surviving painting fragments, discovered in a third century B.C. tomb at Changsha, were executed on silk.

The earliest paintings were of figures, both secular and religious, the latter mostly dealt with Buddhist subjects. Few have survived the ravages of time, although later copies suggest what the originals might have been like. Many of the Buddhist paintings were done as frescoes on cave temple walls in northwestern China along the Silk Road, which also brought Buddhism from India. The frescoes show Indian, Greco-Roman, and central Asian influences.

Landscape painting, which became the most exalted form, did not become preeminent until the tenth century. This subject matter was heavily influenced by Taoist philosophy and Ch'an Buddhism (Zen in Japan), which emphasized meditation and communing with nature. Since the tenth century, nature has been the main inspiration to Chinese painters, be it the majestic and austere mountain landscape of north China; the misty and softer, though no less grand, landscape of the Yangtze valley and southern China; or the intimate study of nature on the small scale of flowers, birds, and animals that first became popular in the court-patronized academies of the Sung dynasty in the eleventh century. Since then, Chinese paintings have been divided into these three large categories: figures; landscapes; and animals, birds, and flowers. Critics tended to consider the last group as trivial, but it has remained popular nevertheless.

Each of the three genres of painting has evolved during the past millennium according to trends and stylistic changes, which were the result of internal developments and external influences. Because even a short discussion of these evolving trends is beyond the scope of this book, those who wish to learn more should consult the references cited.

Much more than with other cultures, Chinese painting is closely linked with calligraphy, or the art of writing and penmanship. The artist and calligrapher used the same media for their works: brush, ink, paper, and silk fabric. Indeed, the accomplished calligrapher was also often an artist and vice versa, for the two fields were considered to be inexorably linked. Most paintings have space reserved for inscriptions. The inscriptions are often poetry composed by the artist and dedications to friends. Distinguished later collectors and connoisseurs might also have added their appreciation or research findings by writing on the reserved spaces of the painting itself or on paper attached to it. In addition to their signatures, artists and connoisseurs also affix their seals to paintings. Seals are most often made of stone and engraved with the owner's names or a motto, generally in an archaic script; the seal impressions are usually red and are made from a paste of red dye mixed with an oil-based substance. Painters and calligraphers were sometimes also seal engravers.

While some painted for pleasure in their leisure time and did not rely on the sale of their works for income, other artists relied on the sale of their paintings for livelihood. Thus painters needed patrons. Cultured rulers were often lavish patrons on a large scale. Hui-tsung, emperor of the Northern Sung dynasty during the early twelfth century, founded a painting academy in his court at Kaifeng and was himself a noted painter of birds and flowers, and a calligrapher. He cultivated the arts and neglected the empire's defences; his reign ended in disaster. He and most of his court were taken prisoners by the northern nomads, and north China was conquered by the nomadic invaders; the remnant Sung government eventually reestablished itself in southern China, never to regain control of the north. While Hui-tsung was an extreme example of a ruler who patronized the arts and culture at the expense of practical matters, many rulers did encourage the arts and artists, if only to give luster to their courts.

Rulers also formed large collections. The most illustrious ruler-collector was the eighteenth-century Emperor Qianlong, who added vastly to what generations of his predecessors had accumulated. What remained of the imperial collection forms the nucleus of the National Palace Museum in Taipei and the Palace Museum in Beijing. Members of the imperial family, officials, and wealthy merchants emulated the rulers and vied with one another as patrons of the arts. The merchant princes of Yangchow in the seventeenth and eighteenth centuries took pride in their lavish lifestyles and their luxurious houses and gardens and patronized painters and formed collections.

An uneasy relationship often existed between artists and patrons; artists needed patrons, but sometimes also felt constrained and stifled by their patronage. Tensions were particularly acute during the early Yuan and Qing dynasties when some Chinese painters took special pains not to be associated with the non-Chinese ruling houses. The most notable artist who chose retirement devoted to poetry and painting to serving the Mongols was Ch'ien Hsuan in the thirteenth century. K'un-ts'an, Shi-tao, and Chu-ta refused to serve the new Manchu government in the late seventeenth century, sought protection in Buddhist and Taoist monasteries, and painted in eccentric and individualistic styles.

The disintegration of traditional Chinese culture that resulted from Western intrusions in the nineteenth century led to the development of two new schools of painting, one in Shanghai and the other in Canton. Both metropolises were the focal points of China's contact with the West. The Shanghai school produced such masters as Jen Hsiung, Jen Po-nien, Hsu Ku, Wu Ch'ang-shuo, Ch'i Pai-shih, Huang Pin-hung, and Hsu Peihung. The most notable masters of the Canton school were Kao Chien-fu and Ch'en Shu-jen. Many from both schools had studied in Japan and France and all were influenced by Western trends, most notably Impressionism.

The tortuous path of reinterpreting their tradition and shaping a synthesis or finding a place in a world influenced by the West was affected and determined by political events—the revolution that overthrew the monarchy and its Confucian social and political base in 1911, the social revolution that followed the May Fourth Movement of 1919, the Japanese invasion that lasted between 1937 and 1945 and that became part of World War II, and the Communist triumph in 1949.

The government of the People's Republic of China has since 1949 put restraints on artists to paint in the "correct" manner of socialist realism and to serve the people. The restrictive and ideologically motivated attitude toward art has been much modified since Mao Ze-dong's death in 1976. In Taiwan, and among the Chinese in diaspora in Europe and North America, painters have continued to respond to the continuing crisis to their cultural identity by experimenting in new media and/or reinterpreting the traditional. Notable among this group are Zao Wou-ki and Liu Kuo-sung in Europe, and C. C. Wang and Tseng Yu-ho in the United States.

Chinese paintings are mounted in the passepartout manner, that is backed by thick paper and banded with thin strips of silk damask. They most frequently take the form of the hanging scroll, which is rolled up when not hung. Long, horizontal paintings are mounted as hand scrolls that are unrolled from right to left and viewed on a table. Small pictures are grouped into albums that are folded concertina fashion. Folding, oval, or circular fans with pictures and inscriptions were popular personal accoutrements of ladies and gentlemen. They too are mounted as small scrolls or to form albums.

References: Laurence Binyon, *Painting in the Far East*, third ed., Dover Publications, 1959; James Cahill, *Chinese Painting*, Rizzoli International Publications, 1977; Joan Lebold Cohen, *The New Chinese Painting, 1949–1986*, Harry Abrams, 1987; Marilyn and Sheng Fu, *Studies in Connoisseurship, Chinese Paintings from the Arthur M. Sackler Collection in New York and Princeton*, Princeton University Press, 1973; Josef Hojzlar, *Chinese Watercolors*, translated by Till Gottheinerova, Octobus Books Ltd., 1980; Chu-Tsing Li, *Trends in Modern Chinese Painting*, Artibus Asiae, 1970; Max Loehr, *The Great Painters of China*, Harper and Row, 1980; Osvard Siren, *Chinese Paintings, Leading Masters and Principles*, 7 vols., Lund Humphries London, 1956, 1958, reissued 1973 by Hacker Art Books, Inc.; Michael Sullivan, *Symbols of Eternity: The Art of Land-*

scape *Painting in China*, Stanford University Press, 1979; Arthur Waley, *An Introduction to the Study of Chinese Painting*, Charles Scribner's Sons, 1923.

Museums: M. H. de Young Memorial Museum, San Francisco, California; Nelson Gallery—Atkins Museum, Kansas City, Kansas; Boston Museum of Art, Boston, Massachusetts; Fogg Museum, Harvard University, Cambridge, Massachusetts; Princeton University Museum, Princeton, New Jersey; Metropolitan Museum of Art, New York, New York; Cleveland Museum of Art, Cleveland, Ohio; Arthur M. Sackler Gallery, Smithsonian Institution, Washington, D.C.

Reproduction Alert: The authentication of Chinese paintings is a most difficult and inexact science. For almost 2,000 years and even now, students begin their studies by copying the works of masters, and only when they have mastered the techniques and styles of masters can they begin to think of developing their own styles. Even renowned painters show their respect for past masters by making copies of their paintings or painting in their style. Unscrupulous men and women faked or forged paintings of the masters to sell for gain or for vicarious fame. Calligraphy can be imitated and seals can be forged in a manner that is difficult to distinguish from the genuine. Thus copies and fakes abound, even for famous living and recently dead artists. Experts frequently disagree on the authenticity of a work. There is no certainty unless one buys directly from a living artist or buys paintings of sure provenance only. Major auction houses and dealers are more likely to stand behind their paintings than less reputable dealers, but as always, caveat emptor. Read and learn as much as you can before buying; look at exhibitions, books, and catalogs.

Advisor: Jiu-Hwa Upshur, PhD

Anonymous
"Egret and kingfisher with lotus flower," ink and colors on silk, $57\frac{7}{8}$" x 16", 19th century **1,500.00**
"Lady with fan," ink and colors on silk, bearing spurious signature of Chou Wen-chu (10th century) and eight spurious collectors' seals, $63\frac{1}{8}$" x $38\frac{3}{4}$" **1,300.00**
Chang Dai-chien (1899-1983)
"Poet composing a poem along the Lakeside," ink and colors on paper, $31\frac{1}{2}$" x $15\frac{3}{4}$", inscribed, dated 1945, signed and two seals of artist **2,000.00**
"Mountain flower and bamboo,", a fan painting in ink and colors on paper, $7\frac{5}{8}$" x $21\frac{7}{8}$", dated to 1947, signed with two seals of artist . . . **1,200.00**
"The Wei River winding through a

Mountain," ink and colors on paper, $38\frac{1}{2}$" x $24\frac{3}{8}$", entitled and inscribed, signed by artist with three seals **25,000.00**
Ch'en Shi-fa (b. 1921), "Banana palm and chicks," ink and colors on paper, signed, with dedication and two seals of artist, $28\frac{3}{4}$" x 16" **1,000.00**
Ch'en Shu-jen (1883-1948) "Bees drawn towards cottonwood blossoms," ink and colors on paper, $49\frac{5}{8}$" x $20\frac{1}{2}$", inscribed with poem, signed and dated to 1926, with one seal **3,200.00**
Ch'i Pai-shih (1864-1957)
"Gourds," ink and colors on paper, signed and with four seals of artist $40\frac{1}{2}$" x 13" **2,000.00**
"Morning Glories," ink and colors on paper, signed and with two seals of artist, $37\frac{1}{4}$" x $13\frac{5}{8}$", ... **8,000.00**
"Three peaches," ink and colors on paper, entitled, signed and with two seals of artist, $39\frac{3}{8}$" x $13\frac{3}{4}$", **9,000.00**
Fu Pao-shih (1904-1965)
"Echoes of Mount Omei," 13" x $17\frac{3}{4}$", ink and colors on paper, inscribed and signed by artist with one seal. **8,000.00**

Left, **Ch'i Pai-shih (1863-1957), "Morning Glories," 53" l. x 13$\frac{1}{4}$" w., ink and colors on paper, signed by artist with four seals. $5,000.00;** *right,* **Lo Chien-ku (Qing Dynasty), "Landscape," 46" l. x 11$\frac{1}{2}$" w., ink and colors on paper, signed with one seal of artist and one collector's seal. $1,500.00**

Chu Chao (19th century), "Landscape," 7¼" l. x 19½" w., folding fan on bamboo ribs, ink and colors on paper, signed by artist with one seal, the reverse with calligraphy of a poem. $600.00

"Landscape with figures," ink and colors on paper, signed dated to 1945, inscribed and with four seals of the artist, 54" x 15¾", . . . **27,000.00**

Ho Wei-pu (1844-1925), "Landscape after Wang Shih-min," ink on paper signed inscribed and with two seals of artist, 59" x 15¾", ... **500.00**

Hsieh Chi-liu (b. 1909)
"Mynah Bird on a red leafed branch," ink and color s on paper, 33½ x 13", with poem, signed and seal of artist **1,000.00**
"Pavilion sheltered under hanging cliff," 76⅜" x 36⅝", ink and colors on paper, dated 1979, signed and seal of artist **3,000.00**

Hsu Pei-hung (1895-1953)
"Willow and magpie," ink and colors on paper, signed, with dedication, dated to 1937 and with one seal of artist, 42" x 15¼" **7,000.00**
"Eagle," ink and colors on paper, signed, dated to 1939 and with one seal of artist, 26¾" x 32½" . . . **14,000.00**

Jen Hsiun (1825-1893), "Lady playing flute," fan painting, ink and colors on paper, signed and with one seal of artist, 7" x 20½" **1,400.00**

Hsieh Chi-liu (b. 1909), "Bird on Branch," 9" l. x 17¾" w., ink and colors on paper, signed by artist with three seals. $1,000.00

T'ing Yen-yung (1902-1978), "Figures," 27" l. x 18" w., ink and colors on paper, signed by artist with one seal. $2,000.00

Jen Yi (1840-1895), "Pheasant under a fruit tree,", ink and color on paper, inscribed, signed, dated to 1876 and with one seal of artist, 42½" x 20½". . **19,000.00**

Kao Chien-fu (1879-1951), "Blue peony," ink and light color on paper, signed, with dedication, dated to 1928, and with one seal of artist, 37¾" x 21¼" **5,000.00**

Li Ko-jan (1907-1989) "Young herder and buffalo under a willow tree," ink and colors on paper, 19⅝" x 18" **5,000.00**

Lin Feng-mien (b. 1900), "Lake scene,", ink and colors on paper, signed and with one seal of artist, 27" x 26¼" **5,500.00**

Li Shan (1686-1756), "Five pine trees," ink on silk, siscribed with long poem, signed and dated to 1747, two seals of artist, 78" x 41½". **26,000.00**

Pu Chuan (b. 1919), Set of four horse paintings, ink and colors on paper, each signed and with two seals of artist, each 39¼" x 12⅝" **1,600.00**

Pu Hua (1830-1911) "Plum blossoms, Peonies, Lotus, and Chrysanthemums," set of 4 scrolls in ink and colors on paper, each 54⅛" x 13⅛" each inscribed, signed and with one seal, dated to 1904 . . . . **10,000.00**

Pu Ju (1896-1963)
"Washing the ink stone," ink and colors on paper, signed, inscribed

Jen I (1840-1895), "Swimming Ducks," 45½" l. x 20" w., ink and light colors on paper, signed and with one seal of artist, one collector's seal. $4,500.00

and with five seals of artist, 36¾" x 13⅜" **5,500.00**
Pu Ju (1896-1963), "Scholars on a bridge watching a waterfall," ink and colors on paper, 26¼" x 9" . . **1,800.00**
Ting Yen-yung (1902-1978) "Lady Yang After a Bath," ink and colors

Pu Ru (1896-1957), "Lotus and Dragon-fly," 28½" l. x 11" w., ink on paper, signed with two seals of artist. $3,500.00

Pao Chun (active mid-19th century) "Prunus," 45½" l. x 26" w., ink on paper, signed by artist with one seal. $800.00

on paper, 32¼" x 19⅝", with inscription, signed by artist and with one seal, dated to 1978 .... **2,500.00**
Wang Chen (1866-1938), "Boating on a river on a spring evening," ink and colors on paper, inscribes, signed, dated to 1926 and with two seals of artist, 25¾" x 50½" **5,000.00**
Wang Chi-chien (C.C.Wang) (b. 1907) "Mountain village," ink and colors on paper, 15½" x 23½", signed and dated to 1983, two seals of the artist **2,000.00**
Wang Yuan-chi (1642-1715), "Landscape after Huang Kung-wang," ink and colors on silk, entitled and inscribed, signed and with four seals

Wang Chen (1866-1938) "Landscape," 7¼" l. x 19" w., folding fan with ivory ribs, ink and colors on gold paper, signed with one seal of artist, the reverse with calligraphy of a poem also on gold paper. $750.00

of artist and two other seals, 60¼″ x
30½″ **10,000.00**
Wu Chang-shuo (1844-1927), "Chry-
santhemums," ink and colors on paper, signed, entitled and inscribed,
with two seals of artist, 27⅛″ x 13¾″ **3,000.00**
Wu Chou (Ming dynasty), "Scholars in
autumn landscape," ink and colors
on silk, dated to 1651, signed with
two seals of artist, 39¾″ x 21¼″ **2,500.00**

PEKING GLASS

History: Recent excavations in China have revealed that there has been a continuous tradition
of glass-making dating from 403 to 221 B.C. It is
supposed that the earliest glass items were used
for ornamentation to imitate jewels as a substitute
for precious stones. Documented records indicate that glass was imported from Rome as early
as the third century A.D., when it was used as a
jade substitute for the production of ritual tomb
objects.

During the Han through Yuan Dynasties some
flasks, cups, and bowls were produced. There is
little known of glass production during the Ming
Dynasty. It was not until the beginning of the
Qing Dynasty that conditions were right for the
development of a flourishing glass industry.

The Emperor Kangxi (1662–1722) set all the
creative arts in motion with the establishment of
imperial workshops for the development of the
arts. Glass-making was encouraged to develop
along with the porcelain industry, cloisonné, and
other crafts. The glass house differed from all the
other creative workshops, since it was the only
one to be founded by Jesuit missionaries. It is
supposed that they influenced the chemical composition of the glass metal and taught techniques
of glass blowing. Apparently they had little influence on the early glass shapes produced.

Glass began to be created in forms that copied
ceramics, lacquer, and jade as well as new forms
of decoration that were taken from porcelain.
During the Kangxi period, monochrome opaque
glass was created in green shades to imitate the
Yuan and Song celadons. Glass shapes from older
times influenced the production of mallet-shaped
vases and foliate dishes. Transparent glass was
also produced. This period also saw the development of cased glass (otherwise known as overlay
or cameo glass), which was carved back to form
designs. The earliest of these techniques used
multifaceted cuts (honeycomb patterned) and
fluted cutting from the outer cased color to the
base-colored glass below. These appeared with a
blue or red casing over a white base. Relief carving, using lapidary techniques became an established technique throughout the 18th century and
was later produced with many different styles and

color combinations. Carving with multiple colors
of casing was developed in the early eighteenth
century. The glass form had blobs of different
colored glass applied in certain areas, which
were then cut back in a design over the base
color. Carvers that had previously worked with
jade were employed to carve both monochrome
and cased glass. Cased glass, was also produced
to simulate hornbill by using a red overlay on a
yellow body. Some of the monochrome motifs
were taken from nature (flowers and birds), some
came from mythology (dragons), and some depicted human figures (children playing).

One of the areas for glass manufacture by imperial decree, was the glass factory established at
Peking. Peking glass has become the presently
accepted term for all handmade glass produced in
China, even though other factories in different
locations have produced glass products since the
name was first applied.

In the mid-eighteenth century, the palace
workshop, influenced by the Jesuit missionaries,
employed foreign craftsmen from the West. The
influence they exerted lead to the development of
Western-style shapes and articles, which were
created to please the emperor. Enameled glass
was also being produced in the early eighteenth
century as a result of this influence. Western style
rooms created in the Yuamning Yuan summer
palace housed some of the products of these en-
deavors. The early glass products that were manufactured during this stage have suffered through
the years by the development of "crizzling," a
decomposition of the glass that causes internal
cracks and surface flaking due to an excess of
alkali in the glass recipe. The presence of crizzling is a sure sign of manufacture during the late
seventeenth to early eighteenth centuries.

Many of the glass colors evolved from attempts
to copy naturally occurring stones that were used
for gems, including lapis, malachite, turquoise,
and carnelian. Even amber and coral were imitated. As the glass formulas improved, different
colors appeared, including transparent reds,
blues, greens, ambers, and purples as well as a
gold-flecked blue glass, carried over from the
Kangxi period. The European color rose pink was
introduced to glass production during the Yongzheng period, and glass production was moved to
the summer palace during his reign. Treatments
were expanded to include gilding (on both
opaque and transparent glass), engraving, and
adding gold flecking to the molten glass metal.

An opaque turquoise blue was used extensively
in the Qianlong period. An opaque to translucent
yellow, which was often produced with carved
decoration, was also featured. Pieces were produced in monochromes, polychromes, and overlay glass. The carving was still being hand done
by jade carvers. Enamel painting on white glass
was also popular.

The early half of Qianlong's reign saw the finest

quality of glass ever produced, and the production of snuff bottles saw its apex in this period. The Emperor Qianlong ordered 500 snuff bottles and 3,000 utensils and glass items in the year 1755. The Xin, Le, and Yuan companies of Peking were the major producers of snuff bottles. They were produced in opaque, cased, and multicolored-cased glass to imitate jade and other stones. Snuff bottles were made in a clear version which was decorated with interior painting and were also produced in overlays of many colors, which were carved back using lapidary techniques.

Techniques less frequently encountered, in eighteenth-century glass production include wheel engraving, diamond point engraving (introduced by the Europeans), and the use of imitation jade-colored glass in the production of jewelry.

In the 1860s, the Jesuit workers left the employ of the imperial glass house. By 1770, the factory was no longer capable of producing the fine ware of its past. It was reduced to the production of snuff bottles and other small items of presentation to the emperor.

The latter half of the eighteenth century saw a slowing down of imperial patronage of the arts due to financial struggles and internal disorder. This was not the end of the glass industry, however. Private factories continued to flourish to meet the demands of the affluent who had long desired products that previously had been made only for the court. Freedom from the influence of imperial tastes lead to imaginative renderings in glass at the independent factories in Boshan and Quangzhou, both of which had coexisted with the imperial factory in Peking. New styles of wares developed into the 19th century, including the production of items for the scholar's desk. Swirled and variegated colored glass was produced. Threaded, or trailed, glass was worked as well, possibly as a result of European influence. Overlay and transparent and opaque monochrome techniques continued through the nineteenth century. (See: Snuff Bottles.)

References: Claudia Brown and Donald Rabiner, *Clear as Crystal, Red as Flame—Later Chinese Glass*, China Institute in America, 1990; the Robert H. Clague Collection, *Chinese Glass of the Qing Dynasty (1644–1911)*, Phoenix Art Museum, 1987; *Chinese Jewelry and Glass*, Spink and Son Ltd., Exhibition catalog, 1989.

Museums: Phoenix Art Museum, Phoenix, Arizona; Los Angeles County Museum of Art, Los Angeles, California; Asian Art Museum of San Francisco, San Francisco, California; Museum of Fine Arts, Boston Massachusetts; Peabody Museum of Salem, Salem, Massachusetts; Nelson-Atkins Museum of Art, Kansas City, Missouri; Brooklyn Museum, Brooklyn, New York; Corning Museum of Glass, Corning, New York; Metropolitan Museum of Art, New York, New York; Toledo Museum of Art, Toledo, Ohio; Chrysler Museum, Norfolk, Virginia; Royal Ontario, Museum, Toronto, Canada; British Museum, London, England; Victoria and Albert Museum, London, England; City of Bristol Museum and Art Gallery, Bristol, England; Tokyo National Museum, Tokyo, Japan; Art Gallery, Chinese University of Hong Kong, Hong Kong; Museum for Far Eastern Antiquities, Stockholm, Sweden.

Reproduction Alert: Cameo (cased) glass overlay is being exported from China now. It is most commonly seen in bowls and vases. The typical ground color is a rather stark opaque milk white without any of the variations of color such as mutton fat, jade white, striated white, or ivory white that were typical of eighteenth-century production. It should be noted that late nineteenth-century products also developed a single white tone as a background color. Modern cased glass overlay employs the colors of red, green, yellow, and blue, which are carved back using modern tools. These pieces show none of the irregularities of surface that are present on eighteenth and early nineteenth-century glass. Modern glass is generally molded rather than blown and reveals less bubbling than its earlier counterparts. These new pieces are lighter in weight and have a thinner casing of glass. The older examples have evidence of the use of hand tools on the edges of the design, while the modern wares have sharp edges, indicating the use of modern machinery in manufacture. The motifs of modern glass are typically cranes, lotus, Mandarin figures, and the One Hundred Antiques pattern.

Collecting Hints: Peking glass is not collected as widely as porcelain, but the market is increasing—especially the interest in eighteenth- and nineteenth-century examples. Eighteenth-century Peking glass is the most expensive because it is the finest and rarest. The prices on all Peking glass have risen recently, but nineteenth-century examples are affordable and are available. The prices will probably continue to rise as the public interest increases and the items become scarcer. Avoid new glass; it is being mass produced in stock patterns that lack the artistic individuality of the older pieces.

Bowl
$2\frac{1}{4}''$ dia., translucent royal blue color, the bell form resting on a short molded foot tapering up sharply to a slightly everted rim, the base impressed with a "shou" medallion **250.00**
$4\frac{3}{8}''$ dia., 19th century, opaque celadon color, bell form tapering to an everted rim and resting on a raised molded foot. **165.00**

Bowl, 6" dia., 19th century, translucent deep red cranberry glass, with two leaf-shaped reserves containing scenes of military figures galloping through mountains, the deep red shading to an opaque purple at the foot. $1,210.00. Courtesy of Butterfield and Butterfield.

Bowl, 6½" dia., translucent white glass with blue overlay, the bright blue carved in layers of multiple facets. $250.00. Courtesy of Butterfield and Butterfield.

4½" dia., 19th century, lavender glass, of deep rounded form on a raised foot, flared rim **375.00**

4⅝" dia., 18th/19th century, red overlay on white, foliate rim, each carved through to the milky white surface with flowering lotus stems issuing from the lotus root-form ring foot, the leaves swirling onto the underside, minute chips **1,800.00**

4⅝" dia., translucent amethyst purple hue, fluted shape with a flared rim over a short ring foot, surface wear **385.00**

4⅞" h., 19th century, opaque white, tulip form **350.00**

5½" l., pair, 19th century, transluscent milky white glass, each of elongated quatrefoil contour separated by raised vbertical ridges flaring to a wide everted foliate-edged rim, the sides tapering sharply to a short diamond-form foot. **2,475.00**

6¼" dia., 19th century, blue overlay white, sharply carved with eight horses grazing in a rocky landscape, all within blue borders, supported on a short foot **650.00**

6½" dia., 19th century, green overlay translucent white glass, with flared rim and curved sides tapering sharply to a bevelled ring foot, the exterior carved in rows of multiple facets **375.00**

6½", Qianlong, carved red glass, the exterior with three pierced rocks rising from waves, divided above three varieties of flowering foliage and birds perched and in flight, four character mark on the base possibly added later **3,300.00**

6⅝" dia., translucent amethyst purple hue, with slightly everted rim

and rounded sides tapering to a high ring foot, the body thickening toward the base, rim and foot chips, surface wear **475.00**

6⅞" dia., emerald green overlay on translucent white glass, with a wide flaring rim and tapering sharply to a ring foot banded in green the exterior sides overlay carved and incised with song birds amid flowering prunus trees issuing from rockwork below a wide green rim band, surface wear **400.00**

7¾" h., pair, 19th century, cranberry red over opaque white, each low-slung ovoid shape resting on a waisted ring base and surmounted by a tall neck flaring slightly to a wide everted rim banded in red, well carved body with meiren in billowing robes gesturing toward a man poling a boat over rhythmic waves, all enveloped by undulating rockwork and extended flora **2,750.00**

7⅞" dia., 19th century, blue overlay on white, with a slightly flared rim and curving sides tapering sharply to a short ring foot, the exterior carved with ribbon-tied linked "cash" emblems, endless knot, and a stylized Chinese character in bright blue, the rim and foot accented with side blue-colored bands **1,320.00**

8" dia., 18th century, opaque turquoise of sky blue, of thick inverted bell shape with countersunk interior, the deep sides tapering to the high ring foot **1,400.00**

8¼" h., 19th century, translucent red overlay on opaque mustard yellow, baluster form, decorated with a continuous band of blossoms and meandering leafy tendrils set between three narrow bands at the shoulders and a lappet band at the base 330.00

9⅜″ dia., late 19th century, fine imperial yellow color, the everted rim and curved sides tapering shaply to a high ring foot, the exterior carved and incised with a continuous scene of waterfowl framed by lotus leaves and blossoms issuing from waves rendered in a stylized pattern and encircling the foot 2,750.00

9½″ dia., Pair, 19th century, translucent dark blue color, foliate rims, bombé quadrefoil form supported on a raised foot with an everted rim 1,100.00

10¼″ h., late 19th/early 20th century, turquoise cut back to white, of baluster form tapering sharply toward the base, overlaid in deep turquoise, cut back in hexagonal facets to reveal the white body . .   950.00

13½″ dia., 19th century, translucent dark blue tone, the deeply set bell form supported by a round foot and tapering to a flattened rim, rim chip 2,200.00

Box and Cover, 4¼″ x 4″, 19th century, rare clear glass of square section, with thick rounded sides tapering to the flat base, on four tab feet, relief carved with a bat in each corner, two sides divided with a "chilong" medallion, with a matching fitted cover, minute chips 2,100.00

Cup and saucer, pair, circa 1900, bright yellow, each of quadrangle section and deep form, on a raised foot with countersunk base, the sides rising steeply to a flared rim and everted lip, the saucers of deep quatrefoil form on a slightly raised foot with a countersunk base, the

Bowl, 10½″, 19th century, foliate rimmed, deep transparent blue color. $775.00

Cup and Saucer, late 19th century, opaque mustard yellow color evenly distributed throughout. $225.00

lobed sides rising up to an outcurved lip 1,540.00

Ginger Jars (with covers), pair, circa 1900, the ovoid sides of each carved in deep relief with a continuous scene of a small bird perched amid flowering peony and prunus branches, one cover depicting a flowering lotus, the other with a peony, one cover restored 1,980.00

Jar

3½″, 18th century, rare opaque turquoise of robin's egg blue tone, with straight sides and gently sloping shoulders, the base with a recessed medallion carved with a four-character hallmark "xing you heng tang" 1,800.00

6⅝″ h., 20th century, red overlay on white, carved with an equestrian warrior and flag-bearing attendant in pursuit of another figure under pine trees in a mountainous setting. 675.00

Plate

8″ dia., opaque yellow, molded with flaring sides slightly curved at the rim, circular foot, recessed base 325.00

8⅛″ dia., opaque celadon hue, molded with a flat circular foot with rounded edge, the recessed center merging into a wide rim thinning slightly at the edge. 165.00

8¼″ h., set of four, muted translucent pink color, each molded with wide flaring rims and resting on a short ring foot, surface wear 935.00

Saucers, 4½″ dia., circa 1900, pair, emerald green color, of shallow form on raised foot, the rounded sides rising up to an everted rim . . .   660.00

Vase

6½″ h., 19th century, thick, opaque

Jar, Covered, 8" h., white glass, bright blue overlay, the cover with a bright blue lotus bud and petals. $750.00

mustard colored body, of high-shouldered ovoid shape, minor surface wear **1,320.00**

6⅝" h., green overlay on translucent milky white glass, melon shaped, the low-slung ovoid body accentuated by eight vertical ridges tapering to a short neck with flared rim, carved with fruiting leafy gourd vines above an irregular band encircling the recessed hexagonal foot, (rim chip, surface wear) **2,200.00**

7" h., opaque brick red color, stick neck over bulbous body, the glass mottled with darker inclusions, (wear) **550.00**

7½" h., cobalt blue overlay, 18th century, the globular body supported on a splayed foot and surmounted by a tall waisted neck with a bulbous mouth, decorated with birds in flight around flowering prunus branches, some casting laws and minor chips . . . **2,750.00**

8" h., late 19th century, red overlayed on clear, carved with bird perched on flowering prunus branches issuing from pierced rockwork extending around the sides, with a thick lip rising from the tiered lobed shoulders **1,500.00**

8¼" h., late 19th century, ruby red, baluster form, carved with plantain leaves above ruyi-lappets and archaistic scrolling motifs, wear to footrim **2,475.00**

8½" h., 19th century, red overlay yellow, of tapered baluster form, depicting a scene of figures in a landscape with pine and bamboo, chips **1,200.00**

9¾" h., 20th century, red overlay on opaque white body, ovoid form, the everted rim banded in red, the

Vases, Pair, 8" h., 19th century, mallet form, yellow glass carved with bands of overlapping lotus petals, the neck carved with qilong amid cloud scrolls, the base inscribed with a four-character Qianlong mark. $8,800.00. Courtesy of Butterfield and Butterfield.

body well carved an incised with a large crane in flight above lotus and other water plants **385.00**

9⅞" h., pair, blue overlay. each of shouldered ovoid section with a wide flared lip, carved through the sky blue with a pair of birds soaring amid flowering plants and plantain leaves, minute chips . . . **1,200.00**

10¼" h., 19th century, sky blue, bottle form, with swirls of darker color. **750.00**

11" h., 18th/19th century, ruby red, bottle form, the globular body

Carved yellow vases, 12" h., ovoid form with short necks and wide everted rims, one carved in relief with cranes in flight and at rest amid pines, the other carved to depict carp leaping over frothing waves, $600.00. Courtesy Butterfield and Butterfield.

supported on a thick ring foot, the tall thick neck of muted burgundy color darkening to ruby at the rim, chips **3,200.00**

12¾'' h., 20th century, cobalt blue overlay, carved with a phoenix perched on large leafy branches with peony blossoms, above lappets encircling the narrow base, with pendent leaves encircling the slightly flared neck **750.00**

QING DYNASTY PORCELAIN

See Appendix I for table of Qing emperors.

History: The Qing Dynasty began in 1644 when the north China Manchus succeeded in deposing the weak Ming rule. The Manchus succeeded in unifying and strengthening the social structure of all of China, creating an atmosphere conducive to the stimulation of art and culture.

The study of Qing porcelain revolves around the production of the ceramic factories of Jingdezhen (Ching-te-chen), located in Kiangi Province, which were reopened during the Kangxi period after a long period of inactivity. The primary focus of attention centers on the years between 1683 and 1750, when the imperial factories established at Jewel Hill were under the supervision of kiln directors Zang Yingxuan, Nien Hsi-yao, and T'ang Ying. Approximately 80 percent of the eighteenth-century porcelain production of China was made at these and the other private kilns located at Chin-te-chen. The provincial kilns of the period (other than those located in Fukien Province) were not producing any porcelain of merit at this time.

The imperial kiln director was directly responsible to the emperor, who in addition to ordering porcelain for the palace and for gifts, was a patron of the porcelain arts. The emperors Kangxi, Yongzheng (his son), and Qianlong (his grandson) were very interested in the production of new glazes and decorative techniques. They instructed the kiln directors to develop new ideas. The staggering amount of porcelain ordered for the imperial household sometimes necessitated the hiring of the private kilns in the area to supplement the production of the imperial factories. These private factories, also located at Ching-te-chen, were primarily devoted to producing export porcelain and fine domestic porcelain for the citizens of China.

The city of Ching-te-chen evolved as a ceramics center from the time of the Han Dynasty. An imperial factory was established there in 1398 during the Ming Dynasty, which continued to produce porcelain (when not ravaged by war) until the close of the Qing Dynasty in 1911. A huge labor force was required to meet industrial needs during the peak of eighteenth-century porcelain production. Hundreds of thousands of laborers drawn from all parts of China, were hired during the summer season. It was said that the firing of the kilns produced a red glow that surrounded the city and could be seen from great distances at night.

When Emperor Kangxi reorganized the imperial kilns after a political revolt and established Zang Yingxuan as kiln director, it marked the beginning of the great innovative period of Chinese porcelain production. Unfortunately for the West, none of the late-seventeenth- and early-eighteenth-century imperial porcelain was exported, except for occasional pieces that were not considered good enough for the palace and were sold off to tradesmen. The influx of wares made to the "Chinese taste" did not reach Europe until the mid-nineteenth century. Until this time most of the porcelain that was exported to Europe was not held in high esteem by the Chinese. Though not satisfactory to the taste of the court, the rest of the world hungered for export porcelains, and the private kilns flourished to accommodate Western demands. Thus the porcelain began to assume Western shapes, colors, and patterns throughout the Qing Dynasty. By the middle of the eighteenth century, the quality of porcelain production suffered from the ravages of the T'aip'ing Rebellion, when Ching-te-chen was destroyed. When the imperial kilns were rebuilt in 1865, they were but a shadow of their former greatness. They continued to produce copies of older wares, but the days of great innovations were over. The People's Republic of China succeeded the last Qing emperor, Xuantong, in 1912. A brief revival of the imperial kilns was seen in 1915 when self-created Emperor Hongxian reestablished some of the kilns that had been deserted in 1911. His reign met with so much resistance that he was forced to resign. He died shortly thereafter in 1916.

Very little is known about ceramic production outside the area of Ching-te-chen during the Qing Dynasty. Tê-hua continued to produce white porcelain, Yi-hsing produced its brown earthenware, Shiwan turned out figures and other objects with its variants of flambé glaze and Tz'u-chou ware (a traditional white glazed porcelain in Sung and Yuan styles).

EARLY QING PORCELAIN

Kangxi Period: The porcelain products made during the reign of Kangxi, both in the imperial factories and private kilns, were of very high quality, although the types of wares produced in each were quite different. The orders from the court consisted of utilitarian wares for the household and were requested in specific styles and colors;

the "imperial yellow" colored monochromes were reserved exclusively for the emperor, his wife, and the empress dowager. Other colors with dragon decorations were assigned to other members of the household according to rank. The lowest level of concubine was presented with polychrome-decorated wares. Other imperial orders were taken for ritual vessels and gifts.

Porcelain of equally high quality but of different taste was produced in the private kilns for the wealthy merchant class and officialdom. These pieces were more flamboyant than the official ware. The use of the nien ho of Kangxi on the base was forbidden during the early years of his reign, but was believed to be reinstated, at least unofficially, during the later years.

Since the use of the characters was forbidden, private kilns often used symbols such as an artemisia leaf, twin fish, a sprig of fungus, a tripod censer, or a rabbit in underglaze blue in the center of the double-concentric circles (executed in underglaze blue). Often the double circles were drawn and left without a central inscription or symbol of any kind. The use of the double circle continued from the early Qing period through the mid-nineteenth century. Other marks used during the period were "place" marks—the names of rooms, studies, libraries, and so forth of the wealthy and aristocratic and also particular halls located in the Imperial Palace. All these marks are otherwise referred to as hallmarks, and their use continued through the Qianlong and into the Daoguang period. Some place marks using the characters for "hall" and "studio" were used by emperors, officials, and artisans; others, including "library," "mountain dwelling," and "rare studio," were used by the aristocracy and officialdom but never by the emperor.

Kangxi appointed several kiln directors during his reign, who were encouraged to develop new colors and painting techniques that became a standard for excellence throughout the Qing Dynasty. Development of finer, whiter clay for porcelain production and new kiln firing techniques were developed. Toward the end of the Kangxi period, rose pink was added to the Chinese enamel palate. This otherwise-known foreign color was introduced from the West as the trade to Europe requested the inclusion of this color on their imports. The use of rose pink lead to the development of the famille rose pattern ware (Rose Medallion and others), which gained great popularity in Europe in the later Qing Dynasty. The use of pink enamel for decoration grew throughout the Yongzheng period and flourished during the reign of Qianlong.

Throughout the Qing Dynasty, it was not uncommon to find porcelain products ("official," popular, and export ware) with the mark of an earlier emperor. This was not an attempt to defraud, but rather to honor the product, which might resemble the style produced during an earlier reign. It also may have been an attempt to give tribute to an exceptionally fine item even if the style was quite different from the original items made in the attributed time period. Kangxi porcelains are frequently found with the marks of previous Ming Dynasty emperors.

The colors and styles attributed to the Kangxi period were monochrome glazes (apple green, sang de boeuf, and peach bloom); powder blue ground decorated vases and bowls with gold tracery designs or reserves in famille verte colors; blue and white decoration featuring the prunis blossom motif; famille verte, famille noire, and famille jaune (all frequently painted directly on the porcelain "biscuit" before firing); revival of the Tang Dynasty splashed glazes (using green, yellow, aubergine, and white [frequently called spinach and egg glaze]); controlled firing of flambé glazes; and pink, white, and other opaque colors included for the first time in the Chinese palette of colors.

Yongzheng Period: The quality of porcelain produced during this short but prolific period was of extremely high quality. Kiln director Nian Hsi-yao was appointed imperial kiln director in 1726. Since additional duties often kept him away from Ching-te-chen, T'ang Ying was appointed by the imperial household in 1728 to act as his assistant at the official kilns. T'ang Ying remained at his post after promotion to supervisor at the beginning of the Qianlong period (with a brief respite from 1750 to 1752) until 1756. Fortunately, in addition to being a talented artist and creative ceramic innovator, he was also an accountant of merit. T'ang Ying kept detailed accounts of the official output of the kilns during his administration. It is because of his meticulous records that we have much information of the quantity and styles of porcelain of this period. During this time the use of famille rose enamels first became widespread. Pink was first introduced into Chinese design, but very soon after, in response to European demands, the motifs began to appear to satisfy European tastes. Scenes of the outdoors, birds, and flowers began to replace traditional Chinese symbols.

Several innovations in porcelain color and technique were developed in these years. The delicate eggshell porcelains, including ruby back plates, first appeared during this reign. Inventive design flourished, including the new technique of continuing a painted pattern over the rim of dishes to the underside. Apple green and bright opaque lime green were popular monochrome colors of the period. A bright opaque lemon yellow was also used, but this color, along with the lime, was not used for a long period due to the presence of lead in the glaze and the difficulties encountered in their production. Doucai enamels, which were being produced at the end of the Kangxi period, were continued in the Yongzheng period, as was the continued improvement and development of flambé glazes. A successful revival of the Chun (jun) glazes of the tenth to fifteenth centuries also took place at Ching-te-chen, as did copies of other traditional glazes from earlier periods. Export wares began to expand.

The most-honored porcelains of this period are the Ku Yueh Hsuan wares "Ancient Moon Pavilion." These porcelains, like their counterparts made in glass, were decorated in a delicate and specific manner with rose and other opaque enamels along with other translucent enamels. The themes consisted of floral designs and landscapes with figures. Porcelains so decorated were small and had, as part of their decoration, a poetic verse painted in black. Period examples of this ware appear with the four-character mark of Yongzheng within double rectangles and applied in blue enamel on the base. Existing examples of this fine porcelain can be seen only at museums.

Qianlong Period: Emperor Qianlong took great pleasure in participating in and encouraging the porcelain production of the imperial kilns. Wares made for the palace were delicately potted, exquisitly painted, and sometimes included poems that Qianlong wrote. His poetry often was placed on Ku Yueh Hsuan-styled porcelain, which he favored greatly. As in the Kangxi and Yongzheng periods, many imperial wares incorporated motifs of dragons (a symbol of the emperor) and phoenix birds (symbolic of the empress) as part of their design.

Porcelain production in general reached one of its highest peaks. Many new glazes, designs, and shapes appeared. Innovative porcelain techniques that imitated the shape, texture, and colors of bamboo, wood, lacquer, and precious metals were created. Gilding was freely used. A new turquoise color was developed, the quality of many other existing colors was improved. The tea dust and iron rust glazes were perfected. The imperial factory first used shading as part of painted decoration. Perfection in the art of piercing to achieve latticework and lacework design was attained. The era also saw the first production of the rice-grained pattern. Lac burgaute, the technique of applying lacquer inlaid in mother-of-pearl, also appeared. Porcelains in the archaic styles and glazes continued to be made.

Although this period saw the highest level of artistic achievement, the quality of the production began to decline after the death of kiln director T'ang Ying in the 1760s. Export of porcelain in the famille rose palette still was very strong and included the manufacture of figures, both molded and modeled. Famille rose pattern wares in whole dinner services were another popular export to Europe, as were Canton and Peking blue and white pattern wares sent to America.

LATE QING PORCELAIN

Jiaqing Period: There were no new innovations in porcelain during this reign, and the quality continued to decline from the end of the Qianlong period. The tradition of giving expensive gifts—which had accounted for a sizable amount of the imperial factories' production—was discontinued by Jiajing. His efforts were directed toward restoring the economic order of his rule, which was left in chaos by the time his father died. Jiaqing's poetic verses were inscribed on porcelains, following his father's tradition.

Daoguang Period: Unfortunately, Daoguang inherited much of the financial woes of his father, Jiajing, and his reign was troubled by both internal upsets and problems related to the opium trade. The quality of porcelain production during Daoguang's reign improved slightly over the Jiaqing period and approached that of the Qianlong era. However, the quality of the porcelain body was not as fine and the glaze flow became uneven—somewhat like the texture of congealed milk, sometimes referred to as a "muslin" glaze. This period is noted for the production of "medallion bowls," which were painted in underglaze blue on the inside and decorated with incised scrolling on the exterior enamel ground color. Enameled medallions of the interior scenes were set in reserves around the exterior. Ground colors used included pink, blue, yellow, and a greyish pink. These bowls were carefully executed and are considered highly desirable.

Xianfeng and Tongzhi Periods: There is no porcelain of distinction attributable to these reigns since political upheaval was preemininent and, eventually led to the destruction of the imperial kilns in 1855. Records are unclear about the reestablishment of imperial kilns, and it is assumed that palace porcelain was produced by better private kilns until the fall of the dynasties. Iron red reign marks, which formally were used solely by the imperial factory, became common after the reign of Xianfeng. It also became a common practice to sign pieces "made in the reign of the Great Qing" during the Tongzhi period. This form of signature continued into the Guangxu period.

Guangxu Period: Guangxu was the only Qing emperor who was not appointed by rights of succession. Instead, he was chosen by Empress Cixi, who continued to dominate the politics of the reign throughout his office.

This era in porcelain production saw some improvement in the quality of wares produced, particularly in the eggshell wares. Although the styles of the Yongzheng period were reproduced, they differed in the use of shading and facial expression. Technically, however, they were perfect.

Xuantong Period: Emperor Xuantong acquired his throne at the age of three. The 1911 revolution deposed both his reign and the production of imperial porcelain at Ching-te-chen. Although this short period of time is not noteworthy in the porcelain history of China, there are examples of copies of Qinglong porcelains made during Xuantong's reign, but their workmanship is obviously inferior to the originals. (See: Armorial Porcelain; Blanc de Chine; Canton and Nanking Blue And White; Chinese Export Porcelain; Fitzhugh Pattern Porcelain; Famille Rose Pattern Porcelain; Monochromes; Shiwan Ware; Yi-hsing.)

References: Gunhild Avitabile, *From the Dragons's Treasure*, Bamboo Publishing Ltd., 1987; John Ayers, *Chinese Ceramics: The Koger Collection*, Sotheby's Publications, 1985; Soame Jenyns, *Later Chinese Porcelain*, Faber and Faber Inc., 1965; Rose Kerr, *Chinese Ceramics: Porcelain of the Ching Dynasty 1644–1911*, Victoria and Albert Museum, 1986; the Chinese University of Hong Kong, *Imperial Porcelain of Late Qing (From the Kwan Collection)*, exhibition from Aug. 13–Sept. 25, 1983; Lady David, *Ch'ing Enamelled Ware: in the Percival David Foundation of Chinese Art*, University of London, Percival David Foundation of Chinese Art, 1973; Jean Martin and S. G. Yeo, *Chinese Blue and White Ceramics* Arts Orientalis, 1978; Margaret Medley, *The Chinese Potter*, Charles Scribner's Sons, 1976; —, *Underglaze Blue and Copper Red: Decorated Porcelains* University of London, Percival David Foundation of Chinese Art, 1976.

Museums: Boston Museum of Fine Arts, Boston, Massachusetts; Metropolitan Museum of Art, New York, New York; Seattle Art Museum, Seattle, Washington; Freer Gallery, Washington, D.C.; National Museum, Singapore; British Museum, London, England; Sir Percival David Foundation, London, England; Victoria and Albert Museum, London, England; Museum fur Kunsthandwerk, Frankfurt, Germany.

Reproduction Alert: It was the custom and tradition of the Chinese to copy the wares of earlier dynasties and to sometimes mark them with the nien hao of earlier emperors. These were not reproductions in the usual sense, but rather commemorative marks giving honor to an earlier reign. This practice has caused a great deal of confusion in attempts to accurately date Chinese porcelains.

For experienced collectors, there are many hints to help separate the "original" porcelains from those using commemorative signatures. To relate them all would be the task of another book. Keep several facts in mind when evaluating the age of any item. Porcelains decorated with opaque "foreign colors," such as the opaque rose pinks, blues, whites, and so forth, cannot be dated before the last years (1715–1722) of the reign of Kangxi regardless of any mark found on the item. The "paste" (clay used to create the porcelain body) used during the eighteenth century is gen-

erally very smooth (somewhat like the silky texture of raw spaghetti), particularly during the Kangxi period. Nineteenth-century and later porcelain is much rougher to the touch. Some early twentieth-century porcelains often are marked with a Qinglong commemorative reign mark. These marks are either stamped or hand-painted in an orange/red seal mark form. True Qianlong seal marks often were carefully hand-painted in blue, less often in a strong iron red (appearing late in the reign), and more rarely in other colors, including gold (seen frequently on porcelains decorated in the style of bronzes, which may have gold lacquer painted on impressed seal marks).

Kangxi porcelain marks were commemorated by the later Qing emperors. Yongzheng marks are found on delicate floral-patterned pieces produced at some commercial factories at Ching-te-chen between 1904 and 1910. Qianlong period porcelains may have commemorative Ming or earlier Qing marks. Current reproductions of eggshell porcelains of the 1920s and 1930s lack the delicate painting techniques of earlier counterparts.

When in doubt, ask your dealer to guarantee the age in writing, a request that will not be denied by any reputable dealer or auction house in the country. When buying from other markets, you are on your own. Thorough studying and museum observation will be your best aides toward a good investment.

Collecting Hints: There is a very strong trend today to collect the mark and period porcelains of the later Qing emperors. One might believe this trend is due to the high prices of older porcelains, which thereby forced the less-expensive later pieces into popularity. While there is, no doubt, some truth to this supposition, it seems that the attraction is forced more by the availability of items on the market. Once again, the law of supply and demand takes hold, and we have seen a phenomenal rise in prices of some of the better quality later Qing ware. Since this is a new trend, there is still time for the collector to find good examples of later porcelain that are "sleepers" on the market.

High-quality eggshell pieces produced in the 1920s and 1930s also are in demand. These items are extremely delicate and transparent, and often are signed with Yongzheng or Qianlong imperial reign marks. The mark is found in light blue enamel or iron red. The painting is very fine and detailed. They are not to be confused with the poorly executed late nineteenth-century eggshell examples with Millefleur decoration and earlier styles of decoration.

QING PORCELAIN—EARLY PERIOD

Basin, Blue and white, 13⅜" dia., Kangxi mark and period, painted in the center with a court lady and attendant under a parasol and an equestrienne, encircled by radiating petal-shaped panels decorated with alternating pairs of women and floral sprays, the exterior with flowerheads and ruyi heads, the underside with a six-character mark, firing cracks, frits, restored chips **1,500.00**

Bowl

Blue and white

6⅞" dia., Kangxi, well painted, the interior painted in the center with a young boy holding a lotus stem while seated within a flower-shaped reserve surrounded by a circular medallion, with a narrow band of lotus scroll below the lipped rim and further boys holding the stems of the dense peony scroll through which they frolic on the exterior, restored rim chips, rim cracks **700.00**

7" dia., Ming-style, Kangxi, painted in deep cobalt tones on the exterior with various flower blooms including lotus, gardenia and peony, borne on a continuous scrolling foliate vine, all above petal lappets encircling the ring foot, the underside with a four-character Xuande mark, rim chips **600.00**

8" dia., well-painted, Kangxi six-character mark a double circle and of the period, painted in intense underglaze blue on the exterior with branches of tree peony extending around the sides from a twister trunk, and with further branches amid

rocks in a medallion on the interior, with decorative bands of chevron and foliate pattern below the rim, all within double-line borders, restoration to foot, crack, rim glaze chip **1,500.00**

9¾" dia., Qianlong six-character mark, and of the period, the interior painted with a medallion of four Buddhist ornaments encircling a flowerhead and separated by trailing ribbons, below the narrow breaking wave band around the rim, the exterior with leafy scrolls centered by a band of eight lotus heads below the eight Buddhist symbols trailing ribbons, all above the cloud collar band encircling the foot with a narrow band of breaking waves. **5,500.00**

10½" dia., scalloped, Kangxi six-character mark within a double circle and of the period, the interior painted with a scene of mounted warriors surrounded by petal-shaped panels depicting further warriors alternating with foliate vignettes rising from the deep well to the everted, scalloped rim, on a wan-fret ground, the exterior with detached foliate sprays above separated ruyi heads, minute hair crack. **1,000.00**

Famille-Verte

5¼" h., Kangxi, the cylindrical body decorated with a continuous scene of a dragon among crashing waves supporting a demon, his body turned to look back at a gate and a leaping carp **650.00**

5⅜" h., 18th Century, the cylindrical form painted with two shaped panels, both boldly painted with scenes of iron-red, black and green carp swimming among various aquatic plants **1,200.00**

Other Decoration

Cafe-au-lait ground, slip-decorated, 7⅛" dia., wood stand, Chenghua six-character mark within a double circle, but 18th century, the deep rounded sides decorated on the exterior with two dragons racing through scattered clouds in pursuit of "flaming pearls" reserved in white slip on a pale cafe-au-lait ground, the interior similarly glazed below the

Bowl, 10" dia., Kangxi period, celadon ground, blue and white decorated with the eight frolicking horses of Emperor Mu Wang. $1,450.00. Courtesy of Butterfield and Butterfield.

white-glazed rim, glaze scratch, small firing fault **650.00**

Bowls, pair, blue and white, conical form, 3¾" dia., Yongzheng six-character mark, and of the period, the interiors with a double-line circle enclosing a lotus head with feathery tendrils, the exteriors with a continuous band of lotus heads on leafy scrolls between a classic scroll band around the rim, a ruyi head band encircling the foot **3,300.00**

Brushpot

Blue and white, 7" h. x 7¼" dia., Kangxi, well-painted on the exterior with two scenes in brilliant cobalt tones, one panel with an interior of officials and dignitaries presenting scrolls, the other with a pheasant perched on rockwork among flowering peony branches, hairline crack at rim, natural firing crack to base **1,200.00**

Yellow-ground

4⅝" dia., iron-red-decorated bowl, Yongzheng mark and period, well-painted around the exterior in tones of iron-red with five sinuous dragons, two pairs confronted, writhing amid clouds and flames, above a band of rolling waves, all reserved on a rich yellow ground, the interior and foot glazed white, the underside with six-character seal mark, cracked, restored **2,200.00**

5¾" dia., green-and-yellow-ground dragon bowl, Qianlong mark and period, incised on the exterior with two scaly dragons in pursuit of the "flaming pearl" amid cloud swirls and flames above crested waves, all in a lustrous green enamel reserved on an egg-yellow ground, the base and interior glazed white, rim restored **3,000.00**

5⅞" dia., dragon bowl, Kangxi mark and period, of deep rounded form with a flared lip, the exterior painted in green with two dragons chasing "flaming pearls" on a yellow ground, the interior glazed white, supported on a low foot, repaired rim chip **3,000.00**

Brushwasher

Blue and white brushwasher and water dropper, 5", Kangxi, the porcelain in the form of a lotus leaf with a lotus bud forming the

dropper, decorated with a small snail in relief **450.00**

Biscuit, grotto group, 7½" h., Kangxi, the base of artemisia-leaf shape with a splashed "egg and spinach" glaze, supporting brown-glazed pierced rockwork, flanked by two pavilions and a central pine tree, the cavity with small fish, lotus plant and crab, chips, cracks, losses **1,300.00**

Charger, blue and white, 18½" dia., Kangxi, with a deep rounded cavetto, the center painted in washy tones of cobalt with deer grazing under a pine tree, with rockwork and flowering plants alongside, the border with flowering branches of prunus, chrysanthemum and peony, with a brown rim **2,200.00**

Dish

Blue and white

6¼" dia., Ming-style, Kangxi mark and period, the deep sides tapering to the high ring foot, painted in deep inky blue tones on the interior with three cranes soaring amid Buddhist emblems, flames and cloud scrolls, all below a band of keyfret at the rim, the exterior with four Buddhist emblems divided by ruyi-centered cloud scroll motifs, hairline cracks **1,000.00**

15⅛" dia., Kangxi, foliate molded, painted in deep blue tones, the center with a leafy lotus blossom within ruyi borders, encircled by radiating petal lappets enclosing floral sprays, all reserved on a diaper ground, within larger petal lappets enclosing rock, floral and fruit sprays including peony, chrysanthemum, peach and pomegranate, also reserved on a diaper ground on the cavetto and rim, rim frits, glaze imperfection, chips to foot **1,320.00**

Coral-ground gilt-decorated, 6½" dia., Kangxi, carved on the interior with a central peony blossom spray under a white glaze, the exterior gilt-decorated with the eight Buddhist symbols borne on a continuous scrolling foliate vine above a classic scroll encircling the footring, all reserved on a coral-red ground, the underside with six-character Jiajing mark, rim chip, restored **500.00**

Doucai decoration, 6⅛" dia., 18th

Dish, 6⅐", commemorative Chenghua mark but Kangxi period, doucai decoration, painted in vibrant enamels, the underside decorated with three fruiting sprigs. $1,200.00

century, decorated on the interior with five stylized lotus blooms borne on a continuous foliate vine within double line borders repeated at the rim, the exterior with a continuous foliate lotus scroll, the underside with six-character Chenghua mark, minute chips to footring.................. **1,000.00**

Famille-rose

4½" dia., pair, Yongzheng, each decorated with a pair of magpies perched on floral sprigs surrounded by a scrolling foliate band in gold, cracks **900.00**

6⅞" dia., famille rose and iron-red dish, molded, fitted box, Yongzheng mark in underglaze blue, and of the period, the fluted ca-

vetto rising to a flared rim, all covered with a brilliant iron-red glaze, the central medallion painted in delicate famille rose enamels with chrysanthemum and a half-open peony **2,200.00**

7¼" dia., saucer dish, Yongzheng mark in underglaze blue within a double circle and of the period, the interior painted in soft-toned enamels with a bird perched on a branch of iron-red leaves, opposite a branch of blossoming tree peony and asters, cracked **3,000.00**

7¾" dia., Yongzheng mark and of the period, decorated in gilt and characteristic colors with a lady and her attendant seated among an arrangement of traditional furniture **5,000.00**

Famille-Verte

8¼" dia., Kangxi, decorated in the center with the Hundred Antiques motif, within five shaped panels enclosing Buddhist emblems reserved on a cell-diaper border, frits to rim and ring foot **800.00**

10½" dia., famille-verte and iron-red decorated, Kangxi, decorated in the center with exotic butterflies amid flowering leafy sprays reserved on a stippled green ground within a band of eight floral medallions reserved on an iron-red decorated ground, traces of gilt, cracks, frits **800.00**

10¾" dia., Kangxi, with a powder-blue ground reserved in the center with a medallion enclosing butterflies over a flowering foliate spray issuing from rockwork, within four

Dish, 7" dia., Qianlong mark and period, the interior painted in iron red with a dragon suspended in a ground of underglaze blue waves, restored rim chips. $1,000.00. Courtesy of Butterfield and Butterfield.

Dish, 12½" dia., Kangxi period, famille verte, decorated with reserves of mythological beasts. $2,800.00

enameled vignettes divided by gilt foliate sprays on the rim, the underside with Ding mark, frits **800.00**

13⅜″ dia., Kangxi, the center painted with a stellate form enclosing flowering plants outlined by an iron red border, the rim with iron-red diaper designs enclosing six panels of blossoms **1,300.00**

16″ dia., Famille-verte/powder-blue-ground, 18th Century, painted in the center with a flowerhead-form panel enclosing flowering and foliate peony branches issuing from rockwork below the rim and decorated with eight barbed quatrefoil panels with floral sprays and landscapes, the underside with wisps of iron-red and green enamel flowering branches, chips to footring, glaze gaps **1,800.00**

Green dragon dish

6¾″ dia., Qianlong mark and period, painted in the center with a spirited scaly dragon pursuing a "flaming pearl" in a medallion within a lined border repeated around the lipped rim, the underside with two further dragons between similar underglaze-blue and green enamel line borders, the decoration in bright green enamel with outlines and detailing drawn in black, crack **1,000.00**

7″ dia., saucer dish, engraved dragon, Qianlong seal mark in underglaze blue and of the period, the interior decorated with a scaly dragon leaping in pursuit of the flaming pearl amid flames, with a frieze of two further dragons pursuing pearls on the wave-carved ground of the exterior, all in bright green enamel with black details within similarly enamelled line borders **2,400.00**

Figure

Guanyin, famille-verte

9½″ h., biscuit, Kangxi, modeled seated with arms at her sides, her long floral-decorated robes falling over her knees and forming a base, her hands resting in her lap with one slightly raised, her hair tied up in a chignon, a square aperture on the reverse, cracks, restoration to hands . . . **1,000.00**

14½″ h., enamelled biscuit, on a pedestal base, Kangxi, the Goddess of Mercy shown seated in padmasana with the figure of a small child seated in her lap between her hands, wearing full robes and a cowl variously decorated with scattered flowers, the separate base of hexagonal form pierced and decorated with diaper pattern below a pierced balustrade surrounding the lotus throne, all in green, yellow, aubergine and black, chips, restoration **1,300.00**

Ginger jar

Blue and white

7¾″ h., Kangxi, of ovoid form decorated with boys enclosed within lozenge panels, reserved on a diaper cell ground, the body further painted with sprays of flowers **800.00**

8″ h., Kangxi, in bright cobalt tones and decorated with quatrefoil panels of archaic vessels on a "cracked ice" and prunus flower ground **800.00**

Jar and cover, 7″ h., Café-au-lait-ground famille-rose, 18th Century, of deep U-shape decorated in famille-rose enamels with four leaf-shaped panels of insects hovering above flowering lotus, peony, and chrysanthemum, all reserved on a coffee-colored ground, the domed cover similarly painted with a central ring knop, glaze gaps **1,100.00**

Jars, covered, 17½″ h., Kangxi mark and period, blue and white, decorated with motif of children enjoying various games in a garden setting. $4,675.00. Courtesy of Butterfield and Butterfield.

Jardiniere
 9″, blue and white, Kangxi, baluster form with an everted rim, decorated with the longevity symbols of stags, lingchih fungus, pine trees, cranes and rocks, below is a border of eight Buddhist symbols **800.00**
 18″ dia., famille-Verte, Kangxi, the tapered body with a cushion molded lip in a diaper pattern above a wide frieze of birds perched among flowering gnarled branches and rockwork, the slightly spread foot with panels of auspicious emblems. **5,000.00**
Lamps, pair, 17″ h., famille-verte, hexagonal vases, Kangxi, each decorated with alternating panels of flowers and antiques, the neck with floral sprays, some enamel chipping **4,500.00**
Moon flask, large yellow-ground blue and white moon flask, 19½″ h., Yongzheng seal mark, each side decorated with eight petals radiating from a raised boss centered by a flowerhead, with bands of lotus scroll on the narrow sides below the leaf-form handles and lingzhi scroll on the neck and foot, all within keyfret borders, and painted in blue wash on a pale yellow ground, mouth rim ground **8,000.00**
Rice bowls, pair, blue and white, 2¾″ x 4″, Kangxi, decorated with a pencilled seated figure drinking and preparing tea in a garden landscape, the foot with the six-character Zhenghua mark. **600.00**
Rosewater sprinklers, pair, blue and white, 9⅜″ h., Kangxi, each of spherical section decorated around the sides with four stylized lotus blossoms, the tapering slender neck and splayed base with foliate scroll, with pendent and upright foliage within narrow unglazed bands washed brown, pinhole glaze gaps **1,800.00**
Scrollpot, blue and white, 11¼″ h., 18th Century, each side painted with pavilions and gardens nestled among mountainous landscapes along a riverbank with ships and figures, with monster-mask handles, all below a slightly raised band of diamond diaper, later etched around the neck with inscriptions **1,600.00**
Vase
 Blue and white
  10″ h., mallet vase, Ming style, Xuande Six-character mark, but Kangxi, painted all over with a dense pattern of leafy lotus

Vase, 4½″, 18th century, underglaze red and blue decoration of dragon chasing flaming pearl above a stylized wave border. $850.00

scroll executed in pencilled line with a narrow band of foliate scroll on the shoulder and a band of classic scroll below the lipped rim, the apocryphal nien hao in a line around the base of the tall, cylindrical neck, raised on a grooved footrim, minute glaze chip on mouth rim **1,500.00**
 17⅜″ h., Yen-Yen shape, Kangxi, painted with an interior scene of ladies, court and military officials, and attendants, divided

Left, Vase, 7¼″ h., Kangxi period, blue and white, double-lobed form, decorated with floral pendents below a waisted neck. $450.00; *right,* Vase, 18″ h., Kangxi period, beaker form, decorated with a continuous figural scene of court officials, the base encircled by a band of pendent stiff leaves. $3,000.00. Both courtesy of Butterfield and Butterfield.

by an exterior view of rocks, plantain and willow trees, the neck decorated with military officials under the moon and willow trees, chips on footrim . . .   **2,750.00**

17½″ h., ovoid vase, Kangxi, of high shouldered form tapering slightly toward the base, painted in bright cobalt tones with pavilions nestled in a mountainous landscape with pine trees, bordering a large expanse of water with boats and a solitary fisherman, below a short neck decorated with bamboo sprays, divided by a crenelated band within double-line borders at the shoulders, the underside with a six-character Chenghua mark, glaze scratches **4,000.00**

18″ h., Rouleau shape, Kangxi, painted with two confronted writhing scaly four-clawed dragons chasing a "flaming pearl," surging up from turbulent waves around the base, amid a background of flame scrolls and another "flaming pearl," all below a waisted neck decorated with cross-hatching on the galleried rim, the underside with an artemisia leaf, some brown speckling, glaze gaps, restored chip at base **1,500.00**

Famille-Verte

7⅝″ h., beaker-form, 18th Century, decorated with various flowers between diaper bands, crack, chip. **300.00**

9¾″ h., baluster form, underglaze-blue, Kangxi, decorated with a phoenix, a soaring bird and a butterfly among leafy flowering peony branches extending around the body and issuing from pierced rockwork, all below a diaper band at the shoulder, the neck decorated in sepia with a spray of bamboo, gilt remains, cracks, losses to enamel   **900.00**

12½″ h., gu-form vase, Kangxi, of hexagonal section, the center panels decorated with stylized shou characters reserved on a stippled green ground, between petal borders and decorated panels of butterflies and birds among various flowering branches on the neck and vase, glaze chips, rim repainted **3,000.00**

17¼″ h., pear-shaped vase, Kangxi, the sides decorated in bright enamels with three large peach-shaped panels, one framing a tiger confronting an airborne dragon, the other two with kylin, with flower-filled leaf-shaped panels above, all reserved on a green ground stippled in black and scattered with blossoms and butterflies, with three smaller panels of fantastic animals reserved on a cell diaper ground on the splayed foot, and with two rows of iron-red and blue shou medallions evenly spaced on a ground of foliate diaper on the neck, crack in base, interior crack to neck **4,000.00**

Guan-type

11″, cong-form vase, Qianlong seal, mark and period, of archaic jade shape molded on each side with the "Eight Trigrams" beneath a pale gray glaze with an even network of darker gray and beige crackle in imitation of Song guanyao **8,000.00**

13⅞″, glazed hu-form vase, Qianlong seal mark and period, two sides molded with large peach-shaped panels, the neck with re-entrant corners and two rectangular pierced handles, the glaze of even pale green color   **7,500.00**

Other glazes and decoration

Celadon-ground underglaze-blue and copper-red-decorated, 16⅛″ h., 18th Century, of hexagonal section surmounted by a tall ribbed neck flaring

Vase, 20¼″, Qianlong mark and period, famille rose, decorated with three medallions depicting pavilions and pagodas, reserved on a Millefleur ground. $4,400.00. Courtesy of Butterfield and Butterfield.

Waterdroppers, Pair, 4″ l., Kangxi period, in the form of crouching rabbits, covered all over with a spinach-and-egg glaze. $800.00

toward the slightly everted rim, decorated on one side with flowering chrysanthemum plants in underglaze-blue with copper-red blooms, the reverse with flowering lotus plants, divided by underglaze-blue bamboo sprays, set with pierced molded handles **1,400.00**

Vases, pair, Doucai decoration, bottle-form, 7¾″ h., Kangxi, decorated at the shoulders with a yellow and green scrolling dragon chasing a "flaming pearl" above a band of crashing waves encircling the base, the underside with four-character Chenghua mark. **3,000.00**

Water coupe, blue and white, 4½″ dia., Yongzheng Six-character mark within a double circle and of the period, painted in the Ming style with a composite floral scroll between lappets at the foot and a ruyi-cloud collar at the shoulder, the rim with small pouring indent, minor frits . . . **2,500.00**

Wine cup, deep conical, famille verte, 4¼″ h., Kangxi, painted with a solitary bird flying above pale yellow, aubergine and iron-red peony and chrysanthemum and rockwork **1,500.00**

Wine cups, pair, iron-red and underglaze blue, 3¼″ dia., Qianlong underglaze blue seal marks, and of the period, the elegantly potted sides rising to a flared mouth, each with four hibiscus flowerheads in iron-red and foliage in underglaze blue between an underglaze blue double-line band encircling the rim and a single line around the foot **1,400.00**

QING PORCELAIN—LATER PERIOD

Bowl

Blue and white

4¼″ dia., Daoguang six-character seal mark in underglaze blue, and of the period, elegantly potted on a raised footring and

with gently curving sides, painted on the exterior in shades of cobalt blue in outline and wash with the eight Taoist Immortals depicted holding their various attributes and standing on a sea of stylized waves, the center of the interior with a circular panel enclosing Shoulao and fellow Immortals at ease beneath a pine tree, all within double lines at the base and rim **800.00**

10½″ dia., 19th century, thickly potted flared shallow bowl, painted on the exterior with a dense band of phoenix and scrolling lotus, the interior with bats **150.00**

6⅛″ dia., yellow-ground underglaze-blue-decorated, Guangxu mark and period, decorated on the interior with a central lotus blossom issuing leafy vine tendrils reserved on a yellow ground within double line borders similarly repeated at the rim, the exterior with five lotus blossoms borne on foliate vines above a band of lappets, all reserved on a yellow ground **700.00**

6¾″ dia., yellow ground famille rose decorated, Jiaqing iron-red six-character mark, and of the period, finely executed, the interior painted in iron-red with the wufu (or five bats), the exterior enamelled in a famille rose palette with lotus, peony, aster and lily blossoms on leafy scrolling stems, all on a rich yellow ground **1,500.00**

8⅞″ dia., turquoise-ground, Empress Dowager foliate, 19th Century, enameled on the exterior en grisaille with a bird perched amid flowering peony branches entwined with fruiting leafy grape vines extending around the sides

Bowls (one of a pair), 6⅞″ dia., Jiaqing mark and period, coral red ground with motif of cranes in flight. $1,000.00. Courtesy of Butterfield and Butterfield.

Bowl, 9⅛″ dia., Daoguang mark and period, deep coral red ground, painted in multicolor enamels, showing a child riding a hobby horse and encircled by five other children standing with various attributes. $600.00. Courtesy of Butterfield and Butterfield.

Dish, 8½″ dia., Guangxu mark and period, blue and white, showing stylized flowers and scrolling vines. $475.00

and below the flaring everted scalloped rim, all reserved on a pale greenish-turquoise ground, inscribed in iron-red Da Ya Zhai and with a seal mark on the exterior, the underside with an iron-red Yong Ching Chang Chun inscription, minute glaze chips . . . **2,500.00**

Bowls (pair)
Famille-rose, 5″ dia., Guangxu mark and period, each decorated on the exterior with four precious items interlaced with colorful ribbons against a white ground and between a brick-red fret border at the rim and a ruyi border at the base **2,000.00**

Brushpot, 4¼″ h., blue and white, 19th century, Cantonese, cylindrically painted and molded with a deer, birds and butterflies among flowers, bamboo and rockwork. **150.00**

Candleholders, (figural), 5½″ l., early 19th century, in the form of Kylins, each in recumbent position with its head slightly turned to one side, the holder rising from the middle of the back. **1,200.00**

Dish
Blue and white, soft paste, saucer dish, 5¾″ dia., Jiajing Six-character mark within a double circle, 18th century, the slightly recessed center painted in deep shades of inky blue with a medallion of a woman seated on a terrace, an attendant holding a vase beside her, within a double-line border repeated at the lipped rim and above and below a continuous series of vignettes of court ladies and their attendants in garden settings on the exterior, crack **500.00**

Doucai decorated saucer dish, 8¼″ h., Daoguang mark and period, painted in the center with two formal C-scrolls and feathery foliage, symmetrically divided by two green leaves, within double line border, the exterior with six formal motifs, cracked, underside with six-character mark **600.00**

Dishes (pair)
Iron-red and yellow-glazed circular saucer dishes, 6¾″ dia., box, Jiaqing/Daoguang, each gilt and painted on the exteriors with four circular panels enclosing characters and reserved on a lemon ground covered in a dense iron-red key-fret between ruyi lappets, the tomato-colored interiors enamelled throughout with flowering gourd in yellow, white and green, below further ruyi, tasseled and dotted and picked out in gold, one with hair rim crack. . . . **1,000.00**

Dragon dish, 14″ dia., yellow-ground famille-verte decorated, 19th century, the rounded sides rising to an everted rim, the interior decorated in the Kangxi style with two dragons contesting a "flaming pearl" amid clouds and flames encircled with a border of assorted flowers, the exterior painted with a running frieze of further dragons chasing "flaming pearls" amid flames and clouds . . . **750.00**

Figure
Buddhist lion with cub, 6½″ h., 19th century, famille verte green-ground figure on brown base. . . . **225.00**

Buddhistic lions, pair
8½″ h., 19th century, blue-ground, shown seated, one with a cub, the other with a brocade ball, with yellow-glazed backs, brown glazed joss-stick holders and on brown rectangular bases **150.00**

Left, Boy attendant, 19th century, holding rose basket, famille rose decorated. $750.00; *right,* Guanyin, 18" h., 19th century, polychrome enameled, shown holding an amphora in her left hand $825.00. Courtesy of Butterfield and Butterfield.

11½" h., 19th century, turquoise aubergine and yellow glazed, shown seated, one with a cub, the other with a brocade ball, looking to the right and left, supporting candleholders on their backs, on yellow-ground drum-shaped bases 450.00

Immortal, 8" h., famille rose palette, 19th century, the boy seated wearing a colorful floral pattern jacket, holding a ruyi staff in one

arm, a foliate stem (one missing) in the other hand, mounted on brass base for electricity 600.00

Official, famille verte enamelled, 30" h., 19th century, the standing figure shown holding a cloth-wrapped gift, wearing a short yellow jacket decorated with green dragons and sprigs of flowers in blue, green and mauve interspersed with mauve clouds, and a long green skirt similarly decorated but with butterflies rather than dragons, with long green ribbons trailing from his blue cap 3,500.00

Phoenix, (pair), 32½" h., famille verte, 19th century, each tall bird with colorful long plumage, perched on a rockwork base issuing peony 2,500.00

Garden Seat

17¾" h., famille rose, 19th century, barrel shaped with bands of molded raised bosses, the sides covered with pairs of confronting dragons and phoenixes amid continuous bands of stylized flowers, the top and sides cut with coin ("cash") emblems 1,500.00

18" h., (pair) celadon glazed garden stools in hexagonal shape, widening slightly toward the center, the sides molded to resemble bamboo, the top and sides pierced with "cash" motifs 1,600.00

19" h., (pair) turquoise-ground, barrel-form in the Da Ya Zhai style, 20th century, each painted with a gilt scaly dragon among enamelled white blossoms, between rows of raised bosses and yellow

Scholar, 7¾" h., 19th century, famille verte decorated. $425.00

Garden Seat, 16" h., 19th century, blue and white decoration of a variety of blossoms and leafy tendrils $1,200.00. Courtesy of Butterfield and Butterfield.

ground foliate borders, the top and sides with pierced "cash" motifs **900.00**

19¼" h., (pair) 20th century, tobacco-leaf pattern, barrel-shaped, colorful enamels with veined leafage and flowers between rows of raised bosses, the sides pierced with double "cash" motifs, the top with a single cash **850.00**

jardiniere, 13¾" h., Crackle-ground famille-verte decoration, late 19th century, the exterior well-painted with a continuous frieze of the One Hundred Antiques, between borders of floral sprigs and bamboo **950.00**

Lantern

7" h., late 19th century, broad oviform lantern, famille rose painted with a procession of boys with banners. **195.00**

11¼" h., late 19th century, rose/verte, pierced hexagonal oviform shape, painted with roundels of boys at play in landscapes reserved on pierced yellow or aubergine panels surrounded by famille verte trellis-pattern **350.00**

Pilgrim bottle, 12¼" h., blue and white, 19th century, with dragon handles painted with two roundels of figures below trees and a ground of scrolling foliage. **95.00**

Plaque, 21" h., 19th century, porcelain, fan-shaped, blue and white, framed, painted with numerous figures and boats before buildings in a river landscape **675.00**

Punch-bowl

14½" dia., blue and white, 19th century, painted on the exterior with

buildings in a continuous mountainous landscape below a band of ruyi heads **450.00**

14¾" dia., blue and white, 19th century, painted on the exterior with figures seated around tables and panels of river landscapes **750.00**

Vase

9" h., blue and white, five-lobed tulip vase, 19th century, with tall cylindrical neck, painted with a continuous river landscape below a band of royal heads **175.00**

13" h., (pair) pink-ground bottle vases, 19th century, the globular body and tall cylindrical neck decorated with two medallions of a peacock and a bird of paradise amid flowering branches of peony and prunus separated by a pomegranate-shaped panel of flowering stems, all reserved on a pink ground incised with floral scrolls and enlivened with flowering branches, the underglaze blue mark reserved on a pale turquoise ground **1,000.00**

17½" h., famille verte, rouleau shape, 19th century, enameled in the Kangxi style with seasonal flowers divided by a lotus trellis, the shoulder with a band of scrolling flowerheads and quatrefoil panels below further formal lotus scroll at the neck **795.00**

17½" h., famille noire, hexagonal form, 19th century, enameled in famille verte colors on a black ground with birds among leafy stems of peony below a wide ruyi collar band all between diaper and iron-red chrysanthemum

Teapot, 6½" h., impressed commemorative Kangxi mark but 19th century, famille noire with coiled green dragon whose head forms the pouring spout. $675.00

Vase, 6⅞" h., Daoguang period, pear shape, blue and white, decorated with banana palms and bamboo growing beside rocks in a fenced garden. $1,750.00. Courtesy of Butterfield and Butterfield.

head bands, the flaring cylindrical neck with phoenix and foliate meander **975.00**

18" h., blue and white, 19th century, baluster form with domed cover, painted with flowering prunus on a washed blue-ground **750.00**

18" h., (pair), lime-ground, famille-rose decorated, 19th century, each of ovoid form, the sides decorated with rounded rectangular panels containing scenes with Shoulao and the Eight Immortals, reserved on a lime-green ground containing lotus blossoms, peaches, bats and other scrolling blossoms, the waisted neck with four quatrefoil panels of immortals, the base and interior glazed turquoise, gilt highlights **3,800.00**

20½", (pair) famille noire, Hu-form, 19th century, each painted with two famille verte landscape reserves on a black ground patterned with stylized animal motifs, gilt fu lion and ring handles **2,200.00**

23¼" h., famille verte, rouleau shape, 19th century, enameled with an interior court scene depicting a seated dignitary receiving a military entourage, above a green lotus meander band, the neck with stylized ruyi collar and leaf blades **1,200.00**

24" h., (pair), blue and white, slender baluster form with domed covers, 19th century, with lion mask and ring handles, painted

Vases, Pair, 9½", commemorative Qian-long seal mark (coral red) but 19th century, each with two reserves of maidens in a garden setting, the yellow grounds decorated with floral patterns in famille rose colors. $475.00

Vases, Pair, 11¾" h., Guangxu mark and period, rectangular form with elephant head handles, decorated in shades of black with birds on a light turquoise blue ground. $1,850.00. Courtesy of Butterfield and Butterfield.

with Ming-style scrolling flowers and leaves among ruyi heads, one small chip **1,200.00**

ROBES AND TEXTILES

History: Sericulture, the raising of silkworms, spinning silk, and weaving silk textiles, began in China during Neolithic times. Earliest extant evidences of sericulture are found in Shang Dynasty (circa 1700–1122 B.C.) tombs in the form of jade carvings of the silkworm crystallis and from impressions of silk wrappers on buried bronze ritual vessels. Many actual samples of silk fabrics that date to the Han Dynasty (202 B.C.–220 A.D.) have been excavated in tombs in China, central Asia, and Soviet Siberia. Surviving frescoes in Italy that date to the early Christian era show Roman ladies wearing dresses of Chinese silk. In fact, the ancient Greeks called China *Seres*, which means "the Land of Silk," and the thousands of miles long caravan route that connected the Han empire of China and the Roman empire was called the Silk Road.

In ancient China men worked in the fields, and women tended the silk worms, spun the thread, and wove the silk fabric. Taxes were assessed in grain and fabrics, evidence that both men and women contributed to the economy. Standard bolts of silk were equated with currency in trade. The huge demand for silk fabrics for domestic and international trade resulted in the establishment of workshops at which hired laborers produced fabric to specification.

Silk textiles were luxury fabrics for the rich; people of lesser means wore clothes spun from hemp (a type of linen) and cotton (after its introduction from India). In addition to many different techniques of weaving (many names of different types of silk fabrics are derived from their places of production in China, for example, nankeen, satin, shantung, and honan) that produced a wide array of silk textiles, the Chinese have also embellished their silk fabrics with embroidery since the Shang Dynasty.

Embroidery was considered a womanly skill, so that young girls, even from wealthy families, were taught to sew and embroider. However, the heavy demand for embroidered clothing for court and religious occasions, as well as for clothes and furnishings for the homes of the well-to-do, resulted in the establishment of workshops where men were also hired to embroider with silk and metallic threads. Frames were used to keep the material taut, and large frames were manned by two people. The chain stitch, satin stitch, counted stitch, and Peking knot were commonly used.

The abundant use of embroidery in the daily life of the well-to-do means that a great deal has survived to the present. However, because most textile items were made for use and wear, few of the surviving textile pieces are in pristine condition. The bulk of the robes and textile objects date to the nineteenth century, eighteenth-century pieces are rare, and even earlier ones are almost never seen outside of museums.

Chinese robes on the market belong to several categories. Dragon robes, or chifu, were worn by men who served the Ch'ing, or Manchu (1644–1911), government on semiformal occasions. Most are in blue and are decorated with either woven or embroidered symbols that include nine dragons (hence their name), clouds, waves, and other objects as specified. Summer robes were made from gauze and other light silk materials, while winter ones were made from satin, brocade, and koss'u (silk tapestry).

Officials also wore a plain surcoat in dark blue, embellished with a square over the chest and back. The square is decorated with one of nine birds or beasts to denote the rank of the wearer: birds for civil and beasts for military officials. Wives and mothers of officials also wore rather similarly decorated dragon robes for formal occasions, with similar rank badges affixed to long-sleeved or sleeveless surcoats.

In addition, one may find a wide variety of women's informal robes. They vary enormously in design, colors, decorations, and fabrics according to means, fashion, and taste. There are long robes with side slits worn by Manchu women; the ankle-length skirts and hip length jackets of Chinese women; and various coats, waistcoats, and capes in fabrics that range from gauze to velvet— some were fur lined. The fabrics may be of plain or jacquard weave. The entire garment may be embroidered with flora and fauna and auspicious symbols in addition to the embroidered borders. Taste and the wealth of the wearer were the deciding factors. The well-dressed men and women also wore hats and embroidered shoes and carried kerchiefs, fan and spectacle cases, purses, and pouches, most of which were also made of silk and embellished with embroidery. Occasionally, one can also find robes and regalia for Buddhist and Taoist priests.

Finally, the homes of the well-to-do were usually furnished with many rich textiles. They contained woven as well as embroidered daily-use items such as sheets, pillow cases, quilt covers, cushions, bed curtains, tablecloths, and hangings. The variety of items is almost too much to enumerate. Temples, too, contained many hangings, cushions, and banners. Again, the quality of these furnishings vary greatly.

While all the silk textiles from China in recent centuries were produced in factories and while many embroidered pieces were done by professionals, the majority must have been produced in millions of homes, where fine needlework was admired as a womanly accomplishment.

References: Schuler Cammann, *Chinese Mandarin Squares: Brief Cataloque of the Letcher Collection*, University of Pennsylvania, 1953; Xun Chou and Gao Chunming, *Five Thousand Years of Chinese Costumes*, China Books and Periodicals, Inc., 1987; Gary Dickinson and Linda Wrigglesworth, *Imperial Wardrobe*, Bamboo Publishing Ltd., 1990; Walter A. Fairservis, Jr., *Costumes of the East*, The American Museum of Natural History, 1971; Hao-tien Ho, ed., *Chinese Costumes, Brocade, Embroidery*, National Historical Museum of Taipei, 1977; R. Soame Jenyns, *Chinese Art* Vol. III (Chapter 1 is on textiles), Rizolli, 1981; Jean Mailey, *Embroidery of Imperial China*, China Institute of America exhibition catalog, New York, 1978; *Masterpieces of Chinese Silk Tapestry and Embroidery in the National Palace Museum*, National Palace Museum, Taipei, 1971; John Vollmer, *In the Presence of the Dragon Throne: Ch'ing Dynasty Costume (1644–1911) in the Royal Ontario Museum*, Royal Ontario Museum (exhibition catalog), 1977; Verity Wilson, *Chinese Dress*, Victoria and Albert Museum, 1986.

Museums: Metropolitan Museum of Art, New York, New York; The Textile Museum, Washington, D.C.; Royal Ontario Museum, Toronto, Canada; Victoria and Albert Museum, London, England; National Museum of History, Taipei, Taiwan; National Palace Museum, Taipei, Taiwan. In addition, many museums throughout the United States have Chinese robes and textiles and have pieces on exhibition in galleries devoted to Chinese art.

Collecting Hints: Chinese robes and textiles are widely available through dealers and from auction houses. Considering the labor spent on the fine weavings, tapestries, and embroideries, their prices are extremely reasonable and affordable. Because most of the pieces were made for wear, personal adornment, and for decoration and because of the nature of the meduim, few pieces earlier than the eighteenth century are available outside museums. The majority of the pieces one is likely to encounter belong to the nineteenth and early twentieth centuries. Thus the quality of the embroidery and the condition of the piece are of prime importance. Prices vary greatly, depending on rarity, age, and condition. An item of fine workmanship and in excellent condition can be more than ten times the price of a mediocre or worn piece. Good embroidery is still made in China, in Suzhou, Hunan, Guandong, and Sichuan. Here again, look for quality and workmanship.

Advisor: Jiu-Hwa Upshur, PhD

ROBES

Men's Wear
  Dragon robe
    Yellow koss'u, 54", very finely woven with the twelve imperial symbols of authority, perfect condition **6,000.00-12,000.00**
    Blue satin ground, the nine dragons, waves, clouds etc. worked in gold metallic thread, 53", perfect condition **1,500.00-2,500.00**
    Blue silk ground, the nine dragons worked in metallic threads, the remainder embroidered in colored silks, 54", good condition. **1,000.00-2,000.00**
  Priest's robe of blue-grey brocade, the robe is applied on the back

with a couched gold panel with the sun and moon symbols above a pagoda medallion, with a wide embroidered border of dragons, 52", excellent condition **1,500.00-2,000.00**
Ladies' Wear
  Coats
    Blue satin sleeveless coat, embroidered overall with white flying cranes amid blue clouds in satin stitch, 58" . . . **1,200.00-2,000.00**
    Brown silk coat, the coat has an elaborate ruyi shaped collar and borders worked with small medallions of figures in Peking knots, reserved on flower stitched ground, excellent condition, 44" **600.00-1,200.00**
  Jacket
    Blue-black gauze, the gauze is plain, with sleeve bands worked in Peking knots, good condition, 39" **400.00-800.00**
    Turquoise silk, the jacket is covered with embroidered exotic birds, flowers and butterflies in colors, similarly decorated collar and borders, 38", good condition **350.00-600.00**
  Miscellaneous
    Informal koss'u robe in sky blue, Decorated with sprays of exotic flowers and butterflies in gold and colors, the black border with similar design, 50", excellent condition **2,500.00-4,500.00**
    Informal summer robe in blue gauze, Woven with dragon medallions, the black gauze border and white gauze cuffs worked in counted stitch with

Dragon Robe, 55", 19th century, blue satin, the dragons embroidered in couched gold, amid clouds, waves, medallions, and auspicious symbols in bright colors. $4,200.00

Woman's Jacket, 38", 19th century, dark blue satin, with borders embroidered with flowers in light blue, and light blue sleevebands embroidered in black. $850.00

Woman's Paired Apron Skirt, 33", late 19th century, of red satin, the accordion-pleated sides and the front panels embroidered with multicolored flowers. $400.00

Woman's Collar, 28", 19th century, with cut-out shapes of clouds, cranes, lotuses, and peaches in pastel colored satin, bordered with multicolored tassels. $700.00

butterflies and flowers in colors, excellent condition, 53" 700.00-1200.00
Informal robe in embroidered red silk, the all-over embroidery of flowers and butterflies done in satin stitch in various colors, the black border worked with matching motifs, excellent condition, 53" 1,000.00-3,000.00
Fur-lined informal robe, the heavy silk fabric embroidered with overall sprays of peonies in satin stitch, interspersed with "shou" medallions in couched gold, the black borders and white cuffs with similar motifs, lined in white fur, 54", excellent condition 1,500.00-3,000.00
Apron skirt in yellow figured silk, the pleated skirt is embroidered with floral roundels above a border of

blue silk similarly decorated, good condition 200.00-500.00
Purple-blue silk vest, the plain vest has a white border and collar that is intricately embroidered with a continuous riverscape scene in couched gold and Peking knots, excellent condition, 28" . . . 400.00-900.00

TEXTILES

Coverlet, embroidered in pale ivory silk, finely embroidered with brightly colored pheasants, peacocks and other birds, some perched, other in flight, amidst bamboos and flowering trees, good condition, 157" x 80" 2,000.00-3,500.00
Hanging, embroidered, red satin, the center panel is embroidered with exotic birds perched amid rocks and trees, within borders of flowers, groups of dignataries, and

Woman's Informal Robe, 57", late 19th century, in pink jacquard woven silk, with black satin border and white sleeve bands embroidered with multicolored flowers and butterflies. $850.00

Woman's Vest, 29", 19th century, in dark blue satin, embroidered all over with medallions in shades of blue, the border similarly embroidered with flowers. $750.00

Detail of Ivory Satin Coverlet, 96" w. x 96" l., 19th century, embroidered in delicate colors with the Hundred Birds pattern, with elaborately knotted tassel border. $4,000.00

trees, excellent condition, 138" x 130" **1,500.00-2,500.00**
Koss'u chair panel
Finely woven in gold ground, with dragons rising from waves, pheasants flying in the sky amidst clouds and flowers in various colors, all enclosed in a floral border, perfect condition, 63" x 20" **1,500.00-3,000.00**
Gold ground koss'u panel, landscape scene with pairs of exotic birds perched on flowering trees above a spotted deer in various colors, perfect condition, 50" x 14" **400.00-700.00**
Mandarin squares or rank badges
Made for officials, these are woven in koss'u, or in silk cloth embroidered in counted stitch, satin stitch or Peking knots; they have at the center one of nine birds for a civil official or one of nine beasts

Detail of Red Jacquard Silk coverlet, 80" l. x 53" w., 19th century, embroidered all over with flowers and butterflies in pastel colors. $750.00

for a military officer, approx. 12" square **40.00-300.00**
Pair of panels, embroidered, the mauve satin embroidered in identical fashion with a pair of elephants supporting a vase on its back, amid vases of flowers and Buddhist symbols, excellent condition, 29" x 29" **400.00-800.00**

SHIWAN WARE (Kuangtung Stoneware)

History: Shiwan is the name of a small town of Nanhai County located twenty kilometers to the southwest of Guangzhou (formerly Canton), the capital city of Guangdong Province. The town is situated on a tributary of the West River, which forms part of the delta that runs into the sea at the Pearl River estuary. With the alluvial ground supplying indigenous clays, the excellent water supply, and a prime location for the transportation of goods, Shiwan was destined to become an important pottery center.

The area around Shiwan had been producing pottery since Neolithic times (3000 B.C.). Many kiln sites have been found in the area that date back to the Han and Tang Dynasties. Shards revealing Song Dynasty reign marks recently have been uncovered. Most of the Song pieces were coarse, utilitarian household wares. Some shards appear with a yellow-green or brownish glaze, though most seem to have been unglazed.

The wares produced at Shiwan consisted of three main groups: pieces used for architecture, daily household items, and artistic creations. In the collecting world, we focus on the work in the last category. The production of the decorative ware as we know it started sometime in the later Ming Dynasty. With the withdrawal of sea trading prohibitions, optimistic capitalistic enterprise resulted in private overseas trade.

The construction of the Temple of the Pottery Master in the Shiwan area circa 1528 was also a major turning point. During its construction, various guilds were initiated and each guild produced its own type of ware. The scope of the potters' industry was widely expanded as a result of this structure. Creativity was encouraged, which resulted in new glazing and sculpting techniques as well as an increase in the variety of products. Pottery was produced both for trade and local consumption. The demand for Shiwan pottery expanded greatly during the Ming Dynasty.

All the kilns were privately owned and operated. The owners had total creative control of their production and responded to the public's desires. The potters began large-scale reproduction of all types of northern kiln wares from all previous Chinese dynasties. Chun, Tzu-chou, Ju, and Ching-te-chen wares all were imitated. Shang and Chou bronzes were copied along with the Tang Dynasty San-ts'ai wares.

Shiwan potters are most famous for their imitation of the Chun-yao glazes. In their attempts to improve development techniques for these glazes, they inadvertently invented new color formations. The resultant glazes, although similar to the Chun-yao glaze, had their own color formations that are highly distinguishable from other colored Chinese glazes. They have received names such as purple Chun-yao, betel nut red, tortoiseshell, crab green, pomegranate red, feathered Mohammedan blue, sea green, and aubergine. The colors run from the rims of the pots and often are feathered with rich colors of purple and blue blending in "flambé" effects. The thick, rich glaze often pooled in heavy globules at the foot rims. The glaze often had an oily appearance; the potting was heavy and somewhat clumsy. The clay itself, ranging from a heavy greyish color to deep red or dark brown, was rich in iron oxides.

Though early production seemed to concentrate on vases and other vessels, the eighteenth century saw increased production of the Shiwan potters' most remarkable achievement: the modeling of both animal and human artistic pottery sculptures. It is in this aspect that people are most familiar with Shiwan wares. They probably rank as the finest pottery figures created in China and are remarkable for their expressive, lifelike features. Figure production does not seem to have started until the late eighteenth century. Early figures appear to have been entirely glazed, but this did not satisfy the potters' desire to portray a truly lifelike piece. They discovered that a much more detailed expression would be revealed if they left the facial and all flesh areas unglazed. The first creations were of images of worship that tended to exaggerate the human anatomy, but the influx of Western art changed their emphasis. The eyes, skin, and facial expressions were modeled to take on an absolutely realistic human appearance. The remainder of the piece, especially the back, was of secondary importance.

During the eighteenth century Chinese export porcelain reached its peak. The early decades of the nineteenth century were the beginning of the end for the ceramics industry of China. Foreign economic imperialism and corrupt and reactionary officials at home caused the entire industry to face a desperate struggle for survival. The Japanese established porcelain factories in southern China which produced cheap utilitarian wares. With the onset of the Sino-Japanese War in the late 1930s, the decline of the Shiwan pottery industry was at a crisis stage. By the end of World War II, only about twelve kilns were still in working condition.

Of interest to some collectors is the production of "mud figures" otherwise know as "mud men" or "mud people" that were made in the Shiwan area between 1910 and 1940. These are small figures usually depicting Chinese elders. They have glazed robes typically colored yellow with green or blue, with unglazed hands, faces, and feet. These late mud figures usually were signed with an impressed mark "CHINA." These figures were exported and used to decorate flowerpots that were decorated as Chinese gardens. Although glaze color, subject, and size vary, the figures are easily identified as mud people.

From 1949 on, the new government reestablished the pottery industry to generate needed revenue. A ceramics insulator industry was developed with a total workforce of 3,000. From these basic roots has developed a new, large pottery industry to rival the output of ancient times. The main aim of the industry today is mass production and profit, not the artistic skill of past generations. The old-time potters still were producing on a small scale, but their work was done for their own enjoyment or to fill local demands for inexpensive and attractive pieces. Their art never was intended for the rich, but rather for the enjoyment of the common folk of China.

References: Nigel Cameron, "Rustic Wares of Guangdong," Orientations Magazine, February 1980; Hong Kong Museum of Art, Shiwan Pottery, 1968; University of Hong Kong, Shiwan Wares, exhibition catalog, October 5 to December 19, 1980, Fung Ping Shan Museum.

Museum: Hong Kong Museum of Art, Hong Kong.

Reproduction Alert: Pottery in the old style is still being made at Shiwan. Many of the old figues in familiar poses are being produced with intense concentration on details of expression. The colors of the clays are also the same. What clearly indicates the difference between the old and new is the types of glazes being used. Since most stores that focus on Oriental giftware will, no doubt, have some of these figures displayed for sale, the collector has the opportunity to study the differences in glaze techniques. On a more sophisticated level, there are more subtle distinctions that will be noticed. Overall, the older figures are more roughly made, without the perfectionistic finishing techniques that are demanded of today's giftware. Even the common mud man is being reproduced, but generally in larger sizes than its earlier, diminutive counterpart. The early Shiwan vases and pots that possess thick, unctuous, streaked and flambé glazes are not currently being produced.

Collecting Hints: With the exception of mud men, Shiwan pottery never had a great impact on international tastes. I assume this is because it was basically a provincial art form and never had been widely disseminated. Today, the collecting of mud men has been for the most part a nostalgic undertaking. Those of us who are old enough may remember them decorating the flowerpots of the average household in the 1930's and 1940's. They are very affordable as a collectible, and because of their size they make good cabinet pieces. Partly because of size, and also because of craftsmanship, these very late Shiwan figures are not of very good quality. This does not pose a problem for the average collector, who focuses on the variety within a collection rather than the quality of individual pieces.

The older artistic wares of Shiwan are attracting a different public. Primary among collectors are the Japanese, who have long admired the irregular and spectacular glaze effects on Shiwan pottery. After the 1980 Fung Ping Shan Museum exhibit of wares in Hong Kong, the prices of the pottery rose sharply. Attractive jars, vases, and bowls that would have sold for $100 ten years ago are now in the $400 to $600 price range. Although the early pieces (eighteenth century and older) are avidly sought, it is the nineteenth-century figural form that is becoming the most collectible.

Advisor: Martin Webster

Bottle, 11⅛", late Ming, raised on a
  slightly inset foot with an elongated
  baluster body with a flaring foot and
  mouth, purple/blue flambé glaze ..   **850.00**
Figure
  Bodhidharma
    Seated, 12" h., early 20th cen-
      tury, pomegranate red glaze ..   **350.00**
    Standing, 18" h., early 20th cen-
      tury, blue jun-type glaze **375.00**

Figure, 8" h., late 19th century, shown seated on rockwork, his robes with a purple to crimson flambé glaze, the dark clay face highlighted with black painted hair, eyebrows, and whiskers. $475.00

Figure, Lohan, 7½" h., shown with arms raised above his head and open mouth, the brown stoneware body covered with a spotty cream colored glaze. $400.00

Elder, seated, 6" h., early 20th century, white glazed robes, potter's
  mark of Hou Jin 250.00
Incense burner, 8" dia., late 19th century, "tiger skin" glaze. 350.00
Vase
  8" h., Qianlong, meiping form, the
    slender body covered with a pur-
    ple glaze suffused with lavender
    falling down the shoulders in
    feathery cascades. 1,200.00
  10⅝" h., 19th century, Junyao type,
    double gourd shape, covered un-
    evenly with a crackled milky blue
    glaze, pitting 850.00
  12" h., 16th century, square shape,
    three color glaze 1,200.00
  Pair, 12¼" h., circa 1900, cylindri-
    cal bodies, covered all over with a
    mottled green glaze draining at
    the rim to a dark brown. 440.00
Mud figures (Animals, bowls, ashtrays,
  and fish bowl items [glazed bridges
  and huts] were also manufactured in
  the 1920's.)
Elders
  1" h., circa 1920s, marked
    "China," white beard and hair,
    brown and green glaze attire   15.00
  1" h., circa 1920s, green glaze at-
    tire 10.00
  2" h., two elders, circa 1910,
    shown playing a game, various
    colored attire 35.00
  2" h., female figure, circa 1920s,
    shown holding a fan, pink,
    brown and yellow glazed attire   35.00

Vase, Bottle, 11¾" h., 16th century, dark blue to purple mottled glaze. $975.00

3" h., circa 1920s marked "China," shown holding a bowl, green glaze attire	25.00
3" h., woman, circa 1920s, marked "China," shown holding a peach, green and blue attire	35.00
3½" h., circa 1920s, marked "China," shown holding a fan, green glaze attire	30.00
4" h., circa 1920s, marked "China," shown holding a fishing pole, blue glaze attire	35.00
5" h., marked "China," white beard and hair, coin carrier, green and brown glazed attire	55.00
9" h., woman, circa 1920s, marked "China," shown holding a teapot, pink and blue glazed attire	225.00
14" h., circa 1920s, marked "China," shown holding a bowl, turquoise and blue glazed attire	225.00
Vase, 9" h., circa 1920s, marked "China," elders applied, brown, green and blue glazes	125.00

SNUFF BOTTLES

History: Snuff—tobacco ground into a very fine powder and enhanced with flowers, spices, or herbs—was consumed by sniffing it into the nostrils. Its use in China spread slowly during the later part of the seventeenth century and early eighteenth century. Consumption of snuff became widespread after Emperor Qianlong (1736–1795) declared it fashionable for himself and his court. The pervading belief of the time was that snuff had medicinal qualities and could cure colds, indigestion, and other illnesses. The emperor treated himself with snuff as a headache cure.

Tobacco was introduced to China by the Europeans at the end of the sixteenth century and became very popular despite the edicts pronounced by the Ming emperor against its use. The Europeans carried their snuff in small boxes, which proved to be very inconvenient in the Chinese climate, because the snuff often caked or lost its fine texture. The natural solution was to store the snuff in medicine bottles that were adapted for snuff use by attaching a small spoon with a cork to the top.

Eventually, the shape of the bottles (cylindrical at first) evolved into many different types as their size was adapted to their use. Men would carry regular bottles of 2½" to 3½" size; ladies would have small bottles of 1½" to 2¼" size; and table bottles might attain a height of 5" to 6". Some people carried twin or multiple bottles in order to enjoy their various aromas. Snuff bottles soon became precious objects in and of themselves, and rules of etiquette were developed as to their use and the style of taking the snuff. Jade and porcelain were used in winter, glass and agate in the spring, bamboo in the summer, and so forth. Snuff bottles were given as gifts, often to buy the favors of court officials. They became collector's items in their time, and huge collections were amassed during the eighteenth century.

The production of snuff bottles was done by skilled workers in workshops, some of which were established in the Imperial Palace by Emperor Kangxi and his successors. The production involved several workers: apprentices to cut the stone and shape the bottle, specialists to hollow the cavity (a very important task), others to polish it, and the most skilled workmen to create the decoration. All materials from precious jade to lowly bamboo were utilized.

CERAMIC BOTTLES

The Chinese were very pleased with their glass and stone snuff bottles, and the production of porcelain snuff bottles lagged, and did not reach its peak until the beginning of the nineteenth century (during the Jiajing period).

Snuffs could not be thrown by a potter in the manner of a vase or bowl. They had to be modeled by molds in one or several parts and assembled. Typically, the body would be made by joining two separate pieces with a slip of the same material. Any imperfection, inside or outside, would be cut and polished away. A neck and a foot would be added using the same technique. The bottle was then fired, decorated, and refired one or more times according to the glazes.

Classifications for porcelain snuffs are made according to decoration. Monochromes, typically cylindrical in shape, were decorated with a single glaze, sometimes applied over relief decoration. Underglaze-decorated bottles were adorned on the biscuit after the first firing and then reglazed and refired. Underglaze decoration featured blue or red, which sometimes appear in combination.

Enameled bottles were decorated after the first glaze had been fired. The number of refirings was governed by the requirements of the glazes. Enamels were used to decorate plain bottles, those with relief decoration (dragons, lohans, and children playing), and molded figural bottles (fruits, animals, and so forth). Relief-molded bottles also are found reticulated, with holes in the outer surface showing an inner bottle which contained the snuff.

Some bottles in relief—often glazed in white, lime green, or pale yellow—are of great quality. The relief decoration on these bottles was carved and not molded. Such bottles were produced in Jingdezhen from the Daoguang period until the beginning of the twentieth century. The best examples are signed by master craftsman Wang Bingrong, and his associates Li Yucheng and Chen Guuozhi among others.

Ceramic and stoneware bottles also were produced. Of specific merit are the stoneware bottles of Yixing (Yi-hsing) that were made in the Yangtze Valley (Province of Jiangsu) during the nineteenth century.

EMBELLISHED BOTTLES

Sometimes older bottles have been redecorated to enhance their beauty. This redecoration was done by both the Chinese and Japanese, but always upon Chinese bottles.

ENAMELED BOTTLES

Enameled snuffs can be separated into four different categories: cloisonné enamels, enamel on glass, enamel on metal, enamel on porcelain (refer to ceramic snuff bottles).

Cloisonné decorated wares were produced in China during the late Ming and throughout the Ching Dynasties, although it was rarely used on snuff bottles. What is available generally was made after World War II. This rule also applies to champlevé and repoussé bottles as well.

Enamel on glass snuff bottles were developed at the end of the reign of Emperor Kangxi. Many bottles of this category were made by the imperial workshop and bear an imperial mark, particularly those made during the reign of Qianlong. Bottles of this type continued to be made throughout the nineteenth century. Some of the finest examples are the work of the artist Ye Zhongsan, his two sons, and their pupil, Wang Xisan, all of whom worked in this century.

There are many myths concerning the production of interior painted snuff bottles, but in reality the production was quite simple. The artist would sit at a table and hold the undecorated bottle in one hand. In the other hand he would hold a bamboo pen that had been angled in order to reach the inside walls of the bottle through the opening at its top. Modern artists (post-1949) also have employed the use of brushes. The first interior-painted bottles were crystal with finely polished interiors that would allow the paint to stick to its walls. Watercolor paints were used. Later, during the nineteenth century, the insides of glass bottles were acid-etched to promote paint adherence. The production of interior-painted snuff bottles is usually divided into three periods.

The early school covers the nineteenth century through the year 1880. The most well-known artist is Gan Xuanwen, whose signature appears on a very well documented bottle produced in 1816. This artist is known to have signed his work with different names.

The middle school began in 1882 when Zhou Leyuan first appeared. The quality of the production of the school peaked around 1915 and then declined except for the work of masters established prior to this date. The following is a rundown of masters established by Hugh M. Moss and published in his book *Snuff Bottles of China* (Bibelot Publishers, London, 1971): "Zhou Leyuan (1882–1893), the inspirer of most of the artists of the school; Zhang Baotian (1891–1904) made very few bottles; Li Shouchang (1892–1895), minor artist, very few bottles; Tang Zichuan (1892–1896), minor artist, very few bottles, dates doubtful; Ye Zhongsan (1892–1912 or later), one of the greatest artists, name signed by his sons until 1949; Bi-Rongjiu (1893 to present), leader of a school within the school located in Shantung Province; Sun Xingwu (1894–1900), rare very fine artist; Ma Shaoxuan (1894–1925), the most popular and successful artist; Gui Xianggu (1895–1900), very few bottles of high quality; Ding Erzhong (1895–1905), a scholar, rare work, extreme quality; Yan Yutian (1895–1918), a prolific artist, capable of the best and the worst; Zi Yizi (1899–1907), a superb artist whose works are extremely rare; Ma Shaoxian (1899–1939), little work, may have signed some of the bottles signed Ma Shaoxuan; Zhou Shaoyuan (1903–1909), a minor artist; Kui Detian (1904), rare bottles; Meng Zhonxan (1907–1918), another unequalled artist, much of his work has been lost; Chen Zhongsan (1907–1918), a specialist of landscapes; Ye Hsiao Feng (1912 onwards), youngest son of Ye Zhongsan; Ye Bengqi (1920 onwards), oldest son of Ye Zhongsan."

Both sons of Ye Zhongsan signed his name until 1949. They created their own studio, using their own names, after the Communists came into power. This list does not include other artists who also worked as contemporaries of the middle school.

The modern school was founded to revive the traditional arts of China upon the reunification of the continental part of China under Communist rule. The modern Peking school has produced some notable artists, among them Ye Bengqi (carrying on his father's tradition); Yeh Shu-Ying (a female artist known for flower and bird subjects), Liu Shaopen, and Wang Xisan (famous for lifelike painting) who recently has been transferred to Tientsin to establish his own school.

From 1966 to 1972 many new contemporary subjects were introduced as themes for painting, incorporating the themes of communism. Since that time students have been allowed to return to traditional themes.

A new school, the Peach River Painting Studio, located in Swatow, is also producing contemporary bottles using old techniques on new shapes.

GLASS BOTTLES

Glass was known in China for a long time, but its use spread considerably at the end of the seventeenth century after Emperor Kangxi established an imperial glass workshop under the direction of the German Jesuit father Stumpff (1680). Contrary to European development, glass was very rare in China and therefore was considered the equivalent of a semiprecious stone. It remained an expensive material throughout the nineteenth century.

Glass was produced in Poshan in Shantung Province and most of it was brought to Peking in the form of bars to be formed into a finished product. Thus the name "Peking glass" became associated with it. Later, other centers of manufacture developed, particularly in Canton.

Glass was a prime material for the production of snuff bottles and was either molded, blown, or carved. It was appreciated both for its own attributes and also as a medium to imitate other materials (precious or semiprecious stones) through the mixture of metallic oxides into the glass paste. Monochrome jadelike and agatelike bottles were produced as well as those imitating other various stones. Coral was imitated, since it was difficult to shape into a snuff bottle. A specific mineral called realgar was highly regarded but could not be used because of its poisonous nature. It, too, was imitated in glass snuff bottles.

Glass was used for snuff bottles in single colors (monochromes), multiple colors mixed together (swirled), and overlay (cased) colors (colors laid one over the other in two or more layers). Overlaid bottles were hand carved using the same lapidary techniques developed over the centuries for hardstones. These bottles were carved in great quantities by the imperial workshop as well as private workshops in Peking and other locations.

One monochrome color deserves specific mention. Through many centuries, yellow had been the favorite color of the emperors. During the reign of Emperor Qianlong, a specific shade of rich egg yolk yellow was reserved, by edict, for the exclusive use of the emperor and his close family. This edict ended with the death of the emperor.

JADE BOTTLES

The Chinese have revered jade for thousands of years. For them it is precious beyond all jewels and gold. Jade represents virtue and humanity and is attributed with many curative powers. Chinese people often wear jade as a symbol of good fortune.

What we call jade is in fact two different minerals. The first one is nephrite, which has a hardness of 5.5 to 6.5 on the Mohs' scale. It is mined in China and has been carved there for more than 2,000 thousand years. The second mineral is jadeite and has its origins in Burma. It was imported to China sometime in the late seventeenth/early 18th century. Its hardness is rated at 6.5 to 7 on the revised and expanded Mohs' scale. Both nephrite and jadeite appear in a wide range of colors. Nephrite, however, is most appreciated when it is pure white (considered imperial jade until the reign of Emperor Qianlong). Jadeite is most appreciated when it appears in a dark emerald green (imperial jade during the nineteenth century).

Because of their hardness and the physical characteristics of their structures, both jades are extremely difficult to carve. On the other hand, the very same characteristics make it possible to carve very fine and intricate designs with very little risk of breakage or fracture. Producing a jade snuff bottle was a very long and difficult procedure. First the boulder of jade had to be cut into small blocks with special tools and abrasives. Slow grinding reduced the block to bottle form, after which it had to be hollowed. The criteria for hollowing required that the volume weight of water poured into the hole be equal to the weight of the bottle, thus allowing it to float. The carved or incised decoration was the last process. All this was accomplished before the introduction of diamond point tools, an amazing achievement. However, huge quantities of jade carvings were produced through primitive methods, particularly during the Qianlong period.

Special mention must be made of the bottles that were carved in Suzhou from the mid-eighteenth century to approximately 1904, toward the end of the reign of Emperor Guangxu. In addition to jade the Suzhou school of carvers worked in chalcedony and other minerals of the quartz family. Their superior carvings are three-dimensional, like sculpture, and utilize all the natural flaws of the stone. Variations of color are carefully incorporated into the design. Frequent motifs were rocks and clouds and include inscriptions.

METAL SNUFF BOTTLES

Metals were used to produce some of the earliest snuff bottles. The most common material was brass, but it is also the most commonly reproduced since a mold can be made from the old bottle. Aside from brass, bronze, silver, and gold were used to make bottles.

ORGANIC MATERIAL BOTTLES

Organic materials may be of vegetal or animal origin or include fossilized materials. Amber is a fossilized material of vegetal origin, originally the resin of coniferous trees during the Tertiary period. Agate was available to China in translucent brown from Burma and in golden brown from the Baltic area. The most interesting snuff bottles are made of "root" amber, which contains impurities of earth, stones, and so forth. Amber snuff bottles have been made since the end of the eighteenth century. They feel supple and warm, unlike their glass imitations, and have been carved with ornate embellishments. Jet, a fossilized wood, is rare in snuff bottles. It is very black and shiny. These snuff bottles were manufactured only after 1850.

Mammoth tooth is a fossilized material of animal origin that was seldom used as snuff bottle material. Snuff bottles that appear on the market made of this material have been produced during the last thirty years.

Coral came to China from Japan, and snuff bottle production began toward the end of the eighteenth century. Early bottles shade from white to light pink and often show flaws or imperfections. The late nineteenth/early twentieth century era saw an improvement in quality and richer colors of coral used.

Ivory carving was a of long-standing tradition in China. Prior to snuff bottles, ivory had been carved for medicine bottles. Bottles were carved in the simplest to the most intricate forms. Old Hornbill ivory snuff bottles are rare. The Helmeted Hornbill (Ho-Ting) lives in a few islands within Borneo. Its ivory has been the object of an intensive trade with China from the Tang period on. The ivory of the Hornbill was traditionally used to create ornaments for high-ranking male officials. In spite of its availability, it does not seem to have been used much in the crafting of snuff bottles before the end of the eighteenth century.

Mother-of-pearl is the inner coating of the Oriental black pearl oyster, which is fairly large and flat. Carving in this material was easy and lent itself to snuff bottle production during the eighteenth and nineteenth centuries.

Lacquer, the product of resin from the tree *Rhus vernicifera*, is used to decorate supporting material (such as wood, porcelain, or metal) and is applied in layers. It is a very hard and resistant material. It can be inlaid, painted, or carved. Cinnabar is a lacquer with red color added that was applied in thick layers and then carved. Cinnabar snuffs were made dating from the second half of the eighteenth century.

Other organic materials used in the production of snuff bottles include horn, tortoiseshell, coco-nut shells, peach stones, and gourds and other seedpods.

PAINTED ENAMEL ON METAL BOTTLES

Otherwise known as "Peking enamel," these snuff bottles were executed primarily on copper. Those that were made at the eighteenth-century imperial workshop bear imperial marks. Similar bottles were produced in Canton in the nineteenth century as well as in Beijing (the modern name for Peking).

ROCK CRYSTAL, AGATE AND RELATED STONES

This group encompasses bottles made of quartz, a mineral widely found both in its crystalline or vitreous versions (rock crystal, smoky crystal, and so on), and its micro or cryptocrystalline versions (chalcedony, agate, jasper, etc.). Quartz is hard, with a hardness of 7 on the Mohs' scale. Its crystal structure makes it easy to work with despite its hardness; it is much easier to carve than jade. The same materials—quartz powder, corundum, crushed garnet, and in the twentieth century, carborundum—were used to carve both quartz and jade.

Rock crystal was mined in southern China, but it also was imported. Crystal comes in several varieties: pure and totally clear or with impurities, (cracks and pockets of air that the craftsmen would incorporate in the design); "hair" crystal, which includes needles of various colors (black with tourmaline needles, very rare green; red on very old bottles). Gold or silver flecks appear on more modern bottles made after the beginning of this century, these specific varieties of crystal have their origins in Brazil. Amethyst, brown, and rose quartz also belong to the quartz family.

The cryptocrystalline versions of quartz have been used to carve some of the most beautiful snuff bottles; these also exist in large numbers. Their generic name is chalcedony, but they often are better known by their specific names: dendritic chalcedony (characterized by treelike markings); agate (marked by concentric bands); carnelian (with a rich red to yellow color). Chalcedony snuff bottles are most often carved to incorporate the impurities or inclusions in the design. Dentritic chalcedony (moss agate), macaroni agate, thumbprint agate and banded agate were carved into bottles of simple form to reveal the richness of the natural stone. Chalcedony in its diverse varieties was a favored material of the Soochow school of carvers.

Jasper also is included in the chalcedony group, and it too can be found in a variety of colors as well. Jasper is basically quartz with lots of impurities, iron oxides, and clays. Jasper also is responsible for the red inclusions found in bloodstones, as well as the many pebbles included in pudding stones.

References: Schuyler Camman, *Miniature Art from Old China*, Montclair Art Museum, 1982; Emily Byrne Curtis, *Reflected Glory in a Bottle: Chinese Snuff Bottle Portraits* Soho Bodhi, 1980; John G. Ford, *Chinese Snuff Bottles: The Edward Choate O'Dell Collection*, Asia House Gallery, November 1982; Henry C. Hitt, *Old Chinese Snuff Bottles*, Charles E. Tuttle Co., Inc., 1978; Raymond Li, *The Medicine—Snuff Bottle Connection*, Nine Dragons, 1979; —, *Chinese Snuff Bottle Themes: Popular Stories and Fables*, Nine Dragons, 1983; —, *The Art of Imitation in Chinese Snuff Bottles, Masterpieces of Chinese Snuff Bottles in the National Palace Museum*, Taipei, 1974; Hugh M. Moss, *Snuff Bottles of China*, Bibelot Publishers Ltd., 1971; —, *Chinese Snuff Bottles of the Silica or Quartz Group*, Bibelot Publishers Ltd., London, 1971; Lilla S. Perry, *Chinese Snuff Bottles; The Adventures and Studies of a Collector*, Charles E. Tuttle Co., Inc., 1960; Bob C. Stevens, *The Collector's Book of Snuff Bottles*, John Weatherhill, 1976; Susan E. Williams, *Chinese Snuff Bottles: Documentation of World Trade West to East*, The Oakland Museum, 1949.

Museums: Los Angeles County Museum of Art, Los Angeles, California; Chicago Natural History Museum, Illinois; Metropolitan Museum of Art, New York; Philadelphia Museum of Art, Philadelphia, Pennsylvania; Seattle Art Museum, Seattle, Washington; Victoria and Albert Museum, London, England; Hong Kong Museum of Art, Hong Kong; National Palace Museum, Taipei, Taiwan.

Reproduction Alert: The first thing to check in a carved snuff bottle is the size of the interior cavity. Bottles that have a straight bore are not true snuff bottles. The purpose of a snuff bottle is to be a container. As such, the cavity needs to be as wide as possible. Even if a snuff bottle is old, if it has been drilled straight, it was manufactured to deceive. Snuff bottles have been collectible since they first started to be produced. Dealers have been taking advantage of collectors ever since.

The market has been invaded with snuff bottles that have been mass produced in the last forty years, which barely qualify as cheap souvenirs for tourists. Beware particularly of: cinnabar or ivory bottles with a metal plate bearing a mark at the base. They are extremely well done, appear of very good quality, but they are made out of plastic. Many dealers sell these products sincerely believing they are real. Frequently handled old cinnabar will show a sheen (from oils absorbed from handling); signs of age on old ivory include discoloration, yellowing, and sometimes cracks. Many interior painted snuff bottles of poor quality have been produced during this century. The value of the bottle is in the quality of the painting. There are *no* inexpensive interior-painted snuff bottles of quality. Overlay glass bottles that have been molded instead of hand-carved. The apparent carving is slanted rather than straight and the overlay progressively loses its color as it reaches the body of the bottle. Suspect coral bottles that are of brilliant red color. Many coral bottles that have been made recently in the People's Republic of China and Hong Kong may, in fact, be glass. Amber bottles may not be true carved amber at all, but a plastic substance of reddish color. Amber has also been imitated in glass. (A test for true amber is its ability to float in a saline solution.) Newer mother-of-pearl bottles are large and flat, with one side shaped according to the shape of the oyster shell. Hornbill ivory, which is rare in old bottles, started appearing in large quantities several years ago. These bottles sold at very high prices commensurate with the valued old carvings. The market is now differentiating between the "new production" and the legitimate rare old bottles.

In regard to glass bottles of Imperial yellow color, they should be judged by the standards of the hollowness of the bottle and the quality of the workmanship, rather than the color alone.

During the early eighteenth century, selected hardstones were used for snuff bottle carvings and departure from established tradition was rare. After 1850 some other hardstones were carved for bottles, especially aquamarine, tourmaline (in its different versions), lapis-lazuli, turquoise, serpentine, onyx, inkstone, and fluorite, among others. These stones, however, also have been used to carve snuff bottles after 1950. The collector should approach such bottles with caution.

Snuff bottles were widely manufactured throughout the entire Qing Dynasty. The production was interrupted in 1912 at its close. Officially, manufacture was renewed after 1949 in mainland China. The fact that bottles exist which can be dated to the 1920s and 1930s, indicates that production was not interrupted at all.

Collecting Hints: Snuff bottles are, and always have been, a very popular collectible. It is for this reason that so many modern bottles have been produced for today's market. Today's production of mass produced as well as contemporary artist-produced bottles is a response to the old law of supply and demand. It is up to the collector to educate himself so that he becomes an intelligent buyer, able to distinguish between the old and the new.

When considering a glass bottle, special attention has to be paid to quality. It should have a well-raised and formed foot (except in the case of those produced to resemble other materials). The neck needs to be regular without any signs of grinding to eliminate chips. The body should show no damage, especially in the case of overlay carvings.

One would think that the long history of porcelain production in China would encourage the early use of porcelain for snuff bottles, but this was not the case. The production of porcelain bottles was mostly a nineteenth-century development, and those of earlier manufacture are not in large supply. One should almost systematically consider that bottles bearing a seventeenth- or eighteenth-century reign mark are not of the period indicated unless if the bottle is of extreme quality and it is possible to compare its characteristics (particularly its decoration and color) with other dated porcelain ware of the period. Poor-quality porcelain snuff bottles dating from the end of the Ching Dynasty should not be purchased by anyone desiring to assemble a worthwhile and attractive collection.

Nephrite and jadeite snuff bottles are among the most desirable. The highest price ever paid for a snuff bottle was reached in Hong Kong at the end of 1990. An emerald green jadeite bottle sold for well over $500,000.00. Soochow school hardstone bottles are superbly carved and also sell for very high prices. Yixing bottles, made in the province of Jiangsu in the nineteenth century, are rare and desirable investments.

Contemporary snuff bottles produced by master artists using old techniques are considered very collectible in today's market and fetch high prices.

Collector's Club: The International Chinese Snuff Bottle Society was founded in November 1968 by Edward Choate O'Dell, its first president, to "perpetuate the goals of connoisseurship and camaraderie among snuff bottle collectors and other interested persons." It publishes a quarterly bulletin and holds a yearly convention in October/November. The yearly membership fee is $65.00 and includes the price of the journal. The address is

The International Chinese Snuff Bottle Society
2601 North Charles Street
Baltimore, MD 21218
(301) 467-3400, fax (301) 243-3451

Advisor: Francois Lorin

Amber
  Pebble shape
    1¾'', 1780-1850, carved all over
      with leaves and vines **950.00**
    2¾'', 19th century, carved with an-
      imals in a landscape of rocks
      and pine trees. **1,200.00**
  Rectangular with rounded shoulders
    tapering toward a neatly formed
    foot, 2⅛'', early 19th century, the
    shoulders carved with masks and
    mock ring handles **1,000.00**
  Rounded, 1⅞'', 1750-1820, carved
    with a rice pattern **1,500.00**
  Square with rounded shoulders and
    tapering toward the foot, 2'', mid
    19th century, root amber carved
    with figures amid rocks and trees   **1,400.00**

Burgaute lacquer
  Rounded rectangular tapering
    toward the foot, 3'', 19th century,
    inlaid with a landscape on one
    side and birds on the reverse **1,350.00**
  Shield shape
    2¾'', early 20th century, inlaid
      with a landscape on each side   **600.00**
    3¼'', 19th century, inlaid with fly-
      ing cranes **850.00**
  Spade shape, 2¼'', 20th century, Jap-
    anese, inlaid with butterflies and
    flowers on a diaper ground **300.00**
Cinnabar
  Elongated baluster shape, 3¼'', 20th
    century, carved on each side with
    a bird on a tree. **350.00**
  Ovoid shape
    2¾'', 18th century, carved on each
      side with a phoenix. **1,500.00**
    3'', 18th century, carved on one
      side with a scholar and his at-
      tendant and children playing on
      the reverse **1,400.00**
  Shield shape
    3'', 1780-1850, carved on each
      side with children playing in a
      garden. **1,200.00**
    3'', 18th century, deeply carved
      with a scene of a sage and his
      attendant on the terrace of a pa-
      vilion within a mountainous
      landscape **1,800.00**
Cloisonné
  Ovoid shape, 2¼'', early 19th cen-
    tury, decorated with butterflies
    and flowers **700.00**
  Rounded shape, 2½'', early 19th cen-
    tury, decorated with stylized
    dragons around the character
    Shou, scrolls on shoulders, band
    around the neck. **950.00**
  Rounded and elongated, 2½'', late
    19th century, Japanese, depicting
    a bouquet of irises on a pale green
    ground **250.00**
  Rounded rectangular, 2⅞'', 1750-
    1820, decorated with lotuses in a
    pond.   **1,200.00**
  Rounded rectangular tapering
    toward the foot, 2½'', 20th cen-
    tury, decorated with flowers,
    scrolls around the neck and the
    base **400.00**
Coral
  Flattened cylinder, 1¾'', 1780-1850,
    light orange color, carved on each
    side with a boy. **3,500.00**
  Pear shape, 2½'', 20th century, or-
    ange-red color carved as a basket
    with leaves and flowers **650.00**
  Rectangular with rounded shoul-

ders, 2⅜″, mid 19th century, orange color, the sides carved with
flowers and leaves, two boys on
one side 950.00
Rectangular with rounded shoulders
tapering toward the foot, 2½″,
1780-1850, orange color with
light white flecks, carved with the
eight Buddhist emblems 4,000.00
Rounded, 2″, mid 19th century, orange color with white stripes,
carved with a dragon amid the
clouds. 800.00
Embellished
Rounded square tapering toward the
foot, 2½″, early 19th century, embellished amber decorated with
soapstone chips and painted with
lacquer, the sides carved with
shoulder masks and mock rings   1,850.00
Rounded rectangular
2¾″, late 19th/early 20th century,
embellished jade decorated
with soapstone chips of various
colors depicting a scholar with
his attendant 1,500.00
2⅝″, early to mid 19th century,
embellished chalcedony decorated with soapstone chips of
various colors depicting familiar house scenes 1,200.00
Glass Bottles
Interior Painted
Note: Unless otherwise indicated, the interior
painted snuff bottles are made of glass. They
are shaped as upright rectangulars with
rounded shoulders. Height varies between 2¼″
and 3″
Artist signed
By Chen Zhongsan, signed and
dated first summer 1918, depicting a cricket amid flowers
and foliage and a deer with a
monkey in a pine tree 500.00
By Ma Shaoxuan
Signed, depicting a land-
scape with a mountain, a
river, flowers under a
bridge in the valley, pavilion, and tree on a rock in
the foreground. 1,100.00
Signed, seal, and dated first
summer 1899, one side
with an inscription, the
other depicting four boys
seated at a table 1,250.00
Signed and dated 1894, depicting a man under a tree
watching a bird in the sky,
the reverse with a land-
scape 1,000.00
Signed and dated second

spring 1895, depicting the
two Qiao sisters sitting on a
bench and reading...... 3,500.00
Signed and dated 1899 with
the reign mark of Guang-
xu, pear-shaped, painted
on rock crystal, depicting
three goats under a willow
tree 1,600.00
Signed and dated 1903,
painted with three goats,
the reverse with an inscription 2,000.00
Signed and dated 1922, depicting a cricket over a
cabbage on one side and a
young man trying to melt
the snow with the heat of
his body on the reverse .. 1,850.00
By Wang Xisan
Signed, 2″, painted on rock
crystal, depicting a man on
each side 850.00
Signed and dated first winter
1977, painted on rock
crystal, depicting Huang
Chenyen on his donkey
with his attendant walking
beside him 1,500.00
By the Ye Family
Dated 1915, at the Apricot
Grove Studio, painted on
rock crystal, depicting
children at play in very
bright colors 800.00
Dated 1924 at the Apricot
Grove Studio, 2½″, rock
crystal of rounded shape,
depicting a group watch-
ing a lady painting 1,200.00
Dated 1927, at the Apricot

Left, **Glass, circa 1900, the interior
painted with a vase and a small tree in a
pot, signature and seal of Ma Shaoxuan,
$1,900.00;** *right,* **Glass, circa 1850-1900,
Yangzhou school, red overlay on transparent, masks and mock ring handles on
the shoulders, seal. $2,000.00**

Grove Studio, 2⅛", painted on smoky rock crystal, of rounded rectangular shape, narrow at the foot, depicting birds and flowers **700.00**

Dated 1933, at the Apricot Grove Studio, depicting Huang Chenyen riding his donkey with his attendant in a snowy landscape.... **650.00**

By Ye Shuyin, signed, depicting the "Three Friends of Winter" (pine, bamboo and prunus)................. **550.00**

By Yen Yutian

Signed and dated 1895, depicting insects flying over a cabbage and flowers **650.00**

Signed and dated 1897, depicting two swallows flying over lotus flowers **550.00**

Signed and dated 1858, depicting a cat seated on a branch with a background of flowers and butterflies **500.00**

By Ye Zhongsan

Signed and dated 1915, translucent brown agate, one side depicting a woman standing under a flowering tree, the other side showing a man sitting in a pavilion **900.00**

Signed and dated first autumn 1899, depicting a group of boys playing amid rocks and trees **950.00**

Signed and dated spring 1905, depicting Liu Mai, his string of cash and his three-legged toad **1,500.00**

By Zhen Zhongsan, signed and dated 1910, depicting a cat chasing a butterfly along a riverbank.............. **1,000.00**

By Zhou Leyuan

Signed and dated first autumn 1892, depicting a fisherman on his boat.... **1,250.00**

Signed and dated 1892, depicting a landscape in front and a cricket on a cabbage on the reverse **1,200.00**

Signed and dated second winter 1899, depicting two ladies sitting amid rocks and flowers **1,750.00**

Unsigned

Middle school, unsigned, depicting a scholar standing by a pond with an inscription on the reverse **750.00**

Modern school, depicting a young revolutionary holding up a lantern **850.00**

Overlay glass bottles

Circular, 2⅜", 1780-1850, two black overlay medallions of leaves and flowers on milk glass **1,600.00**

Cylindrical, 3¼", mid 19th century, ruby red overlay on snowflake glass, carved with two intertwined dragons chasing a flaming pearl **800.00**

Oval, 2⅞", 19th century, five color overlay on milk glass carved with precious objects............ **800.00**

Rectangular with rounded shoulders, 3⅛", late 19th century, emerald green overlay on transparent snowflake glass, shoulders carved with two mock handles........ **950.00**

Rectangular with rounded shoulders tapering toward the base, 3¼", 19th century, green overlay on same green, carved with a crab amid seaweeds **450.00**

Rounded rectangular, elongated 2¼", late 19th century, Yangzhou (seal school), brown overlay with a demon standing on a cloud, with a seal inscription........ **1,500.00**

Rounded rectangular tapering toward the base

2½", early to mid 19th century, blue overlay carved as fish on ruby red glass with a neat blue overlay foot **1,200.00**

2⅞", 1789-1850, red overlay on snowflake glass, with a carved dragon on each side and a carved bat on each shoulder .. **1,200.00**

Round, 2⅝", late 19th century, blue overlay on milk glass, carved with two squirrels playing amid vines **650.00**

Glass, 18th century, ruby red overlay on snowflake background, depicting Shou Lao riding a mule on the reverse side, one shoulder carved with a pine tree, the other with a monkey. $2,500.00

Miscellaneous Glass bottles
Circular
  $2\frac{1}{2}''$, 18th century, imperial yellow glass incised with a basket weave pattern **3,500.00**
  $2\frac{3}{4}''$, 19th century, imperial yellow glass, plain **800.00**
Cylindrical, $3\frac{1}{4}''$, 1780-1850, imperial yellow glass, ... **2,350.00**
Double gourd shape, $2\frac{3}{4}''$, 19th century, white glass with green shades imitating jade **600.00**
Flattened rectangular, $3\frac{1}{2}''$, late 19th/early 20th century, turquoise color glass, plain **250.00**
Flattened round rectangular, $3\frac{1}{2}''$, 1780-1850, yellow overlay on light amber bubble glass, carved with intertwined dragons **2,000.00**
Oval
  $2\frac{3}{4}''$, 1780-1850, emerald green glass with gold flecks **1,000.00**
  $2\frac{7}{8}''$, 19th century, glass imitating realgar. **750.00**
Round, $2\frac{1}{8}''$, 19th century, flowers and birds enameled on milk glass, four character Qianlong mark . . .   **500.00**
Rounded elongated, $3''$, 19th century, multicolored swirled glass   **1,100.00**
Rounded rectangular, flattened, $2\frac{5}{8}''$, late 19th/early 20th century, blue overlay on bubble suffused glass, carved with flowers **150.00**
Rounded rectangular tapering toward the base
  $2\frac{7}{8}''$, 1780-1850, four colors (red, dark blue, green and yellow) on white glass, carved with "One Hundred Antiques" **1,000.00**
  $3''$, 19th century, pale green opaque glass imitating jade, incised with geometric designs

Glass, late 18th/early 19th century, green with gold flecks. $1,400.00

on one side and carved with a bat on the reverse **1,250.00**
Spade shape, $2\frac{3}{8}''$, 1780-1850, blue glass with gold flecks imitating lapis lazuli **1,800.00**
Upright rectangular
  $2\frac{3}{4}''$, 19th century, glass imitating coral, carved with a dragon and a horse amid scrolls of clouds   **1,100.00**
  $3\frac{3}{8}''$, 19th century, transparent glass imitating a deep red amber, the sides carved with long mock rings. **900.00**
Vase shape, $3''$, early to mid 19th century, plain body shading from clear at the rim to deep red at the bottom **300.00**
Gourd
  Double gourd shape, $2\frac{1}{4}''$, early 19th century **950.00**
  Rounded shape, $2\frac{1}{2}''$, early to mid 19th century, molded on each side with round inscribed panels   **1,250.00**
Hornbill Ivory
  Rectangular tapering toward the foot

Left to right: Glass, early 19th century, three overlay colors on milk glass, the reverse carved with flowers in a pot, masks and mock ring handles on the shoulders, $3,200.00; Glass, early 19th century, mottled red and yellow imitating realgar, $650.00; Glass, 18th century, imperial yellow, $4,500.00.

Glass, imitating aquamarine, transparent, carved in low relief with two pavilions in a mountainous landscape. $1,650.00

2¼″, after 1960, yellow hornbill ivory, red sides with medallions, carved in low relief on each side 750.00

2½″, after 1960, yellow hornbill ivory with red sides, carved in low relief on each side 850.00

Rounded rectangular with well formed foot, 2½″, 1800-1850, rich orange honey color body with red sides, carved with panels in low relief 9,500.00

Inkstone
Ovoid shape
1⅞″, 18th century, decorated with dragons in the archaic style, very worn 650.00

2¼″, 19th century, carved with dragons amid clouds 1,500.00

Rectangular with rounded shoulders and tapering toward the foot, 2¾″, late 18th/early 19th century, very well carved with stylized dragons on one side and a lengthy inscription on the reverse 1,800.00

Ivory
Disc shape, 2¾″, 19th century, ivory medallions with lacquer burgauté body, Qianlong mark on base . . .   1,200.00

Shield shaped, 2″, mid 19th century, carved in low relief on each side, the neck and border incised with scrolls 950.00

Rectangular with rounded shoulders narrowing toward the base, 2¾″, mid to late 19th century, carved with figures in a landscape 500.00

Rounded shape, 2¾″, late 19th century, carved all around in low relief, the shoulders, neck and foot with floral bands 850.00

Rounded rectangular
2½″, late 19th century, carved with a dragon on each side, the

Ivory, mid to late 19th century, commemorative Qianlong mark, polychrome. $1,800.00

ivory stained with gold, red, green, and black, Qianlong mark on base 650.00

2½″, mid 19th century, polychrome ivory with key fret at the base and the shoulder carved in low relief with figures in a landscape 1,500.00

Rounded rectangular tapering toward the base, with flattened body, 2″, 19th century, one side with a lengthy inscription, the other incised with a landscape . .   800.00

2⅞″, 1870-1920, Japanese decorated with flowers, branches and leaves with figures on a boat on a river 850.00

Jade
Bulbous shape, flattened, 2⅝″, 18th century, even yellow nephrite . . .   2,500.00

Double gourd shape
2½″, C. 1780-1850, white nephrite 800.00

Jade, late 19th century, brown and grey nephrite. $800.00

$2\frac{1}{2}''$, 19th century, brown nephrite with white inclusions carved as foliage and fruits **1,200.00**

Figural forms

Eggplant shaped, $2\frac{5}{8}''$, late 19th century, white nephrite with a collar of spinach green leaves **850.00**

Fish, carved, $3''$, 1850-1900, gray and brown nephrite, roughly carved **500.00**

Melon, carved, $2\frac{3}{8}''$, 1780-1850, white nephrite carved with leaves and stalks **1,500.00**

Pear shaped, flattened, with masks and mock ring handles, $2\frac{5}{8}''$, 19th century, off-white jade **900.00**

Stone shape, $3''$, 19th century, pale cream nephrite jade with russet color, uncarved **650.00**

Purse shape, irregular elongated shape, $2\frac{1}{4}''$, early 19th century, light gray nephrite with carved brocade tied around the top, a light brown monkey climbing along the side **1,200.00**

Strawberry shape, $1\frac{1}{2}''$, 18th century, white nephrite **1,250.00**

Hu shaped, $2\frac{5}{8}''$, early 19th century, white nephrite **800.00**

Irregular shape, $2\frac{1}{2}''$, 19th century, white to light green and emerald green jadite with splashes of brown, carved with four acorns and leaves **1,500.00**

Pebble form, $2\frac{7}{8}''$, 19th century, pale celadon green and brown jade, polished and well hollowed **850.00**

Rectangular shape with a very well formed foot, $2\frac{1}{2}''$, 18th century, white nephrite with carved panels on each side. **1,800.00**

Rectangular shape with rounded shoulders

$2\frac{1}{4}''$, 19th century, pale gray to brown skin nephrite jade, carved in low relief **1,100.00**

$3''$, 19th century, celadon green jade with carved brown skin on the front side, with the back simply polished **1,500.00**

Rectangular with rounded shoulders and tapering toward foot

$2\frac{3}{8}''$, 1780-1850, white nephrite carved in low relief **1,500.00**

$2\frac{1}{2}''$ early 19th century, white nephrite carved in low relief on each side with two confronting dragons **1,200.00**

Rounded shape

$2\frac{3}{8}''$, 18th century, pale apple green with splashes of lavender and flecks of emerald green . . . **3,000.00**

$2\frac{1}{4}''$, 19th century, spinach jade **300.00**

$2\frac{1}{4}''$, 19th century, white nephrite carved with fruit, leaves and vines **600.00**

$2\frac{1}{4}''$, late 19th century, white and light green jadeite **350.00**

Rounded circular shape

$2\frac{1}{4}''$, 18th century, white nephrite, uncarved **2,500.00**

$2\frac{1}{4}''$, 1780-1850, mottled dark and light gray nephrite, uncarved **1,200.00**

$2\frac{3}{4}''$, 1780-1850, pale green nephrite, the top carved as a purse and the bottom carved in low relief **2,000.00**

Rounded flattened shape tapering toward the base with wide lips, $2''$, 1780-1850, green jadeite, uncarved **4,500.00**

Rounded rectangular shape tapering toward the foot

$2\frac{1}{4}''$, 19th century, gray and green jadeite with splashes of emerald green **4,500.00**

$3\frac{1}{4}''$, late 19th century, white nephrite carved all over with the same Chinese character . . . **400.00**

Square with rounded shoulders, $2\frac{1}{2}''$, 19th century, spinach green nephrite **600.00**

Square with rounded shoulders and tapering toward the foot

$2\frac{1}{4}''$, early 19th century, yellowish green nephrite with brown skin, carving on both sides depicting two men in a landscape of rocks and trees **1,200.00**

$2\frac{7}{8}''$, 1750-1820, white nephrite **1,500.00**

Metal

Pear shape, $2\frac{1}{4}''$, 19th century, gold decorated with sprigs of bamboo **1,800.00**

Rounded, $2\frac{3}{4}''$, 1750-1820, champlevé enamel. **1,200.00**

Rounded and elongated, $2\frac{3}{4}''$, 19th century, silver with chased panels **900.00**

Mother-of-pearl

Rectangular with rounded shoulders tapering toward the foot, $2\frac{1}{2}''$, 20th century, carved in low relief with stylized confronting dragons on one side and a man sitting on the reverse **850.00**

Square with rounded shoulders tapering toward the foot, $2\frac{5}{8}''$, 19th century, carved with a dragon amid clouds on one side, a man holding a peach on the reverse . . **600.00**

Porcelain

Circular

$2\frac{3}{4}''$, 19th century, porcelain with floral design, famille rose enamel, Qianlong mark **950.00**

2⅝″, tapering toward the base, 19th century, Daoguang period (1820-1850), two groups of dancers on each side, famille rose enamel, Qianlong mark **750.00**

Cylindrical

2¾″, 19th century, with robin's egg glaze **250.00**

2¾″, Guangxu mark and period (1875-1909), white porcelain decorated with a cricket in famille rose palette........... **750.00**

3¼″, 19th century, white porcelain with red dragons design underglaze **350.00**

3⅜″, 19th century, porcelain with black background and decor of green branches and leaves and red flowers............... **350.00**

3⅜″, late 19th century, crackled beige glaze **400.00**

3½″, early to mid 20th century, design of two ladies sitting in a garden, famille rose palette ... **850.00**

Double gourd shape, 2⅝″, early to mid 19th century, flambé glaze **550.00**

Figural

Cabbage leaf shape, 2¾″, mid 19th century, green glaze and red buds **450.00**

Representing Liu Hai with a string of cash over his shoulder, 3″, early 19th century, porcelain decorated in blue, red and green glazes, the hat forming the stopper of the bottle...... **1,200.00**

Representing Li T'leh Kuai with his gourd on his back, 3¾″, mid 19th century, porcelain decorated with green and yellow glazes **1,600.00**

Rectangular

2¼″, mid 19th century, molded in the form of a ritual Tsung, white glaze................... **550.00**

2½″, 19th century, porcelain, decorated with the face of a bearded European man wearing a hat which transforms into the face of a European lady when turned upside down, famille rose enamel, two character mark (medicine bottle) **1,500.00**

Rectangular with rounded shoulders, 2¾″, early 19th century, famille rose flower pattern **800.00**

Rounded

2¼″, Daoguang mark and period (1821-1850), white porcelain decorated with two crickets... **750.00**

2¼″, Daoguang mark and period (1821-1850), white porcelain with eight iron-red fish **650.00**

3″, with elongated neck, second half of the 19th century, pale green glaze in low relief **950.00**

Rounded rectangular tapering toward the base

3¼″, with long neck, 19th century, light green glazed porcelain molded in relief with a crane perched in a pine tree **900.00**

3½″, 19th century, porcelain molded with phoenix and dragon, reticulated to show inner bottle, famille rose enamel **550.00**

3⅜″, 1821-1850, red Daoguang mark under the foot, molded in

Porcelain (left to right), Reticulated, Jiaqing mark and period, molded with a pair of fu dogs contesting a ribbon-tied ball, all in pastel enamels, $825.00; late 19th century, famille rose enamels on a crackle glaze, showing European figures in a landscape, $330.00; early 19th century, blue and white, decorated in underglaze blue and iron red, showing tree peony and stylized rocks, $150.00. Courtesy of Butterfield and Butterfield.

relief with the eighteen Lohans,
famille rose enamel **850.00**

Quartz
  Agate
    Ovoid shape, 2⅜", 20th century,
    transparent grey agate carved
    with a bird under pine trees . . . **450.00**
    Pear shape, 2¼", 20th century,
    two color agate carved with
    fruit and flowers **200.00**
    Rectangular with rounded shoul-
    ders and tapering toward the
    foot, 3⅛", 19th century, opaque
    greyish beige, light brown in-
    clusions carved with a turtle
    amid a landscape of trees and
    rocks **600.00**
    Rounded shape
    2⅜", 1780-1850, translucent
    pale gray striated agate snuff
    bottle with white and red
    bands **1,200.00**
    2¼", early 19th century, grey
    agate with white and dark
    splashes, the shoulders
    carved with masks and mock
    handles **600.00**
    Rounded rectangular tapering
    toward the neatly formed foot,
    2½", early 19th century, dark
    beige and brown agate with a
    white inclusion carved to de-
    pict two monkeys, the shoul-
    ders and the sides carved with
    masks and mock ring handles **2,500.00**
    Spade shape, 2", late 19th cen-
    tury, bright beige agate with
    brown inclusions carved with
    flowers and vines **250.00**

**Porcelain, Jiaqing mark and period,
1796–1821, molded and reticulated,
coral red glaze, the reverse with a dragon.
$850.00**

**Agate, circa 1750-1820, honey colored
with brown inclusions, carved in the
shape of a hawk. $4,000.00**

Banded agate
  Flattened oval shape, 2¼", 1780-
  1850, banded agate of translucent beige color with one light
  white striation encircling the
  body **950.00**
  Rectangular with rounded shoul-
  ders and tapering toward the
  foot, 2¼", 19th century, banded
  agate of brownish beige color
  with white and brown bands in
  the middle **950.00**
  Rounded rectangular tapering
  toward the foot, 2⅜", early 19th
  century, banded agate of light
  grey color with white striations
  encircling the body from the
  bottom two thirds up **900.00**
  Rounded upright shape, 2⅜",
  1800-1850, "macaroni agate,"
  the shoulders and sides carved
  with masks and mock handles,
  dark and light brown colors . . . **800.00**
Chalcedony agate
  Rounded shape, 2", 1800-1850,
  chalcedony agate of dark grey
  color with natural beige inclusions carved with a bear under
  a pine tree **1,500.00**
  Rounded rectangular tapering
  toward the foot, 2½", early 19th
  century, chalcedony agate of
  beige color with darker inclusions carved in the shape of a
  bird sitting on a vase **2,000.00**
Jasper
  Rounded shape, 2½", 19th century, green jasper with red and
  ocher inclusions **1,200.00**
  Rounded rectangular, 2⅞", 1780-
  1850, brown jasper with red
  and green swirls, a green and
  beige inclusion carved on the

front with two monkeys playing under pine trees **3,000.00**

Moss Agate (dendritic Chalcedony)
Flattened disc shape, 2½″ 1800-1850, of light gray color with white, green, brown and red moss inclusions **950.00**

Rounded shape, 2⅛″ 19th century, of grayish color with green, red and brown moss inclusions **750.00**

Rectangular with rounded shoulders and tapering toward the foot
2¼″, 19th century, of translucent beige color with an opaque whitish beige inclusion, carved as a man riding a horse and carrying branches and foliage **2,500.00**

2⅜″, 19th century, with green and russet colors, the shoulders and sides carved with masks and mock handles . . . **950.00**

Rounded shape, 2½″, 1780-1850, beige with green and white moss inclusions, uncarved . . . **600.00**

Square with rounded shoulders and tapering toward the foot, 2¾″, 1750-1850, translucent beige-brown agate with brown inclusions carved to depict a horse with a monkey on its back and another monkey **3,600.00**

Silhouette agate
Rounded shape with well formed foot, 2¼″, late 19th century, light beige color with two splashes of brown lightly carved to suggest butterflies . . **850.00**

Rounded rectangular tapering toward the foot, 2½″, 19th century, pale grey color with a dark

inclusion carved to depict a goose **800.00**

Rectangular with rounded shoulders and tapering toward the foot, 2¾″, 19th century, beige color with two dark splashes carved in the shape of two bats **1,200.00**

Rock Crystal
Rounded rectangular tapering toward the foot, 2⅛″, late 19th century, clear with inclusions of gold rutile needles **850.00**

Rounded, 2¼″, 19th century, clear crystal with inclusions of dense tourmaline needles, the shoulders carved with masks and mock handles **1,000.00**

Plain rectangular, 2⅞″, 19th century, transparent **550.00**

Rectangular with rounded shoulders and tapering toward the foot, 3¼″, 19th century, smoky, the shoulders carved with masks and mock handles **1,200.00**

Semi-Precious Stones
Lapis Lazuli
Shield shape, 2¾″, 19th century, blue color with gold flecks, waisted neck **850.00**

Rectangular, 3″, late 19th/early 20th century, deep blue color, carved with figures and trees **1,200.00**

Ruby matrix
Rounded rectangular, 2¾″, 20th century, deep red, carved in low relief with a group of men riding horses **950.00**

Rounded rectangular tapering toward the foot, 3″, 19th century, carved with a very low relief, masks and mock ring handles on the shoulders **1,600.00**

Turquoise
Elongated melon shape, 1⅝″, date undetermined, carved with leaves, buds and tendrils **650.00**

Moss Agate, circa 1750-1850, the shoulders carved with masks and mock ring handles, well hollowed. $1,000.00

Rock Crystal, 18th century. $1,200.00

Double gourd shape, 2¼", late
19th century, carved with fruits
and vines **850.00**
Flattened round shape, 2¼",
1780-1850, turquoise matrix
with black crackle **800.00**
Pebble shape, 2¼", 19th century,
turquoise of natural shape,
bluish with black crackles **2,500.00**
Tourmaline
Carved Liu Nai and his three
legged toad, 2¼", date undetermined, green tourmaline of
very good carving, the hat of
the figure forms the stopper . . .   **1,500.00**
Rounded rectangular, 2½", early
to mid 19th century, yellow to
pink tourmaline, plain **1,800.00**
Elongated melon shape, 2⅝", mid
19th century, carved with a
cricket and a butterfly amid
flowers and foliage **2,500.00**
Sharkskin, ovoid shape, 2¾", late 19th/
early 20th century, the skin is char-
acteristically raised with small
bumps **550.00**

SONG DYNASTY CERAMICS

See Appendix I for table of Song emperors.

History: The peaceful, cultured life of the Northern Song Dynasty was interrupted by the invasion
of the Tartars in 1127, which forced the reloca-
tion of the Song capital from Honan to Hangchow, where the dynasty continued under the
name of Southern Song. The Song society put
great value on art—writing, poetry, sculpture,
jade carving, and ceramic art. Imperial patronage
of the kilns in the Northern Song supported factories in Ting Chou and Ju Chou. The Southern
Song created an imperial factory named after Emperor Ching-te, which is now known throughout
the world as Jingdezhen (Ching-te-chen), the
home of the imperial ceramic factories of China.

Most of the ceramic wares made during this
great artistic dynasty were created on a high-fired
porcelaneous stoneware body. The clay usually
contained iron and the exposed parts (footings)
often turned a reddish brown in the firing. The
clay colors were white, grey, or buff and were
smooth to the touch, with the exception of the
buff, which was sometimes rough. Song wares
vary in weight from very thin, light, and translucent to heavy and thickly walled. The primary
decoration was the glaze color, with or without
crackle. Incised, molded, and carved decorations
also were used on some wares. Only the produc-

tion of T'zu-chou wares involved painted decoration. There was little influence from the outside
world during Song times, and both form and
glaze were created to the "Chinese taste." The
Chinese still regard this period as their aesthetic
height of ceramic art.

Innovative wares of the Song Dynasty included
Ting Yao (Hopei Province); T'zu-chou wares (Hopei Province); Ju Yao (Honan Province); Chun
Yao (Honan province); Kuan Yao (Hangchow,
capitol of the Southern Song); Ko Yao wares (Chekiang Province); Northern celadons and Lung-ch-
uan celadons (Checkiang Province); Chien Yao-
Temmouku (Fukien Province); Chi Chou wares
(Kiangsi Province); and Ch'ing Pai (Jingdezhen
and elsewhere).

Ting Yao was a white porcelaneous ware characterized by an ivory-colored glaze and had
carved, molded, or incised decorations. Notice-
able on some items were the "tear streaks" or
thickenings in the glaze where it formed in drops
on the surface. The items often were fired upside
down and are sometimes found with a bronze
sheath on the unglazed rim.

T'zu-chou ware, like Ting Yao, was produced
in Hopei Province during the Northern Song. This
porcelaneous stoneware was covered with a
white slip over a grey or brown clay body. The
decoration was enameled, incised, or painted
with brownish black, red, green, or yellow pigments. Sgraffito techniques and brown wash
paintings over a buff-colored glaze were the most
popular styles of decoration.

Ju Yao still remains somewhat of a mystery
since various scholars have supported different
views of the glazes. Some describe it as a celadon, while others elude to it really being a Ying
Ching glaze. We are certain that it existed because it was written about by the scholars of the
day. Unfortunately, the translations are vague.

Chun Yao was characterized by a thick bluish
glaze that had been affected to a greater or lesser
degree by furnace transmutation. The flambé effect (which was far more subtle than modern
flambé), was accomplished by adding a copper
compound to the glaze during firing. The results
of this technique showed splotches of color ranging from green to purple to copper red. The glaze
was thick, bubbly, and runny and often pooled at
the foot, leaving the upper portion of the object
with a thinner glaze coat. The stoneware body
was made of white, grey, yellow, or sand-colored
clays and may have burned to a brownish red
when fired.

Kuan Yao, the official "imperial" ware of the
Southern Song Dynasty, was characterized by its
bright, jewel-like lustrous glaze. The colors
ranged from the preferred blue to greyish green to
a greenish white or a buff or grey shade. The
magnified glaze reveals endless minute bubbles
and was characterized by a crackle of the crab's
claw variety. The bases of Kuan Yao pieces some-

times reveal spur marks which are seldom found on Chinese ceramic wares.

Northern Celadons: see Celadon section.

Lung-ch-uan Celadons: see Celadon section.

Chien Yao stoneware, named Temmouku by the Japanese, who use these Song tea bowls in their tea ceremony, had a lustrous brown/black glaze which may have tints of purple or blue. When these other tones appear in the glaze as mottled streaks, they are referred to as "hare's fur." An "oil spot" glaze occurred when the mottling appeared as silver spotting.

Chi Chou Temmouku tea bowls were similar to the Chien Yao but sometimes had painted decoration. They often had leaves or paper cutouts stuck to the stoneware body under the glaze. These were burnt out during the firing, leaving a faithful design under the glaze. Some vases, jars, and ewers were also produced using this technique.

Ch'ing Pai or Ying Ching (shadow blue as it is now more popularly called) was a true white porcelain, thinly potted, which when fired had a slightly bluish or greenish cast to its transparent, glassy glaze. The decoration consisted of incising, combing, carving, and molding, and the porcelain was very thin and delicate. Bowls were sometimes fired upside down in the kiln, leaving the rim unglazed. The unglazed porcelain body sometimes fired to a pale orange tone at the rim of these pieces (also see Celadon).

References: Andacht, Garthe, and Mascarelli, *Price Guide to Oriental Antiques*, second ed., Wallace Homestead, 1984; John Ayers, *Chinese Ceramics: The Koger Collection*, Sotheby's Publications, 1985; Warren E. Cox, *Pottery and Porcelain*, Crown Publishers Inc., 1970; R. L. Hobson, *Chinese Pottery and Porcelain*, Dover Publications Inc., 1976; Margaret Medley, *The Chinese Potter*, Charles Scribner's Sons, 1976; W. R. Thiel, *Chinese Pottery and Stoneware*, Thomas Nelson and Sons, New York.

Museums: Art Institute of Chicago, Chicago, Illinois; Nelson Gallery of Art, Kansas City, Kansas; Boston Museum of Art, Boston, Massachusetts; Metropolitan Museum of Art, New York, New York; Cleveland Museum of Art; Cleveland, Ohio; Seattle Art Museum, Seattle, Washington; Freer Gallery of Art, Washington D.C.; British Museum, London, England; Sir Percival David Foundation, London England; Victoria and Albert Museum, London, England; National Museum, Tokyo, Japan; National Museum, Seoul, Korea; Rijksmuseum, Amsterdam, the Netherlands; National Museum of History, Taipei, Taiwan.

Reproduction Alert: Kuan Yao was very successfully reproduced in Jingdezhen in the late seventeenth century. Ting ware was made there at the same time but was not as faithfully reproduced. Styles and glazes of the Song Dynasty were copied throughout the Qing period, but were often

marked with the nien ho of the reigning emperor, thereby leaving no doubt as to their age.

Collecting Hints: The prices of Ching Pai wares, shallow bowls in particular, have dropped radically since the large influx of illegal imports from China has risen. Once selling for as much as $3,000.00, each they are now available in the marketplace for as little as $700.00 to $900.00 each. This is a recent development which has made these once precious and scarce items available to the average collector. The same is true of some crudely potted black-glazed Temmouku bowls of the period. As long as looting of the graves in China goes unpunished, we can expect the supply to remain constant. If China puts a stop to the illegal export of such items (including Han and Tang mortuary pottery), one would expect the prices to go up again in response to the diminished supply.

Qing porcelain has risen in price as a reaction to this phenomenon. Since Qing porcelain was not buried with the dead, there is a definite limit to what is now available on the market. Much of it rests in private collections or museum archives, making it relatively scarce in comparison to the large quantities of burial items that can possibly surface in the future.

CHIEN YAO (JIENYAO)—TEMMOUKOU

"Hare's fur" tea bowl

4¼'' dia., Southern Song Dynasty, the conical body plainly glazed on the exterior and in the interior with yellow and brown streaked hare's fur glaze thickly dribbling and ground back in one area on the crisply cut foot **875.00**

4¾'' dia., flaring sides, black glaze streaked with bright iron russet, thinning to dark chocolate at the rim, the thick glaze pooling at the foot. **1,200.00**

Tea bowl, 3½'' dia., temmoku, hare's fur glaze of deep brown with lighter brown streaks on the interior, the exterior glaze pooling irregularly around the foot of the beige color clay body. $650.00

4¾'' dia., conical sides, black glaze streaked all over in iron-russet thinning to reddish brown around the rim, the glaze pooling thickly above the shallow cut brown stoneware foot **800.00**

"Oilspot" teabowl, 4⅞'' dia., the steeply rounded sides incurved beneath the rim, covered overall with a lustrous black glaze evenly speckled with silvery iridescence drained to russet at the rim and falling in streaks down the exterior over a rust-brown glaze, ending well above the unglazed foot, burnt brick-red in the firing **1,200.00**

CH'ING PAI (QINGBAI) also called YING CHING (YINGQING)

Bowl

7'' dia., carved design on interior with a floral motif of radiating petals, conical shape, neatly cut foot, base unglazed, pale bluish green glaze **1,400.00**

7⅛'' dia., molded on the interior with a central lotus medallion below the well, with a band of phoenix flying amid flowering peony stems, the unglazed rim encircled with a trellis patterned band **1,000.00**

7¾'' dia., the thin flaring shallow body with petal cut rim, the interior fluidly carved with a luxuriant blossoming lotus spray, the glaze of classic pale blue translucent color **950.00**

7⅞'' dia., incised, the widely flared sides well-carved on the interior with a single peony

Bowl, 6⅛'' dia., Qingbai, carved with a single peony beneath a transluscent glaze of icy blue tone. $825.00. Courtesy of Butterfield and Butterfield.

spray beneath the petal-shaped rim, encompassed by leafy fronds extending around the sides covered inside and out with a translucent glaze of very pale bluish-green tone, chips   **950.00**

Censer, 4⅛'' h., of compressed globular form, raised on tripod feet, the everted rim with two short braided handles, the censer atop a pierced hexagonal stand, covered save on the interior of the censer and foot of the stand with a pale blue glaze **1,500.00**

Dish

5½'' dia., twin fish decoration, the fish depicted around a central flower head amid lapping waves, covered with a clear blue tinged glaze **900.00**

6½'' dia., carved foliate design, the glaze shading from a pale gray blue to a blue/green, sturdy potting with concave bottom   **1,200.00**

Ewer and cover, 4¾'', unusual, the hexagonal pear-shaped body applied with an arched handle set opposite the slender curved spout, with small cylindrical loops on the cover and handle for attachment, all beneath a translucent glaze of striking blue tone . .   **3,500.00**

Figure, dog, 4⅞'' l., the reclining beast modeled in an alert position with head and tail up, the small ears pricked forward, covered with a pale blue glaze, the underside burnt pink in the firing **1,200.00**

Stem cup on stand, 7'' h., the deep globular bowl on a counter flaring stem the stand with a foliate rim both under a bluish tinged clear crackled glaze **900.00**

CHUN YAO (JUNYAO)

Bowl

3½'' dia., of deep form with steeply rounded sides slightly incurved at the rim, resting on a slightly flaring foot of wedge cross-section, the glaze of a grayish-blue color with small white veining and larger areas of white, draining to a mushroom tone at the rim and falling unevenly to the unglazed foot-rim **1,500.00**

7⅞'' dia., Song Dynasty, of conical form resting on a small foot, the sides slightly incurved at the rim, covered with a thick even milky-blue glaze suffused with small bubbles draining to a

Urns, Pair 10⅝″ h., Yingqing, one urn featuring large figure of a tiger and a dog, the other with a large dragon and a phoenix, painted in iron oxide contrasting with a translucent pale green glaze. $825.00. Courtesy of Butterfield and Butterfield.

mushroom color on the rim and falling unevenly to the unglazed footrim **3,000.00**

Dish

7⅜″ dia., of shallow form, rising to an everted rim, covered with a bubble-suffused lavender blue glaze, draining around the rim to a mushroom tone, the short footrim left unglazed, two foot chips **3,500.00**

Jar, 7⅜″ dia., Song Dynasty, splashed glaze, the globular body modeled with a short wide neck encircled by four lug handles, covered with a lavender-blue glaze drained to mushroom along the rim and extremities, boldly decorated with two crescent-shaped splashes of brilliant pur-

Bowl, 6⅛″ dia., Qingbai, carved with a single peony beneath a translucent glaze of icy blue tone. $825.00. Courtesy of Butterfield and Butterfield.

plish-red and turquoise, the unglazed ring foot burned slightly red in the firing **6,000.00**

Saucer dish

4½″ dia., the shallow dish with an evenly applied lavender glaze thinning around the rim to an olive color, the glaze pooling around the short straight unglazed foot............ **1,300.00**

7¼″ dia., of shallow form, covered inside and out with a milky blue glaze of even tone draining at the rim to mushroom color, the base with three spur marks within the wedge-shaped foot **8,500.00**

Vase

7¼″ on stand, Southern Song Dynasty, rare, the elegant pear-shaped vase with tall cylindrical neck raised on a pierced pedestal base molded with five flanged legs connected to a ring foot, covered with a milky lavender-blue glaze thinning on the rim and drained to a mushroom tone along the extremities of the legs, stopping short of the base showing the ware burnt a reddish-brown in the firing ... **5,500.00**

11⅝″ h., rare, the globular body supported on a hollow splayed foot and surmounted by a flared neck with everted rim, the lip turned over to form five "petals," covered with an attractive milky lavender-blue glaze thinning at the extremities to a mushroom tone and stopping short of the foot to show the ware burnt orange in the firing, interior of base also glazed, minor chips and repair to base of neck **25,000.00**

13⅜″ h., meiping shape, the slender ovoid body tapered sharply toward the narrow base, covered over all with a milky lavender-blue glaze ending in an uneven line above the foot showing the ware burnt orange in the firing, the side with a splash of deep purple, the neck reduced **10,000.00**

HONAN (HENAN)

Bowl, 7½″ dia., the pottery bowl with conical sides incurved at the rim and covered with a rich and glossy black glaze drained to a russet brown at the rim, the interior with a floral spray in russet, the glaze ending in sweeps above the base on the exterior showing the grainy ware **1,800.00**

Censer, tripod, 6" dia., the compressed globular body molded with a row of seven florets encircling the shoulders beneath the rim, the whole raised on three paw feet, covered with an iridescent black glaze drained to russet brown along the rim and bosses **6,000.00**

Jar, 7¾", finely-glazed, superbly potted and applied with grooved loop handles, the lustrous black glaze with russet splashes ending in a sweeping line to reveal the clear brown glaze **7,500.00**

Pillow, 8½", unusual, black-glazed, the dished headrest of shaped ruyi-form above the faceted sides molded with flower-filled jardinieres, covered overall with a thick black glaze shading to brown highlighting the molded decoration **2,500.00**

TING YAO (DINGYAO)

Bowl, 7¼" dia., delicately potted on raised footring and with gently curved sides, lightly carved on the exterior with simplified lotus amid long leafy branches, all under a whitish-yellow glaze pooling in characteristic teardrops in one area above the base **6,500.00**

Dish, 4⅝" dia., of shallow form resting on a wide footring, the slightly flaring sides with a metal-bound rim, the interior carved with a pair of fish swimming side by side on a combed wave ground. **800.00**

Saucer dish

6¼", of shallow form delicately carved on the interior with a lotus in full bloom within a line medallion, the glaze of ivory tint **850.00**

6⅛", finely molded with two scrolling peony stems, the full blossoms and leaves in perfect detail enclosing the central medallion with two further blooms, copper bound rim . . . **9,000.00**

T'ZU-CHOU (CIZHOU)

Figure, ladies (pair), 5" high, each figure depicted with hands together holding a fan in front of chest, covered with pale ivory slip, painted in dark brown, red and brown, with details in black **900.00**

Jar, 9¼", brown-glazed sgraffito, the shoulder unglazed above a wide radial band carved with stylized scrolling leaves, the glaze

stopping well short of the tall flared foot, chips. **1,200.00**

Pillow

8¾" l., painted pottery, of bean shape, the slightly concave surface decorated with a large peony blossom and smaller blossom on a leafy branch on a ground of dense circlets, all in brown on a white slip, beneath a clear glaze, small aperture in rear, unglazed base, minor chips. **6,800.00**

10⅞", carved pottery, the concave surface carved with a large exotic blossom on a leafy branch with incised detail, reserved on a cafe-au-lait ground, all beneath a clear ivory glaze, the base unglazed revealing the buff pottery body, small aperture in rear, glaze abraded on side corners **2,800.00**

MISCELLANEOUS GLAZES

Bowl, 5¼" dia., of deep form with slightly incurved rim covered inside and out with a dark brown glaze splashed with olive yellow, chip **3,800.00**

Pillow

10¼" l., sancai glazed pottery, of ingot shape, each end incised and glazed with a cream blossom with green leaves on an ochre ground contained within brown spandrels and green border, the four sides with central panels similarly decorated and bordered by narrow cream and brown glazed bands, each wide green-glazed border decorated with cream, ocher, and brown-glazed bands of V-shaped stylized flowers and small buds, all beneath a clear glaze, chips and abraded surface at angles **8,500.00**

Pillow, 10" l., Cizhou, pottery, ovoid shape, painted brown with blossoming leafy sprigs on a white slip ground. $600.00.

13", tiger-form, glazed pottery, the recumbent animal glazed in pale brown, crisply modeled with rust-brown stripes, with tail flicked out over its haunches, tail restored **3,800.00**

TANG DYNASTY

See Appendix I for table of Tang emperors.

History: The Tang Dynasty was a period of prosperity in China which led to the "golden age" of art and literature. Unlike the ceramic production during the Han period, outside influences, particularly Hellenistic art, influenced Tang art. The stiff renditions of Han pottery were replaced by an interest in realistic movement and life in the pottery figures, both human and animal, with a greater concern for details. The glazes employed were a purer form of the alkaline glazes used during Han times, which used brown tones (sometimes casting a purplish hue) and greens, with occasional use of cobalt pigments. These typical colors of the period were used in the sansai (sancai) tri-color glaze, which was achieved by first covering the dried molded body with a white glaze that then was covered with brown and green or blue. When these colors were air dried, they were put into the kiln for firing. The heat of the kiln melted and mixed the colors. Sansai glazes appeared both with and without crackle.

The most typical glaze used was the "straw"-colored glaze which was transparent, crackled, and thinly applied. The characteristics of this glaze often resulted in its eventual separation from the body of the ware. Other decoration of the period included lightly fired pigments of red, white, and black used with occasional blue and green.

As in the Han Dynasty, the ceramic pots of the Tang Dynasty closely imitated the form of the old bronzes; however, the method of glazing the wares down to the foot as an imitation of metal changed in the Tang, when the interior glaze frequently just spilled over the top of the pot with drips of glaze falling toward the foot. Many splashed, dripped, and running techniques were decoratively used, sometimes using incised lines to control the flow of the glaze.

The ceramic bodies of the period varied from soft pottery to porcelaneous ware. White clays were employed with a lead-based transparent glaze, which assumed a pale straw color as a result of its iron content. Pale grey, buff, and red clays were also used. Tomb figures produced included musicians, dancers, merchants, entertainers, and men at arms. Ladies were decorated with faces usually left in the biscuit, or with a straw glaze and the typical palette of Tang glaze colors for dress. The ladies were designed to be examples of feminine appeal and were shown in various poses. The early figures show very thin, elegant ladies, but early in the eighth century they began to look fatter and more matronly. The last ones produced in the middle of the century were decidedly fat. One characteristic that is common to all is the look of benign contentment on their faces, a fulfillment of the eighth-century artists' view of ideal womanhood. The Lokapala figure (guardian of a quarter in Buddhist heaven) first appeared with an animallike visage but was also represented with human features. Figures were made in molds and various parts were joined and refined after removal.

Tang horses of various breeds as well as camels and other animal forms were produced. The most familiar was the horse, which was depicted in a variety of realistic poses with or without saddle and rider. Some were unglazed and painted. Others had a straw glaze or were decorated with brown, amber, or green splashes of glaze. Horses and camels, along with other figures, were intended for burial with the dead.

Vases, jars (with and without covers), and ewers were produced. Decoration of jars consisted of differing glaze techniques employing spots, streaks, cross-hatching, and chevrons. They sometimes appeared with three-claw feet, loops on the shoulders, and designs. Large green-glazed ewers were also made along with molded ewers of bronze form.

An interesting technique of the period was imitating stone by combining different colors of clay to form a marblelike look. These "marble" wares were refined to a very thinly potted ware by the end of the Tang Dynasty.

Small objects, such as wrist rests and boxes, reveal decorative incising with glaze applied within the boundaries.

References: Cecile and Michel Beurdeley, *A Connoisseur's Guide to Chinese Ceramics*, Harper and Row, n.d., Stephen W. Bushell, *Chinese Art*, Rare Reprints Inc., 1977; Warren E. Cox, *Pottery and Porcelain*, Crown Publishers Inc., 1970; Seizo Hayashiya and Gakuji Hasebe, *Chinese Ceramics*, Charles E. Tuttle Co., 1966; R. L. Hobson, *Chinese Pottery and Porcelain*, Dover Publications, 1976; Fujio Koyama and John Figgess, *Two Thousand Years of Oriental Ceramics*, Harry N. Abrams, Inc.; Margaret Medley, *The Chinese Potter*, Phaidon Press Ltd., 1976; Albert W. R. Theil, *Chinese Pottery and Stoneware*, Thomas Nelson and Sons, n.d.; *Tri Color Pottery of the Tang Dynasty*, National Museum of History, 1977; Susan G. Valenstein, *A Handbook of Chinese Ceramics*, Metropolitan Museum of Art, 1975.

Museums: Art Institute of Chicago, Chicago, Illinois; Nelson Gallery of Art, Kansas City, Kansas;

Boston Museum of Art, Boston, Massachusetts; Metropolitan Museum of Art, New York, New York; Cleveland Museum of Art, Cleveland, Ohio; Freer Gallery of Art, Washington, D.C.; Seattle Art Museum, Seattle, Washington; National Museum of History, Taipei, Taiwain; British Museum, London, England; Sir Percival David Foundation, London, England; Victoria and Albert Museum, London, England; National Museum, Tokyo, Japan.

Reproduction Alert: Tang figures have always been reproduced because they have traditionally fetched very high prices. The standard for authentication has been and still is the thermoluminescent test, a carbon dating process that has been established as a criterion for dating of ancient pottery. The University of Oxford in England is the accepted source for such testing although it has been done in some major cities in the United States. It is an involved process and quite expensive, costing approximately $250.00 for analysis of a single specimen (a small core drilled out of the body of the piece). Unfortunately, the results of testing, even on authentic pieces, often is inconclusive. This is due to the fact that frequently there are repairs on the items that have been done at a later date. If the core site involves any area of repair, the test may show a later dating than the true age of the item. The answer to this problem is to test several sites on the piece. The cost may seem prohibitive, but since so many Tang items sell in the four- and five-figure range, the assurance provided by the test is worth more than the uncertainty of purchasing a costly item which can be proven worthless at a later date.

To further complicate authenticity concerns, there is a current rumor that shards from tomb burial items are being used as parts around which whole new bogus figures are being built. Apparently the shards are placed at the "belly" sections of horses and camels, a site that is most frequently used for testing. If this rumor is in fact true, the results of a single test in this area could be totally misleading.

Although we believe that the major auction houses and antiques dealers are honest, we also know that identification of age cannot be accomplished by just visually inspecting objects of this vintage. Without a proper thermoluminescent test, no absolute determination of age can be made. Do not buy an expensive figure from this period without such a test, and preferably not unless it has been tested at several sites on the figure itself. If these conditions have not been met at the time of sale, get a receipt guaranteeing a return with full money refund. If the results of your testing do not confirm the proper dating of Han or Tang items, you will then be protected.

Collecting Hints: Ceramics of the Tang Dynasty, which have been scarce and very costly in the past, have been affected in recent years by the importation of tomb items that have dug up and illegally removed from mainland China. This has become a very big business venture for some enterprising Chinese merchants—and a dangerous one—since the Communist government does not sanction the looting of its national treasure.

The result of this influx of all types of early Han and Tang ceramics has been the lowering in price of what once was scarce and rare merchandise and the resulting creation of a larger consumer market who can take advantage of the availability and lower cost of these items. From the amount of goods coming out of China, the supply of Han and Tang ceramics seems endless, which does not bode well for the collector who is buying solely as an investment. The old law of supply and demand takes hold. There is no way of telling if the prices will go down any further. Also, there is always a possibility that the number of collectors will continue to grow, thereby steadying the market. Recent spending trends indicate, however, that collectors are somewhat befuddled by the tremendous amount of goods available and are beginning to become suspicious of the authenticity of the pieces.

Amphora vase, 14¼" h., the high rounded oviform body surmounted by a trumpet neck with cup-shaped mouth, the two studded double strap handles terminating in dragon heads reaching into the mouth, dark brown glaze on mouth and handles, the shoulders splash glazed with brown, green ivory and amber, the lower section unglazed **3,500.00**

Bowl

1¼" h. x 3", brown glazed stoneware, of squat globular form with an olive green glaze over a brown stoneware body, the glaze falling shot of the footless base **100.00**

4" dia., blue glaze, of shallow form with everted lip, covered with a strong blue glaze falling over a raised rim encircling the exterior to reveal the compact white ware, the slightly pared foot with beveled edge **3,000.00**

7½" dia., deep bowl, of compressed globular form, thinly potted with gently incurved rim, the thin khaki-colored glaze covering the interior and falling irregularly down the sides on the exterior, glaze flaking **700.00**

Box, with slightly domed cover, 1¼" h. x 3", creamy white glaze **150.00**

Ewer

7" h., 9th/10th Century, formed as a stylized bird, set with a short cut spout opposite a curled thumbpiece, flanked by a pair of small wings on the shoulder, the layers of plumage drawn in small lines, covered in a crackled pale olive glaze splashed brown and green which stops evenly above the base, mouth rim repaired **1,200.00**

$7\frac{1}{2}''$ h., rare cream-glazed stoneware, the ovoid body surmounted by a flared neck rolled at the rim, connected by a double-strap handle to the shoulders, set opposite an upright short spout, all beneath a translucent and crackled glaze of ivory tone over white slip stopping above the foot to show the grainy ware, crack along side **700.00**

$8\frac{3}{4}''$ h., brown-splashed pottery, the sides decorated with three appliqués splashed in a rich chocolate brown, showing an elaborate floral spray, a beribboned floral medallion enclosing the character zhang, and a figure of a lion with the character zhang, the shoulders applied with a faceted spout set opposite a loop handle, flanked by two smaller loop handles below the cylindrical neck, covered all over with a crackled clear glaze over white slip, restored rim and handle. **2,000.00**

$12\frac{1}{2}''$ h., rare sancai-glazed pottery ewer, the well-potted globular body set beneath a tall waisted and ringed neck flaring to a wide pinched mouth, attached to the shoulders by a strap handle with molded leaf decoration, the whole raised on a high splayed foot, restored crack on the handle and repainting on mouth. **38,000.00**

Figure

Bactrian camel, $14\frac{3}{4}''$ h., shown standing on a rectangular base, its long neck curved upwards, its head raised, its humps protruding from a pleated green saddle cloth, covered in a burnt caramel gaze except for an area of cream covering most of its face, base drilled with a small hole **5,500.00**

Camel

$16\frac{1}{4}''$ h., shown standing foursquare on a rectangular base, with head raised high, a large pack balanced between the humps over the saddle, the slip-covered body with traces of pigment and burial earth adhering **2,000.00**

$17\frac{3}{4}''$, straw-glazed pottery, well-modeled and striding forward

Attendant, $10\frac{3}{8}''$ h., tomb figure, green glaze extending overhead and most of long belted robe, the feet and the square plinth left unglazed, restorations on head and base. $825.00. Courtesy of Butterfield and Butterfield.

on a rectangular base, the heavily laden beast carrying large saddlebags draped across the body and between the humps, the bags hung with water vessels and game birds on a slatted projecting frame, the muscular legs with well-defined padded feet, the glaze partially degraded. **4,800.00**

$26''$ h. x $15\frac{3}{4}''$ l., sancai-glazed, the tall animal standing foursquare on a rectangular base, with head raised up and teeth bared in a braying pose, the body covered with an amber glaze, the mane, humps and underside of neck glazed cream, the saddlecloth of mottled amber and cream, splashed with green **15,000.00**

Court lady

$5\frac{3}{4}''$ h., red pottery, miniatures, the fully formed standing fig-

Boar, $5\frac{1}{4}''$ l., degraded straw glaze. $975.00

Camel, 17" h., painted pottery, the two humps, saddlebag, and neck ruff painted with pale red pigment, the muscular legs splashed brown. $4,675.00. Courtesy of Butterfield and Butterfield.

ures dressed in long flowing robes, hands held together before their chests, elaborate coiffures with hanging topknot, traces of pigments, burial earth impacted **1,600.00**
12⅛" h., painted pottery, standing with hands clasped at waist, wearing a brick red bodice over a long-sleeved dress tied around the hips with a knotted sash, with broad face and upswept hair coiled above each ear, traces of white slip and red, green and black pigment **1,700.00**
16" h., painted pottery, the elegant plump figure standing with

Female attendant, 10" h., tomb figure, degraded straw glaze. $975.00

hands clasped in a long voluminous robe painted orange, falling in crisp pleats to the top of her ruyi-toed shoes, the face very well modeled with haughty, fully rounded features, framed by long hair drawn into an elaborate coiffure showing traces of black pigments **9,500.00**
19" h., pottery, the full figured lady shown with draped in long robes standing with a pronounced forward sway one foot set in front of the other, the hands held together at her waist hidden by the folds of the sleeves of her robe, her hair swept up in an asymmetrical triple coil which reveals long lobed ears, traces of white pigment, the eyes dotted black . . .   **15,000.00**
Courtier, 17⅞" h., unusual painted red pottery, the tall figure shown standing with his right hand raised as if to hold a bird, wearing a long robe draped in folds and belted low at the waist, painted overall in cream with a finely detailed red and black collar, the plump face with extensive pigment remaining beneath a soft cap painted with long black tabs in back **12,000.00**
Dignitary, 17" h., early Tang Dynasty, straw-glazed pottery, well-modeled, the hands clasped together over his chest obscured by the sleeves of a long tunic worn over loose pantaloons, the toes projecting beneath the hem, the face with crisply defined features, covered in an iridescent straw-colored glaze with areas of green, the cloth cap with some black pigment remaining **1,800.00**
Dog, hound
2½" h., partly glazed on the upper body with a degraded cream color, the hound shown recumbent with head held high **350.00**
4½" h., buff pottery, shown seated on his haunches on a U shaped base, the head facing straight ahead, the tail shown curled to one side, a collar tied around the neck **1,500.00**
8⅜" l., painted dark grey pottery, shown in a recumbent position with ears pricked and tail curled, head turned to the side, signs of knife paring beneath the remains of a mottled white

slip, with traces of red pigment on the face and a red collar around the neck, some restoration **1,200.00**

9½" h., pottery, one of twelve Zodiac figures, the human body shown with hands clasped together in front of chest, the modelled canine head on a thick set neck, dressed in draped robes shown belted high at the waist, red and black pigment evident in the floral borders around the collar and sleeves **1,300.00**

Duck, 5" h., pottery with a degraded gesso covering, shown standing head up and facing forward, the feathers detailed by continuous grooves, the eyes pierced **450.00**

Dwarf, 7" h., painted pottery, standing with right hand against chest, wearing a short sleeved shirt under an orange jacket with green lapels, the right sleeve pulled away from the shoulder and the left trailing down the back, the face with broad features beneath a tall cloth cap, traces of black, green and orange pigments **1,000.00**

Earth spirit
9½" h., painted pottery, seated on its haunches on a triangular rockwork base, its head with prominent facial features, a single small horn protruding from the forehead in front of the crest between the pair of ears, the shoulders with wing-like projections, traces of pigmentation, restoration **1,100.00**

11⅞" h., painted pottery, seated on its haunches on a base of bean section, its head with prominent facial features, long ears and a single horn, its shoulders with flamelike projections, traces of black, green, and red pigmentation, restored break across shoulders **1,400.00**

14" h., sancai glaze of amber, cream and green, shown seated, with mouth open in roar, cream glazed horns and mane, restorations **7,500.00**

Equestrian
10" h., painted pottery, the rider wearing a red robe and black boots, his face with painted features beneath a black cloth cap, his right arm raised to strike a small drum strapped to the saddle, the horse standing foursquare with head turned to the left **1,500.00**

12¼" h., painted pottery figure, the rider wearing a loose tunic over boots and a hooded cape, his left hand stretched out and his right cupped over his mouth as if whistling, astride a horse standing foursquare with head slightly bowed, traces of red and black pigment and white slip **4,500.00**

Female musician
5½" h., (four), each figure shown seated with legs tucked under on a square base, wearing double knotted hairdos and long robes, one figure with a reed pipe at her lips, the other two as if singing, traces of red and black pigment, restored **2,800.00**

7½" h., painted pottery, shown seated on a square base playing a *qin*, wearing an orange shawl draped over the shoulders of a long dress painted with red stripes, her hair drawn up into two topknots and her face picked out in red and black pigment, neck repaired **2,000.00**

Foreign soldier, 21⅝" h., shown standing dressed in a breastplate beneath his tunic, his shoulder pads molded as lion masks, his sleeves rolled to the elbows, one hand shown holding a sword (missing) the other with palm held out, his pantaloons tucked above high strapped boots, head shown facing the side with bulging eyes, aquiline nose and lips shown parted in a smile, wearing a close fitting cap with a peaked front and knop finial, traces of orange, red, green and white pigment **6,800.00**

Guardians, 19½" h., (two), sancai glaze of ivory, dark amber and green, with left hands on hips and right arms bent at the elbows, the hands and face left unglazed, one head modelled with a tightly fitting cap, the other with mouth open and fierce expression, with fitted wood stands **10,000.00**

Groom
8½" h., pottery, amber and dark olive splashed glaze, shown standing on a rectangular base, the long sleeves of his tunic

hiding his hands held on a prominent belly, the glaze pooling on the underside of the base **1,100.00**

10½″ h., pair, amber glazed pottery, each tunic clad figure standing on a rectangular base, hand folded in front of chest, wearing high boots and peaked cap, the hands and head unglazed, the amber glaze pooling at the base, one head reattached **1,600.00**

11″ h., standing on a square plinth, with hands folded at chest, the moustachioed face painted in pink below the cap with a bow and double-knot top, the tunic splashed with a leaf-green glaze dribbling onto and stopping irregularly short on his high boots **2,500.00**

16″ and 17″, red pottery, shown standing on square bases with hands outstretched as if to hold reigns, one dressed as a foreigner **6,000.00**

Horse

12½″, well-modeled painted pottery, standing foursquare on a rectangular base, the head turned slightly to the right, the black saddle draped with an orange saddlecloth, the buff ware with an overall pinkish tone. . . **2,800.00**

14½″ h., amber and yellow splash-glazed pottery, well-modeled standing with its head slightly turned, the thick mane covered in a yellow glaze, the saddle unglazed but with a streak of brown. **10,000.00**

15″ h., depicted prancing, painted pottery, shown standing with right leg raised and head turned slightly to the left revealing bulging eyes, flared nostrils and open mouth, the mane combed to one side, a ridged saddle draped across the square saddlecloth, traces of red and black pigment over white slip. **6,000.00**

Lion, 7″ l., grey pottery, shown in crouching posture, legs held close on oval plinth, with striated mane, eyes bulging, ears swept back and mouth open. **1,400.00**

Lokapala, 29″ h., the fierce guardian shown trampling a recumbent beast, the right arm resting akimbo on his hips, the left raised and with fist clenched in a

Horse, 17½″ h., painted pottery, traces of original pigment, restoration. $5,700.00

menacing gesture, wearing an armored breastplate bound with cords extending down over the powerful chest and waist, over a short gathered tunic showing below the fringed leather apron and grazing the top of the boots, the head vigorously modeled with protruding eyes staring intently from beneath furrowed brows and framed by a helmet with upturned rim, traces of red and black pigment.................... **20,000.00**

Mythical marine creature, 7½″ h., grey pottery, the fish with elaborate scrolling gills and incised scales and fins, its human head turned sharply to its left, its lower edge supported on an irregular base with wave-like striations . . . **900.00**

Princess, 15″ h., rare painted pottery, the slender lady standing wearing an elaborate high-waisted gown tied in front with a yellow cord the back with long yellow double sashes looped through a pendent jade disc and knotted in four places, traces of painted black and red decoration on the layered skirt and streamered front panel above the ‘“cloud”-toed shoes, the aristocratic face delicately modeled with small features, the hair pulled back to reveal her high forehead and sculpted into a winged coif **12,000.00**

Ram, 4″ h., buff pottery, shown recumbent with horned head held high, painted black spots **500.00**

Rooster

3½″ h., unglazed red pottery,

standing with a long tail and head held high **400.00**

4'' h., glazed on the upper body with a degraded cream glaze, shown standing supported by a cylindrical petal on a circular foot **400.00**

Warrior

14½'' h., buff pottery, modelled standing in a three-quarter length coat, wearing a helmet, with hands held together, mounted on wood base **1,400.00**

16'' h., sancai-glazed, shown standing atop a buffalo, his right arm with raised clenched fist, his left hand resting on his hip, wearing a sancai jacket over an amber shirt and green trousers, the cow also covered with amber glaze, the face with traces of pigment **2,800.00**

Granary jar, 5½'' x 4'', unusual yellow glaze, modelled in cylindrical form with a simulated dome cover and a pearl shaped finial, the glaze falling short of the foot at one side **500.00**

Jar

4'' x 3½'', stoneware, yellow and green, the globular jar with two handles and a short waisted neck, the streaked glaze terminating midway down the body **800.00**

4½'', sancai splashed glaze of ivory, green and amber, globular body below the thickened ring around the wide mouth attached with the short cylindrical spout, all supported on a low spreading foot, large chips on foot and mouth . . . **1,100.00**

7¾'', phosphatic-splashed stoneware, of Huangdao type, solidly potted and applied with curled loop handles, the chalky blue glaze liberally splashed shading to olive with robin's-egg streaks . . . **4,850.00**

8'' x 7'', green and cream glaze, of ovoid form with a short neck and everted rim, the glaze stopping just short of the foot leaving a white underglaze **1,800.00**

8½'' x 4'', Cizhou, white glazed and of bluster form with a waisted neck, the loop handles finger pressed on the shoulder **160.00**

9'' dia., on tripod feet, sancai glaze of cream, green and amber, globular form, applied with three winged lions soaring between foliate medallions placed above each of the three tripod feet which are modelled as paws **4,500.00**

13'' with cover, straw-glazed pottery jar and cover, of globular form set on three tripod feet which are modelled as paws, glaze degraded, crack **1,600.00**

Offering set, circular tray and eleven wine cups, sancai splashed glaze of green, cream and chestnut, the splashed glaze revealing the buff body, small chips to cups and tray **2,000.00**

Vase

10½'' x 8'', grey glazed baluster body with a faint incised band around the shoulder and a good greyish white glaze with brown crackle stopping just short of the foot. . . . **1,300.00**

13'' h., unusual green-glazed pottery, the slender ovoid body supported on a high pedestal, a ring encircling the shoulders beneath the waisted neck, the whole splashed with a finely crackled blue-green glaze, restored rim. . . **4,500.00**

Water pot, 5½'' dia., green and straw glaze, globular form, deep rounded sides on a low spreading foot, short cylindrical spout below the wide thickened mouth, straw glazed interior, exterior in a crackled green glaze stopping short of the foot **2,000.00**

TRANSITIONAL PERIOD PORCELAIN

See Appendix I for table of related emperors.

History: Transitional Period Porcelain dates from the end of the Ming Dynasty (the death of Emperor Wanli in 1619) to the reign of the second emperor of the Qing Dynasty (Emperor Kangxi, in 1662). It was doubtful that the imperial kilns were supported by the court at this time because of the rapid succession of emperors. This gave the master potters of China a chance to express their initiative in the creation of experimental techniques. The resulting nontraditional designs paved the way for the new decorative treatment of porcelain in the Kangxi years. Hobson described the quality of the porcelain of this period as ''of strong build, suitable for export and of good material, with a clear white body often left unglazed on a flat base. The glaze is thick and rather bubbly. . . .'' According to Michel Beurdeley, the shapes of the period are also distinctive: ''a slender cylindrical vase with a small neck, precursor of the mallet or rouleau vase, ovoid jars, wine bottles, various bowls and, of course, some purely European shapes such as tankards, mugs, goblets, large handled vases, candlesticks, teapots, etc. Particularly to be noted is one special shape: the 'hookah' or *kendi* made for the Near East and the Malay Archipelago, which continued in production for a long period. A few are zoomorphic, in the shape of frogs or elephants.''

Tea ceremony ceramics were also made in response to the Japanese demand in the early seventeenth century. Kosometsuke wares (''old blue and white'') were produced during the Tianqi and Chongzheng reigns. These somewhat crude, casual ceramics were decorated and modeled to the Japanese taste. Another blue and white export of the Transitional Period, produced a bit later, was Shonsui (tea ceremony) porcelain. Made to order for the tea masters, Shonsui also was produced in Japanese patterns and shapes. It employed the finest of craftsmenship and utilized the refined violet blue pigment of the era.

European demands for blue and white Kraak porcelain continued from the late Ming Dynasty throughout the Transitional Period. The geometric design of radiating panels of flowers and birds was most often produced on large deep dishes. Kraak design was distinctively Chinese. Demand for this ware in the Qing Dynasty was soon to be replaced with requests for porcelain of more European shape, color, and motif.

Other Transitional period designs featured landscapes, including figures, rocks, clouds, and grass. Landscapes became the popular motif of the Western exports. Scenes were boldly drawn around the surface of the new vases of the period. Legendary, historical, and romantic scenes also flourished. Dated inscriptions were not uncommon. In answer to the demands of the export trade, the shape of some of the porcelains became more Western, and the scheme of using flowers to separate landscape panels revealed a decidedly European influence. Generally, the decorations employed during the Transitional period tended to be large in scale, unregimented, smooth flowing, well executed, and brightly colored.

It was during this time that the potters succeeded in refining their native cobalt blue to approximate the quality of the imported pigments. The blue and white porcelain of this time featured a bright blue violet color otherwise known as ''violets in milk.'' The enamels, particularly the wu ts'ai five-color ware, show the influence of the Wanli era but the underglaze blue occupied larger areas of the surface than either the Wanli or later Kangxi periods. Overglaze enamel pieces with green as the predominant color became the prototype for the famille verte porcelains of the Kangxi period.

Monochrome-glazed porcelains showed little or no change from the preceding Ming production, as engraved, slip-decorated, and pierced white porcelains continued to be made. (See Chinese Export Porcelain; Ming Dynasty Ceramics; Monochrome Glazes.)

References: C. and M. Beurdeley, *A Connoisseur's Guide to Chinese Ceramics*, Harper and Row, n.d.; Daisy Lion-Goldschmidt, *Ming Porcelain,* Rizzoli International Publications, 1978; Duncan Macintosh, *Chinese Blue and White Porcelain,* Charles E. Tuttle Co., Inc., 1977; Margaret Medley, *The Chinese Potter,* Phaidon Press Ltd., 1976; Suzanne G. Valenstein, *A Handbook of Chinese Ceramics,* Metropolitan Museum of Art, 1975.

Museums: Asian Art Museum, San Francisco, California; Chicago Art Institute, Chicago, Illinois; Indianapolis Museum of Art, Indianapolis, Indiana; Nelson Gallery of Art, Kansas City, Kansas; Boston Museum of Fine Arts, Boston, Massachusetts; Museum of the University of Michigan, Ann Arbor, Michigan; Detroit Institute of Arts, Detroit, Michigan; Saint Louis Art Museum, St. Louis, Missouri; Metropolitan Museum of Art, New York, New York; Cleveland Museum of Art, Cleveland, Ohio; Philadelphia Museum of Art, Philadelphia, Pennsylvania; Seattle Art Museum, Seattle, Washington; British Museum, London, England, Sir Percival David Foundation, London, England; Victoria and Albert Museum, London, England; Gemeente Museum, Leeuwarden, the Netherlands; Rijksmuseum, Amsterdam, the Netherlands.

Collecting Hints: The most frequently found forms of Transitional porcelains are vases, which appear in a variety of shapes not found in earlier periods. This change in shape heralded the innovative departure from tradition that took place as the Qing Dynasty assumed its throne. New vase shapes that appeared during this period included tall, cylindrical vases that narrow into a short, flared rim; oval vases on flat unglazed foundations; cylindrical forms with thickened midsections; tall vases with flared mouth rims; and rectangular vases. Motifs of stiff leaves were sometimes painted at the lip and base of vases.

Other products from this period are domed round boxes, incense burners, brush pots, and bowls. Many of these items were exported to Japan.

Bowl
  2'' h. x 6'' w., blue and white, wide
  mouth, rounded, painted with Fu
  Dogs interspaced with peony
  blooms, short foot with the Jiajing
  six-character mark **500.00**
  7¾'' dia., Xuande mark, Transitional,
  copper-red and underglazed-
  blue, of deep form with steeply
  rounded sides, the interior decorated with a central medallion depicting a carp leaping out of a
  circle of lotus blossoms floating
  on rippling waves beneath a band
  of clouds partially blocking the
  sun, surrounded by a frieze of
  assorted fish and crustaceans, fantastic seashells and bubbles be-

Bowl, 9″ dia., wucai colors, all over continuous decoration showing Middle Eastern influence, exceptionally fine painting, along with carved wooden stand. $4,500.00

neath a band of stylized waves and lotus heads at the rim, the exterior decorated with a frieze of various fish swimming among rolling waves and lotus blossoms above an undulating rocky sea-bottom sprouting long swaying seagrasses, chips **1,400.00**

11¾″ dia., circa 1640, blue and white, deep, flared, painted on the exterior with numerous figures seated below trees at various leisure pursuits in a continuous rocky fenced landscape near swirling clouds and below a band of ruyi heads at the rim, (three small rim hairlines, two chips). . . **2,600.00**

Brushpot, 6¾″ h., fitted box, blue and white, circa 1650, the high cylindrical sides painted in varied blue tones with a garden scene featuring rocks and plantains, two boy attendants waiting on a scholar-official by a terrace **1,000.00**

Censer, 6¼″ h., x 8⅝″ dia., blue and white, wide mouth with an unglazed rim, painted on the bombé sides with a continuous scene of two warriors, one on horseback, in a rocky landscape with swirling clouds and waterfalls, underglaze firing cracks, chips to rim and foot **1,100.00**

Charger, 14¼″ dia., famille verte, bearing Chenghua six-character mark within double rings, the well painted in iron-red with chrysanthemums, fruiting foliage and other flowers within striped and diaper borders all enclosed by a wider border of flowerheads in iron-red, aubergine and yellow reserved on a dense foliate ground **1,800.00**

Dish
5⅝″ dia., Tianqi, thinly potted and decorated on the interior with a long robed figure seated in the moonlight on a squat stool holding a pipe, all within a single blue line repeated on the exterior above four cloud scroll motifs, the underside with spurious seal mark, rim frits, restored foot ring chip **1,200.00**

5¾″ dia., pair, blue and white, 17th Century, of small saucer shape, similarly painted on the interior with a flower, curling leaves and a hovering butterfly, encircled by dots, with a single large peony near a low fence, frits, glaze gaps, sand grits on back **200.00**

9″ w., blue and white, shallow with a thick rim, painted in primitive style with two horses standing beneath a windblown willow and rocks, the reverse with a bamboo motif and an unglazed foot **1,000.00**

11″ w., blue and white, the shallow dish with a thick rim, painted with dragon and clouds, the reverse with dragon's tail and two clouds, the foot ink wash **800.00**

11″ w., blue and white, deep sided with a thick rim and a boldly painted swirling dragon amid clouds, the reverse with the dragon's tail and clouds, the foot unglazed. **1,000.00**

11″ w., blue and white, deep sided with a thick rim, decorated with a sinuous dragon and clouds, the reverse with the dragon's tail and clouds, engraved with a collection mark **1,200.00**

Jar
4¾″ h., pair, wucai, tapering oviform, painted with scrolling peony. **495.00**

5″ x 4″, Ming/Transition Period, blue and white, baluster form and decorated in a Transitional style with figures in a landscape divided by rocks and palm tree, the shoulder of the jar with a dragon-scroll on a blue ground, the foot with the seal mark Xi Ju. **400.00**

8″ dia., wucai, globular, painted with yellow Buddhistic lions among dense scrolling peony below a cracked-ice pattern band (rubbed) **600.00**

8″ dia., wucai, globular, painted with horses leaping among iron-red swirling clouds, green breaking waves and underglaze rockwork below an iron-red band of flames at the neck **875.00**

Jar, 8″ dia., Ming Dynasty/Transitional period, wucai colors, flat globular form, continuous scene of children at play below stylized stiff leaves at the neck. $3,500.00

9¼″ h., blue and white, oviform, painted with a group of figures gathered in a fenced rocky landscape watching a water buffalo near swirling clouds 725.00

10″ h., blue and white. oviform, with short cylindrical rim painted with scattered sprays of fruit and flowers 850.00

10¾″ h., pair, polychome enamelled, baluster form each painted in iron-red, green and yellow with a similar pattern of quatrefoil panels enclosing lotus heads, below a wide ruyi-collar border enclosing chrysanthemum and peony, reserved on an iron-red scale or diaper pattern ground, the wood covers with carnelian finials (old damages). 2,200.00

11¼″ h., with cover, wucai colors, decorated with galloping horses among flowerheads and beribboned precious objects, divided by massive rocks and waves, all reserved on an iron-red swirling line ground, the domed knopped cover with waves and beribboned objects, firing cracks, glaze chips, restoration to cover 1,600.00

15¼″ h., wucai-decorated, mid-17th century, baluster form, painted in the characteristic palette with a dignitary receiving a group of warriors with scholar officials in attendance, before a table on the fenced terrace of a pavilion, a mass of cloud at the rear partially enveloping rockwork and trees emerging on the sides, a band of peony and chrysanthemum and further rockwork encircling the

waisted neck, the cover with three boys at play on a further fenced terrace 2,800.00

15½″ h., blue and white, baluster form, 17th Century, the stoutly potted jar decorated in brilliant cobalt tones with a continuous dense flowering lotus and foliate scroll, below a band of geometric scrollwork and pointed petal borders at the neck, the bud-shaped knopped domed cover similarly decorated, glaze gaps, chip to cover 2,200.00

22″ h., blue and white, baluster form, painted in underglaze blue line and wash with alternating circular and square panels depicting different scenes of a court lady and her attendants, separated by T-shaped cloud scrolls and set between a collar of conjoined ruyi heads above and a band of stiff upright leaf tips below, which are repeated at the base of the neck below a double line border encircling the molded mouth rim, minor fritting to rim 5,500.00

Saucer dish, 7½″ dia., blue and white, Tianqi, the sides petal molded, the center painted with a lotus head, the petals enclosing key-scroll in the center with a brocade ball enclosed by tied scrolls 450.00

Stem cup, 3″ x 3″, blue and white, round, pedestal stem, motif of pencil drawn dragons and flaming pearls, foot with the four character marks of Zhenghua. 800.00

Tray, 6″ x 6″, blue and white, decorated in the Tianqi style, with cranes circling a central crane medallion intertwined with a lotus and scrolage motif, the everted sides have floral reserves, the exterior has a motif of floral sprays, unglazed foot 800,00

Vase

6″ h., blue and white, pear-shaped, painted in pencilled line with two scholars seated on the ground conversing, with a willow tree growing from the bank behind and flowers in the foreground, the reverse with palmette-form plants beside a pool of water, all within single and double-line borders below a band of upright leaves evenly spaced around the flared neck, firing cracks in foot 300.00

6¼″ h., blue and white, circa 1650, meiping shape, painted underglaze with birds flying amid or

Vase, 6½" h., wucai colors, showing a boy, rockwork, trees, and mountains in the distance, stylized stiff leaves at the neck. $1,400.00

YI-HSING WARES

History: During the mid-seventeenth century, the Europeans developed a passion for drinking tea. The Dutch East India Company developed a brisk trade in "Boccaro" (Yi-hsing) teapots through the Netherlands. The pots were made of unglazed red stoneware and originated in Kiangsu Province, China, where the mountain clay for its production was found. The district of Yi-hsing was naturally suited for pottery production, having abundant clay deposits and fuel in the nearby hills. It was also located close to the cities of Shanghai and Nanking, facilitating the possibility of trade.

Prior to trade with the Europeans, the Yi-hsing area produced pottery objects for utilitarian purposes for local use. Other fine wares such as vases, flowerpots, scholars' desk items, dishes, and teapots were exported at first to Thailand and Japan. The most prolifically produced item, however, was the teapot.

At first the artist formed the entire teapot by hand, but by the start of the Qing Dynasty, a method using sectional molds was introduced. At the end of the eighteenth century, a few artists, namely Yang P'eng-nien, Shao Erh-Ch'wan, Feng Tsai-hsia, and Huang Yu-lin, returned to the old hand-modeled techniques, but the vast majority of artists preferred quicker production using molds and wheel finishing. From the time of the growth of European trade in the seventeenth and eighteenth centuries, the potters of Yi-hsing proceeded to create teapots of fanciful design shaped in the form of fruit, gourds, bamboo trunks, birds, and so forth. They also produced tea caddies, vases, and other small items, although the teapot (sha-hu) was and still is the most important export item from this area.

Although the color of the clay used was typically a brownish red, other clays from this area were often blended to produce a dark brown or purplish color. This highly prized color, called Tzu-sha or "purple sand," is due to the high iron content of the clay. Items were also produced using a yellowish clay, sometimes in combination with a darker color. Occasionally, quartz particles were applied to the clay surface to create a "pear skin" appearance.

The teapots produced were typically small, somewhat squat, and had a straight spout. Applied decoration was common and fruit finials often were applied to the lids. Calligraphy was etched into the sides of some simple pots. Painted decoration using opaque famille rose colors did not come into vogue until the late eighteenth/early nineteenth century. Teapot fanciers in Europe sometimes created silver gilt mounts for their favorite pots.

Yi-hsing wares won many gold medals at international exhibitions in the first quarter of the twentieth century. Trade remained steady until

perched on a bough of flowering foliage growing near pierced rockwork, wood lid **750.00**
6½" x 4", blue and white, baluster form, painted with a warrior, horse and courtier on a landscape with castle and rocks, incised border on the shoulder, foliage motif around the short neck **800.00**
7" x 3", blue and white, waisted cylindrical form with a motif of birds, peachtree and rocks **700.00**
7" x 4", blue and white, baluster form with a painted horned kylin, terrace and mountain view interspersed with palm trees, the shoulder with an incised border, the neck with pendent palmettes   **1,000.00**
9" h., famille verte, globular, painted in green, yellow, iron-red and aubergine with clusters of fruit on a scale-pattern ground, drilled for electricity **850.00**
9¼" h., circa 1640, blue and white, exaggerated baluster form with two lizard handles applied to the bulbous garlic-shaped neck and on spreading foot, painted on each side with a dignitary and attendant in a fenced wooden garden between bands of stylized flowers **1,100.00**
9½" h., pair, circa 1635, blue and white, hexagonal pear-shaped, with slender flared necks painted with scenes of figures in rocky wooded landscapes near swirling clouds, one neck with stylized foliage **1,800.00**

the start of World War II. At this point production ceased entirely. The revival of Yi-hsing wares took place in the early 1950s, when the Shu Shan Workshop was set up as part of the Cultural Revolution.

References: Terese Tse Bartholomew, *I-Hsing Ware*, China Institute in America, 1978; D. F. Lunsingh Scheurleer, *Chinese Export Porcelain (Chine de Commande)*, Pitman Publishing Corp., 1974.

Museums: Asian Art Museum of San Francisco, San Franciso, California; Yale University Art Gallery, New Haven, Connecticut; Art Institute of Chicago, Chicago, Illinois; Nelson Gallery of Art, Kansas City, Missouri; Newark Museum, Newark, New Jersey; Philadelphia Museum of Art, Philadelphia, Pennsylvania; Seattle Art Museum, Seattle, Washington.

Reproduction Alert: Oddly, it was the inventor of porcelain in Europe, Bottger of Meissen (who died in 1719), who copied the red stoneware of Yi-hsing. Copies were also made in Japan. The most important reproductions to date still come from the Yi-hsing kilns themselves, since the kilns have never ceased to produce teapots and other stoneware products. For many years they have been making red "dragon and cloud" vases, the newest versions of which can be found in the gift shops of the Chinatowns of the United States and Europe.

Since Chinese custom required that the Yi-hsing teapot not be washed but merely rinsed (in order to preserve the fragrance, color, and taste of the tea), the patina that the pot acquired from handling is one sure tip-off as to the age of the piece. Newer pots have a rather matte finish, or have a sheen that appears to be lacquered on.

Distinguishing the age of Yi-hsing stoneware is difficult. Even when marked, potters' seals have been know to be false. The more famous artists' seal marks have been outrageously duplicated. The following artist marks have been known to be extensively copied on teapots: Ch'en Ming-yuan; Shih Ta-pin, Ch'en Man-sheng and Hui Meng-ch'en on miniature teapots.

Collecting Hints: Of all the products made at Yi-Hsing, it is the teapot that has attracted the most attention. They are collected here, in Europe, and in Japan, where they are used in the tea ceremony. Collectors are charmed by their variety of interesting shapes. The older ones, made in the eighteenth century and earlier, are eagerly sought after and fetch prices in the thousands of dollars. Early pots with known potter's marks are, of course, the most expensive. (See Marks section.)

If the age of a pot is of primary concern, don't forget to check the interior of the spout. The late nineteenth-century potters introduced the practice of piercing the interior spout with many small filtering holes to catch tea leaves. Prior to this time there was but one single hole. Mass-produced teapots, with the exception of some very small ones made especially for the Fukien district, have multiple holes from this time forward. Contemporary "master artist" potted teapots made in the old style may still appear with one hole.

Colored enamel painting first became popular as a form of decoration during the eighteenth century. Encasement in pewter dates a pot to no earlier than the Daoguang (1821–1850) period. These teapots are often found with jade spouts or knops on the lids. More elaborate mountings may indicate European additions to favored pots.

Those who gather Yi-hsing teapots as a collection rather than as an investment will be content to seek out the unusual forms and mixed clay colors rather than concentrating on rare early signed pieces. Nineteenth-century and later pieces can most often be found at antiques shows and shops. They are not outrageously priced and are lots of fun to find. One can never anticipate what charming shape or clay color is going to be next on the teapot shelf!

Ewer, late 19th century, pale orange color, in shape of water well, incised with scene of scholar in garden, other side with eight character inscription, impressed seal on base and under cover, minor chips **450.00**

Covered teapot

   2½" h., 19th century, miniature, compressed pear shape, red-brown color, seven character inscription on base, chips **200.00**

   2¾", 19th century, miniature, squat melon form, stalk cover, dark stoneware body **225.00**

   3¾" h., 19th century, styled like a pine tree trunk, pale yellow with dark brown wash, modeled with

Teapot, 3" h., tan body with multicolored clay applied fruits and nuts, an upside-down mushroom forming the cover, supported on nut and fruit feet, a caltrop fruit forming the handle and a tuber for a spout, with other nuts and seeds on the shoulder. $495.00.

gnarls, branch form handle and spouts, impressed seal mark on base **400.00**

4'', 19th century, bronze kettle form with dragon head spout and kylins on the loop handle and cover, impressed leiwen band around midsection, supported on tripod feet, seal mark on base. **375.00**

4⅜'', chrysanthemum form, the lobed sides forming 6 large petals radiating from the mouth curving down to meet six matching petals rising from the base, matching cover and pierced flower knop, impressed seal on base, chips . . .   **350.00**

4½'', in the form of bamboo stalks bound with raised cord in the middle, bamboo branches forming the handle and spout, impressed Yixing mark on the base   **450.00**

4⅝'', 19th century, lobed shape with prunus branches in relief flanking the branch form handles and spout, impressed seal mark under cover, chips **375.00**

5'', 19th century, hexagonal, with lion on cover facing a loop handle with a loose bead, impressed seal mark under cover, chip **350.00**

5½'' h., 19th century, the irregular tree trunk body applied with a gnarled branch spout and split branch handle, the sides carved in crisp relief with squirrels clambering on leafy berried branches, the flat cover with a recumbent deer finial.   **450.00**

5⅝'' h., Late 18th/early 19th century, pale brown, globular body, slip decorated in reddish brown clay with scholars and their ladies with attendants in a garden, the slip incised with details, chip to the insert of cover **550.00**

6⅞'', early 18th century, globular body with domed cover, knop fin-

Teapot, 2¼'' h., with an inscribed poem and a prunus sprig as decoration, signed with the impressed potter's seal Yang Pengnian. $900.00

ial, lobed body with loop handle and short spout **650.00**

7'', Daoguang, square body with curved spout and handle, set of four bracket feet, covered with a robin's egg glaze **800.00**

7½'' l., 18th century, brown stoneware, compressed body and domed cover, entirely plain, polished dark surface **700.00**

7⅞'' l., 19th century, the compressed body relief molded with overlapping lotus petals, the cover formed as a leaf with a frog finial.   **375.00**

8'' l., circa 1800, modeled as two cojoined hexagonal cylinders, fluted sides, the front top modeled as bamboo, the other with a detachable pine twig cover, restoration to rim **550.00**

Waterdropper, 3¾'' l., peach form, yellow clay, the fruit shape brushed with red slip toward the tip and applied with two chocolate brown leaves lightly incised with veins, connected by a slender twig to the hollow stem forming the spout also in dark brown, pierced with a small hole on top **400.00**

YUAN DYNASTY CERAMICS

See Appendix I for table of Yuan emperors.

History: Since the ceramic history of China is closely related to its political history, we find the productive years of the Yuan Dynasty (1280–1368) disrupted by the Mongol leadership that survived the death of Kublai Khan, the founder of the Yuan Dynasty. The Jingdezhen (Ching-te-chen) potteries were subjugated by the Mongol commissioner and much of its production was directed elsewhere. Many other kilns wasted away under the heavy taxation levied by their landowners.

Most ceramic objects of the Song Dynasty continued to be made in the Yuan, i.e. dark brown ware, Ting (Ding) ware, Tz'u-chow (Cizou), Chun Yao (Junyao), Ying Ching (Yingqing), white wares (with the first appearance of An Hua "hidden" designs), Honan (Henan) temmoku, and southern celadons (see Song Dynasty).

Some historians of Chinese ceramics insist that there was a radical change, not in the types of wares made in the Song and Yuan Dynasties but in the quality of the production. They note that there was no patronage of the Yuan kilns and that the Mongolian influence shifted the emphasis from simplicity of form and color to one of more elaborate decoration and shape.

Blue and white ware (thought by some to have made its initial appearance in the Song Dynasty) production was increased; it was often made in Mongolian shapes. The techniques of painting in underglaze blue were perfected during this time period; however, the blue pigments were unreliable in the firing, leading to some interesting characteristics of Yuan Dynasty blue and white wares. The ceramic body of the pieces were heavy, had a light blue cast, and contained a small amount of iron. In the firing, the cobalt changed in shade to a darker blue or sometimes to a greyish tone, thus presenting various grades of shading. If the blue pigment was applied too thickly, black spots appeared in the blue. The bases of the porcelains were left unglazed but turned to rusty red in the firing. Bases were slightly concave and set on a wide, shallow footrim.

The use of underglaze copper red was a expanded during this period. Yuan Dynasty technique used the painting of copper oxide under the glaze in the same manner as the underglaze blue technique.

Lung Ch'uan celadons, including the spotted celadons of Song Dynasty, were exported to Central Asia and Mongolia. The shapes and decoration of these wares were more elaborate than they were in the Song Dynasty.

In the north, the Tz'u-chow kilns were still producing. However, it has been noted by several historians that the Yuan techniques in the manufacture of this ware, were greatly inferior to the Song. The same may be said of Chun ware.

The production of Ying-ch'ing (Ch'ing Pai), otherwise called shadow blue, continued from the Song, but had a somewhat denser body while maintaining the translucent glaze. These wares were heavily exported to Southeast Asia and Japan.

A ware which can be specifically attributed to the Yuan Dynasty is Shu-fu ware; the Chinese characters mean "central palace." These wares were produced with the Shu-fu mark as part of molded relief decoration, which is not always easy to spot in an elaborate background. These porcelains resemble the Ying-ch'ing in shape and decoration but differ in their glazing. Shu-fu porcelain has a heavy, oily semiopaque glaze of a bluish white color.

One other ceramic art form characteristic of the Yuan Dynasty and influenced by the Mongol occupation of China was pottery figures of actors, dancers, and musicians. These figures were portrayed in casual shapes.

Marks are not known to appear on porcelain of this period. (See: Song Dynasty Ceramics.)

References: Cecile and Michel Beurdeley, *A Connoisseurs' Guide to Chinese Ceramics*, Har-

per and Row, n.d.; Warren E. Cox, *Pottery and Porcelain*, Crown Publishers, Inc., 1970; Seizo Hayashiya and Gakuji Hasebe, *Chinese Ceramics*, Charles E. Tuttle Co., Inc., 1966; R. L. Hobson, *Chinese Pottery and Porcelain*, Dover Publications, Inc., 1976; John Alexander Pope, *Chinese Porcelains from the Ardebil Shrine*, Sotheby Parke Bernet Publications, 1981.

Museums: Avery Brundage Collection, M. H. de Young Museum, San Francisco, California; Museum of Fine Arts, Boston, Massachusetts; Brooklyn Museum, Brooklyn, New York; Metropolitan Museum of Art, New York, New York; Cleveland Museum of Art, Cleveland, Ohio; Freer Gallery, Washington, D.C.; British Museum, London, England; Sir Percival David Foundation, London, England; Victoria and Albert Museum, London, England; Archaeological Museum, Teheran, Iran; Royal Palace Museum, Ayuthia, Thailand; Topkapi Saray Palace Museum, Istanbul, Turkey.

Collecting Hints: There are very few remaining examples of Yuan underglaze red porcelain as contrasted with the amount of blue and white wares that have survived to this day. You can expect to find these copper oxide porcelains only in museums. Although a piece of blue and white ware of this period surfaces from time to time, this porcelain is considered to be extremely rare. The copper oxide experimentation progressed into the Ming Dynasty when the technique was blended with underglaze blue; a combination which continued in popularity into the Qing Dynasty.

Shu-fu ware was sometimes made without the central palace mark. It may also be marked with other greetings and salutations. It too, is likely to be found only in museums.

Of all the wares of this period, the collector has the best chance of finding the Lung Ch'uan celadons. These appear at auctions, antiques shows, and shops. Tz'u-chow ware can also be found occasionally. Earlier Tang and Song porcelains are more plentiful and available to the collector, especially since they have arrived in this country in large quantities in recent years. These early wares, which once were sold only at the most sophisticated auction sales, can now be found at antiques shows and shops.

Bowl
2½" h. x 6" dia., junyao, conical with a vertical rim, the glaze a pale blue grading to grey around the rim, stopping short of the foot   **500.00**
4⅛" dia., junyao, aubergine-glazed, circular form, on slightly waisted circular foot, covered on the exterior in a pale purple glaze faintly mottled with white, the interior covered in a crackled turquoise glaze **1,400.00**
4½" x 4½" h., cizhou, rounded with a ribbed rim, painted with florets

of iron rust on a crackled cream ground, the glaze falling just short of the foot **500.00**

5½″ x 3″ h., Henantemmoku, wide-mouthed conical shape with a thick vertical rim, black glaze with iron rust spotting and streaks, the exterior graded to a cafe'-au-lait color falling short of the foot **500.00**

7″ x 3″ h., Henan temmoku, wide conical form with a teadust glaze falling short of the foot **400.00**

7⅛″ dia., Yingqing, the interior crisply molded with a pair of phoenix birds in the central well, enclosed by six radiating panels of flowers in vases and jardinieres, all beneath a clear blue glaze, the unglazed rim burnt a slight orange in the firing **2,200.00**

8″ dia., shufu, subtly molded with a classic flowering branch scroll surrounding a foliate meander under a typical creamy glaze **725.00**

9″ dia., Southern Yuan Dynasty, junyao, the minutely pitted interior glaze of brilliant milky-lavender color with four purple, lavender, and green splashes, the interior rim of greenish hue blending into the violet and lavender exterior, the thick glaze coagulating and stopping short of the knife-pared foot, restorations . . . **3,800.00**

Brushrest, 4⅛″, Yingqing, rare, of "five peak" form and slightly curved, molded on each side with horses grazing and rolling beneath a willow, the glaze of good pale blue color **950.00**

Censer

3½″ h., junyao, of flat and slightly hollow shape with a round everted rim, the smooth glaze is olive green in tone with pale blue

clouding to one side, the exterior an unglazed reddish-brown stone-ware **300.00**

3½″ x 8″ dia., Ding, shallow with an everted rim, grey white tone glaze **300.00**

5½″ w., incised gray pottery, tripod form, the bombé body supported on three cabriole legs and surmounted by a low neck with wide everted rim, incised with a continuous band of three mythical animals striding forward amidst scrolling clouds **1,000.00**

9½″ dia., tripod form, late Yuan/early Ming, 14th/15th Century, molded on the exterior with the eight trigrams on a carved cursory foliage ground and simple bands on the tapering cylindrical body, standing on short feet, the interior with "waster" remnants, large firing crack **2,400.00**

Cup stand, 6⅛″ dia., Yingqing, the center finely molded with a continuous leafy tendril bearing four lotus blossoms between double thread-relief borders, the well fluted and the everted rim with scalloped edge, covered in a matte, pale blue glaze stopping short of the flat, unglazed base **950.00**

Ewer, 5⅛″ h., blue and white, double-gourd shape, the upper and lower bulbs decorated on each side with a foliate spray below decorative borders and interrupted by a curved strap handle on one side opposite an upright spout on the other, all under a bubble-suffused glaze of grayish tone **600.00**

Figure, Buddhistic lion, 9¼″ h., Henan temmouku, brown-glazed, the lively beast modelled crouching on a steep rectangular base, turned slightly to the right and with a paw resting on a ball, beside a molded cylindrical joss-stick holder under a deep, metallic brown glaze, minor chips **1,200.00**

Jar

5¼″ h., cizhou, blackish-brown glaze, squat baluster form, applied at the short neck with a pair of double looped handles, covered in a rich, dark brown glaze stopping above the base and revealing an underglaze of greenish olive **1,000.00**

12½″ h., cizhou, carved and painted Guan, the solidly potted body with high rounded shoulders tapering to the small foot with countersunk base, surmounted by a

Bowl, 11½″ dia., Tz'u-chow freely painted in brown with abstracted foliate patterns. $300.00. Courtesy of Butterfield and Butterfield.

low waisted neck and covered in an ivory slip overpainted in brown with a band of two shaped panels of phoenix in flight amid cloud forms separated by smaller panels of overlapping petals, the details of the birds and clouds carved through the slip to show the buff stoneware, covered all over in a clear transparent glaze, the neck restored **6,000.00**
13″ h., painted cizhou, heavily potted and surmounted by a cup-shaped mouth applied with two pairs of thin loop handles at the neck, freely painted with floral sprays divided by line borders on the angled shoulder in brown slip on a pale olive ground beneath a clear glaze. **2,000.00**

Vase

6⅞″, pair, yingqing, each of ovoid form with tapered neck and flared mouth, with scrolling loop handles, attached to a hexagonal plinth, the body with two phoenixes above vertically swirled lines, covered with a pale greenish-blue glaze pooling in the recesses **1,400.00**
7″ h., Henan temmouku, bottle vase, slightly-flattened ovoid shape with a short narrow neck and a round everted rim, the glaze a black luster with color falling short of the foot. **600.00**
7″ h., pair, blue and white, baluster, each painted around the body in inky-blue tones with an arching lotus scroll within bands of classic scroll, all between lotus panels above the foot and a chrysanthemum scroll at the shoulder, beneath a band of trellis-pattern below acanthus leaves at the tapering neck. **30,000.00**
11¾″ h., blue and white, octagonal pear-shaped, rare and exceptional, molded in horizontal tiers, the facets around the base painted as lotus panels enclosing flaming pearls, the body painted with lotus or fruiting and flowering pomegranate alternating with geometric designs including lozenge, trellis and interlocking brocade-pattern and concentric quatrelobe pattern, the neck with further flaming pearls below a band of trellis-pattern and upright stiff leaves, the interior of the flaring neck with trefoils, all resting on a spreading foot painted with classic scroll. . **100,000.00**

JAPANESE ANTIQUES

ARITA PORCELAIN

History: Arita is a town in what is today Saga Prefecture (earlier Hizen Province) on the island of Kyushu (the southernmost island in the Japanese archipelago). It has been the center of Japanese porcelain production since the seventeenth century. From the various Arita kilns have come Imari porcelain, Kakiemon, Nabeshima, and Arita porcelain. Japanese porcelain terms are used somewhat inconsistently, causing great confusion. The term Arita porcelain is variously used to refer to two distinct but related entities: (1) only the blue and white products of the Arita kilns that are not Kakiemon, Hirado, or Nabeshima and (2) all the porcelains (blue and whites, celadons, underglaze blue, and overglaze polychrome enamel decorated pieces) from the Arita area kilns that do not fit the Imari, Kakiemon, Hirado, or Nabeshima categorizations. This article will deal with only those Arita products which are decorated solely in underglaze blue.

With Arita blue and whites, the blue is produced from a cobalt or indigo pigment and is painted straight onto the biscuit (perhaps, after a preparatory firing), after which the vessel is glazed and refired. Called gosu blue in Japan, the blue varies. It can be anything from a grey-blue, a purple-blue verging on black, or the sapphire blue associated with Ming and Qing blue and whites. Note also that Arita blue and whites are sometimes referred to as "Sometsuke," which simply means blue and white porcelain.

Japan derived its blue and white ceramic tradition first from Korea and then from China. The dating of Japanese porcelain depends in part on this history. During the Momoyama Period (approximately 1568 to 1615), pottery and the art of glazing made steady progress in Japan. Cha-no-yu, or the Japanese tea ceremony, encouraged pottery making and, a half century later, porcelain production. The earliest Japanese porcelain showed no trace of Chinese influence. It appears to have been the product of Korean potters living in Japan. The earliest shards that have been found bear a striking resemblance to contemporaneous Korean wares of the time and to previously made Karatsu pieces.

Korean potters had been active in the Kyushu area of Japan (directly across from the Korean peninsula) for some time. Many of them were involved in making old Karatsu, a pottery tradition highly influenced by Korean ceramics. With Hideyoshi's invasion of Korea at the end of the sixteenth century, many more Korean potters were brought to Kyushu. These new émigrés were educated in the most modern techniques of porcelain production. Once porcelaneous clay was discovered in the Arita area of Hizen Province on Kyushu (1616), porcelain production was ready to begin. In effect, the pottery kilns used for Karatsu were gradually transformed into kilns for blue and white porcelain.

By the mid-seventeenth century, Japanese blue and white porcelain showed the marked influence of Chinese wares. The simple Korean designs, consisting of sketchy floral designs, drawn from the Karatsu and Korean ceramic tradition, gave way to the more elaborate Chinese style, with landscapes, flora, and fauna predominating, along with conventional Chinese patterns. These were copies of Wanli (1573–1619) period, Transitional period, and Swatow porcelains. Wanli blue and whites were made at Ching-te-chen in China and were exported to Japan and Europe. These pieces typically had a Wanli border (fuyode in Japan): panels on the rim with alternating Chinese symbols and flowers with a central focus in the middle. Transitional period Chinese porcelain (1619–1644) was also very popular in Japan. Japanese Transitional imports were often made specially for the Japanese market. Designed to be used in the tea ceremony, they were roughly made in the Japanese taste; in Japan these porcelains are called ko-sometsuke. In the Chinese porcelains, male figures, floral motifs, and landscapes predominated. Swatow ware was characterized by thick walls and a thick crackled glaze. It was probably made in Fukien, China, and was shipped from the port of Swatow to Japan and Southeast Asia.

All of these styles dominated Japanese porcelain production. This was partly due to the popularity of Chinese wares in Japan, but the sudden impetus in the middle of the seventeenth century to produce massive numbers of Wanli and Transitional-style porcelains lay outside of Japan. By 1653, the civil war in China and the effective blockade by opposition forces prevented the importation of Chinese blue and white ceramics to Europe. The Dutch East India Company attempted to fill the gap by purchasing Japanese copies. It commissioned the Arita kilns to make blue and white porcelain in the Wanli and Transitional period styles. The company provided wooden models and other designs. Interestingly, some of these models incorporated European design elements, especially in terms of forms. The golden age of this trade was between 1663 and 1672. When Ching-te-chen resumed production under Emperor Kangxi in 1683, China once more became the favored source of blue and white porcelain, although Chinese merchants continued to transport Japanese blue and whites to Europe. (The Chinese bought great quantities of Arita ware for resale to European nations).

By the late seventeenth century, there was a decrease in trade and an increase in Japanese isolationism. Native Japanese design elements began to resurface in Arita porcelain, and by the eighteenth century, Japanese indigenous designs began to predominate: arabesques, botanical motifs, human figures, and other decorative elements taken from contemporary copybooks and costume designs.

Arita became the center of this early blue and white porcelain production and remains so today; thus the term Arita is used for these wares. The very earliest blue and white Arita wares that have survived are crudely made; they are often termed Old Imari or Shoki Imari, after the port from which they were shipped, or Early Hizen, after the province in which they were made. Rims have a deep orange tint. The glaze has a strong greenish tinge and blemishes are common. Sand often adheres to the footrim, because they were fired on sand. They do not have spur marks. The most common decoration is sketchy foliage, in the Korean manner. Examples of these are scarce and exist mainly in Japan.

Seventeenth-century Chinese-influenced Arita wares, which exist in some numbers in the West due to the heavy export in the seventeenth century, show a perceptible difference from their Chinese counterparts. First of all, although the Arita pieces were copied from Chinese models, close examination often reveals stylistic differences in particular motifs. When the Japanese potters worked from a Dutch wooden model (perhaps painted by a Delft potter) rather than the Chinese original, the figures show a strange awkwardness and a European influence. Even when a Chinese original appears to have been used, however, particular flower motifs are more elongated or abstracted in the Japanese versions. Except in the finest late seventeenth and early eighteenth century pieces, Arita potters did not seem to mix their clay very well, which produced a body with a greyish or bluish cast. The iron in the clay also was a factor in this bluish cast. The potters had less control of the cobalt blue used for decoration, often producing a darker blue, or even violet, pigment. The painting itself is much more fuzzy—again a difference attributable to the surface itself.

It is important to note that the Japanese and Chinese glazes differed. The Japanese glaze was distinguished by small irregularities; many small pinholes are visible in good light. In addition, the edges of pieces were thicker and more rounded than their Chinese counterparts. The footrims differed as well. Japanese porcelains usually had a square-cut rim (rather than beveled), and until the mid-nineteenth century, spur marks exist on most pieces of more than moderate size. The body showed the effects of being thrown or press molded. Cast molds were not used until the nineteenth century.

As the styles diverged in the eighteenth century, the Japanese potters become more inventive, and one sees striking Japanese forms of animals, courtiers, and asymmetrical abstractions. Output increased in the nineteenth century with the advent of mass production. Technical brilliance became the standard, but spontaneity was lost with an overemphasis on form and formalizing. For the first time, porcelains had the potter's signatures or marks indicating the locality or kiln from which they came.

References: John Ayers, Oliver Impey, and J. V. G. Mallet, *Porcelain for Palaces*, Oriental Ceramic Society, 1990; Hazel H. Gorham, *Japanese and Oriental Ceramics*, Charles E. Tuttle Co., Inc., 1971; Soame Jenyns, *Japanese Porcelain*, Faber and Faber, 1979; Tsugio Mikami, *The Art of Japanese Ceramics*, Weatherhill/Heibonsha, 1972; Maria Penkala, *A Survey of Japanese Ceramics*, Interbook International B.V., 1980; P. L. W. Arts, *Japanese Porcelain*, Lochem-Poperinge, 1983; William Tilley and Peter Bufton, "Japanese Blue and White Porcelain," *Arts of Asia*, March to April 1984.

Museums: Los Angeles County Museum of Art, Los Angeles, California; Center of Asian Art and Culture, Avery Brundage Collection, M. H. de Young Memorial Museum, San Francisco, California; Honolulu Academy of Arts, Honolulu, Hawaii; Art Institute of Chicago, Chicago, Illinois; Nelson Gallery-Atkins Museum, Kansas City, Kansas; Baltimore Museum of Art, Baltimore, Maryland; Museum of Fine Arts, Boston, Massachusetts; University of Michigan Museum of Art, Ann Arbor, Michigan; Detroit Institute of Arts, Detroit, Michigan; City Art Museum of St. Louis, St. Louis, Missouri; Brooklyn Museum, Brooklyn, New York; Metropolitan Museum of Art, New York, New York; Cleveland Museum of Art, Cleveland, Ohio; Philadelphia Museum of Art, Philadelphia, Pennsylvania; Eugene Fuller Memorial Collection, Seattle Art Museum, Seattle, Washington; Royal Ontario Museum, Toronto, Canada; Fitzwilliam Museum Cambridge, England; British Museum, London, England; Victoria and Albert Museum, London, England; Ashmolean Museum, Oxford, England; Burghley House Collection, Stamford, England; Porzellansammlung, Dresden, Germany; Kyushu Ceramic Museum, Arita, Japan; Kakiemon Museum, Ashikaga, Japan; Kurita Museum, Ashikaga, Japan; Saga Prefectural Museum, Saga, Japan; Idemitsu Museum of Art, Tokyo, Japan; Rijkmuseum, Amsterdam, the Netherlands; Groningen Museum, Groningen, the Netherlands.

The best source for information about temporary exhibitions is probably the "Calendar of Exhibitions and Seminars" in *Orientations*, a periodical put out in Hong Kong but widely available in the United States, which lists Asian art exhibits around the world on a monthly basis.

Reproduction Alert: You do not want to buy a reproduction unknowingly or even a late emulation that can unintentionally fool. The paste and painting, the motifs and style can be quite good on these. Look for a lack of spontaneity in the composition and an hardness in the drawing.

Above all, look at the foot. Does it look like it has never been set down? Is the surface of the piece without the slightest scratch in the glaze? Even a fifty-year-old piece should show some wear. Often a brown discoloration has been added to the base and sometimes the body to disguise its freshness. This stain does not wash off with soap and water, but it can be cleaned off with paint remover. After the eye becomes accustomed to this particular hue, it is a good indicator of a reproduction.

Collecting Hints: Since the early 1970s, there has been an increasing enthusiasm for early and interesting Arita blue and whites, among Japanese, European, and American buyers. Prices, on the whole, however, are moderate when compared with their Korean and Chinese counterparts and even many twentieth-century Japanese porcelains. The most expensive Arita blue and whites, not unexpectedly, tend to be rare examples of late seventeenth-century or eighteenth-century wares. Prices for these run into thousands of dollars. Nineteenth-century Arita ware, in contrast, is very affordable. Since there are so few collectors that understand and thus collect Arita, it is undervalued.

In forming a collection of Arita several questions have to be kept in mind: How much discretionary income is available for your collection? How large a collection do you desire? How quickly do you want to put your collection together? If you want rare examples of seventeenth-century blue and white Arita, you will amass a small but important collection; however, it will take some time and/or a large sum of money. Since seventeenth-century and eighteenth-century Arita ware is still relatively rare in this country, forming a collection will probably necessitate trips to Europe or paying a dealer to buy overseas for you. If on the other hand, the amount you wish to spend is less and you would rather do your hunting nearer home, you would be well advised to buy good examples of nineteenth-century Arita. If you prefer a smaller collection, you can limit your purchases in some manner (by era, form, artist, motif, and so forth), or if you want an encompassing collection, you will find all sorts of interesting examples.

If you are a beginning collector and if you do not feel you are yet able to judge the quality of pieces, you would be wise to buy from a knowledgeable dealer who will guarantee the authenticity of the pieces you are buying in writing and over time. Knowledgeable and reliable dealers have usually done considerable research on their pieces and will have no difficulty in giving you a meaningful guarantee. They will also give you a hands-on education, and once they see you are serious about collecting, they will be on the lookout for pieces for you. You don't always have to pay a premium for buying from the knowledgeable specialist, but even if you do, it's well worth it. The money you will save in avoiding buying spurious or mediocre pieces will buy the piece of your dreams.

Whoever you buy from, but particularly if you are making your purchase based on your own expertise, you want to do as much reading as possible and you should visit fine museums that house good collections of blue and white Arita ware. In judging a potential purchase, keep what you have learned clearly in mind. Consider the following questions. Is the piece offered really Arita in contrast to an Arita look alike, for example, a Chinese Kangxi blue and white? This book and other books indicate telltale differences. In general, you need to look at spur marks; the type of foot, the quality of the glaze, clay, potting, and underglaze cobalt and painting; motifs; and stylistic elements, marks, and forms. Pay particular attention to the exposed paste on the base.

Is the piece actually from the period you desire or it is purported to be from? Again, you must examine the piece carefully looking for telltale signs. Keep the above criteria in mind. Take the piece on approval, if you have to, and examine it with the books in front of you.

Further questions include the following. Is the piece of the quality you desire? Is the body pure white? Is the cobalt vivid? Does the painting excel? Is the piece in good condition? Has it been repaired? Is there a chip? Is there a glaze imperfection? Is the piece rare? The size and form, certain symbols and motifs, or a particular signature can make a piece rarer and more valuable. Is the piece a reproduction or a very late emulation?

Advisors: Stewart and Barbara Hilbert

Apothecary bottle, blue and white, 8½", birds among peony and pomegranates, the base with a medallion containing the letters IC, circa 1665-1685 . . . . **24,000.00**
Bottle, 7½" h., 19th century, with pale grey glaze, inscribed in underglaze blue ISTE SOORT, JAPANSCH ZOYA **975.00**
Bowl
    Namban bowl, 10" dia., Edo period, 19th century, set on a high ring foot molded in the well with a

Bottle, 8⅞″ h., circa 1665-1685, apothecary, broad oviform shape with a wide band of birds among tree peony and pomegranates, the base with a medallion containing the letters IC. $23,254.00. Courtesy of Christie's, London.

herd of horses covered in a celadon glaze surrounding a gourd form panel of cherry trees in underglaze blue, the exterior painted in underglaze blue with figures of foreigners and panels of foreign ships above waves, underglaze blue Fuku mark. **2,640.00**

Blue and white, 14½″ dia., early 19th century, the interior with two panels obtruding onto a ground of flowers and foliage with depictions of seashore landscapes with rocky islets, the rim with roundels of the swastika pattern, the exterior with scrolling foliage and flowerheads, Fuku mark **4,350.00**

17½″, 19th century, underglazed blue garden landscape with peony among rocks, the base with a six character apocryphal Chinese reign mark, kiln flaws and wear   **750.00**

Brushpot

Blue and white

5⅞″ h., late 17th century, cylindrical, carp ascending a waterfall   **550.00**

6″ h., late 19th century, cylindrical, bamboo design **125.00**

Censer, 9″, Meiji, tripod ovoid form on three cylindrical supports, keyfret handles, high domed lid, underglaze blue shishi and peony, seal-form Fuku mark, restoration to handle . . .   **900.00**

Charger

16½″, 19th century, underglaze blue carp amid water weeds, signed Kameyama-sei, crack, rim frits, surface wear **1,300.00**

18″, early 19th century, blue and white, peonies among rockwork   **2,204.00**

21¾″, late 17th century, decorated in deep underglaze blue with a pair of ho-o birds beside pomegranates, within a band of stylized peonies **45,540.00**

Dish

5″, early 18th C., in Dutch Delft style, molded form raised on three conical feet, underglaze blue decoration with Chinese figures on a bridge **2,050.00**

6″, late 17th/early 18th century, deep rounded form with petal-lobed rim, underglaze blue ho-o bird on a blue wash ground, running Fuku mark. **1,250.00**

8¼″, late 17th/early 18th century, after a Dutch Delft original, simply painted in underglaze blue with buildings in a landscape, the base with biscuit ring and three spur marks, without a foot rim **3,650.00**

10¾″, Meiji period, of irregular shape, decorated in underglaze blue with a mountain landscape, seals in iron-red and gilding, marked Dai Nihon, Bunsei nen sei   **475.00**

Serving dish, 12½″ w., late 19th century, decorated with a center panel in the Chinese manner with a boy dancing before a lady, the border with butterflies interspersed among flowers and foliage and brocade designs, the reverse with an underglaze blue bird **1,300.00**

Blue and white

8″, 18th century, center with prancing kylin surrounded by a border of geometric pattern, the reverse with a pattern of stylized flowerheads **600.00**

Charger, 18⅛″, Meiji period, showing a large carp emerging from crested waves ascending a waterfall, surface wear, spur marks. $550.00. Courtesy of Butterfield and Butterfield.

Charger, 18⅞″, Meiji period, shade of underglaze blue with occasional underglaze green accents, bird in a prunus tree with surrounding flowers, surface wear, rough foot, spur marks. $250.00. Courtesy of Butterfield and Butterfield.

8½″, late 17th century, Kraak-style, the center with branches of pomegranates surrounded by alternate panels of Buddhist emblems and stylized flower-heads and foliage linked by narrower panels of single flower-heads **550.00**

14″, late 17th century, Kraak-style, central roundel of flower sprays, surrounded by panels of flower sprays and bamboo **2,750.00**

15″, 2nd half of 17th century, of shallow form with wide everted rim, sketchily painted in pale underglaze blue with pomegranates and peonies with

Dish, 15½″ dia., late 17th century, decorated in underglaze blue with the central monogram VOC surrounded by a ho-o birds, camellias, and pomegranates, the rim with panels of bamboo and peony. $27,985.00. Courtesy of Sotheby's, London.

panels of Buddhist objects and flowers **325.00**

18½″, 18/19 century, decorated in Kakiemon style with a fan and lobed-shaped panel alternately depicting Fukurokuju astride a flying crane above mountains, pine trees and a rocky lakeside landscape, surrounded by as geometric design, cursive Fuku mark **7,250.00**

V. O. C. dish, 8½″, late 17th century, rounded form, underglaze blue V. O. C. insignia bordered by sprays of pomegranates and persimmon, the base with a second V. O. C., small rim chip ... **15,485.00**

Dishes

5″, pair, 18th century, octagonal, underglaze blue with Kinko seated on a carp, reverse with landscape, Chinese Chenghua mark **902.00**

6″, set of five, 19th century, square shape, interior with underglaze blue dragon among scrolling clouds, the base with a six character inscription **1,000.00**

8″ dia., pair, 18th century, blue and white, shallow form, design of the Hall of One Hundred Boys **1,900.00**

Ewer

10″, mid-17th century, ovoid form with underglaze blue figures in a landscape, hairline crack **1,320.00**

10½″, circa 1680, blue and white, decorated with a continuous and of figures among rocky outcrops, the loop handle with a dash and dot design **2,021.00**

Figure, Bijin, 6″ h., 18th century, standing holding the hem of the kimono, painted in underglaze blue, her robes with pine needles **1,050.00**

Garniture set, blue and white, 24½″ h., late 17th century, comprising 3 jars and covers and 2 trumpet shaped vases, decorated with a ho-o bird hovering above the rockwork, another perched among peonies and chrysanthemums, the shoulders with a band of lappets alternately containing hares among grasses, the domed covers with a large knop finial, the trumpet vases similarly decorated, some restoration **24,400.00**

Jardiniere, 14½″, late 17th century, everted rim, underglaze blue dragon amid clouds, restored chip **3,762.00**

Kendi, 8″, late 17 C.,, globular form, underglaze blue panels of figures and birds, frits on spout **2,049.00**

Plaque, rectangular, $8\frac{3}{4}''$ x $7\frac{1}{2}''$, Meiji/
Taisho period, decorated in various
colored enamels and gilt with a
panel depicting Kato Kiyomasa
fighting a huge bird, slight rubbing ... **260.00**

Plate
$8\frac{1}{2}''$, early 19th century, foliate
edged, decorated in shades of underglaze blue with a central floral
medallion surrounded by four
panels, two depicting "Dutchmen" standing against a diaper
pattern ground and separated by a
scene of frolicking karako and a
panel of leafy scrolls, signed
Sentoku nensei **1,200.00**
10'', 19th century, underglaze blue
rockwork and a peony blossom, a
floral scrolling border, foliate
edge **250.00**
10'', 19th century, underglaze blue
rockwork and a peony blossom, a
floral scrolling border, foliate
edge **250.00**
Ship's tureen and cover, $11\frac{1}{2}''$, late
17th century, the bowl with an
everted spill rim decorated with peony sprays and foliage in underglaze
blue beneath a band of foliage lappets, the domed cover with birds
among branches of plum blossoms
in a vase beneath a large pierced
tear-shaped knob **6,050.00**
Shoki-Imari, early Arita
Shallow dish
6'', circa 1650, decorated in underglaze blue, the center depicting a waterfall in a forested
mountain landscape, the rim
with a band of lappets **10,350.00**
$6\frac{1}{2}''$, circa 1650, decorated in underglaze blue with an iris spray
with a band of hatch design to
the rim, slight hairline **3,800.00**
8'', 17th century, shallow dish on
a recessed ring foot decorated
in underglaze blue with a spray
of flowering camellias with butterflies flying beside, rim chips,
fitted wood box **3,080.00**
Tankard, $8\frac{3}{4}''$, late 17th century, finely
painted in underglaze blue with
panels of figures and birds in a landscape, reserved on karakusa, handle
repaired **850.00**
Teabowl, 3'', early 18th century, underglaze blue figures punting on a
canal, blue washed rim, four character Ming mark **600.00**
Tokuri, $8\frac{1}{2}''$, 19th century, cylindrical
form, underglaze blue bird on a
pine, iron-red seal mark, firing
cracks, rim chip, one body crack ... **683.00**

**Tankard, late 17th century, dated 1698,
baluster form, the silver-mount inset with
a single taler of Ernst Brauschweig-Lune-
burg. $7,475.00. Courtesy of Christie's,
London.**

Tray, rectangular, 12'', 19th century,
decorated with a crane in flight
above and below a minogame
swimming above stylized waves,
restoration to corner **400.00**
Vase
10'' h., late 17th century, oviform
decorated with fishing boats
among rocks near a fishing village, the neck with a band of geometric design, firing crack to base **3,100.00**
10'', late 17th century, bottle form in
the form of a bamboo tea whisk,
underglaze blue birds and peonies **25,047.00**
$18\frac{1}{2}''$, beaker form, late 17th/early
18th century, of tall cylindrical
form with flared foot and rim, decorated in underglaze blue with a

**Vase, $23\frac{1}{2}''$ h., late 17th/early 18th cen-
tury, ovoid form with a cylindrical neck,
decorated in underglaze blue with ho-o
birds among peonies. $1,615.00. Cour-
tesy of Sotheby's, London.**

continuous band of mountainous landscape above a glade, a band of stylized leaf design towards the foot **11,650.00**
24½", with cover, late 17th century, octagonal form, underglaze blue 3 figure set in a garden, the cover with a domed form and a molded knop, cover repaired, neck with a small chip **56,925.00**
31", Meiji, baluster vase, elongated ovoid body, with fan-shaped reserves of floral sprays and butterflies **600.00**

BANKO WARE

History: The Paris exhibition of 1878 brought the West's attention to a uniquely styled and executed ware produced in Japan which was introduced under the name Banko. The name was taken by the potter Mori Yusetsu. He bought the *Banko* and *Fuyeki* seals and formulas from the grandson of Numanomi Goyzayemon (the original Banko who also worked under the name Fuyeki). Yusetsu, using the *Banko* seal, founded a factory at Kuwana in the province of Ise in 1850. His brother Yohei, using the *Fuyeki* seal, also started production of Banko wares.

The Banko factory ware that was exported to the West by Yusetsu and Yohei used hand-modeled or molded natural clays (created by the formulas of Goyzayemon) to form both utilitarian and decorative objects. Multiple molds were used and combined to create novelties. Natural clay colors were generally used as a background for other decorative techniques that included applied slip, applied molds, relief molding, hand painting, enameling, and occasional glazing. Incised or impressed decoration could be used alone or in conjunction with the other techniques.

Banko wares also employed another technique: a marbleized tapestry or Millefleur appearance was achieved by combining different colored clays. These multicolored clays were rolled very thinly. The kiln-fired finished product had a delicate translucency when held to the light.

The wares of the original Banko are unknown in the West. It is the later Banko wares made by the Yusetsu brothers, and others that followed their style, that have gained acclaim and are collected in our country. The Banko factories are still in production.

References: Sandra Andacut, "Will the Real Banko Stand Up" *The Orientalia Journal, Annual of Articles on Oriental Antiques and Collectibles,* Vol. 1, 1981; Hazel H. Gorham, *Japanese and Oriental Ceramics,* Charles E. Tuttle Co., Inc.,

1971; Irene Stitt, *Japanese Ceramics of the Last 100 years,* Crown Publishers, 1974.

Museums: Metropolitan Museum of Art, New York, New York; Victoria and Albert Museum, London.

Reproduction Alert: Wares using the known *Banko* seals continued to be made during the Nippon period until after World War II. Small brown stoneware teapots are still being made at the Banko factory.

Collecting Hints: Original Banko ware produced by Goyzayemon is rarely found outside Japan. His wares did not resemble what is currently known as Banko ware at antiques shows. Goyzayemon, in his capacity as official potter to the shogun, produced wares influenced by the Chinese and Raku ware used for the tea ceremony. His original and innovative use of natural colored clays of beige, brown, yellow, white, and marbleized combinations are now called ko Yaki to distinguish it from the later Banko ware produced by the Yesetsus and later potters of the Meiji period.

Some of the most collectable later Banko wares are miniature teapots, which are available in a large variety of shapes and sizes. They are often found in animal figure form. The animals portrayed may be inspired by reality or taken from mythology.

Entire tea sets were also frequently produced using marbleized clay (Mokume Yaki). It would be difficult to find an entire set intact. Creamers, sugar bowls, teapots, and cups and saucers can be collected separately to accumulate a set.

Box and lid, 1¾" h., grey clay, three heavily enamelled flowers on lid . . .   **95.00**
Creamer
    1¼" h., dark brown clay, modelled as lily leaf with a dark brown oil resist glaze, signed **100.00**
    2¼", blue clay, with blue and green marbleized millefleur design, applied coil handle, signed **100.00**
    3½", blue and green marbleized design **85.00**
    5" h., marbled clay **95.00**
Cup and Saucer (handled cup)
    1¾" cup, 3½" dia. saucer, thin, translucent marbleized clay, with enamelled gold flowers on fluted cup **115.00**
    1¼" cup, 3½" dia., saucer, thin translucent marbleized clay **95.00**
Cup and saucer (handless cup), 3¼", marbleized patchwork design on blown out quilted cup, signed **100.00**
Pitcher, 7", grey clay, formed in vase shape with long neck forming the spout, the handle in the form of a tree branch ending on the body with

Humidor, Figural 7", grey clay, the top formed as the elongated head of the god of knowledge, the body depicting the faces of the Seven Immortals, all enameled in bright colors. $450.00. Courtesy of Wayne Williamson.

Teapot, Figural 8" l., 20th century, in the form of a badger, the animal's nose forming the pouring spout, painted in enamel floral design. $125.00. Courtesy of Wayne Williamson.

hand painted leaves of yellow, white
and pink 225.00
Teapot and lid
2½" h., fluted sides, brown clay, enamelled flowers, wicker handle   100.00
3¼" h., grey clay, heavily enamelled
flying crane decoration, applied
clay roping, wicker handle,
signed 250.00
3¼" h., beige clay, hand potted with
modelled side pouring handle,
flying crane design, signed 250.00
3¾" h., beige clay, fluted body, applied roping, design of walking
crane in flower garden, wicker
handle missing, signed 250.00
3¾" h., dull white clay, fluted body,
modelled side pouring handle,
enamelled all over with a bird in a
garden scene, gold highlights,
signed 250.00
4" h., blue tapestry design, tree
branch knop on lid, heavy slip
flowers and birds painted in bright
enamels, wicker handle 185.00
Teapot (figural)
6" h., 19th century, shaped like
Mount Fuji, the white en-
amelled peak forming the lid   195.00
6" h. x 7" l., grey clay, shaped as
elephant with rider as finial on
lid, the rider and blanket saddle
decorated in bright enamels,
the lifted trunk forming the
spout, rattan handle missing . . .   450.00
6¼" h., form of cat, with orange
band and gold bell around neck
above which the face forms the
lid of pot, the raised paw forms
the spout and the tail circles to

form a handle, decorated with
enamel flowers on the body . . .   475.00
Vase
5" h., beige clay, narrow neck
with bulbous body, enamelled
flying cranes on body 120.00
Pair, 5½" h., beige clay, pear
shaped, enamelled butterflies   75.00
6½" h., gourd shaped, decorated
in floral enamels 375.00
Wall Pocket, grey clay, shape of a lotus
blossom with a applied in relief frog
chasing hand painted and en-
amelled flying insects, signed 475.00

BASKETS

History: Basketry has existed in Japan in one form or another since the Jomon Period (prior to 200 B.C.). Earliest baskets were of a utilitarian type and were used to store grains, carry farm produce, act as sieves, and so forth. These utilitarian baskets are still made today. Later, baskets were woven in box-shaped form and used to store clothing, papers, and personal articles. Bamboo is the principle component, but wisteria, rattan, vines, and tree roots are also used. Collectors are mainly concerned with the ikebana, or flower-arranging basket.

There were three distinct influences on Japanese basket making. In the fifteenth century in Kyoto, the imperial capital, the educated class, or literati, began to import various arts and crafts from China. Scrolls, ceramics, art objects, and baskets were considered de rigueur for cultured people to have in their homes. Chinese baskets are symmetrical, finely woven, elaborate, and elegant items. They have fine knots and many details. They usually have a handle. In time, Japanese basket makers in the Kyoto area began to copy the Chinese examples. A certain Japanese feeling and taste crept in, but they retained the fine detail and workmanship of the Chinese originals. Many of the finest examples of this formal, elegant style come from the Kyoto area today.

A second influence appeared in the sixteenth century with the development of the tea ceremony. The principal influence on the tea ceremony was Zen Buddhism and its philosophy of simplicity of purism. Aesthetically, it emphasized a refined poverty. The early tea master Sen no Rikyu incorporated simple flower arrangments into the tea ceremony. A more natural and simple container than the Chinese examples was sought to display flowers in the tokonoma, or alcove. "Found" objects, natural materials, and baskets borrowed from the humble peasant were used. For instance, a fishing creel, or winnow, was considered to be very charming with a single flower or two placed in it. This simple, natural influence on basket making produced baskets in the true Japanese aesthetic. Asymmetry, vacant spaces, and understated refinement are the characteristics of the basket for the tea ceremony. The quiet beauty of these Zen-influenced baskets complemented the natural beauty of the flowers. Quietness and harmony were preferred over ostentatiousness.

The third influence on basket making was the arts and crafts movement of the late nineteenth and early twentieth centuries. Many international exhibitions were held in Europe and the United States, and Japanese products were exhibited for the first time. The flow of ideas and the meeting of craftsmen from other cultures prompted an explosion of ideas. The basket became freer and more experimental and was regarded as an art rather than just a craft. Unusual materials and original shapes are characteristics of this period. Baskets were signed for the first time in the nineteenth century. Coincidentally, there was a tremendous surge in the popularity of the tea ceremony and flower arranging among the growing merchant class, and demand for baskets grew. The Meiji period (1868–1912) until World War II was one of the most prolific and creative periods in Japanese basketry.

References: Victor and Takako Hauge, *Folk Traditions in Japanese Art*, Kodansha, 1978; Toshiko M. McCallum, *Containing Beauty*, University of California at Los Angeles Museum of Cultural History, 1988; Patricia Salmon, *Japanese Antiques*, Art International Publishers, 1975; —, *Japanese Bamboo Baskets*, Kodansha, 1980.

Reproduction Alert: The Chinese have begun to reproduce Japanese ikebana baskets in recent years. These baskets are made for commercial reasons. They tend to be simply made using labor-saving styles rather than using complicated techniques. There is no attempt at creativity or refinement. They also lack the characteristic patina of an old basket.

Collecting Hints: There are several important points to look for when collecting baskets: (1) The overall shape and design should be pleasing. Unusual shapes are desirable. Many basket designs were repeated over and over so it is exciting to see an original and creative form. (2) The condition should be excellent. There are many fine examples available, so avoid baskets that are damaged. Check the bottom in particular for breakage or worm damage. (3) Good patina is also important. An extremely dirty basket can seldom be satisfactorily cleaned up and will not have the same warmth as one that has been well taken care of. (4) Look for fine work and pride of craftsmanship. Intricate wrapping, attention to detail, interesting combinations of stitches and weaves, and handles that are integrated into the overall design and not just stuck on the basket show planning. If a signature is present, it rarely will be on the bottom, and it indicates the maker's pride of workmanship. Incidentally, many wonderful baskets were never signed. Important names are Shokosai, Chikuhosai, Chikuyusai, Kochikusai, and Rokansai.

Advisor: Janet Lashbrook

14", double gourd shaped basket with branch base	**395.00**
18", double weave basket with tightly woven inner core covered by a hexagonal weave outer layer, handle finished nicely at the top with a knot	**450.00**
20", in form of a boat with natural wood prow and plaited rigging	**700.00**

15", fruit basket, rather low open shape, with reinforced bottom, well-finished rim, bamboo handle crosses over the basket and forms design on the front, good knotting in several places; signed Chikuhosai. $1,200.00

Kyoto Style, 18", with square handle, good knots, signed Kohosai. $1,200.00

Mingei style, 15", with tight and loose weaving, bamboo vines woven through body. $600.00

Kyoto style, 22" very elaborate knots and lacing on the sides, signed Chikushunsai **1,900.00**

23", tightly woven cylindrical shape, Branch handle interwoven with bamboo which continues drown the front of the basket forming a bamboo leaf design **500.00**

CORALENE

History: China and pottery items that have been decorated in the coralene manner are easily recognizable by the iridescence of a design that is made up of tiny glass beads. Japanese coralene on china and porcelain was made in Japan for exportation to the United States and the United Kingdom from the late 1890s to the post—World War

II era. Several American and English companies have also made glass coralene since the 1800s.

The coralene finish is achieved by firing small, colorless beads on either a glass, porcelain, or pottery body. The process was perfected and patented in 1909 by Alban L. Rock, an American citizen who lived in Yokohama, Japan.

The main components of the fusing substance were silicate of albument and flux, which was added to a dry porcelain color pigment and water for mixing. This mixture was applied to the predetermined design on the porcelain body in a wet state. The tiny, round, colorless, and transparent beads were placed on top of the fusing mixture which held them in place. Great care had to be taken so that the coating of beads was uniform in order to obtain a smooth finish. The decorated piece was then fired in the usual manner so that the beads were permanently fixed to the body.

Backstamps frequently found on Japanese coralene include United States Patent number 912-171, dated February 9, 1909, with the word *Japan*. The patent number 16137 is a British Patent Office registration number. Some pieces are marked "Patent applied for number 382-57" or "Patent Pending," with or without the word *Japan*. The word *Kinran* can also be found accompanied by Japanese characters and sometimes with the patent number. These marks are usually green or magenta in color.

There are known to be a few pieces of coralene which are marked "RC Nippon," accompanied by a mark similar to the rising sun mark. These pieces are decorated in the same manner as the Japanese coralene but lack the plushness of color and iridescence found on Japanese coralene pieces. The shapes of the body are simple and without trim.

Sometimes Nippon porcelain blanks were used for coralene decorating. The background finish on most of these pieces is typically a matte glaze with soft shading of color. There are some found occasionally with high-glaze backgrounds.

References: Kathy Wojciechowski, *The Wonderful World of Nippon Porcelain*, Schiffer Publications, 1991; Joan Van Patten, *The Collector's Encyclopedia of Nippon Porcelain*, Series 1, 2, 3, Collector's Books, 1986.

Reproduction Alert: There is a small quantity of reproductions on the market that are executed on old glass bases. The beaded decoration on new coralene has been glued on and not refired. As a result, the glass beads can be easily scratched off.

Advisor: Kathy Wojciechowski

Biscuit Jar

6" h., Blue beading on a matte finish, outlined in gold, sterling silver lid and bail **535.00**

6" h., blue background, gold foliage, silver plate rim and handle **475.00**

Bowl, 8" dia., circa 1910, purple plums and green leaves on a blue background, patent mark 250.00

Box

1½" x 2" x 3", lavender, pink and green thistle design on a copper matte background, marked Kinran Patent #16132 Japan 145.00

5" h., yellow and pink flowers and light green foliage on a pale blue background 100.00

Ewer, 5" h., pale pink and green fruit on a green background outlined in gold 295.00

Ferner, footed, 7" w., dogwood pattern in shades of yellow on a shaded brown to yellow background, with gold beading 245.00

Pitcher

4½" h., beaded yellow daffodils on a red and brown background, 1909 patent mark 325.00

4½" h., pink red and yellow flowers, outlined in gold on cobalt background and trim, gold handle, 1912 patent mark 345.00

Plate

7¾" dia., orange to rust poppies on a shaded green to pink background, gold beaded rim, patent mark . . . 110.00

10½" dia., yellow and blue butterflies on a shaded yellow to green background, blue flowers. 325.00

Rose bowl, 5" dia., melon ribbed and footed, dark turquoise to lavender irises 135.00

Sugar shaker, 5" h., orange seaweed design on white background, silver plated original lid, Patent applied for mark 195.00

Sweetmeat jar, 5", seaweed pattern in shades of coral 245.00

Vase

4½" h., tiny blue morning glories on a tan background, patent mark . . . 210.00

5" h., fat and round shape, hand painted roses and lavender with pink coralene roses on a shaded lavender to pink backgound. 225.00

5" h., coralene rose and foliage front and back on a shaded brown to rust background, gold beaded fluted rim and handle 225.00

6½" h., large blue and pink flowers rising out of foliage on a burnished gold background, gold beaded trim, marked 100.00

6½" h., daisy and leaf design on a shaded green to brown background, gold handles, Kinran patent #16132 Japan 450.00

8" h., dogwood design, gold bead-

Vases, Pair, large open flowers, buds and leaves in shades of pink blue and yellow on a bright cobalt background, Patent applied for mark. $550.00

ing on brown shaded background, loop handles, patent applied for Japan mark 425.00

8½" h., yellow dragonflies on a green background 295.00

8½" h., yellow floral with beading, raised gold and cobalt blue trim on a green background, patent mark 450.00

8½" h., bulbous shape with scalloped and fluted rim, multicolored snapdragons on a shaded light blue to lavender background 275.00

11" h., large yellow flowers with long tan stems and foliage on a tan to brown background, Kinran mark 625.00

HIRADO PORCELAIN

History: Hirado is the name of a Japanese porcelain produced at Mikawachi near Arita, and for much of its history made under the patronage of the lords of Hirado. It consists of a very pure, high-quality white porcelain, usually decorated in cobalt blue under the glaze, sometimes in combination with dark brown, blue, and/or black enamels.

Hirado wares became known to Europe in the eighteenth century when the kilns came under the institutionalized patronage of the lord of Hirado, but actually its history goes back further and is intertwined with the history of the first Arita products. As with Arita, the early ceramic tradition of the Hirado area starts with the importation of Korean potters. Foreign potters were brought in by an early lord of Hirado who founded a kiln in the village of Nanko in 1598, which then began producing a type of Karatsu ware. In the second quarter of the seventeenth century, porcelaneous clay was found near Mikawachi and several of the Nanko potters were moved to the village, which was six miles south of Arita. Thus Hirado porcelain production was begun.

Initially, the kiln was not very successful: utilitarian tea ceremony wares for the domestic market were made, and the Dutch showed little interest in importing that ware. In 1662, a porcelain stone of very good quality was found on Amakusa Island, in the Hirado domain. This stone displayed amazing qualities of plasticity: it produced porcelain of striking fineness and purity. Still, in 1751, the Hirado kilns were not competing well. When the kilns were all but failing, the Hirado daimyo (lord) took over the kilns completely, putting them under his family's official patronage.

Hirado porcelain became restricted to the Matsuura family, the lords of Hirado, and Hirado wares were commissioned for the use of the daimyo in his domain and for presentation gifts for other members of the Japanese aristocracy. The kilns remained under this patronage until 1843, producing what has often been called the best Japanese porcelain ever produced.

In 1830, with the decline of feudalism, the kilns were encouraged to go commercial. Overall quality declined, but the removal of restrictions on the potters also gave rise to a different kind of creative inspiration. At first both the Chinese and the wealthy Japanese provided the market for these pieces, but soon the kilns began to produce commercial wares for the Dutch market. Large quantities of white eggshell coffee sets, in particular, were exported. With the Meiji restoration (1868), commercial expansion was given an impetus, and for a time the Hirado kilns prospered. However, around the turn of the century, more modern production-line manufacturers proved to be too much competition for the Mikawachi/Hirado potters, and the business was taken over by the Fukugawa Porcelain Company.

Seventeenth-century Hirado ware is difficult to distinguish from early Arita. What was produced was a rough and undistinguished blue and white porcelain. In contrast, the eighteenth-century wares, especially under the patronage of the Matsuura family, were excellent.

The body was milk white, with a lustrous glaze which had a very fine-grained texture. The painting was done in miniature. Landscapes with figures, trees, and flowers were typical designs done in pencil-thin pale silvery blue—an odd number of boys at play being perhaps the most popular subject. Often the border of these dishes had a cord and tassel pattern on the rim. Typically, overglaze enamels were not used until late in the nineteenth century, though a blue, brown, and/or black glaze was sometimes used as a ground

color or to highlight the effect of relief carving, modeling, or the piercing that was also typical of Hirado ware. Most of the pieces were small and modest and related to the tea ceremony. None of these pieces had marks on the bases.

Traditionally styled Hirado continued to be made into the nineteenth century, but with the commercialization of the kilns and the end of aristocratic patronage, a whole new range of articles were produced. Larger, highly ornate vases and censors, with elaborate animal-head handles and pierced basket-weave interiors were created. The malleability of the Amakusa clay allowed intricate modeling, piercing, and deep carving—retaining the potter's details after firing. This experimentation explored the full potential of the clay. Animal and floral subjects became more common than landscapes. Animals and figures modeled in the round also became very popular, as were pitchers and teapots modeled as animals and humans.

Eggshell pieces were produced, often for the export market. They were usually unpainted. With all of this experimentation, Hirado even began producing red and green overglaze-decorated porcelain, Kutani-styled eggshell porcelain, and finally, a rice-grain porcelain (like that of China) in an attempt to gain more of a share of the market.

After 1843, potter and factory marks on the base often indicated the piece's origin. Some of these potters were quite distinguished, others were minor. Many commercialized pieces were produced in the nineteenth century, but so were some extraordinary works of art.

References: P. L. W. Arts, *Japanese Porcelain*, Lochem-Poperinge, 1983; C. Philip Cardeiro, *Japanese Hirado Porcelain*, Art Asia Museum, 1989; R. Cleveland, *200 Years of Japanese Porcelain*, St. Louis City Art Museum, 1970; Hazel H. Gorham, *Japanese and Oriental Ceramics*, Charles E. Tuttle Company, Co., Inc., 1971; Soame Jenyns, *Japanese Porcelain*, Faber and Faber, 1979; David King, "Hirado Porcelain: Its Dating," *Transactions of the Oriental Ceramic Society*, Vol. 45, 1982; Adalbert Klein, *Japanese Ceramics*, translated by Katherine Watson, Alpine Fine Arts Collection (U.K.) Ltd., 1987; Louis Lawrence, *Hirado Porcelain*, Tempus Antiques, Ltd., 1981; Tsugio Mikami, *The Art of Japanese Ceramics*, Weatherhill/Heibonsha, 1972; Maria Penkala, *A Survey of Japanese Ceramics*, Interbook International B.V., 1980; Laurence Smith, "Japanese Porcelain in the Early 19th Century," *International Symposium on Japanese Ceramics (Seattle Art Museum)*, 1972.

Museums: Los Angeles County Museum of Art, Los Angeles, California; Center of Asian Art and Culture, Avery Brundage Collection, M. H. de Young Memorial Museum, San Francisco, California; Honolulu Academy of Arts, Honolulu, Hawaii; Art Institute of Chicago, Chicago, Illinois; Nelson Gallery-Atkins Museum, Kansas City, Kansas; Baltimore Museum of Art, Baltimore, Maryland; Museum of Fine Arts, Boston, Massachusetts; University of Michigan Museum of Art, Ann Arbor, Michigan; Detroit Institute of Arts, Detroit, Michigan; City Art Museum of St. Louis, St. Louis, Missouri; Brooklyn Museum, Brooklyn, New York; Metropolitan Museum of Art, New York, New York; Cleveland Museum of Art, Cleveland, Ohio; Philadelphia Museum of Art, Philadelphia, Pennsylvania; Eugene Fuller Memorial Collection, Seattle Art Museum, Seattle, Washington; Royal Ontario Museum, Toronto, Canada; British Museum, London, England; Victoria and Albert Museum, London, England; Kyushu Ceramic Museum, Arita, Japan; Kakiemon Museum, Ashikaga, Japan; Idemitsu Museum of Art, Tokyo, Japan.

The best source for temporary exhibitions is probably the "Calendar of Exhibitions and Seminars" in *Orientations*, a periodical put out in Hong Kong but widely available in the United States, which lists Asian art exhibits around the world on a monthly basis.

Reproduction Alert: You do not want to buy a reproduction unknowingly or even a late emulation that can unintentionally fool. The paste and painting, the motifs and style can be quite good on these. Look for a lack of spontaneity in the composition and an awkwardness in the drawing. Above all, look at the foot. Does it look like it has never been set down? Is the surface of the piece without the slightest scratch in the glaze? Even a fifty-year-old piece should show some wear.

Collecting Hints: A Hirado porcelain collection makes a favorable statement about a collector's discernment and sophistication. Hirado is an exceptionally fine porcelain, clearly one of the best porcelains ever made in Japan, but it takes a certain sophistication to collect in a field that is still so relatively unknown in this country and Europe. It also takes a love of the hunt. Hirado ware is not plentiful in this country. Pre-nineteenth century examples are almost nonexistent. Remember, Hirado ware was not allowed out of the Hirado nobility's intimate circle until well into the nineteenth century. Although late-nineteenth century production was ample, it was relatively short lived. For every fine example of nineteenth-century Hirado, there are enumerable fine Chinese blue and white examples, but that is part of the enjoyment in putting together a fine Hirado collection.

If you are a beginner collector or if you do not feel you are yet qualified to judge the quality of pieces on your own, you would be wise to buy from a knowledgeable dealer who will guarantee, over time, the authenticity of the pieces you are buying in writing. Knowledgeable and reliable dealers have usually done considerable research on their pieces and will have no difficulty in giving you a meaningful guarantee. They will also give you a hands-on education, and once they see you are serious about collecting, they will be on the lookout for pieces for you. You don't always have to pay a premium for buying from the knowledgeable specialist, but even if you do, it's worth it. The money you will save in avoiding buying spurious or mediocre pieces might buy a museum-quality piece—the best of your collection.

Whomever you buy from, but particularly if you are making your purchase based on your own expertise, you want to do as much reading as possible and to visit fine museums housing collections of Hirado ware. In judging a potential purchase, keep what you have learned clearly in mind. Consider whether the piece offered is really Hirado. In general, you need to look at spur marks; the type of foot; the quality of the glaze, clay, potting, underglaze cobalt, and painting; the motifs; and the stylistic elements, marks, and forms. Pay particular attention to the exposed paste on the base. Is the piece of the period you desire or it is purported to be? Again, you must examine the piece carefully looking for telltale signs of period. Keep the above criteria in mind. Take the piece on approval, if you have to, and examine it with some good books on Japanese porcelains in front of you.

Other questions to ask yourself are the following. Is the piece of the quality you desire? Is the body pure white? Is the cobalt vivid? Does the painting excel? Is the piece in good condition? Has is been repaired? Is there a chip? Is there a glaze imperfection? Is the piece rare? Size, form, certain symbols and motifs, or a rare signature can make a piece rarer and more valuable. Is the piece a reproduction or a very late emulation?

Advisors: Stewart and Barbara Hilbert

Box and cover, $5\frac{1}{4}''$ l., late 19th century, modelled in the form of a peach, decorated with brown, blue and black enamels, the interior with numerous cranes in flight, the exterior with applied flowering twigs and leaves, wear on applied decoration **1,400.00**

Brushrest, 3″ l., 19th century, modeled as a lotus leaf with undulating edges and curving up to one side, the veined surface with two applied frogs, blue and white decoration . . . **350.00**

Brushwasher, $3\frac{5}{8}''$ l., 19th century, formed as an eggplant with an oval opening to the side of a figure of a small boy seated near the top stem, the figure and leaves painted in underglaze blue, minor restoration to figure **715.00**

Censer, 12″ h., 19th century, double-wall construction, a pierced dome-shaped lid surmounting a pair of re-

Bowl, 3" dia., 19th century, eggshell, decorated in underglaze blue with a continuous scene of Chinese boys playing under a fir tree, marked Mikawachi kiln. $900.00

Dishes, 6" dia., late 19th century, set of three, in the Nabeshima style of shallow rounded form on a raised foot, decorated in underglaze blue and polychrome enamels, the foot decorated with a band of Comb pattern. $1,800.00

ticulated lobes of graduated size alternating with a stylized chrysanthemum with everted petals, the first supported by a row of down turned leaves and applied with two pairs of peony scrolling handles, signed. . . .   975.00

Chopstick rests, pair, 3", circa 1900 modeled as small recumbent Chinese boys, decorated in underglaze blue 180.00

Dish

5¼" dia., melon-form, Meiji, shallow bowl of circular shape slightly pinched to either side and applied with low-relief scrolling leafy tendrils, painted with washes of underglaze blue and a large unglazed leaf serving as the base, signed 715.00

5½" dia., 19th century, square, lobed shape, decorated in Nabeshima style in underglaze blue with a Chinese style landscape, back, stylized spray of peonies, the foot with a "comb" design 1,237.00

8" dia., blue and white, Meiji, in the Nabeshima style of rounded form on a raised foot, painted with a clump of primula, the exterior with three groups of shippo, foot with band of "comb" pattern 575.00

8½" w., late 19th century, shallow dish, decorated in underglaze blue with chrysanthemums among swirling waters, the inverted edges with chrysanthemum flowerheads and foliage in applied relief, slight damage to the petals 950.00

Ewer

10½" h., Meiji period, bottle form with tall cylindrical neck fitted with a bud-form stopper, molded with a dragon painted in underglaze blue and similarly painted around the body with landscapes   2,640.00

10⅞" h., Meiji period, of globular form with cylindrical neck entwined with a dragon forming the handle and spout, the cover in the form of a tama, painted in underglaze blue with a landscape, one flame with a small chip 2,330.00

6½" h., 19th century, with cover, flattened globular form, S spout and strap handle with thumbpiece, underglaze blue figures in a garden, domed cover, inscribed box 10,246.00

Ewer, 10" h., Meiji period, a dragon forming the spout, painted in underglaze blue with figures under a fir tree. $1,800.00

Figure

Group of fighting shishi, 12'', Meiji, one shishi pinning the other to the ground, mane, tail, and other details picked out in underglaze blue, traces of gilding and black enamel, two ears restored, old firing cracks filled with blue enamel **3,415.00**

Horse, $9\frac{1}{4}$ ''', 19th century, recumbent, glazed white, nostrils flared **2,854.00**

Puppy, 6'' h., 19th century, white glazed, eyes picked out in black, recumbent, tailed curved around **950.00**

Tiger, $8\frac{1}{4}$'', Meiji period, standing with its tail raised and its head turned to the right, covered with a clear glaze **1,450.00**

Hahaike, $8\frac{1}{2}$'' h., late 19th century, modeled as a hawk perched on a gnarled branch, its feather details in underglaze blue and brown enamels, slight crazing to tail feathers **1,475.00**

Hibachi, 15'', 19th century, globular body decorated in underglaze blue with three-petal blossoms decorated with geometric designs, drilled **900.00**

Incense burner and cover, $7\frac{1}{2}$'' h., early Meiji, in the form of a human skull with serrated holes in the crown, pink tinge, the teeth glazed white, with wood box **3,400.00**

Jar

$8\frac{1}{8}$'' h., Meiji period, of squat ovoid form painted in shades of underglaze blue with a continuous scene of shishi frolicking under a fir tree with peonies and a stream in the background, bordered by a cross-hatched band and ovals depicting origame swans **3,225.00**

9'' h., with cover, Meiji, cylindrical form decorated in underglaze blue with crowds of boys pulling Hotei in a hand cart, the low cover with a reclining figure applied, finial added **2,275.00**

$9\frac{1}{2}$'' h., with cover, Meiji period, of rounded ovoid form, decorated in shades of blue under a thick green-tinged glaze with a continuous mountain landscape, the foreground with two small figures on a promontory watching boats sailing in the distance **1,975.00**

Koro

12'' h., with cover, Meiji period, the reticulated censor set on a till base of chrysanthemum buds and a smaller reticulated basin above a stylized lappet tripod base, the pierced cover surmounted by a

shishi, fitted with detachable porcelain bells and chain **2,200.00**

$13\frac{1}{4}$'' h., Meiji period, in the form of a brocade ball held aloft by three small boys and surmounted by a shishi, decorated in underglaze blue, base cracked, signed **1,075.00**

Lanterns, pair, 24'' h., Meiji, blue and white, three sections: a stepped hexagonal base supporting a tall cylindrical shaft with a central bulb, the top surmounted by a hexagonal light-well with pierced panels, below a high roof-shaped top with curving ridges, center drilled, electrified **1,045.00**

Pomander, 19th century, tripod feet, domed cover pierced, base with underglaze blue decoration of small boys **575.00**

Teapot

4'' h., globular body, late 19th century, white glazed, the lid with pale blue chrysanthemums and a single butterfly in relief, losses and restoration **350.00**

6'' h., late 19th century, underglaze blue decoration of painted flowers, peony flowers in relief on body and lid, minor restoration on some petals **875.00**

Tokuri

$5\frac{7}{8}$'' h., 18th century, tapering octagonal form with a short cylindrical neck, underglaze blue mountain landscape **5,266.00**

$6\frac{1}{2}$'' h., 19th century, of impressed triangular section, applied in relief and painted in underglaze blue with kiku reserved on pine trees **850.00**

Wine Ewer, $8\frac{1}{4}$'' h. x 9'' w., Edo period, decorated in underglaze blue with four distinct landscape scenes, the top with quatrefoil stylized decoration of ships at sea and birds in flight. $2,600.00

Vase

6" h., 19th C., flaring beaker form, the interior and exterior decorated with the branches of a blossoming tree, a bird flying nearby, ring foot   **780.00**

8¾" h., dated 1835, bottle form, rounded body with a long neck, painted in underglaze blue with a continuous scene of boys waving fans and chasing butterflies, the reverse with a square mon enclosing a triangle, the base signed Wakigawa ke den Tempo 6 Mikawachi sei. **13,090.00**

10½" h., 20th century, blue and white, in the shape of a bronze gu, the central knop painted with shishi playing among tama, the flared neck bearing a dragon and ho-o bird, the foot with peonies **2,200.00**

12⅛" h., Meiji period, bottle form, rounded body with a long slender neck, decorated in underglaze blue with a large ho-o bird hovering above a branch of paulownia, the mouth with a foliate border, impressed double gourd mark **3,400.00**

12¼" h., pair, 19th century, bottle form, each with a rounded body and long neck, slightly flared at the mouth, painted in underglaze blue with seven boys running around trying to catch butterflies beneath a spreading pine, the neck with a key border, one chipped at the mouth **9,535.00**

16¼" h., 19th century, in the shape of a bronze gu, the ribbed waisted form with flared rim and foot, two hexagonal handles, painted in underglaze blue with a flight of cranes above waves **3,150.00**

Vessel, in the form of mandarin duck, 9⅝" h., 19th century, the duck on a rocky outcrop beside a cylindrical container, painted with underglaze blue and brown details, firing cracks and chips **1,236.00**

Waterdropper, 3", late 19th century, squash-shaped with open fluted mouth, decorated in underglaze blue **275.00**

INRO

History: The literal translation of *inro* is "seal container." The earliest inros (late fifteenth century) were standing boxes that were part of the furniture of a Japanese room. During the Keicho era (1596–1614) the portable inro came into use.

As we know them today, inros are mostly cylindrical containers, usually rectangular in shape, generally about 3" to 4" by 2" to 3" and about 1" deep. Inros are divided into a series of boxes, each fitting snugly into the other in layers. These boxes are referred to as cases. There are inros that consist of one case and a lid, and some can have as many as seven cases. The usual number is four or five. They are held together by a cord running down the sides and across the bottom. The cord can run down through tubes along the sides or through channels inside the case. The cord and the case are worn suspended from the sash (obi) of the kimono.

Inros were used to carry seals and seal paste in early times and later for various powders and herbs used as medicines. The Japanese were very enthusiastic about carrying medicines with them. The tight-fitting sections kept materials fresh.

The Japanese kimono has no pockets and many types of "sagemonos" (hanging objects) were carried from the obi. A slide bead (ojime) is threaded on the cord which allows the inro to be held closed; the ojime is moved up to allow the inro cases to be opened. The end of the inro cord is attached to a netsuke (toggle) which is slipped behind and over the top of the obi to keep the inro from falling.

The earliest inros were probably red or black lacquer; many had inlays of mother-of-pearl and abalone shell. This method came from China, as did the use of the standing inro. The early inros in the Japanese style reflected the simple designs in the taste of the nobility and upper classes. In the late sixteenth and early seventeenth centuries, when inros were adopted by the merchants and townspeople, more elaborate and innovative designs were begun, and greater strength of design and decoration were accepted.

During the Tokugawa (Edo) Period (1615-1868) inro use spread to all segments of society, both in cities and provinces. They were displayed to attract attention and became more lavish and ornate. It became fashionable to collect them and special chests were made to hold them. Inros became an indication of the wearer's taste and affluence. They gradually lost their function and became primarily decorative.

It is not possible to assign a specific design or shape to any particular time during the less than 300 years that inros were produced. Many were made in round shapes, from a complete circle to a thick or slender ellipse. To find inros in square sections is a rarity. One of the earliest fashionable shapes in the eighteenth century was the tall, narrow cylinder with few deep cases. A few were made in squat horizontal shape. In the late Meiji Period, the preference was for flat shapes and large sizes. Very large ones were used by wrestlers and actors. A few had the boxes in a sheath or outer casing which had cutouts to show the design on the boxes.

Different shapes seemed to give impetus to the variety of design. In the early seventeenth century artists broke away from the Chinese style of inlay and carved lacquer and the style became ornate with finely executed techniques in powdered gold. Great displays of technical skill were produced, such as inlays in the Shibayama form in the nineteenth century. The inside of the sections also changed from the early red lacquer and plain gold to the nashiji finish. (See: Shibayama)

References: Raymond Bushell, *The Inro Handbook*, John Weatherhill, Inc., 1979; Melvin and M. C. Champoud, "A Few Notes on Inro," *Journal of the International Netsuke Collectors Society*, Vol. 2; Melvin and Betty Jahss, *Inro and Other Miniature Forms of Japanese Lacquer Art*, Charles Tuttle and Co., Inc., n.d.; 1981; Trudel Klefisch, "Inro," *Netsuke Kendyukai Study Journal*, Vol. 6; E. A. Wrangham and the Ashmolean Museum, Oxford, *An Exhibition of Japanese Inro*, 1972; Catalog of the Inro Museum of Takayama City, Takayama City, Japan, 1990.

Museums: Most museums in the United States do not have permanent exhibits of large numbers of inros. A few pieces will be found in the general exhibits of Japanese items. Special collections are occasionally exhibited in some of the larger museums such as Los Angeles County Museum of Art, Los Angeles, California; San Francisco Asian Art Museum, San Francisco; Newark Museum, Newark, New Jersey; Metropolitan Museum of Art, New York, New York; the Inro Museum, Takayama City, Japan.

Reproduction Alert: Very few fine inros are made today. The exquisite, time-consuming processes required do not conform to modern manufacturing philosophy. A number of versions, mostly from Hong Kong, have surfaced. Among these are inros made of amber (pressed or synthetic), ivory, bone, and wood. Technically, they are not very fine, and they should be very inexpensive.

Collecting Hints: Collectors should be aware that the condition of the inro has a great influence on its value. Lacquer, especially, is easily subject to cracking, rubbing, and chipping. It is important to check that the sections come apart without seizing or binding. Damage from old adhesive labels is a common difficulty. Wood or ivory inro are subject to cracking as a result of temperature and humidity variations. Pieces in pristine condition command extremely high prices. It is possible, however, to build a very fine collection economically, if the emphasis is on aesthetic quality rather than on perfect condition. Signatures can be verified in the books by Jahss and Bushell, but should not be a major factor.

Cleaning of inros (lacquer or ivory) should be done without the use of solvents. Dust should be removed with a sift brush or cloth. Only in severe cases, should one use a damp cloth (squeezed almost dry) and mild Ivory soap, which then must be wiped dry very quickly. Collectors are urged to store and exhibit inros in enclosed environments, away from radiator heat, sunlight, and the possibility of accidental breakage.

A very desirable state of affairs is one in which the ensemble of inros, ojimes, and netsukes are harmoniously chosen. The sizes of the pieces should look in proper proportion, and the theme or motifs should be related. Such an arrangement, called "en suite," is the ideal of many collectors and sometimes creates a large challenge. Since most inros became separated from the original combinations, the search for compatible components becomes difficult, but can be very rewarding.

Note: A glossary of descriptive lacquer terms used in the inro listings will be found in the sections on Japanese lacquer.

Advisors: Bernard and Irene Rosett

One case
    Inro and Ivory Netsuke, signed Hakukinsai/Shirokamesai 19th century, the one case inro with a fitted interior compartment and of convex lozenge shape, decorated to either side with a writhing dragon with inlaid eyes emerging from cloud scrolls, executed in shades of gold takamaki-e, hiramaki-e, iro-e togidashi on a kinji ground, together with an agate bead ojime and ivory netsuke of seven theatrical masks, including Okame, Hannya, Okina and others, signed Togyokusai **1,100.00**
    Unsigned, 4" x 3½", mid-19th century, made of tightly woven narrow strips of bamboo, lacquered

One case, 3", early 19th century, brown lacquer, deeply carved in wave design, en suite with bronze spherical ojime and ivory manju netsuke. $1,600.00

designs very worn, en suite with woven ojime and woven netsuke in the form of a double gourd **425.00**

Two case

Inscribed Sekiran, inro and netsuke, 2¼″ l., ebony, depicting a stag passing by a temple gate with a doe and fawn on the reverse resting near a stone lantern, all on a finely pitted ground with stag antler and copper-wire inlay ojime and ebony netsuke carved as a pavilion in a landscape setting with a couple walking on a bridge, ...   **375.00**

Signed Togi, 2¼″ 18th/19th century, decorated in iro-e aogai and stag horn with three fish swimming near water weeds and kelp, the eyes inlaid in horn and lacquer against a roiro ground, (chips to one runner), signed Togi with kakihan, stag antler vase-form ojime and inlaid ivory manju with butterflies and bugs, unsigned **1,050.00**

Unsigned, decorated with a crane in flight before a moon, above crested wave splashed rocks, in togidashi, kirikane and taka-makiye, on a roiro ground **700.00**

Unsigned, 19th century, fashioned as a leather tonkotsu (tobacco pouch) with the shaped front flap applied with a silver clasp featuring a recumbent tiger, the leather-like textured surface heightened with a dark brown lacquer, together with a nut-like textured bead ojime and a green-lacquered wood netsuke of a comic demonic mask **550.00**

Unsigned, 19th century, fashioned from a flattened length of bamboo decorated to the front with a large bear growling at a pair of crabs biting at its rear haunches, its paws resting on a rocky outcropping extending to the reverse and bordering a cascading stream, the design elements rendered in silver and gold hiramaki-e, together with an oval agate bead ojime and a wood netsuke carved as two chestnuts, stained and incised for effect. **1,000.00**

Three case

Signed with scratched characters Hokkyo Korin with seal, 2¼″, Late 17th/Early 18th century, bearing a fundame ground and decorated with a grasshopper on a flowering plant beneath a formalized fence,

Three case, 19th century, decorated with gold and silver takamaki-e, hiramaki-e, joined to a carved wood bark form netsuke. $770.00. Courtesy of Butterfield and Butterfield.

in colored takamakie, pewter and mother of pearl, the interior of kinji **650.00**

Signed Kanshosai, 3⅛″, Early 19th century, decorated on the roiro ground in gold and black takamakie and hiramakie, roiro interior with fundame risers, with a gold lacquer Manju decorated with a rake and Buddhist objects **575.00**

Signed Koju, 4″, 19th century, ivory, one side carved in high relief with Benten, Ebisu, Daikoku, Fukurokuju, bishamonten, and Kishijoten standing with their attributes, the reverse showing Hotei dragging his bag of goods, a young karako peering out of his bag all rendered in shishiabori technique, with ivory ojime of puppies and ivory manju carved with a young karako dancing in front of a bijin, the details inlaid in multicolored aogai, signed Gyokkosai Morimasa **950.00**

Signed inlaid cartouche reading Masamitsu/Shoko, late 19th century, Shibayama School, the front featuring a hanging flower basket issuing sprigs of flowering cherry, wisteria and peony, reversed by a rooster and hen walking amid blossoming chrysanthemum bushes below a butterfly, executed in incised mother-of-pearl, aogai, tortoise shell, and stained ivory, together with an ivory bead ojime inlaid with leafy cherry blossoms and an inlaid ivory manju netsuke featuring auspicious emblems **3,000.00**

Signed Ritsuo on a mother-of-pearl plaque, 4½″, 1½″, Late 19th century, applied on the gold hiramakie, kirigane and kinji ground with Ryujin, accompanied by his daughter Otohime who carries the tide jewel, walking upon turbulent waves before the castle of Ryugujo, which appears amid clouds above them, the reverse with three attendants, details in mother-of-pearl, coral, horn and colored ivory, the interior of nashiji, an Ivory Netsuke of a man standing looking into a large wooden tub, and a Good Ivory Ojime in the form of a Monkey, dressed in a short coat, seated with his arms and legs wrapped around the inro cord **8,000.00**

Unsigned, 19th century, flattened barrel form, roiro ground with tiger amid bamboo on front and reverse, inlaid in aogai and gold foil, brown lacquer interiors, faded and dulled **950.00**

Unsigned, 3″, circular, 18th century, tsuikoku, heavily carved with stylized scrolling flowers and a family crest, the edges with brocade design, runners slightly chipped, with coral bead ojime **1,700.00**

Unsigned, roiro lacquer on a red ground, carved with Komaku on his crane, the reverse with Chokwaro and his horse **400.00**

Four case

Inscribed Hokkyo Korin with seal, 3⅜″, 19th century, gold lacquer, bearing a fundame ground and decorated with formalized flowering plants and grasses in gold takamakie, pewter and aogai, the interior of kinji **1,000.00**

Signed Kajikawa with seal, 3″, 19th century, decorated in gold hiramakie, togidashi, and kirigane with willows and bridge, the reverse with cottages beside a lake, nahiji interiors, with ivory netsuke of a karako riding a hobby horse **1,200.00**

Signed Kajikawa saku, 3¼″, 19th century, kinji ground, decorated in gold, silver and colored takamakie with three horses on one and two on the reverse, very minor chips, en suite with gold lacquer ojime and lacquered wood netsuke of a horse **4,000.00**

Signed Kanshosai with kakihan, 3⅛″, 19th century, of four cases, decorated on the kinji and fundame

Four case, circa 1800, lacquer, black ground, inlaid silver dragon and gold and red low-relief clouds on front, reverse with high-relief gold tiger and red and gold bamboo forest, en suite with ojime and ivory netsuke of bamboo slice, some rubbing and wear. **$1,200.00**

ground with the seven gods of good fortune at various pursuits, finely worked in shades of gold and slight colored takamakie with details of e-nashiji and kirigane, the interior of nashiji **3,800.00**

Signed Koma saku, 3¼″, 19th century, of wide form, the roiro ground with sparse gold flakes, decorated with a family of minogame around a winding stream in gold takamakie with details of e-nashiji and kirigane **750.00**

Signed Seimin, 4″, 19th century, gold lacquer bearing a kinji ground, showing a metal figure of a courtiere among large shells and trailing weeds in gold and colored takamakie and aogai, the interior of nashiji **800.00**

Signed Shiomi Masanari in seal form on the side, 3¾″, Late 18th century, the ground of roiro and shaded kinji, decorated with two pheasants among kadomatsu in shades of gold takamakie, the interior of roiro with kinji edges. . . . **3,000**

Signed Yamada saku, 3¼″, 19th century, decorated in gold and colored hiramakie, kirigane and gold foil, two pheasants amid peonies and trees, nashiji interiors, wear and small chips, with ivory netsuke of a shojo signed Rakumin **1,300.00**

Unsigned, 2¾″, 18th century, bearing a roiro ground and decorated with the Moon seen beyond a pine tree in gold and silver takamakie with details of kirigane and aogai. **475.00**

Unsigned, 2¾″, 18th century, of ribbed form, bearing alternating bands of various designs in gold, red and black lacquer, with a wood Netsuke of a Tiger on a base, lacquered in Negoro style   525.00

Unsigned, 3⅜″, 19th century, bearing a mura-nashiji ground and decorated with two inlaid metal figures of a nobleman and lady meeting in a landscape, a waterfall to one side, the figures of gold, silver and shakudo, the background of gold takamakie with details of e-nashiji, the ends with a rinzu pattern and the interior of nashiji, with a tsuishu lacquer Manju, carved with a crane, minogame and kadomatsu and inlaid with a metal kanermono depicting two Manzai dancers, and a very rare wood Ojime in the form of a circular temple bell, signed with ukibori characters Tadatoshi   3,500.00

Unsigned, 3½″, 19th century, ivory, the cylindrical inro finely etched with landscape vignettes of scholars seated and walking through mountainous trails, inscribed with poems, composition Daruma ojime, carved ivory netsuke of an old man holding a lantern and leaning down to pat a young pup, inscribed Kogyokudo on the underside   475.00

Unsigned, 4½″ x 3″, early 19th century, blue and white ceramic, floral and bamboo motif, en suite with blue and white ceramic netsuke in manju form and blue and white ceramic ojime.   650.00

Unsigned, 3¾″, Meiji Period, Shibayama Style, decorated on one side with a cockatoo perched on a plum branch gazing at butterflies in flight near by, reversed by a hanging basket filled with peonies, chrysanthemums and plum blossoms, all inlaid in multicolored aogai, ivory, and coral, the ojime and manju en suite   2,100.00

Five case

Signed Jokusai, 3⅛″ x 1⅞″, 19th century, shaped as a wrapped saki bottle, decorated in hiramakie, the aogai details as festival masks and implements, with fine nashiji interiors, coral bead ojime   2,800.00

Signed Kajiwara-zukuri, 19th century, with an overall design of a grove of pines emerging from billowing clouds beneath a silver full moon, executed in gold hiramaki-e and takamaki-e with okibirame accents, and with one seal, together with a black bead ojime and an ivory netsuke of Hotei standing with a small child resting on his right shoulder   400.00

Signed Koma Koru saku, 19th century, roiro ground, warrior on horseback, with fallen warrior on reverse both in silver, gold and red takamakie, sime rubbing, nashiji interiors, en suite with silver ojime and wood netsuke of a warrior helmet   2,000.00

Signed Koma Kyuhaku-zukuri, 19th century, decorated with silver sparrows in flight over stylized pine trees, rendered in silver and gold takamaki-e, hiramaki-e with togidashi accents on a roiro ground scattered with sparse nashiji, with carnelian bead ojime and wood netsuke carved as a boy with an ox, bearing the signature "Tomoji"   1,450.00

Signed Masanori on a pearl tablet, 3⅜″, 19th century, bearing a nashiji ground and decorated with lines of pine trees in gold takamakie divided by diagonal kinji bands, decorated with flowering plants in applied pear, horn, coral and other materials, the interior of nashiji, with a good ivory Ojime of oval form, carved in relief with a bird and lilies, and a stag antler netsuke in the form of a bamboo section, lacquered with a snail and grasses in colored hiramakie   3,400.00

Signed Shori, 19th century, featuring the legendary beauty, Ono no Komachi, attended by and elderly courtier and a youth holding an umbrella as the group battles a rain storm buffeting a large pine and raging sea to the reverse, executed in gold and silver takamaki-e, hiramaki-e and togidashi on a kinji ground   1,050.00

Signed Suichikuken and sealed Tsunehide, mid-19th century, featuring a rear view of a mounted Tartar under a vine-wrapped pine tree extending to either side, the warrior dressed in exotic armor and turning back with a bow in his outstretched left arm, his arrow lodged in a group of rocks to the opposite side, executed in gold and silver hiramaki-e, takamaki-e, okibirame with red lacquer accents on a roiro ground, together with a cylindrical silver ojime with a shakudo mon and an ivory netsuke of a Benkei-like warrior in armor and wielding a long halberd 700.00

Unsigned, lobed sections, decorated with two hounds seated, the reverse with peonies growing before a house 400.00

Unsigned, decorated in relief with a woman seated in a boat, in aogai, kirikane and taka-makiye on a mura-nashiji ground 350.00

Unsigned, decorated with a fern-like bush growing before rocks, in kirikane and hira-makiye on a roiro ground 500.00

Unsigned, decorated with a traveller resting on a river bank, with a pine tree on the opposite bank, in mura-nashiji and silver on a fundame ground 225.00

Unsigned, decorated with an insect hovering over lotus flowers, pod and leaves, in oxidized metal, mother-o'-pearl, coral and taka-makiye on a roiro ground 600.00

Unsigned, decorated with Shoki pursuing Oni in aogai and mura-nashiji 250.00

Unsigned, decorated with tortoise-shell panels of houses on river bank, on a hira-makiye rinzu ground 225.00

Unsigned, parquetry, with a sliding side panel revealing five drawers and compartments 100.00

Six case

Unsigned, 4¼", 18th century, of slender form, bearing a roiro ground and decorated with a carp leaping a waterfall beneath overhanging pine branches in gold and silver takamakie with details of e-nashiji and kirigane 950.00

Unsigned, decorated on both sides with cherry blossom, in red lacquer taka-makiye and kirikane on a roiro ground 750.00

JAPANESE CLOISONNÉ AND CHAMPLEVÉ

CLOISONNÉ

History: The art of enameling in glass, which is the foundation of cloisonné enameling, came to the Orient long after European and the Near Eastern craftsmen had developed it as an art form. China saw its rise to popularity during the Ming Period (see Chinese Cloisonné). Japan did not produce cloisonné, except for sword furnishings and small ornaments created for the shogun and samurai classes, until the nineteenth century. There is some speculation regarding where the influence for its production came from—the West or China. The most collectable cloisonné products of Japan however, are quite different from either source. The Japanese, although motivated by the techniques and styles of other nations, took the idea, developed it, and turned cloisonné into something that is purely Japanese in nature.

One reason for the late development of cloisonné in Japan was the country's deliberate policy of isolationism, which kept out foreign influence (Christianity in particular) and trade during the years of its feudal military dictatorship (the Tokugawa period). During this period of domestic stability, arts and crafts flourished, particularly the art of lacquering, which no doubt influenced the early cloisonné artists. During the late Tokugawa period (1615–1868), the ruling class and rich merchants encouraged the development of decorative objects.

The earliest documented evidence of the establishment of cloisonné as an art comes from the chronicles of the Hirata family. Hirata Hikoshiro (better known by his artistic name of Donin) produced decoration for sword furnishings for Shogun Tokugawa Ieyasu. His family of artists produced cloisonné medallions to decorate sword accoutrements, using gold or silver wire cloisons and transparent enamels in their work. Donin died in 1646, leaving behind a family of cloisonné artists working for the shogun, all of whom continued to work in the Hirata cloisonné style. In 1874 the tenth Hirata was appointed to make medals, thus the family's traditional line of cloisonné production came to a close. Another family that produced cloisonné for seven generations until the mid-nineteenth century was founded by Takatsuki of Kyoto. This family produced small items such as medallions, rollers for hanging scrolls, and door pulls in the Hirata style.

An entirely different school of cloisonné art, one that focused on the production of freestanding cloisonné objects was started in 1838 by Kaji Tsunedichi of Nagoya. He came to cloisonné production as a result of his experimentation with a Chinese cloisonné plate he had purchased from a Nagoya antiques dealer in 1832. In 1838 he had produced his first plate based on the Chinese model. He is credited with the reinvention of cloisonné in Japan, because his work was done without any knowledge of the earlier work done for the shoguns. He had never seen or learned of any foreign cloisonné methods other than the single Chinese dish he had examined. Within a few years he was producing writing accessories made entirely of cloisonné, and by 1850 he was appointed as a cloisonné artist to the daimyo of Owari Province. One of his pupils Hayashi Shogoro, who later founded the cloisonné village of Shippo-mura just outside Nagoya, became the teacher of some outstanding cloisonné artists. One pupil, Tsukamoto Kaisuke, produced a hexagonal bowl on which he depicted the Nagoya castle in a traditional painting style. He is also credited with being the first to use cloisonné on a ceramic body. Tsukamoto also worked with Gottfried von Wagner, a foreigner who had been hired to work on ceramic enamels for the government. In 1875 they created special enamels to be used for cloisonné production, which resulted in new opaque enamels that were both brilliant and glossy.

The export of cloisonné items to Europe marks the second important period of cloisonné art in Japan. The palette used for cloisonné employed four basic colors: turquoise, white, red, and black; yellow and yellow-green were added later. The first pieces were on copper, which was enameled on both sides. Motifs were heavily influenced by Chinese Ming Dynasty styles.

After 1868, with the destruction of the shoguns and the return to power of the emperor, the conditions were right to rekindle the old arts and to develop new ones that would be valuable as trade. As a result of Commodore Perry's visit to Japan in 1853, the port city of Yokohama was built to accommodate the export industry. The port was opened for trade in 1859, and all cloisonné destined for the West was shipped from Yokohama.

Although the very first cloisonné products produced in Japan are so similar to the Chinese that they can hardly be differentiated, the Japanese cloisonné—or shippo nagashi, as it was named, meaning seven precious things—responded to the growing export trade. These changes were the results of the Westernization of Japan following the Meiji takeover in 1868. Export to the West was further promoted through Japan's participation in the Paris Exposition of 1867. The primary motif of cloisonné during this period was textile designs. The use of brocade patterns was easily accommodated by closely placed cloisons that ensured the security of the fired glass enamels. By 1870, Japan was exporting cloisonné to Europe and the United States. The cloisonné village of Shipp-mura began mass production for export. Different craftsmen and their families devoted themselves to their own secret formulas and styles of production.

Although export demands tended to lower the standards of workmanship, some artists still continued to experiment and develop quality cloisonné techniques on a high level. By the end of the century, three different styles, or schools, of ware had developed. One school, which stressed flowers, birds and landscapes, was headed by Namikawa Yasuyuki of Kyoto, who began working in 1873. His wirework was flawless and his pieces represented technical perfection both in geometric designs and the subjects from nature. His designs were graceful and far superior to the early export ware. His fine work was sometimes executed with silver wire and silver bodies (ginjippo). He is credited with the invention of a mirror black enamel that revolutionized the look of cloisonné.

Yasuyuki's work influenced Inaba Scichiho who established the Inaba Cloisonné Company, a business that is still producing cloisonné today. The company developed plique-à-jour cloisonné (shotai-shippo) between 1903 and 1910. This method used wires that were attached to each other instead of the base metal. After firing, the base metal was removed, revealing translucent or transparent enamels contained by the wires, an appearance akin to stained glass.

In 1880, Namikawa Sosuke started a company in Tokyo and proceeded to invent the "wireless" cloisonné art. This technique was the first developed to avoid breaking up the picture with the cloisons. The method, called musen-jippo, stressed a scenic or pictorial result. In this type of work the cloisons were removed before firing. The resulting colors were neatly separated without obvious wires. In another type, the cloisons were covered with enamel and hidden. Both these techniques left a perfect surface of harmonious colors joining to form the picture.

The third school went one step further and treated the surface of cloisonné in a manner that imitated painted Chinese porcelain. Translucent as well as opaque enamels were used. Transparent colors of yellow, green, red, and purple were developed. These were applied over a carved (or chiseled bas taille) base as a background, and the opaque design in cloisons (oftentimes flowers) seemed to be suspended on the transparent ground (Hirado-jippo). Some were produced in bas taille only, without any other ornamentation (gin-zuki-jippo). Red is the favored transparent color, which when used in this technique is called pigeon blood cloisonné (asasuke). Gin-bari cloisonné is a variation of this technique, using a thin layer of silver foil under the transparent enamel. These foils were typically tinted in pink, aqua, or other tones. The Paris Exhibition of 1900 featured gin-bari cloisonné, which then became a popular export item. Sometimes the foil was used in combination with enamels.

The application of goldstone, bluestone, and greenstone was used frequently in the years 1885 to 1887. Goldstone was achieved by adding pyrite and copper filings to translucent enamel. Color was added to the translucent enamel to achieve the green and blue varieties.

The Ando Company created moriage cloisonné. The moriage technique had been previously used on ceramics and consisted of piling up enamels in relief above the surface of the piece.

This technique was first applied to cloisonné in the 1903 to 1910 creative period.

Two other unusual types of cloisonné were cloisonné on pottery or porcelain (totai-jippo) and a type called tree bark cloisonné. The artist Kinkozan is credited with the creation of wired cloisonné on faience wares, which employed the shapes and crackled glaze of Satsuma ware. The artist Kenzan also worked in this medium in the 1870s. Rarer than this, is cloisonné on true porcelain. This resembles the Satsuma type but is transparent in undecorated areas when held to the light. Tree bark cloisonné on porcelain features a black or more typical brown background, which is textured to look like the bark of a tree. The cloisonné areas are raised above this background and decorated in deep green, orange, and other dark tones.

Openwork cloisonné was a variety produced using cloisonné on only a part of the body of a piece, the rest of the surface was left free of cloisons or had cloisons that were not filled with enamel. Cloisonné was also used on lacquer for a very brief period of time and then abandoned.

Although cloisonné was directly traded with Europe and America from 1880 on, the opening of tourist stores in Japan that catered to foreign tourists aided the worldwide spread of cloisonné. Foreign auctions were also held. The finer pieces of cloisonné reached the West through these means. The shippo-mura factories were exporting the cheaper mass-produced wares at the same time and are still in operation. By 1918 only three of the factories that produced the finest wares remained in operation.

CHAMPLEVÉ

Like cloisonné, champlevé was a European art style before it was adapted by the Orient. Champlevé bronzes bedecked with added jewels began production in Europe in the ninth century. The Chinese made few champlevé pieces. The Japanese, however, produced many heavy champlevé decorated bronzes in the early twentieth century.

Champlevé is similar to cloisonné in its technique of filling partitioned cells with colored glass enamels. The champlevé cells were created by chiseling, acid etching, or molding a body of cast bronze. Wires (cloisons) were not used to create the divisions. The bronze had to have heavy walls to accommodate the hollows that were created.

In most Japanese examples, champlevé decoration was limited to bands of enamels that were archaic in design and color. The enamels were limited to the colors of brown, red, white, and blue in most examples. The bronze was treated to give it an ancient appearance. In some examples, the champlevé decoration was created independently of the ware and was later applied by solder.

References: W. F. Alexander, *Cloisonné and Related Arts*, Wallace-Homestead Book Co., 1972; W. F. Alexander and Donald K. Gerber, *Cloisonné Extraordinaire*, Wallace-Homestead Book Co., 1977; Arthur and Grace Chu, *Oriental Cloisonné and Other Enamels*, Crown Publishers, 1975; Lawrence A. Coben and Dorothy C. Ferster, *Japanese Cloisonné*, John Weatherhill Inc., 1982; Sir Harry Garner, *Chinese and Japanese Cloisonné Enamels*, John Weatherhill, Inc., 1982.

Museums: Asian Art Museum of San Francisco, San Francisco, California; Lowe Art Museum. Coral Gables, Florida; Art Institute of Chicago, Chicago, Illinois; Walter Art Gallery, Baltimore, Maryland; Fogg Art Museum, Cambridge, Massachusetts; George Walter Vincent Smith Museum, Springfield, Massachusetts; Detroit Institute of Arts, Detroit, Michigan; Minneapolis Institute of Art, Minneapolis, Minnesota; Walker Art Center, Minneapolis, Minnesota; Brooklyn Museum, Brooklyn, New York; Metropolitan Museum of Art, New York, New York; Cleveland Museum of Art, Cleveland, Ohio; University Museum, Philadelphia, Pennsylvania; Philadelphia Museum of Art, Philadelphia, Pennsylvania; Virginia Museum of Fine Arts, Richmond, Virginia; Freer Gallery of Art, Washington, D.C.; Seattle Art Museum, Seattle, Washington; Royal Ontario Museum, Toronto, Canada; Palace Museum, Beijing, China; British Museum, London, England; Victoria and Albert Museum, London, England; Tokyo National Museum, Tokyo, Japan. National Museum of Western Art, Tokyo, Japan; National Palace Museum, Taipei, Taiwan.

Reproduction Alert: Copies of Chinese cloisonné were made during the period of 1850–1870 by artist Maizono Genwo and also by other artists at the end of the century. These are very difficult to distinguish from the originals. Recently, a new plique-à-jour cloisonné has been exported from Japan. The work is shoddy in comparison to earlier exports of this type. The surface is irregular and lacks grace. Small vases of this type show the Japanese mon on the base.

The products of the Inaba Company are still being exported and are of good quality. Some modern cloisonné novelties are selling for very modest prices.

Collecting Hints: The wares of Manikawa Yasuyki, which are represented in many museum collections, are considered to represent the highest criteria of workmanship. Since most Japanese pieces are not signed, cloisonné should be judged primarily by the quality of work.

The last twenty years has seen an explosion in Japanese cloisonné prices, particularly in the styles developed in the late nineteenth/early twentieth centuries. Prior to this time, Chinese cloisonné was more popularly collected. Prices peaked on Japanese items in the 1980s and have fallen since then. Collectors have been cautious in their recent buying, hoping the prices will go down even further. This is likely to happen, particularly on the highest ticketed items, which seem to have been priced above the means of the available market of collectors. (See: Chinese Cloisonné.)

JAPANESE CLOISONNÉ

Beaker, 3¾″, Meiji Period, with a slightly waisted body and silver interior, worked in silver wire with chrysanthemums floating on a stylized stream, on a black ground between floral borders, the underside enamelled with flowers and flecked with aventurine, signed in the enamel Nagoya, Suzuki tsukuru ...   750.00

Bowl, 4½″ dia., Meiji Period, the interior decorated in colored enamels with stylized blossoms amid scrolling tendrils on a muted green ground, the exterior rim edged with a scale-patterned black band suspending flowering peony and cherry sprigs on a green ground with abstracted leaf patterning above further black scale-shaped bands, the base with a modified Hayashi studio mark, silver banded rim and foot ...   220.00

Box and Cover
  4″, Meiji Period, of rounded rectangular form worked in silver wire with an egret wading among water lilies, on a pale blue ground, applied with silver mounts, stamped jun gin, seal of Ando ...   550.00
  5¼″ w., Meiji Period, of rounded rectangular form decorated in silver wire with four butterflies in flight on a midnight-blue ground   750.00
  7⅝″ dia., Circa 1900, of circular form resting on a high ring foot and fit-

ted with a flattened lid, decorated in bright polychrome enamels with a phoenix medallion reserved on a turquoise-blue ground with an all over pattern of fronted lotus blossoms, linked by scrolling leafy tendrils repeated on the lower section, the base with an enamel cartouche reading Da min keitai. 425.00

Coffee Set, 6¼″, Meiji Period, comprising coffee pot and cover, sugar bowl and cover, cream jug, two cups and two saucers, decorated in gilt wire with butterflies, peonies, larch and karakusa on a slightly mottled yellow ground between formal borders, signed Namikawa 2,800.00

Dish
  14⅜″, Meiji Period, decorated with a bowl containing a crayfish and a fish, a dragonfly flying overhead   550.00
  23⅝″, Meiji Period, of octagonal form, worked in silver wire with a fishergirl wearing a kimono and straw apron, standing on a shore with two water buckets beneath a pine tree, watching a wave breaking over a rock 900.00
  24″, Meiji Period, decorated with birds flying above numerous flowers including peony, orchids, daisies and lilies on a riverbank, on a blue ground within a lozenge border 1,600.00

Jar, 15″ h., Meiji Period, of large globular contour with faceted sides resting on three bronze hemispherical supports and fitted with a circular lid

Bowl, 4¼″ dia., plique-à-jour, silver wire, raised on three short feet, depicting various bright flowers on a cream-colored ground, silver rim. $550.00. Courtesy of Butterfield and Butterfield.

Charger (one of pair), 24″ dia., floral design on black background, the rim showing chidori in flight. $3,300.00. Courtesy of Butterfield and Butterfield.

surmounted by a ball finial, the body decorated in polychrome enamels with a central band of shaped butterfly reserves on a floral-patterned ground and suspending stiff-leaf leaves of ho-o bird and dragons, the sloping shoulder encircled by a ruyi-color garland, the lid decorated en suite 1,750.00

Koro and Cover

4″, Meiji Period, of ovoid form decorated on a brown and aventurine ground with shield-shaped panels of ho-o bird and dragons, the cover with a kiku-form knop 250.00

7¼″, Meiji Period, of globular form decorated with shield-shaped panels of ho-o bird and bands of dragons and floral design on a red ginbari ground, the cover with spherical knop 650.00

Panel, 15″ x 12″, framed, Meiji Period, worked in silver wire with an eagle perched on a rock above foaming waves, signed Shippo Kaisha. 650.00

Plaque, 20 x 12¾″, 20th century, featuring three small sparrows flying toward another perched on bamboo stake supporting a flowering spider chrysanthemum, further blossoming chrysanthemums within a bamboo enclosure to the left, all in polychrome enamels on a peach-colored ground, set in a wooden frame. 600.00

Plate

9¾″ dia., Meiji Period, Circa 1870-1880, decorated in muted polychrome enamels with an interior medallion featuring a stylized dragon with large wings and bird-like scaly body flying amid cloud scrolls within a narrow geometric-patterned band, the sloping sides divided into four sections of abstracted flowering tendrils on a dark green ground, the exterior encircled by leafy tendrils bracketed by bands of geometric mokko and heart shapes. 110.00

9⅝″ dia., Meiji Period, the interior well decorated with blossoming sprigs of morning glory, hinaginu and bush clover rendered in polychrome enamels on a deep blue ground, all surrounded by a wide band with irregular reserves of geometric and floral design on a ground scattered with leafy chrysanthemum blossoms and set off by two yellow-beaded bands, bronze edge 330.00

Tray, 10¾″, Meiji Period, the lobed body worked in silver wire and musen-jippo with two birds perched on a flowering cherry branch, on a graduated pale blue and grey ground, the reverse decorated in tones of brown enamel with scattered flowers, applied with a shakudo rim, seal of Namikawa Sosuke 1,200.00

Vase

3½″ h., Meiji Period, of modified mei-ping shape resting on a splayed foot, the sides decorated in translucent colored enamels with three goldfish swimming below a flowering wisteria vine, silver foot and rim band 220.00

4″ h., Meiji Period, pair, each of slender ovoid form surmounted by a small waisted neck flaring toward the rim and resting on a short ring foot, each decorated on the front with swimming goldfish executed in color-tinted transparent enamels revealing the textured silver ground and set against a background of dark opaque blue, bronze fittings. 220.00

4¼″ h., with copper overlay, Meiji Period, cast as two tapering bamboo joints with slender stalks forming irregular-shaped handles to either side, the sides featuring a small sparrow in flight above sprigs of leafy bamboo, the bird and some leaves executed in copper takazogan with incised details, the reverse with a two character cartouche incised "Shigeaki" 425.00

4½″ h., ovoid, Meiji Period, the globular body tapering sharply to a short ring foot and surmounted by a short waisted neck flaring at the rim, the front featuring a hawk perched on a rock above cresting waves encircling the body, the bird and rock in colored opaque enamels defined by silver cloisons and the waves and sky in translucent shades of blue enamel revealing an undulating pattern of waves below a granulated overall ground for the sky, silver banded foot and rims. 300.00

4½″ h., Meiji Period, the ovoid body decorated with swallows flying among trailing blue, white and pink wistaria, leaves and tendrils, on a black ground, the foot with kiku and scrolls. 800.00

4¾″ h., with a small waisted neck

flaring slightly at the rim and globular body tapering to a high pedestal foot, decorated in colored enamels with three cranes in flight over an inset bordered by lush vegetation silhouetted against a shaded pink ground, bronze-edged rim and foot **400.00**

5'' h., Meiji Period, with an ovoid body and short neck finely worked in various thicknesses of tapering silver wire with five large butterflies in flight on a midnight-blue ground, the neck and foot with borders of butterflies and prunus blossom, stamped mark of Ogasawara Shuzo **1,200.00**

5¼'' h., Meiji Period, Ogasawara Shuzo, the high-shouldered globular body designed with an elegant cluster of nadeshiko (wild pinks), the white flowers and bamboo-like leaves set against a dark-blue sky below an elaborate geometric collar of multi-colored enamels below the chrysanthemum decorated neck, signed with a two character cartouche on the silver mounted footrim **650.00**

5¾'' h., Meiji Period, of slender ovoid shape tapering to a high ring foot and surmounted by a narrow waisted neck flaring at the rim, the body decorated to the front with a crane amid flowering chrysanthemum, reversed by a delicate blossoming water plant, the motifs defined in silver cloisons and executed in various colored enamels on a deep blue

Vase, 5½' h., gin-bari decoration, with lilac colored morning glories on a blue foil background which fades to white at the base. $300.00

ground, gilt brass rim and foot, the base stamped with Takeuchi Chubei studio mark **300.00**

5⅞'' h., pair, Meiji Period, of hexagonal form, each worked in silver wire on the midnight blue ground with butterflies above hydrangea, the foot and neck with formal design and sentoku rims, with mark Miwa Tomisaburo **900.00**

6'' h., Meiji Period, each vase of ovoid form and decorated with three birds in flight above a blossoming chrysanthemum bush, the base with a lappet band, all on a cobalt blue ground **720.00**

6'' h., Meiji Period, each high shouldered ovoid vase decorated with a solitary writhing dragon rendered in blue and white enamels with red flames on a cobalt blue ground **400.00**

7⅛'' h., Meiji Period, the slender ovoid body with a high shoulder and short waisted neck flaring at the rim, decorated on the front in colored enamels with a wild goose in flight above wind-blown reeds on a muted green ground, rim and foot banded with bronze   **450.00**

7⅛'' h., Late Meiji Period, Hayashi School, of high-shouldered ovoid shape tapering toward the base and surmounted by a waisted neck with an everted rim, the front minutely decorated in polychrome enamels with small birds cavorting near a large blossoming chrysanthemum bush issuing from rocks near a meandering stream bordered by further flowers and sprigs of leafy bamboo on a black ground, all set off by narrow keyfret bands to the top and bottom, executed in gold and silver cloisons with some wires of uneven thickness, rim bands to the rim and foot **900.00**

7⅛'' h., pair, each of slender ovoid contour with a waisted neck and tapering to a slightly flared foot, the front decorated with a small bird perched on a lush flowering chrysanthemum spray in bright colored enamels on a translucent deep red ground revealing a secondary design of a sparrow amid bamboo set against a granulated pattern **250.00**

7¼'' h., Meiji Period, pair, each with a shouldered slender body worked in silver wire with a cock and hen beneath purple and white wistaria, the base with brocade borders, applied with silver mounts **1,000.00**

7¼″ h., Meiji Period, of rounded square section delicately worked in silver wire with numerous flowers including chrysanthemums, daisies, lilies and hydrangeas among wild grasses, on a midnight-blue ground between brocade borders, applied with silver mounts, signed Aichi, Hayashi Ko   **1,800.00**

7⅞″ h., Meiji Period, of high-shouldered flattened ovoid contour tapering to a splayed foot and surmounted by a tall slender neck flaring toward the rim, the body decorated in polychrome enamels with a production of flowering plants and trees delicately defined by silver cloisons set against a deep blue ground, the rounded rectangular foot with a geometric-patterned band, a jewelled garland band suspended from the rim, with silver edge bands **825.00**

7½″ h., Meiji Period, of hexagonal ovoid form resting on a splayed foot and decorated with a rooster and a hen under a blossoming cherry tree reversed by a iris, all on a cobalt blue ground, the base with studio mark **375.00**

8¼″ h., Meiji Period, with an ovoid body and tall neck decorated in silver wire with butterflies in flight on a black ground, the neck and foot with formal borders, applied with silver mounts, signed on a silver plaque Kyoto, Namikawa   **2,200.00**

Vase, 7½″ h, early 20th century, green bamboo on a white ground. $275.00

8½″ h., Meiji Period, of high-shoulder globular contour tapering to a high ring foot and surmounted by a short waisted neck flaring to a wide mouth, the body decorated all over with a pattern of flowering prunus in bright opaque enamels on a translucent red enamel ground revealing a pattern of horizontal striations, silver-banded rim and foot, the foot impressed with Ando Jubei studio mark **700.00**

8¾″ h., stick neck, Meiji Period, the low-slung ovoid body tapering to a very small foot and surmounted by a long slender neck flaring to a wide everted rim, the sides decorated in multicolored enamels with reserves of dragon and ho-o bird separated by bird-and-flower motifs superimposed with truncated floral roundels, an ornate garland band encircling the base of the neck scattered with butterfly, bird and floral medallions on a dense scroll ground **360.00**

8¾″ h., Meiji Period, the slender tapering body with a squared contour resting on a high splayed foot and surmounted by a tall waisted neck flaring at the rim, each of the four sides decorated in polychrome enamels with an ovoid reserve featuring various types of flowering plants on a grey ground and within a frame suspended from a stylized butterfly, all on a dark blue ground scattered with chrysanthemum blossoms and a dense pattern of scrolling tendrils, the high pedestal foot with an ornate stiff-leaf band, and elaborate jewelled garland suspended from the rim with a silver edge, the base incised Dai Nihon Hayashi Kodenji-sei **1,500.00**

9¼″ h., Meiji Period, of ovoid contour tapering to a recessed circular foot and surmounted by a short waisted neck flaring to a dished mouth, the sides with shaped cloisonné enamel decorated panels featuring birds and flowers reserved against a flowering prunus tree on a brown wood-textured ground, the muted enamel colors repeated in the floral and geometric patterned bands encircling the foot and neck **275.00**

9½″ h., Meiji Period, the slender body worked in silver wire yusenjippo and gin-bari with purple, yellow and red convolvulus, on a scrolled blue ground, engraved mark of Hayashi Hachizaemon ... **350.00**

9½" h., of elongated ovoid form decorated with a kingfisher perched in a blossoming wisteria bush, reversed by a smaller blossoming vine, all on a powder blue ground ... **550.00**

9⅝" h., Early 20th century, the tapering ovoid body with high shoulders and a waisted neck flaring at the rim, the front decorated in opaque colored enamels with a pair of birds amid flowering chrysanthemum bushes silhouetted against a translucent ruby-red enamel ground revealing further blossoming chrysanthemum sprigs and granulated silver base, the base inlaid with the studio mark of Ando Jubei, with silver bands to the rim and foot, one impressed jungin **1,000.00**

9¾" h., Meiji Period, the gently rounded hexagonal form and long narrow neck decorated with light blue panel depicting various blossoming flowers and light green panel with herons and ducks in a stream surrounded by flowers and trees, all on a deep blue ground ... **800.00**

9¾" h., Meiji Period, the gently rounded hexagonal form and long narrow neck decorated with light blue panel depicting various blossoming flowers and light green panel with herons and ducks in a stream surrounded by flowers and trees, all on a deep blue ground ... **800.00**

9¾" h., of elongated ovoid form resting on a splayed foot and decorated with a fierce dragon depicted in icy-green on a cobalt blue ground, impressed with mark of Adachi Kinjiro **450.00**

10⅝" h., Meiji Period, the ovoid midnight-blue body intricately worked in varying thicknesses of tapered silver wire with seventeen large butterflies in flight, between formal borders of flowers and foliate scrolls, applied with silver mounts, stamped jun gin, signed on a silver plaque Aichi, Hayashi yaki **6,000.00**

12" h., Meiji Period, the shouldered body worked in gold and varying thicknesses of silver wire with birds and flowering prunus, on a blue ground between formal borders, applied with silver mounts, stamped jun gin **1,000.00**

12" h., of elongated ovoid form decorated with birds resting in a blossoming plum tree, another in flight, the base of the tree decorated with colorful chrysanthemum blossoms repeated to the reverse, the neck and base banded with floral lappets, the base applied with a plum blossom-form cartouche reading To **1,100.00**

12" h., Meiji Period, the slender tapering body with a high shoulder and surmounted by a waisted neck flaring to a wide mouth, the upper body decorated in brightly colored enamels with butterflies and flowering sprigs on a turquoise blue ground set off by patterned bands, the lower suspending stiff-leaf reserves of ho-o bird and dragons over a mottled-brown ground, a smaller stiff-leaf band encircling the neck ringed by small blossoms, double-leaf bands at the bronze-edged rim and foot, the base with Ando Jubei studio mark................. **715.00**

12" h., Meiji Period, the ovoid body surmounted by a waisted neck and decorated with lappet-shaped reserves of ho-o birds and abstract dragons encircling the teadust colored body, the shoulder banded by floral and dragon reserves below a scrolling tendril ground, the neck with further lappets........................ **650.00**

12⅛" h., Meiji Period, each of slightly squared ovoid shape surmounted by a long waisted neck flaring to a wide mouth, the slender tapering body featuring a yusen-jippo design of flowering magnolia branches in opaque colored enamels on a dark blue ground and set off by multicolored floral-patterned bands at the rim and foot **300.00**

12¼", beaker form, Meiji Period, in the style of Hayashi Kodenji, with a flared body worked in varying thicknesses of silver wire with numerous sparrows perched and flying among leafy stems of bamboo, above purple and white daisies on a midnight-blue ground **950.00**

12⅜" h., Meiji Period, with a flared body and tall bulbous neck, worked in varying thicknesses of silver wire with branches of trailing white wistaria, on a midnight-blue ground **750.00**

Vases, Pair, 12¼'' h., Meiji period, the sides decorated with birds and butterflies hovering above plants, the shoulder, neck, and base with geometric and floral patterned bands of muted hue, bright-colored enamels on a turquoise ground, cracks, wear. $770.00. Courtesy of Butterfield and Butterfield.

13¼'' h., ovoid form, Meiji Period, pair, each of high-shouldered slender ovoid contour with a waisted neck flaring to a wide rim and tapering sharply to a high stepped foot, the body decorated with birds and butterflies amid flowering sprigs in bright enamels on a black ground and flanked by two wide floral-patterned bands on a translucent brown ground, the neck with further stylized blossoms below a wide linked shippo-tsunagi band repeated on the high flaring foot, bronze rim and foot 750.00

14¼'' h., of elongated ovoid form decorated with a pair of cranes standing in front of a bamboo bush, reversed by a smaller bamboo sprig, all on a royal blue ground, silver rims 650.00

14⅜'' h., Meiji Period, pair, each of slender ovoid contour with lobed sides tapering to a short ring foot and surmounted by a tall waisted neck flaring toward the rim, the sides decorated in polychrome enamels with a wide band of pendent stiff leaves featuring dragon and ho-o bird below a ruyi-head cloud-collar at the shoulder, the neck and central band of linked diamonds and flower-heads, all on a deep blue ground 550.00

14½'' h., Early 20th century, of slender ovoid form tapering to the foot and surmounted by a waisted neck flaring to a dished mouth, the body decorated in multicolored enamels. with various types of chrysanthemum blossoms issuing from leafy stalks silhouetted against a dark blue ground and set off by geometric-patterned bands at the foot and rim, bronze bands encircling the rim and foot 900.00

14¾'' h., Meiji Period, pair, each of slender ovoid form with flared neck and foot, decorated with panels of dragons and ho-o bird on a red ginbari ground 750.00

15½'', Meiji Period, each of rounded square section, decorated in silver wire with alternate panels of landscapes and birds among flowers and branches, the landscapes extending from one vase to the other, the ground and borders scattered with shells, the shoulder worked in gilt wire with diaper and ho-o bird panels and the neck decorated with dragon roundels   2,500.00

16½'' h., Meiji Period, the tall baluster form with gently everted rim is decorated with two large turquoise-blue panels containing pheasant, quail, swallows, hummingbirds and butterflies among flowering trees flanked by elaborate geometric and floral decorated spandrels 700.00

18⅛'' h., Meiji Period, pair, each of

Vase, 15'' h., cloisonné on porcelain, totai-jippo, dense design of harbor surrounded by mountains and rockwork, the neck and foot with brocade patterns, bold multicolored enamels on a turquoise ground, the interior rim decorated with an underglaze blue border pattern, the base left white, unsigned. $1,250.00

slender high-shouldered ovoid shape tapering sharply to a splayed foot and surmounted by a tall waisted neck flaring toward the rim, decorated in multicolored enamels with a central band of butterflies and blossoms bordered by a pair of abstracted floral bands flanked by larger lappet and stiff-leaf bands with further butterflies and blossoms on a black spiral-patterned ground extending over the neck, green fish scale-patterned bands at the rim, shoulder and foot **1,300.00**

18⅛″ h., Early Meiji Period, pair, each of baluster form with flared rim and foot, decorated on a blue ground with sea eagles watching a flight of chidorii above waves . . .   **950.00**

19⅛″ h., baluster form, Early Meiji Period, the slender ovoid body surmounted by a large trumpet-form mouth and tapering to a high waisted circular pedestal resting on three shaped supports, the body decorated in polychrome enamels with two mokko-form panels of birds and flowers reserved on a bright green ground with a dense pattern of flowers amid leafy tendrils repeated on the pedestal and set off by geometric-patterned bands, the high shoulder with a stiff-leaf band below circular and diamond-shaped floral reserves on a neck beneath further patterned bands at the rim   **525.00**

CHAMPLEVÉ

Figure, Manjusri, 16½″ h., late Tokugawa period, the figure seated on the back of a roaring fu lion, enamels of blue and yellow on the garment, saddle and harness, unsigned **1,430.00**

Urn with domed shaped lid, 20¾″ h., Meiji period, featuring a stylized figure of a standing kirin on a compressed ovoid body tapering to a pedestal base composed of two horizontal lobes, the slightly splayed floriform foot cast with small animal heads, with a wide multicolored bird shaped reserves around the sides with floral inlaid bands around the shoulder and base, oversize bird form loose ring handles flanking the waisted neck **770.00**

Vase

8″ h., handled, early 20th century, with a band of birds and floral

Vases, Pair, 13¾″ h., pear-shaped with two polychrome enamel decorated bands of floral and taotieh design, the base with a two-character studio mark. $775.00. Courtesy of Butterfield and Butterfield.

around center, multicolored enamel inlay. **120.00**

11½″ h., pair, parcel gilt champlevé enamel, 18th century, each of lobed gu form, with flared neck and base encircled by tall enamel lappets, between recessed floral bands, the cental bulb decorated with lotus scroll repeated below the lipped key-fret rim, the exterior covered in gilt, casting flaw   **3,500.00**

JAPANESE FURNITURE

History: Historically, Japan has a very limited furniture culture. Both upper and lower classes have always sat on the floor, slept on the floor, and taken their meals at low tables while sitting on the floor. Their homes have built-in areas for storage of personal items. Chairs were used on a limited basis by priests, samurai, and the nobility. Coffers and trunks (nagamochi) were used to store clothes and were kept out in the family warehouse. Various small boxes known as temoto dansu were kept in the house for small personal items. They were often made of quite beautiful and highly grained woods such as black persimmon and mulberry. Cosmetic boxes, sewing boxes, and mirrors in lovely lacquered boxes stored other items needed on a daily basis. Wooden and ceramic hibachis contained small charcoal fires to provide heat in the cold months.

It was only with the rise of the merchant class in the late Edo Period that furniture became popular. Good-looking, well-made furniture in the shop area became a status symbol. Later, this desire for conspicuous consumption carried over into the merchants' and wealthy farmers' homes. At least one beautiful chest of drawers (tansu) was displayed prominently where everyone could see it. They were limited by the shogunate to natural wooden finishes or simple black lacquer finishes. Only the samurai class was allowed the fancy gold maki-e lacquer finishes. As a result, more and more highly grained woods were sought out, and elaborate iron hardware was applied to these merchant chests. The golden era of Japanese furniture making occurred in the mid-Meiji period (1880–1900). Communication between various regions was limited, and distinct styles of furniture developed in each locale. Every region had a particular style of tansu dependent on the availability of certain hardwoods in that area and the presence or lack of skilled ironworkers to make the hardware.

The most commonly found tansus are for clothing. They may be one, two, or three pieces stacked one on top of another. Most tansus have a cryptomeria case with hardwoods used only for the drawer fronts. Only a small percentage of chests are 100 percent hardwood. Combinations of four large drawers with one or two small drawers and a small compartment with a door are common. Locks range from simple to extravagant. In the Sendai area, locks in the shape of flowers, birds, and dragons are common. The hardware varies so much from area to area that it is a reliable indicator of the origin of the piece. Early pieces frequently had a locking bar across two of the drawers. This proved to be so inconvenient that it was later abandoned.

In addition to storing clothing, there were tansus for several special uses as well. The kuruma dansu was a heavy utilitarian chest with wheels on it. It was first used by officials to store documents; later it was used by merchants to store records. The wheels were to facilitate moving the documents in case of fire. Early kuruma dansus were heavy, functional pieces. Later kuruma dansus have highly grained zelkova drawer fronts and elaborate hardware.

In the merchant's shop were storage chests with sliding doors (todana dansu) for inventory; shop chests (choba dansu) for storing papers, account books, and tea items; and sometimes a stair chest (kaidan dansu). The stair chest served as stairs to the upper floors or loft and was completely built in underneath with multiple drawers and doors to provide storage for shop inventory and account books. These were also popular in large farmhouses. Various money boxes (zeni bako), writing boxes (suzuri bako), and seal boxes (in bako) were also present in the shop.

Sea chests (funa dansu) are the most intricate and complex pieces of Japanese furniture. They are made of very durable woods and are bound with heavy iron hardware to hold up under hard use. They frequently have elaborate locks and secret hiding places to discourage anyone from going through the captain's papers. Because they were often carried ashore as the captain went about his business, they are made of beautifully grained zelkova wood and heavy, elaborate hardware with a family crest. These chests were both impressive and practical.

Another interesting chest is the kitchen chest (mizuya). Many of these were made in the Hikone area. Mizuyas consist of two pieces stacked one on top of the other and vary in length from 36" to 110". They are composed of various sizes of drawers and sliding doors for utensils. There is frequently a cupboard with a screened-door for storing food items.

With the beginning of mass-production techniques in the 1920s, the golden era of Japanese furniture making came to an end.

References: Victor and Takako Hauge, *Folk Traditions in Japanese Art*, Kodansha, 1978; Ty and Kyoko Heineken, *Tanzu*, Weatherhill, 1981; Kazuko Koizumi, *Traditional Japanese Furniture*, Kodansha, 1986; Hugo Munsterberg, *The Folk Art of Japan*, Charles E. Tuttle Co., Inc., 1958.

Museum: Tokyo Furniture Museum, Tokyo, Japan.

Reproduction Alert: In recent years, reproductions of the most desirable and expensive pieces of Japanese furniture have appeared on the market. Most of these reproductions are made in Korea from old wood and old hardware. The most commonly reproduced items are sea chests, small wheeled chests, and stair chests. Stair chests in particular are popular. The reproductions are usually small in size and not really tall enough to serve as stairs to a second floor. Stair chests normally break down into two—only occasionally three—pieces, which are not finished on the unexposed portions. The reproductions have been finished on all sides to increase their versatility and can be used stacked or individually. Be wary of stair chests with drawers and doors on both sides that can be used as a room divider. Common woods in stair chests are zelkova, cryptomeria, and cypress. Reproductions are frequently made of paulownia, a very lightweight wood that would not hold up under the heavy use a stair chest would normally receive. The steps should be thick enough and strong enough to hold your weight without shoes. Above all, stair chests should be heavy, sturdy, bulky pieces of furniture. The same holds true for wheeled chests. They were normally very heavy utilitarian pieces. Only a few were small in size.

Collecting Hints: From a resale standpoint, refinished pieces are best avoided. A certain amount of restoration is allowable, but large amounts of wood should not be replaced, nor should the hardware be altered in any way. Cryptomeria has a tendency to shrink in a dry climate and develop spaces between adjoining boards. This can be filled in with wood by a skilled craftsman. Cracks across the grain of a single board are more problematic. Avoid pieces with worm damage. Look for pieces that are attractive, with good patina and a minimum amount of restoration. Hardwoods such as zelkova or keyaki wood are most desirable and will cost twice as much as a similar chest in a softwood.

Most people do not buy furniture as an investment. Their main goal is to buy attractive pieces that are functional. However, we have seen the price of good-quality tansus double in the last five years.

Sea chests if they can be found at a reasonable price are a good investment. They can sometimes be found in New England in areas where the sea trade was once important. Because of their small size and rarity, the Japanese collect sea chests. This keeps prices relatively high and resale quite good. Sea chests may also be available at auction. In general, auction prices for furniture tend to be fairly reasonable, but shipping from the auction house to your area may add several hundred dollars to the final price. We have also noted Korean reproductions being sold as Japanese in the auction houses from time to time, so be aware that this is happening.

Advisor: Janet Lashbrooke

HIBACHI

Edo style
    15'' x 29'' x 16'', Meiji era, zelkova wood, three drawers with iron handles, metal liner **550.00**
    15'' x 27'' x 16'', Meiji era, three drawers to one side, well grained zelkova wood. **1,300.00**
Kyoto style, 12'' x 22'' x 15'', Meiji era, zelkova wood. **1,300.00**
Porcelain hibachis
    16'' dia. x 10'', late Meiji era, hand painted wisteria design with some stencilled trim along the borders **900.00**
    24'' dia. x 12'', late Meiji era, hand painted chrysanthemum design **1,200.00**
Smoking hibachi, 13'' x 9'', Meiji era, burled grape root, good patina **900.00**

TANSU

Clothing chest
    44'' x 37'' x 17'', late Meiji era, paulownia wood, two pieces, round iron lock plates **2,000.00**
    Matsumoto, 41'' x 32'' x 15'', late Meiji era, cryptomeria wood with black lacquer finish, two drawers covered with locking bar, iron locks in shape of money bags **3,000.00**

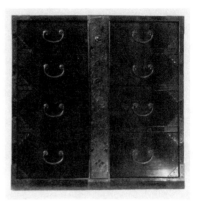

Kodansu, Taisho period, black lacquer with cryptomeria case, from Shonai area, $1,500.00

Nihonmatsu
    44'' x 44'' x 17'', Taisho era, two pieces, zelkova drawer fronts with cryptomeria case, round iron lock plates with crane, turtle, pine, plum, and bamboo in brass **5,000.00**
    46'' x 36'' x 18'', late Meiji era, two pieces, rectangular iron lock plates trimmed with yellow brass in the three friends design with brass butterfly escutcheon cover, zelkova drawer fronts with cryptomeria case. **3,500.00**
Sendai
    45'' x 33'' x 17½'', signed Taisho 15, zelkova drawer fronts cryptomeria case, iron repoussé hardware in shape of chrysanthemum **4,000.00**
    46'' x 34'' x 17½'', signed and dated Meiji 25 by Shibataro, zelkova drawer fronts with cryptomeria case, unusual iron repoussé hardware with parasol, fan, and top hat **3,000.00**
    47'' x 40'' x 17½'', Meiji era, all zelkova case with highly grained drawer fronts, iron repoussé hardware in peony design **8,000.00**
    32'' x 41'' x 18'', Meiji era, chestnut drawers with cryptomeria case, chrysanthemum hardware rimmed in white brass . . . **1,540.00**
Shonai, 34'' x 39'' x 16'', late Meiji era, zelkova drawer fronts, cryptomeria case, heavy iron kakute handles. **7,500.00**

Sendai, clothing chest, zelkova and cryptomeria wood, signed Taisho 15, $4,000.00

Sendai, Meiji period, clothing chest, highly grained zelkova drawers with zelkova case, separate base, $8,000.00

Yamagata
    39" x 40" x 17", late Meiji era, two pieces, zelkova drawer fronts with cryptomeria case, round iron lock plate trimmed with brass pine and turtle motif **3,500.00**
    37" x 47" x 17", Taisho era, two pieces, zelkova drawer fronts with cryptomeria case, round iron lock plate with paulownia design................... **2,100.00**
Futon chest
    69" x 74" x 27", Meiji era, zelkova doors and drawers, cryptomeria case, brass and iron hardware ... **4,200.00**
    70" x 71" x 22", Meiji era, cryptomeria and cypress, iron hardware **2,800.00**
Kitchen chest
    106" x 69" x 23", signed Taisho 5, cedar and cypress case with zelkova drawers and doors **12,000.00**

60" x 69" x 23", late Meiji era, cedar and cypress case with zelkova drawers and doors, from Hikone **4,000.00**
61" x 69" x 22", late Meiji era, burled zelkova door fronts with cryptomeria and cypress case, from Kanazawa **4,500.00**
40" x 60" x 22", late Meiji era, zelkova drawer fronts with cryptomeria and cypress case........ **3,000.00**
Kodansu (small chest)
    From Shonai, 23" x 23" x 14", Taisho era, stained cryptomeria case with black lacquer front, locking bar across four drawers **1,500.00**
    18" x 20" x 16", Meiji era, paulownia wood, iron mokko handles... **1,200.00**
    21" x 20" x 12", Meiji era, cryptomeria with black lacquer finish, six drawers covered by locking bar **600.00**
Sea chest
    Chobako style
        21" x 10" x 11", late Edo era, all zelkova wood.............. **5,000.00**
        21" x 21" x 12", Meiji era, burled zelkova drawer fronts with cryptomeria case **4,000.00**
        10" x 23" x 13", Meiji era, all zelkova, fitted with new stand **3,500.00**
    Kakesuzuri style, 17" x 15" x 19", Meiji era, all zelkova wood, heavy iron hardware with brass family crest on door................. **4,200.00**
    Hangai style, 18" x 32" x 16", Meiji era, zelkova chest with paulownia drawers behind a drop door..... **4,700.00**
Sendai office chest, 26" x 69" x 16", Meiji era, all zelkova case with burled zelkova drawers and iron repoussé hardware in peony design,

Kodansu, Meiji period, paulownia wood, $1,200.00

Wheeled chest, Meiji period, zelkova and cryptomeria, from Ishikawa, $10,000.00

unusual design combining drawers
with large door opening to reveal file
storage **8,000.00**
Stair chest
54" x 95" x 30", Taisho era, cryptomeria and cypress with zelkova
drawers and doors, latches in the
shape of Mt. Fuji and chess piece **8,000.00**
106" x 92" x 30", Taisho era, cy-
press drawers and doors with
cryptomeria case **9,000.00**
Wheeled chest
54" x 46" x 26", Meiji era, zelkova
face and structural pieces with
cryptomeria case, one locking bar
over two drawers over another
locking bar over two drawers,
small door to one side, beautiful
wood grain with excellent lacquer
finish, excellent hardware, from
Ishikawa area **10,000.00**
54" x 44" x 25", Edo era, zelkova
face and top with cryptomeria
sides, locking bar (replaced) over
two drawers over sliding doors
and three small drawers to one
side **4,000.00**

JAPANESE IMARI

History: The port of Imari on Kyushu Island is the
channel through which all Arita ware porcelain
products were shipped, either to other Japanese
ports or abroad. Technically, the ware we Western collectors usually call Imari should be termed
Arita, but through custom, the term Imari is generally reserved for the underglaze blue, overglaze
red, gilt, and/or polychrome enameled ware produced in Arita; the term Arita being reserved generally for the blue and white wares exported from

this region. The following are generally accepted
as Imari wares by current definition: three-color
Imari (old Japan), five-color Imari (gosai), or brocade Imari (nishikide); and Kinrande Imari (gold
designs on a ground color of red enamel).

It was in the area of Arita that the first true
porcelain clay was discovered in Hizen Province.
Although the exact date for this discovery is still
unknown, the evidence currently places it in the
early seventeenth century. Until that time, the
Japanese people used earthen ware and lacquered ware for dining.

It was the Dutch traders that created the export
market for Imari porcelain. Though the first orders
were for blue and white wares (the production
from China lagging because political upheaval at
the end of the Ming Dynasty), these were quickly
supplanted by European orders for polychrome
enamel pieces.

The color palette of underglaze blue and overglaze red on a white ground were the first two
styles of Imari to be produced. The blue was a dull
purplish hue and the red had a decidedly orange
cast. The most frequent design used with this
combination was a flower basket. Another type
used the enamel colors of red and green on a
white ground. The sparse decoration was limited
to designs of birds, flowers, fish, and occasionally
human figures.

The use of five colors (green, yellow, aubergine, blue, and black, along with gold embellishment) combined with patterns of flowers and
landscapes became the standard for what we now
recognize under the heading of brocade ware.
The first motifs were taken freely from the Chinese
palette of colors and designs and included the
Flower Basket pattern which was influenced by
Chinese art. The porcelains, however, took on a
decidedly Japanese character. The most distinctive character of brocade Imari porcelain was its
dense overall design, which covered so much of
the surface that the background color was hardly
visible. The presence of the Dutch traders encouraged the incorporation of Western figures and
sailing ships into the decoration, and some of the
traditional designs included Western motifs.

Gosai Imari, which was more popular in Japan
than in the West, used the same palette of colors
as the brocade ware. It differed in design, however; the painting was less complicated and much
of the ground color remained visible. Flowers
were the favored motif. The central Flower Basket
was still used but the basket shape was typically
Japanese as opposed to earlier basket renderings
that were clearly influenced by Chinese designs.

Kinrande Imari very closely resembled the later
Kutani wares, but the color used beneath the gold
design was typically Imari red, and the designs
employed were executed in traditional Imari
style.

Unfortunately for Arita and the Japanese export
trade, the Kilns at Jingdezhen (Ching-te-chen) in

China were again supplying the world with large amounts of porcelain by the end of the seventeenth century. Chinese porcelain production included deliberate copies of Japanese brocade Imari which they were able to sell at a much lower price to the Dutch East India Company traders. As a result, the Dutch did not renew their formal trading contracts with Japan, which expired in 1795. Although some private trading continued to furnish Europe with Japanese Imari, the supply all but ceased by the end of the eighteenth century. Production of Imari wares continued for local use until the nineteenth century, when trade was resumed with the West.

Among today's most sought-after pieces of Imari porcelain are those produced by the Fukagawa family, who started their own porcelain factory in Arita in 1875 and subsequently exhibited at both the Centennial Exhibition in Philadelphia in 1876 and a private exhibit in Paris in 1878. In 1894, Chuji Fukagawa, one of the sons of the family, started the Fukagawa Porcelain Manufacturing Company, which was geared to the Western export market and reflected European tastes. He excelled in his brocade Imari designs, and subsequently, the factory was the recipient of numerous international awards. The company began exporting in 1900 and is still in business.

It is interesting to note that Japanese porcelain took its influence from the Chinese designs from the outset of its porcelain industry. The use of underglaze blue with overglaze enamels is only one example. However, the Japanese departed from the Chinese in their use of innovative shapes (fish-shaped dishes for example) and their nontraditional use of color for decoration rather than realism. It is this difference that makes Imari so distinctively Japanese. (It is of interest, that the only time the Chinese ceramicists copied the Japanese, was in the area of Imari wares, and this was done deliberately and competitively in order to recapture their export market from Japan at the beginning of the Ching Dynasty. (See: Chinese Imari; Arita; Kakiemon; Nabeshima.)

References: Hazel H. Gorham, *Japanese and Oriental Ceramics*, Charles E. Tuttle Co., Inc., 1971; Soame Jenyns, *Japanese Porcelain*, Fredrick A. Praeger, 1965; Roy Andrew Miller, *Japanese Ceramics*, Toto Shuppan Co., Ltd., 1963; Nancy Schiffer, *Japanese Porcelain*, Schiffer Publishing Ltd., 1986; Irene Stitt, *Japanese Ceramics of the Last 100 Years*, Crown Publishers, 1974.

Museums: Los Angeles County Museum of Art, Los Angeles, California; Stanford University Art Museum, Stanford, Connecticut; Honolulu Academy of Arts, Honolulu, Hawaii; Nelson Gallery, Kansas City, Kansas; Baltimore Museum of Fine Arts, Baltimore, Maryland; Museum of Fine Arts, Boston, Massachusetts; University of Michigan Museum of Art, Ann Arbor, Michigan; Detroit Institute of Arts, Detroit, Michigan; City Art Museum of St. Louis, St. Louis, Missouri; Newark Museum, Newark, New Jersey; Metropolitan Museum of Art, New York, New York; Cleveland Museum of Art, Cleveland, Ohio; Dayton Art Institute, Dayton, Ohio; Philadelphia Museum of Art, Philadelphia, Pennsylvania; Seattle Art Museum, Seattle, Washington; Royal Ontario Museum, Toronto, Canada; Art Gallery of Greater Victoria, Victoria, Canada; British Museum, London, England; Victoria and Albert Museum, London, England; Tokyo National Museum, Tokyo, Japan; Topkapi Saray Palace Museum, Istanbul, Turkey.

Reproduction Alert: Imari porcelains have been in production in Japan since the early seventeenth century. The earliest pieces are unmarked and may have spur marks on the base. Latter pieces can be found with potters' marks (after 1868), and "Made in Japan" marks appear in the early years of this century. These latter marks have sometimes been removed. (It was not unusual to have the marks scrubbed out during World War II, when it was not popular to own items that were made in Japan.)

The early Imari wares were carefully executed. The quality of work declined during the Meiji period. During the twentieth century, all qualities have been exported. The most recent exports are perfect in design and shape, and it is this perfection that is the tip-off that the piece is not old.

The early eighteenth century saw copies of Imari designs on European porcelain. Meissen was the first factory to create porcelain in the Imari style, but it was soon followed by other porcelain manufacturers: Worcester, St. Cloud Chantilly, Mennecy Villeroy, Samson, and others also produced in the Imari style. Examination of these European pieces and their distinctive markings should not confuse the collector.

Collecting Hints: Imari porcelains are a hot item in the collector's market and have commanded increasingly high prices. Reasons for its collectablity include its availability in the West, the distinctive palette of colors employed, the ease of dating the ware, and its decorative value. Many of the most avid collectors are the Japanese people themselves. Since Imari was not just an export item but was used domestically since the beginning of its production, a taste for fine examples have always existed. At first it was only available to the wealthy who chose it for tableware over the pottery and lacquer products of the early seventeenth century. It was made affordable to the general population when the export market dropped at the end of the eighteenth century. The factories reduced the prices for the local population rather than abandon the kilns altogether. Because the ware was made for such a diverse consumer market over the years, there are a great many styles and qualities of Imari available. Of course, signed pieces from the Fukagawa family and other major artists will be at a premium both in Japan and in the West. Pieces depicting Dutch ships and European figures are also high on the collector's list. Large pieces such as export chargers and tall vases are commanding thousands of dollars, whereas small pieces from the late nineteenth and early twentieth centuries are still available at less than $100.

Bottle
11⅜", pair, late 17th century, each of triple-gourd form molded in relief and painted in underglaze-blue, iron-red, green and aubergine enamels and gilding with two small boys playing with kites among clumps of kiku and camellia. **12,000.00**
12" h., 19th century, the conical body tapering to a short ring foot and with a long waisted neck surmounted by a dished rim, the sides decorated gilt and polychrome enamels with a continuous scene of karako and han aguruma in a flowering landscape set off by floral bands, the neck encircled by a stiff-leaf border below linked hexagons **550.00**

Bowl
Barber's, 11" dia., circa 1700, decorated with a quatrelobed jardiniere containing peonies and prunus, the cavetto with stylized flowers and chrysanthemums . . . **1,300.00**
Fish, 15¾", Meiji Period, Fukagawa, the interior painted in underglaze-blue and black with a carp beneath rippling water, the exterior with a central panel of children playing, the blue ground deco-

Bottle, 6¾" h., 19th century, triple gourd form, decorated all over with a cobalt blue pattern of blossoms and scrolling leafy tendrils on a red enamel ground. $275.00. Courtesy of Butterfield and Butterfield.

rated with peony, painted Fuji mark **1,200.00**
8¼" dia., 19th century, of compressed ovoid shape resting on a short ring foot, painted in gilt, underglaze blue and shades of red enamel with shaped floral panels linked by smaller stylized flower reserves on a blue ground with gilt-accented floral roundels, the low conical lid decorated en suite and surmounted by a large jewel-form finial **650.00**
9¾" dia., Meiji period, this unusual piece of deep, rounded form with gently everted rim resting on a high foot, the interior decorated in red, green and gilt with cranes in flight and stylized floral panels encircling blue and white well depicting sailing ships, the exterior decorated with hanging foliage against a black ground **350.00**
9¾" and 10", pair, Meiji Period, each of inverted bell form and resting on a short ring foot, the interior well painted in the characteristic palette with a medallion of confronted ho-o bird below a wide rim band featuring floral and zoomorphic motifs, the exterior with further ho-o bird medallions alternating with landscape scenes on a diaper-patterned ground above stiff-leaf and linked-spiral bands encircling the base **450.00**
10" dia., late 19th century, floral and geometric interior design, the exterior with floral motif, executed in blue, green, red, yellow and blue enamels **600.00**
11" dia., 19th century, with steep fluted sides tapering sharply to a short ring foot, the interior well decorated in the characteristic palette with a medallion featuring a vase with blossoming sprigs encircled by three shaped bird-and-flower reserves separated by vertical panels of various design scattered with ho-o birds and dragon roundels, the exterior painted en suite **775.00**
11⅞" dia., 19th century, with straight sides and resting on a double-ring foot, the interior painted in gilt, underglaze blue and polychrome enamels with overlapping shaped reserves of geometric, "cracked-ice and prunus," and floral design surrounded by irregular shaped reserves of karashishi in a

flowering landscape separated by geometric-patterned vertical panels and small diamond shaped floral reserves, the exterior with a wide band of shippo-tsunagi design...................... **725.00**

12'' dia., 19th century, the steep sides resting on a raised foot, the exterior decorated in polychrome enamels and gilt depicting peonies and cranes in a landscape and stylized ho-o bird, the cavetto painted en suite with roundels of gilt dragons encircling a central blossom medallion............ **1,200.00**

12½'' dia., 19th century, with low straight sides and resting on a double-ring foot, the interior well painted in the characteristic palette with a pair of pheasants feeding in a flowering landscape encircled by an irregular geometric patterned border, the sides with further geometric bands alternating with floral motifs and scattered with fan-shaped reserves, the exterior painted en suite.......... **725.00**

14⅜'' dia., Meiji Period, with steep sides tapering to a high ring foot and decorated in underglaze blue, green, white and shades of red enamel with a large central medallion of stylized dragons amid leafy floral sprays encircled by a shippo-tsunagi band beneath three oval panels featuring abstracted birds reserved on a ground of blossoming peony and scrolling leafy tendrils intersected by three vertically linked mokko-bands on an arabesque-patterned red ground, the exterior with an overall cobalt blue design of scrolling tendrils, the base with a six-character inscription reading Daimin seika nensei............. **1,050.00**

19'' dia., well painted in gilt, underglaze blue and polychrome enamels with a scene of a court lady seated in an open pavilion shaded by lush blossoming trees and a cliff overhanging a stream winding into the distance, the foreground showing a large folding screen with a mountain landscape and three court attendants kneeling as they present various gifts, all surrounded by a wide border band of plovers in flight above stylized waves extending up the curved sides and continued on the exterior.................... **1,750.00**

Canisters, 8'' h., a pair of Imari canisters, covers and liners, the bodies of rectangular section, painted with panels of peonies and chrysanthemums, in iron-red, gilt and underglaze blue.................... **2,000.00**

Charger

14½'' dia., Meiji Period, painted in underglaze blue, gilt and bright enamels with a central roundel of carp amid cresting waves surrounded by a narrow floral-patterned band and three large reserves featuring a court lady's apartments alternating with shaped floral reserves on a gilt diaper-patterned blue ground..... **475.00**

14⅜'' dia., 19th century, with shallow sides and molded with lobes radiating from the center, the interior well decorated in underglaze blue, gilt and shades of red enamel with a hexagonal floral reserve surrounded by large shaped panels of flowering trees and plants alternating with smaller reserves of plovers and cresting waves on a blue ground, the exterior with ribbon-tied shippo-tsunagi clusters.............. **715.00**

17⅛'' dia., 19th century, the octagonal shape well painted in underglaze blue, polychrome enamels and gilt with large blossoming peony sprigs on a garden terrace near a meandering stream below brocade-patterned clouds, the cavetto with a narrow band of alternating floral reserves and roundels below shaped reserves of karashi-

Charger, 17¾'' dia., Meiji period, decorated in gilt, underglaze blue and polychrome enamels, twenty-four diaper- and brocade-patterned bands, spur marks, rough foot, surface wear. $1,430.00. Courtesy of Butterfield and Butterfield.

shi with peonies alternating with flowering chrysanthemum on the wide flaring rim **1,600.00**

17⅝" dia., Circa 1990, decorated in the typical palette with a small central peony medallion encircled by a kinrande peony band bordered by a narrow cobalt-blue hanabishi band flanked by four petal-shaped landscape reserves alternating with smaller floral reserves on a kinrande karakusa ground, the exterior with a wide band of scrolling tendrils above a lappet band encircling the low foot, the base with a kiln mark . . . **800.00**

17⅞" dia., Late Meiji Period, the interior medallion painted in the characteristic palette with sprays of momiji and flowering peony within a narrow band with oval floral reserves, the sloping sides painted with shaped blossoming peony panels separated by reserves of further flowers or karashishi reserved on a diaper-patterned ground overlaid by areas of kinrande floral brocade, the exterior with ho-o birds and reishi-fungus set off by narrow blue bands **600.00**

18¾" dia., 19th century, painted in gilt, underglaze blue, and polychrome enamels with a large floral medallion surrounded by eight foliate-shaped panels featuring a crane on a flowering prunus, karako, shochikubai, and Mandarin ducks reserved on ground of blossoming leafy tendrils, the exterior with three chrysanthemum sprigs **900.00**

Charger, 17⅞", circa 1900, decorated in gilt, underglaze blue and shades of red, kiln mark, spur mark, minor surface wear. $825.00. Courtesy of Butterfield and Butterfield.

21" dia., Meiji period, well painted in gilt, underglaze blue and bright polychrome enamels with a large fan-shaped reserve of birds and flowers partially overlapped by a scroll-form reserve depicting a hawk on a pine overhanging a garden in bloom, a small cherry-form reserve of sparrows and bamboo featured toward the bottom, all on a ground of gilt scrolling tendrils on underglaze blue and scattered with geometric and floral patterned hexagons, the exterior with three large flowering sprigs, the base with spur marks **1,200.00**

23⅝" dia., Meiji Period, decorated in gilt, underglaze blue and multicolored enamels with a central medallion of chrysanthemum blossoms with a hexagonal border intersected by three feathers joined to a feather-patterned border, all encircled by a narrow undulating floral band surrounded by large ogiwa-shaped reserves depicting ho-o birds above paulownia alternating with cranes in a landscape on a blue ground with gilt foliate sprays, the base with a kiln mark **2,000.00**

23⅞" dia., Meiji Period, carefully painted in gilt, underglaze blue and bright polychrome enamels with a large unfolding scroll featuring panels of longevity motifs or karashishi in a landscape within diaper-patterned borders, the scroll's underside with a crane-and-cloud design contrasting with a brocade ground scattered with ho-o bird and dragon medallions, a wide hanabishi band at the rim, the exterior with clusters of floral sprays **5,500.00**

24⅜" dia., Meiji Period, decorated in gilt underglaze blue and multicolored enamels with three large stylized ho-o bird medallions separated by abstracted dragons flanked by "flaming jewels" on a dense foliate ground, the center with a fronted blossom framed by a pair of long-tailed birds, the exterior with discontinuous floral scrolls, a maple-leaf cipher on the base **3,800.00**

Dish

11¼" l., 19th century, with shallow curving sides converging to a point toward the bow and flattened at the stern, the interior painted in gilt, underglaze blue and colored enamels with irregular bird- and floral-patterned radiating reserves bracketed by foliate-patterned "cloud collars" to the top and bottom, all below a rim band of scattered flower heads on a blue ground, the exterior with a stylized wave design **1,050.00**

13" dia., 17th century, a deep dish, painted in underglaze blue, iron-red and gilt with a circular panel of a boat in a rocky river landscape, surrounded by panels of flowers **900.00**

13$\frac{3}{4}$" l., 19th century, the interior decorated in the typical palette with a shallow flower container set with lush flowering sprays and surrounded by a diaper-patterned band overlaid by shaped dragon and karashishi reserves, the latter extending to the rim and bracketing large flowering landscape scenes, the exterior with cobalt blue floral sprigs **1,000.00**

18$\frac{3}{8}$", Meiji Period, boldly decorated in enamels with prunus among rocks, the underglaze-blue ground stencilled with bamboo, within a brocade border, bearing a Chinese inscription and dated Meiji tsuchinoto tora (1878), signed Hizen, Arita, Fukagawa sei **1,400.00**

20$\frac{1}{4}$", 17th century, of deep rounded form with narrow everted rim, decorated in underglaze-blue, iron-red and gilding with a circular panel showing a bridge and a building by a lake bordered by panels of kiku, peonies and cherry blossom, the reverse with a band of scrolling cherry **3,500.00**

21", Late 17th century, of deep rounded form, decorated in underglaze-blue, iron-red and green, yellow and aubergine enamels with a circular panel showing tasseled cords hanging before a weeping cherry within a broad band of clumps of kiku, peonies and camellia, the reverse with interwoven pine and prunus **4,800.00**

Figure, female

Bijin

14$\frac{1}{2}$" h., standing demurely, holding a baluster vase, her kimono decorated in iron-red, blue, green and gilt with chrysanthemums and cloud scrolls **700.00**

Bijin, 17" h., Meiji period. $900.00

17" h., Meiji period, the stately figure posed stroking a small animal held in the crook of her right arm as she pats the animal with her other hand, the elegant bijin dressed in dark blue floral kimono decorated with kiku blossoms scattered over a meandering stream, her hair brought up in an elaborate headdress framing her white-painted face **900.00**

Dancer, 13$\frac{3}{4}$" h., standing in an elaborate brocade-patterned kimono and floral-embroidered over-robe, her left hand holding a small drum, her slightly turned head with delicate facial features and framed by a floral headdress **400.00**

Geisha, 13$\frac{1}{2}$" h., standing holding a small drum, wearing a kimono decorated in red, shades of blue, gilt and green with large blossoms **500.00**

Girl, 14$\frac{1}{2}$" h., standing in a green kimono decorated with flowers and autumn motifs, her left hand hidden in one of her long sleeves, the other holding a small battledore, the youthful face turned to the right and framed by a classical coiffure **600.00**

Kambun Era beauty, 11$\frac{1}{2}$" h., standing in a boldly patterned kimono with a design of blossoms and stylized waves, a small puppy held in her hands to the front, the smiling face turned slightly to one side and framed by short tresses cascading from her characteristic hair style **275.00**

Musician, 7$\frac{1}{2}$" h., shown in a kneeling posture with her left knee slightly raised to support a cord-tied double-headed drum, her right hand about to strike another drum resting on her shoulder near her delicately painted face framed by an elaborate coiffure, the lithe body wearing a kimono decorated in bright enamels with scattered "Genji"-ciphers and cherry blossoms on an emerald green ground 200.00

8¼″ h., shown in a youthful kimono with a dramatic pattern of maple leaves floating on a meandering stream, her right hand to her side, the other petting a small dog resting on her lap, the sensitively painted face accented by a jet-black Shimada-style coiffure, on a metal base 475.00

8⅜″ h., the molded figure seated in a brightly patterned kimono and over-robe, her hands holding a long love letter which curls down toward the floor, her sweet visage accented by an elaborate coiffure ornamented with combs and hairpins. 525.00

11⅝″ h., shown walking with a lantern held in her left hand, the right with a fan held near her face turning slightly to the right and framed by tresses falling from her distinctive hair style, her deep blue kimono with cherry blossom pattern in bright polychrome enamels . . . 400.00

Ginger jar, 16″ h., 19th century, the ovoid form well decorated in gilt and colored enamels with a multitude of blossoms in vases, the dome's cover decorated en suite and the finial formed as a grinning shishi with his "brocade" ball 1,200.00

Jar

6½″ h., 19th century, of ovoid form, painted with peony and chrysanthemum blossoms, the shoulder with three reserves depicting a garden terrace, the neck painted with floral reserves 450.00

6¾″, pair, late 17th/early 18th century, each of slender ovoid form, molded in relief and painted in underglaze-blue, iron-red and gilding with panels showing a small boy holding an uchiwa beside clumps of kiku and peonies 1,200.00

Jardiniere

8¾″ h., 11⅛″ dia., of cylindrical form tapering slightly toward the base resting on three short shaped supports, decorated in gilt, underglaze blue and shades of red

Jardiniere, 13½″ h., 16″ dia., Meiji period. $1,450.00. Courtesy of Butterfield and Butterfield.

enamel with three shaped reserves of a vase issuing flowering sprigs separated by alternating vertical bands of floral design, all overlapped by two horizontal raised floral-patterned bands encircling the upper section 825.00

12″ h., Meiji period, decorated with three polychrome and gilt cloud collar reserves depicting a party of courtiers, lush chrysanthemums, bamboo and cranes against an underglaze blue and iron-red ground of peony sprays, neck with dragons and cintamani 1,200.00

13″ h., 15½″ dia., Meiji period, the high-shouldered body with a recessed rolled rim and fluted sides tapering sharply to a recessed ring foot, well decorated in the characteristic palette with a pair of large shaped reserves featuring an imaginary landscape alternating with smaller figural reserves, all on a blue ground scattered with blossoming leafy tendrils above a stylized lappet band encircling the foot, the shoulder molded with a "brocade square" decorated with shaped reserves of seashells on a patterned ground 1,875.00

13½″ h., 16½″ dia., ovoid, Meiji period, the high-shouldered body tapering sharply to a recessed ring foot and surmounted by a cylindrical neck set with a wide everted rim, the sides painted in the characteristic palette with two large shaped figural reserves of dancing bijin alternating with shaped landscape reserves, all on a blue ground with gilt scrolling tendrils below a shoulder band of cranes in flight, the neck with scattered kikko floral lozenges on a gilt-accented blue ground repeated on the rim with small floral reserves separated by chrysanthemum blossoms **1,450.00**

14½″ h., Meiji period, pair, each of tapered form with wide, slightly flaring rim, decorated with four shaped panels depicting paired male and female pheasants sitting among flowering magnolias, crab apple and peony issuing from squat blue vases, all against a varied geometric and foliate ground with small roundels of ho-o birds and blossoms **2,750.00**

8½″ h., Jubako two tiered, 19th century, the cylindrical sides and slightly domed lid decorated with polychrome reserves depicting butterflies, blossoms and landscapes against an iron-red and gilt fern-patterned ground **300.00**

Temple Jar, 31½″ h., late 17th/early 18th Century, the ovoid-form octagonal jar painted with upraised lappet-form landscape reserves issuing from a band of smaller lappets enclosing peony and nadeshiko blossoms, all on a dense ground of cherry blossoms intersected by bamboo, the neck painted with alternating ho-o birds and nadeshiko lappet form reserves, the high-dome form lid decorated en suite, and now mounted with a wooden finial, (cracks and restorations, lid of later date) **1,750.00**

Koro and Cover, 17″, Meiji Period, the ovoid body decorated with panels of flowers and foliage on a floral ground, the sides with panels of ho-o birds, the pierced cover surmounted by a shishi finial **3,500.00**

Plate

9⅛″ and 9⅜″ l., Meiji period, pair, each fashioned as a stylized fish, its head, fins and tail juxtaposed with floral reserves on a foliate-patterned ground executed in gilt, underglaze blue and colored enamels **500.00**

11¾″ dia., 19th century, the interior decorated in the typical palette with a central landscape motif surrounded by four large medallions of boats and blossoming flowers, all over four partially obscured floral reserves at the corners beneath a gilt-accented blue band **330.00**

Wedding lamps, 14″ h., Meiji period, decorated with white cranes in relief and underglaze blue, iron red and gilt flowers. $2,100.00. Courtesy of Butterfield and Butterfield.

12″ dia., Meiji period, delicately painted in gilt, underglaze blue and shades of red enamel with butterflies and scattered peony blossoms, together with decorated fans, books and scrolls, the base impressed with a studio mark. . . . **275.00**

13⅜″ dia., 19th century, the interior well decorated in gilt, underglaze blue, green and shades of red enamel with lush flowering sprigs issuing from a container on a garden terrace, surrounded by kinrande reserves of butterflies and blossoms alternating with shaped floral panels reserved on a gilt-accented cobalt blue ground **400.00**

Platter

14″ l., Meiji period, decorated in gilt, underglaze blue and colored enamels with a central cloud-form medallion painted with floating maple leaves, surrounded by four radiating shaped reserves with lush blossoming sprigs below ho-o birds or butterflies on a gilt-accented blue ground **525.00**

14¾″ l., 19th century, the interior well painted in the characteristic palette with a scene of cranes in a blossoming autumn landscape near a garden fence surrounded by a kinrande floral border band with stylized pine-cones at each corner, the flared sides with stylized shaped floral reserves on a diaper patterned ground. **1,200.00**

15½″ l., oval, 19th century, the interior well painted in gilt, underglaze blue and shades of red enamel with a scene of birds-and-flowers bracketed by two stylized floral reserves, the flared rim with molded fan-shaped reserves of rabbits alternating with blossoming sprigs on a dense floral patterned ground scattered with pierced shippo-tsunagi executed in underglaze blue on the reverse   **825.00**

18½'' dia., 19th century, the deep, circular platter resting on a recessed foot, the cavetto painted in iron-red, blue, turquoise and gilt with four alternating panels depicting cranes and bamboo on a blue ground, kirin and peony sprays on a white ground, the well decorated with swirling leaves and blossoms **950.00**

Urn

14½'' h., 19th century, of slender ovoid contour with vertical flutes stopping short of the high ring foot, decorated in the characteristic palette with dense irregular reserves featuring flowering chrysanthemum alternating with pavilions amid blossoming sprigs bracketed by flora bands on a dark blue ground to the top and bottom, the tall dome-shaped lid with a wide rim and oversize knob finial **825.00**

16¾'' h., 19th century, the slender fluted body with a rounded shoulder and tapering to a high ring foot, the body painted in the typical palette with shaped landscape reserves alternating with floral re-

serves on a blue ground with gilt scroll work above a lappet band encircling the base, the shoulder with further lappet-shaped design accented with figural and floral motifs, the high dome-shaped lid with a wide rim and oversize knob finial, decorated en suite **950.00**

Vase

9'', bottle vase, early 18th century, in the form of a leather flask decorated in underglaze-blue, iron-red and gliding with clumps of flowering peony and kiku. **900.00**

10'' h., pair, Meiji Period, Fukagawa studio, each of ovoid contour tapering to a short slightly splayed ring foot and surmounted by a waisted neck flaring toward the rim, the sides painted in underglaze blue, gilt and shades of red enamel with two large floral reserves alternating with smaller panels of stylized butterflies, all on a foliate-patterned ground, the neck with further shaped reserves featuring ho-o bird and paulownia, each base with orchid cipher, on inscribed Fukagawa-sei. **1,100.00**

10'' h., an Imari baluster vase and cover, painted with panels of phoenix, reserved on a ground of scattered flowerhead and lotus roundels **600.00**

12'' h., pair, beaker vases, octagonal, of squat shape with tall trumpet necks, painted in underglaze blue, iron-red and gilt with vases of peonies **700.00**

12⅜'' h., 19th century, each of high-

Punch Bowl, 18½'' dia., 19th century, steep fluted sides and set on a high ring foot, the interior painted in gilt, underglaze blue and shades of red enamel, crack, old restoration, extensive wear. $1,430.00. Courtesy of Butterfield and Butterfield.

Umbrella Stand, 24'' h., Meiji period, decorated in gilt, underglaze blue and shades of red, wear. $1,000.00. Courtesy of Butterfield and Butterfield.

shouldered ovoid form tapering to a recessed circular foot and surmounted by a long waisted neck flaring to a dished rim, decorated in underglaze blue, gilt and red enamel with large reserves of ho-o birds above blossoming bushes on a dense ground of flowering peony below a floral-patterned petal band suspended from the rim **1,450.00**

14⅛", Meiji Period, of baluster form, decorated in underglaze-blue, iron-red, enamels and gilding with a dragon and ho-o bird, both passing over vertical panels variously decorated with flowers, foliage, stylized waves, birds amid clouds and diaper design, the neck with roundels decorated with various formal patterns, signed Fukagawa **950.00**

15" h., late 19th century, baluster form, floral reserves on a floral background, blue, red and gilt palette. **800.00**

16½" h., Meiji Period, the slender body with a tapering diamond contour surmounted by a waisted neck flaring to a wide diamond-form mouth, the sides painted in underglaze blue, gilt and colored enamels with two large shaped reserves, each featuring the Chinese sennin Gama and Chokaro on a dense floral-patterned ground scattered with small geometric and floral reserves below a molded foliate-patterned shoulder band beneath mokko-shaped landscape panels on the neck decorated en suite **1,100.00**

21¼", Meiji Period, boldly decorated in underglaze blue, colored enamels, iron-red and gilt with numerous cranes, standing among stylized waves, pine branches and flowers, the ground gilt with cloud scrolls **1,400.00**

23" h., the high-shouldered body set with a tall cylindrical neck and tapering sharply to a high ring foot, the sides well painted in gilt, cobalt blue and polychrome enamels with three large shaped reserves featuring bijin in a flowering landscape, all on a dense ground of chrysanthemum blossoms above a lappet band encircling the base, the neck with a band of writhing dragons amid cloud scrolls **1,200.00**

Vase, 24½" h., Meiji period, ovoid body, drilled and converted to lamp base, decorated with reserves of blossoming peony and chrysanthemums in colors of red, blue, yellow and gilt. $3,300.00. Courtesy of Butterfield and Butterfield.

24¼", beaker vase, late 17th/early 18th century, of octagonal section with flared rim, decorated in underglaze blue, iron-red, gilding and black enamel with a panel showing a man and two ladies with two horses and a foal, the reverse with a panel showing an elaborate vase of flowers, all bordered by bands of floral design. . . **3,500.00**

42¼", Meiji Period, with a slender body and flared neck, decorated in underglaze-blue, iron-red, colored enamels and gilt with panels of birds among flowers and foliage

Pair, 30½" h., Meiji period, unusual, decorated in the familiar palette, decorated in dense floral patterns, restorations and wear. $5,225.00. Courtesy of Butterfield and Butterfield.

above minogame, the sides with
scrolling foliage and dragon
roundels **4,200.00**
Vegetable dish with cover, 10½″, oval
shape, late 19th century, pomegranate finial, vine and flower design,
blue red and gilt decoration **450.00**

KAKIEMON PORCELAIN

History: Kakiemon is a type of Japanese porcelain ware made in the Arita area that is decorated
with polychrome enamels over the glaze. The
body of this ware is pure white porcelain, the
enamel overglaze motifs incorporate Japanese
design elements, leaving much of the surface unpainted. It has long been associated with the Kakiemon family of potters.

The history of Kakiemon porcelain is somewhat
clouded. Today, there is no real concensus about
its origins or that of Japanese polychrome porcelain itself. This was not true a decade ago. According to traditional accounts, Kakiemon porcelain and the technique of enamel decoration on
porcelain in Japan itself were invented by Sakaida
Kizaemon, known as Kakiemon I (1569–1666),
who learned the technique from a ceramics
dealer in Imari who had learned it from a Chinese
potter at Nagasaki. The Sakaida family kiln in the
Nangawara Valley near Imari was then given over
to the production of this new type of porcelain.
The new porcelain so pleased the daimyo of
Nabeshima that when a piece in the shape of two
persimmons (kaki) was presented to him, he
asked Kizaemon to change his name to Kakiemon, a great honor. From then on the oldest son
took the name of Kakiemon and the family continued making Kakiemon wares down to the present.

In recent years, some serious doubts have
arisen about the reliability of this account. First,
no shards in polychrome enamels have been
found at the sites of early Kakiemon kilns; only
blue and white porcelain fragments have been
discovered. Second, those pieces that have been
attributed to the first three Kakiemons show
marked Kangxi influence and, therefore, are more
likely to have been produced by Kakiemon IV
(1641–1674) or Kakiemon V (1660–1691). The
first three Kakiemons had all died by 1672, and
they would have been influenced by Ming styles,
not Kangxi. What is clear is that polychrome
enamel decoration came directly to Japan from
China (wu ts'ai, Wanli red and green enamel, and
Swatow examples had been exported to Japan)—
and not through Korea—and that a number of
pieces were being produced in the mid-seventeenth century. Dutch records note the export of
such pieces in 1659. The Kakiemon family was

involved in its production by this time, but so
were other Arita area kilns.

Actually, despite the excitement about learning
the Chinese secret of polychrome enamel decoration, once the Japanese learned the technique of
blue decoration under the glaze fired at high temperatures, it should not have been very difficult
for them to learn to add and fire polychrome
enamels in a muffle kiln. The secret would have
spread quickly. Certainly, polychrome enameled
wares were being produced in Arita by the 1660s.
Japanese documents note that authorities gathered enamel painters into one part of Arita
(Akemachi) from 1661 to 1672, prohibiting others
from practicing the art. By 1672 the secret had
become common property.

Some authorities have argued that it is possible
to distinguish the Arita Kakiemon-style wares
from those produced by the Kakiemons, but because there is no agreement on this point, it is
probably better to speak of Kakiemon porcelain
as a style rather than as the product of a particular
kiln.

What made Kakiemon porcelain so prized was
the perfection of the pure white body and the
brilliance of both the enamel colors and the design. Eliminating the excess iron in the clay and
glaze produced the milky white color—the glaze
was almost transparent, although full of bubbles.
The clay was kneaded thoroughly, and the pieces
were finished on a treadle wheel by shaving or by
molding. There were two to three firings. If there
was a preparatory firing, it was to firm up the
unglazed body and the second was for the glaze.
Afterward, the pieces were enameled and fired in
a muffle kiln. Red, green, yellow, blue, aubergine,
and later, gold made up the typical Kakiemon
color scheme. Usually the hues were softer than
that of ordinary Arita porcelains. Some pieces
were also decorated in underglaze blue, in combination with polychrome enamels, and sometimes by itself. However, the peculiar persimmon
(kaki) color orange-red and the brilliant overglaze
blue are the colors that are most characteristic of
Kakiemon wares. Whichever of the Kakiemon
colors were used, however, usually one or two
colors were key to the scheme, accentuating the
composition. The overglaze cobalt pigment is
said to have come from the Near East rather than
China, and was even more brilliant than the
Kangxi blue. An iron brown was often used on the
rim of dishes, but this was not exclusively a Kakiemon device.

The style of decoration was completely new to
porcelain. It appears to have derived from Kano
(Chinese influenced) and Tosa (native element)
painting styles, which in turn were derived from
Chinese Sung Dynasty bird and flower painting.
Designs were simple, and instead of decorating
the whole surface in the Chinese manner, artists
left blank spaces to balance the painting. The

naturalistic designs represented spring and autumn as depicted in Japanese painting. The brushwork was beautiful itself, showing a strength and fluency associated with fine painting. Among the motifs typically used were the ho-o bird, shishi (fu dog), dragon, crane, tortoise, deer, and horse, along with bamboo, pine, prunus, grasses, peony, and chrysanthemum. Often famous motifs from the Japanese repertoire were used in combination with each other: a tiger curled around bamboo with a plum tree and/or brushwood fence, quail with millet, squirrels among vines, deer cantering under maples, cranes fishing from rocks, birds with flowering plums and bamboo, and rocks with trees. Male figures were rare but Chinese boys were commonly depicted, especially the famous Chinese story of Si Maguang who shattered a barrel to rescue a friend. The undersides were usually decorated with simple tendril or peony scrolls mostly in underglaze blue.

In the late seventeenth and early eighteenth centuries, textile designs appeared, often on pieces that were geometrically shaped. In addition, pieces molded in the round were also made, especially in the form of women (bijin), boys, ducks, elephants, tigers, and shishi. These proved very popular.

Early pieces of Kakiemon did not have a mark of any kind. Even later, marks on fully fledged Kakiemon pieces were rare. When they did appear, they were not particularly reliable. Underglaze blue decorated Kakiemon sometimes had Chinese dynasty marks, usually Ming or Qing six-character marks. Around 1690, the fuku (good fortune) mark started occasionally appearing on Kakiemon wares, as on Arita and Kutani porcelains. Often it was written in a running script, called a running fuku mark. In the early eighteenth century, these characters became boxed in a double square. Some pieces inscribed kaki have been attributed to the late seventeenth century—a few of them have reign marks as well, indicating they were made in 1695 and 1699. The Genroku era (1688–1704) was considered the golden period of Kakiemon porcelain, but the reign marks are not totally accepted. The kaki mark continued to be used in the eighteenth century as well. In the mid-Meiji Period, the Kakiemons sold their mark. From 1928, to the 1950s, their pieces were marked "made by Kakiemon" or incorporate the kaki mark on a double ring in light green enamels.

Nineteenth-century Japan saw rapid economic growth and porcelain production increased as well. In 1810, a revival of Kakiemon ware took place, as many new Nabeshima designs were incorporated. Many traditionally styled pieces continued to be made, although experts would argue that the milk white quality of the body had declined and the fineness of design had deteriorated. In the early twentieth century, two generations of the Kakiemon family (Kakiemon XII and Kakiemon XIII) attempted to recreate the glory of Kakiemon wares, relearning the secret of the pure white body. Kakiemon XIII and Kakiemon XIX, in particular, have been very inventive and were recognized by the Japanese government as an Important Intangible Cultural Treasure, a supreme honor.

Kakiemon wares were tremendously popular in Europe where they were imitated by the leading European porcelain manufacturers. Kakiemon designs and forms were copied by Delft in Holland; St. Cloud, Mennery, and Chantilly in France; Meissen in Germany; Bow, Chelsea, and Worcester in England; and later Samson in France. A very important collection was formed by Augustus the Strong, elector of Saxony and king of Poland who in 1717 began housing his collection in Dresden. The inventory of this collection is an important guide to dating early Kakiemon pieces. Great collections house seventeenth- and eighteenth-century examples of Kakiemon wares. Much less attention has been paid to nineteenth-century wares.

References: John Ayers, Oliver Impey, and J. V. G. Mallet, *Porcelain for Palaces*, Oriental Ceramic Society, 1990; R. Cleveland, *200 Years of Japanese Porcelain*, St. Louis City Art Museum, 1970; Soame Jenyns, *Japanese Porcelain*, Faber and Faber, 1979; Adalbert Klein, *Japanese Ceramics*, translated by Katherine Watson, Alpine Fine Arts Collection Ltd., 1987; Tsugio Mikami, *The Art of Japanese Ceramics*, Weatherhill/Heibonsha, 1972; Takeshi Nagatake, *Kakiemon, Famous Ceramics of Japan*, Vol. 5, Kodansha International Ltd., 1981; Maria Penkala, *A Survey of Japanese Ceramics*, Interbook International BV, 1980; P. L. W. Arts, *Japanese Porcelain*, Lochem-Poperinge, 1983.

Museums: Museums that house the best Kakiemon collections are in Japan and Europe. In Japan these include Kyushu Ceramic Museum, Arita; Kakiemon Museum, Ashikaga; Kurita Museum, Ashikaga; Saga Prefectural Museum, Saga; and Idemitsu Museum of Art, Tokyo.

Museums in Europe include Musees Royaux d'Art et d'Histoire, Brussels, Belgium; Fitzwilliam Museum, Cambridge, England; British Museum, London, England; Victoria and Albert Museum, London, England; Ashmolean Museum, Oxford, England; Burghley House Collection, Stamford, England; Musee du Louvre, Paris, France; Porzellansammlung, Dresden, Germany; Residenzmuseum, Munich, Germany; Stichting Twickel, Delden, the Netherlands; and Groninger Museum, Groningen, the Netherlands.

Museums in North America include Los Angeles County Museum of Art, Los Angeles, California; Center of Asian Art and Culture, Avery Brundage Collection, M. H. de Young Memorial Museum, San Francisco, California; Honolulu

Academy of Arts, Honolulu, Hawaii; Art Institute of Chicago, Chicago, Illinois; Nelson Gallery-Atkins Museum, Kansas City, Kansas; Baltimore Museum of Art, Baltimore, Maryland; Museum of Fine Arts, Boston, Massachusetts; University of Michigan Museum of Art, Ann Arbor, Michigan; The Detroit Institute of Arts, Detroit, Michigan; City Art Museum of St. Louis, St. Louis, Missouri; Brooklyn Museum, Brooklyn, New York; Metropolitan Museum of Art, New York, New York; Cleveland Museum of Art, Cleveland, Ohio; Philadelphia Museum of Art, Philadelphia, Pennsylvania; Eugene Fuller Memorial Collection, Seattle Art Museum, Seattle, Washington; Royal Ontario Museum, Toronto, Canada.

The best source for temporary exhibitions is probably the "Calendar of Exhibitions and Seminars" in *Orientations*, a periodical put out in Hong Kong but widely available in the United States, which lists Asian art exhibits around the world on a monthly basis.

Reproduction Alert: Tin-glazed earthenware, a soft pottery ceramic covered with a lead glaze that makes it appear somewhat like porcelain, was already widespread in Europe when Kakiemon burst on the scene. Since Kakiemon's popularity threatened this industry's profitability, European factories were quick to copy Kakiemon. Some of the Delft copies are particularly good. Fortunately, many have the correct potter or factory mark, and of course, close inspection reveals that they are not porcelain. Harder to detect are the Ching-te-chen or Arita blanks enameled in the Kakiemon style by Dutch enamelers in the early eighteenth century. The famous Kakiemon collection of Augustus the Strong at Dresden contains some of these pieces. There also are the European porcelain copies of Kakiemon. Meissen, Chantilly, St. Cloud, Chelsea, Bow, and Samson copied Kakiemon well enough to fool the novice. Most of these had a potter or factory mark, but it sometimes was erased or covered over when an unscrupulous individual saw a quick profit in selling a piece as Kakiemon. An example is the infamous case of Lemaire and the Meissen factory in the eighteenth century. For a short period (1729–1731) Lemaire managed to convince the Meissen factory to produce Kakiemon copies (copied from genuine pieces in Augustus the Strong's collection) without the usual crossed swords mark, which was sometimes replaced with a pseudo-Oriental mark or it was put over the glaze where it could be easily taken off. Even if you were to be fooled by such a piece, you would have an interesting and early piece, valuable in its own right. This would not be true if it were a Samson copy, a nineteenth-century porcelain that often fools the unwary.

Collecting Hints: Kakiemon caused a sensation in Europe in the seventeenth century and makes a striking and important collecting field today. Fine nineteenth-century examples are widely available as are, of course, twentieth-century pieces. With the official government recognition of the Kakiemon potters, Kakiemon XIII and Kakiemon IV, one would not do badly collecting contemporary Kakiemon porcelains. If you wish to collect late seventeenth- and early eighteenth-century Kakiemon, you are in for a more difficult time. You will probably need to travel to Europe, in particular England, Germany, and France (or have a dealer buy for you there), and you will need to set fairly large sums of money aside for your collection. Furthermore, you will need to educate your eye to the European copies of Kakiemon. Fortunately, most of these are valuable in their own right.

With Kakiemon, its always wise to buy from a knowledgeable and honest dealer who will guarantee the authenticity of the pieces you are buying in writing and over time. Knowledgeable and reliable dealers have usually done considerable research on their pieces and will have no difficulty in giving you a meaningful guarantee. They will also give you a hands-on education, and once they see you are serious about collecting, they will be on the lookout for pieces for you. You don't always have to pay a premium for buying from the knowledgeable specialist, but even if you do, it's well worth it. The money you will save in avoiding buying spurious or mediocre pieces might add up to the purchase price of a museum-quality Kakiemon porcelain piece.

Whomever you buy from, but particularly if you are making your purchase based on your own expertise, you want to do as much reading as possible and to visit fine museums housing collections of Kakiemon. In judging a potential purchase keep what you have learned clearly in mind. Consider whether the piece offered is really Kakiemon. In general, you need to look at the type of foot; the quality of the glaze, clay, potting, enamels, and painting; motifs and stylistic elements; marks; and forms. Pay particular attention to the exposed paste on the base. Is the piece of the period you desire or it is purported to be? Again, you must examine the piece carefully looking for telltale signs of period. Keep the above criteria in mind. Take the piece on approval, if you have to, and examine it with the books in front of you.

Other questions to ask are the following. Is the piece of the quality you desire? Is the body pure white? Are the enamels vivid? Does the painting excel? Is the piece in good condition? Has it been repaired? Is there a chip? Is there a glaze imperfection? Is the piece rare? Size, form, certain symbols and motifs, or a rare signature can make a piece rarer and more valuable.

Advisors: Stewart and Barbara Hilbert

Beaker, tapering, octagonal, $3\frac{1}{4}''$ h., late 17th century, decorated in iron-

Beakers, Pair, late 17th century, octagonal tapering form, decorated in blue, yellow, and black enamels, one with two chips to the rim. $6,342.00. Courtesy of Christie's, London.

Bottles, pair 10½" h., late 17th century, set in Louis XV gilt bronze mounts, painted in iron red, green, blue, and black enamels, one bottle with old repair, and one body crack, the bases struck with the crowned C. $87,450.00. Courtesy of Sotheby's, London.

red, green, blue, yellow and black enamels, each with an exterior of chrysanthemum sprays, the everted rim with plum blossoms, slight chip to rim **3,490.00**

Bottle, Kakiemon-style, 9" h., late 17th/early 18th century, octagonal with a tall cylindrical neck, decorated in underglaze blue, iron-red, blue, green, and yellow enamels and touches of gilding, panels of formal floral design, small restored rim chip **27,325.00**

Bowl
4½" dia., late 17th century, on a ring foot decorated in iron-red, green, blue and black enamels with a bird on branches of peony in a banded hedge. **4,400.00**

6" dia., mid-19th century, square form with indented corners and tapered sides, short ring foot, decorated with a peach and cherry sprigs alternating with blossoming chrysanthemums, the exterior with flowering branches and birds   **850.00**

6" dia., molded, circa 1900, shallow tapering to a short ring foot, flaring sides and a foliate-edged rim molded with a continuous keyfret pattern, the interior sides with molded interlocking pattern alternating with shaped floral reserves surrounding a central medallion of auspicious fungus, lily and fruiting branches **600.00**

7½" dia., blue and white, 19th century, foliate-edged molded with faceted sides, the interior painted in underglaze blue with dragons and blossoms, scrolling tendrils

below the brown foliate-edged rim, spur marks, stylized mark . . .   **400.00**

8⅛" dia., 18th century, flaring sides, high foot ring, interior painted in polychrome enamels and gilt, kirin below three sho-chiku-bai, exterior with three fruiting pomegranate trees, cracks, gilt restoration **1,100.00**

Censer, with a reticulated silver lid, 4½" h., 20th century, cylindrical shape on three short feet, cobalt painted dragon-form handles, the exteriors with a polychrome enamel design of two ho-o birds, pierced low domed silver top **770.00**

Bowl, 8½" dia., late 17th century, deep multilobed form, decorated in iron red, blue, green, and yellow enamels and gilding, small chips, one crack. $10,494.00. Courtesy of Sotheby's, London.

Cup

2⅝" h., late 17th century, octagonal form, iron-red, green and blue enamels and touches of gilding, floral sprays **4,140.00**

4" h., with cover, 19th century, steep flaring sides tapering to a short splayed ring foot and decorated on the exterior in underglaze blue, gilt and polychrome enamels with scattered ho-o birds and stylized floral motifs, repeated on the domed lid, the foot encircled by double rings, stylized fuku mark **1,200.00**

Dish

3⅝" dia. and 5¾" dia., two floriform dishes, 19th century, painted in gilt and polychrome enamels, the first fashioned as a five-petal blossom, the interior with a small leafy blossoms encircled by a ho-o bird, the second a small scallop-edged multi-lobed dish with a ho-o bird   **330.00**

4" dia., and 6⅞" dia., two dishes, 19th century, the first a deep bowl with an everted rim, a short ring foot, decorated to either side in gilt and polychrome enamels with leafy flowering springs, hairline crack, the second, a small triangular dish on three short supports, floral scrolls beneath two pierced holes on each side, the interior painted with a fruiting peach spray. **935.00**

4¾" dia., saucer dish, circa 1670, decorated in iron red, green, blue and black enamels and gilt with butterflies hovering above chrysanthemum sprays among banded hedge, slight chip to foot **500.00**

6", set of four, oval shape, early 20th century rounded sides, mons in polychrome enamels **800.00**

8" dia., enamelled, foliate-rimmed, circa 1660, decorated in iron-red, green, blue, yellow and black in the Kraak manner, the center with a grasshopper on rockwork beneath peonies, bordered by panels of Buddhist emblems and flowers, lacquer repair to rim **4,400.00**

8⅜" dia., late 17th century, shallow rounded form, decorated in underglaze blue, iron-red, green and yellow enamels, spray of kiku, a border of a band of flowers among rocks, foliate scrolls in a band on the reverse **3,000.00**

8½" dia., pair, circa 1700, blue and white, foliate rimmed, decorated

Molded Dish, 7½" dia., circa 1860, foliate rimmed, decorated in iron red, green, blue, yellow, and black enamels and gilt, chocolate rim. $46,508.00. Courtesy of Christie's, London.

with a band of lozenge-shaped panels containing flowerheads among lotus sprays beneath another band of flowerheads, the reverse with scrolling karakusa, fuku mark **4,775.00**

8¾" dia., foliate-rimmed saucer dish, circa 1680, decorated in iron-red, green, yellow, blue and black enamels with a bird in the bowing branches of bamboo among pine and plum blossom issuing from banded hedges, chocolate rim, enamels rubbed, rim chips restored **16,535.00**

Set of eight Kakiemon chrysanthemum dishes, 20th century, each oval bowl with a scalloped edge and radiating lobed sides, the interior painted in underglaze blue and colored enamels with a fruiting pomegranate tree and blossoming prunus **825.00**

Figure

Bijin, 15½" h., circa 1680, decorated in iron-red, green, blue, yellow and black enamels with scattered blossoms and scrolling foliage on her outer kimono, her under robe with cherry blossoms and ribbons **128,600.00**

Tiger, seated, 7½" h., late 17th century, its yellow body painted with brown fur marking, the mouth and ears detailed in iron-red, the eyes in green with black pupils, restoration to ears and tail **58,775.00**

Jar, Kakiemon-style, 7¾", late 17th century, ovoid form decorated in underglaze blue, iron-red, deep yellow and green enamels, a continuous band of butterflies among clumps of

Ewer, 12" h., late 17th century, Middle Eastern–inspired form, painted in iron red, blue, green, yellow, and black. $48,975.00. Courtesy of Sotheby's, London.

kiku and prunus, slight firing crack within the base **66,600.00**
Kendi, 8½" h., late 17th century, decorated in iron red, blue and green and black enamels, the ovoid body with karashishi prowling among peony   **8,600.00**
Koro and cover, 4½" h., 19th century, kakiemon-style of hexagonal form with two curved handles, decorated in iron red, enamels and gilding with prunus and pomegranates, the pierced cover with floral designs and surmounted by a kiku form knop . . .   **720.00**
Mukozuke, pair, 4⅛" dia., 19th century, floriform, each with a foliate edge and steep sides tapering to a ring foot, the interior with four styl-

ized floral springs in polychrome enamels, the exterior with four blossoming plants, foot chip **550.00**
Pillow, 4¾" x 3⅜" x 2⅝", late 17th/early 18th century, rectangular form, decorated in underglaze blue, iron red and enamels, with two peacocks and a small boy among sprays of kiri, the base has bands on enamel on the biscuit **6,470.00**
Plate, early 20th century, iron red, green, yellow, blue and black enamels with a bird in the bowing branches of bamboo among pine and plum blossoms issuing from banded hedge **750.00**
Saucer, 3" dia., 19th century, underglaze blue and polychrome overglaze enamels **385.00**
Teapot, 7½" h., 19th century, Kakiemon-style polychrome and gilt decorated, rectangular shaped with a slender cylindrical neck, S-curved squared spout and large C-form handle, the front painted in gilt and polychrome enamels with blossoming branches, small dome-shaped lid with a large knob finial **450.00**
Tokuri, 7¼", late 17th/early 18th century, in the form of a well bucket, decorated in iron red and enamels, additional flowers and shrubs, a shishi, and birds in Dutch enamels and gilding, handles missing, cracks and repairs **2,500.00**
Tureen, 10¾" h., circa 1680, Kakiemon-style blue and white decorated with a continuous band of pavilions beneath pine trees, domed cover similarly decorated and surmounted by a gilt-metal finial **10,360.00**
Vase, trumpet shaped, 18", circa 1680, decorated in iron-red, green blue, yellow and black enamels with peonies among rockwork intertwined with bamboo among brushwork fences, restored **45,925.00**

KIMONO AND OBI

History: The Japanese verb *ki* "to wear," and the noun *mono* "a thing," provide us with the literal translation of the word *kimono*. Kimono in current usage is a general term applied to the many types of robe-type garments worn by the Japanese. However, in the sixteenth to nineteenth centuries these robes were known as *kosode*, and this term is still often used to describe the robes of this period. Here, we will use the more common term, *kimono*.

Stag, 7" h. x 8½" l., circa 1860, decorated in dark yellow, iron red, and blue enamel, some restoration. $306,075.00. Courtesy of Sotheby's, London.

Excavations of tombs of the Kofun period (250–552) have produced terra-cotta figures wearing crossover necklined robes decorated with designs and patterns. These are believed to have been the forerunner of today's kimono. The earliest of recorded kimonos were dyed with natural elements of bark, roots, and leaves in designs expressing an appreciation for the freedom and beauty of nature. It was thought that the artistry, patience, and skill required to produce these masterpieces imbued each textile creation with a spirit of its own.

The dichotomy of the Japanese character—reverence for discipline versus attraction to the ornate—is reflected in the kimono. By the twelfth century the kimono became a standard part of court dress. Rank and season of the year dictated exactly the type of clothing to be worn and by whom. In an effort to express individuality, court members adopted a motif from their favorite textile pattern and used it to symbolize their family name. This practice led the tradition of applying mons (family crests) to the kimono as well as virtually any family possession. Wealth was displayed by multilayers of silk robes, which were thought to add dignity to the floor-seated silhouette. During this period, court members would wear up to twenty layers of robes. However, this practice changed after a fire broke out and most of the court perished because they could not move quickly enough to escape.

The shogun soon after pushed fashion into austerity, with simplicity of design reigning. Patterns fell to the hemline and elaborate brocades and colors were hidden inside the kimono. The concept of reserved elegance has remained the hallmark of the kimono through the centuries.

By the seventeenth century, the Japanese weaving industry was able to copy complex fabrics from China, but they did not know how to manufacture metallic yarns. They duplicated them by applying gold and silver leaf directly on the fabric. It was during this era that the Kabuki theater had its greatest influence on fashion. For example, a famous Kabuki female impersonator was credited with the introduction of the modern obi (a wide sash worn around the waist). He was so tall that in an attempt to avert attention from his height he used a very wide obi instead of the standard thin tie around his waist. The new style was soon popular throughout Japan. It was also common at that time for patrons of the theater to throw their own kimono onto the stage as a gift to the actors. The actors would recycle these gift robes, thereby reviving past styles and creating new styles, which the women quickly adapted and copied.

With the innovation of woodblock printing, books were complied by vendors to sell their kimonos and obis. Some famous artists supplemented their incomes by designing textile pattern books and even hand-painting the kimonos themselves.

The Japanese of today believe that the kimono and obi symbolize both tradition and discipline. Cloth brocades will often be given to a new bride by her in-laws as a sign of acceptance into the family. Even today, wedding kimonos (uchikake) made by top Tokyo artists command prices of $20,000 to $60,000. Consequently, many brides can not afford one and must rent the traditional robes for the occasion.

The obi has become as important to Japanese women as the kimono itself. The obi was always tied in the back with one major exception—courtesans traditionally tied the obi in front, presumably for convenience. The obi makes a fashion statement as important to the Japanese woman as jewelry is to the Western woman.

References: Reiko Mochinaga Brandon, *Country Textiles of Japan*, Weatherhill, 1986; Ishimura Hayao and Maruyama Nobuhiko, *Robes of Elegance Japanese Kimonos of the 16th–20th Centuries*, North Carolina Museum of Art, 1988; Jill Liddell, *The Story of the Kimono*, E. P. Dutton, 1989; Norio Yamanaka, *The Book of Kimono*, Kodansha International, 1982.

Museums: Santa Barbara Museum, Santa Barbara, California; Textile Arts Center, Chicago, Illinois; Japanese Galleries, Newark Museum, Newark, New Jersey; Japan House Gallery, New York, New York; Metropolitan Museum of Art, New York, New York; Virginia and Bagley Wright Permanent Exhibit, Textile Study Center, Seattle Art Museum, Seattle, Washington; Arthur M. Sackley Gallery, Smithsonian Institute, Washington, D.C.

Reproduction Alert: The collector of Japanese textiles need not worry about encountering reproductions. However, the vast majority of kimonos on the market will be of this century. The most common kimono found in the United States today is the hand-painted floral design on silk made from the 1930s to the 1960s. A whole industry was set up after World War II just to repair old kimonos to sell to U.S. soldiers. Wedding kimonos from the 1920s to the 1950s also are easy to find. These are often kimonos that have been retired from rental agencies. The age of these textiles may often be exaggerated.

Collecting Hints: There are relatively few ardent kimono collectors today. Consequently, an antique kimono in excellent condition can be had for a relatively reasonable sum considering their beauty and artistry. The Japanese have little interest in all but the finest and rarest pieces. Obis are seldom sold at auction and in retail shops they rarely command more than a few hundred dollars, particularly for obis of this century. Kimonos are occasionally offered at major auction houses, but seldom bring more than a few thousand dollars for fine examples and often are sold for much less. Today one can put together a marvelous collection of Japanese textiles for a minimum investment.

The collector will encounter four basic types of obi: (1) maru, the ceremonial obi, 12" wide and patterned on both sides; (2) fukuro, the formal obi, 12" wide but patterned only on one side; (3) han haba, the casual obi, 6" wide; and (4) nagoya, the casual obi, half 12" wide and half folded and stitched to 6" wide and patterned on one side (after 1920).

There are several different types of kimono that are commonly collected: (1) uchikake, the ceremonial robe (usually wedding), 70" long, sleeves 40", and weighted at hemline; (2) tomesode, the formal kimono for married women, 60" long, sleeves 20"; (3) furisode, the formal kimono for a single person, 60" long, sleeves 30 to 40"; and (4) haori, a lightweight coat 30 to 60" long.

Advisors: Paul and Janiece Knutson

KIMONO

Haori
  38" l., 1930-1940's, thin black gauze-like silk so loosely woven that one can see through this summer jacket, five family crests the only design, good condition. **200.00**
  39" long, 1930-1940's, black silk exterior, brocade landscape on interior, minor fraying **350.00**
Miscellaneous
  45" l., 19th century, Ainu robe of natural weave bordered at the hem, sleeves and neck with navy cotton embroidered in cotton with geometric patterns, mounted in Plexiglas frame **4,000.00**
  74" l., 19th century, finely woven priest's robe, rectangular robe decorated with a stylized floral pattern and an elaborate brocade design, with ring fitting and purple linings. **1,000.00**
  80" l., 19th century, embroidered priest's robe, rectangular ocher silk priest's robe embroidered with a maple leaf design **1,500.00**
  82" l., late 18th/early 19th century, finely woven priest's robe, rectangular robe decorated with stylized pattern of scrolling paulownia leaves and applied with brocade patches with salmon pink linings **2,500.00**
  85" l., 18th/early 19th century, brocade priest's robe, rectangular robe woven with a design of stylized peony and chrysanthemum,

with applied brocade patches, with salmon silk linings **2,500.00**
Tomesode
  58" l., 1930-40's, Iro Muji Kuro Tomesode with subtly embossed floral design on royal blue crepe material, with five mons, soiled. **150.00**
  58" l., 1920-30's, Iro Tomesode pink and blue chrysanthemums and plum branches, hand painted on black crepe background, pattern repeated on inside green crepe background lining, soiled and minor stains **150.00**
Uchikake
  72" l., 1940-1950's, wedding kimono in gold, silver, cadmium red and power blue brocade, design of traditional mons, weighted at hemline, fraying of collar area . . . **750.00**
  72" l., 1940-1950's, white silk embroidered with gold and silver thread outlined flying cranes, dark greens used in pine tree decoration, and subtle browns in bamboo design, thicker and weighted at hem line, red silk lining, worn and stained **850.00**
  72" l., mid 19th century, cadmium red colored silk with gold dipped silk thread used in the turtle with a tail, silver dipped thread used in the swan outline, soft emerald green colors in a pine design, seagreen, salmon-pink, and cadmium orange used in the rest of the decoration of the beautiful wedding kimono with a rich red silk lining, weighted hemline, some fading and a few loose threads **1,500.00**

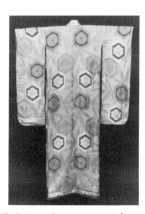

Uchikake, 72" l., 1940–1950, brocade of gold and silver, some fraying. $750.00

Uchikake, 72" l., 19th century, embroidery on patterned silk, soiled and frayed. $1,500.00

OBI

Fukuro
  164" l. and 12" w., 1930-1940's, silk brocade of landscape scenes in silver and gold on shrimp colored background, minor soiling   175.00
  164" l. and 12" w., 1930-1940's, dark blue background with gold threads detailing tree, branches leaves and birds in soft running display, solid black crepe back, some loose gold threads and soiling 200.00
Han Haba, 125" l. and 6" w., 1940-50's, brocade of floral pattern with cranes in orange, green, white, and plum, fraying at seams 75.00
Maru
  164" l. and 13" w., 1940-1950's, heavy stiff silk brocade with pattern of floral fans in orange, rust, blue and white, soiled throughout especially around seams 200.00
  164" l. and 13" w., 1930-1940's, heavy stiff silk brocade of fans and floral patterns in orange, gold, blue, black, and silver, good condition with little soiling. 300.00
  164" l. and 13" w., 19th century, heavy stiff silk embroidered with gold, white , green, and orange thread on a pale green background, seamed on one side folded on other, pattern flows continuously side to side, soiled and worn edges 500.00
  Child's, 160" l. and 12" w., 1930-1940's, brocade of cadmium orange and silver thread in fish and shrimp design, silver discolored   150.00

Maru, 160" l., 1930–1940, child's, brocade in silver and cadmium orange, silver tarnished, $150.00

Nagoya
  140" l. and 12" w., 1930-1940's, Fukuro Nagoya Obi of lightweight gold silk background with orange maple leaves, detailed with black branches, folded and sewn on one end, minor soiling 75.00
  140" l. and 12" w., 1930-1940's, soft pale golden green crepe with gold, orange, tan, and blue crest displayed between gold crisscrossed weave, one end folded and sewn together, spectacular color, minor soiling 150.00

KOMAI WORK

History: Japanese metalwork, technically and artistically, has been unrivaled by that of other cultures for many centuries, mainly as a result of emphasis on the Samurai swords and related objects. In 1868, the Meiji restoration curtailed the power of the warrior class, prohibited the wearing of swords, and greatly reduced the income of swordsmiths and related artisans. These skilled and creative people turned their efforts to peaceful products.

In Kyoto, the Komai family, traditionally involved in the work on sword ornaments, then turned their efforts to other decorative work. Their most successful products were mostly small items such as boxes, dishes, trays, and miniature chests made by a very difficult process of metalwork. A base of iron or steel was decorated with minute bits of gold and silver to form designs of leaves, flowers, houses, landscapes, mountains, and such.

The process consisted of preparing the base metal by chiseling a cross-hatched groundwork of grooves in the metal. The intersections of the grooves provided minute burrs which were able to secure the inlays of silver and gold which were hammered in to form the design. The design was drawn by a fine, needle-pointed scribe. After the gold and silver had been applied, many layers of lacquer (black) were applied, cured, and burnished.

References: Henri Joly and Kumasaku Tomita, *Japanese Art and Handicraft (The "Red Cross" Catalogue)*, Charles E. Tuttle & Co., Inc., 1976; Kyoto Commercial Museum, Catalog, 1910; Bernard Rosett, "Komai Work," *The Orientalia Journal*, Vol. 3, January 1981.

Museums: Museum collections of Komai work are not known at this time. Occasional pieces might be found in auction catalogs of fine Orientalia or special exhibits of Japanese metalwork.

Collecting Hints: The collector should be wary of the crude Damascene work, which can simulate Komai work at first glance. However, it lacks the exquisite sharp detail of genuine work and very often is done on a brass base. A magnet will aid in determining the nature of the base metal, and the work should be inspected with a 3x to 5x magnifier. Much of the true Komai pieces have signatures or a seal mark, but there are some fine unsigned items as well.

Old pieces of Komai work will have tarnished silver areas. Sometimes finger rubbing is sufficient to bring up the luster. If polish is needed, it should be handled gently, applied with a cotton swab.

Large pieces of Komai work are not often encountered and are spectacularly expensive when found. Smaller examples, such as dishes of 3" to 4" can still be found at prices within reason.

Advisors: Bernard and Irene Rosett

Cabinet, miniature, 2⅛", signed Koma Meiji, late 19th century, gold inlay on iron, 4 drawers, panels of flowers and foliage, irises, phoenix bird, landscape, butterflies, vines **1,800.00**
Chest, miniature, 3¼" h., signed Koma Meiji, late 19th century, gold and silver inlays on iron, 3 drawers with

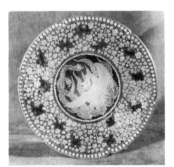

Dish, 3¾" dia., circa 1875, gold and silver inlays on iron, scalloped rim, phoenix bird in central circle surrounded by grapes and grape leaf motif, unsigned. $850.00

Watch Fob, 3½", circa 1890, in brass, with black background in the designs of flowers, temples, birds, and waterwheel, in six hinged sections, short brass chain and clip for the watch, stamped To on the back of each section. $250.00

chrysanthemum knobs, one with decorated inner cover; decorated overall with geometric designs, temples, landscapes, vine leaves, butterflies, foliage **3,600.00**
Dish, 3½" dia., signed Nihon-koku Kyoto Ju Komai sei, late 19th century, cranes and Mt. Fuji motif, silver and gold inlays on iron **1,200.00**
Vase, 4", signed Nishiko Inoue sei, late 19th century, cylindrical shape, inlaid gilt on iron, landscape, flowers, grapevines **1,200.00**

KUTANI WARE

History: Kutani is the name of a small village in Kaga Province, now called Enuma County, Ishikawa Prefecture, which is located on the northwest coast of the main island of Japan. Recent excavations in the area have produced evidence that Kaga had been operating kilns since the twelfth century. Apparently the region dominated the production of stoneware in the northern coastal area until the sixteenth century. By the seventeenth century, the commercial success of porcelain production in Japan lead to the establishment of the "old Kutani" kilns.

In the seventeenth century, Kaga Province was a rice-producing land under the feudal control of the wealthy Maeda family. The history of "old Kutani" or "ko Kutani" is cloudy, and what exists is a combination of speculation and fact. It is believed that the discovery of porcelain stone in Kutani inspired the Maeda clan to send Goto Saijiro to Arita to learn porcelain techniques from the master Kakiemon. When he returned to Kutani in the mid-seventeenth century, he brought Chinese potters with him. The kiln was shut down sometime after 1690, presumably because of political disfavor between the shogunate and the Maeda family. The enameled wares produced at Kutani during this relatively short period (approximately sixty years) is what we currently consider to be ko Kutani. Later production in the same area (which produced a porcelain of different appearance) is now called by the name Kutani.

The ceramic body of ko Kutani ware, generally a greyish white in color, varies from stoneware to porcelain. The variety suggests that some of the ceramic blanks may have been brought in from other kiln sites, possibly in Arita, to be decorated in Kutani by the Chinese artists. The wares made included dishes, plain and footed bowls, sake bottles and footed sake servers, containers with lids, and vases. Of these, the most plentiful were the dishes and bowls. The decorative polychrome enamel colors used are thought to have come from China and included Persian blue, a vivid green, yellow, purple, and a variety of reds. They were applied heavily as overglazes achieving a visual effect of dark and somber color. The reds were not always used, and when they appeared, they were scantily applied. Underglaze blue, when used, was limited to outlines of design or light decoration on the sides or undersides of dishes and bowls.

Subjects from nature were painted in a free handed style using birds, flowers, and natural settings as motifs. The general style of dishes and bowls included a picture in the center, with or without decoration on the rims. Sometimes the rim decorations were quite complex, consisting of diaper patterns and medallions. Another type of ko Kutani decoration was to cover the entire surface with geometrical patterns. These wares, if signed, show the Chinese good fortune (fuku) mark within a square. The mark was generally painted in black and covered with a thick layer of transparent green or purple glaze. Occasionally, blue glaze was used but it is not considered typical.

Also included in the production of this period was what we now call ao Kutani (green color) which generally has a heavy stoneware body. Ao Kutani wares employed the general palette of ko Kutani colors, with green predominating; there was a notable absence of the color red. The colors were applied in expansive washes and were decorated with black lines.

Little is known of the ceramic production in Kutani during the eighteenth century. The early nineteenth century brought a revival of the Kutani kilns. Wares signed with the Kutani seal rather than the fuku mark appeared at this time. The Kutani ceramic industry was concerned with two different styles of production. The first concentrated on producing wares in the traditional style. The other focused on the development of a decorative scheme in which red was the predominant color.

It was not until the middle of the century however, that the kilns expanded their output. Under the direction of Iidaya Hachiroemon, a new decorative technique was innovated, employing fancy gold patterns on a red enamel ground which were called aka-e (red) Kutani. This style was continued by the artist Eiraku Wazen and his brother Nishimura Sosaburo (Kaizen) in the 1860s after Hachiroemon's death (in 1849). Wazen also continued to work in the Kaga aka-e style of red and/or gold design on a white background, sometimes used in conjunction with underglaze blue. His pieces were often signed "Made by Eiraku at Kutani" or stamped "Eiraku." The European demand for the Kinrande (gold brocade) style wares was so great that many new kilns were founded in Kaga Province to fill the persistent orders. Many of these wares contain potter's marks along with the traditional Kutani mark.

After a short inactive interval at the beginning of the Meiji period the Kutani-yaki kilns went back to active export production.

Kaga-style ware is a general term for the late nineteenth- to twentieth-century porcelain production of the Kutani wares of Kaga Province, which is now Ishikawa Prefecture. Late Kaga-style porcelain had its origins in the red Kaga designs of the mid-nineteenth century but differed in the employment of gaudy colors derived from Western pigments. Some greyish bodied Kaga ware was also produced with underglaze blue transfer decoration. One Kaga-style pattern, which features girls in various settings, is usually signed in Japanese with a symbol or factory name. Some of the twentieth-century Kutani porcelain was also made in the Satsuma style, using designs that formerly appeared on Satsuma ware.

Many different porcelain products were made, including tea, coffee, and chocolate sets; dishes and bowls; incense burners; and small decorative objects. Signatures on Kaga-style wares were marked Kutani in Japanese characters. The potter's name appeared painted in gold on top of a red brushstroke. Later marks, such as the t in the cherry blossom mark, were followed by "Nippon" (1891–1921), and "Made in Japan." Generally, the quality of this late Kaga-style ware is very poor. (See: Twentieth Century Japanese Porcelain; Nippon.)

References: Stephen W. Bushell, *Oriental Ceramic Art*, Crown Publishers, Inc., 1980; Sensaku Nakagawa, *Kutani Ware*, Kodansha International Ltd. and Shibundo, 1979; Maria Penkala, *Far Eastern Ceramics*, Charles E. Tuttle Co., Inc., 1963; Nancy Schiffer, *Japanese Porcelain 1800–1950*, Schiffer Publishing Ltd., 1986; Irene Stitt, *Japanese Ceramics the Last 100 Years*, Crown Publishers, Inc., 1974.

Museums: Museum of Fine Arts, Boston, Massachusetts; Fogg Art Museum, Cambridge, Massachusetts; Peabody Museum, Salem, Massachusetts; Metropolitan Museum of Art, New York, New York; Philadelphia Museum of Art, Philadelphia, Pennsylvania; Seattle Art Museum, Seattle, Washington; British Museum, London, England;

Victoria and Albert Museum, London, England; Ishidawa Prefecture Art Museum, Japan; Komatsu Municipal Museum, Komatsu City, Japan; Nakamura Memorial Art Museum, Nakamura, Japan; Japan Folk Art Museum, Tokyo, Japan; Tokyo National Museum, Tokyo, Japan.

Reproduction Alert: A new kiln was created in Kutani in the early 1900s in the Bunka era (1804–1817) where copies of old traditional wares were produced. Although imitations of the old Kutani wares were made, the bulk of production in the later nineteenth century (encouraged by the rising export market), generally confined itself to red or polychrome and gold enamels on a white ground (with or without the combination of underglaze blue drawing) and Kinrande techniques. When the old color combinations were utilized, the painters employed new pigments and techniques that should serve to separate the old from the new to the experienced eye of the collector. Kutani kilns still are producing porcelain for export.

Collecting Hints: It is not difficult to distinguish the old Kutani styles from those produced in the nineteenth century and later. Of the ko Kutani wares surviving today, the bowls and dishes are most likely to be found. Dishes come in all sizes and may be of several shapes, including round, octagonal, square, hexagonal, and gourd. They may have foliate rims or be footed. Bowls also vary in size from large to small and may be deep or shallow, with or without handles and matching stands. Spouted sake servers and bottles, primarily of gourd shape, appear both in ribbed and spiral form. Containers with lids were also produced. These forms are found in both the ko and ao Kutani palette of colors and styles. The many red colors, when used, were very understated, unlike those found in Imari or Nabeshima wares. Generally, these old wares give an impression of heavy subdued color, as opposed to the nineteenth-century Kutani wares which use bright coral red as a predominant color. Also, gold decoration, which is a familiar component in the nineteenth century Kutani ware, is totally absent in ko Kutani.

The later Kaga-style Kutani porcelains exported in the late nineteenth and early twentieth centuries should be classified under the heading of collectables, since they bear little resemblance to the original output of the Kutani kilns. The ko Kutani and ao Kutani ceramics, created as individual works of art, are much valued and sought after by the Japanese, whereas the late Kaga-style pieces were inspired by, and created for, the commercial export market. Americans apparently admire these later designs and style which do not really reflect the Japanese taste at all. They are considered highly collectable as nostalgic items from the earlier part of this century.

Since some of the old-style wares were brought back from Japan in the nineteenth century as sou-venirs, there are pieces that show up from time to time at local markets and antiques shows, sold by uninformed dealers who do not recognize the ware for its aesthetic properties or monetary value. Interested collectors should study the research material so that they can become familiar with these wares and be able to recognize a bargain when they see one. Ao and ko Kutani and nineteenth-century revival pieces can occasionally be found for mere dollars, even though they are actually worth thousands to a serious collector.

Bottle
    With Stopper, 18″, 19th century, of double-gourd form decorated in yellow, green and aubergine enamel with dragons among clouds on a "Y" diaper ground, marked Kutani **1,200.00**
    13⅛″ h., pair, Meiji Period, each of double-lobed gourd shape resting on a high splayed foot and surmounted by a cylindrical neck fitted with a cap molded with a foliate-form finial, the lower lobe with shaped reserves of birds-and-flowers alternating with iris amid flowering grasses below further reserves of ho-o birds on the upper section, all on a gilt-accented red enamel ground, the base inscribed Kutani-zukuri **1,050.00**

Bowl
    Ao Kutani, 6″ dia., Meiji Period, with steep sides tapering to a short ring foot, the interior well painted in polychrome enamels with a sparrow flying toward a clump of flowering plants, one edge featuring lengths of variously patterned brocade cloths, the exterior with scrolling leafy vines in black on a bright green ground, the base with a cartouche reading Kutani **200.00**
    7½″ dia., Meiji Period, the square form bowl with rounded corners and raised on a ring foot, the sides split, overlapped and applied with small circular bosses, decorated to the interior with poets in an abstract landscape setting, four character mark to base reading Kutani Mokubei **475.00**
    18″, Meiji Period, decorated in iron-red and gilt with Sciobo accompanied by two attendants, one of whom carries the dish of peaches, the other fanning the goddess with a large uchiwa, the border with cloud-shaped panels of flowers, the exterior with panels of flowers,

Punch Bowl, 14⅛" dia., the center with a dragon and cloud scrolls on gilt ground surrounded by a row of arhats, the exterior with arhats, painted in bright enamels, the base inscribed Kutani-zukuri Akiyama-sei. $1,540.00. Courtesy of Butterfield and Butterfield.

signed Oite Kutani Watano sei
Hongen ga 950.00
Box, 5½" h., fashioned in the form of
Hotei emerging from his large sack,
the lid depicting his face peering out
of his sack and the bowl decorated
with whorl patterns on a green
glazed ground 375.00
Censer, 11" h., Kutani kinrande globu-
lar tripod censer and pierced cover,
the body decorated with panels of
villages and families on river banks,
on a ground of scattered flowers and
trailing wind 900.00
Charger, Ao Kutani, 15½" dia., Meiji
Period, the interior well painted in
gilt and polychrome enamels with a
large hawk perched on a pine tree
entwined with vines, the regal bird

Charger, 19" dia., Meiji period, the interior painted with bright enamels, the scene of swimming carp on a brick red ground, the exterior with scattered floral sprigs. $2,750.00. Courtesy of Butterfield and Butterfield.

gazing intently at a pair of swallows
flying past a distant lieh en-studded
pine with gilt needles, all encircled
by a geometric-patterned rim band
featuring shaped reserves of ho-o
birds, dragon, and "auspicious motifs," the exterior with three peonies
amid stylized leafy branches, the
base with cartouche reading Kutani
and potter's name. 475.00
Compote
9½" h., 11¾" l., Mid-19th Century,
the upper section of diamond
shape tapering sharply to a
stepped waisted pedestal flaring at
the base, the exterior body
painted in bright colored enamels
with squared molded floral reserves on a kinrande ground below a recticulated band of elongated ovals within shaped
patterned reserves below the scalloped-edge rim with gilt knob-like
projections on the four corners,
the slender pedestal encircled by
writhing dragon in relief against a
kinrande ground extending to the
boat-shaped foot with circular
pierced accents, the base inscribed "Saichoku-tei Keiko sei"
Ao Kutani, 12" dia., Meiji Period,   750.00
the large bell-form bowl tapering
to an everted rim and raised on a
tall tapering foot, decorated to the
interior two scholars on a garden
path depicted in green, ocher,
blue and aubergine, the exterior
decorated with scrolling tendrils,
Fuku mark on base 475.00
Dish
8¼", Late 17th/Early 18th century, of
shallow rounded form decorated
in iron-red and blue, green, aubergine and yellow enamels with a
flowering cherry tree beside rocks
within an underglaze-blue band   450.00
14¾", 19th century, of rounded form,
decorated in green, aubergine,
yellow and blue enamels with a
central panel of a monkey
perched in a banana tree, the border with panels of circles upon diaper design, the reverse with
scrolling foliate design, with Fuku
mark 650.00
Figure
Dog
10¼" h., pair, each molded in the
Chinese style and resting on a
plinth, one with its front paw on
a "brocade ball," the other with
a pup, each with mouth agape

Male, 16" h., early 19th century, ao Kutani, shown seated with shishi at his feet, his robes glazed in green blue, red, and gilt enamels, age crackle, chips. $3,200.00

Maidens, Pair 15⅜" h. and 13⅝" h., a high-ranking courtesan and a maiko, each wearing brocade robes and sensitively rendered facial features, elaborate coiffures. $2,750.00

exposing tongue and teeth, impressed Kutani mark on base **350.00**
10" h., 11" l., each dog painted with yellow and gilt sunbursts and black mane and tail on green ground, fiercely playing with its blue incised "brocade" ball, one with mouth open, one with mouth shut, inscribed and incised seals **1,300.00**
Shishi, 8¾", 19th century, seated with its head raised and turned slightly to the left, details painted in iron-red and gilding **850.00**
Kannon, 14" h., Meiji Period, the deity wearing phoenix-patterned brocade robes and standing on a writhing dragon wreathed in undulating cloud scrolls, her hands hidden by long sleeves beneath her elaborate necklace framing her sensitively modelled face with a high chignon covered by a cowl, all decorated in gilt and bright colored enamels, the base inscribed Kutani-sei **500.00**
Jardiniere, 12" h., Kutani kinrande baluster-shaped, painted with panels of flowers and religious figures, on a ground of scrolling foliage **850.00**
Koro and Cover, 5¼", Meiji Period, in the form of a thatched hut, painted with colored enamels and gilt with ivy growing over the roof and walls, the base pierced with a circular window **875.00**

Plate, Ao Kutani, 14" dia., Meiji Period, decorated on the interior with a central landscape scene surrounded by triangular reserves of brocade patterns alternating with leaves and tendril reserves all painted in green, ocher, aubergine and blue, the exterior painted green with a scrolling tendril design, Fuku mark on base **500.00**
Tokkuri, 9¾" h., 19th century, of ovoid form narrowing to a tall slender neck and tapering slightly to a recessed ring foot, the body decorated in col-

Plate, 14½" dia., Meiji period, showing a sage near a waterfall, encircled by peony blossoms and fans, the decorative palette consisting of green, ocher, aubergine, and blue, with a fuku mark on the base. $800.00. Courtesy of Butterfield and Butterfield.

ored enamels with blossoming peony bushes below an underglaze lappet band on the neck, the base with fuku cartouche **1,150.00**

Vase

8¾'' h., Meiji Period, trumpet-mouth, of low-slung ovoid contour resting on a high slightly splayed foot and tapering to a waisted neck encircled by a raised band and flanked by a pair of animal-mask handles below the wide dished mouth, the body well painted in gilt and polychrome enamels with shaped figural and bird reserves on a dense kinrande foliate-patterned ground above a raised band set with four mock animal-mask handles, a raised keyfret and taotieh band encircling the foot, the base inscribed Kutani shoin-do sei **900.00**

10⅞'' h., pair, Meiji Period, each with a tall waisted neck flaring to a wide mouth and slightly tapering to a short recessed foot, the sides decorated in gilt and polychrome enamels with pairs of long-tailed birds on a dense millefleur ground and applied with a pair of fans below the narrow sloping shoulder with a shippo-tsunagi band repeated at the base, the neck with a kinrande band of butterflies amid scrolling leafy tendrils, the base with Kutani studio mark **975.00**

12½'' h., kinrande double vase, molded in high relief with Ashinaga and Tenaga, the oviform bodies painted with the foxes' wedding **850.00**

12½'' h., pair, Meiji Period, double gourd form, both vases decorated with a patchwork of triangular reserves, each painted with a different brocade pattern, with further brocade decorated textile forms overlapping the reserves, the base with a lappet band and the neck with a cloud collar, the small lids decorated en suite, nine character inscription to base reading "Kaga-WkuniWatano-sei Hakuken-byo"   **1,200.00**

13⅛'' h., pair, 20th century, each of slender ovoid contour tapering to a recessed circular foot and surmounted by long waisted neck flaring at the rim, the body painted in polychrome enamels with two large bird-and-flower panels re-served on a kinrande patterned ground below further shaped floral panels on the neck, and overlapping lappet band encircling the foot, the base with Kutani mark   **420.00**

13¼'' h., pair, each baluster-form vase resting on a splayed foot and tapering to a trumpeted mouth, molded at the shoulders with opposing dragon-form handles, decorated in gilt and copper-red enamel with floral reserves on a brocade decorated ground, the base with mark reading kutani . . .   **725.00**

14'' h., 20th century, with sloping shoulders and tapering to a recessed circular foot, the sides well painted in polychrome enamels with Buddhist arhats dressed in monastic robes and holding various attributes above a lappet petal band at the base, an elaborate wide band featuring dragon and ho-o bird panels reserved against a floral garland beneath a stylized foliate-patterned band encircling the short waisted neck and flared rim, the base inscribed Kutani-zukuri Akiyama-sei **475.00**

14¼'' h., Meiji period, pair, each of ovoid form and decorated with birds in flight and resting in a blossoming peony bush and cherry tree, banded at the waist with a gilt lotus scroll and at the neck with further leafy scrolls encircling diaper-patterned medallions, the base with an inscription reading Kutani Yukiyama sei **1,300.00**

Vase (one of pair), 14½'' h., Meiji period, each decorated in polychrome and gold on a white background, bird and floral decoration with diaper patterns at the neck and foot. $1,320.00

14⅝" h., pair, 20th century, each of slender ovoid contour tapering to a slightly splayed foot and fashioned with a long waisted neck flaring to a dished rim and flanked by a pair of wave-shaped handles, the body painted in polychrome enamels with a continuous scene of women and children viewing chrysanthemums along a river bordered by a distant village, the sloping shoulder with an undulating band scattered with shaped geometric-patterned reserves below stylized ho-o bird reserves on a ground on clouds and momiji at the neck, a lappet band suspended from the rim, the base inscribed Kutani ni oite Ota/Orita-sei 475.00

14¾" h,. pair, baluster form, Meiji Period, each of ovoid form tapering to a high banded foot and surmounted by a waisted neck flaring to a rolled rim and flanked by a pair of elaborate animal-mask handles, the sides well painted in gilt, black and shades of red enamel with frolicking karako, reversed by various birds in a flowering landscape, each ovoid panel framed by confronted ho-o bird and reserved on a gilt ground randomly scattered with floral, geometric and zoomorphic medallions extending over the neck below a linked floral-accented kikko band at the rim, the base inscribed Dai Nihon Kutani-zukuri 1,350.00

15" h., Meiji period, pear shaped, each elongated ovoid body decorated with two scalloped edge reserves of cranes and lotus separated by fronted lotus and foliate tendrils on an orange ground below a stiff-leaf collar band at the neck under a wide band of flying cranes 775.00

15⅝" h., the elongated vase painted in gilt and copper-red with two scalloped-edge reserves, one of court figures enjoying a plate of pomagrantes reversed by three small birds resting in blossoming peony and cherry branches, on a diaper patterned ground alternating with smaller reserves of karashishi, the neck decorated with phoenix medallions below a band of lotus blossoms 775.00

Vase (one of pair), 15½" h., Meiji period, double-gourd form, painted with scalloped reserves of birds resting on branches, along with an abstract butterfly and phoenix medallion, one restored, the base with inscription Dai Nihon Kutani Tsukuru. $1,210.00

LACQUER

History: Oriental lacquer differs from what we know as lacquer in the West. We think of it as a resinous material suspended in a solution such as alcohol which dries by solvent evaporation. Oriental lacquer is a nonresinous sap derived from the *Rhus vernicifera* tree, which hardens in an atmosphere of high humidity (65 to 85 percent) and temperature of 75 to 85°F. This tree is related to poison ivy, poison oak, and poison sumac, and many people have toxic reactions to the raw lacquer.

The trees are tapped from late spring to early fall. Sap oozes out very slowly and an average tree produces only six or seven ounces per season. The raw material must then be refined. The trees are found in Japan and China and are less common in Korea, Vietnam, Cambodia, and Burma.

The history of lacquer use begins in ancient China, where it was used to protect and beautify the wood used in constructing homes in approximately 2000 B.C. By 1000 B.C. lacquer objects were used as tribute or gifts to the court. Chinese lacquer dated to about 400 B.C. has been found in Korea, over which China had established control. In about 300 A.D., Chinese lacquerers left Korea and settled in Japan, where Chinese style was adopted. Early Chinese lacquer was used to cover large wooden statues and for cups, wine beakers, small boxes, which were mostly undecorated. Later on, in the fourteenth century, decorated pieces were made with inlays of mother-of-pearl. Deeply carved cinnabar lacquer was begun in the sixteenth century. In the seventeenth century the decoration we call coromandel was begun, as well as painting on a black background. All these techniques are still in use today.

By the sixth century, the Japanese had begun to produce lacquer objects (learning from the Chinese and Koreans), and by the eighth century they had developed their own techniques and styles. Lacquer was first used to decorate statues, interiors of palaces, and furniture. Later on came boxes of all kinds, bowls, trays, utensils, small cabinets, writing desks, inro, and netsuke.

Most lacquer pieces have a core of wood, although the core can be bamboo, animal hide, layers of fabric, or paper. The refined lacquer is applied to the core and then hardened, It seals the surface, making it completely resistant to all liquids and even to some acids. Japanese lacquerers use a wide variety of techniques and materials to make their exquisitely fine lacquer objects. The most commonly seen materials and techniques are described below along with the Japanese terms, which are usually used in the literature and auction catalogs.

Aogai: Blue-green iridescent abalone shell.

Fundame: Thinly ground gold powder sprinkled on heavily. The surface is duller than other gold powders because it is not polished.

Hira maki-e: Low or flat sprinkled picture (low relief).

Kin ji: Heavily sprinkled powdered gold ground that takes a very shiny finish when polished.

Kiri-gane: Decorative technique employing thin pieces of gold leaf in various shapes, often forming a mosaic.

Maki-e: The technique of sprinkling metallic or pigmented powders to form a design on wet lacquer ground.

Mokume: A finish resembling natural wood grain.

Nashiji: Small irregular gold flakes are sprinkled in several layers in an orange-toned lacquer medium, then polished to resemble "pear skin."

Negoro-nuri: The ground is first lacquered black and then red. It is polished to a mottled effect so the black shows through in some places.

Raden: Mother-of-pearl inlay technique.

Roiro: Shiny black waxy ground, used in highest-quality pieces.

Taka maki-e: High relief. The design is built up in layers of lacquer.

Togidashi maki-e: A design is drawn in wet lacquer, then pigmented or metallic powders are sprinkled on and layers of black lacquer are added to coat the surface. The surface is then ground down until the original design is revealed.

Tsui koku: Carving in multilayered black lacquer.

Tsui shu: Carving in multilayered red lacquer.

References: E. Ehrenkrantz and J. Epstein, "A Glossary of Japanese Lacquer Techniques and Terms," *Netsuke Kenkyukai Study Journal*, vol. 4, n.d.; Melvin and Betty Jahss, *Inro and Other Miniature Forms of Lacquer Art*, Charles E. Tuttle Co., Inc., 1981; Oscar Luzzato-Bilitz, *Oriental Lacquer*, Paul Hamlyn Publishing Group, 1969; Barbara Teri Okada, *A Sprinkling of Gold*, the Newark Museum, 1983; Andrew J. Pekarik, *Japanese Lacquer 1600–1900*, The Metropolitan Museum of Art, 1980; Staff of Tokyo National Museum, eds., *Textiles and Lacquer*, Toto Shuppan Co. Ltd., 1958; Harold P. Stern, *The Magnificent Three: Lacquer, Netsuke and Tsuba*, Japan Society, Inc., 1972.

Museums: Los Angeles County Museum of Art, Los Angeles, California; Asian Art Museum, San Francisco, California; Boston Museum of Art, Boston, Massachusetts; Newark Museum, Newark, New Jersey; Metropolitan Museum of Art, New York, New York; British Museum, London, England; Victoria and Albert Museum, London, England; National Museum of Art, Tokyo, Japan.

Reproduction Alert: There are few lacquer reproductions of old items in the art market. Collectors should not easily be fooled by the souvenir-type items made of bakelite forms of plastic that are being produced now. In some cases, the crudeness and mass-produced look and synthetic coloring of the imitation lacquer proclaim the modern origins of these pieces. There are some fairly high-quality pieces, newly made of plastic, that can be very attractive, but the collector should be aware of the differences.

Collecting Hints: Without a sizable bankroll, the collector is bound to be traumatized by the prices reached at auction of lacquer objets d'art. Condition greatly influences the value of most of these items. It is amazing how some have retained their pristine condition over the years. Many collectors have acquired excellent pieces by accepting items with small defects such as dings, chips, rubs, and the like, as long as the artistic highlights have not suffered; The Venus de Milo (without arms) is frequently noted as such an example.

While the collector of today cannot undo the "slings and arrows" of history, he or she can certainly take precautions to maintain the proper conditions of temperature and humidity and to avoid strong light. Carelessness in transporting items is one of the chief causes of damage, including dropping, which causes cracks and dings. Contact and friction from other objects are responsible for a lot of trouble. Museum curators have almost unanimously set forth rules about carrying no more than two objects at a time. The use of carrying trays is suggested. Museums and auction houses require the wearing of soft cotton gloves when handling very fine lacquer.

Advisors: Bernard and Irene Rosett

Basins, 6" dia., pair, each of low cylindrical contour with raised horizontal bands to the exterior and resting on three short supports, the interior well and sides featuring clumps of flowering iris in gold hiramaki-e and takamaki-e on a roiro ground **250.00**

Bowl

4¼" dia., set of six, all with steepsides resting on a slightly recessed foot, the interior of black lacquer, the exterior a peacock blue painted over silk **250.00**

4¾" dia., with covers, set of six, the inside of the lid decorated with cherry petals fluttering down toward a striped curtain, the reverse with a partial view of an ox cart opposed by a Genji cipher, executed in colored and gold hiramaki-e on a roiro ground **200.00**

4¾" dia., trays-14¼" l., covered bowls and two trays, set of eight, the lid of each bowl painted with scattered momiji and sakura in colored and gold hiramaki-e on a roiro ground, each tray of square shape, the first lacquer a plain black, the other painted with blossoming prunus and a pair of birds in colored, black and gold hiramaki-e on a roiro ground **200.00**

5" dia., set of eight, each bell form bowl fitted with lids painted in hiramaki-e and e-nashiji with butterflies, one with mother-of-pearl inlay, the interior painted in takamaki-e with stylized chrysanthemum and leaves **400.00**

10¼" dia., the well rounded form resting on a high, splayed foot and set with paired foliate-shaped handles trimmed in gilt-metal, decorated en suite with hiramaki-e and e-nashiji blossoming tendrils **600.00**

Box

2¾" x 2⅜" x 1½", with cover, 19th century, of rectangular form, the cover carved with flowering kiku, the base with geometric design **325.00**

4¾" x 6" x 2", 19th century, decorated in gold and silver high relief, with wisteria hanging over a fence, on roiro and gold ground, silver interior **1,000.00**

13" h., with Stand, late 19th century, three tiers of square sections with cover, decorated in gold low relief with scrolls on a black ground, red interiors, stand similarly decorated **850.00**

Document Box

11" x 4½" x 2⅞", late 19th century, rectangular with rounded corners, decorated in gold low relief with blossoms on nashiji ground, nashiji interior, silver fanform mounts for cord **700.00**

10¾" x 11¼" x 5", of square shape with chamfered corners and resting on four short shaped supports, lid decorated with different types of musical instruments associated with traditional gagaku music, flowering lotus, cherry, peony, wisteria and pine branches on the sides, executed in gilt hiramaki-e and togidashi maki-e with okibirame and nashiji accents on a roiro ground, dense nashiji on the interior **600.00**

15⅝" x 12½" x 4⅞", of rectangular

Left to right: **Box, 2" x 1½", 19th century, brown lacquer ground with mother-of-pearl inlays showing various Buddhist symbols and butterfly. $200.00; Box, Incense, 3½" x 2¾" x 1½", 18th century, shaped as a radish, negoro-nuri. $700.00; Box, 1½", late 19th century, carved red lacquer. $600.00**

shape with a fitted lid, decorated to the top with Mount Fuji emerging from stylized clouds and being circumnavigated by a flock of wild geese flying over a placid lake bordered by shoal of pines to the front, the front and one side with further pines, the remaining sides with clumps of reeds, executed in gilt hiramaki-e, with silver and nashiji accents on a roiro ground **715.00**

Food Box, 11½" h., 14¼ dia., raised on a high splayed foot and decorated on the cover with a large abstract blossom medallion in hiramaki-e on a raised black lacquer ground, the interior painted in red lacquer with deep green and yellow leaves................. **550.00**

Hinged Box, 8½" l., of rectangular form, the lid painted with cranes in a village, the sides with insects and flowering sprigs, executed in red and gold hiramaki-e and takamaki-e on a dark textured ground **110.00**

Jubako, Three-tiered box 12¼" h., Two-tiered box 8¼" h., pair, both 12" w., Meiji Period, the lids featuring a large hiramaki-e central mon depicting crossed feathers against a roiro ground, rims highlighted with hiramaki-e interior painted with dense nashiji, the slightly recessed bases with nashiji..................... **1,200.00**

Picnic Box, 13⅛" x 12½" x 7¼", 19th century, of characteristic openframe rectangular construction with two interior shelves, one side with a pair of squared ovoid sake containers fitted into the lid of a small rectangular box with chamfered corners, each piece decorated with leafy blossoming peony sprigs on an undulating fish-net ground, executed in gilt hiramaki-e and takamaki-e and applied with gold and silver-foil accents **375.00**

Scroll Box
2¾" x 15" x 3", 19th century, of rectangular contour with rounded edges, the upper section ornamented all over with a design of flowering chrysanthemum branches rendered in shades of gold hiramaki-e and e-nashiji on a roiro ground, with gilt metal fittings **1,100.00**

2¾" x 15¾" x 3⅞", 20th century, of rectangular shape with rounded

edges, each section scattered with sho- chiku-bai medallions in gold hiramaki-e and takamaki-e on a roiro ground, goldflecked paper lining and metal fittings.................... **1,450.00**

Storage Box, 4⅝" x 10" x 10¾", Meiji Period, of basically square shape with chamfered corners and bevel- edged lid, scattered on the exterior with floral roundels delicately rendered in gilt hiramaki-e, takamaki-e, togidashi and okibirame on a dark lacquer ground, the interior plain nashiji **550.00**

Brush Holder, 5½" h., fashioned as two joined lengths of bamboo, the exterior painted with a sparrow in flight above snow-covered bamboo and stylized clouds at the base, executed in gilt hiramaki-e, takamaki-e and e-nashiji on a roiro ground, the interior lined with gilt brocade **250.00**

Brushpot, 4¾" h., 19th century, inlaid in aogai and goldfoil with birds and butterflies, diaper borders on roiro ground **750.00**

Bunko with Inlaid Accents, 16½" x 13" x 5½", of rectangular shape with rounded corners and a fitted lid, the top with a Korin-style design of bamboo sprigs below a large maple tree with some leaves overlaid with mother-of-pearl or pewter, executed in gilt hiramaki-e, takamaki-e and e-nashiji on a dense nashiji ground, with interior fitted tray **600.00**

Cabinet
Miniature, 3½" x 2¾" x 3¼", 19th century, rectangular form, with hinged door opening to three drawers, decorated in gold takamakie, jiramakie and kirigane with silver and red lacquer details, houses and pagoda by a waterfall in a mountain landscape, interior in togidashi maki-e with flowers, silver mounts **5,500.00**

20¾" x 15½" x 13", Momoyama Period, of rectangular form, the drop-front converted to two hinged doors, enclosing an arrangement of nine drawers, decorated in gold hiramakie, and inlaid raden with panels of birds among flowers and foliage and circular geometric designs on a nashiji ground, gilt metal mounts engraved with floral designs..... **3,500.00**

with stand, 24⅝" x 19" x 13", 19th century, of rectangular form with one drawer and two hinged doors

opening to reveal six drawers, the
whole decorated on the nashiji
ground in gold hiramakie with
aoi-mon reserved on scrolling foliage, the stand similarly decorated...................... **1,600.00**

29¾'' x 29¾'' x 16½'', 19th century, of
rectangular form with two hinged
doors enclosing nine drawers
(three missing), the exterior of the
doors with one barbed quatro-foil
panel decorated in gold and silver
takamakie, hiramakie, togidashi
and gold leaf with a busy fish market on the shores of Lake Biwa, a
flight of cranes against Mt. Fuji
towering on the horizon, the top,
sides and back with cranes above
flowering prunus on a nashiji
ground, the interior with cranes
and bamboo on a nashiji ground,
copper mounts chased with scrol-
ling foliage, later wood stand **6,500.00**

Cake Container, 10'' h., the deep bowl
resting on a high, splayed foot, the
interior decorated with green and
gold leaves on a red ground....... **450.00**

Censer, 3½'' dia., 19th century, lacquer
and silver of lobed form, decorated
in gold hiramakie and gold foil with
peonies and bamboo nashiji ground,
with pierced silver cover and liner **1,300.00**

Coffer, 8⅝'' x 6¼'' x 5¼'', Momoyama
Period, circa 1600, of rectangular
form with domed cover, decorated
on the roiro ground in gold lacquer
and inlaid raden with panels of flowers and grasses divided by bands of
shippo and geometric designs, later
gilt-bronze corner mounts and feet **4,800.00**

Comb
3½'' l., 19th century, with straight
sides and a curved top, the outer
edges decorated to either side
with a flock of cranes flying amid
clouds over an incised feather-
patterned ground, rendered in hiramaki-e, takamaki-e, e- nashiji
and kindameji, the central section
with sparse nashiji **225.00**

Set, 19th century, the upper edge of
the rounded comb featuring a pair
of Mandarin ducks beneath a
flowering cherry tree extending to
the opposite side, well executed
in gold hiramaki-e, takamaki-e,
kirikane, aogai inlay and accents
of red lacquer and sparse nashiji
on a roiro ground, the kanzashi
(hair pin) decorated en suite and
signed..................... **475.00**

Set, 3⅜'' and 5⅞'' l., 19th century, the

comb with squared sides and decorated with sprigs of flowering
bagi (bush cover) executed in gilt
hiramaki-e, takamaki-e and okibirame on a fundame ground, the
two section kanzashi with a
slender shaft bracketed by two
slightly flaring rectangular termi-
nals decorated en suite........ **250.00**

Cosmetic box, 4'' dia., 19th century,
circular, decorated in gold and silver
takamakie, hiramakie and kirigane
showing a house in woods, on kinji
ground with nashiji interiors fitted
with seven small circular boxes,
each decorated in gold hiramakie in
geometric patterns **9,500.00**

Cosmetic Stand, 10¾'' h., Meiji Period,
set with a recessed tray to the top,
supported by a tall pedestal with cut-
out sides and painted in hiramaki-e
and nashiji with leafy tendrils on a
brown lacquer ground, the interior
of tray lacquered red **350.00**

Dish, 21'', Meiji Period, decorated in
colored takamakie with Benekei
fighting a crocodile, signed Kajkawa
Choka....................... **500.00**

Floor screen, 45'' x 50'', signed Taiya,
sealed Koma, early 19th century,
one side decorated in gold, silver
black and green lacquer of a bamboo forest, reverse decorated in gold
and silver nashiji on roiro nuri
ground with a moon rising among
clouds, in wood and soft metal
frame, some old damages **7,500.00**

Hibachi, 19¼'' dia., 19th century, of
compressed ovoid contour with
thick walls and rounded rim, the
sides encircled by the blossoming
plants and grasses of autumn, including mukuge, kiku, obana (su-
suki), ominaishi and kikkyo, rendered in gold takamaki-e with inlay
of pewter and mother-of-pearl on a
natural wood-grain ground, with a
copper liner and resting on a roiro
lacquered circular base **1,100.00**

Hinamatsuri Set, 1½'' l., Meiji Period,
consisting of emperor and empress
dolls and a rectangular tatami-like
platform, each of the figures seated
in stylized poses in brocade patterned robes rendered in gold hiramaki-e and e-nashiji with red lacquer accents on a kinji ground, the
roiro platform with iro-e hiramaki-e
geometric-patterned edging....... **1,300.00**

Jubako (circular), 8¼'' h., three-tier,
each section decorated in gold hiramaki-e, the bottom with persimmon-

shaped landscape reserves, the middle with various fans, and the top with diamond-shaped landscape reserves, each on a different diaper patterned ground, the lid decorated with abstract dragons encircled by alternating mon 500.00

Kimono tray, 14″ x 19″, signed Heian Yokodo, 19th century, shallow tray decorated in gold hiramakie and togidashi on nashiji ground, with sprays of chrysanthemums and rockwork, with silver mounts, in fitted and inscribed wooden box. 800.00

Kobako
2¼″ x 5½″ x 3¾″, Meiji Period, the rectangular top decorated with a lush landscape scene of a waterfall cascading through a hillside thick with blossoming plum trees, the sides decorated with a multitude of brocade patterns all rendered in gold hiramaki-e, takamaki-e and togidashi on a shaded nashiji ground, the interior dense nashiji and signed Shoei tsukuru, slightly faded 500.00

3¼″ x 3″ x 2″, 19th century, of square shape, the lid decorated in gold hiramaki-e with matsu and kiku on a ground of dense nashiji, mounted with pewter rims 900.00

3½″ x 3″ x ⅞″, 17th century, of shallow rounded rectangular form, bearing a roiro ground and decorated all over with scattered cherry blossoms inlaid in gold and silver foil and aogai, the interior of nashiji and the rims mounted with pewter 700.00

Kodansu, 9″ x 7½″ dia., Late Meiji Period, the small cabinet with two hinged doors enclosing three small drawers, is decorated with gold hiramaki-e, red accents and rich nashiji on a black lacquer ground depicting pavilions amidst pine trees in a mountainous landscape, metal foliate hinges and central clasp 1,100.00

Kogo (incense container), and cover, 2¼″, late 19th century, compressed globular form on short tripod foot, modeled as a split bamboo basket and cover, stylized chrysanthemums on the sides, cover with New Year decoration 1,000.00

Quiver (bamboo), 36¾″ l., 2⅞″ dia., Momoyama Period, the cylindrical section of bamboo decorated in gold and colored lacquer with trailing vines hung with bunches of grapes, either end with an undulating roiro

band decorated in gold hiramakie with suwama-mon and maru-ni-futatsu-mon reserved on scrolling foliage, two metal loose-ring handles with floral bosses 2,500.00

Smoking Set, 10⅝″ l., 19th century, consisting of a rectangular box with a hinges brass rectangular handle and open to one side, the recessed top inset with two floral patterned brass containers, one a small tobacco holder, the other a larger pierced ash receptacle, all above a pierced front and two small drawers, the exterior sides decorated with gold takamaki-e plovers in flight above undulating waves in hiramaki-e on a natural wood-grain ground, the front with two hooks suspending a long kiseru (pipe) painted with bush clover, the motif repeated on the silver mouthpiece and bowl 950.00

Stand, 5¾″ x 14½″, square with recessed top painted in dense nashiji, the rim highlighted in gold hiramaki-e and resting on black lacquer rectangular cutout sides 330.00

Storage chest, 33″ x 14″ x 11″, late 18th century, decorated in gold hiramakie with foliate scrolls and roiro ground, engraved gilt bronze mounts, minor cracks and wear. . . .   5,500.00

Suiban, 5″ x 31″ x 23″, 20th century, of rectangular form with short slightly tapering sides and resting on four short shaped supports, each exterior side featuring a Tokugawa mon centered by a dense pattern of scrolling leafy tendrils executed in golden yellow on a roiro ground, the interior with copper liner 475.00

Suzuribako (writing box), 7½″ x 6½″ x 1½″, late 19th century, well decorated in gold hiramakie and togidashi on nashiji ground depicting ferns, the interior and base in sparse nashiji, with silver water dropper formed as cherry blossoms, ink stone, silver mounts, old chips to the foot. 2,000.00

Table Cabinet, 11⅛″ x 9⅜″ x 7¾″, 19th century, of rectangular form, the frame enclosing two compartments with doors, four drawers and two shelves, decorated on the sparse nashiji ground in gold and colored takamakie, hiramakie, togidas hi, kirigane and foil with roundels of birds and sprays of flowers reserved on butterflies, metal mounts in the form of butterflies 1,800.00

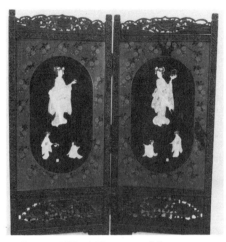

Screen, 71½" x 32", two panel, ivory over-laid, with two attendant figures set within a lacquer frame of blossoming sprigs, the reverse with a hawk perched in a gnarled tree. $2,200.00

Tea Caddy, 2½" h., 18th century, deco-rated in gold foil, low and high re-lief, inlaid with silver studs, chrysan-themums and rockwork on nashiji ground bronze liner 1,500.00

Trays
14¼" dia., set of five, each square-form tray set upon four curving legs and decorated to the interior with incised graining and keyfret border on a brown lacquer ground, the exterior in black lac-quer 500.00
18⅓" l., set of five, each individual setting composed of five vermil-ion lacquered dishes, including a small circular compote, a covered rice bowl, a covered soup bowl, one tea cup and one small sake cup, all on a low-sided square tray resting on four slightly curved sup-ports with modified hoof termi-nals, together with a wooded box with exterior label and place of manufacture 200.00

Zushi
2¼", Edo Period, the gilt interior con-taining a carved wood figure of a priest seated holding a rosary, the inside of the doors painted with attendants, the exterior with gold hiramakie in the form of metal mounts 500.00
2⅞", Meiji/Taisho Period, the gilt in-terior containing a figure of Kan-non standing on a lotus pedestal,

slight details in gilt, the exterior of black lacquer 395.00
4", Edo Period, the gilt interior with a figure of Jizo Bosatsu on a re-placed base, the robes with gilt details, the interior of the door painted with scattered lotus blos-som, the exterior with good gilt-metal fittings engraved with but-terflies and scrolling foliage 650.00
4⅛", Edo Period, the gilt interior con-taining a figure of Fudo Myoo seated among flames on an elabo-rated pedestal, the details painted in gold and colours, the interior of the doors painted with two attend-ants doji, the black lacquered ex-terior with gilt metal mounted engraved with scrolling kiku 475.00
9¼", Edo Period, containing a gilt wood figure of yakushi Nyorai seated on a lotus pedestal behind a rinzu - carved screen, the inte-rior of the doors with Buddhist in-scription, the exterior with gilt-metal mounts 1,200.00

MODERN STUDIO CERAMICS

Introduction: There are basically four distinct pe-riods in the history of Japanese ceramics. First is the traditional era with its emphasis on utilitarian items basically for the cha-no-yu (Japanese tea ceremony) and ikebana (Japanese flower arrang-ing). This historical period dominated Japanese crafts for hundreds of years until Commodore Perry's 1853–1854 "opening" of Japan to the industrialized West. The second period was one of Westernization or the wholesale adoption of a national export-oriented market and the subse-quent demise of regional styles and traditional methods of production. This era was in ascen-dancy during the Meiji period (1868–1912). The third period was the mingei, or folk craft, move-ment that formed as a national response to the mass assimilation of Western ideas and the over-emphasis on techniques and designs. This move-ment emphasized functionality and the tradi-tional. It dominated Japanese crafts until 1960 and is still strong in many quarters. The last period should be called the contemporary period as op-posed to the modern period. Many of the craft artists (potters) since 1960 have emphasized non-functional, nontraditional avant-garde sculptural pieces, some of very large size. That movement is in harmony with other worldwide trends in the arts.

This short article will not deal with contemporary artists as defined above, nor will it deal with the traditional. Out of necessity, artists of the Meiji period will briefly be dealt with because some of those artists worked simultaneously during the mingei movement. Furthermore, the artists of the folk craft movement can best be defined by what they reacted against. It is also important to recognize that there are several studio potters who cannot be put under any rubric—they are the true eccentrics that every society and every period create to the ultimate delight of the collector of subsequent generations.

The modern period is best defined as the period from 1912 to 1960, and, as we will see, the term is a misnomer, because although the period in question is the twentieth century, the output of the potters was very traditional. Studio ceramics are best defined as the output of potters (whether porcelain, stoneware, or pottery) who either participated in, or closely supervised, most of the processes of craft production at their kilns.

History: During the Edo period, daimyos (clan lords) patronized the arts. In Japan, craft production had long been considered a fine art—the distinction between craftsman and artist did not exist. Unlike the West, potters had substantial followings and the sale of their utilitarian products offered them comfortable lives. Various ceramics from famous kiln sites such as Shino, Hagi, and Bizen, for example, were known, recognized, and supported widely throughout Japan. Such regional styles relied on tried kiln and glaze techniques, usually inspired from early Chinese or Korean examples. Potters also sought a harmony with nature. International events were to change that traditional value system; potters had to undergo the same kind of socioeconomic changes as the whole of Japanese society.

Commodore Perry's "black ship" visits of 1853–1854 clearly demonstrated to the Japanese that the West was a superior military power and that the Industrial Revolution in the West had brought profound socioeconomic changes to those societies. The resulting fall of the Tokugawa shogunate in Japan and the restoration of the emperor in 1868 was accompanied by the disenfranchisement of the feudal clan lords and their well-established patronage system, and a deliberate government attempt to assimilate everything Western. The result for crafts was devastating—many of the traditional clan kilns were abolished and many potters were forced to seek a new means of livelihood. The Meiji government, in search for a model to compete with the West, totally challenged traditional Japanese values and traditional artistic approaches. Emperor Meiji went so far as to set up the Technical Art School in Tokyo whose faculty, by directorate, could be composed only of Westerners. In addition, the government in 1868 hired Gottfried Wagener, a German chemist, to modernize craft production

and introduce Western production methods. The raison d'être was to encourage craft production for mass export. In 1904, a ceramic factory, based on the standardization of the original factory in Germany, was set up in Nagoya. By 1907, the Meiji government announced that ceramics would be totally excluded from the Bunten (the Ministry of Education Art Exhibition). This was the low point for the traditional Japanese potter.

Mass commercialization, and its corollary the profit motive, led the Japanese to participation in world expositions. Commercial and individual craft products were entered into the Vienna World Exposition in 1873. This exposition was quickly followed by the Paris Exposition of 1873; Philadelphia, 1876; Paris, 1878; Chicago, 1893; Paris, 1900; St. Louis, 1904; and London, 1910. As a result of the first few expositions, a few potters quickly gained recognition in the West and were able to challenge the prevailing trends and become independent studio potters.

Out of the expositions arose a master studio ceramist Miyagawa Kozan also known as Makuzu Kozan (1842–1916), who began his career in the Kyoto area with pottery, but moved to Ota near Yokohama. In 1871 he began producing hardpaste porcelains in a variety of glazes and techniques (including some sculptural pieces). Makuzu's hand-thrown pieces clearly exhibited Western influence: they were incised, carved, and decorated in both underglaze blue and overglaze enamels. He used forms that were often very nontraditional, but he is most famous for his semitraditional Chinese red and peach-bloom monochromes. His pieces were well received at the international expositions in Philadelphia, Chicago, and Paris. He was honored in 1896 by being appointed as a member of the Art Committee of the Imperial Household.

Seifu Yohei III (1851–1914) rivaled Makuzu in producing hardpaste studio porcelains. He stayed in Kyoto and was trained by his father who studied under Dohachi. His major design influence came from Chinese shapes and glazes. However, like Makuzu, Seifu made few nontraditional sculptural ceramics. Seifu excelled in Chinese-style blue and whites, but went a step further—by adding molded and carved designs to Chinese shapes. He finished them with rich celadons or pastel and cream-colored glazes. On occasion, he would use multicolored glazes to accentuate his designs. Those designs were normally in relief taken from plant life, usually flowers.

Other notable potters of this period are Shofu Katei (Meiji/Taisho), Suwa Sozan (1852–1922), and Denshichi Kanzan (1821–1896). (Yabu Meizan [1853–1934], a satsuma style decorator, is not included in this section because he did not throw his own pieces.) Katei excelled in hardpaste porcelains with underglaze blue designs and even made pieces with a silver resist on a midnight blue background. He was also known for blowout designs in multicolored glazes. Sozan, a member of the Imperial Fine Arts Academy, elaborated on Korean-style mishima (carved and inlaid pieces) often finished in a rich celadon glaze. Leaving behind his early Kyoto pottery training, he became inspired by Chinese Ting wares, Kutani wares, and the Koryo Dynasty wares of Korea. Kanzan, noted for his Kyoto decorated pottery, also moved into decorating porcelains.

Although many other studio potters of this period could be mentioned (including important potters such as Inoue Ryosai, Komamitsu Shozan, and Ito Kozan), it is important to identify the main potters who reacted to Westernization and modernization with its overemphasis on technique and design.

An individually inspired potter who crossed all kiln lines (Oribe, Bizen, Shigaraki, Iga, Seto, Karatsu, and Shino) and methods was Kitaoji Rosanjin (1883–1959). He was perhaps as great a potter as Hokusai was a print artist—and just as eclectic. He generally did not prepare his own clay or pot his own pieces, but he did finish them and give them shapes and glazes. He was one of the last great independent craftsmen who worked across movements, styles, designs, and glazes. He was influenced by Kyoto pottery and held to the dictum that pots should be utilitarian. He actually made numerous pieces for the gourmet restaurant he was running. Thus Rosanjin communicated with some of the principles of the following folk art movement. He could justifiably be ranked as the most important potter of the twentieth century.

Rosanjin largely stood alone among potters in Japan, while many others were questioning the governments' emphasis on technique and design. Their inspiration, strangely, came from abroad—specifically England.

William Morris (1834–1896), one of the proponents of the English arts and crafts movement, and the works and ideas of the great English potter Bernard Leach (1887–1979) were to leave an indisputable influence on subsequent Japanese potters. The somewhat parallel movement created in Japan as a result became known as the Nihon mingei-kei (Japanese folk craft movement) founded by philosopher and potter Yanagi Soetsu (1889–1961). His colleagues and fellow potters were Hamada Shoji, Kawai Kanjiro, and Tomimoto Kenkichi. This movement became so strong that its proponents were able to eventually establish the Folk Art Museum in 1936—a must for the collector and visitor to Japan.

Itaya Hazan (1872–1963) was one of the truly great ceramacists but very little of his work ever reached the West. In addition, his total oeuvre was very small. He studied Kutani and also taught sculpture. At his kiln in Tabata, Toyko, he excelled in under-the-glaze floral relief carving of celadons and white porcelain wares. He fused both Western and Chinese traditional influences, excelled in temmouku tea bowls and the use of polychrome enamels. He was the first ceramic artist both to design and to execute his ceramics and the first to receive the Order of Cultural Merit. Indeed, he had a lasting influence on ceramic greats Hamada Shoji and Kawai Kanjiro and others of the folk art movement.

Hamada Shoji (1894–1978) graduated from the ceramic department of Tokyo's Technological High School, worked with Kawai Kanjiro in Kyoto and traveled to St. Ives, Cornwall, to work with Bernard Leach. He stayed in Cornwall for almost four years and forged a deep friendship with Leach. Hamada returned to Japan in 1924, settling at now-famous Mashiko. As the foremost proponent of the folk art movement, he embodied its values: (1) pots should be functional, utilitarian, and traditional so that the spirit of the piece is in harmony with the natural environment; (2) prices should be kept low so that the masses, or common people, could afford them; and (3) an artist should remain anonymous and not sign his pieces. The foregoing premises are great in theory, but in practice even Hamada signed the rare occasional piece, and almost all his major pieces that were boxed had his signature on the box. He was well aware of the practical necessity of signed boxes, particularly if the pots themselves were not signed. For his role in the "modern" ceramic history of Japan, Hamada was named a "national treasure" (Important Intangible Cultural Property) in 1955. Shimaoka Tatsuo (b. 1919), Hamada's most famous student, makes pottery in the folk craft style, but unlike his master, he signs his pieces. Those pots are largely inspired by Korean mishima traditional types. Another potter influenced by Hamada was Yanagi Muneyoshi (1889–1961) who also was made a living national treasure.

In sum, the important point is that where the potter got his inspiration, East or West, was the basic dividing line—not his day-to-day adherence to the founding principles espoused by Hamada. Those who were inspired by traditional Eastern forms—whether Chinese, Korean, or earlier Japanese—were more ethnocentric than those who turned to the West. Japanese society as a whole supported the traditional approach. With many regional kiln sites spread throughout Japan and the accretion of long historical associations of region to kiln, it seems natural for that support to occur. Even today, Japanese society offers a very good living, perhaps the best, to those who follow Eastern traditional forms.

Kawai Kanjiro (1890–1966) went to the same technical ceramic high school that his good friend Hamada did; both claimed it took a lifetime to cast off the few years' training in Western methods learned there. Kawai, a great potter, took his inspiration from ancient Chinese ceramics and Korean wares of the Yi Dynasty. His later works were much more abstract under "contemporary" international art pressures. He worked hard politically with Yanagi and Hamada to establish the folk art movement.

Tomimoto Kenkichi (1886–1963) rounded out the famous four. He went to the design school of the Tokyo School of Fine Arts, but was from Nara. He subsequently went to France to study—as did many artists of the day—and when he returned established a friendship with Bernard Leach in Japan. After making pottery early in his career, he turned to porcelain decorated in bright overglaze enamels, often with underglaze blue designs. He became known for his multicolored wares iro-e, his five-color wares gosai, and his red wares aka-e. He strongly felt that his designs had to be by direct observation. He received the Order of Cultural Merit in 1961, but not before he was made a living national treasure in 1955. One of his students, Kondo Yuzo (b. 1902), also was named a living national treasure. These artists were instrumental in reviving the traditional, but they infused it with new heart, spirit, or simply, inspiration. They took studio ceramacists in a new direction for almost half a century.

The following artists will only be briefly mentioned. They are either Holders of Important Cultural Properties (living national treasures) or were highly honored in their lifetimes and made significant contributions to Japanese studio ceramics.

Kato Hajime (1900–1968) is known for his utilitarian porcelain objects with yellow, Ming reds, and overglazes in reds and greens. He also used gold-leaf decorations applied with lacquer and exhibited great technical skill. He was named a living national treasure in 1961.

Fujiwara Kei (1899–1983) is known mostly for his Bizen tradition of cha-no-yu utilitarian objects and was a native of that same province. Pottery was a strange profession for a man who started out in literature, poetry, and theater. He was named a living national treasure in 1970.

Kaneshige Toyo (1896–1967) was best known for his Bizen tea ceremony objects of art, but his son Michiaki (b. 1935) is known for his unorthodox seven-sided bowls. The father was unconventional, drew his inspiration from Japanese tradition, and used an ash glaze.

Takahashi Rakusei (1898–1976) and Takahashi Rakusei III (b. 1925) produced traditional ware in the Shigaraki tradition. Traditional production of large vessels often using a design of horizontal rows of engraved parallel lines.

Miwa Kyuwa (b. 1895) makes irregular modern shapes and scores the sides, unlike the former traditional Miwa's tea ceremony objects in the Hagi and Shino traditions. In 1970, he was named a living national treasure.

Arakawa Toyozo (1894–1985): was from Gifu and became skilled in both the Shino and the Seto-guro traditions of the seventeenth-century Momoyama period. He began his career, however, in Kyoto doing traditonal ceramics. His tea ceramics have irregular tops and are painted in an unorthodox Shino tradition. He became a living national treasure in 1955.

Kusube Yoichi (1897–1984) was from Kyoto and came to love porcelains, particularly those with light celadon glazes and flowers picked out in multicolored hues. His pots were inspired from Japanese and Chinese traditional forms. He received the Order of Cultural Merit in 1978.

Imaizumi Imaemon XII (1897–1975) and Imaizumi Imaemon XIII (b. 1926): In 1971 the iro Nabeshima style, instead of a specific person, was registered as an important cultural property. The colored Nabeshima tradition still continues today, with multiglazes used with underglaze blues. The Imaizumi Imaemon XIII introduced new and novel designs to these traditonal wares.

Sakaida Kakiemon XII (1878–1963), Sakaida Kakiemon XIII (1906–?), and Sakaida Kakiemon XIV (b. 1934) continued the Kakiemon technique and retained the milky white bodies of the wares. The former was registered as an important cultural property in 1971; the body being protected in 1955. Both Sakaida Kakiemon XIII and XIV modernized the designs and decorations of this fine porcelain.

Ishiguro Munemaro (1893–1968) was inspired by iron glazes, particularly Chinese Song Dynasty temmouku ware. These were largely applied to traditional cha-no-yu ceramics.

There are many, many other artists that deserve recognition here—perhaps more than 5,000. Of those, many have received extensive international recognition. The collector should refer to the references for further information on the artists mentioned here as well as data on the many other potters of the era.

References: Adalbert Klein, *Japanese Ceramics*, Alpine Fine Arts Collection Ltd., n.d.; Musée des Beaux-Arts, *Ceramiques de l'ere Showa*, Europalia, 1989; Amaury Saint-Gilles, *Earth 'n' Fire*, Shufunotomo Co., Ltd., 1978; Tokyo's National Museum of Modern Art, *Japanese Painted Porcelain: Modern Masterpieces in Overglaze Enamel*, translated by Richard L Gage, Weatherhill/Tankosha, 1979–1980.

Museums: Museum of Fine Arts, Boston, Massachusetts; Philadelphia Museum of Art, Philadelphia, Pennsylvania; Freer Gallery of Art, Washington, D.C.; British Museum, London, England; Victoria and Albert Museum, London, England; Ashmolean Museum, Oxford, England; Museum fur Ostasiatische Kunst, Berlin, Germany;

Deutsches Keramik Museum, Dusseldorf, Germany; Hetjens Museum, Dusseldorf, Germany; Museum fur Volkerkunde, Freiburg, Germany; Museum fur Kunst and Gewerbe, Hamburg, Germany; Staatliches Museum fur Volkerkunde, Munich, Germany; Ohara Museum, Kurashioki, Japan; Museum of Modern Art, Kyoto, Japan; Folk Art on Mingei Museum, Tokyo, Japan; National Museum of Modern Art, Tokyo, Japan.

Reproduction Alert: When artists' works reach astronomical prices, such as Rosanjin's, or good prices like Hamada's and Kanjiro's, reproductions will always arise. The pots are not always difficult to imitate. For example, when Hamada was asked about his numerous students' (and imitators') works, he is supposed to have said that in 100 years the best would be attributed to him, the worst to his students and imitators.

Tongue in cheek as it is, Hamada did box his pieces and sign them. They, therefore, are relevant in pricing. An unboxed Hamada (boxes got destroyed for one reason or another, and he gave many pieces away) is generally worth only a fraction of a boxed and signed piece. Rosanjin put such stock in signed pieces and boxes that I would not buy his ceramics without both being signed. Generally, however, I have not seen reproductions good enough to fool the collector on the market.

Collecting Hints: I would reiterate that a collector would be best served by getting the signed box with the ceramic piece. When buying from an unknown dealer—to save embarrassment if it's necessary to return a pot—be sure to get in writing the right to an unconditional return and a full refund. Many dealers will tell you buyer beware or give a thirty-day grace period. In sum, make sure you purchase your pots from a reliable dealer who will help you build an important collection over time.

In any case, be sure to analyze signatures and chops with known museum examples. Be very aware that size is important but that condition is even more important. In addition, shape is relative to price: vases are in greater demand internationally. The most likely pieces to be found by the collector in the United States are pieces that were exhibited at the many expositions. In general, Meiji period ceramics made for Western export are likely to be more plentiful in the United States and Europe than in Japan, whereas Showa period folk art ceramics are most likely to be found in Japan or at international auction houses. There is no collecting hint that can surpass the following: there is no substitute for reading all the available material and then handling important pieces.

Advisors: Stewart and Barbara Hilbert

Arakawa Toyozo (1894-1895)
 Shino ware pottery tea bowl, 4½'' h.,
  the deep, cylindrical bowl set on

Eiraku, probably Tokizen (1854-1910), 6'' dia., late 19th/early 20th century, five-lobed dish, decorated in underglaze blue with stylized pine trees in a double circle, underglaze blue mark Eiraku on base. $750.00

an unglazed ring foot decorated with a grey heron and grasses on bubbly white ground, with wood storage box inscribed Shino cha-wan Toyozo **9,350.00**
Circular pottery deep dish, 2½'' dia., the coarse pale grey body burnt to a brick-red and glazed Ki-Seto style with patches left unglazed and pooling in the well (gold lacquer Naoshi in the rim), signed ''To'' **1,300.00**
Denshichi Kanzan (1821-1896), pair of Kyoto porcelain vases, 27½'', Meiji period, each of ovoid form with flared neck, the shoulders with shishi and ring handles, painted in enamels and gilding with ducks and

Denshichi Kanzan (1821-1896), 4½'' h., vase with cranes flying on shoulder, with red sun setting in background, signed Kanzan in underglaze blue on base. $850.00

small birds beneath snow covered blossoms by a pond, signed Dai Nihon Kanzan sei 6,900.00

Hamada Shoji (1894-1978)

Contemporary stoneware bottle (tokkuri), 9″ h., the slab- sided tall bottle with recessed foot and short neck with flared rim decorated with thick colored glazes over a thick grey glaze with crosses and stylized plant motif 3,520.00

Contemporary cup, 3¾″, the cylindrical stoneware body set on a raised ring foot decorated with stylized raindrops in alternating grey and iron-brown on a clear glaze, with temmoku rim 715.00

Contemporary charger, 17¾″ dia., the large shallow stoneware bowl with flared rim and on raised ring foot decorated in the "flambe" style in a opalescent glaze of turquoise, white, brown, and lavender tones with three quatrefoils in the well 7,150.00

Contemporary stoneware dish 10½″ dia., the shallow dish on a raised ring foot simply decorated with a green glaze beneath a thin white glaze pooling in small areas 1,320.00

11½″ dia., square, on a raised foot and with sharply everted rim and impressed cross-hatch design, decorated with iron-brown and white on a green ground beneath a clear fine glaze 3,850.00

Contemporary jar (kabin), 8¼″ h., the cylindrical stoneware jar with sharply cut shoulders and with short neck with everted rim and set on a raised ring foot decorated with a temmoku glaze with a resist flower spray 2,200.00

Contemporary teabowl, 4¾″ h., the deep stoneware bowl tapering inward above a ring foot incised about the walls with wavy parallel lines glazed blue on a ground of mottled grey-brown, the area above the foot a grey salt-glaze, with wood storage box inscribed Shoji saku kushime ranmaki chawan Shinsaku shiki "Made by Shoji, a tea bowl with lines glazed blue, box by Shinsaku" 7,150.00

Inoue Ryosai (b. 1828)

porcelain vase, 6⅞″ h., Meiji period, the baluster body painted with pinkish-mauve persimmons and green leaves, signed Inoue Ryosai in underglaze blue 575.00

Vase and cover, 6½″ h., 19th century, oviform vase on tripod feet molded in relief with flowering roses and foliage in underglaze green and pink on a white ground, the cover with knop finial, signed Inoue Ryosai 1,650.00

Isamu Noguchi (1904-1988), contemporary Iga-style bowl, 9½″ dia., signed with maker's mark, the ribbed ovoid bowl decorated in a thin Iga-style celadon glaze richly pooling to a crackled and translucent emerald in the well 16,500.00

Attributed to Kanashige Toyo (1896-1967) contemporary Bizen style dish, 11¼″ dia., the roughly potted rectangular stoneware body with raised cup corners decorated in typical Bizen style with a natural ash glaze 1,800.00

Kawai Kanjiro (1890-1966)

Contemporary stoneware bottle (tokkuri), 6⅛″ h., the short slab-sided stoneware bottle with short rectangular neck and everted rim and set on a flat base decorated with red and green stylized plant design on a blue ground 8,800.00

Contemporary stoneware cup, 3⅛″ h., the cylindrical cup on a raised ring foot simply decorated in blue beneath a thin crackled and bubble suffused white glaze 935.00

Contemporary stoneware sake cup (sakezuki) 3″ h., with a box sealed Kawai Kan No In , the cup of cylindrical form with sharply cut foot and recessed base decorated in relief with scrolling abstract flower forms and covered with blue beneath a thin, crackled and bubble-suffused glaze 1,300.00

Contemporary stoneware teabowl (chawan)

3⅛″ h., the stoneware bowl on raised ring foot decorated in iron-red and blue with stylized flower sprays on a thick pale, crackled ground, crack to the rim 990.00

5″ dia., the stoneware bowl set on a raised, sharply cut ring foot decorated with copper-red and iron-brown stylized flower forms beneath a thick bubble suffused and crackled pale grey glaze 4,620.00

Kawamoto Masukichi, vase, 12⅛″ h., 19th century, oviform vase decorated in underglaze blue with a continuous design of puppies playing in a snowfall among snow-covered

flowers and foliage, signed Seto Kawamoto Masukichi Sei. **880.00**
Kitaoji Rosanjin (1883-1959)
Bowl
Contemporary bowl (hachi), 8½″
dia., on raised ring foot decorated in iron and blue beneath a
thick crackled glaze and gold
and silver overglaze depicting
the moon over the Musashin
grasses, signed "Ro", in fitted
wood box inscribed Musashin
hachi and signed Ro in kata-
kana **22,000.00**
Contemporary Shino style bowl
(hachi), signed in Kanji "Ro",
the deep bowl sloping to a short
ring foot decorated with underglaze iron with a trellis design
beneath a white, bubble-
suffused glaze burnt orange in
places during the firing, with
wood box **11,000.00**
Oribe-style bowl (hachi), 10″
dia., fan-shaped stoneware set
on three loop tripod feet and
decorated in typical Oribe style
with underglaze iron brown
textile pattern of drying persimmon juxtaposed against a crackled, copper-green glaze pooling in the well and other
recesses, signed below, Rosanjin, in fitted wood box inscribed
Oribe hachi and signed Rosan-
jin and sealed Ro. **33,000.00**
Contemporary Shino-style cup (mu-
kozuke), 3⅞″, the deep stoneware
cup decorated in underglaze iron
with a cross hatch pattern above
vertical parallel lines under a
bubbly white overglaze, scorched
orange where thin, the foot
unglazed, signed "Ro". **8,250.00**
Set of five contemporary porcelain
cups, each 3″, signed in Kanji
"Ro", the cups of cylindrical form
sloping to raised ring feet and decorated in iron-red and colored enamels with vari-colored stripes, in
fitted wood box inscribed Iro-e
yunomi gonin, signed Rosanjin
and sealed Hoshigaoka yo **33,000.00**
Set of five contemporary porcelain
dishes, 8⅜″ dia., each signed Rosanjin, each dish with raised rim
and set on low ring feet and decorated in underglaze blue with
boldly inscribed fuku characters
beneath a thick white glaze,
signed below--each in wood stor-
age box **27,500.00**
Pair of contemporary large dishes,

**Kitaoji Rosanjin (1883-1959), set of five
red and blue enamel decorated fish-form
plates, 20th century, with studio mark
and signed box, the base with a cartouche
with the character Ro. $12,000.00**

10¾″ each, signed "Ro", the shallow stoneware dishes with raised
rims decorated in iron-brown beneath a thick crackled and bubble-suffused celadon glaze pooling to a blue tinge in the recesses
and with stylized autumn grasses **7,700.00**
Koji, vase, 13′h., oviform, 19th century, decorated in shaded underglaze grey and pink with two hares
beside morning glory and grasses in
the moonlight, signed Koji **1,650.00**
Kondo Yuzo (1902-), contemporary
tea bowl, 4⅜″, the deep bowl set on a
splayed ring foot decorated in underglaze blue with sprigs of pomegranates and a ring at the base above
two rings encircling the foot, with
wood storage box inscribed Zakuro
sometsuke chawan Yu saku "tea
bowl with pomegranates in under-
glaze blue by Yu(zo)" and sealed. . . **3,520.00**
Kozan oviform vase, 11½″ h., 19th
century, with everted neck decorated in underglaze brown and black
with a deep blue ground with pig-
eons strutting, striking poses or fly-
ing, signed Kozan sei **850.00**
Makuzu Kozan (1842-1916)
Koro and cover, earthenware, 6″,
Meiji period, in the form of a ka-
buto, decorated in the Satsuma
palette, the tall pointed hachi
pierced and painted with gilt
dragons, the base realistically
modeled, impressed mark Ma-
kuzu, one string reglued **2,450.00**
Vase
Baluster vase with tall tapering
neck, 12″ h., Meiji period, decorated in Satsuma style in various colored enamels and gilt on
a crackled white ground with
stylized grotesque animals
holding scrolls above a band of

Makuzu Kozan, (1842-1916), celadon-glazed karashishi, 4½" h., x 6" w., impressed mark, eyes and feet in biscuit, the celadon draining to reveal the fine modeling and details. $3,400.00

alternate leaf-shaped panels containing dragons, signed on the base Makuzu-yo Kozan sei **6,000.00**
Blue and white molded vase and cover, 9½" h., late 19th century shaped as a closed chrysanthemum, the lobes outlined in a petal pattern, the cover similarly molded, signed inside the cover and on the base within an incised double line circle **3,650.00**
Broad oviform vase, 8" h., late 19th century, decorated in underglaze blue and black enamels on a white ground with cranes taking off into flight, signed Makuzu Kozan sei **2,500.00**
Porcelain vase, 6", Meiji period, rounded body decorated with a large branch of persimmons in orange and brown enamels, the foliage painted in underglaze blue, signed in blue Makuzu

Makuzu Kozan (1842-1916), small vase with Chinese-style flambé glaze draining from neck to shoulder, underglaze blue signature on base in characters Makuzu Kozan Sei. $1,500.00

Kozan sei, with original box signed "Makuzu Kozan: Blue and white persimmon vase". . . **3,740.00**
Water pot, molded porcelain, 4", Meiji period, of squat rounded form with a wide mouth, molded with a double band of key-pattern between formal underglaze blue borders, all on an iron-red ground, signed in blue Makuzu yo Kozan sei **850.00**
Mino Nishiura porcelain vase, 12" h., Meiji period, of ovoid form, with narrow cylindrical neck and slightly flared rim, decorated with a tiger lily spray and molded bud and blossom in pale yellow, green, blue, purple and black on a pale lavender ground, the base w ith an underglaze blue mark Mino Nishiura, small chips to molded areas **1,650.00**
Seifu Yohei (1851-1914)
Set of six porcelain bowls, Meiji period, each of deep rounded form, one larger than the rest and with an everted rim, all painted in shades of underglaze-blue with a continuous mountain and lake landscape with fishermen, sages, and shrines, incised signature, one chip on foot ring, a wooden box fitted with six shelves and bearing the artist's name Cho Rokuyo and the potter's name Teishitsu Gigei-in Seifu Yohei zo **6,600.00**
Celadon censer, 4⅛" h., Meiji period, globular form raised on three feet, the rim with two rope-work handles, covered with a pale celadon glaze, impressed seal Seifu **400.00**
Porcelain jar and cover, 11¼" h., Meiji period, impressed signature Seifu, the large globular jar molded with lush peony blossoms and covered with a shiny transparent glaze over the white porcelain body, the matching cover with bud form knop **8,250.00**
Koro, tripodal, 3½" h., dark green simulating bamboo ribs, a pierced silver plate cover decorated in shishiaibori with cranes among cloud, signed on the base Seifu, the metal cover signed Koroku, inner wood box and cover, signed and sealed Seifu **1,650.00**
Porcelain vase, Chinese style, 14¾" h., the oviform body on raised ring foot and with short, cylindrical neck with slightly flared and inturned rim, decorated in underglaze blue with dragon

Left, Miyagawa Kozan (1842-1916), vase, 14" h., early multiglazed Satsuma-style, Kyoto kiln period, molded aquatic plants in relief, impressed Miyagawa Kozan Sei in double-gourd mark on base. $3,800.00; right, Seifu Yohei III (1851-1914), vase, 14" h., celadon glazed, molded and carved with scrolling chrysanthemum pattern, two-character Seifu mark etched in the paste on the foot. $3,500.00

roundels and stylized flower-heads, the base and neck with stylized floral design signed Dai Nihon Seifu Zo 900.00

Seifu II (1844-1878), porcelain vase, 9¾" h., Meiji period, of ovoid form with wide circular mouth, molded in relief with three geese in white, yellow and black against a pale lavender ground, the base with an underglaze blue mark, Seifu II 2,750.00

Shofu Katei, porcelain vase, 4½" h., Meiji period, the oviform vase, tapering to a narrow and recessed ring foot and sloping to a short raised and flared neck, decorated with white egrets on a green ground signed Shofu 1,980.00

Tomimoto Kenkichi (1886-1963)
Contemporary porcelain box and cover, 3½" x 2¾" x 2⅛", the rectangular box and cover simply decorated in underglaze blue and a flower within a rectangular border, with fitted box inscribed Hana mon ryoho kogo and signed Kenkichi zo and sealed Tomi 7,700.00

Contemporary blue and white porcelain dish, 8½" dia., the circular dish with recessed well set on a ring foot painted in underglaze blue with a dwelling, plum trees and the moon within a blue border on the flattened rim, the underside painted with birds, in wood

box inscribed Bai rin tsuki zo "Plum grove and moon" and the numeral Shi "Four" 14,300.00

Pair of contemporary porcelain dishes, 6⅝" dia., shallow on raised ring feet decorated in underglaze blue and iron red depicting a house in a landscape signed with Kakihan 7,700.00

MORIAGE

History: Moriage (pronounced *mor-ee-AH-ga*) is an art technique used to decorate Japanese ceramics (porcelain, softpaste wares, and pottery) that were produced for export to the United States and United Kingdom during the Nippon era (1891–1921).

The word *moriage* translates loosely as "to pile up" and refers to applied relief motifs, affixed to ceramic works to create a design with a three-dimensional quality. The raised decoration was applied either before or after glazing in any of three ways: (1) slip was rolled and shaped, then put manually on the object in one or more layers, with thickness and shape depending on the desired design; (2) tubing or slip trailing was applied from a tube in a manner similar to that used today to decorate cakes; or (3) slip was reduced to a liquid and applied with a brush. The Japanese word for this technique is hankeme.

The moriage technique had been used by Japanese porcelain and pottery factories since the mid-1700s for domestic ceramic production. During the Nippon era, however, moriage techniques became popular for export wares.

Many moriage items bear a variety of Nippon marks, which include the letter M in wreath, blue maple leaf, Oriental china Nippon, pagoda, royal nishiki mark, and royal Moriye mark. Items bearing the royal Moriye mark confuse some collectors. The word *Moriye* does not refer to the form of decoration, rather it is the name of a company that produced moriage decorated items. Most moriage pieces are unmarked or are stamped with Oriental characters alone or are encased within a square or circle. These characters designate the production company.

References: Joan Van Patten, *The Collector's Encyclopedia of Nippon Porcelain*, Collector's Books, Series 1, 2, and 3, 1986; Kathy Wojciechowski, *The Wonderful World of Nippon Porcelain*, Schiffer Publishers Ltd., 1991.

Collecting Hints: Though the moriage technique was used to decorate softpaste and pottery in addition to porcelain wares, it is the porcelains that are the most sought after by collectors. The quality of the artwork and application of moriage is noticeably finer and has greater detail on porcelain objects than on softpaste or pottery. Because of this, porcelain items generally command higher prices.

For many years, collector's views toward the unmarked moriage wares were somewhat mixed. In the last forty years, however, collectors have shown new interest in the collectability of Nippon marked and unmarked moriage wares.

Three of the most important things collectors look for when adding a new moriage item to their collections are (1) that the item be free from cracks, chips, or restoration; (2) that there is little or none of the moriage design missing; and (3) that the quality of the workmanship and art is up to their standards. These three aspects affect the price structure greatly. The appreciation of items made with the moriage technique is growing in leaps and bounds, and prices have skyrocketed in the last five years.

Advisor: Kathy Wojciechowski

Basket
  9" h., blue background, light blue peony pattern, heavy white moriage trim, unmarked **275.00**
  9" h., pink background, pink and white irises **285.00**
Box
  2" x 2¾", club shaped, scenic lid, moriage trim **45.00**
  3½" l., blue background, pale pink, blue and white moriage design, center portrait medallion, Nippon green M in wreath mark **225.00**
Bowl, 6½" w. x 4" h., pale green background, white moriage Japanese figure kneeling on front, back shows Japanese figure running, all outlined in gold, unmarked **255.00**
Candlestick, 8¼" h., triangular in shape, hand painted forest scene in shades of brown and yellow, white

Basket, 10" h., slate grey background, large moriage seagulls, marked Nippon. $375.00

Cake Plate, 11" h., pierced handles, large moriage palm trees, moriage beaded trim. $185.00

  moriage trees and beading, Nippon blue maple leaf mark **285.00**
Chocolate pot, 9" h., pale green background, large floral medallions front and back, all over white lacy design   **285.00**
Chocolate set, pot 13" h., RS Prussia shape, footed, melon ribbed base, four cups and saucers, thin fine porcelain, moriage dragons with jeweled eyes, Nippon M in wreath mark   **975.00**
Cookie Jar
  6½" h., lavender background, with pastel geometric designs, unmarked **190.00**
  6½" h., turquoise background, loop type handles **210.00**
  7¼" h., square shape, metal rim, lid and bail, moriage water lillies, oriental symbols **245.00**
Cracker Jar, handles, 7½" h., lavender background, melon ribbed pink and white roses, unmarked **130.00**
Creamer and Sugar Bowl, Marbleized green and pink background, pink hand painted flowers outlined in white moriage, unmarked **75.00**
Ferner, 4" h., four footed, ruffled top opening, yellow and green background, large oak leaves done and outlined in white moriage, beaded top and feet, unmarked **285.00**
Humidor
  5½" h., large moriage skull and crossbones, marked Nippon **485.00**
  6¼" h., dark green background with center medallion of flowers, all over white lacy moriage design, signed Nippon **585.00**
  6" x 7", brown background, moriage matches, pipe, cigar, and cigarettes, lid has hand painted deck of playing cards **475.00**

7¾″, marbleized background, with allover design 325.00
Perfume, 3¼″ h., wheat pattern, Nippon mark 135.00
Pitcher
  6″ h., pink on white handles with green slip-trailing, gold handle, marked Nippon 175.00
  6″ x 6½″, squat shape, rose panels with heavy beading and slip-trailing, unmarked 175.00
Salt and Pepper Shakers, 3″ h., gold background with all over moriage decoration, marked Japan 35.00
Spitoon and Underplate (rare), brown background with moriage brown stems and white dogwood flowers   400.00
Tankard
  10¼″ h., orange and rust background with white moriage flying geese, marked Nippon 325.00
  10¼″ h., front medallion scene of house and trees, floral back medallion, both medallions surrounded by moriage trim and flowers, marked Japan 285.00
  10¼″ h., hand painted large orchids and moriage flowers and leaves, unmarked 235.00
  15¼″ h., heavily decorated with the peony pattern, unmarked 325.00
Tea Caddy, 6″ h., triangular shape, footed, cover and lid, hand painted mountain scene with large white trees, marked Nippon 250.00
Tea Pot, 6½″ h., Oriental design, unmarked 65.00
Tea Set, consisting of tea pot, creamer, sugar bowl, five cups and saucers, dark mauve background with pink and mauve flowers 675.00
Urn
  10″ turquoise background with white moriage birds, leaves and buds, marked Japan 265.00
  11¾″ h., two piece bolted urn with dome lid, moriage slip decorated with enamelled jewels and bands of enameled beads, unmarked . . .   465.00
Vase
  4¼″ h., three handles, three feet, very fine Wedgwood type decoration, unmarked 135.00
  6¾″ h., mottled green and pink background with hand painted pink flowers, Oriental mark 145.00
  9″ h., moriage slip and enamelling combination, unmarked 255.00
  10½″ h., small handles near neck, white moriage butterfly and bouquet of lilacs, marked Nippon . . .   335.00

12″ h., soft paste, unmarked 95.00
Wine Decanter, 16″ h., moriage ho-o bird 225.00
Wine Jug, 9½″ h., original matching stopper, green background with white moriage wheat, marked Nippon 150.00

NABESHIMA PORCELAIN

History: Located between the Port of Imari and Arita, the Nabeshima family kilns were founded in 1660 in Okawachi. The products of this kiln (which employed the most talented workman from the Hirado factories) were produced for the feudal lord Nabeshima to be used as presentation pieces for the shogun or other feudal lords. It was for this impressive hierarchy that the Nabeshima porcelain was made, and as a result, the wares were of extremely fine quality. Products of the kiln that were thought to be less than perfect were discarded. Production was limited to about 5,000 pieces a year, and none was made available for export or for sale to the common people. Great pains were taken to keep the location of the factory obscure and the area was well guarded against the removal of any pieces from the factory.

Many dishes were produced in standardized sizes. They were made of extremely fine clay and possessed a pale greenish glaze that distinguishes them from the finest of the old Kakiemon plates of that period. This fineness was also extended to the smoothness of the glaze, which never revealed any pitting on the surface. The shallow dishes were set up on a high foot (takadaizara). The outside of this footing reveals an underglaze blue serrated line design called kusitadake (comb base). Although this design also appears on the bases of some Arita and Kutani porcelain, it was officially licensed to the Nabeshima kilns in the eighteenth century. Patterns, evenly distributed in three places, appeared on the underside of dishes. There were also some dishes made in octagonal shapes as well as occasional melon and leaf shapes.

Besides the dishes, cups were frequently produced. The form was small and narrow with high straight sides in a pentagon shape. Sometimes the rims were petal shaped and the sides were ribbed. Another cup form (appearing in the early eighteenth century) that seems to be particularly identified with Nabeshima has a narrow base flaring to a wide top.

Decoration of dishes, which was done by the Imaizumi family of Arita, consisted of underglaze blue and white (sometsuke) and an overglaze enamel technique (iro Nabeshima) very much like the Chinese doucai (tou-ts′ai) enamels. Outlines were presented in underglaze blues and then filled with colored enamels: iron red, soft green, transparent lilac purple, and pale translucent yellow. Unlike the Chinese doucai and Kakiyemon decoration which it resembled, the Nabeshima enamels were applied in washes that could not be felt above the surface of the porcelain. The subjects chosen for the designs were primarily fruits and vegetables or flowers. Repeating brocade patterns were thought to have appeared on some early pieces.

Celadon wares (Nabeshima seiji) were also made, often with underglaze blue decoration. The kilns' production of celadon wares was not restricted to cups and dishes and represents a greater variety of subject matter. Figures, incense burners, relief-molded dishes, vases, and cups appear on the lists of celadon-glazed wares of the Nabeshima kilns.

The finest period of production is said to have been between the years 1715 and 1735. The quality of work went into decline after 1775 when the Nabeshima family started to withdraw its support of the kiln.

In 1867 some Nabeshima pieces appeared in the Paris International Exhibition. It was not until 1868, however, that Nabeshima wares were allowed to be officially sold outside the "family." The clan system was abolished in 1871, leaving the Imaizumi family of decorators free to carry on the Nabeshima tradition using their own clay and kilns. Twelfth-generation Imaizumi Imaemon, a student of kiln construction and ceramics was responsible for keeping the family tradition alive. The Nabeshima kilns are still producing porcelain. (See: Modern Studio Ceramics.)

References: Hazel M. Gorham, *Japanese and Oriental Ceramics*, Charles E. Tuttle Co., Inc., 1971; Soame Jenyns, *Japanese Porcelain*, Frederick A. Praeger, 1965; Irene Stitt, *Japanese Ceramics of the Last 100 Years*, Crown Publishers, Inc., 1974;—, *200 Years of Japanese Porcelain*, City Art Museum of Saint Louis, 1970.

Museums: Los Angeles County Museum of Art, Los Angeles, California; Honolulu Academy of Arts, Honolulu, Hawaii; Art Institute of Chicago, Chicago, Illinois; Nelson Gallery of Art, Kansas City, Kansas; Baltimore Museum of Art, Baltimore, Maryland; Museum of Fine Arts, Boston, Massachusetts; University of Michigan Museum of Art, Ann Arbor, Michigan; Detroit Institute of Arts, Detroit, Michigan; Brooklyn Museum, Brooklyn, New York; Metropolitan Museum of Art, New York, New York; Cleveland Museum of Art, Cleveland, Ohio; Philadelphia Museum of Art, Philadelphia, Pennsylvania; Seattle Art Museum, Seattle, Washington; Royal Ontario Museum, Toronto, Canada; Fitzwilliam Museum, Cambridge, England; British Museum, London, England; Victoria and Albert Museum, London, England; Ashmolean Museum, Oxford, England;

Idemitsu Museum of Art, Tokyo, Japan; Kyushu Ceramic Museum, Arita, Japan.

Reproduction Alert: Though not reproductions in the contemporary sense, the late nineteenth century and early twentieth century saw a great influx to Europe of Nabeshima dishes using old designs. The use of dark violet blue and some silver is certainly a late nineteenth century innovation. Later pieces often show glaze defects; their bodies are somewhat thick and clumsy. Oftentimes the comb pattern around the base is irregular in comparison with the delicate and even application of eighteenth-century products. Frequently, the blue outlines around the design are missing or the decoration appears to be very crowded.

An exception, are the wares of Imaizumi Imaemon, who worked in the old tradition and produced technically perfect pieces. He died in 1975. Imaizumi Yoshinori, born in 1926, continues the tradition.

Collecting Hints: Nabeshima porcelains are not usually marked. The earliest wares were decorated solely in underglaze blue. Celadons were also produced during this period. The eighteenth century saw the advent of colored wares (iro Nabeshima). Since the earliest wares were not exported to Europe until after the decline of the clans and the selling off of wares by the impoverished nobility, most of what is available on today's market will be of nineteenth- and twentieth-century origin.

Advisors: Stewart and Barbara Hilbert

Bowl, 7¾" dia., Tokugawa Period, of characteristic shape resting on a high ring foot, the well potted body decorated in multicolored enamels and shades of underglaze blue with a flowering clump of narcissus silhouetted on a divided ground of white and blue, the exterior with discontinuous foliate scrolls above a comb-pattered band on the foot, wear extensive gold lacquer restorations **1,320.00**

Dish
  8 '" dia., 18th century, rare , of rounded form and everted rim, decorated in deep underglaze blue with a branch of camellia, the reverse with three groups of shippo design, the foot with comb design **1,800.00**
  6½", late 19th century Nabeshima style, round form with everted rim, underglaze blue decoration of a sake jar on a stylized wave ground **700.00**
  7½" dia., late 19th century Nabeshima style, decorated with underglaze blue, iron-red showing

Dish, 8" dia., late 18th/early 19th century, underglaze blue and white design of flowering branch, the reverse with three groups of shippo design, the foot with comb design. $1,400.00

scrolling foliage and peonies, the reverse with three groups of shippo design, the tall foot with a comb design. **550.00**

8½" dia., late 19th century Nabeshima style, typical form, decorated in underglaze blue, iron-red and enamels, showing two vases on a stylized wave ground, the reverse with foliate scrolls and a comb on foot **900.00**

NETSUKE

History: A netsuke is a form of miniature sculpture that developed in Japan over a period of more than 300 years. Netsuke served both functional and aesthetic purposes.

The kimono, the traditional form of Japanese dress had no pockets. Women would tuck small personal items into their sleeves, but men suspended their tobacco pouches, pipes, purses, or writing implements on a silk cord from their sash (obi). These hanging objects are called sagemono. To stop the cord from slipping through the obi, a small toggle was attached. This toggle is called a netsuke. (The most popular pronunciation is net-ski, while the actual Japanese is closer to net-skeh). A sliding bead (ojime) was strung on the cord between the netsuke and the sagemono to tighten or loosen the opening of the sagemono. The entire ensemble was then worn at the waist and functioned as a sort of removeable hip pocket. All three objects, the netsuke, the ojime, and the different types of sagemono were often beautifully decorated with elaborate carving, lacquer work, or inlays of rare and exotic materials, including wood, ivory, precious metals, shell, coral, and semiprecious stones. All three items

have developed into highly coveted and collectible art forms, but it is the netsuke that has by far most captivated the collector.

Netsuke are essentially toggles, which at first were not carved or adorned in any way. Most were merely found objects such as roots, shells, gourds or pieces of wood that were selected for their pleasing shapes. Toggles had been used for this purpose in other countries such as north China, Tibet, Mongolia, and Hungary, but it is only in Japan that the toggle developed into an art form. Its development as a great art form resulted from the natural aesthetic genius of the Japanese people to apply beauty to all aspects of their surroundings, even mundane, utilitarian objects.

The custom of wearing netsuke flourished in Japan during the three centuries of the Tokugawa era and Meiji Period (1603–1912). One of the major reasons for the development of the netsuke was the widely practiced custom of smoking tobacco. This custom was first introduced by the Portuguese in the sixteenth century and increased greatly in the seventeenth century, and thus necessitated the wearing of tobacco pouches or pipe cases to carry the loose tobacco. These were carried by every man of means—merchants and farmers as well as the samurai class. Netsuke were carved in quantity to fill this need. The tobacco pouch with its accompanying netsuke reached its height of production in the first half of the nineteenth century, often referred to as the "golden age of netsuke." Many fine carvers devoted their talents exclusively to creating this unique art form. However, the demand was so great, that other artisans such as lacquerers, metal artists, mask carvers, and potters produced netsuke in addition to their main pursuits.

Both internal and external events affected Japan and contributed to the gradual decline of netsuke as a functional art form. Commodore Perry's opening of Japan in 1853 ended almost 300 years of peace and isolation in Japan under the Tokugawa shogunate. Japan had been free from outside influences, thereby giving netsuke, as well as other art forms, the chance to flourish and be uniquely Japanese. But by 1867 great political upheaval ended the Tokugawa era and restored the emperor to power. After trade was reestablished in 1853, the Japanese were very receptive to Western ideas. They soon discarded their traditional garb for western dress. Moreover, cigarettes replaced pipes with their loose tobacco, which obviated the need to wear tobacco pouches. Soon there were many netsuke available that no longer needed to be used for their original function.

These fascinating objects soon caught the eyes of Western collectors who were captivated by the incredible beauty of the miniature masterpieces. Great collections were formed, at very modest prices, during that period of time. Thousands of netsuke poured out of Japan. The Japanese showed little interest in collecting them as art objects. When they were fashionable to wear, people vied for the finest specimens, but when they went out of style, interest was lost among the Japanese. A small coterie of serious collectors was able to form great collections of netsuke, undervalued and underpriced. Of course, with such low prices many netsuke were also collected as trinkets and souvenirs by foreigners.

The period between 1875 and 1925 called the postrestoration period was a rather confusing one in the netsuke world. The supply of great antique netsuke disappeared form Japan. Many carvers began to produce cheap, quick imitations for export. However, even during this period of mass production, several great netsuke artists did flourish. Several of these artists created dazzling displays of technique, often utilizing unusual combinations of materials. Popular subjects for these netsuke were ordinary objects and scenes from everyday life. Freed from the constraints of having to be worn, the best netsuke of this period are often incredible displays of intricacy and workmanship. At one time criticized by collectors as too fussy or too intricate for practical use, Meiji Period netsuke have recently enjoyed a renaissance of popularity with collectors.

With a few exceptions, the following fifty years, until about the end of World War II, was a rather weak period in the quality of netsuke production; mass-produced, quickly executed, and inexpensive netsuke carved for export dominated the scene. However, by 1960 a whole new group of young, serious netsuke artists began to emerge. They were encouraged by a small group of collectors who took great interest in their work and encouraged them with both books on the subject and purchases.

Netsuke have been carved from a wide variety of materials; however, the majority were made of wood or ivory (primarily elephant or marine ivory). Other materials used included stag antler, lacquer, various stones, walnuts, pottery and porcelain, sea pine, and metals. Since the ban on elephant ivory imports in May 1989, many contemporary netsuke carvers are working in exotic woods and fossil ivories with excellent results and without a threat to endangered species. The most popular of the fossil ivories are mammoth and mastedon ivory, found in Alaska and Siberia. Most of this material is between 10,000 and 50,000 years old. It looks very much like elephant ivory but possesses rich, unique properties. Since the material has been buried in the permafrost for thousands of years, it has usually absorbed minerals from the surrounding areas and it takes on a subtle, and occasionally dramatic, coloration. This has added a whole new dimension to the art of netsuke. Another popular material is fossil walrus ivory, which polishes to a magnificent luster. Many collectors enjoy these fascinating new materials. In fact, the variety of materials used

today has added such an interesting dimension to the netsuke world, it is unlikely elephant ivory will ever be used to the degree that it was in the past. Whatever the material, the artistry is the most important factor in determining the appeal of the netsuke.

There are many different types of netsuke. Not only do netsuke vary in their subject matter and material, but they also vary in form and in style. Style developed from large, powerful, simplified forms of the seventeenth and eighteenth centuries to more detailed, intricate designs of the nineteenth and early twentieth centuries. Styles also varied greatly from one artist to another and one region to another. It is a great challenge to the collector to try to identify artists' styles, because over half of all antique netsuke, including many great ones, were unsigned, according to the custom of the day. Contemporary netsuke are a little easier to identify since the twentieth-century custom is to sign the netsuke, and most of the leading artists' signatures are listed in good reference books or are well known to serious dealers in contemporary netsuke.

There are several major forms of netsuke, all equally valid. By far, the most popular form with collectors is a type known as katabori, which means carving in the round. Katabori netsuke represent human figures, animals, mythological creatures, vegetable groups, and all aspects of everyday life and legends. The second largest group of netsuke and probably the earliest form is the manju, named for the small rice cake or bun it resembles. Generally, it is flat and round, although it is sometimes oval or rectangular. A manju may be in one piece, or it may be divided into two halves that fit into each other, sometimes with an additional design on the inside. A variant of the manju is the kagamibuta, or mirror lid. It is round and bowl shaped; is usually made of ivory, bone, horn, or wood; and has a metal disk insert, in most cases made by a famous metal artist. Another variation is the ryusa, named for an eighteenth-century artist who originated the type. The surface is pierced, and the core has been hollowed out. These are usually elaborately carved. There are also long and sashi netsuke, which were thrust into the sash or had a hook, top, and bottom for the obi to pass through. (See: Inro; Ojime)

References: Raymond Bushell, *An Introduction to Netsuke*, Charles E. Tuttle Co., Inc., 1964; —, *Collector's Netsuke*, Weatherhill, 1971; —, *Netsuke Familiar and Unfamiliar, New Principles for Collecting*, Weatherhill, 1971; —, *The Wonderful World of Netsuke*, Charles E. Tuttle Co., Inc., 1964; Neil Davey, *Netsuke*, Faber and Faber, 1974; Bernard Hurting, *Masterpieces of Netsuke Art: One Thousand Favorites of Leading Collectors*, Weatherhill, 1973; F. M. Jones, *Netsuke*, Kegan Paul, London, 1928; reprinted by Charles E.

Tuttle Co. Inc., 1960; Miriam Kinsey, *Contemporary Netsuke*, Charles E. Tuttle Co., Inc., 1977; —, *Living Masters of Netsuke*, Kodansha International, 1983; George Lazarnick, *The Signature Book of Netsuke: Inro and Lacquer Artists in Photographs*, Reed Publishers, 1976; Masatoshi, *The Art of Netsuke Carving*, as told to Raymond Bushell, Kodansha International, 1981; Frederick Meinertzhagen, *The Art of the Netsuke Carver*, Routledge and Kegan Paul, 1956; Mary Louise O'Brien, *Netsuke: A Guide for Collectors*, Charles E. Tuttle Co., Inc., 1965; Egerton Ruerson, *The Netsuke of Japan*, G. Bell and Sons, 1958, reprinted by A. S. Barnes, 1958; Michael Spindel, *Netsuke Newsletter* (see Board of Advisors for address); Edwin C. Symmes, Jr., *Netsuke: Japanese Life and Legend in Miniature*, Charles E. Tuttle Co., Inc., 1991; Reikichi Ueda, *The Netsuke Handbook of Ueda Reikichi*, Charles E. Tuttle Co., Inc., 1961; Masayoshi Yamada, *Netsuke: Modern Masterpieces*, family publication, available from Michael Spindel, Ltd. (see Board of Advisors for address), n.d.

Museums: Los Angeles County Museum of Art, Los Angeles, California; Asian Art Museum of San Francisco, San Francisco, California; Cummer Gallery of Art, Jacksonville, Florida; Field Museum of Natural History, Chicago, Illinois; John Hopkins University Evergreen House, Baltimore, Maryland; The Walters Art Gallery, Baltimore, Maryland; Museum of Fine Arts, Boston, Massachusetts; Newark Museum, Newark, New Jersey; American Museum of Natural History, New York, New York; Margaret Woodbury Strong Museum, Rochester, New York; Seattle Art Museum, Seattle, Washington; Birmingham Museum and Art Gallery, Birmingham, England; British Museum, London, England; Victoria and Albert Museum, London, England; Pitt Rivers Museum, Oxford, England; Canterbury Museum, Christchurch, New Zealand; Rohss Museum of Arts and Crafts, Goteborg, Sweden; Museum of Far Eastern Antiquities, Stockholm, Sweden; Collections Baur, Geneva, Switzerland.

Collector's Club: Netsuke Kenkyukai Society, P. O. Box 11248, Torrance, California 90510-1248 publishes the *Netsuke Kenkyukai Journal* four times a year. The organization was founded by collectors for the purpose of promoting the study of netsuke and their related appurtenances, the artists who created them, and the society from which they evolved. Such study is accomplished through conventions; exhibits; lectures; workshops; and the dissemination of written materials, photographs, and its journal. Local chapters are in Los Angeles, San Francisco, Washington D.C., Ohio, Michigan, New York, Chicago, and London.

Reproduction Alert: Many people first encounter netsuke in tourist areas and hotel shops. While a few of these places have some authentic netsuke, it has been our experience that the stock is usually made up of mass produced reproductions from Hong Kong, China, or Taiwan. These pieces can be appealing because of their diminutive size, their varied subject matter, and their apparently intricate carving. If the collector knows that he or she is buying a reproduction, no harm is done, as long as the price is fair and the pieces are not misrepresented as original works of art. Unfortunately, this is not always the case, and many people have purchased these commercial-grade pieces thinking they were getting the real thing. We offer the following advice to avoid getting caught with a misrepresented netsuke. Many of these guidelines will be useful to collectors of other art forms as well.

First, good netsukes are fairly expensive. There is hardly anything on the market of decent quality, whether antique or contemporary, for less than $1,000. It is in the $100 to $500 range that the collector is most likely to be stung with a misrepresented reproduction. The following guidelines will help avoid this trap.

Ask a lot of questions. Does the seller seem to be knowledgeable about the art form, the subject matter, and the artist? If you do make a purchase, get the following information on your receipt:

1. The subject of the netsuke.
2. The material: is it wood, ivory, etc? Some collectors are worried about whether a netsuke is of real ivory. Most of the reproductions in the price range discussed are of real elephant ivory. There are even molded pieces made of resin or other synthetic compounds, but it is rare that the dealer will write ivory on your receipt if it is not, although it can happen. Ivory has a natural grain pattern that is readily identifiable. Ivory pieces are also usually heavier than those made of resin.
3. The approximate date when it was carved. For an antique, this could be a "circa" date to a quarter of a century: for example, mid-nineteenth century. On authentic contemporary pieces, the dates may be a little more specific because the dealer often knows the artist personally.
4. The country of origin of the carver. Be cautious about miniature mass-produced carvings being represented as authentic netsuke. Most of these are from Taiwan, Hong Kong, or China. They may look like netsukes, as many are copies of authentic pieces, but a true netsuke is one that is designed, carved, and signed by an individual artist. Most original fine art netsukes are carved in Japan. But there is a growing number of talented netsuke carvers outside the Orient (for example, in England, Australia, and the United States). These artists are doing serious netsukes and

are accepted as netsuke artists by the Japanese Netsuke Carver's Association and the established netsuke collecting community.

5. The name of the carver. This is most important. With a signed netsuke you must get the name of the artist. Most of the known artists are listed in books or known to established collectors and dealers. We strongly suggest that if you cannot get the name of the artist in writing from the seller, you do not buy the piece. Antique pieces can be a little more difficult to pin down, as many were not signed and sometimes signatures were added over the years by apprentices to honor the master or sometimes by unscrupulous dealers to enhance the value of the piece. In that case, you have to rely on your own judgment as to quality and the integrity of the dealer from whom you are making a purchase.

6. Reliable dealers will fully guarantee the authenticity and condition of any piece they sell. Their reputation is their most valuable asset. Should a piece prove to be other than as represented, the reliable dealer should give a full refund of the purchase price. Some dealers also permit a collector to trade in or upgrade a purchase as their knowledge and confidence grows. When done, this is usually as a courtesy, and we recommend that the collector refrain from doing this too often.

7. Reliable dealers can also help you with resales, for a commission fee, should you wish to sell. They can also refer you to reliable appraisers for insurance and estate purposes.

Collecting Hints: A netsuke is a sculpture, but one that is truly unique. Although miniature, a netsuke offers a format for the artist to portray, in sculptural form, an astonishing array of subject matter, including legends, folklore, history, studies of animals, insects, mythological and imaginary creatures, and everyday life. The netsuke collector enters a magnificent miniature world, where the philosophy, customs, and culture of the artist are conveyed in an art form that is often overwhelming in its emotional power and beauty.

Today, contemporary netsukes of the finest quality are still being carved, as highly respected, original works of art. While not intended to be worn, they adhere to all the standards of a true netsuke. There are several dozen highly successful netsuke artists, many of whom have been apprentices to great carvers of the past who are currently creating modern masterpieces. Another fascinating aspect of these contemporary netsukes is that they reflect the time and place in which the artist lives. In the early part of this century, dealers advised netsuke carvers to emulate antique netsukes both in style and subject matter. These had a charm of their own. Most working netsuke artists are exploring new techniques, new subject matter, and new materials. This vibrant approach to the netsuke has captured the interest of both old and new collectors throughout the world. Also, netsuke carving is no longer confined to Japan. There are talented, enthusiastic carvers excited by worldwide collector interest, museum exhibits, collector organizations, and a wealth of books on the subject; they are creating netsukes in many parts of the world. Some use traditional Japanese themes, others explore themes indigenous to their own areas. There are now talented and respected netsuke carvers in Japan, England, the United States, Canada, Africa, Australia, New Zealand, Belgium, and Germany. Interest in collecting netsukes and in creating them is enjoying a strong renaissance. There are active collector's groups that are expanding the knowledge of netsuke carving and advancing the art form. This is an exciting time for both the established and the new collector to be involved with netsukes.

In all good netsukes, form has to follow function. This poses a tremendous challenge to the artist. Designs have to be compact, with no protruding or sharp edges that would either snag a beautiful kimono or break off in use. Netsukes are usually between 1″ and 2″ in size but some unusual pieces could be as long as 8″ or 9″. A good netsuke must be completely carved on all sides, including the top and bottom. Though many netsukes will stand—and this is considered desirable by some collectors—it is not imperative, as they were not originally intended to be viewed this way. Netsukes must have holes (himotoshi), or natural openings formed by the design of the piece, through which a silk cord can be passed to be attached to the sagemono. The placement of holes is important because it determines how well the netsuke will hang. A good netsuke will usually hang with its best side facing forward. The netsuke must be light enough to be comfortably worn yet sturdy enough to withstand the rigors of daily use. Netsukes should feel good, be comfortable when handled, and should be aesthetically pleasing from every angle. With an antique netsuke, one of the most appealing aspects of the piece was put there not by the carver but by the wearer and by time, which added a lustrous and mellow patination known as aji. This is the owner's contribution, which adds warmth, charm, and even a sense of history to the work of art, without which an antique netsuke would not be complete. Interestingly, collectors of contemporary netsuke often like to handle their netsuke, and the natural oils of the skin add a patina to these pieces as well.

Today, netsukes are important, highly coveted works of art. Their tremendous appeal has to do with many factors, including their size. They are easily carried on one's person, transported over great distances, displayed, and stored. They take up very little space. When created by a true artist, they can be the finest miniature sculptures in the world. When at their finest, netsukes can have all the power, strength, and artistry of a Michelangelo or Rodin. Yet, you can carry it in your pocket and share it with other admirers by placing it in their hands. The netsuke lends itself to informal enjoyment and communication. There is a certain intimacy one can feel about a netsuke that does not apply to any other form of sculpture. Collectors can satisfy their senses of sight, touch, and even smell at the same time. It is difficult to describe the excitement the collector feels on holding a masterpiece and knowing that a netsuke carver's finest achievement is in the palm of his or her hand.

Many potential collectors are fascinated by netsukes but are reluctant to become involved with them because they feel that the field is too complicated to learn. This is not the case. Netsukes are no more difficult to collect than any other fine art form. All it takes is some common sense, a keen eye, and some knowledge. Fortunately for new and established collectors, there are many excellent books on netsuke collecting as well as knowledgeable and reliable dealers.

Netsuke collecting requires a substantial investment. We suggest that you read some of the fine books available and look at netsukes in museums, in galleries, and at fine art and antiques shows. Try to meet other collectors and get to know the reliable dealers in the field who can guide you with your purchases and stand behind what they sell. There is a lot of competition for good to great netsukes in the marketplace. It is a field of growing worldwide interest and demand. Therefore, there are few "sleepers," or undiscovered bargains, in the field. Of course, the final choice as to what to purchase will depend on your own tastes and interest. All art is subjective. It must say something to you. Go with what your instincts tell you is right, with what you love. Then go with a reliable dealer who will make sure that you are treaty fairly. Buy the best quality you can afford and have an open mind. Remember, a great netsuke does not have to be signed. Some of the finest early netsukes were not signed and some record prices have been realized on unsigned netsukes. There are fine antique netsukes on the market, but antique is not always better. Netsukes were functional objects and many of the old netsukes are of rather mediocre quality. There are great pieces in both antique and contemporary netsukes. You may be able to purchase a contemporary masterpiece for much less than an antique of comparable quality. You do not have to be Japanese to carve a great netsuke. During the past twenty years, talented carvers have been noted in many parts of the world. These artists have a deep understanding of the unique nature of netsuke art and have been accepted enthusiastically by established carvers and collectors worldwide.

Price is always a factor in choosing a work of art. Expect to pay between $1,000 and $5,000 for a good netsuke, whether antique or contemporary. Many fine netsukes go into five figures and record prices of over $200,000 have been realized, but this is very rare. Outstanding contemporary netsukes can be found in the $5,000 to $10,000 range with some extraordinary pieces going for as much as $25,000. All these prices are likely to go higher as the number of collectors increases and fine netsukes are absorbed into collections. The demand for all netsuke of high quality has been strong for many years. No one can predict the art market with any guarantee, but if the rules of supply and demand and past performance are any indicators of future performance, the outlook for fine antique and contemporary netsukes appears bright, both as art treasures and as good economic investments.

Advisors: Michael Spindel and Elaine Ehrenkranz

IVORY CARVINGS, EIGHTEENTH CENTURY

Boar (wild), 2", asleep on a bed of leaves, engraved hairwork, unsigned, Kyoto school **8,200.00**
Deer, 1⅞", late 18th C., slightly worn and well stained, inlaid pupils, signed Okatomo in rectangular reserve **45,750.00**
Dog, 2", late 18th C., well patinated and worn, slight age crack, signed Okatomo within an oval reserve . . . **18,700.00**
Drummer (South Sea Island), 5¾" tall, shown standing and holding a drum and drumstick, well patinated, singed Shugetsu, important and rare! **85,300.00**
Dutchman, 2⅞" tall, late 18th C., stand-

Boar, 1⅞" l., 18th century, reclining on a bed of autumn leaves, ivory with mellow patina Kyoto school, signed Tomotada in reserve. $8,000.00

Deer, 1¼" l., 18th century, stained ivory, inlaid eyes, unsigned. $7,500.00

ing and holding a trumpet and supporting a child on his shoulders, lightly stained, patina, unsigned ... **3,250.00**

Fox, 4⅜" tall, the magic fox dancing on his hind legs, lightly stained, patina, unsigned, rare............ **19,050.00**

Fox Priest, 4", medium stained, unsigned...................... **16,500.00**

Goshisho Hoisting an Incense burner, 1¾", late 18th C., lightly stained, signed Hidemasa.............. **1,540.00**

Kwan Yu, 4½", lightly stained, unsigned...................... **1,760.00**

Monkey showman (Sarumawashi), 3" l., late 18th C., reclining with a monkey holding a peach at his feet, stained with dark stained details, unsigned...................... **1,725.00**

Ox and young (reclining), 2¼" l., stained and patinated with incised hairwork and inlaid eye pupils in horn, signed Tomotada.......... **5,500.00**

Quail (pair), 1⅜" h., late 18th C., shown on two large millet heads and leaves, dark stained feather work,

signed Okatomo in rectangular reserve....................... **4,350.00**

Rat, 1¾", well worn and patinated, signed Okatomo in an oval reserve **9,900.00**

Shoki and Oni, 5½", late 18th C., stained, some age cracks, repair to one foot, unsigned............. **4,125.00**

Stag (reclining), 1¾", incised hairwork and eyes inlaid in horn, signed Oka, Kyoto school................. **3,000.00**

Sparrow, 1½" h., late 18th C., shown with a tiny man on its back, lightly stained, patina, signed Hidemasa in a reserve...................... **2,100.00**

Tiger, 1½" h., shown seated on bamboo, well patinated and worn, several age cracks, unsigned......... **2,420.00**

Tiger on Bamboo, 2", late 18th C., slightly worn, well stained and patinated, unsigned.............. **4,150.00**

WOOD CARVINGS, EIGHTEENTH CENTURY

Badger, seated, (Tanaka no hara tsuzumi), 1⅛" h., stained with incised hairwork and inlaid eye pupils, signed Minko with kakihan ... **1,550.00**

Handaka Sonja, 6¼", late 18th/early 19th C., well patinated stained boxwood, eyes inlaid with horn, unsigned...................... **14,300.00**

Frog, 1⅞", shown on a sandal, darkly stained wood, signed Kokei in rectangular reserve................ **825.00**

Horse, 2⅛", richly patinated wood, eyes inlaid with horn, fine and rare, signed Tomotada in rectangular reserve...................... **45,750.00**

Lotus Seed Pod, 1½", late 18th C., well stained, moveable seeds of wood and horn, signed Temetaka **1,550.00**

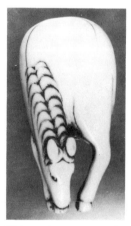

Horse, 2" h., 18th century, grazing, ivory with rich patina, unsigned. $3,500.00

Shishi Head, 1⅛" h., 18th century, stained ivory, articulated jaw, rich patina, signed by the great Kyoto school carver Tomotada. $8,500.00

IVORY CARVINGS, NINETEENTH CENTURY

Arhat, (Manju netsuke) 1¼" dia., the Arhat shown holding a bowl, stained, unsigned **600.00**

Bamboo shoot, 2⅜" l., late 19th C., stained, unsigned **1,275.00**

Branch with two loquats and a leaf attached, 2¼" l., stained and stippled, signed in gourd shaped reserve, Mitsuhiro and kakihan **2,700.00**

Clam Dream, 2⅛", showing the clam half open, the interior delicately carved with a domestic scene, signed Gaho **1,870.00**

Daruma
   1½" h., shown seated in meditation, Narwhale ivory, signed Sharaku with seal **3,000.00**
   2" h., shown standing with folded arms holding a Hossu, lightly stained, signed Masatsugu **1,050.00**

Fisherman, 3¼" h., shown with a basket supporting a small boy on his back, lightly stained, signed Senshusaku **10,900.00**

Fisherwoman (ama), seated beside large octopus, 1⅝" l., late 19th C., stained, signed Shuraku **5,450.00**

Fukurokuju (happy God), 2" l., shown laughing and leaning against his reclining stag, stained with incised hairwork, signed Yoshitomo in oval reserve **2,250.00**

Ghost Lantern, 1¾", mid 19th C., darkly stained, eyes inlaid, signed Ryumin. **2,200.00**

Goose, 1¾" l., 19th C., shown with its head turned back, engraved plummage, eyes inlaid in horn, signed Hidemasa.   **1,300.00**

Hares (two), 1⅝" l., early 19th C.,

Two boys, 1¾" h. × 1⅞" l., 19th century, romping on a grinding stone, lightly stained ivory, signed Shokyosai. $1,800.00

lightly stained with incised hairwork and eyes inlaid in horn, signed Rakuzan **5,200.00**

Hotei
   1⅜", late 19th C., inlays of various materials, signed Yasuaki (homei) with inlaid seal reading Kodama   **3,100.00**
   1½" h., late 19th century, shown standing while holding a Chinese fan and a sack suspended from his shoulder, lightly stained, signed Hidekazu on a red lacquer tablet   **700.00**

Man
   1⅜", late 19th/early 20th C., shown seated painting a Daruma doll, light unstained Ivory, signed Komei and kakihan **12,700.00**
   2" l., late 19th C., shown polishing the character Shin, dark stained details, unsigned **1,200.00**

Masks (cluster), 2", lightly stained, unsigned. **1,760.00**

Mermaid, 2" l., early 19th C., shown reclining clasping a seashell, stained with dark details, inscribed Okakoto   **1,275.00**

Monkey
   1½" h., late 19th C., shown seated, holding a persimmon between its feet and wearing a Shishimai headdress, incised hairwork, signed Masatami **2,600.00**
   1¾", shown with young, lightly stained and worn, signed within oval reserve Masatsugu **6,050.00**

New Year's Dragon Dancer, 1¾", late 19th C., jaw moves to reveal a face underneath, lightly stained, inlays, unsigned.   **1,980.00**

Pheasants (two part Manju Netsuke), inlaid with shell, coral, lacquer, horn, engraved details, signed Shibayama on a pearl tablet **950.00**

Quail (two), 1½", early 19th C., Slightly worn, well stained and patinated, eyes inlaid, signed Okatomo in rectangular reserve **3,750.00**

Rats
   Group of three, 1⅜" w., late 19th C., lightly stained with eyes inlaid in dark horn, signed Masaka **5,650.00**
   Two, 2⅜", late 19th C., shown on a bucket, lightly stained, dark horn inlaid eyes, signed Masaka. **21,850.00**

Shepherd Boy on an Ox, 1⅞", lightly stained, signed Tomonobu. **1,550.00**

The Three Long-lived Men Seated in a Sake Cup, 1½", mid 19th C., stained, signed Hojitsu **1,980.00**

Three Sake Tasters, 1½", mid/late 19th C., lightly stained, signed Tomochika **1,870.00**

Tortoise, 2" l., early 19th C., shown

with young on its back, lightly stained, signed Garaku **2,050.00**
Tongue-cut Sparrow, $1\frac{3}{8}$″, late 19th C., lightly stained, signed Naoaki **935.00**
Twelve animals of the Oriental Zodiac (Manju Netsuke), $1\frac{3}{4}$″, well stained, inlaid eyes, signed Kaigyokusai Masatstugu in well polished reserve **11,550.00**

WOOD CARVINGS, NINETEENTH CENTURY

Ashinaga and Tenaga (figures), $4\frac{3}{4}$″, early 19th C., well stained and patinated, unsigned **4,800.00**
Baby Crawling, $1\frac{7}{8}$″, well stained wood with lacquer details, signed Hojitsu **1,975.00**
Boar, $1\frac{3}{8}$″ l., circa 1850, shown seated, stained, incised hairwork and inlaid eye pupils, unsigned **4,400.00**
Chinese boy (Karako) $1\frac{3}{4}$″ l., shown lying on his stomach, stained, signed Hozan **800.00**
Chinese Sennin (Manju netsuke), $1\frac{1}{2}$″ dia., stained, signed Toyomasa **2,900.00**
Cockerel on well bucket with hen at its side, $1\frac{5}{8}$″, tall, stained, incised hairwork, inlaid horn eyes, unsigned . . . **650.00**
Stylized Chrysanthemum (ryusa manju netsuke), $1\frac{1}{2}$″ dia., stained, unsigned **1,000.00**
Daruma, $2\frac{1}{2}$″, mid 19th C., stained Boxwood, signed Tomotoshi **3,650.00**
Fox Woman and her child, $1\frac{1}{2}$″, lightly stained, signed Masakazu **4,400.00**
Gorilla, $1\frac{3}{4}$″, late 19th C., well stained boxwood with shell inlaid eyes, signed Masami **1,200.00**
Kappa on a Clamshell, $1\frac{3}{4}$″, early 19th C., well-stained boxwood, eyes inlaid, himotoshi ringed **7,700.00**
Kiojime with Bell, $1\frac{5}{8}$″, darkly stained, signed Masakazu in oval reserve . . . **3,550.00**
Locust, $1\frac{1}{2}$″, late 19th/early 20th C., lightly stained, signed Gyokuso **7,100.00**
Mask netsuke, $1\frac{5}{8}$″ h., composed from parts of the crab, a reference to the Heike crabs of Dan-no-ura, stained boxwood, unsigned **1,550.00**
Mushroom and Two Chestnuts (grouping), $1\frac{7}{8}$″, early 19th C., well patinated and stained, unsigned **1,500.00**
Oni
- $1\frac{1}{2}$″ l., shown trapping Shoki beneath a large basket, stained, eyes inlaid with horn and ivory, signed Romokazu in oval reserve **2,250.00**
- $1\frac{1}{2}$″, shown carrying a huge mask, well stained and patinated, signed Minkoku **3,750.00**

Ox with goat on back, $1\frac{1}{2}$″ h., stained, signed Masamitsu **2,200.00**
Rat (coiled), $1\frac{5}{8}$″, stained, incised hairwork, eyes inlaid with horn, signed Masanao **3,000.00**
Samboso Dancer, $1\frac{1}{2}$″, lightly stained, with lacquer details, unsigned **2,310.00**
Shoki, $1\frac{3}{4}$″ l., shown sharpening his sword on a rock, stained, signed in ukibori characters Tadaroshi of Nagoya **5,100.00**
Skull with entwined snake, $1\frac{3}{8}$″ h., stained, unsigned **2,600.00**
Snail and Aubergine on a Pumpkin, $1\frac{3}{4}$″ h., early 19th C., stained, signed Shigemasato **2,400.00**
Snake (coiled), $1\frac{3}{4}$″ l., ebony wood with double tortoise inlay in eyes, unsigned **1,250.00**
Sumo Wrestlers, 3″ h., early 19th C., shown posed in the Kawazu throw, red lacquered wood, unsigned **2,900.00**
Rat, $1\frac{3}{4}$″, mid 19th C., well patinated and slightly worn wood, signed Tomokazu within an oval reserve **2,475.00**
Terrapins (group), $1\frac{5}{8}$″ l., late 19th C., shown in an old basket, signed Chichi in oval reserve **1,550.00**
Tiger, $1\frac{1}{8}$″ h., shown sitting with its long tail curled across its back, stained with eye pupils inlaid in black horn, signed Masanobu **1,200.00**
Toad, $1\frac{1}{2}$″ l., shown with baby toad on back, black inlaid eye pupils, signed Masanao **1,500.00**
Wolf, 2″ l., early 19th C., shown holding a venison leg in his paws, eyes inlaid with horn **7,700.00**

OTHER MEDIA

Coral Fisherman, $2\frac{1}{2}$″ h., ebony, ivory, coral, various woods, shells, metal inlays, signed Ikko in oval reserve **9,350.00**
Horse grazing, $2\frac{5}{8}$″ h., stag antler, shell inlaid eyes, signed Koku(sai) in a carved plaque **6,050.00**
Kagamibuta netsuke
- Decorated with Takamono (treasures of good fortune articles), $1\frac{1}{2}$″ dia., cloisonne enamels on a iron plate in a bowl, unsigned **800.00**
- Three Sake Tasters, $1\frac{7}{8}$″, ivory bowl with plate of Shibuichi, copper and gold, unsigned **375.00**
- The plate decorated with Taishin Fujin playing a Koto, and the bowl carved with Chinese figures, 5 cm. dia., late 19th C., the bowl in wood, plate in metals, signed Setsuga **4,150.00**

Standing boy doll, $2\frac{1}{8}$″ h., gold and colored lacquers on wood, unsigned **3,650.00**
Women of the Gay Quarter, $2\frac{1}{8}$″, late

Real Gourd, $2\frac{3}{8}$" l., 19th century, decorated with gold lacquer, silver metal ring screw top, ring around center, unsigned. $2,500.00

19th/early 20th C., ivory, various woods, inlauys of lacquer and metal, signed Kinkosai with inlaid gold tablet with Kakihan of Hoshu **17,675.00**

IVORY CARVINGS, TWENTIETH CENTURY

Actor, $1\frac{3}{8}$", mid 20th C., lightly stained, signed Masatoshi **7,900.00**
After the Bath, $2\frac{3}{8}$", late 20th C., lacquer details, signed Ryushi **12,500.00**
Cat, $1\frac{1}{2}$", late 20th C., stained with sumie details, signed Yukimasa **975.00**
Cicada on a Biwa, $1\frac{5}{8}$", late 20th C., stained, shell inlays, signed Senpo **4,500.00**
Cherry Blossom, $1\frac{1}{2}$" l., late 20th C., signed Kosei Hideyuki in 18k gold plaque **4,500.00**
Figure seated with frog, $1\frac{1}{2}$" h., late 20th C., lacquer details, signed Hodo **2,800.00**
Fish, $1\frac{1}{4}$", late 20th C., with sumie details, signed Ryoshu III **975.00**
Frogs (two), wrestling on a lotus leaf, $1\frac{3}{8}$", late 20th C., colored stone inlays, signed Koetsu **975.00**
Go Players (two) in a pumpkin, $1\frac{1}{2}$", stained details, pumpkin opens and closes, signed Shodo **2,500.00**
Horse (ceremonial), $1\frac{3}{8}$" l., mid 20th C., inlays of shell, lacquer and sumie details, signed Meigyokusai **3,000.00**
Octopus in a shell, $1\frac{3}{8}$", late 20th C., with shell inlay, signed Seigyoku . . . **2,000.00**
Man
Playing with child and a noh mask, $1\frac{3}{8}$", late 20th C., signed Gyokusho **2,400.00**
Teaching himself to play Go, $2\frac{1}{4}$", late 20th C., lacquer details, signed Koyu **3,000.00**
Men playing go, $1\frac{3}{8}$", late 20th C., sumie details, signed Keigyoku **750.00**
Monk with rosary beads, $1\frac{3}{8}$", late 20th C., lacquer details, signed Hozan . . **2,800.00**
Noh Dancer, $1\frac{1}{2}$", mid 20th C., with brightly painted enamels, signed Ichiro **3,000.00**
Nude
$1\frac{1}{2}$", late 20th C., signed Sumi **3,800.00**
With large hat, $2\frac{3}{8}$", late 20th C., signed Ryushi **12,500.00**
Oni looking at a mirror, $1\frac{3}{8}$", mid 20th C., sumie details, silver inlay, shell inlaid eyes, signed Meigyokusai . . . **3,000.00**
Peacock, 2" l., late 20th C., lacquered, signed Shingetsu **4,200.00**
Porpoises, $1\frac{3}{4}$", late 20th C., signed Godo **1,800.00**
Praying Mantis on bamboo, $1\frac{1}{2}$", late 20th C., stained, signed Senpo **3,800.00**
Shochukubai (Three Friends of Winter) $3\frac{1}{8}$", late 20th C., signed Kosei Hideyuke in 18k gold plaque **6,500.00**
Squirrel, $1\frac{5}{8}$", late 20th C., shell inlaid eyes, signed Ikumi **1,800.00**
Swallows (pair), $1\frac{1}{2}$", late 20th C., shell inlays, signed Ranjoh **3,000.00**
Swan (abstract carving), $1\frac{1}{2}$", late 20th C., signed Bishu **4,500.00**
Traveler, $1\frac{3}{4}$", late 20th C., lacquer details signed Koyu **3,000.00**
Woman, cutting her toenails, $1\frac{3}{8}$", late 20th C., inlays of shell, signed Yusufusa in 18k gold signature plaque . . . **2,500.00**
Woman of Edo, $1\frac{1}{2}$", late 20th C., with polychrome lacquer details, signed Ryosei **2,500.00**

PREHISTORIC IVORY, TWENTIETH CENTURY

Boar and three young, $1\frac{5}{8}$", late 20th C., shell inlaid eyes, signed Kangyoku Risshisai **7,500.00**
Dancing Fox, 3", late 20th C., mammoth ivory with shell inlaid eyes, Sashi style, signed Bishu **4,200.00**
Duet for Carp, $1\frac{1}{2}$", late 20th C., lacquered, shell inlaid eyes, carved in Ryusa style, signed Shingetsu **4,500.00**
Kirin (mythical beast), $3\frac{3}{8}$", late 20th C., mammouth Ivory, shell inlaid eyes, signed Kangyoku Risshisai . . . **6,800.00**
Leda and the Swan, $1\frac{1}{2}$", late 20th C., signed Sumi **4,500.00**
Mandarin Duck, $1\frac{5}{8}$" l., late 20th C., lacquered with gold leaf and brilliant multicolors, shell inlaid eyes, signed Shingetsu **4,200.00**

Mare with Foal, 1½″ w. x 1¼″ h., late 20th century, prehistoric ivory, translucent shell inlaid eyes, signed Kangyoku Risshisai. $6,500.00

Skull with Raven, 1⅜″ h. x 1⅛″ w., late 20th century, prehistoric ivory and ebony, signed Tanetoshi. $6,000.00

Cat, 1½″ h., late 20th century, prehistoric ivory with shell inlaid eyes, 18k bell, signed Sumi. $4,000.00

Tiger with Cub, 1¾″ h., late 20th century, prehistoric ivory, shell inlaid eyes, Kangyoku Risshisai. $6,500.00

C., mammoth ivory, shell inlaid eyes, signed Kangyoku Risshisai . . . **6,500.00**

WOOD CARVINGS, TWENTIETH CENTURY

Baboons, mother and baby, 1½″, lightly stained boxwood, double shell inlaid eyes, signed Nick Lamb in 18k gold reserve **3,800.00**

Beetles, 1⅜″, late 20th C., stained boxwood, shell inlays, signed Akihide **4,200.00**

Bobcat with a snake , ojime to match, 1⅝″, and ¼″, late 20th C., boxwood, sumie details and shell inlays, signed Nick Lamb in 18k gold reserve. **3,800.00**

Cowboy leaning on a Grave Post, 2″, late 20th C., boxwood, stained with many colors, signed David Carlin **3,000.00**

Daikiku, one of the Seven Gods of Good Fortune, 1¼″, early 20th C., lightly stained boxwood, signed Gyokuso. **5,775.00**

Drunken Frog, 1⅝″, late 20th C., Ma-

My Nymph, 1⅞″ h., late 20th century, prehistoric ivory, signed Ryushi. $12,500.00

Three eyed bag ghost, 2½″, late 20th C., shell inlaid eyes, signed Kansui **3,800.00**

Twelve Animals of the Zodiac, 1½″, late 20th C., shell inlaid eyes, signed Tanetoshi **6,000.00**

Water buffalo with calf, 2″ l., late 20th

Nue, 4" h., late 20th century, mythological beast with head of lion, body of tiger, tail is a snake with head at the end, Sashi style, stained boxwood, shell inlaid eyes, stag antler inlays for teeth, signed Ikku. $10,000.00

Hotei, God of Good Fortune, 2", early 20th C., various woods, ivory inlay, signed Sosui **8,800.00**

Kamaitachi (mythical Creature who Causes Typhoons), tall netsuke, $4\frac{3}{4}$", late 20th C., Ebony with inlays of stag antler and horn signed Ikku **10,000.00**

Kappa on Earthquake Fish, $1\frac{7}{8}$", late 20th C., boxwood, shell inlays, signed Hidefumi. **2,800.00**

Komoso (Mendicant Monk) $2\frac{1}{4}$", mid 20th C., lightly stained and tinted, signed Ichiro. **2,100.00**

Legend of Shisui, $1\frac{1}{2}$", late 20th C., boxwood, signed Seiho **4,500.00**

Log Bundle, bound with rope, realistically carved, $1\frac{3}{4}$", early 20th C., boxwood, signed Soko in an inlaid ivory plaque **17,600.00**

Nio on a Saddle, $1\frac{1}{2}$", early 20th C., boxwood, lightly stained, signed Sosui. **12,100.00**

Chimpanzee with Persimmon, $1\frac{5}{8}$" h., late 20th century, boxwood, stained details, double inlays of horn, signed Nick Lamb. $3,800.00

Toy Vendor with Fox, $1\frac{7}{8}$" h., late 20th century, boxwood, inlays of shell, coral, and 18k gold, signed Seihosai Meikei. $25,000.00

hogany with shell inlaid eyes, signed Kansui **3,600.00**

Dutchman (tall standing figure) 3", late 20th C., stained Boxwood, inlays of ebony, ivory and onyx, signed Akihide. **5,000.00**

Ghosts of Oiwa and Kihei, $2\frac{1}{4}$", late 20th C., stained boxwood, shell inlaid eyes, 18k gold details, signed Meikei **25,000.00**

Gorilla, $1\frac{3}{4}$", late 20th C., ebony with horn inlaid eyes, signed Nick Lamb in 18k gold reserve. **3,800.00**

Haniwa figure of a General, $1\frac{3}{8}$", late 20th C., mahogany, signed Bradford Blakely **2,500.00**

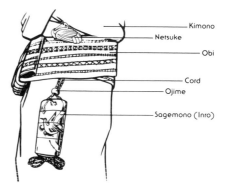

Placement of a netsuke with Japanese clothing. Illustration by Thomas Aquirri.

Oni laughing with head of Shoki, $2\frac{1}{8}''$, late 20th C., stained Boxwood with shell inlays, signed Kosei Hideyuki **4,200.00**
Rolling shishi, $1\frac{1}{2}''$, late 20th C., stained boxwood, shell inlaid eyes and moveable ivory ball, signed Seiho **4,500.00**
Sumo Wrestlers, $2\frac{3}{8}''$, late 20th C., stained boxwood, shell inlaid eyes, signed Meikei. **25,000.00**
Tennin Angel, $1\frac{7}{8}''$, early 20th C., well stained boxwood, signed Sosui **9,900.00**
Winter Peony, $2\frac{1}{4}''$, late 20th C., stained boxwood with inlays of pre-historic ivory and coral, signed Ikku **9,500.00**

OTHER MEDIA

Basket of Flowers, $1\frac{5}{8}''$, late 20th C., stag antler, inlays of various natural materials, signed Shubi **3,000.00**
Duck, $1\frac{3}{8}''$, late 20th C., Amber with shell inlaid eyes, signed Kenji **1,800.00**

NIPPON PORCELAIN

History: Nippon hand painted porcelain was made for export from Japan between the years of 1891 and 1921. In October 1891, the McKinley Tariff Act was passed by Congress, proclaiming, "All articles of foreign manufacture, be stamped, branded, or labeled and all packages containing such or their imported articles shall, respectively be marked, stamped, branded, or labeled in legible English words so as to indicate the country of their origin; and unless so marked, stamped, branded, or labeled they shall not be admitted to entry." The Japanese chose to use "Nippon," which is the English equivalent of "Japan," as their marking.

The McKinley Tariff Act also set rules and regulations on the marking system, stating, "all articles of foreign manufacture which are capable of being marked without injury shall be marked with country of origin in legible English words and marking shall be nearly indelible and permanent as the nature of the article will permit." Paper labels were excepted and in the case of small articles shipped together, only the inside and outside packages were required to be marked with the country of origin.

Decoration of Nippon ware was, for the most part, dictated by the styles of the Western world. Porcelain objects were painted in the Victorian, art nouveau, Edwardian, and art deco styles. Many Nippon pieces resemble their European counterparts so strongly in style, decoration, and quality that it is necessary to check the base mark to verify that they are indeed Nippon in origin. Most Nippon hand-painted porcelain copied the

styles of the china ware of Europe. Tapestry techniques, achieved by pressing linen cloth on the soft clay and Wedgewood cameo techniques were occasionally used but are considered scarce by collectors. Sometimes the colorful and bold art nouveau designs of Gouda ware from Holland were copied. A notable exception to this adoption of European motif, are the Nippon items found decorated in the primitive motifs of South America or with ancient Middle Eastern–style decoration. These pieces are considered oddities and were decorated with incised, stamped, or impressed designs along with classical hand-painted work; they rank among the most unusual of Nippon marked items.

The majority of Nippon items are those employing hand-painted techniques, particularly stressing floral, natural, and landscape design. Animal motifs were also popular, especially on male-oriented items such as cigar humidors. Frequently, the animals (or the nuts painted on nut bowls) were molded in relief, giving the object a three-dimensional appearance, a style considered very collectable in today's market. Moriage techniques and coralene decoration were sometimes used as embellishments on Nippon marked porcelain. (See: Coralene; Moriage.)

In 1921, the government reversed its position and decided that the word *Nippon* was no longer in compliance with the law: "After examination into the history and derivation of the word 'Nippon,' and lexicographers of recognized standing, the department is constrained to the conclusion that 'Nippon' is a Japanese word, the English equivalent of which is 'Japan' and the weight of authority does not support the earlier view that the word has become incorporated into the English language. All Japanese items must now be marked in English 'Japan.' " Thus the Nippon era came to an end.

There are more than 221 known and recorded Nippon backstamps or marks. The three most common are the M in wreath, the maple leaf, and the rising sun. Marks were applied by under glaze decal sticker or direct imprinting. Paper labels were also used, but these were eventually lost, resulting in the large number of unmarked pieces found today.

References: Harry Rinker, ed., *Warman's Antiques and Their Prices* Wallace-Homestead, 1991; Joan Van Patton, *The Collectors Encyclopedia of Nippon Porcelain*, Series 1, 2, and 3, Collector Books, 1986; Kathy Wojciechowski, *The Wonderful World of Nippon Porcelain*, Schiffer Publications, 1991.

Reproduction Alert: There are many Nippon reproductions on the market today. These items are made in Taiwan but are marked with a version of an original Nippon backstamp. In addition to the bogus Nippon mark, a paper label, saying "Made in Taiwan" is affixed to the bottom, which properly indicates the country of origin. Once the porcelain object clears U.S. Customs, the paper label is removed. Therefore, it is possible that an unsuspecting buyer may buy one of these pieces thinking that it dates from the "Nippon" era, even though some items do not even resemble the porcelain of that period. U.S. Customs agents are actively seeking help in identifying and prosecuting the large importing firms that are illegally falsifying Nippon marks.

The three Nippon marks that are being reproduced are variations of the M in wreath, maple leaf, and rising sun. An authentic M in wreath mark has an *M* in the center of a wreath that is open at the top. The bogus mark has an hourglass in the center of a wreath which is open at the bottom. In the reproduction rising sun mark, the rays extending from the sun are connected, whereas the authentic rising sun mark has open rays. The bogus maple leaf mark is quite large compared with the mark that collectors recognize as authentic.

Collecting Hints: The wide range of types of decoration found on Nippon porcelain items account for the many specialties found in Nippon collections. Since collecting is somewhat of an extension of oneself, collectors should concentrate on what is most appealing to them and their lifestyles. Nippon collectors should educate themselves before making purchases by reading everything they can and familiarizing themselves with the three bogus Nippon marks. Once familiar with the authentic marks and their imitations it is very easy to see the differences.

Damaged and repaired items should only be purchased at reduced prices. Remember that a damaged item today, is still a damaged item ten years from now, whereas an undamaged, high-quality item today, will escalate in value.

Collector's Clubs: International Nippon Collector's Club, 46-45 188th Street, Flushing, NY 11358 (quarterly newsletter, annual convention); Great Lakes Nippon Collector's Club, Kathy Wojciechowski, P.O. Box 230, Peotone, IL 60468; Ark-La-Tex Nippon Club, Debra Tuttle, 1021 Summer Place, Southlake TX 76092; Buckeye Chapter, Jenny Foster, 164 West Lakeview Ave., Colombus, OH 43202; Dixieland Nippon Collectors, Polly Frye, Route 1, Box 361, Keezletown, VA 22832; Long Island Nippon Club, Rhonda Perroncino, 72 Hewlett Ave., Merrick, NY 11566; Maryland-Pennsylvania Collectors Club, Russ Heckman, 2511 Village Bridge, Lyndenwald, NJ 08021; New England Collector's Club, Stephen Costa, 145 Londonberry Rd., Windham, NH 03087

Advisor: Kathy Wojciechowski

Ashtray
    4½" l., shinny finish, scenic lake and trees, wreath mark **65.00**

    5", colorful playing cards on brown background, wreath mark **135.00**
    5¼", molded in relief dog with scenic earth tones, wreath mark **425.00**
    5¼", Moriage dragon design, grey background, Royal Moriage **175.00**
    6" w., triangular shape, decal of moose, wreath mark **90.00**
    With attached Match Box, 7", hand painted cigar in center of ashtray, Rare molded in relief Indian profile on match box **800.00**
Basket
    4" h., garlands of tiny flowers on a white background, Sun mark **45.00**
    5¼" h., heavy all over moriage decoration, unmarked **300.00**
    7½" h., large moriage sea gulls on a grey background **350.00**
    7½" h., loop handle, cobalt blue with central portrait medallion, maple leaf mark **425.00**
    8" h., bisque scenic of bridge over lake, painted in blue and orange tones, fancy moriage handle, maple leaf mark. **325.00**
Berry Bowl (pierced with underplate)
    8¼" dia., heavy pink and dark pink roses with gold, fancy scroll feet, band of gold, maple leaf mark . . .   **125.00**
    8¾" dia., scalloped edges, wide top band of bright green with heavy gold overlay designs, maple leaf mark **125.00**
Berry Set (master bowl and six small)
    10" master, 5¼" small, medallions of swans on a lake on a cobalt blue background, heavy gold beading, wreath mark **345.00**
    10¼" master, 5" small, bands of yellow and blue roses on a white background, rising sun mark **125.00**
    10½" master, 5" small, all over geometric design, executed in red, black and gold, gold beading on rims, maple leaf mark **300.00**
    11" master, 5¼" small, scalloped edges, heavily decorated with large red and white roses and gold   **300.00**
Blotter (rocking), 6", pink, yellow and blue flowers, gold handle, original brass insert, Paper label inside "compliments of the Morimura Bros. 1903," wreath mark **175.00**
Bouillon Cup (two handled cup, lid and underplate)
    4" h., bands of pink roses on red background, maple leaf mark. . . .   **85.00**
    5" h., cobalt blue, white and gold, wreath mark **120.00**
    5" h., all over gold design on a white background **85.00**

Bowl

5½'', bisque scenic of lake windmill and trees **25.00**

5¾'', footed with pierced handles, berries and leaves all outlined in gold, RC mark **50.00**

7½'', pink flowers with green garlands **25.00**

7¾'', geometric designs **65.00**

9¾'', bisque scenic of house and trees, wreath mark **90.00**

9'', 3 footed, molded in relief squirrel eating nuts, wreath mark **375.00**

10'', yellow daisies on dark green background, Kinran mark **165.00**

10¾'', footed, wide band of colorful fruit on a white background, gold handles, wreath mark **85.00**

12'', R.S. Prussia mold, with blown out sides, heavy red and white roses traced with gold, wreath mark **225.00**

Box

Cigarette

4¾'', side profile of moriage Indian in brown on a earthtone background, wreath mark **200.00**

5½'', enamelled, Japanese pagoda scene done in bright blue, green and gold, wreath mark **135.00**

Stamp Box

2¼'', shinny windmill scene, wreath mark **85.00**

2¾'', geometric designs, black and white **85.00**

Trinket Box

3'', pedestal base, orange flowers, RC mark **45.00**

3½'', pastel shades of moriage surrounding center portrait on a pale blue background, wreath mark **235.00**

6½'', Rare, butterfly shaped box, dark magenta and light pink roses, gold, wreath mark **185.00**

2½'' x 6'', Rare, shaped as a baby grand piano on tall thin legs, pink bands with multicolored jewels, hold legs, scenic lid . . .   **350.00**

Powder Box, 8'', large pink flowers and buds all outlined in gold on a pale pink background, maple leaf mark **265.00**

Butter Tub (with lid, insert and underplate)

7¼'', Bisque scenic, TEOH mark **85.00**

7½'', orange and green floral on cream background, wreath mark   **125.00**

7½'', Heavy red roses on a red background, wreath mark **165.00**

Cake Plate (pierced handles)

10'', yellow roses with garlands outlined in gold, wreath mark . . .   **115.00**

Cake Plate, 12'' dia., pierced handles, large red and magenta roses, heavy gold overlay and beading, unsigned. $175.00

11'', bisque scenic of barn on country road, wreath mark **85.00**

12'', Band of fruit, Kinran mark **150.00**

Cake Set (master and 4 or 6 small)

Scenic of birds on lake, TEOH mark   **75.00**

Floral on cream background, wreath mark **95.00**

Scenic with windmill, lake house . .   **125.00**

Floral with heavy gold overlay on cobalt blue background, wreath mark **450.00**

Candle Lamp, 15'' h., Rare, white doves on base and shade, robin's egg blue background, wreath mark   **1,400.00**

Candlestick

5½'' h., child's, decorated with bunnies, wreath mark **100.00**

6¼'' h., Nile scene, with ship and moriage flowers **110.00**

7'' h., Gouda type decoration **95.00**

7'' h., square base, decorated with Oriental flowers, wreath mark . . .   **95.00**

7½'' h., (pair) Rare Lavender Wedgewood, wreath mark **525.00**

8'' h., (pair) triangular shape, tiny gold handle, bisque scenic of camel and rider at camp fire **485.00**

10 h., triangular base, Galle scene, tall trees in a forest, moriage floral trim, maple leaf mark **275.00**

Celery Set (master and 4 or 6 salts)

11'' master, 3¾'' (6) salts, heavy band of cobalt blue and gold on white background, heavy gold wreath mark **145.00**

12'' master, 6 salts, tiny bands of violets, TEOH mark **65.00**

12½'' master, 5 salts, open pierced handles on master, yellow band with roses on a white background, rising sun mark **65.00**

13½'' 4 salts, pastel Geisha girls with red trim, mountains in background, Royal Kaga Nippon mark   **115.00**

Child's Feeding Dish
   8" dia., children playing with dog,
     rising sun mark **135.00**
   8" dia., girl with book, rising sun
     mark **150.00**
Child's Tea Set, 3¼" tea pot, cream
   sugar bowl, 3 cups and saucers, two
   geese with blue top and bottom
   bands, rising sun mark **250.00**
Chocolate Pot
   9" h., pastoral scene, TEOH mark   **85.00**
   10" h., center floral medallion, gold
     background with heavy turquoise
     beading, graceful shape and han-
     dle, maple leaf mark **375.00**
   10" h., top and bottom bands of
     geometric design, sun mark **145.00**
   10¼" h., cobalt blue with heavy gold
     overlay designs, wreath mark. . . .   **400.00**
Chocolate set
   9" pot, six cups and saucers, large
     poppies on a cream background,
     top and bottom bands of gold,
     wreath mark **375.00**
   9½" pot, four cups and saucers, top
     and bottom bands of pink blos-
     soms with garlands of foliage, ris-
     ing sun mark **275.00**
   10" pot, six cups and saucers,
     shinny finish scenic of house, lake
     and trees, wreath mark **275.00**
   10" pot, six cups and saucers, Prus-
     sia mold, fancy handles and feet,
     large orchids on a shaded pale
     green background, heavy multi-
     colored jewels in gold design, ma-
     ple leaf mark **1,400.00**
   12½" pot, six cups and saucers, Prus-
     sia mold, fancy handle, blown out
     sides, large magenta and pink
     mums, heavy gold trim, maple
     leaf **1,400.00**
Desk Set, rare, triangular shaped ink-
   well, envelope holder, calendar
   holder, pen rest, rocking blotter,
   stamp box, two ink pad corners,
   scene of Indian in canoe, wreath
   mark **1,250.00**
Dresser set
   11" tray, open hat pin holder, footed
     powder box and hair receiver,
     Nile scene with ship and palm
     trees, wreath mark **375.00**
   11" tray, open hat pin holder, pow-
     der box, hair receiver and trinket,
     bands of violets on white back-
     ground, spoke mark **165.00**
   12" tray, closed hat pin holder, two
     perfume bottles with stoppers,
     open trinket, cobalt and gold de-
     sign on white, wreath mark **650.00**
Dutch Shoe, 3" l., heavy turquoise and
   gold floral design **145.00**

Ewer
   7½" h., footed, pastoral scene, ma-
     ple leaf mark **425.00**
   8" h., all over moriage design on
     pale blue background **245.00**
   9½" h., all over design of grapes on
     muted background, wreath mark   **175.00**
   10" h., bisque scenic, wreath mark   **175.00**
   13" h., bolted, large roses in cobalt
     background **375.00**
   13" h., center medallion of Count-
     ess Anna Potcka on a cream back-
     ground, heavy all over raised gold
     design **625.00**
Ferner
   4½" h., footed, ruffled, large moriage
     leaves **325.00**
   5" across, molded in relief, front
     panel of horse, back of elephant,
     decorated with a brown wash,
     wreath mark **195.00**
   5½" across, triangular in shape, sail-
     ing ships in front, windmill in
     background, earth tone colors,
     wreath mark **145.00**
   8" across, gold handles and feet,
     large pink and yellow roses and
     foliage, wreath mark **250.00**
Hat Pin Holder
   4½" h., triangular in shape, open top,
     bands of orange and blue flowers,
     wreath mark **65.00**
   4¾" h., closed top, maple leaf mark   **175.00**
   4¾", top and bottom bands of design,
     white background, R.C. mark. . . .   **85.00**
   4¾" h., footed, closed top, turquoise
     background with heavy pink floral
     decoration, maple leaf mark **165.00**
   4¾" h., attached rocking bottom,
     closed top, cobalt blue, gold and
     white decoration, maple leaf mark   **375.00**
   5" h., attached rocking bottom,
     closed top, portrait with heavy
     hold overlay design and beading,
     Rare, maple leaf mark. **375.00**

**Humidor, 6¾" h., molded in relief lion
and serpent, brown wash, wreath mark.
$900.00**

Humidor

4½" h., playing cards on rust background, wreath mark **250.00**

4½" h., mile scene, moriage palm trees, wreath mark **250.00**

5" h., colorful geometric designs, wreath mark **350.00**

5½" h., bisque windmill scene, wreath mark **275.00**

6" h., pipe and smoke, smoke forms ladies head on lid, brown background, Rare, wreath mark. **1,300.00**

6" h., three gold handles, bisque windmill scene, with person walking in lane, moon in sky, wreath mark **675.00**

6½" h., molded in relief, four dogs in profile, wreath mark **750.00**

6½" h., molded in relief, Indian on horseback, brown wash, wreath mark **575.00**

7" h., jockey on race horse, wreath mark **450.00**

7½" h., desert scene with palm trees and people, top and bottom band of deco design, wreath mark **450.00**

9" h., hexagon shape, four ball feet, brown moriage Indian on front, pipe with smoke on back, wreath mark **650.00**

Inkwell, 4" x 4", triangular in shape, Indian in a canoe scene, wreath mark **250.00**

Mug

4½" h., pink floral design, white background, wreath mark **135.00**

5" h., sailing ships with full sails, wreath mark **225.00**

5" h., moriage dragon on grey background, wreath mark **245.00**

Mustard

3½" h., underplate and spoon, floral design wreath mark **35.00**

3½" h., shinny scenic, spoon, wreath mark **35.00**

Humidor, 6" h., roses and gold on dark green background, wreath mark. $375.00

3½" h., underplate, spoon, heavy gold design on red roses **65.00**

Napkin Ring

Triangular shape, magenta and pink roses with gold on a forest green background **70.00**

Scenic, wreath mark. **55.00**

Nut Set, master and four or six small

5½" wide master, six small, footed melon ribbed, gold overlay designs on a cream background, leaf mark **175.00**

6" master, 4 small, floral design, leaf mark **95.00**

Plaque

8½", wide moriage trim border, dog profile in center **395.00**

9", bisque courtyard scene, ducks in lane, wreath mark. **225.00**

10", camel and rider desert scene, palm trees, wreath mark **225.00**

10", floral wisteria, with heavy gold leaves, wreath mark **285.00**

10" rectangular, Indians on horseback, wreath mark **750.00**

10", sailing ships done in oranges, wreath mark **225.00**

10", wide green and gold border with center of two deer in forest, maple leaf mark **275.00**

10", cream background with heavy hold overlay and beading, central portrait medallion, maple leaf mark **400.00**

10¼" rectangular, saint bernard, wreath mark **750.00**

10¼", shinny scenic, stone bridge over lake, house and trees, wreath mark **225.00**

10¼", handkerchief center medallion of horse and two dogs, marbleized background, wreath mark **145.00**

10½", molded in relief, black horse head, wreath mark **850.00**

10½", molded in relief, moose, wreath mark **400.00**

10½", molded in relief, apple and dogs, wreath mark **1,200.00**

11½", wide gold and jeweled border, large white sea gull over large ocean waves, maple leaf mark . . . **375.00**

12", still life with lobster, wreath mark **275.00**

12", turquoise background with heavy gold beading, center medallion of Indian princess, maple leaf mark. **650.00**

Plate

6½" dia., bisque scenic, wreath mark **45.00**

6¼" dia., blown out child's face, rising sun mark **75.00**

7½" dia, floral border, wreath mark **65.00**

Plate, 9" dia., pink and blue roses with cobalt and gold trim, leaf mark. $125.00

Sugar Shaker, 5" h., violets with gold, wreath mark. $125.00

Stein, 7" h., molded in relief owls, rare, wreath mark. $1,300.00

$7\frac{1}{2}$" dia, heavy geometric designs,
wreath mark 65.00
9" dia., souvenir of Washington,
D.C., gold trim, wreath mark 145.00
$10\frac{1}{2}$" dia., mountain scene, cobalt
blue and gold trim, ... 225.00
Punch Set, banquet size punch bowl,
footed pedestal base, 6 pedestal
based punch cups, scenic in blue
tones, leaf mark 1,400.00
Salt and Pepper Shakers
Bisque scenic, wreath mark 25.00
Cobalt blue, gold, with roses, leaf
mark 55.00
Bands of orange flowers on white
background, sun mark 25.00
Sugar Shaker
5" h., hexagon shape, bands of floral, gold handle, wreath mark . . . 95.00
5" h., floral with cobalt blue trim on
a pale green background, gold
handle 95.00
Stein (all measure 7" h.)
All over floral design, wreath mark 375.00
Dancing pheasants, marbleized
background wreath mark 450.00
Enamelled Oriental design in blue
and reds, wreath mark 325.00
Monk with beer stein, enamelled
flowers, wreath mark 450.00
Molded in relief, owls, Rare, wreath
mark 1,300.00
Scenic with top and bottom bands of
owls, wreath mark 425.00
Tankard
$10\frac{1}{4}$" h., tapestry of pink and yellow
roses, leaf mark. 650.00
12" h., forest scene, matte finish,
wreath mark 175.00
13" h., moriage flowers and trim . . . 395.00
$13\frac{3}{4}$" h., heavy floral and gold on
dark green background, leaf mark 450.00
14" h., cobalt blue, gold and roses,

full figure portrait of lady with the
doves, Rare, leaf mark 1,300.00
Tea Set (six cups and saucers)
$5\frac{1}{2}$" h. tea pot, footed, melon ribbed,
short and squat, gold on white de-
sign, wreath mark 225.00
$5\frac{1}{2}$" h. tea pot, cream, sugar, hexagon shaped saucers, floral design,
gold handles, maple leaf mark . . . 285.00
$5\frac{1}{2}$" h. tea pot, bisque forest scene 285.00
6" h. tea pot, cream, sugar, oriental
Satsuma type decoration, TEOH
mark 285.00
$7\frac{1}{2}$" h. tea pot, cream, sugar, RS
Prussia shape, footed melon
ribbed, gold feet and handles,
center medallions of ladies in garden on a pale green and blue
background, Rare 1,100.00
Tea Strainer
5", round shape, small bands of flo-
ral, wreath mark 75.00
5", bisque scenic with white underplate, wreath mark 75.00
6" footed base, yellow and white
daises, wreath mark 95.00
6", cobalt blue, gold and white decoration with white roses, leaf mark 135.00
Hexagon shape, large pink and red

roses with heavy gold on a turquoise background, maple leaf
mark **225.00**
Toothpick Holder, 3″ h.
　Barnyard scene, wreath mark **65.00**
　Three gold handles, band of Indian
　deco design, wreath mark **95.00**
　Pedestal base, fruit, rising sun mark   **45.00**
　Small stand up handles, white
　cranes on a blue background, leaf
　mark **45.00**
　Rocking bottom, ruffled top, pink
　and red roses, leaf mark **75.00**
Urn
　9¼″ h., footed with lid, scene of for-
　est and lake with birds in flight,
　heavy gold and jewels, wreath
　mark **375.00**
　9½″ h., covered, fancy handles, pink
　and white flowers outlined in gold
　with gold leaves on a turquoise
　background, maple leaf mark **450.00**
　11″ h., bolted two piece, dome lid,
　pastel moriage flowers on a pink
　marbleized background **1,500.00**
　14″ h., bolted two piece with lid,
　center portrait on Anna Potocka,
　heavy gold overlay design and
　beading on a cream background,
　maple leaf mark **2,800.00**
　17½″ h., bolted two piece urn with
　dome lid, scene of lake, heavy
　white enamelled jewels, heavy
　gold overlay design and beading
　on a green background, maple
　leaf mark **2,300.00**
　18″ h., bolted two piece, central
　bisque scene of people walking
　up lane, cobalt blue and gold
　background, maple leaf mark **1,900.00**
　9½″ h., bolted two piece with lid,
　loop handles, forest scene in
　shades of orange with cobalt blue
　and gold background, wreath
　mark **2,300.00**
Vase
　5½″ h., lady, child and dog, moriage
　trim leaf mark **155.00**
　5½″ h., floral on green background,
　wreath mark **85.00**
　5½″ h., footed, pink and blue roses,
　wreath mark **125.00**
　5½″ h., art nouveau type flowers,
　wreath mark **65.00**
　5½″ h., windmill scene with earth
　tones, wreath mark **85.00**
　6″ h., center tapestry of swans on
　lake, heavy moriage grapes and
　leaves, maple leaf mark **750.00**
　6½″ h., bottle neck, cobalt blue with
　gold overlay, wreath mark **300.00**
　6½″ h., stand up gold handles, yel-
　low daisies on blue background   **90.00**

Vase, 8″ h., footed with loop handles and ruffled top, pink and red roses, gold beading, leaf mark. $185.00

　7″ h., pink flowers, gold back-
　ground with turquoise beading,
　leaf mark **350.00**
　7″ h., coralene, floral on shaded
　background, patent mark **350.00**
　7½″ h., lavender violets on blue
　background, wreath mark **135.00**
　8¼″ h., dancing pheasants on mar-
　bleized background, jeweled,
　wreath mark **325.00**
　8½″ h., white treed woodland scene
　on pale green background **325.00**
　8½″ h., moriage owl on branch,
　wreath mark **750.00**
　8½″ h., scenic tapestry of man, lady
　and boat, leaf mark **750.00**
　8½″ h., poinsettia on blue back-
　ground, wreath mark **135.00**
　Bisque sailing ships, wreath mark   **250.00**
　8½″ h., grapes and vine on blue
　background, wreath mark **175.00**
　8¾″ h., bisque scene, wreath mark   **185.00**
　8¾″ h., colorful deco design on
　cream background, wreath mark   **150.00**
　8¾″ h., Wedgwood with griffin base,
　wreath mark **650.00**
　9″ h., sailing ships, cobalt blue and
　gold, wreath mark **350.00**
　9¼″ h., center medallion of sail boats
　on a green background, wreath
　mark **210.00**
　9½″ h., molded in relief strawberries,
　wreath mark **450.00**
　9½″ h., desert scene of man on
　camel, leaf mark **425.00**
　9½″ h., geisha girls in blue and red,
　gold handles, wreath mark **200.00**
　10″ h., poppies on gold background   **145.00**
　Footed, winter scene, gold and pink
　background, leaf mark **250.00**
　11½″ h., chrysanthemums and gold
　overlay, wreath mark **265.00**
　11½″ h., ribbon handles, wisteria

flowers on a gold background,
leaf mark. **300.00**
12" h., silhouette on cowboy on
horseback, wreath mark. **325.00**
12" h., Jack Armstrong shape,
plushy roses, heavy gold, leaf
mark. **235.00**
12" h., stick vase, front panel of
roses with heavy gold. **325.00**
12" h., hand painted lavender flow-
ers along with moriage flowers. . .   **225.00**
12" h., center portrait, heavy gold
overlay and multicolored jewels
on a robin's egg blue background,
leaf mark. **750.00**
9½" h., large white moriage sea gulls
on a gray background, leaf mark   **275.00**
10" h., scene of forest, lake and
birds, heavy bands of gold **350.00**
10" h., ring pretzel handles, ruffled
top, large red and pink roses with
heavy panels of gold, leaf mark   **850.00**
12½" h., molded in relief, two chil-
dren under a tree, Rare, wreath
mark. **1,600.00**
13" h., bisque scene of fisherman
and cart, wreath mark. **750.00**
13" h., scissor handles, large white
orchids, leaf mark. **345.00**
14" h., mountain scene with cobalt
blue and heavy gold, wreath mark   **550.00**
15½" h., large urn of pastel roses in a
garden scene with gold overlay,
leaf mark. **1,300.00**
24" h., trumpet shaped floor vase,
red and yellow roses and foliage
on a dark background, leaf mark   **1,300.00**

OJIME

History: The traditional Japanese dress style does not have pockets. In the late sixteenth and early seventeenth centuries pouches and cases of all kinds were worn suspended from the waist sash (obi) by a cord. At one end of the cord was a toggle (netsuke) and strung on the cord below it was a slide bead—the ojime. The ojime served to keep the case or pouch closed; it could be loosened to open the case.

Ojimes were fashioned with the same care and fine techniques of carving and metalwork as any inro or netsuke. The styles and designs of ojimes also followed the changes in tastes over the years. Ojimes were made of ivory, metal, wood, ceramic, coral, and semiprecious stones. In many cases, the netsuke, inro and ojime were made by the same or related artists so that the component parts were related in style and motif. Simple beads of spherical or ovoid shapes were often used, as well as intricately worked and decorated types.

References: Frederick Chavea, "Japanese Ojime—An Historical Perspective," *Netsuke Kenkyukai Study Journal*, Vol. 4 n.d.; Melvin and Betty Jahss, *Inro and Other Miniature Forms of Lacquer Art*, Charles E. Tuttle Co., Inc., 1981; Robert Kinsey, "Ojime Masterpieces," *Journal of the International Netsuke Collectors' Society*, Vol. 12, 1985; —, "Ojime," *Journal of the International Netsuke Collectors' Society*, Vol. 2, n.d.; Barbara Okada, *Japanese Netsuke and Ojime from the Herman and Paul Jaehne Collection of the Newark Museum*, Newark Museum, 1976.

Museum: Newark Museum, Newark, New Jersey.

Collecting Hints: True ojimes have a rather large bore (himotoshi), 3 to 4 mm or at least ⅛", since a double thickness of fairly thick cord must go through. Beads with small openings are sometimes represented as ojimes. There are plastic and composition beads which resemble ojimes, but these are molded and the work is generally crude when compared with hand-carved pieces. With small objects and minute detail, the use of a magnifier is recommended.

Advisors: Bernard and Irene Rosett

Copper, 19th century, signed gyokuzan, flat drum shape, engraved with
a phoenix bird and passion flower   **200.00**
Inlaid ivory, 19th century, signed Masakazu, inlaid in Shibayama style
with mother-of-pearl, floral design   **275.00**
Ivory
19th century, signed Shozan, carved
with a series of rabbits **325.00**
19th century, signed (unread),
deeply carved man and pine trees   **275.00**
19th century, signature plaque
worn, depicting a young girl
seated by a pine in a large forest,
carved and undercut with good
patina. **358.00**
19th century, unsigned, deeply

Bone, ¾" h., late 19th century, bell shaped with working compass, $225.00.

Left to right: Ivory, ¾" dia., mid 19th century, deeply carved man and pine trees, **$250.00;** Lacquer, ¾" dia., late 19th century, carved red lacquer with mother-of-pearl inlay of leaves, **$295.00;** Brass, 1" dia., mid-19th century, gilt wash, openwork design of bird and passion flower, in drum form. **$400.00**

carved with dragon covering the entire surface	185.00
19th century, unsigned, double masks set back to back, good patina	250.00
Silver, ¾", signature plaque worn, molded in the form of a cylindrical basket, applied with plum branch	140.00
Silver, copper, gold, 19th century, unsigned, shaped as a rock with inlaid crab	295.00
Silvered Metal	
19th century, signed Tomoyuki, in seed form with high relief hawk, snake, and flower with gilt highlights	175.00
19th century, signed (unread), very small form of a begging dog with a gold collar	575.00
Wood, 19th century, signed Akimin, deeply carved dragons, sennin, coral inlay of pearl of wisdom	375.00

OKIMONO

History: The word *okimono* refers to Japanese sculptural pieces, most often of wood, ivory, or bronze, and rarely stone. As far back as the Asuka Period (522–646), when Buddhism was introduced from China via Korea, bronze and wooden images appeared in temples, many of which still exist. Early sculptural examples were the life-size versions of larger masterpieces featured in the decoration of these temples. Some non-Buddhist images, also carved by Buddhist sculptors, were Shinto icons, sculptural portraits, and masks for drama and dance. At the end of the Kamakura Period (circa 1333) the art of the great Buddhist sculpture had unfortunately declined. By the end of the sixteenth century, art and sculpture began to reflect the patronage of secular groups such as warlords and merchants.

In 1605, Shogun Hidetada ordered every household to have its own Buddhist image, which caused the carving trade to flourish for a time. By the end of the eighteenth century, the demand was over, and many sculptors turned their talents to carving netsukes, the miniature sculptures used as toggles, as well as pieces of larger sizes called okimonos, using the same techniques and materials for both genre. These okimonos were displayed in the home in an alcove called the *tokonoma*. They were usually shown one at a time with scroll paintings, flower arrangements, and other things of beauty, especially pieces for the tea ceremony (cha-no-yu). Some truly elegant wooden sculpture as well as the more exotic ivory carvings and fine examples of bronze castings are among these specimens.

These creations, no longer restricted to Buddhist imagery, often show commonplace subjects along with popular mythology, well-known historical events, household gods, and warrior figures. Noteworthy in this genre are the depictions of live creatures like toads and tortoises as well as figures of fishermen and farmers fashioned with extraordinary realism.

Ivory carving in Japan is comparatively recent, the earliest examples are from the middle of the eighteenth century. Most of the ivory pieces that are seen today are considerably later, from the mid-nineteenth and early twentieth centuries. Many of these subjects show great artistry and technique, concentrating on the human and animal forms. Often the ivory is combined with lacquer work and inlays of metal, mother-of-pearl and semiprecious stones.

After the Japanese began to trade with the West in the 1860s, the presence of the U.S. Navy stimulated the creation of erotic figures in okimonos. As a rule, Japanese culture has not shown a great interest in the nude figure as an erotic image. This has not precluded their remarkable expression in sculpture of human anatomy, musculature, and strength, which is seen in the okimonos of sumo wrestlers, folk heroes, and demons. In their characterization of women and children there can be great tenderness expressed by the artistic use of human anatomy.

Many of the sculptures create humorous and satirical situations. The artists seem to delight in revealing unexpected surprises, not noticed until one carefully examines all aspects of the piece, which is carefully sculpted on all sides, including the bottom.

Okimonos are being created currently in Japan by a small group of carvers carrying on the old traditions of excellence in techniques and artistry. However, since they work in the twentieth century, they have adopted some of the aesthetic and artistic modes of our time. The carvers have indeed been innovative in this respect, while still expressing Japanese traditions.

References: National Gallery of Art, *Exhibition of Japanese Painting and Sculpture*, Catalog, 1953; Donald Jenkins, *Masterworks in Wood: China and Japan*, Portland Art Museum, 1976; Miriam Kinsey, *Contemporary Netsuke*, Charles E. Tuttle Co., Inc., 1977; George Lazarnick, *Netsuke and Inro Artists and How to Read Their Signatures*, Reed Publishers, 1982; Alfred Maskell, *Ivories*, Charles E. Tuttle Co., Inc., 1966; Phillip Schneider, *The Japanese Signature Handbook*, Phillip Schneider 1978; F. A. Turk, *Japanese Objects d'Art*, Sterling Publishing Co., 1963; V. F. Weber, *Ko-Ji Ho-Ten*, Haker Art Books, 1965.

Museums: Los Angeles County Museum of Art, Los Angeles, California; Walters Art Gallery, Baltimore, Maryland; Museum of Fine Arts, Boston; Massachusetts; Newark Museum, Newark, New Jersey; Art Institute of Chicago, Chicago, Illinois; Brooklyn Museum, Brooklyn, New York; Asia House Gallery, New York, New York (occasional collections); American Museum of Natural History, New York, New York; Japan House, New York, New York (occasional collections); Metropolitan Museum of Art, New York, New York; Seattle Art Museum, Seattle, Washington.

Reproduction Alert: There have been many attempts in the last century or more at passing off reproductions of desirable okimonos. At one time, there was a manufacturing process that used a pantographic tracing technique, as in a key-making machine, by which one or more replicas of an ivory original could be ground on ivory blanks. Reproductions made by such techniques were not very successful. They revealed themselves by their sharp, angular discontinuities and the "judder," or ripple, in certain areas. The more common fakes were achieved by means of flexible molds; epoxy plastics or ivory dust was used to simulate ivory or even wood. The hot needle test in an inconspicuous area will easily determine such substitutions. (A needle brought to red hot heat in a flame will not affect the surface of true ivory or bone. On other materials it will burn a hole or leave a dark mark).

Hong Kong and, lately, Thailand have been the sources of many art fakes. Caution is strongly advised. Buying from a knowledgeable and reliable dealer is the surest protection against forgeries. A responsible dealer is always ready to back up sales with guarantees.

Collecting Hints: The task of assembling a decent collection of okimonos is sometimes difficult but always rewarding. Samples turn up in the most unexpected places. The charm and appeal of okimonos are such that they have been included in groups of Americana, continental art, curiosa, and general interest. In general, the pickings are best in large cities, especially in ports where sailors and other travelers abound. San Francisco, New York, Boston, and London have been the most fruitful locations in my experience. Hong Kong and Singapore offer some promise, but reproductions must be avoided. Tokyo and Kyoto contain treasures, but only at astronomical prices. Antiques and art publications sometimes provide promising leads. Antiques shows often provide an excellent source, because specialists in Orientalia who buy and sell throughout the country can be found. They will be happy to "scout" for you and bring back items for your collection at their next show in your city.

Some okimonos are of groups of people or animals. Those constructed from several components and glued together should certainly be less expensive than pieces carved from one block. In old pieces, the glued-and-assembled types reveal themselves because they usually had to be reglued one or more times. The seams and glue spills are easily detected, especially with a 3x or 5x magnifier. Careful collectors find the aid of a magnifier vital in all their searches.

Signatures on sculptured pieces can be considered questionable in some cases. Pieces made before the nineteenth century were rarely signed. The trend to provide signatures was pursued mainly in response to Western demands. There are several reference books dealing with signatures of Japanese artists. Authenticity of signatures can be dubious, especially since many of the early artists were illiterate or used the name of a teacher as a mark of respect. In regard to forgeries, the collector is warned that it is much easier to forge a signature than to carve a complex piece of sculpture. Collectors should judge a piece on the basis of quality rather than the signature it bears.

Advisors: Irene and Bernard Rosett

Bronze
   Elephant
      6" l., circa 1900, ivory tusks, signed, fine detail **350.00**
      22" l., late 19th century, ivory tusks, trunk upraised **1,500.00**
      Pair, 13" l., late 19th century, trunks lowered **750.00**

Farmer, 20″ h., x 29″ l., signed on rectangular panel, circa 1900, man seated on a large rock eating rice and holding a teacup....... 8,000.00

Fish and Shrimp, 4½″ l., late 19th century.................... 225.00

Frog, 6″ l., late 19th century, head tilted in whimsical fashion, fine patina.................... 350.00

Lion, 22″ l., late 19th century, mouth wide open, glass eyes, wood base, signed with a square plaque in base 1,200.00

Mice, 10½″ l., late 19th century, two mice on an ear of corn, one on each end................... 400.00

Puppy, 2½″ l., signed in seal form, late 19th century 400.00

Samurai
 8″ h., late 19th century, holding spear, many fine details 850.00
 13½″ h., signed Yoshimitsu, circa 1900, warrior holding sword over his head, excellent detail in the style of Miyao 4,200.00

Shi-shi, 4″ l., 18th century, in jumping position................. 350.00

Shojo, 4″ h., early 19th century, exquisite detail, with long flowing hair, in attitude of dance....... 275.00

Toad
 2½″ l., circa 1850 .... 300.00
 3″ l., circa 1840, head tilted 325.00
 6″ l., 20th century, seared on maple leaf, thin-walled casting, very realistic.............. 200.00

Tortoise group, 9″ l., mid 19th century, signed Seimin, minogame with baby on its back, wonderful detail 3,000.00

Turtle, 3½″ l., mid 19th century, signed, fine detail............ 250.00

Turtle group, 6½″ l., mid 19th century, three figures in pyramid shape 550.00

Warrior, 14″ h., circa 1900, signed

Mask, 8½″ h., late 19th century, wrought iron, representing woman of perfect beauty. $900.00

Miyao, holding five-socle candelabrum, silver and gold inlays on robe 6,000.00

Woman, 13½″ h., circa 1880, ivory hands and head, playing the koto 1,500.00

Ivory
 Blind men, 6″ h., late 19th century, signed Toshiyuki, three blind men one of whom is being bitten by a crab, beautiful patina 2,000.00

Dancer, 3½″ h., late 19th century, lacquer and ivory figure with ivory face and hands, wearing an elaborate gold cape over an salmon and gold lacquer robe 650.00

Dragons, 8″ h., late 19th century,

Blind Men Group, 3¾″ h., mid 19th century, five legendary blind men fighting each other, signed Fyokunori saku. $1,000.00

Turtle Group 3½″ l., late 19th century, large turtle and two smaller ones. $400.00

signed Kiraku, two intertwined dragons forming a cylinder, exceptionally fine workmanship ... **4,000.00**

Duck, 2½" w., circa 1880, mother-of-pearl inlaid eyes, perfectly carved feathers and feet **200.00**

Farmer
4" l., circa 1880, signed cursively, man with two baskets of eggplants sitting and watching a boy catching frogs **950.00**
9½" h. circa 1870, signed Yoshikazu, holding a hen and rooster **1,700.00**

Girl
4½" h., circa 1880, shown holding scythe near corn plants **400.00**
11" h., late 19th century, young girl holding a flower basket with a child holding her skirt **350.00**

Goddess, 10" h., circa 1900, stately figure with a dragon draped over her shoulders, very finely carved details.................... **1,100.00**

Go Game Players, 4" l., circa 1880, signed on inset ivory plaque, three old men sitting around go game table, figures stained except for white hair and beards.......... **900.00**

Laborer, 4½" h., late 19th century, signed on red lacquer plaque, man sitting on tree stump holding his hat, with bundles at his feet, finely detailed............... **1,900.00**

Landscape, 5¼" h., circa 1890, scene depicting a cottage on a cliff overlooking a river where three men sit in a boat, a woman cooking inside the cottage, several figures on the hillside **1,000.00**

Lohan, 2¼" l., late 19th century, signed Muneharu, superbly carved figure seated at a low table burning incense **1,200.00**

Man and Woman, 3¼" h., signed Tomochika, late 19th century, the couple depicted tying a knot in a large sack on which the characters for "patience" are written **650.00**

Man and Boy, 6" h., circa 1880, signed Miyoshi............... **200.00**

Oni, 3" h. x 5" w., circa 1850, signed Hokyudo Itsumin, two oni painting a bad dream for a sleeping Shoki, superb carving **7,000.00**

Oni group
3½" h., late 19th century, signed Masayuki Yasumitsu, two oni carousing with drum......... **900.00**
5" h., late 19th century, signed Masamitsu, three oni fleeing from beans thrown at them at the New Year **600.00**
6" h., late 19th century, signed Gyokku, Shoki chasing an oni up into a tree.............. **1,200.00**

Peasant, 4½" h., late 19th century, signed Gyokuzan, man wearing straw hat calling to a bird **400.00**

Rat Catcher, 4½" l., circa 1880,

Grasshopper on a Radish, 5" l., mid 19th century, exquisite detail, fine old patina. $650.00

Shoki and One, 4" l., mid 19th century, signed Hokyudo Itsumin, completely carved on reverse and bottom, extremely high quality. $7,000.00

Fisherman and child, 6" h., late 19th century, excellent realism. $650.00

squatting man, openmouthed as a rat climbs on his shoulder, superb expressive carving **1,100.00**

Tusk

Section, 6'' l., circa 1870, showing Fukurokuju and children, well carved **550.00**

21'' l., circa 1870, showing a parade of frogs mimicking people, marching with a palanquin having a frog inside, one side carved in relief, the other in intaglio, very humorous subject finely carved **2,100.00**

Warriors

2½'' h., late 19th century, the Soga Brothers in armor with drawn swords **400.00**

7'' h., circa 1860, shown in armor, swords sheathed, fierce expressions, fine patina **800.00**

Woman, 7'' h., circa 1900, woman carrying child on her back with a basket of fruit, extremely well carved to show maternal feeling **950.00**

Multimetal

Crane group, 3½'' h., marked Yoshigin, two cranes standing on rocks, silver, shaduko and gold, on a hexagonal base with chrysanthemum mon **2,100.00**

Nobleman, 20'' h., late 19th century, man holding and umbrella inverted in a stiff breeze, shakudo and shibuichi with gilt details. . . . **800.00**

Oni group, 12½'' h., circa 1880, two oni supporting a large crystal ball, one oni in copper, the other in sentoku (brass-type metal) with silver and gold details **11,000.00**

Silver

Crane group, 9½'' l., circa 1860, two cranes in a rolling wave **2,500.00**

Wood

Ashinaga, 5'' h., late 19th century, boxwood, seated figure, his long arms clasped above his head **500.00**

Blind men, 3'' h., circa 1850, boxwood, six blind men carrying staves, in a circular arrangement, well carved to show the various expressive faces and musculature **1,400.00**

Buddhist Deity, 3'' h., circa 1840, Fudo Mio O, standing on a rock carrying his rope, the sword missing from his other hand **500.00**

Daikoku, 6'' h. x 5½'' w., circa 1900, the household god of abundance holding his large sack, laughing, carved in ittobori style **225.00**

Daruma

6'' h. x 4½'' w., early 20th century,

yew wood, the legless holy man in an unusual pose, laughing **200.00**

6½'' h., mid 18th century, boxwood, seated in the traditional meditation pose, eyes lowered, lovely old patina **1,100.00**

Deer, 2¾'' l., late 19th century, bamboo root, the delicate animal at rest, elegantly carved **550.00**

Fisherman, 4'' h., mid 18th century, bamboo root, stooped over his net with fish, crab and basket **450.00**

Frog, 2½'' w., 20th century, cedar wood, signed Teiji, seated on lily pad **300.00**

Gamma Sennin, 5'' h., circa 1850, boxwood, shown with frog and mugwort cape **450.00**

Kannon, 21'' h., late 19th century, the six inch goddess seated atop a mountain on which a coiled dragon sits, fine patina **400.00**

"Maria" Kannon, 9½'' h., 18th century, signed in archaic seal form, long inscription on one side, the figure dressed in a draped and hooded robe shown standing next to a bonsai plant with eyes lowered, this representation was a "secret Christian" Virgin Mary, disguised as a Buddhist Kannon **1,100.00**

Masseur, 3'' h., circa 1850, signed Masayoshi, boxwood, shown working on the back of a client, fine patina. **550.00**

Monkey, 18'' h., circa 1910, shown seated on haunches holding a peach, Mingei style carving **250.00**

Samurai, 3'' l., mid 19th century, signed Hokyudo Itsumin, box-

Fukurokuju (god of longevity), 10'' h., late 19th century, yew wood, carved in rustic style, some bark remaining at the lower portion. $850.00

Sennin, 20" h., circa 1900, figure standing on a tall rock group wearing a mugwort cape, one hand upraised holding a staff **500.00**

Old Woman, 9" h., circa 1870, boxwood, the 10th-century poetess Ono No Komachi depicted as an old woman with torn straw hat on her back, fantastic detail, extremely high quality, signed Masanori. $4,800.00

Samurai, 5" h., late 19th century, boxwood, warrior atop lion and playing the sheng, fine patina and details, signed Kogetsu. $1,400.00

wood, two hand wrestling Samurai seated on a sandal, exquisite musculature and facial detail **2,000.00**

Scholar, 9" h. x 7" w., early 19th century, signed with kakihan, the bearded figure shown seated wearing an old-style eboshi hat, serene expression **300.00**

Shi-shi, 10½" h., mid 19th century, bamboo, seated on haunches with mouth open **500.00**

Tiger, 4½" l., circa 1900, bamboo, shown seated on bamboo stalk . .   **900.00**

Temple Guardian, 12½" h., circa 1850, angry faced figure with mandala surrounding him, traces of gilt and polychrome, ivory eyes   **600.00**

ORIBE CERAMICS AND THE TEA CEREMONY

History: Before any discussion of Oribe ceramics can begin, it is necessary to understand the environment in which it developed, particularly the development of the tea ceremony as it related to the growth of the ceramic industry in Japan. Tea was introduced to Japan by China during the Tang Dynasty. It was adopted by the Japanese Buddhist monks for its curative powers as promulgated by the Chinese, who used it to cure aches and pains as well as proclaiming it a key to immortality. In the ninth century, Japanese monks planted their own tea seeds, and by the twelfth century the monks were grinding leaves to make tea in the custom of the Chinese. Rules were established for a tea-drinking ceremony (cha-no-yu), which stressed the values of the religious order.

By the fourteenth century the Buddhist priest Murata Juko, acting as tea advisor, presented the rules of drinking tea to Shogun Ashikaga Yoshimasa. These rules were based on poverty, humility, and simplicity. Ironically, at first, the nobility engaged in the tea-drinking ritual to show off their material wealth, which consisted primarily of ceramics and other arts imported from China. Although the practice of drinking tea was first restricted to the clergy and the nobility, by the Momoyama period (1568–1615), it was secularized. This allowed the samurai and merchant classes to participate in the developing tea ritual. Thus the tea ceremony was established as a way of life in Japan. Official "tea masters" were appointed, and tea wares were created especially for the drinking of tea.

The practice continued to develop, and by the late sixteenth century, the rules for proper tea etiquette were observed. The formal rules for the tea ceremony were put into writing by Rikyu (1521–1591) at the order of Shogun Hideyoshi. The rules covered the serving of food, the hours to be devoted, the time of day, the way to prepare the tea, the types of ceramics to be used to create harmony with the food and so forth. Buddhist thought encouraged the aesthetics of crudity and simplicity in ceramics and drew attention away from the Chinese ceramic imports, which were regarded as status symbols at that time. Korean ceramics, which were simple and were irregular in shape and glaze became more influential.

Two tea masters were established during this time period, who set the standard for tea ceremony ware and changed the utilitarian ceramic industry of Japan into one that was primarily concerned with pottery as works of art.

Because of the evolving ceremony of serving tea, the Japanese tradition of art pottery had its origins in the production of tea bowls. Deep ones were used in winter and shallow ones, that would cool the tea faster were used in warm weather. Other pottery utensils (cha ki) were mandated. The two tea masters whose names have come to be associated with the first production of pottery made especially for the tea ceremony were Shino Soshin and Futura Oribe-no Sho. The attribution of the name Shino to sixteenth-century white-glazed tea bowls that employed a milky white feldspathic glaze over a white clay body (supposedly made in Seto, though new evidence points to Mino as the actual kiln site) was not actually made until the early eighteenth century. The Korean influence was apparant in the irregularity of form, which was right in line with the Buddhist thinking of beauty in imperfection. Shino wares were either undecorated or had a iron wash design under the white glaze, which fired to a red or sometimes grey tone. Birds, trees, and other natural subjects were depicted in painted-on designs that are typical of this ware. Red Shino, grey Shino, and marbleized Shino were all variations of an iron ore slip combined with white feldspathic glaze.

Futura Oribe was born near Seto in 1544. He became a samurai in 1582. In 1585, Shogun Hideyoshi proclaimed him a lord responsible for a castle located near Kyoto. During this period, he became a pupil of Rikyu. Later on, one of Oribe's students became the second Tokugawa shogun. When he gained power, the second Tokugawa shogun appointed Oribe as an official tea master (chajin).

Oribe's influence over the pottery production of his day lead to the development of a certain type of ware that was later named after him. The pottery that was made under his authority was untraditional, stressing irregularity of form in deliberate strange and distorted ways. These unusual shapes required hand modeling or molding rather than wheel-throwing techniques. A great variety of wares was made, all related in some way to the tea ceremony. Teahouses for the ritual of cha-no-yu were also built according to his specifications.

Dishes were made in deep rectangles or a new form of joined rectangles. Fan shaped dishes were also produced. Sake bottles (choshi), incense burners (koro), sweetmeat jars, water jars (mizusashi), waste water containers (koboshi), tea bowls (cha wan), and jars (cha-ire) for the powdered teas that were used in the tea rituals, were all produced. Oribe's preferred shapes were dented or appeared to be bent in one direction or another.

Decoration was done in copper green glaze (its first use as a glaze in Japan), sometimes along with simple underglaze designs in iron oxide.

Green glazes were used over white slip (ao Oribe yaki). Black glazed wares (kuro Oribe yaki), and a red type (aka Oribe yaki) were also made. Shino/Oribe wares were made in the later Shino style.

At first, to Western eyes, the glazes all seem to be pretty much the same. They are however, subtly different. A dark green glaze, which may thin out at the edges to a peacock blue and purple-red, is present on all pieces to some degree. Some are entirely green glazed. A heavy grey glaze is on the items categorized as black or green Oribe, while a reddish brown glaze appears on the red group.

It is sometimes difficult to tell the difference between Shino and Oribe wares since both were made by some of the same potters and at the same kilns. The influence of Oribe ware is still felt on the modern ceramic art scene of Japan.

References: Ryoichi Fujioka, *Shino and Oribe Ceramics*, Kodansha International Ltd. and Shibundo Publishing, 1977; Hazel H. Gorham, *Japanese and Oriental Ceramics*, Charles E. Tuttle Co., Inc., 1971; Soame Jenyns, *Japanese Pottery*, Faber and Faber, 1971; Adalbert Klein, *A Connoisseur's Guide to Japanese Ceramics*, translated by Katherine Watson, Alpine Fine Arts Collection, 1984; Irene Stitt, *Japanese Ceramics of the Last 100 Years*, Crown Publishers, Inc., 1974.

Museums: Brooklyn Museum of Art, Brooklyn, New York; Cleveland Museum of Art, Cleveland, Ohio; Philadelphia Museum of Art, Philadelphia, Pennsylvania; Seattle Art Museum, Seattle, Washington; British Museum, London, England; Victoria and Albert Museum, London, England; Kyoto National Museum, Kyoto, Japan; Nara National Museum, Nara, Japan; Fujita Art Museum, Osaka, Japan; Goto Art Museum, Tokyo, Japan; Suntory Art Museum, Tokyo, Japan; Tokyo National Museum, Tokyo, Japan.

Reproduction Alert: Many modern kiln sites in Japan are producing Oribe yaki as well as copies of early Shino wares. Copies were made in the Momoyama Period as well, which are probably much more difficult to distinguish from the original. Modern pottery pieces are produced with the Oribe color formula and designs, but lack the bizarre shapes of the early tea ceremony items. Their lack of symmetry is a clue to their modern derivation, as is their function as items apart from the tea ceremony.

Collecting Hints: Oribe wares and Oribe-styled wares are particularly Japanese in taste and were never made for export from the country. Although they were being made during the same time period that Japanese porcelain was starting to be produced for export purposes, they were then, and remain now, a prime example of the true art form of Japanese ceramics.

Gold lacquer repairs on old tea ceramics are not considered a detriment but rather an enhancement, proving that the value attached to the item is undiminished and that restoration and veneration were warranted.

Since Oribe and Shino wares were produced in modern times, many of the items have found their way into Western collections. They are collected worldwide by potters who admire and attempt to copy their glazing techniques. The Japanese themselves are the largest collectors of their old tea ritual utensils.

ORIBE

Basin, 22½″ dia., late 18th/early 19th century, the thickly potted, irregular sides curving to a slightly raised foot, decorated in Oribe taste with brown flowers and calligraphy against an olive green, blue and cream glazed ground **1,500.00**

Bottles, 5¼″ h., Meiji Period, pair, each of cylindrical shape resting on a recessed circular foot and tapering to a tall neck flaring at the rim, the horizontally ribbed body painted with an abstract iron-oxide design on a cream-colored ground, the neck and sloping shoulder glazed a translucent dark green................ **450.00**

Cake dish and cover, 8½″ l., rectangular, slab construction with each corner differently shaped, loosely decorated with scattered motif of formal pattern, with irregular splashes of turquoise and spinach green glaze in the Momoyama taste **2,500.00**

Chawan (pottery bowl)

3⅜″ h., black oribe, 17th/18th century, raised on a thin footring, the cylindrical bowl decorated with a vicous black glaze highlighted by

Basin, 22½″ dia., late 18th/early 19th century, the thickly potted, irregular sides curving to a slightly raised foot, decorated in Oribe taste with brown flowers and calligraphy against an olive green, blue and cream glazed ground. $1,500.00. Courtesy Butterfield and Butterfield.

a mountain, moon and flower scene in white and erupted black, wood box **2,000.00**

6½″ dia., 18th century, irregular waisted oval body on a roughly cut circular footring decorated with a splashed brown glaze on a grey flecked ground, the glaze falling irregularly toward the foot **1,200.00**

6⅜″ l., 18th century, irregular oval form with rich black-brown glaze surrounding a panel of red grasses on a cream ground **1,300.00**

Dish

4¼″ square, late 19th century, decorated with a landscape scene in brown and green **85.00**

4½″ dia., set of five, 18th/19th century, painted with brown flowers and splashed with green........ **750.00**

5¼″ dia., set of five, 18th/19th century, painted with brown designs between two green splashes..... **1,200.00**

7″ l., Mid-19th century, of square form with chamfered corners and resting on three short "strap" supports, the exterior of the lid and body decorated with floral and abstract motifs in iron-oxide and white on a mottled gray-brown ground with two large splashes of translucent green glaze **350.00**

8⅜″, square, 18th century, with low vertical walls decorated in overglaze green and brown with chidori in flight over fence and large field of green below, the design continuing to the exterior, gold lacquer repairs **750.00**

Mizusashi (water vessel), 7⅛″ h., 19th century, barrel form, jar with inset foot and one-sided depression splashed to one side of the mouth with a grey/green glaze, lacquered wood cover **1,650.00**

Oribe mukozuke

5½″ l., Tokugawa Period, of irregular keyhole shape with a curved top merging into a rectangle, the sides and interior decorated with abstracted iron-red designs and splashes of translucent green glaze..................... **725.00**

10¾″ dia., Pair of, each fan-shaped dish raised on three short floriform feet and glazed to one corner with a deep sea-green, the interior painted tin a brown iron glaze with floral medallions and on the exterior with stripes **275.00**

Eight 4⅛″ x 4⅛″, Late 18th/19th century, each of square form with slight irregularities and decorated with splashes of spinach-green and freely painted design of spring ferns in iron oxide on a cream-colored crackled glaze, signed Rokubei **600.00**

Teapot, 13¼″ h., 20th century, the globular body with horizontal ribs and applied with a stout curved spout and two lug handles for the bound twine loop handle, the sides painted in iron-oxide with abstract motifs partially overlaid by translucent green glaze on the neck and sloping shoulder, the lid with a large pierced knob and decorated en suite   **350.00**

Vase, 8⅜″ h., Meiji Period, of pear shape resting on a short ring foot and tapering to a long neck flaring toward the mouth, the sides freely painted in iron-oxide with geometric and floral motifs, some partially obscured by the translucent green glaze applied to the rim and neck, the base impressed with a two character mark reading Shun **150.00**

SATSUMA WARE

History: Satsuma Province is a peninsula-shaped projection of land located at the southwestern tip of Kyushu Island in Japan. At the beginning of the seventeenth century, the feudal lord of Satsuma, attached to the affluent and important Shimazu clan, invited twenty-two Korean potters and their families to the area where they settled in two towns and began small kilns. Their first products, now known as old Satsuma (ko Satsuma) were articles made for the cha-no-yu (tea ceremony). When white clay was discovered in the nearby town of Naeshirogawa, the potters resettled there and proceeded to develop the ware that was called white Satsuma (haku ji). In the 1790s an artist named Kimura Tangen was hired to paint designs on the white clay wares and the Satsuma tradition as we know it was begun.

Satsuma ware was not a true porcelain but rather a faience ware (soft-paste porcelain), which was characterized by a fine crackling in the transparent creamy colored glaze. Old Satsuma consisted of overglaze decoration in soft enamel colors. The decoration was sparse; was generally limited to flowers, scrolls, and occasional animal figures; and was not painted in perspective. The fine crackle glaze was the predominant feature. Production was limited to small items such as incense burners, bowls, dishes, and teapots.

Kilns were set up in other areas under the control of the lord of Satsuma. For many years thereafter, the Satsuma potters sent representatives to

other ceramic centers in Japan to learn enameling techniques. It was not until the end of the eighteenth century that techniques were refined enough to produce the type of decoration that became popular in the West. The Chosa kiln site developed a style of brocade decoration (Satsuma nishikide) in the late eighteenth century, using the enamel colors of iron red, blue, blue green, light purple, black, and a bit of yellow.

During the first half of the nineteenth century, potters produced decorative motifs, including birds, animals, flowers, and insects along with geometric textile designs. The second half of the century, saw the first appearance of human figures on Satsuma ware. The Seven Lucky Gods was a popular motif. As the century progressed, the use of perspective and the introduction of shading became part of standard decoration.

The nineteenth century also saw the rising of other kiln sites that produced Satsuma-type wares. At the Awata kilns near Kyoto they had been producing this ware since the mid-eighteenth century. Here the local clay was a yellowish color rather than white, and the crackled glaze was clear rather than creamy. Floral decoration predominated. Human figures and animals appeared toward the close of the nineteenth century. Kyoto became the major site of Satsuma production from the Meiji period onward. When the old feudal system was replaced with a more structured executive-type of government, the production of private kilns and studios was augmented by the opening of large factories for the purpose of mass producing ceramics for the growing middle class and exportation.

When Satsuma became a desirable export, the styles changed to suit the West. Pieces became larger and more colors were added for decorative purposes. Enormous vases were created for the Philadelphia Exposition in 1876 and the London exhibit in 1880. Raised enameling (jeweled) pieces were produced to satisfy Victorian tastes. Small items such as buttons and belt buckles were also made.

The nineteenth century also saw the growth of other kiln sites devoted to the production of Satsuma-type wares. Potters on Awaji Island produced the ceramics of Kashiu Mimpei, a ware created for export which resembled the Satsuma produced at Awata. In 1869 a kiln was established at Ota near Yokohama, when the port was opened to foreign trade. The potter Miyakawa Kozan and his son moved there and established themselves as Satsuma potters in the Awata style. Kozan received world acclaim for his work, which was shown in several international exhibits. He was elected to membership in the Imperial Academy of Tokyo in 1896. Tokyo had also become a center for international trade and established its own kilns for the purpose of decorating and firing Satsuma blanks (undecorated Satsuma white ware). Decoration kilns were established in other areas as well.

A peculiar situation arose in the early twentieth century regarding the use of Satsuma blanks. Up until World War I, hobbyists in the United States had been importing blank porcelain from Europe and hand painting the pieces themselves. Their supply vanished with the onset of the war. As a consequence, the suppliers began to import blank Satsuma from Japan, which was subsequently hand painted here by amateur artists for their own enjoyment.

After World War I, Japan began exporting large quantities of Satsuma-type wares to the West. The styles and shapes were a reflection of the taste of the time. Many of the wares appeared with the entire surface enameled. The outlines of decoration were drawn in black, and raised gold enamels were used as embellishments. A matte black background color was popular in the 1920s, and red became predominant in the 1930s. Brown was also used as a background color. The familiar Satsuma crackle is completely hidden under the decoration and can only be seen on the base of the object. These later pieces can sometimes be found with "Made in Japan" and "Occupied Japan" marks.

References: S. W. Bushell, *Oriental Ceramic Art*, Crown Publishers, Inc., 1980; Soame Jenyns, *Japanese Porcelain*, Frederick A. Praeger, 1965; Louis Laurence, *Satsuma*, Dauphin Publishing Ltd., 1991; Nancy Schiffer, *Japanese Porcelain 1880–1950*, Schiffer Publishing, Ltd., 1986; Irene Stitt, *Japanese Ceramics of the Last 100 Years*, Crown Publishers. Inc., 1974.

Museums: Boston Museum of Fine Art, Boston, Massachusetts; Brooklyn Museum, Brooklyn, New York; Metropolitan Museum of Art, New York, New York; British Museum, London, England; Victoria and Albert Museum, London, England; Tokyo National Museum, Tokyo, Japan.

Reproduction Alert: Satsuma kilns are still operating in Japan and are exporting their wares to the United States and Europe. One type of ware is still being made to resemble the early wares in color and design. It has a creamy colored surface that is covered with crackle and painted decoration (mostly flowers and birds) using colored enamels and gold. The most frequent forms are vases, plates, and tea sets with handless cups. It is not very difficult to see the differences between the old and new Satsuma wares. The potting of the ware is very mechanical compared with the hand-potted pieces of the past, and the enamels used are not as textured as the old. The surface has the appearance of being flat. The gold is very thinly applied and very bright. The crackle also is not as fine as old Satsuma. They are usually marked in red calligraphy on the base. The prices for these objects are low, and the pieces can be found in gift shops and department stores everywhere.

Another type of Satsuma product that is imported to the West today is much more difficult to distinguish from the old. These pieces are very imposing; they tend to be large and very ornately decorated. Large vases, bowls with scalloped edges, and punch bowls are the favored forms. The two patterns that are predominant in the designs are the Millefleur and Thousand Flying Cranes. Primary colors are used in the decoration. Red, bright green, and royal blue are found accented with black, white, and a touch of gold. The prices for this new Satsuma product are high, from the upper hundreds into the thousands, no doubt resulting from the amount of time and skill it takes to decorate the heavily enameled ware. These items are lovely, but they are not antiques.

The quickest way for the novice to tell if an item is old, is to look at the mark. The new Satsuma of this type is signed underneath with a gold square as opposed to the old Satsuma mark, which was signed with gold on a black square. Exposure to a few pieces will be enough to school any collector in the more subtle differences of color and enameling between these items and old Satsuma.

Collecting Hints: Satsuma and Satsuma-style wares are highly collectable. Westerners tend to lump all the finely crackled enamel decorated pieces under the heading of Satsuma, even if the pieces were made in Kyoto or another area that produced Satsuma-style ware, rather than identifying pieces according to their geographic origin. Prices generally depend on the name of the artist or studio responsible for the item and not location. It is sometimes very difficult to determine area of origin so we must rely on the quality of the work if a signature is absent.

In recent years, the focus of attention of the sophisticated collectors of Satsuma has focused on the work of several artists who worked out of studios that exhibited in the Paris Exhibition of 1867. The most notable of these, Yabu Meizan (1853–1934), was renowned for his exquisite painting. His works are currently fetching the highest market prices for wares of the Satsuma type. Meizan, however, is not technically considered to be a studio potter, because he did not throw his own pots. The Kinkozan family had been Satsusma potters from the seventeenth century. Kinkozan Sorbei (sixth generation) began the Kinzozan Pottery in 1877, which was continued by his son until it closed in 1927. He is credited with having been the first to use cobalt blue backgounds with overlaid gold or silver tracery designs on Satsuma style wares. The Kinkozan workshop exhibited wares at all the major international exhibitions.

Other Meiji period studios and artists have become important names in the field of collecting. Some studios are Makuzu Kozan, Ryozan, Seikozan, Kaizan, Shizan, Taizan, Bizan, and Kinkozan Pottery; and Sozan, Itozan, Semiishi, and Shisui are some of the well-known artists. There may be other workshops and artists that have not yet been researched who will become popular in the future.

Westerners show a preference for the highly decorated pieces of the late nineteenth century over the earlier simple faience wares—our preference aided, no doubt, by the shapes and decorations deliberately employed to please us. Signed pieces by renowned artists are in the highest price category, even though they may be of diminutive size. The large palace vases that graced many Victorian homes can be found both here and in Europe, but the work on these is not as fine as some of the smaller items. Hand-painted Satsuma blanks, with art nouveau designs are a sought-after novelty as are the scarce undecorated blanks themselves.

The mass-produced Satsuma-type wares of the 1920s through the 1940s also attract a large group of collectors. The overall quality of these pieces is coarse and sometimes sloppy, but their decoration is very colorful. Their prices still range from thirty-five dollars to the low hundreds. They are often purchased as part of a "Made in Japan" or "Occupied Japan" collection.

Bottle, 5¼", Meiji Period, of pear shape with small waisted neck, decorated with two rectangular panels, one with a warrior at a palace garden, the other with figures on the shore of a lake, all in enamels and gilding on a ground of floral designs in silver on blue, signed Kinkozan tsukuru **700.00**

Bowl
  4¾" dia., Meiji period, the deep bell-form bowl on short ring foot elaborately decorated in gilt and colored enamels with fan shaped reserves of figures in a garden, a blossoming plum branch, and ducks in a pond, all on a ground of

Charger, 17¾ dia., Meiji period, heavily potted, decorated with a scene of women on a seaside outing, signed Kyusan sei. $5,225.00. Courtesy of Butterfield and Butterfield.

flower blossoms, the exterior painted with various flowers and butterflies, rectangular seal to base **550.00**

  5¼", Meiji Period, of flared form, decorated in enamels and gilding with panels of sennin and karako bordered by brocade designs, the interior with a band of cranes within a band of butterflies, signed Hokuzan. **895.00**

  6" dia., painted on the interior with a river landscape scene, the bank lined with buildings and famed by wisteria blossoms repeated to the exterior, the base signed Koshida **300.00**

  7¼" dia., Meiji Period, the shallow bowl resting on a short ring foot and molded to the cavetto with eight petal-like segments each painted with matsubishigawa above a lappet band encircling a center decorated with further blossoms amid a swirling wave pattern, the exterior painted in gilt with scrolling tendrils and stylized flowers, signed Nihon Yamashita Tsukuru **400.00**

  7¼", late 19th century, with ceremonial and floral scenes on the interior and a wide floral border, character marks on base **650.00**

  13⅛", Early Meiji Period, with a flared lightly fluted body boldly decorated in colored enamels and gilding with two cranes standing behind a fence beneath bamboo and chrysanthemums and with numerous further chrysanthemums growing behind a wicker screen, between formal brocade borders, signed Satsuma yaki, Kinzan **9,500.00**

  14¾", Meiji Period, of lobed form decorated in enamels and gilding with a dragon coiled among immortals, signed Satsuma-mon, Dai Nihon Satsuma yaki, Hododa . . . **950.00**

  15⅜" dia., Meiji Period, the deep steep-sided bowl with a scallop-edged rim and tapering to a high ring foot, the interior painted in gilt and bright polychrome enamels with a depiction of the wife of Kamatari rescuing the sacred jewel from Ryujin (The Dragon King), her right hand brandishing a dagger above a large octopus emerging from the sea with the Ryugu-jo Castle in the distance, the central medallion bordered by a narrow gilt band and surrounded with further waves and Ryujin accompanied by his army of fantastic sea creatures, the exterior encircled by a multitude of butterflies above a flock of cranes amid clouds, the base with a central gilt cartouche reading Satsuma bordered by the inscription Dai Nihon-kuni Meiji-seizo **2,000.00**

Box and cover

4½" dia., the lid painted with three bijin strolling along a river bank underneath a blossoming cherry tree, the sides decorated with diaper patterns, the interior painted with various blossoms, the base signed Masayoshi gashi/Sho ko gashi **525.00**

6", Meiji Period, the body of circular section on three squat feet, painted and gilt with two bijin, one standing and the other kneeling beside a shodana, the sides with scrolling lotus leaves, signed Nihonzan **550.00**

Censer

4" h., Meiji Period, of compressed ovoid contour resting on three short shaped supports, the sloping shoulder applied with a pair of small scroll-form handles below the fitted dome-shaped lid decorated in gilt with patterned bands and two large Satsuma mon alternating with pierced floral design below the round knob, the body with two colorful figural reserves on a cobalt blue ground with further gilt floral and geometric motifs, the base with a cartouche reading Chozan/Asayama **450.00**

4⅝" h., signed hotoda, the tripod censer raised on a stem painted with blossoming cherry trees and extending upward to a short cylindrical body flanked by squared handles and painted with quail and peony bushes, reversed by further blossoms on a river bank, the lid pierced by three heart-shaped cut-outs on a densely patterned brocade and floral ground and surmounted by a pierced triangular finial, signed Satsuma Hotoda **550.00**

Cup and Saucer

Demitasse, 2½" and 3⅞" dia., Meiji Period, the small deep cup with a curved handle and minutely painted in gilt and multicolored enamels with birds in a lush blossoming landscape above a narrow floral-pattern gilt band, another band of butterflies encircling the short foot rim, the sloping saucer decorated en suite center with a hanabishi motif while a band of shippo-tsunagi encircles the rim, each with a two character cartouche reading Shizan **300.00**

2¼" h., Meiji Period, the saucer decorated with figures frolicking on a beach, the horizon extending out to a rocky sea, the small but deep cup decorated en suite, rectangular seal to bases. **250.00**

Dish

8½" dia., Meiji Period, of rounded rectangular form, with upswept rim, the interior painted in enamels and gilt with floral and diaper design on a tomoe mon, signed **750.00**

8½" dia., decorated with three women on a veranda preparing for the Tanabata festival by hanging poems in a bamboo bough, with cartouche reading Fujin fuzoku shichigatsu, the base impressed with seal reading Kinkozan-sei **550.00**

Figure

Ebisu, 9", Meiji Period, he sits cross-legged, his robes decorated in enamels and gilt with a scrolling foliate design, and open fan in his right hand and a creel to his left, signed Kagoshima Genzan. **1,400.00**

Buddhist Saint, 14⅜" h., Meiji Period, depicting the rakkan Chuda handaka Sonja seated rajalilasana

Covered Censer, 18¾" h., circa 1900, scene of Five Hundred Rakan, wear to gilt, inscribed Shunzan. $1,050.00. Courtesy of Butterfield and Butterfield.

on a rocky plinth, his slightly turning body wearing thick multi-layered monastic robes of various brocade designs executed in gilt and bright polychrome enamels, further gilt applied to the rosary held in his right hand and to his earrings framing his other-worldly face with an oversized cranium, furrowed brows and open mouth   **1,650.00**

Figural Group, 11⅞" h., Meiji Period, well molded and decorated in gilt and polychrome enamels as Bukkan (Feng Kan) seated on a large crouching tiger, the immortal's emaciated body partially exposed with his elaborately patterned monastic garments draped over his left shoulder and falling in gentle folds over his pendent legs, his right hand holds a flywhisk while the other rests on the head of his ferocious mount with large eyes and open mouth framed by an uncharacteristic curly mane, the striped marking alternating with star-patterned whorls extending over its body.....................   **715.00**

Jar

With cover, 4", Meiji Period, of polyhedrons form, decorated in enamels and gilding with panels of stylized kiku and butterflies and kiri reserved on scrolling foliage, the cover of shallow cylindrical form, painted mark Satsuma-mon, Satsuma-yaki **900.00**

17½", Meiji Period, of shouldered form, molded in relief with a dragon in a stormy sky, decorated in green and black glaze........   **450.00**

Koro and Cover

3", Meiji Period, the bulbous body painted in enamels and gilt with two panels, one with figures seated on a balcony, being entertained by a dancer and musician, the other with figures in a landscape, reserved on a floral and formal ground, the pieced cover surmounted by a kiku knop, signed Gyokushu **1,500.00**

6¾" h., late 19th century, decorated with hiking figures on one side, and a waterside scene on the other, the figural finial showing a scholar, with molded elephant handles....................   **800.00**

10", Meiji Period, raised on three mask feet, painted in enamels and gilt with four panels, one with Handaka Sonja holding aloft the bowl from which issues the dragon, upon whose back stands

Benten, another with courtiers, and two with birds on a woven ground, with two handles, the pierced cover surmounted by a shishi knop.................   **475.00**

Libation Cup, 4⅞" l., Meiji Period, of flattened ovoid contour flaring toward the rim with a wide pouring spout opposed by a C-shaped handle, the interior well painted in gilt and bright polychrome enamels with an allover pattern of butterflies on a granulated gilt ground and encircled by diaper-patterned gilt band at the rim, the exterior with two figural reserves, one of heart shape featuring samurai and attendants in a landscape, the other a roundel with children playing, each superimposed over blossoming plants and grasses above a geometric-patterned lappet band encircling the low oval foot, the base with a four character cartouche reading Hankinzan-do   **1,000.00**

Plate

7¼" dia, Meiji Period, the shallow plate glazed in a fine crackled creamy white color and decorated with a blossoming cherry tree in bright enamels and gilt, base with seal of Yabu Meizan..........   **600.00**

8¾" dia., Meiji Period, the slightly sloping dish with a central cherry-shaped panel delicately painted in gilt and polychrome enamels with a bijin and Japanese children in a spring landscape within a narrow gilt border, reserved on a deep blue ground scattered with leafy berry sprigs in gilt, the base with a four character cartouche reading Shozan Nampo..............   **900.00**

10" dia., Meiji Period, the sloping interior minutely painted in gilt and polychrome enamels with a comic rendition of a writhing dragon above a gathering of Buddhist rakan in a mountainous landscape fed by streams and dotted with trees and pavilions, the top with a partial cloud-collar border with a large Satsuma mon on a seigaiha-patterned ground, two further mon contested by a pair of writhing dragons on the exterior, the base with a large cartouche inscribed Dai Nihon "Rohaku"-an Satsuma-kuni Kinkoku-yaki Nakashima-zukuri **475.00**

Tea Caddy, 6¼" h., Meiji Period, of globular form surmounted by a domed exterior lid and a fitted interior lid, decorated with a procession

of women and children walking in
the streets of a village, the neck and
lid decorated with a brocade motif 475.00
Teapot, 4″ dia., Meiji Period, the small
squat form teapot resting on three
short feet and painted to the top with
three fan shaped reserves, two of
various figures, the third of a landscape, all on a ground of peony blossoms and minute butterflies, signed
below in a rectangular seal 550.00
Tea Set
6¾″ teapot handle to spout, late 19th
century, teapot, covered creamer
and sugar, six cups and saucers,
gilt and polychromed tropical bird
motif, signed Shinzan 1,500.00
7⅛″ dia. tea plates, Meiji Period,
comprising tea pot, sugar bowl
and milk jug, all with lids, six
cups, saucers and tea plates, all
decorated in enamels and gilt with
various scenes of children's festi-
vals, signed Shinzan 750.00
Tray, 13¾″ dia., Meiji Period, the interior decorated in gilt and polychrome enamels with a group of
karako playing musical instruments,
dancing, playing go, or lounging on
a grassy slope toward the bottom,
the low slightly-curved sides with an
exterior band of abbreviated cranes
and scrolling tendrils 220.00
Urn, 19½″ h., Meiji Period, of ovoid
form tapering to a splayed rolled foot
and surmounted by a waisted neck
flaring toward the rim, the high
shoulders applied with a pair of handles of dual U-shaped straps joined
by an upstanding loop, the front
painted in gilt and polychrome enamels with a figural scene of buddhist saints, reversed by birds in a
blossoming landscape, each reserved on a brocade-patterned
ground repeated near the foot and
on the neck, the high domed lid decorated en suite and surmounted by a
large sculptural karashishi seated
with its forepaw on a brocade ball 450.00
Vase
2⅜″ h., Meiji Period, of globular
form, painted in gilt on the blue
ground with a rain dragon, the
shoulder with formal design,
signed Dai Nihon Kyoto Kinkozan
tsukuru 295.00
4″ h., pair, baluster form, with short
waisted necks, decorated with
panels of children, reserved on a
ground of flowers 700.00
4½″ h., Meiji Period, painted and gilt
with a scene of travellers on a

mountain path above a river and a
small village, the blue ground gilt
and painted with flowers and
leaves impressed mark Kinkozan
tsukuru 1,800.00
4¾″, pair, Meiji Period, each well
painted with rural scenes of rice
pickers and others preparing corn,
the reverse with birds and flowers,
the necks with butterflies, applied
with ring handles, signed Meizan
sei 2,600.00
6″ h., ovoid, Late Meiji period,
ovoid, painted centrally with two
rectangular panels of a court procession reserved on a gilt floral
and geometric patterned brocade
ground, the neck molded to either
side with butterfly-form handles,
signed kaga taniguchi 200.00
6″ h., square shape, continuous
scene of Arahats with an entwined
dragon throughout, Shimazu
creast and character marks 450.00
6½″ h., pair, each of ovoid form resting on a splayed foot and tapering
to a waisted neck and painted
with a playful scene of a maiden
and her attendants walking next to
a patch of blossoming bushes in
the gusty wind, which has blown
some of their hats off, the base
inscribed Kinkozan-zukuri 475.00
6⅝″ l., pair, early 20th century, each
fashioned as a row of six cylindrical tubes with linked flattened
flared rims and all supported on
an oval base, the front painted in
gilt and polychrome enamels with
a flower basket amid birds and
fluffy gilt clouds, reversed by butterflies, the front signed Kinkozan
in gilt, the base impressed Kinkozan 800.00
7½″ h., pair, early 20th century, each
of slender ovoid shape with a high
shoulder and hexagonal faceted
sides, decorated in gilt and bright
colored enamels with two large
bird-and-flower reserves on a
deep blue ground scattered with
gilt geometric and floral motifs repeated on the band encircling the
short neck with a rolled rim, the
base with a Satsuma mon and cartouche reading "Ban"-zukuri. 525.00
7½″ h., discus form, Meiji Period,
with a long waisted neck, painted
in enamels and gilt with a profu-
sion of flowers beneath a
flowering cherry tree, the underside of the body with a formal
hanging blade design, the neck

with geometric and formal design, signed Kinkozan tsukuru **950.00**

7½″ h., oviform, decorated with a continuous scene of women and children at leisure in a bamboo grove before a winding stream, above and below petal bands of flowers on a gilt network ground, fine quality **2,200.00**

8″, bottle form, Meiji Period, painted with a central band of figures at a festival, the neck with fan shaped panels scattered among scrolling foliage beneath birds and cherry blossom, signed within a floral medallion Yabu Meizan   **3,800.00**

8½″ h., baluster form, Meiji Period, painted in brightly colored enamels with two reserves depicting court women and children walking through blossoming gardens reserved on a cobalt blue and gilt ground of floral scrolls and medallions, the neck with abstract phoenix medallions, the base with cartouche reading Kyozan **700.00**

9¾″, Meiji Period, painted in colored enamels and gilt with a scene from the Chushingaru, the revenge of the forty seven ronin, the neck with various mon on a stylized ground, signed Nihon Seirindo. **850.00**

10″ h., Meiji Period, with globular body and short neck, decorated on the brown ground in gilt, silver and blue enamel with a grasshopper and dragonfly before fruiting vines, the shoulder mounted

Vase, 9¾″ h., Meiji period, painted in brightly colored enamels on a finely crackled cream-colored ground, scene of court maidens, signed on the base with a cartouche reading Kozan. $1,550.00

with petal-shaped panels of diaper and floral roundels, signed Kinkozan tsukuru **750.00**

12″ h., pair, Meiji Period, each molded as section of bamboo resting on a tall ring foot and with each joint accentuated by an incised horizontal line repeated below the slightly flaring rim, the exterior finely painted in gilt and polychrome enamels with Chinese sages engaged in elegant pursuits in a bamboo grove set off by two narrow foliate-patterned bands at the rim and foot **800.00**

12″ h., the long cylindrical vase molded with rounded shoulders and tapering to a waisted neck, decorated overall with scrolling chrysanthemum blossoms and leafy tendrils on a chocolate brown ground, the neck with brocade diaper patterns, the base with inscription reading Dai Nihon hozan **165.00**

12½″ h., Meiji Period, intricately painted in enamels and gilt with four large shaped panels, one depicting a procession, one with figures in a pleasure garden, another with numerous toys and a fourth with fish and vegetables, smaller panels decorated with figures, landscapes and flowers, all reserved upon bands of flowers, butterflies, diaper and formal design, signed Matsumoto Hozan **6,500.00**

14½″ h., Meiji Period, painted and gilt with panels of immortals and karako, the sides with butterflies and diaper panels **450.00**

14½″ h., high waisted ovoid body, Meiji Period, decorated with two fan-shaped reserves of immortals engaged in conversation in a landscape setting and a group of samurai on a pavilion terrace separated with gilt and floral bands below a molded ring neck and modified trumpet mouth **1,350.00**

14½″ h., pair, 20th century, slender ovoid shape, each of tapering to a splayed foot and narrowing to a tall waisted neck applied with a pair of dragon-form handles beneath the flared rim, the sides painted in gilt and colored enamels with two large figural reserves depicting samurai being entertained by elegant bijin, all on a brocade-patterned ground repeated on the neck accented with two floral roundels below a lappet band at the rim, the base with Satsuma mon and inscribed Dai Nihon Satsuma-yaki Hanrin-ga **775.00**

14¾" h., Meiji Period, of slender tapering form, painted in colored enamels and gilt on the graduated yellow and blue ground with a kitten, seated before an exotic flower, looking upward at a butterfly, the shoulder and foot with floral and diaper design, signed Dai Nihon Taizan tsukuru **650.00**

15¼" h., Taisho Period, decorated in underglaze-blue and green with leafy stems of bamboo, impressed Kinkozan tsukuru **1,250.00**

16½" h., pair, late Meiji Period, each raised on a flared ring foot depicting Benten surrounded by a group of rakkan and immortals in a stylized landscape below a tapered-spiral decorated neck with satsuma mon, sealed on the underside Kinkozan Tsukuru with Dai Nihon, also inscribed with satsuma mon on the footrim **3,000.00**

16½" h., Meiji/Taisho Period, with a pair of pierced ear-shaped handles flanking a tall neck with central bulge above a small compressed ovoid body resting on a short ring foot, decorated in gilt and polychrome enamels with a shaped reserve of a celestial maiden and attendants reversed by a scalloped-edge floral reserve, all on a ground of Western-inspired scrolling leafy tendrils on a dark blue ground, the rolled rim with gilt edge, the base with model number **300.00**

17½" h., stick neck, Meiji Period, Kinkozan studio, the bulbous ovoid body resting on a short ring foot and surmounted by an extremely long slender neck flaring toward the rim, the sides well painted in gilt and polychrome enamels with clumps of flowering iris and wild pinks amid gilt-flecked patches of mist, the base both impressed and inscribed Kinkozan-zukuri **1,450.00**

17½" h., stick neck, Meiji Period, the globular body resting on a ring foot and tapering to a tall cylindrical neck, decorated in gilt and polychrome enamels with a scattered pattern of birds, bamboo, flowering and fruiting sprigs flanking a central band of birds and flower roundels linked by stylized floral motifs, all on a shaded blue ground below a scalloped-edge brocade-patterned band encircling the neck decorated en suite, a lappet band at the rim. . . . **330.00**

21½", pair, Meiji period, brightly enamelled and gilt with Ryujin and an army of fantastic sea creatures armed with swords and spears and dressed in patterned robes, chasing the fishergirl who rescued the precious jewel for Kamatari, the Riu Gu Jo castle in the dis-

Vase, 15⅝" h., Meiji period, ovoid shape, decorated in gilt and multicolored enamels with two large rectangular reserves, one depicting the Seven Lucky Gods and other historical figures, the other with the Seven Sages of the Bamboo Grove, Satsuma mon and signed Hokoku. $2,750.00. Courtesy of Butterfield and Butterfield.

Vase, 18½" h., Meiji period, decorated with a continuous scene of the Five Hundred Rakan and two dragons, wear to gilt and polychromes, Satsuma mon at the shoulders, inscription to the base reading Kinkozan - zukuri. $1,650.00. Courtesy of Butterfield and Butterfield.

tance beyond foaming waves, inscribed Tokyo, Matsumato Yoshinobu and Yoshikirimon, signed Nihon, Tokyo Kyugawa sei **7,000.00**

22⅛" h., baluster form, Late Meiji/Taisho Period, the ovoid body tapering to a high pedestal foot and applied with a pair of scrolling zoomorphic handles bracketing the tall waisted neck with a raised central band and terminating in an irregular rim fashioned as an open brocade bag, the sides decorated in raised gilt and polychrome enamels with a large reserve of samurai reversed by iris and set off by a brocade-patterned ground repeated on the neck and pedestal   **500.00**

22" h., pair, Taisho period, each elongated ovoid body decorated with a continuous scene illustrating chapters form the founding of Japan, one showing Amaterasu surrounded by a sun-halo, the other showing Taka-no-uchi bowing before her, the dynamic figures set against a background of shadowy foxes and blowing bamboo, all below a gilt floral decorated shoulder band, signed Soun Yoshiyuki, each base signed Uchigawa tsukuru **3,000.00**

Vases and Covers, 34", pair, Meiji Period, each with an ovoid body and domed cover painted in gilt, with warriors, courtier and attendants,

Vase, 42" h., late 19th/early 20th century, decorated in a subtle palette of brown, blue, red, and pink, the scene showing a mother and children in front of a flowering cherry tree and warriors preparing for battle. $880.00. Courtesy of Butterfield and Butterfield.

the foot with a stiff leaf border the neck with brocade and foliage **9,000.00**

Water pail, 14½" h., late 19th century, decorated with central panels of scholars and Arahat figures, floral and geometric borders. **850.00**

Wine Pot, 3" dia., a miniature Satsuma wine pot and cover decorated with two panels of villages on river banks, on a blue and gilt ground, signed Kinkozan **400.00**

SHIBAYAMA

History: The family name Shibayama has become the generic term for a style of decorative inlays of mother-of-pearl, tortoise shell, ivory, coral, semiprecious stones, and metal. The decoration was originally done on lacquer surfaces, but spread to ivory and metal as well. In the early nineteenth century, when the wealthy merchant class began to patronize the arts, the decorative arts became more technically detailed and ornate to satisfy the luxurious tastes of the newly established moneyed class. One type of decorative inlay took the name of the family that did the early work. At this time, many Japanese considered Shibayama style to be in poor artistic taste.

During the mid- and late nineteenth century, much of the Shibayama-style inlays were done for commercial purposes by special workers, rather than lacquer artists as in the early times. Most of the later work was unsigned. Many fine examples of early work still exist, signed by the Shibayama family. By the late nineteenth century, these articles were commonly made for export to the West where they had become very popular.

Reference: Melvin and Betty Jahss, *Inro and Other Miniature Forms of Japanese Lacquer Art*, Charles E. Tuttle Co., Inc., 1981.

Museums: Examples will be found in some exhibits of lacquer, inro, and Meiji Period articles; no special exhibits are known.

Collecting Hints: It is not unusual to find pieces in which some of the inlays have been lost, so that one must examine all the details very carefully. The missing pieces may have been replaced in some cases, and much of the time it is possible to detect such repairs. The pieces with missing inlays and/or good repairs can still be of value and bring enjoyment to the collector, but he or she should be prepared to pay accordingly.

Advisors: Bernard and Irene Rosett

Dish, 7" dia., signature unread, late 19th century, gold lacquer and metal filigree; central lacquer area

Card Case, 2¼" x 4", late 19th century, signed in seal form, ivory covers with cloth pockets, inlaid with mother-of-pearl, coral, and tortoise shell. $950.00

decorated in shibayama style inlays of birds and flowers **1,300.00**
Inro
  3 case, 3" h., signed Kazuyauki, late
    19th century, ivory inlaid with
    mother-of-pearl, horn, colored
    stones; flowering hydrangea and
    cherry trees, the reverse with wis-
    teria and stream, ensuite with sim-
    ilarly inlaid ivory ojime and
    manju netsuke **1,800.00**
  4 case, signed Seigyoku, late 19th
    century, ivory inlaid with mother-
    of-pearl and colored stones, phea-
    sant on branch and on the reverse
    a tiger lily **1,400.00**
Ojime, ⅝" dia., signed Kozan in
  mother-of-pearl plaque, late 19th
  century, ivory, incised floral motif
  with mother-of-pearl inlays **150.00**
Tusk vases, pair, 9¾" h., late 19 cen-
  tury, signed Masanaga; curved cylinder form elaborately inlaid with
  several floral arrangements, birds

Netsuke, 2" h., late 19th century, ivory elephant with multicolored semiprecious stones and glass, signed Masaharu. $1,400.00

Parasol Handle, 10" l., late 19th century, ivory, inlaid with mother-of-pearl, coral, tortoise shell, and semiprecious stones, unsigned. $1,250.00

and plants; wood bases, some losses
  to inlay **3,000.00**
Vase
  6¾" h., pair, signed Masatomo, late
    19th century, inlaid in Shibayama
    style with flowers and foliage **4,000.00**
  8¼" h., late 19th century, signed Bai-
    setsu, lacquer decorated in gold
    and inlaid in Shibayama style with
    scenes of birds, butterflies, fish,
    flowers, foliage; hexagonal with
    tall neck, everted rim and stepped
    foot **4,000.00**

SUMIDA GAWA

History: In the past, Sumida ware has been erroneously called Banko ware, Korean ware, and Poo ware by collectors. They were misinformed, however, as to its proper name and its place of origin. Sumida pottery and porcelain wares were created not far from the city of Tokyo near the banks of the Sumida River by a potter named Inoue Ryosai I and his son Inoue Ryosai II around 1895. The ware has come to be known as Sumida Gawa (Sumida River) ware.

    Fine examples have beautiful flambé drip glazes usually adorning the tops and sides of vases and bowls of all shapes, both classical and asymmetrical. Areas free of flambé glaze reveal background colors of reddish orange, black, brown, and dark green, which over time, may peel away leaving the tan ceramic body exposed. This background, most frequently found in the red, set the stage for the most outstanding feature of Sumida Gawa ware: the molding and/or application of modeled figures most often of children and monks or elders. These figures are sometimes applied in full relief, giving a full three-dimensional view of the subjects. Children are sometimes depicted hanging over the edge and peering into glazed bowls as if something special was about to happen. Elders and monks are arranged in mysterious stances and postures.

Signatures are normally incorporated on cartouches of various shapes and sizes that are applied to the body of the individual work of art. Signatures also appear, at times, on the bottom of smaller pieces, but one will also come across works which do not have any maker's marks. We can only assume that some paper labels were used after 1900 in accordance with the McKinley Tarriff Act, which required imports to include a country of origin. Paper stickers that may have been marked "Made in Japan" could have been removed or have fallen off, leaving the object unmarked.

Reference: S. Andacht, N. Garthe, and R. Mascarelli, *Price Guide to Oriental Antiques*, 2nd ed., Wallace Homestead, 1984.

Museum: Leitner Museum, St. Augustine, Florida.

Collecting Hints: Sumida Gawa is enjoying tremendous popularity and has been rapidly escalating in price. People are discovering the unique quality of these dramatic works of art that seem to enhance any decor. There is a growing number of collectors who are quickly gathering up the best examples of the ware. The supply of the superior pieces diminishes every day. Collectors should look for pieces that have sharp details.

Pieces can be found in the United States and Europe but rarely if ever in Japan. This clearly indicates that the ware was intended for export only. A striking example of Sumida Gawa ware can be seen at the Leitner Museum in St. Augustine, Florida. The museum features a Sumida vase which is 30" tall and has hundreds of monkeys applied to the top and sides.

Advisor: Shane Lyons

Ashtray, 3" h., red background, applied relief figure of a frog upon a rock 295.00
Bowl
  6" dia., green background, applied relief figures of three children at play. 350.00
  7" dia., red background, shallow with small lip, applied relief children and monkeys playing together, a grass hut shown to one side. 800.00
  9" dia., red background, showing ten children peering over the sides of the bowl 1,250.00

Bowl, 4" h., three flesh-colored monkeys astride a green-glazed rim. $475.00. Courtesy of Butterfield and Butterfield.

Mug, 5" h., red background, monkey in relief. 300.00
Pitcher, 12" h., red background, applied relief figure of bullfrog. 850.00
Pitcher and mugs, 16" h., red background, pitcher, six mugs with handles 5" h., applied dragons and clouds, chips 975.00
Planter on stand, 30" h., dark background, the stand showing a coiled dragon creeping up to the planter bowl. 4,000.00
Teapot, 4" h., flat crescent form, red background, two children on either side. 390.00
Vase
  $3\frac{1}{2}$", in the form of child climbing bamboo, tan background, flambé highlights 180.00
  $4\frac{1}{4}$" h., late Meiji Period, the indented ovoid body covered with a translucent, crackled white glaze and yellow spots, decorated with a small crab climbing out of a crevice, studio mark to base 195.00
  7" h., red background, applied relief figure of an Oni. 275.00

Vase, $6\frac{1}{8}$" h., two children one holding flag, dark brown-black background, with a greenish foamy drip glaze at the neck, signed on porcelain cartouche. $375.00

Left, **Vase, 12" h., four children climbing in play, red background, unsigned. $495.00;** *right,* **Vase, 13" h., of dented form with flowering branch of prunus on red background, signed on base. $395.00. Both courtesy of Jan-tiques.**

9", with cover, red background, squat form on four legs showing relief applied elders and children on the sides.	2,400.00
10" h., shape of pilgrim bottle, red background, showing relief applied children on a mountain side	1,500.00
12" h., circa 1900, ovoid form, red background, with a procession of monkeys in human clothing shown crossing a bridge, the neck and shoulders streaked with a purplish grey glaze.	1,600.00
17¾" h., late 19th century, ovoid form, showing hoards of monkeys scrambling over one another on rocky outcroppings, red background, dark rim glaze turning to celadon green and purple at the edges	2,750.00
25" h., red background, with a coiling dragon encircling the vase	3,000.00

TOBACCO RELATED ITEMS: TONKOTSU AND KISERU-ZUTSU

History: Tobacco, pipes, and the smoking habit were carried to the Orient by Portuguese and Dutch traders and swiftly spread to China, Korea, and Japan. The Portuguese brought tobacco into Japan toward the close of the sixteenth century, and by 1605 tobacco plantations were established. In Japan, smoking soon became a national mania, indulged in by men, women, and even children. About ten years after it was introduced, the daimyo of Hirado ordered all tobacco to be destroyed because the habit had become so pervasive. The ban on smoking was largely ignored and had to be rescinded. From the middle of the seventeenth century, smoking was an extremely popular activity among all classes of society, especially well-to-do merchants.

The Japanese pipe (kiseru), consisting of a small thimblelike bowl of silver or silver-related alloy and a stem of metal or bamboo connecting to a mouthpiece of metal, was carried in a pipe case (kiseru-zutsu), most commonly made of stag antler, ivory, or wood. It was necessary to have a storage container for tobacco. Boxes (called tonkotsus) or pouches (called tabako-ires) were the two types in general use.

The materials used in tonkotsus were varied and included every type of wood, bamboo, ceramic, gourd, metal, tree bark, tortoise sell, woven rattan, reeds and grasses, and animal skin. The tonkotsus were decorated with carving, inlays of ivory, semiprecious stones, mother-of-pearl, pottery, and lacquer. Pouches were made of tooled leather, printed fabrics, and brocades. The shapes of the tonkotsus were boxlike or made in the shape of monkeys, frogs, and other animals; skulls; shells; pumpkins; and so forth. By 1900, tonkotsus were made commercially in mass production. These are generally not of interest as artistic works. Earlier on, people took great pride in the artistry and individuality of their tobacco boxes and pipe cases, and many of the finest carvers, lacquerers, and artisans of all types produced these items.

The tonkotsus and kiseru-zutsus were worn suspended from the waist sash (obi) by means of a woven silk cord, since kimonos do not have pockets. The generic term *sagemono* is applied to all suspended objects. They were provided individually with a toggle (netsuke) to prevent them from slipping out from the obi. A slide bead (ojime) also was used to keep the container closed. It is desirable to have the box or pouch, or case; the ojime; and the netsuke all present and compatible or original; this is known as en suite (tomozutsu). Ideally, the same artist was responsible for all the components. In many cases the pipe case served as the netsuke; the tonkotsu was hung directly from it and the pipe case was kept behind the obi.

The Japanese traditionally made their functional appurtenances into items of artistic beauty, and that temperament reveals itself in some of the wonderful designs of the kiseru-zutsus. This occurred in spite of the restrictions imposed by the long, narrow shape of this piece. The inventiveness of the artisans is shown by the many forms of the pipe case that have evolved. Typically, the Japanese have given each style a name.

The two-part style in narrow cylinder form is

called muso-zutso. The lower section takes the pipe (bowl down) and is closed with a narrower and shorter cylinder. A one-piece case, called otoshi-zutsu, is shaped like a scabbard, narrowing at the top. The bowl of the senry-zutsu (also one piece) fits into a curved area and the mouthpiece end of the pipe fits into a rounded aperture. The aikichi-zutsu is two pieced; the two parts abut each other. Another one-piece form is the wari-zutsu; its springy walls keep the pipe secure.

Stag antler is one of the commonly used materials, since its natural shape is well suited to this purpose. As with the tonkotsu, the materials can be extremely varied: woven basketry, wood of all types, bamboo, ivory, leather, metal, and combinations of these. Many are in rustic style to complement simple tonkotsus, and others become increasingly elegant to match the finer tonkotsus. Here again, the decorative materials are wide-ranging: lacquer, carving, metal, mother-of-pearl, and so on.

References: Raymond Bushell, *The Inro Handbook*, Weatherhill, 1979; —, "Kiseruzutsu," *Arts of Asia*, November to December 1980; Fumihito Ido, *Nihon Fukuromono Shi (History of Japanese Bags)*, 1919; Bertold Laufer, *Tobacco and Its Uses in Asia, Anthropology Leaflet 18*, Field Museum of Natural History, 1924; Bernard Rosett, article written for the *Orientalia Journal*, January 1983.

Museums: These pieces are not usually exhibited, except when included with groups of inro or in specialized exhibits.

Collecting Hints: In the past, tonkotsus and kiseru-zutsus as collector's items have been overlooked and underpriced. Lately there is greater interest, and the prices have begun to surge. However, the number of collectors has not grown too rapidly and sanity has prevailed so far. When signatures are present, the artists are often familiar as netsuke and inro artists and lacquerers. Most dealers specializing in Orientalia usually have a small number of tonkotsus, and kiseru-zutsus, and tabako-ires. The admonition to consider quality rather than signature cannot be repeated too often.

Advisors: Bernard and Irene Rosett

KISERU-ZUTSU

Aikuchi-zutsu

8" l., Mid 19th century, wood and stag antler, the long portion carved with pine, bamboo and crab 850.00

9" l., late 19th century, red lacquer (tsueshi), carved in stylized wave design. 800.00

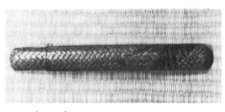

8" l., 19th century, muso-zutsu, woven bamboo strips with lacquered leaves of bamboo, silver band. $400.00

9½" l., mid 19th century, lacquer, leaf and eggplant design in gold, mother-of-pearl inlays, some damage. 350.00

Muso-zutsu

8" l., 18th century, signed Setsudo, ivory, elegantly carved with ducks and water plants, cracks repaired in the Japanese manner with silver staples. 650.00

8¼" l., woven rattan, lacquered, with lotus and bamboo in black and gold 350.00

9" l., 19th century, wood, carved to imitate woven bamboo 275.00

Otoshi-zutsu

8" l., mid 19th century, signed Soko, Morita seal, cherry wood in the shape of a long bean pod with stem and leaves 900.00

8" l., mid 19th century, dark wood, one side highly polished, the other carved with peonies 225.00

8" l., late 19th century, stag antler, detailed carving of Chinese landscape scene 400.00

8½" l., circa 1870, wood, detailed carving of houses and landscape with mother-of-pearl moon inlay   275.00

9" l., 18th century, stag antler, carving shows a masked Samurai hiding behind a tree, well worn, fine age patina 450.00

Senry-zutsu

8" l., 19th century, umimatsu (black coral), natural shape with reddish markings, highly polished 375.00

10" l., senry-zutsu form, ebony wood, elongated gourd shape, beautiful old patina. $350.00

9" l., 19th century, wari-zutsu, stag antler with floral and geometric openwork. $375.00

8" l., 19th century, formed as a bonsai clipper, carved with an oni holding a hammer **750.00**

8" l., early 19th century, stag antler, delicately carved to resemble the stem and seed pod of a lotus, with movable seeds, inserts of mother-of-pearl simulate water droplets on the stem **450.00**

8" l., early 19th century, stag antler, unadorned, pipe mouthpiece held in hollowed out section of antler **275.00**

8" l., circa 1860, signed Harumitsu, wood, a long-legged frog on a lotus, pipe mouthpiece extends through the frog's open mouth . . . **900.00**

8" l., late 19th century, wood, carved in the form of a long, thin fish, pipe mouthpiece extends through the open mouth of the fish **450.00**

Wari-zutsu, 9" l., circa 1850, stag antler, with open work lozenges and carved flowers **375.00**

TONKOTSU (TABAKO-IRE)

Box

$3\frac{1}{2}$" dia. x $1\frac{1}{2}$" h., early 19th century, kiri wood, drum shaped, with bone "nailheads" around drum, cover is in the form of a man lying prone on drum, together with a

plain wood ojime bead and ebony wood kiser-zutsu, in rustic style, uncarved **375.00**

3" x 1" x $2\frac{1}{4}$" h., circa 1850, stag antler, in the form of a temple bell, with a hinged front opening, and dragon handle **650.00**

3" x 1" x $2\frac{1}{4}$" h., mid 19th century, persimmon rind, folded into pouch shape, then dried to become woodlike, together with a bone ojime bead and a carved bone mask netsuke **950.00**

3" x 3" x $2\frac{1}{2}$" h., circa 1850, wood, unadorned with very fine old patina, with ceramic ojime bead . . . **250.00**

4" x 3" x 3" h., late 19th century, wood, in the shape of an elephant, various inlays of mother-of-pearl, ivory, coral, en suite with ivory ojime bead, and kiseru-zutsu inlaid with an elephant trainer in ivory **1,200.00**

$3\frac{1}{2}$" x $1\frac{1}{4}$" x 3" h., mid 19th century, wood and lacquer, one side showing two crabs, the other with grasses and flower inlaid in mother-of-pearl, in inro form **500.00**

$3\frac{1}{2}$" x 2" x 3" h., late 19th century, wood, inlaid with mother-of-pearl, ivory and some lacquer, showing a man wrestling a turtle, reverse side with inlaid calligraphy in mother-of-pearl, signed . . . **800.00**

$3\frac{1}{2}$" x 1" x 3" h., mid 19th century, iron, in shape of a pouch, with a hinged lid, raised deer design, rustic style **225.00**

$3\frac{1}{2}$" x 2" x 3" h., early 19th century, kiri wood, uncarved rustic style, en suite with plain wood bead and flat leather pipe case, hand stitched along one side **275.00**

4" x $1\frac{1}{2}$" x 3" h., 19th century, bamboo strips, woven, unadorned, with stone ojime bead **325.00**

Box, 5" w., wood, carved turtles in waves on front and back, along with turtle netsuke. $975.00

Box, 4" h., mid 19th century, formed from bitter orange rind (dai-dai) which hardens when dry, carved wood Daruma faced cover, seed ojime, wooden senry-zutsu-type pipe case. $800.00

2'' dia., 3'' h., cylinder, mid 19th century, separate cover, fine old patina, with large stone ojime bead 325.00

3½'' x 2½'' x 3'' h., early 19th century, bamboo, carved peonies and leaves, cover with raised archaic symbol 400.00

3'' x 1½'' x 3'' h., early 19th century, bamboo root, basket shaped, rustic style, unadorned, with small cylinder attached for matches . . .   300.00

3'' h., ovoid, 19th century, boxwood, cover carved with shi-shi, inlaid horn eyes 375.00

4'' x 2'' x 3'' h., late 18th century, frogskin leather, from Ainu Tribe, very rare 500.00

3½'' x 2'' x 3½'' h., mid 19th century, rootwood, natural style, unadorned 200.00

4½'' x 2'' x 3½'' h., late 19th century, wood, surface carved to resemble tree bark, with oni head on one side, en suite with large wood ojime bead in form of Daruma and eggplant shaped cigarette holder with ivory collar to hold cigarette, very unusual 1,000.00

4'' x 2'' x 3½'' h., circa 1850, wood, with inlays of insects and ginkgo leaves in ivory, mother-of-pearl and wood 500.00

4'' x 2'' x 3½'' h., late 19th century, dragons carved front and back, en suite with ceramic ojime bead, stag antler kiseru-zutsuu with silver metal dragon 850.00

3'' x 2'' x 4'' h., early 19th century, briar root, en suite with agate ojime bead and rootwood kiseruzutsu, rustic style with natural finish 325.00

3'' x 1'' x 4'' h., early 19th century, signed Hikkyo Korin, cherry wood, showing the thunder god in raised pewter, gold and black lacquer, and the reverse side showing the wind god in thick pearl and gold and black lacquer, along with an agate ojime 1,500.00

3'' x 1½'' x 4'' h., 20th century, chrome finish, mass produced in inro style, en suite with glass ojime bead and chrome kiseruzutsu 70.00

Pouch

4'' x 2½'', late 19th century, printed cloth, envelope form with silver floriform clasp, felt lined, en suite with natural seed ojime bead and netsuke formed from the eye socket bone of a stag 400.00

3'' x 5'', late 19th century, leather, reptile, with shakudo and fold dragon clasp signed on back, containing finely cut tobacco, en suite with agate ojime bead and finely woven kiseru-zutsu with gold trim   500.00

3'' x 5'', late 19th century, leather, worn, some gilt remaining, crab clasp signed on back, with bone ojime bead 375.00

late 19th century, brocade cloth, with overall design of Kabuki characters, silver dragon clasp, together with netsuke, manju type, ivory owl and silver disk showing carved shi-shi, the netsuke attached to pouch with multiple chains 1,500.00

4'' x 4½'', circa 1850, leather, drawstring type, unadorned, rustic style, together with an agate ojime bead and a wood netsuke, Manju style with a dragon carved on one side, brass trim 350.00

Box, 4½'' l., mid 19th century, carved red lacquer on wood, dragon draped around bottom, brass fittings on lid opening on back, en suite with lacquer ojime and lacquered manju netsuke. $1,300.00

Pouch, 4'' w., late 19th century, tooled leather, silver dragon-form clasp, kagamibuta netsuke with ivory bowl and silver disk of repoussé dragon. $475.00

TWENTIETH CENTURY JAPANESE PORCELAIN

Included here are Geisha Girl porcelain, Made in Japan, Occupied Japan, and Phoenix Bird chinaware.

Introduction: Twentieth-century mass-produced collectibles in all fields and of all origins, including Orientalia and Americana, have enjoyed a resurgence of popularity over the past ten years. The decrease in availability of antiques (literally those items with an age equal to or exceeding 100 years) makes it more difficult to amass a collection, and the accompanying price increases mean antiques are affordable only to a relative few. Today's collectors, in turning to items more abundant in the marketplace and within reach of their pocketbooks, have found items reminiscent of the heydays of their parents, grandparents, or their own early childhood appealing. These items bear value not only due to sentiment but because, for the most part and aside from any current reproductions, they are not being made in their original form or of their original quality. These collectibles are diverse enough to provide a wealth of opportunity for enthusiasts, allowing them to specialize in favored areas or explore a wide swath of history.

Within the field of Orientalia, certain categories of Japanese collectibles have developed an ardent following. Not only are these collected wares known for their beauty and quality but they have other traits that have endeared them to large segments of the collecting populous. Nippon wares, covered elsewhere in this volume, and the Occupied Japan products detailed below are noted for their time stamp. It is verifiable that marked Nippon wares were produced in Japan between 1891 and early 1920. Wares marked Occupied Japan were manufactured during the years succeeding World War II (1945–1952). Alternatively, Geisha Girl Porcelain is known for its colorful depiction of the kimono-clad Japanese ladies in scenes of premodern Japanese life. Phoenix ware is loved for its classical underglaze blue and white depiction of the many-tailed ho-o bird of Japanese lore. Other twentieth-century collectibles, including moriage, Noritake, and Kutani wares (also predates this period) are detailed elsewhere in this volume. And, of course, there are the "Made in Japan" wares—a wide array of styles and forms produced after the Nippon period, which don't necessarily fall under any categorizable heading but, even so, have found a small niche in the marketplace.

What do all these collectibles have in common, besides their Japanese heritage? They were all mass produced in the twentieth century. Mass production implies volume produced under more or less automated procedures. It does not mean that all these items were machine reproduced or decorated. To the contrary, many of these wares were the result of small cottage industries which relied heavily on human labor. It is important to understand that the collectibles considered here were made for export, i.e., they were made with Western tastes and utility in mind even though many bear designs that are Oriental in nature. The intended consumers were not the Japanese; rather the china was shipped to other countries, including America, England, Germany, and Switzerland. On Japanese soil, these pieces were sold in gift and military shops catering to foreign trade.

What follows are detailed descriptions and exemplary items of some of the popular twentieth-century Japanese porcelain collectibles. (See: Kutani; Nippon; Noritake; Satsuma.)

Advisor: Elyce Litts

GEISHA GIRL PORCELAIN

History: Geisha Girl porcelain is a Japanese export ware the production of which commenced during the last quarter of the nineteenth century and continued heavily until World War II. Production waned during the occupational period and proceeded on a very limited basis until the mid-1980s. There are significant differences between the prewar and postwar wares (see: Reproduction Alert).

Geisha Girl porcelain features kimono-clad women and children amid Japanese gardens and temples. There are almost 300 brightly enameled pattern variations depicting premodern Japanese life. These patterns, or scenes, explore all manner of topics, including Japanese mythological characters, bicycle races, child's play, flower arranging, and the West's influence on Japan.

Geisha ware may be completely hand-painted, hand-painted over a stenciled outline, or occasionally, decaled. The stenciled underlying design is usually red-orange but is also found in brown and black and rarely green.

All Geisha Girl items are bordered by one or a combination of the following colors: blues, reds, greens, rhubarb, yellow, black, brown, and gold. The most common is red-orange. Borders may be wavy, scalloped, or banded and range from $\frac{1}{16}$" to $\frac{1}{4}$" thickness. The borders themselves are often further decorated with gold, white, or yellow lacings and flowers, dots, or stripes. Some examples even display interior frames of butterflies or flowers.

Geisha Girl ware is found in many forms, including tea, cocoa, lunch, and children's sets; dresser items; vases; and serving dishes. The diversity of Geisha ware is due in part to the more than 150 known manufacturers of Geisha Girl porcelain. Some collectors prefer to accumulate a single pattern, while others may concentrate on a particular border color.

References: Elyce Litts, *Collector's Encyclopedia of Geisha Girl Porcelain*, Collector Books, 1988; *Geisha Girl Porcelain Newsletter* (1982–1990), P. O. Box 394, Morris Plains, NJ 07950.

Reproduction Alert: Geisha Girl porcelain produced after World War II generally had a red-orange border without gold embellishment, although a set of demitasse cups and saucers was produced, each bearing a different border color, including green, blue, and black. Modern porcelain bodies are a pure, smooth white when compared with the rougher, grey bisque of older items. Coloring and detail of modern items are sparse, and use of gold is almost nonexistent. Examples with a blue underlying stencil are believed to be from the postwar period. Reproduced items include a three-piece dresser set (hair receiver, powder jar, and tray), tea and sake sets, toothbrush holder, table plates, and small vases.

Several Geisha-style tea items with decal-applied designs were made in Czechoslovakia. Faces on these items will look more European than Oriental, and the overall effect is often more Chinese than Japanese. The base may have an unusually large pseudo-Japanese mark, occasionally accompanied by a Czechoslovakian factory mark.

Collecting Hints: Tea wares, hair receivers, and powder jars are the commonly found forms. Dinner plates, large platters, candlesticks, and mugs are difficult to locate. Souvenir and advertising items are highly desirable. Buy only good to mint condition examples.

Advisor: Elyce Litts

MADE IN JAPAN

History: Made in Japan generally references the post-Nippon period, after 1921. The U.S. government had decided that *Nippon* was a Japanese word and that imported wares had to be marked in the English language, thus the birth of the phrase "Made in Japan." It appeared as a backstamp, impression, or label and might have been accompanied by a handwritten signature, a Japanese trademark, or the name of the Occidental importing company.

Except for the time frame, Made in Japan wares has no succinct description. Made in Japan wares included the same types of ware that had been produced during earlier periods: hand-painted Nippon-style items, Geisha Girl, Phoenix Bird, Noritake, and moriage, Satsuma look-alikes, and Kutani productions. They included deco-styled pieces which became the rage in the 1940's, luster wares, replications of American 1950s dinnerware, and imitation English and Italian wares, for example, ceramic house teapots and faux majolica. The forms were endless—a virtually infinite list, ranging from dinner and tea wares to decorative wares to figurines and lamps.

Reproduction Alert: Since the Made in Japan period includes modern-day items, collectors should avail themselves of local gift shops to learn what is in current production versus what is fifty to seventy years old. Many recently produced Made in Japan items find their way into antiques and collectible markets.

Collecting Hints: Collectors should pay particular attention to quality. Because of the relative lack of age and large volume production of these items, only excellent to mint condition items should be purchased. There is no specific or generic "hot" category within the Made in Japan arena; the most popular collectibles from or spanning this period have a dedicated section in this volume.

Advisor: Elyce Litts

OCCUPIED JAPAN

History: Of utmost importance to the Japanese after World War II was the revitalization of their economy. One of the most logical means to that end was the restoration of the many porcelain manufacturing centers to their former rate and quality of production. With aid from the United States, the recovery was initiated and Japan began to turn out all imaginable forms of china for sale to U.S. personnel stationed in Japan and for export to the United States and other countries. From 1945 to 1952, while U.S. forces held sway in Japan, porcelain wares were, by law, supposed to have been marked Made in Occupied Japan, Occupied Japan, Made in Japan, or Japan. Only those items marked Occupied Japan or Made in Occupied Japan are sought by collectors as memorabilia verifiable from this period. These attributions may be accompanied by factory trademarks or Japanese artisan signatures.

Occupied Japan cup and saucer sets and figurines are the most well-known of the offerings, but all manner of dinnerware, vases, miniatures, ashtrays, souvenir items, lamps, and so forth can be found.

Reference: Gene Florence, *The Collector's Encyclopedia of Occupied Japan Collectibles*, Collector Books, 1982.

Reproduction Alert: Watch for overglaze marks that wash off or smear when rubbed with your finger; these are fake marks added to modern wares. Look for quality. Japan worked hard to bring its production up to par, but lack of available resources lead to some wares which were not of top quality. Condition is also of vital importance when considering value.

Collecting Hints: While the focus of this article has been Occupied Japan porcelain, the reader should be aware that other Occupied Japan items, including dolls, metals, and toys are highly collectible. According to the trade press, a March 1990 Christies's auction garnered $9,680 for a celluloid toy of Mickey Mouse riding Pluto Pup, marked Occupied Japan.

Collector's Clubs: Occupied Japan Collectors Club, 18309 Faysmith Avenue, Torrance, CA 90504; O.J. Club, 29 Freeborn St., Newport, RI 02840.

Advisor: Elyse Litts

PHOENIX BIRD CHINAWARE

History: Phoenix Bird is a blue and white porcelain dinnerware pattern dating to the early 1900s. The phoenix is a mythical bird of Egyptian culture that, according to legend, lived in the Arabian desert for 500 to 600 years and consumed itself in fire; it then arose renewed from the ashes to start another long life. The phoenix remains a symbol of immortality and spiritual rebirth. To the Japanese, it is an emblem of wise and good government and good fortune; a symbol of energy; and a harbinger of happiness, friendship, and affection. The phoenix was proudly adopted as the crest of the Japanese empress. It is this crest that provides the Phoenix Bird pattern's main motif. The secondary motifs are the Mikado's two crests—the underside of a chrysanthemum (kiku, in Japanese) and the three leaves and blossoms of the *Paulownia imperialis*, or kiri. A meandering vine and its leaves (kara kusa grass) completes the pattern.

The term Phoenix Bird is used to describe one of five unique but similar patterns, each of which includes a particular style of phoenix. The other four are named Flying Turkey, Flying Dragon, Howo (Bird of Paradise), and Twin Phoenix. The majority of Phoenix Bird patterns carry the cloud/mountain border, which looks like a blue horseshoe with a blue bar between each shoe. The rest carry a blue border the inside edge of which resembles the top part of a heart; each heart has a blue circle in its center. The latter border, borrowed from the Flying Turkey pattern, is called Ho-o. It is referenced in *The History of Exporting Pottery of Japan* as "representative [of an] exporting item in the ending decade of the Meiji era (1868–1912) and is called Sometsuke Ho-o."

The earliest documentation concerning Phoenix Bird has been found in the 1914 and 1916 catalogs of A. A. Vantine, Inc. of New York. One page from each of its catalogs lists from thirty-five to sixty-five pieces of the pattern. Some of the dishes speak for themselves, however, by being marked Nippon. In 1921, a catalog by one of the pattern's makers—Morimura Brothers, Inc. of New York—listed some eighty pieces in the Howo and Flying Dragon patterns, pricing them

by the dozen for wholesale to various stores and restaurants. Both patterns were listed as stock number 228. The patterns were intermixed in the lots; thus a customer ordering stock number 228 could have received either or both patterns.

Phoenix Bird came in diverse body thicknesses, from eggshell thin to restaurant weight; in varied quality of workmanship, from placement of transfer print to the exceptional hand-painted piece; and in an array of forms, plain edge versus scalloped edge, for example. This is due, in part, to the large number of manufacturers of Phoenix Bird. Over 100 backstamps have been cataloged to date. The most common are the Morimura M in Wreath or concave M within crossed stems, Tashiro Shoten's petaled flower with T in the stamen, and "Made in Japan."

A select number of pieces were made during the occupation of Japan, mostly cups and saucers for tea or coffee. There are two different styles of coffee sets which carry the Occupied Japan marking. Child-size cups and saucers are occasionally found as well.

References: J. C Oates, *Phoenix Bird Chinaware* Books I, II, III, and IV, published by the author; *Phoenix Bird Discoveries Newsletter*, J. C. Oates, 5912 Kingsfield, West Bloomfield, MI 48322

Reproduction Alert: Around 1936 the English company Myott and Son produced Phoenix Bird earthenware, calling and marking it Satsuma. The blue designs are not as intense as the Japanese-produced version and the pieces are not as varied in shape.

The Phoenix Bird patterns continue in production today on china, glass, and other accessories. Approximately thirty shapes are known to have been produced since the late 1960s, the most prevalent is ginger jars. These came with paper labels, but no backstamps. The blue is very harsh and the background is milk white. The vinework is less profusive on later items, especially near the bottom of demicups and ginger jars. From 1975 to 1978, a few ginger and temple jars as well as three styles of coffee mugs were produced using a grey speckled pottery ware. A mustard yellow paint has been noted on some of the post-1970 ginger jars. The blue line border has been made up into a tea set of small plates, sugar, creamer, and possibly a teapot.

Collecting Hints: Ho-o bird bordered examples are coveted because the pieces are less abundant than those with the standard Phoenix Bird border. Rarely found in Phoenix Bird are items in green and white, which might also have a bit of gold leaf embellishment. (One should not confuse these rarities with the green and white Flying Dragon patterned items which are as prevalent in green as they are in blue. In addition to the standard Phoenix Bird motifs, the Flying Dragon variant has a pinwheel design and varied border as its own distinction.) A minority of extant examples also include items with a simple, solid blue or green line border with multicolored designs; mosaic-style design in lieu of vinework; an orange line border overlaid with yellow designs; a border of small circles, and in reserve with a Geisha Girl Porcelain pattern.

Advisor: Joan Collet Oates

GEISHA GIRL PORCELAIN

Biscuit Jar, Vantines Blue, pale blue, Vantines stamp mark	55.00
Candlestick, 6½″, Lantern A, red, Kutani mark	75.00
Cocoa Pot, 6½″, Basket A, light apple green	45.00
Creamer and Sugar	
Bulbous, Parasol C, red	18.00
Fluted, Silhouette of ho-o bird	35.00
Cup and Saucer Sets	
Boullion, with lid and saucer, Mother and Son C, pattern in reserve on beige ground, allover decor of mums, coins	55.00
Demitasse, Carp A, apple green with red	15.00
Tea, Elegance in Motion, Paulownia Blossom mark	23.00
Tea, Child Reaching for Butterfly, red	4.00
Hair Receiver, Garden Bench C, apple green	25.00
Matchholder	
Hanging, Parasol C, red	35.00
Round from smoke set, Parasol C, red	10.00
Mug, Parasol C, red	45.00
Nappy, leaf shape, 7″ x 5½″, Parasol D, multi-color	25.00
Pin Tray	
Geisha in Sampan B, multicolor zigzag border	14.00
Pitcher, 2″, Garden Bench B, red	12.00

Serving Platter, 8¾″, Gardening pattern, blue-green border, $35.00

Plate	
9¾″, scallop fluted, Battledore, apple green	35.00
6″, scallop fluted, Geisha Dance, cobalt blue	14.00
Ring Tree, Flower Gathering B, red border, stem and hooks	35.00
Salad Set, 10¼″ master, five individual bowls, So Big, multicolor border . . .	110.00
Sugar Bowl, Rendevous pattern, multicolor border	25.00
Sweetmeat Set, Torii, orange luster, ship trademark, in laquer box	55.00
Toothpick, Courtesan Lady, red with roses	12.00

MADE IN JAPAN

Figure, beaver chewing pencil	4.00
Lamp Base, Satsuma style, horse drawn coach	39.00
Luncheon Set, service for eight complete, red ground with gold dragons and border design	425.00
Matchholder	
3″ h. x 4″ w., form of seated girl . . .	19.00

Hatpin Holder, Long Stemmed Peony pattern, cobalt blue with gold, $45.00

Teapot, 6″, footed, Battledore pattern, apple green and gold, $50.00

Liquor decanter, porcelain, screen-printed multicolor scene of Mt. Fuji one one side, boat caught in waves on other side, both from Hokusai prints, decoration, plastic cap, $10.00

Deco, wide mouthed bird with outspread wings	20.00
Pincushion, small lion	8.00
Pitcher, 4", cream color crackle ware with hand painted flowers, signed Kinkozan	45.00
Sake Set, whistling pitcher, six cups, gray moriage dragon on white ground, Geisha lithophane in cups	65.00
Sugar and Creamer, 4", form of Dutch girl and boy	40.00
Teapot	
Deco form, luster ground with bluebird decor	10.00
House shape, majolica style	25.00
Satsuma style, dragon spout, elephants molded in relief on body, green ground, moriage trees	40.00
Urn, lidded, cobalt ground with floral design, brass mounted base and neck handle attachment of Greek key design	55.00
Wallpocket, deep brown tree bark-type finish with red flowers	12.00

Salt and Pepper Shakers and Spoon Rest, gold decoration on cream ground, $12.00

Tea Cozy with tray, nested, black and red on off-white ground, $20.00

Vase, 4", bulbous, Sumida style with poorly defined figures	25.00

OCCUPIED JAPAN

Cup and Saucer Set

Coffee, cream ground, red roses	16.00
Tea, Blue Willow pattern	12.00
Tea, white ground, violet decor	22.00
Miniature, moriage dragon, grey ground	8.00
Demitasse Set, 15 piece (pot, creamer, sugar, six cups/saucers), cream ground, floral decor	55.00
Figurines	
Boy with sack slung over shoulder, 5"	12.00
Cherub playing violin, 3"	6.00
Colonial man and woman, 7", pair	25.00
Hummel reproduction, Well Done	19.00
Oriental man and woman, 8" pair	28.00
Woman playing cello, 3¼"	10.00
Lamp, 8", figural, colonial man and woman	30.00
Matchholder, double hanging, man and woman holding baskets	35.00
Mug, Toby, 3¼"	14.00
Planter, donkey cart	15.00
Planter, boy seated by tree trunk	12.00

Vase, 7¾", yellow ground with gold and pink floral and vine decor surrounding portrait of Oriental lady, $35.00

Ashtray, 2¾″ h. x 4″ w., art deco style cat of white, tan, orange, and black, yellow luster tray with blue luster border, $7.00

Planter, 4″, Hummel look-alike, $10.00

Left, post-1970 flowerpot, 4½″ h. x 4½″ dia., without traditional border design, $22.50; right, post-1970 utility or florist's bowl, 6½″ dia. x 2¾″ h. $20.00. Also available in 7½″ dia. x 3″ h. size, $22.50

Child's playtime tea set #2, one of six different styles available, $80

Salt and Pepper shakers, figural deer,
   seated **10.00**
Teapot, 5″, clay with brown glaze and
   floral designed front panel **37.00**
Tea set
   Child's, floral design, original box   **65.00**
   Figural cottage, 3 piece (pot,
     creamer, sugar). **48.00**
   Tomato shape, 13 piece (pot,
     creamer, sugar, five cups/saucers)   **65.00**
Umbrella Stand, green and yellow bor-
   ders, floral and bird design **150.00**
Vase
   Cherub sitting on book attached to
     bud vase, 3″ **12.00**
   Vase, fluted with bunnies at base, 3″   **8.00**

PHOENIX BIRD

Bowl
   Cereal, 6″ dia. **15.00**
   Fruit, large, round. **55.00**
   Soup, 7¼″ **40.00**
Cup and Saucer
   Boullion **22.00**
   Child's **18.00**
   Tea/Coffee **9.00**
Chocolate Cup **18.00**

Coffee mugs of pottery weight, circa 1975–1978. *Left:* dark blue designs on grey ground; *center:* blue designs on white ground; *right:* brown designs on white ground. All have brown rims and handles and brown flecks throughout, $10

Water tankard, 6½" h. x 6" dia. with average size, traditional border. $110

Chocolate Pot, scalloped base.......	**125.00**
Custard Cup, 5 oz................	**15.00**
Eggcup, double size..............	**15.00**
Gravy boat and underplate	**65.00**
Muffineer.....................	**125.00**
Pancake Server, covered	**145.00**
Plate	
Bread and butter, 6"............	**6.00**
Dessert, 7¼"..................	**9.00**
Dinner, 9¾"	**45.00**
Luncheon, 8½"	**15.00**
Platter	
12½" x 8¾"	**48.00**
14½" x 10"	**75.00**
Ramekin with underplate..........	**38.00**
Shortcake Dish..................	**25.00**
Teapot, medium.................	**45.00**
Tile, 6" dia.	**45.00**
Vegetable Tureen with cover.......	**95.00**

WOODBLOCK PRINTS (UKIYO-E)—EARLY

History: The decline of the medieval feudal society in Japan began at the onset of the Edo Period (1615–1868). Educational developments and changes in popular culture resulted in diminished emphasis on agriculture as the source of income for the samurai (warrior) class. The old rural culture of the farmers gave way to a new urban focus. The life and needs of city people gave rise to a new culture. Development of a different economic system was associated with enhanced social status of the urban merchants. In essence, the burgeoning of a respected middle class was a vital factor in the flowering of intellectual activity. The increase in prosperity and heightened social status of the merchants led to a remarkable increase in the urban population, unavoidably accompanied by development of intellectual, artistic, and hedonistic goals and pursuits. (Many of the terms that will be used in this section are defined in Appendix IV.)

As Jenaga states in *Japanese Art: A Cultural Appreciation*, "In the arts, Sarugaku Noh and the painting style of the Kano School, both of which enjoyed the protection and patronage of the military class, lost vitality and merely repeated and preserved old traditions. Furthermore, given the restrictions imposed on them by Confucianism, the Samurai code, the formalities and ceremonies of feudal morality and demands for suppression of emotions, it is scarcely to be wondered that the warriors lost the ability to contribute to the development of the arts." As a result, cultural leadership became centered in the town, and an age of remarkable artistic development ensued, the peak of which appeared in the Genroku era (1688–1704). In the words of Richard Lane in *Images from the Floating World*, "Ukiyo-e represents a unique development in Japanese art. A great renaissance based upon a largely popular foundation, whereas the earlier pinnacles of Japanese civilization had been due primarily to the aristocracy, the Samurai or the priesthood."

A number of art forms were created and began to mature at this time, including haiku (poetic form); genre literature (ukiyo-zoshi), which ultimately developed into a way of depicting the realities of the new urban world; puppet drama (ningyo-joruri); kabuki drama; and finally, ukiyo-e paintings and woodblock prints. Ukiyo-e have been defined as "pictures of the floating world" and "pictures of popular manners and mores."

What did the expression *floating world* really mean to the people of the period? Richard Lane answered this question in a most insightful and expressive way in *Images from the Floating World*: "It is rare to find a single term that expresses the changing concept of an age, but ukiyo-e is such a term. In medieval Japan it appeared as a Buddhist expression which connoted first 'this world of pain,' with the derived sense of 'this transient, unreliable world.' Thus, etymologically it meant, 'this fleeting, floating world.' But for the newly liberated townsman of the seventeenth-century Japanese Renaissance, 'floating world' tended to lose its connotations of the transitory world of illusion and to take on hedonistic implications. It denoted the newly evolved, stylish world of pleasure, the world of easy women and handsome actors; all the varied pleasures of the flesh. The novelist Ryoi, in his Ukiyo monogatari (*Tales of the Floating World*), ca. 1661, gives his own apt description of this concept; 'Living only for the moment, turning our full attention to the pleasures of the moon, the snow, the cherry blossoms and the maple leaves; singing songs, drinking wine, diverting ourselves in just floating, floating; caring not a whit for the pauperism staring us in the face, refusing to be disheartened like a gourd floating along with the river current: this is what we call the floating world. . . .'

By the time the suffix -e (meaning pictures) had been added, around the year 1680, to form the new compound ukiyo-e (floating-world pictures), this hedonistic significance had become predominant. Thus ukiyo-e meant something like the following to the Japanese of the age that engendered it: a new style of pictures, very much in vogue, devoted to depicting everyday life; particularly fair women and handsome men indulging in pleasure, or part of the world of pleasure pictures, as often as not, of an erotic nature."

The ukiyo-e style was, in a sense, originated by Hishikawa Moronobu in 1681. Following some works of earlier yamato-e painters and artists of the Kano school, great interest was shown in ordinary ways of life among the townspeople, including depiction of beautiful women, courtesans, and prostitutes; actors; wrestlers; and so on. The woodblock print's popularity arose out of this subject matter, plus the fact that the prints were cheap, easy to obtain, and could be produced in fairly large numbers. The first ukiyo-e prints were monochrome (black ink). Later on the polychrome print appeared.

Awareness of the existence of Japanese woodblock prints in the United States was one result of Commodore Perry's expeditions of 1853 and 1854. Perry brought back fine examples of prints by Hiroshige and others. And, as part of the account of his mission, U.S. Congress released the first color reproductions of ukiyo-e prints to appear outside of Japan. Within a few years of their appearance in the West, ukiyo-es were to become an important influence on the work of artists around the world.

One of the first artists to discover ukiyo-e prints was Whistler, followed shortly after by a large group, including Monet, Degas, van Gogh, Gauguin, Toulouse-Lautrec, Cassatt, and others. As Munsterberg points out in The Japanese Print: A Historical Guide, they admired and often imitated "the sense of design exhibited by the great Japanese printmakers, their emphasis on two-dimensional space, their strong feeling for decorative pattern, the boldness of their composition, their clearly defined forms and their subtle colors." It has been suggested that the peak of the outstanding French contribution to the art of the poster (in the 1880s and 1890s) was the result of Japanese influence.

It is interesting to take a moment to look at the origin of woodblock printmaking. Printmaking began in China as a manifestation of Buddhism; printed sheets of inscriptions date back to the Nara Period in Japan (646–794), although existing prints date back only to the Heian Period (794–1185). According to Munsterberg, the oldest surviving printed images are dated to 1162. Most of the remaining examples are from the Kamakura period (1185–1333). The images of Bud-

dhist and Shinto deities were supposed to bring good luck, ward off evil, and help the dead enter paradise. Such prints are still being sold today. Although of interest (and old ones are sought after by museums), they are not of the quality of later Edo period (1615–1868) prints. Both technically and conceptually, later ukiyo-es are related to the early black and white prints. Munsterberg (in The Japanese Print) stressed, for example, the "vivacious genre scenes" printed on a set of fans during the Heian period, "as a landmark in the development of wood-block printing, which foreshadows the kind of genre prints depicting scenes from ordinary Japanese life that were to be the most characteristic subject matter of the prints of the ukiyo-e school."

Gradually the meaning of ukiyo shifted from its original Buddhist sense of the fleeting secular world, to the (in the Edo period) floating world of pleasure. In 1680 the word ukiyo-e appeared and became the definitive term of reference for this school over the following 200 years. This school thus developed not only out of cultural factors but also as the unique progeny of the combined creations of the Kano, Tosa, and Yamato-e schools of painting as well as those of the illustrated book— in particular the erotic pillow books which appeared in 1660.

The first prints considered to be definitive ukiyo-e were produced by Hishikawa Moronobu. Although his first dated print was in 1672, most of his great work appeared during the 1680s. His genius was largely responsible for the founding of the ukiyo-e school of printmaking. He was intrigued by the people and life of the Yoshiwara, and created numerous erotic scenes (termed spring pictures, or shunga) as well as depictions of courtesans and their lovers. All the prints were done in black and white. Moronobu died in 1694. None of his followers, including Morofusa (his son), Moronaga (his son-in-law), and Moroshige (his best pupil), could produce prints of equal quality to his. Only one, Sugimura Jihei, became outstanding and has been considered by some to be as brilliant.

The influence of Moronobu continued into the eighteenth century, as reflected by the work of Kiyonobu, Kiyomasu, Masanobu, and Kaige-tsudo.

The number of artists from the beginning of ukiyo-e to the Meiji period totals between 600 and 700. Those of major interest, however, are only about half that many or less. The art can, in general, be chronologically divided into several periods: (1) the primitives, from the founding of the school by Moronobu and Matabei to the appearance of the color print at the time of Harunobu (circa 1765); (2) from 1765 to the death of Utamaro in 1806; (3) the period from 1806 to 1825; and (4) the period from 1825 to 1860, after which the art seemed to decline, regaining some of its former glory only with the appearance of the

Masanobu, 21⅞″ x 12¼″, a sumizuri-e depicting a young man seated on the veranda of a house, playing the shakuhachi, a landscape beyond, kakemono-e, signed Okimura Masanobu-ga, sealed Masanobu, published by Igaya

Harunobu, 10¾″ x 8¼″, the teahouse beauty Osen at the Kagiya Teahouse at the gate of the Kasamori Shrine, offering a cup of tea to the rival beauty Ofuji, who in turn offers Osen a wrapper of toothbrushes from her father's shop, chuban, Motoyanagiya, signed Harunobu-ga

masters of landscape, Hokusai and Hiroshige. (In the next section of this book there is some discussion of the resurgence of the art in the twentieth century.) The period from 1765 to 1860 yielded the color print at its best.

Following the early shunga and prints of courtesans, the most popular subjects included scenes of Kabuki theater, actors, beautiful women, mythological and legendary figures, and ultimately landscapes. We do not have the space, in the present volume, to dwell at any length on all these topics and the many artists depicting them. However, certain major steps in the development of the art and the important contributions of some of the most outstanding artists cannot go without specific mention. Particular note will be taken of those principal artists with whose work collectors most often will be involved.

Following Moronobu and Matabei, major interest focuses on Torii Kiyonobu (1664–1729) and the Torii school he founded, which was primarily concerned with theatrical subjects. His contribution was continued by Kiyomasu (1679–1762) and his son Kiyomitsu (1735–1785), whose work bridged the period between the two-color and polychrome print originated by Suzuki Harunobu (1725–1770).

Kiyomine, the fifth leader of the school, sometimes used the signature Kiyomitsu. His work is clearly different, however, since he used all the color available at his time. A third Kiyomitsu (actually Kiyofusa) died in 1892. There is, on occasion, some confusion as to whether a particular work is that of Kiyonobu or Kiyomasu. The works of the latter are all printed black and white (sumizuro-e), although hand coloring was added in many cases. In the words of Munsterberg (in The Japanese Print), "Kiyonobu towers above most of his later followers in the boldness of his lines, the strength of his designs and the grandeur of his conceptions. . . . He is today regarded as one of the greatest and most influential of all ukiyo-e artists." A number of followers used the same names; in fact, as many as five took over the Kiyonobu signature. Their work is never of the same quality.

The next great steps are associated with Masanobu and Harunobu. Before their contributions, however, mention must be made of the most outstanding images of the courtesans of the Genroku period: the work of Kaigetsudo Ando (1671–1743) and his school. Although he confined himself to painting and the prints were by his followers, today the prints are considered more valuable than the paintings. The prints were by three artists: Anohi, Doshin, and Dohan. Only forty-three of their prints still exist—their rarity being responsible for the high prices they command. These works are particularly remarkable for the beauty of the kimono designs.

The work of Orumura Masanobu (1686–1764) occupied most of the period during which the print changed from black and white (sumizuri-e) to the color prints of the benizuri-e type. He produced hashira-e as well as urushi-e and uki-e. The colors were predominantly rose-pink and a green derived from the initial washing of verdigris. Up to four colors were being used by the late 1750s. Other great printmakers of this period include Nishimura Shigenaga and Ishikawa Toyonobu (1711–1785).

Full development of the multicolored print dates from 1765, with the appearance of the first polychrome prints (nishiki-e), created by Suzuki Harunobu (circa 1725–1770). He was one of the giants of the art, and it is not actually known how many prints he made, in part because others such as Harushige (later known as Shiba Kokan) and Koryusai signed his name to their prints to enhance their own reputations. Nonetheless, his output was amazingly large. His work is noted for its charm and poetic sensitivity. It is vital, in forming a collection, to beware of modern (late nineteenth- and twentieth-century) forgeries of Harunobu's work. It is essential to be critical about the quality of the colors; compare the piece with a print of undoubted authenticity. The condition is of prime importance; changes in color can be much more detrimental than in prints of less sensitivity and refinement.

One of the most important of Harunobu's contemporaries was Katsukawa Shunsho (1726–1792) whose Kabuki prints have been thought by many to be the most outstanding of their type. Perhaps the greatest contribution of his talent was the introduction of a quality of realism; for example, actors were depicted as recognizable personalities—as human beings. He also portrayed courtesans, sumo wrestlers, and shunga. He had many followers, including Shunko, Shun'ei, Shuncho, and Shunro (known as Hokusai).

Shunko's major contribution was the okube-e (big head or close-up portrait), developed later by Sharaku.

Between the time of Harunobu's death and that of Kiyonaga, the Kitao school flourished and a marked change in the style of bijin-ga. For the first time women were depicted not as fantasies, but as the average Japanese woman in the street.

The major figure in the 1780s was Torii Kiyonaga (1752–1815), the last of the Torii school. Technically, he developed the form of the triptych printed from three full-size sheets. He also changed, once more, the representation of female beauty. His women were neither frail (like Harunobu) nor earthy (like Shigemasa). Some authors have compared his portrayals with those of Greek goddesses—a combination of fantasy and reality, resulting in what has been described as a "classic perfection." Kiyonaga's prints are rare and in great demand.

Although he had several followers (including Shuncho and Shunman), Utagawa Toyoharu (1733–1814) was most notable as the originator of pure landscape in ukiyo-e. One of his pupils (Toyohiro) trained Hiroshige and others (Toyokuni and his followers) helped to move ukiyo-e into the modern era.

With the retirement of Kiyonaga comes the period of the great master Utamaro (1754–1806). His figure studies made his early work famous. His later prints were marked by certain anatomical exaggerations, regarded by many as a decline in quality. His style is well described by von Seidlitz (in *History of Japanese Color Prints*): "He created an absolutely new type of female beauty. At first he was content to draw the head in normal proportions and quite definitely round in shape; only the neck on which this head was posed was already notably slender. . . . Towards the middle of the tenth decade these exaggerated proportions

Sharaku, 15″ x 10″, an okubi-e portrait of the actor Sakata Hangoro III in the role of the villain Fujikawa Mizuemon, from the plan Hana-ayame bunroku Soga, oban tate-e, signed Toshusai Sharaku-ga and published by Tsutaya Juzaburo, Kiwame seal

Utamaro, 15″ x 9⅞″, circa 1791, woman adjusting her sidelock in a mirror, from the series Sugatami Shichinin gesho, Seven Women Making up with a Mirror, oban tate-e, signed Utamaro-ga and published by Tsutaya Juzaburo, Kiwame seal

of the body had reached such an extreme that the heads were twice as long as they were broad, set upon slim, long necks, which in turn swayed upon very narrow shoulders; the upper coiffure bulged out to such a degree that it almost surpassed the head itself in extent; the eyes were indicated by short slits, and were separated by an inordinately long nose from an infinitesimally small mouth; the soft robes hung loosely about figures of an almost unearthly thinness." It is of uncommon interest to consider the possibility that this radically different vision of Utamaro's was purposeful and remarkably creative. It could have evolved from the more classical view, such as did Picasso's later work, and ultimately exerted a marked influence on other artists and sculptors such as Madigliani and Marini.

Somewhat later these differences became even more accentuated. The degree of exaggeration helps to distinguish his early from his late work, as does the form of his signature. As pointed out by Stewart in *A Guide to Japanese Prints*, in the early period the signature "is small, compact and carefully written; in the later it tends to sprawl, is written larger, and the character for 'uta' is finished off with a long tail." The latter style also appears on work of his pupils. A great many forgeries were produced by lesser artists of the time, ultimately leading him to sign some of his prints "the real Utamaro" (Shomei Utamaro). Both Toyokuni and Eizan were responsible for some of these fakes, as was Utamaro's pupil Koikawa Shuncho, who upon Utamaro's death married his widow and assumed his name (Utamaro II).

Some of his most talented contemporaries and followers were Chobunsai Eishi, Kikugawa Eizan, Keisai Eisen, and Eishosai Choki. The most influential of the group was Utagawa Toyokuni (who himself was influenced by Sharaku, an artist about whom little is known). His bijin-ga have been very important to collectors, as well as his early Kabuki prints. His late work, however, was of much lesser quality. He was of great importance as a teacher; among his students were Toyokuni II, Kuniyoshi, and Kunisada (1785–1864)—also called Toyokuni III. Toyokuni's fellow student Toyohiro was also an important teacher; his outstanding pupil was Hiroshige, who with Hokusai became one of the greatest masters of the landscape.

Although Kunisada produced an enormous amount of work, most of it was not considered of the finest quality demanded in the eighteenth century. Because of the quantity, however, he was looked on as the head of the Toyokuni school, despite the superior artistry of Kuniyoshi (1798–1861). The latter's fame resulted from a number of series, the most important of which dealt with heroic events in Japanese history and legends.

Space does not permit discussion of their many

pupils. Many of the names can be recognized by the use of syllables taken from the name of the teacher: Kuniyasu, Kunimasa, Sadahide, Sadamasu, and so on. Kuniyoshi's pupils all started their names with *yoshi:* yoshi-tora, yoshi-kuni, and yoshitoshi. The Osaka school was formed in 1825 by the pupils of Kunisada and Hokusai. It was the first time print making emanated from a place other than Edo.

With the death of Utamaro, artists began to seek subjects other than bijin-ga, and landscape became the predominant theme of the period. The artist most responsible for the flowering of the landscape print was Katsushika Hokusai (1760–1840). In discussing his place in the art of Japan, Munsterberg (in *The Japanese Print*) quotes Nuneshige Narazaki as saying, "Hokusai stands alone among the artists of ukiyo-e. No other artist can be compared with him. He called himself Sori from age thirty-six to thirty-nine, and around this time he succeeded in blending three styles—Japanese, Chinese and Western—into one unified individual, and highly personal style. From that time on he became the most famous ukiyo-e artist of the time." Working over a period of seventy years, he produced an astonishing number of prints, paintings, drawings, and illustrated books, and used thirty-one different artist names over the years. His masterpieces include fifteen volumes of sketchbooks, called *Manga*, that depict every aspect of Japanese life and, especially, a number of series, including "The Thirty-Six Views of Fuji." Furthermore, as so admirably stated by Munsterberg (*The Japanese Print*), "The decorative quality of the Korin School, the narrative emphasis of yamato-e (native style Japanese painting), the brush drawing of the Kano School, the interest in genre scenes reflected in his ukiyo-e background, as well as the greater realism and emphasis on spatial depth derived from Western sources, and the influence of Chinese art, are all

Hokusai: 10⅛″ x 15″, **Kanagawa oki nami-ura, Under the Wave off Kanagawa, from Fugaku Sanjurrokei, The Thirty-six Views of Mt. Fuji series, oban yoko-e, signed Hokusai oratame Jitsu hitsu and published by Eijudo**

found in these magnificent prints." This is the most famous series and early copies in good condition are among the most desirable masterpieces of ukiyo-e. Although most of his famous prints are rare, many reproductions and reprints can be found, and care must be exerted by the collector.

Under the influence of Hokusai, the other great ukiyo-e master of landscape—thought by many to be the most remarkable of the printmakers—began to create prints that had a major influence on Western art. Ando Hiroshige (1797–1858), as no one before him, managed to convey the physical and emotional content of the Japanese landscape. He portrayed nature during different seasons and was preeminent in the depiction of rain, snow, fog, mist, sunrise, sunset, leaves, and trees. The foremost example of this focus of his work (although not the rarest) is the series of prints titled, "The Fifty-Three Stations on the Tokaido" (the road from Edo to Kyoto), published in 1833 and 1834. With the publication of this album, his reputation was established. The most famous print from this series is the one, so often reproduced, of travelers caught in a sudden shower at Shono, with its masterful rendition of mist and rain. Its incredible popularity has led to endless reprints, even today, and consequently, the availability of a large number of prints of inferior quality.

Other series include "The Sixty-Nine Stations on the Kiso Highway" and "One Hundred Views of Famous Places in Edo" (1856–1858). One of the most remarkable of the latter series is "Sudden Shower at Ohashi": the rain, the bridge, and the figures crossing the bridge in the face of the downpour are astonishing.

Numerous other series testify to his incredible talent and sensitivity. Detailed discussion of these works can be found in Stewart's *Guide to Japanese Prints.*

Hiroshige had numerous followers, none of whom were at his level of artistry or productivity,

not even Shigenobu, who married his daughter and assumed the name of Hiroshige II. Later, a second student came to call himself Hiroshige III. The work of neither is of very great consequence.

By the time of Hiroshige III's death in 1894, the Tokugawa era had terminated and the Meiji Period had begun. The work of the ensuing period is the subject of another section of this book. It seems appropriate to conclude this brief outline of ukiyo-e with a quotation from E. F. Strange in reference to the reason why Hiroshige's landscapes have been the basis for the attraction of collectors to these prints. In *Japanese Colour-Prints*, Strange says, "Japanese colour-prints devoted to landscape form a class apart in the art of the world. There is nothing else like them; neither in the highly idealistic and often lovely abstractions of the aristocratic painters of Japan, nor in the more imitative, and, it must be said, more meaningless transcripts, from nature of European artists. The colour-print, as executed by the best men of the Japanese popular school, occupies an intermediate place; perhaps thus furnishing a reason why we Westerners so easily appreciate it. Its imagery and sentiment are elementary in the eyes of the native critic of Japanese high art; its attempts at realism are, in his eyes, more evidence of vulgarity. On the other hand, these very qualities endear it to us. We can understand the first without the long training in symbolism which is the essential of refinement to an educated man of the extreme East. And the other characteristic forms, in our eyes, a leading recommendation. In short, the landscapes of artists such as Hiroshige, approach more nearly to our own standards, and are thus more easily acceptable to us than anything else in the pictorial arts of China and Japan. While they have all the fascination of a strange technique, a bold and undaunted convention, and a superb excellence of composition not too remote, in principal, from our own".

References: Saburo Jenaga, *Japanese Art: A Cultural Appreciation*, Weatherill, 1979; Richard Lane, *Images from the Floating World*, Chartwell Books, Inc., 1978; Hugo Munsterberg, *The Japanese Print: A Historical Guide*, Weatherill, 1988; Muneshige Narazaki, *The Japanese Print: Its Evolution and Essence*, 1966; W. von Seidlitz, *History of Japanese Color Prints*, 1910; Basil Stewart, *A Guide to Japanese Prints*, Dover Press, E. F. Strange, *Japanese Colour-Prints*, 4th ed., Victoria and Albert Museum, 1913.

Museums: Chicago Institute of Art, Chicago, Illinois; Museum of Fine Arts, Boston, Massachusetts; Detroit Institute of Art, Detroit, Michigan; Minneapolis Museum of Art, Minneapolis, Minnesota; Metropolitan Museum of Art, New York, New York; Cincinnati Museum of Art, Cincinnati, Ohio; Toledo Museum of Art, Toledo, Ohio; Seattle Museum of Art, Seattle, Washington; Fukuoka Art Museum, Tokyo, Japan; MOA Museum of Art,

Hiroshige, 9⅛″ x 15¼″, Oi, station forty-seven from the series Kisokaido rokiyukyu no uchi, The Sixty-nine Stations of the Kisokaido, oban yoko-e, signed Hiroshige-ga and published by Hoeido/Kinjudo

Tokyo, Japan; The National Museum of Modern Art, Tokyo, Japan; Tokyo Metropolitan Museum of Art, Tokyo, Japan; Tokyo National Museum, Tokyo, Japan.

Reproduction Alert: There is never a time when even the most celebrated auction houses or dealers can be presumed to be completely reliable, and not infrequently, sources of lesser stature and/or knowledge may mistake reproductions, reprints, or forgeries for originals. In some cases, as with so many human enterprises, simple greed rears its ugly head. Let the collector beware!

The most important factor, of course, is the genuineness of the print. There are prints made during an artist's lifetime, prints made after the woodblocks are no longer in their original condition—made even after the original artist has died, reprints, and reproductions. Reprints are prints taken off the original woodblock, but so late that the outlines are blurred or fuzzy and the colors have deteriorated. Reproductions are copies from a new block or made by a photographic process. Since reprints were frequently made after the artist had died, in some cases the prints were artificially aged. Consequently, without definitive characteristics of genuineness—discoloration or worm holes—a print should be looked at with a jaundiced eye.

It should be noted that a date seal by itself is not convincing evidence that a print is a first edition example. The seal was cut into the block when it was made, and gives no information concerning the actual time at which the print was taken from the block. Whether or not it is an early copy is to be judged by the quality—by the sharpness, clarity, and intensity of the colors.

In determining the genuineness of a print, the quality of the paper is of great importance. In the search for paper with the necessary characteristics to give the desired quality of color, many types were used. For example, the paper employed in the period of Hokusai and Hiroshige is thinner and harder than that used earlier. The genuine papers absorbed the colors so that when the print is held up to the light and looked at from the back, the entire design can be seen. If the color is broken up or spotty, it gives rise to grave questions concerning the origin of the print. In addition, before the use of aniline dyes, colors were more mellow.

Collecting Hints: The formation of a collection of ukiyo-e essentially is based on a combination of knowledge, experience, taste, sensitivity, opportunity, luck, and finances. Perhaps one other factor should be added without which the attainment of this goal often becomes highly improbable—namely, paranoia. It is extremely difficult to say anything definitive about the prices of prints. To some extent, like other art forms, prices fluctuate with the times and with location. In addition, different examples of the same print may be priced at very different levels. In fact, two copies of the same print may be listed, for example, at $1,000 and $10,000, depending on the condition and the quality. In this regard, the collector must take a series of factors into account, including beauty, provenance, presence or absence of the artist's signature (plus such things as censor's and publisher's seals), rarity, and condition (i.e., the state of the print relative to color, fading, stains, tears, worm holes, repairs, trimming, and other imperfections). As stated very succinctly by Munsterberg in *The Japanese Print*, the most important criteria in judging the quality and value of a specific print "are its condition, the sharpness of impression and the beauty of the colors." Other factors of undoubted importance relate to whether the print is early or late, if it is from a famous series, and if it is very rare.

A few words should be said concerning the handling and preservation of prints. Perhaps the briefest summary is that of Munsterberg in *The Japanese Print*: "Never hold a print so that your fingertips grip the surface, and never let moisture of any kind touch it. Do not fold any print even if it is so large that it does not fit into your portfolio or storage cabinet. Never glue a print to a cardboard backing, but use a bit of paste or film paste. Prints should be placed in a mat or folder made of acid-free paper and must always be stored in a cool, dry place. If you frame them for display, be sure they are not exposed to direct sunlight, for this will cause the colors to fade."

Sizes of woodblock prints in the following listings are noted as chuban (medium-size vertical prints), koban (approx. 5" x 3"), oban (15" x 10" or 22¾" x 12½" for large oban), surimono (small size), or tanjaku (15" x 5").

Advisors: Robert A. Wittman and Robert E. Grenell

CHIKANOBU
Woman and girl by planter, Snow
Moon Flower, 1900, Oban **150.00**
Woman and child in snow, Snow
Moon Flower, 1900, Oban **175.00**
EISEN
Courtesan Yosooi of the Matsuba
House, C. 1825, Oban **1,550.00**
Courtesan Oyodo of the Tsuru
House, Annual Events in the Yo-
shiwara, C. 1830, oban **1,300.00**
GAKUTEI Suikoden Hero. Series: 10
Heroes of Suikoden, C. 1820, Suri-
mono **950.00**
HIROSHIGE
Boat at Honmoku, 36 Views of Fuji,
1858, Oban **1,950.00**
HIROSHIGE HAKONE Kale in Sa-
gami, 36 Views of Fuji, 1858,
Oban **1,950.00**

Kitagawa Utamaro II, circa 1806, featuring a high-ranking coutesan with an elaborate butterfly coiffure, and seated with her left sleeve raised toward her face, the figure identified as Shigeoka from the house of Okamoto-ya, fair impression, very good to good color, toned, stained, rubbed, otherwise good state, signed Utamaro (II) hitsu, with kiwame negitsu and publisher Kozu-yu seals, aiban, tate-e. $1,210.00. Courtesy of Butterfield and Butterfield.

Two Actors and lotus, Popular actors paired with flowers, 1854, Oban	450.00
Funabashi at Toyama in Etchu Province, Famous Views in 60-Odd Provinces, 1853, Oban	1,500.00
Hasu Lake in Kaga, Famous Views in 60-Odd Provinces, 1853, Oban	1,450.00
Chikugo Province, Famous Views in 60-Odd Provinces, 1855	1,450.00

Hiroshige, Night Snow, number 16, Fifty-three Stations of the Tokaido Road, middle impression (second state), fair color, faded, slightly trimmed, center crease, slightly stained, tape to reverse, otherwise good state, signed Hiroshige-ga with publisher's seal of Takeuchi, oban, yoko-e. $8,250.00. Courtesy of Butterfield and Butterfield.

Hodogaya Station, Hoeido Tokaido 53 Stations, C. 1832, Oban	1,500.00
Miura in Sagami Province, 36 Views of Fuji, 1858, Oban	1,450.00
Tsuchiyama Station, Kyoka Tokaido series, C. 1840, Chuban	250.00
Zojoji Pagoda, 100 Famous Views of Edo, 1857, Oban	1,850.00
Miyato River, 100 Famous Views of Edo, 1858, Oban	4,500.00
Takata Riding grounds, 100 Famous Views of Edo, 1857, Oban	3,300.00
Robe hanging pine, 100 Famous Views of Edo, 1856, Oban	1,400.00
KUNICHIKA Actor Nakamura Shikan as Toyama Kasuminozo, 1862, Oban	225.00
KUNIHISA Sumo match at Spring Tournament, 1862, Oban triptych	950.00
KUNISADA	
Actor Bando Mitsugoro IV as Mitsuhide, C.1835, Shikishi size	175.00
Actor Iwai Kumesaburo as Ono no Komachi, 1820's, Oban	250.00
Actor Iwai Tojaku as poetess Suo no Naishi, C. 1835. Shikishi size	175.00
Actor Nakamura Shikan	
As Otomo Kuronushi, 1820's, Oban	175.00
As Ariwara Narihira, 1820's, Oban	200.00
As Bunya no Yasuhide, 1820's, Oban	200.00
As Kisen Hoshi, 1820's, Oban	175.00
As Sojo Henjo, 1820's, Oban	200.00
KUNISADA II Ch. 48, Sawarabi, Series: 54 Chapters of Tale of Genji, 1857, Oban	150.00
KUNIYASU Memorial portrait of actor Segawa Kikunojo. 1832, Oban	200.00
KUNIYOSHI	
Geno Ikkatsu destroys wicked fox. Magic Fox of the 3 Countries, 1849-50, Oban	1,250.00
Dutiful Karumo, 24 Paragons of Filial Piety, 1842, Chuban	575.00
Sekishogun Sekiyu, 108 Heroes of Suikoden, 1840's, Chuban	850.00
Oishi Seizaemon Nobukiyo, True portraits of faithful Samurai, 1853, Oban	750.00
Empress Jingo watching return of fleet from Korea, Virtuous Women for the 8 Views, 1842, Tanzaku	1,550.00
Gentoku, Kanu and Chohi taking their oath of Loyalty in the Peach Orchard, 1853, Oban triptych	2,350.00
Kabuki scene, Late 1840's, Oban triptych	750.00
Takuma Morimasu, Heroic stories of Taiheiki, 1848, Oban	775.00
Kido maru tying to reach Minamoto Raiko, 1851, Oban triptych	4,150.00

Kuniyoshi, Surugadai, circa 1834, Toto Meisho, featuring travelers looking at a rainbow, middle impression, good to fair color, toned, stained, patched, otherwise fair state, with kiwame and publisher kaga-ya Kichiemon seals, signed Kunioshi-ga, oban, yoko-e. $1,980.00. Courtesy of Butterfield and Butterfield.

Fuwa Katsuemon Masatane, True
Portraits of the Faithful Samurai,
1853, Oban 750.00
Binshiken sweeping snow, Mirror of
24 Paragons of Filial Piety,
c.1840, Oban 2,500.00
47 Ronin seizing Moronao, Chu-
shingura, 1851, Oban triptych . . . 1,900.00
Gentoku, Kanu and Chohi visiting
Komei, Romance of 3 Kingdoms,
1853, Oban triptych 2,600.00
Tokuzo confronted by umi bozu's
apparition, 53 Parallels for the Tokaido, c.1845, Oban 1,950.00
Wife of Onodera Junai, Stories of
Faithful hearts and true Loyalty,
1848, Oban 900.00
Inukai Kenpachi wielding trunch-
eon, Abridged stories of our country's Swordsmanship, 1845, Oban 750.00
Takagi Oriemon recording his de-
struction of robber gang, Abridged
stories of our country's swordsmanship, 1845, Oban 550.00
Nikki Danjo, Ukiyoe comparison to
cloudy chapters of Genji, 1845,
Oban 350.00
Villain Takumi standing on Okiku's
sword, Ogura Imitation of 100
Poets, c.1845, Oban. 300.00
Jakuren Hoshi in rain, 100 Poets,
1840-42, Oban. 950.00
Nakamasa inspecting severed head,
Heroic stories of Taiheiki, 1848-
49, Oban 750.00
Ashikaga Takauji at preparation of
feast, 1852, Oban triptych 1,250.00
Chinese hero Choryo at Kutsukake
station, 69 Stations Kisokaido,
1852, Oban 450.00
Matabei at Bamba Station, 69 Sta-
tions of Kisokaido, 1852, Oban 500.00

Benkei at Seba Station, 69 Stations of
Kisokaido, 1852, Oban 400.00
Famous artist Matabei and his draw-
ings, 1853, Oban diptych. 850.00
Kintsura driven from Masakado's
court, 1851, Oban triptych. 1,250.00
Arakage killing giant salamander,
1834-35, Oban. 4,300.00
Woman in striped haori, Late
1820's, Oban, Aizuri-e(blue print) 950.00
KUNIYOSHI CHUSENKO Teitoku-
son spearing serpent, 108 Heroes
of Suikoden, 1840's, Chu 850.00
KUNIYOSHI KAMADA Matahachi
fighting wolves, 24 Paragons of
Filial Piety, 1842, Chuban 750.00
KUNIYOSHI SHIGEMORI at screen,
Stories of 47 Ronin, 1847-48,
Oban 450.00
SENCHO Courtesan Onoyama of the
Sugata Ebi House, Views of the Pros-
perous Capital, C. 1830, Oban 950.00
SHOSON
Reeds and Geese, 1928, Oban, Pub-
lisher-Watanabe. 675.00
Cranes on the Seashore, 1933,
Oban, Publisher-Watanabe 675.00
SHUNTEI Warrior on horseback in wa-
ter, C. 1795. Oban 275.00
TOYOHARU, People walking in Ka-

Katsukawa Shunsen, depicting a high-ranking courtesan standing in elaborate brocade kimono and obi, fair impression and color, faded, toned, wrinkled, stained, backed, otherwise fair state, signed Karsukawa Sunsen ga, kakemo-no-e. $440.00. Courtesy of Butterfield and Butterfield.

meido Shrine Garden in 4th month, Series: 12 months, C. 1780, Koban **1,500.00**

TOYOKUNI I Actors Seki Sanjuro and Onoe Kikugoro, C.1800, Oban diptych...................... **550.00**

TOYOKUNI II Actor Seki Sanjuro II in 3 roles, Late 1820's, Oban **375.00**

TOYOKUNI III
Ch. 11 from Tale of Genji series, 1858, Oban diptych........... **550.00**
Ch. 18 from Tale of Genji series, 1858, Oban diptych........... **550.00**
Ch. 33 from Tale of Genji series, 1858, Oban diptych........... **550.00**
Tattooed actor in kabuki scene, 1858, Oban diptych........... **475.00**
Actor as Yaegiri, 1852, Chuban **250.00**
Actor Arashi Kichisaburo at Okabe Station, Series: Tokaido Portraits, 1852, Oban **275.00**

YOSHIIKU Picture of Foreign men and women of all Nationalities, 1861, Oban triptych................. **2,250.00**

YOSHIKAZU General Uesugi Kenshin, Series: Images of Famous Commanders of our Country, 1858, Oban **300.00**

YOSHIMORI Various foreigners shown at Nihombashi, 1861, Oban diptych...................... **2,750.00**

YOSHITORA
General Oda Nobunaga, Series: 60 or so Generals of Japan, 1866, Oban **350.00**
General Ashikaga Takauji, Same series as above, 1866, Oban **350.00**
Hideyoshi watching his troops blow up a ship in Korea, 1863, Oban triptych.................... **750.00**
Battle between Nitta Yoshisada as Ashikaga Takauji at Yahagi River in 1335, 1840's, Oban triptych **650.00**

YOSHITOSHI
Poetess Akazome Emon, 100 Moons, 1886, Oban........... **275.00**
Great battle of Ane River in Taiheikik, 1867, Oban triptych **3,400.00**
Woman holding bonsai, Collection of desires, 1878, Oban........ **475.00**
Moonlight at Lonely house, 100 Moons, 1890, Oban........... **625.00**
Chinese Beauty, 100 Moons. 1888, Oban **475.00**
Warrior Shigeyuki at Battle of Tobisu Mtn. 100 Moons, 1887, Oban ... **750.00**

Toyokuni I, featuring a man standing on the deck of his boat as it passes beneath a bridge, good to fair impression, fair color, faded, stained, toned, wormage, creased, glue at top back corners, overall fair state, signed Toyokuni-ga, with kiwame and publisher Oyama-ya Hangoro seals, oban, tate-e. $248.00. Courtesy of Butterfield and Butterfield.

Utamaro, circa 1797–1798, Twelve Forms of Woman's Handiwork, featuring a half-portrait of a youth approaching a toothbrush saleswoman at the stall, good impression and color, laid down (dry mounted), slightly soiled and faded, otherwise good state, signed Utamaro hitsu, with publisher Wakasa-ya seal, oban, tate-e. $3,300.00. Courtesy of Butterfield and Butterfield.

Yugiri Pounding Cloth, 100 Moons, 1890, Oban **475.00**

Battle of Sanno Shrine, 1874, Oban triptych **1,250.00**

Enlightenment 6f Jigoku-dayu, 36 Ghosts, 1890, Oban **1,250.00**

Spirit of Tengu, 24 Accomplishments in Imperial Japan, 1881, Oban **550.00**

Emperor rewards Tawara Toda, Mirror of Famous Generals of Japan, 1880, Oban **275.00**

WOODBLOCK PRINTS—MODERN

History: The Japanese word for print is *hanga*. The traditional print developed since the seventeenth century is ukiyo-e hanga, or simply ukiyo-e. *Ukiyo* literally translated means "fleeting or floating world," and e means "pictures of." Traditional ukiyo-e, therefore, depicted genre scenes of the floating world or, in modern terms, the more colorful scenes from the nonprivileged urban world of work and play in Kyoto, Osaka, and Edo (present-day Tokyo). The eclipse of traditional ukiyo-e is generally accepted as coinciding with the end of the Meiji Period (1912)—challenged by two competing movements in the print world: the shin hanga, or new print movement, and the sosaku hanga, or creative print movement. Shin hanga artists followed a traditional ukiyo-e framework in the carving and printing of their designs, but the designs themselves clearly showed Western influence, mixed with the eighteenth-century Utagawa tradition. Utamaro's bijin-ga, or paintings beautiful women from the entertainment districts, came from that earlier period as did traditional Japanese views of urban and rural landscapes. In addition, traditional Kabuki theater and noh drama inspired several shin hanga print artists.

The competing movement of sosaku hanga artists, which actually began before the new print movement but did not reach ascendancy until after World War II, emphasized original designs, the carving of one's own blocks, and the printing of one's own designs. Complete control of the total artistic process was the movement's goal. Most of these artists were also influenced by Western, that is European (in particular, French), design methods. This movement was itself eclipsed after 1970 by the contemporary print movement, which has gone in many directions but has been primarily influenced by movements in the United States. Collectors interested in this latter period need only consult the references given below. There are many graphic media for the collector to choose from; one of the most important is designs influenced by the pop art movement.

When Commodore Perry's black ships arrived in Japan in 1853, the Tokugawa government was forced to open Japan to Western trade. The influx of foreigners and their ideas into the port of Yokohama sped up the process of modernization and social change and led to the Meiji restoration of 1868. Although traditional ukiyo-e artists such as OHARA Koson (1877–1945: OHARA Shoson after 1926) seemed immune to new influences in his designs, Tsukioka Yoshitoshi (1839–1892) and Kiyochika KOBAYASHI (1847–1915) were not. In this section family names are capitalized. They are generally used by Western-trained artists such as sosaku hanga artists. But it should be noted that shin hanga artists generally use their given names in the traditional ukiyo-e style.

Yoshitoshi and Kiyochika helped make the transition from the traditional to the modern period. In Yoshitoshi's work, one can detect elements of a synthesis between traditional and modern methods that became conscious and deliberate in Kiyochika KOBAYASHI's (1847–1915) work. Kiyochika clearly exhibited a fusion between Western and Japanese styles and methods. He experimented with the modern, or Western, concepts of shadow, light, and perspective as well as Western subject matter. His early career training mirrored his later print output—he studied Japanese painting under Zeshin and Western oil painting under the Englishman Charles Wirgman. In addition, he had been formally trained in methods of Western photography.

The move to Westernization in all things eventually led to a reactive period in the 1890s and a sharp increase in nationalism. Even though the sosaku hanga movement was in full swing, it was the more traditional neo-ukiyo-e shin hanga movement that benefited from the upsurge in nationalism. This latter movement came to dominate the period between World Wars I and II.

Hashiguchi Goyo (1880–1921) became one of the most notable shin hanga artists of the interwar period. Although partially trained in Western art methods, he was deeply inspired by Utamaro's depictions of beautiful women. Goyo copied his idol's previous prints until the publisher Watanabe in 1915 put him under contract. Goyo subsequently produced fourteen bijin-ga prints through 1921 that ensured him a permanent place in the history of the Japanese print. Two other artists produced similar designs: ITO Shinsui (1898–1972) and TORII Kotondo (1900–1977). Many of the artists of this period began their training under KABURAGI Kiyokata (1878–1972), a famous ukiyo-e painter, in the Utagawa tradition. Kiyokata was famous for his depictions of bijin-ga and trained great bijin-ga artists such as Shinsui, Kotondo, and YAMAKAWA Shuho (1898–1944). He also trained KASAMATSU Shiro (b. 1898) and, strangely, the Hiroshige landscape specialist of the modern period, KAWASE Hasui (1883–1957). Other artists of this genre were ISHIWATA Koitsu (1897–1987), YOSHIDA Toshi (b. 1911), and YOSHIDA Hodaka (b. 1926), who has moved toward abstract designs in recent years.

The father of the last two Yoshidas was one of the giants of the shin hanga movement: YOSHIDA Hiroshi (1876–1950). The elder Yoshida oversaw the printing of his own blocks, which was one of the premises of the competing movement. Yoshida's late prints were, in fact, closer to the ideas of sosaku hanga artists than shin hanga artists. Although Goyo, like Yoshida, also oversaw the printing of his own blocks, he remained firmly in the shin hanga tradition. Yoshida, however, moved closer and closer to the creative print movement, embracing many of its primary principles and designs. This was not totally surprising, though, since the elder Yoshida's father had studied under Antonio Fontanesi at the Technical College Art School in Tokyo. That school allowed only Westerners to be on its faculty and was the bastion of Westernization in Japan until its forced closure in 1883. Indeed, Yoshida traveled extensively and frequently exhibited abroad. Today, the youngest of the Yoshidas, YOSHIDA Ayomi (b. 1958), daughter of Hodaka, works in the print medium producing interesting asbstract graphics.

YAMAMURA Toyonari (1885–1942) and NATORI Shunsen (1886–1969) focused neither on bijin-ga nor on landscapes, but on' Kabuki portraits and large actor portraits, respectively. Both these artists worked in the conservative new print movement tradition.

In between the two movements fall a number of print artists who have reached international prominence. They will be mentioned briefly: (1) URUSHIBARA Mokuchu (1888–1913); (2) FUGITA Tsuguji, known as Leonard Foujita in the West (1886–1968); and (3) Paul Jacoulet (1896?–1960). Urushibara and Fugita were Japanese natives who traveled West: the former to many European capitals, the latter mainly to Paris. Jacoulet, in contrast, spent his adult life in Japan. Urushibara, although he spent most of his creative life in the West, never used oil and canvas but pursued the traditional medium of the Japanese woodblock, although his landscapes did not escape Western influence. Foujita, who eventually became a French citizen, used French methods of design, yet his prints are infused with an intangible Oriental touch, partially because of his traditional use of the woodblock medium. Jacoulet, a Frenchman who went in the opposite direction—West to East—also used the traditional Japanese woodblock medium. He liked portraying beautiful women, but not women from the Utagawa ideal. He presented his own view. His works were technically superb and very colorful. His editions were limited—his total oeuvre is

known by the various seals he used for different editions. These three artists made an incalculable contribution to graphic arts, but defy any real means of categorization.

Sosaku hanga artists, unlike their competing colleagues, wanted control of the entire artistic process from start to finish. Influenced by Western methods and the mingei, or folk art movement begun by Japanese potters, these artists also took to the Western convention of becoming known by their family or surnames. Their designs were different, as were their sense of perspective, color, and shading. Many of them exhibited in the West, and all were aware of foreign movements in the graphic arts.

Although YAMAMOTO Kanae (1882–1945) is generally considered to have founded the Nihon Sosaku Hanga Kyokai (Japan Creative Print Association) in 1918, ONCHI Koshiro (1891–1955) is considered to have been its moving force. He was an outstanding abstractionist and greatly influenced SEKINO Jun'ichiro (1914–1988). ONCHI was very highly regarded in Japan, but MUNAKATA Shiko (1903–1975), with his abstract black and white Zen Buddhist images derived from Japanese folk tradition (mingei), became better known in the West. His prints have a strange intensity and power that comes from his style and method; his inspiration is often from traditional subjects. Furthermore, when Munakata used colors, that they were often hand applied from the back of the print, which was not traditional.

Other important sosaku hanga figures included HIRATSUKA Un'ichi (b. 1895); who delighted in using black and white (sumi-e), and found his inspiration in the architecture of Japan. Saito Kiyoshi (b. 1907) became known in the West for his unusual designs, which found their inspiration in nature and the snows of his native Aizu. Maekawa Senpan (1888–1960) preserved some form of "Japaneseness" in his creative prints, whereas Kawanishi Hide (1894–1965) looked to past Nagasaki-e prints for inspiration. Yamaguchi Gen (1903–1976) often used the same natural objects (leaves, twigs, flowers, and so on) in his prints that Onchi used.

Of the hundreds of sosaku hanga artists, Munakata Shiko is generally recognized as the most important artist of the group, just as Hashiguchi Goyo is recognized as the most prominent figure of the shin hanga movement.

References: Francis Blakemore, *Who's Who in Modern Japanese Prints*, Weatherhill, 1975; Margaret K. Johnson and Dale K. Hilton, Japanese Prints Today, Shufunotomo Co., Ltd., 1980; Julia Meech-Pekarik, *The World of the Meiji Print, Impressions of a New Civilization*, Weatherhill, 1986; Helen Merritt, *Modern Japanese Woodblock Prints*, University of Hawaii Press, 1990; James A. Michener, *The Modern Japanese Print*, Charles E. Tuttle Co., Inc., 1968; Kawakita Michiaki, *Modern Currents in Japanese Art*, Weatherhill/Heibonsha, 1974; Richard Miles, *The Prints of Paul Jacoulet*, Robert E. Sawers Publishing Co., 1982; M. Narazaki, *Kawase Hasui Mokuhangashu*, Mainichi Shimbun, 1979; Irwin J. Pachter, *Kawase Hasui and His Contemporaries: The Shin Hanga (New Print) Movement In Landscape Art*, Everson Museum of Art, 1986; J. Thomas Rimer and Shuji Takashima, *Paris in Japan: The Japanese Encounter with European Painting*, Toppan Printing Co. Ltd., 1987; Lawrence Smith, *The Japanese Print Since 1900*, Harper and Row, 1983; —, *Contemporary Japanese Prints*, Harper and Row, 1985; Oliver Statler, *Modern Japanese Prints*, Charles E. Tuttle Co., Inc., 1956; Abe Yuji, *Modern Japanese Prints, A Contemporary Selection*, Charles E. Tuttle Co., Inc., 1971.

Museums: Chicago Institute of Art (Buckingham Collection), Chicago, Illinois; Museum of Fine Arts, Boston, Massachusetts; Detroit Institute of Art, Detroit, Michigan; Minneapolis Museum of Art, Minneapolis, Minnesota; Metropolitan Museum of Art, New York, New York; Cincinnati Museum of Art (the largest collection), Cincinnati, Ohio; Toledo Museum of Art, Toledo, Ohio; Seattle Museum of Art, Seattle, Washington; Fukuoka Art Museum, Fukuoka, Japan; MOA Museum of Art, Shizvoka prefecture, Japan; The National Museum of Modern Art, Tokyo, Japan; Tokyo Metropolitan Museum of Art, Tokyo, Japan; Tokyo National Museum, Tokyo, Japan.

Reproduction Alert: Many of the more famous shin hanga have been reproduced—new editions have been made from the original blocks that have been recut, new woodblocks have been cut, and more modern means of reproduction have also been used. It is important to note, however, that, to my knowledge, none of these latter editions were meant to deceive. Unscrupulous dealers and, in particular, unknowledgeable dealers have sold many of these as originals. It is important to read and reread the introduction and notes to Pachter's book (see listing) on marks and editions. The seals listed therein are invaluable for understanding and dating the majority of shin hanga prints.

In addition, the novice absolutely must understand the jizuri seal—the two-character seal in the margin of a print. For example, on a Yoshida print it indicates that the artist "self-printed" his own designs. Without such a jizuri seal, a YOSHIDA Hiroshi print would not be an original and would, therefore, be worth only a small fraction of a print with a jizuri seal. If the circular seal by the publisher Watanabe is on a shin hanga print made between the great earthquake of 1923 and the advent of World War II (1939), it is probably a postwar reprint, *not* an original.

Fortunately, most artists of the sosaku hanga movement are not subject to the same scrutiny,

and the collector or dealer need basically memorize the style of the signature. But it is imperative to mention that nothing can replace the knowledge that comes from handling an original print and from reading about the style and oeuvre of an artist. Visit different print dealers and galleries, but most of all do not overlook your local museum as a potential resource. Most museums have a representational array of modern prints or are actively seeking to acquire them.

Collecting Hints: Shin hanga and sosaku hanga have always been generally more popular in the West than in Japan. In the past few years, however, several artists have been seemingly more appreciated than others, and their prints have appreciated accordingly. HASHIGUCHI Goyo's and MUNAKATA Shiko's prints have risen astronomically. The result has been a sharp rise in price for lesser artists as well. The collector should, of course, like a print before purchasing it, and if he or she could foresee which artists will eventually be collected by the Japanese, then both art and investment could be served.

Advisors: Stewart and Barbara Hilbert

Azechi Umetao (1902-) 13⅝" x 18⅞"; Koshu no yama "Kofu mountain," dated Kigen 2600 (1940) signed Azechi Umetaro saku and Umetaro Azechi in pencil good impression, color and condition **1,100.00**
Hashiguchi Goyo (1880?-1921)
    Tanzaku, 19½" x 5⅝", a young woman tying the obi of her underrobe, signed Gogo ga and sealed Gogo, dated Taisho 9 (1920), 5th month, stamped on the reverse Hashiguchi hansho-very good impression and color, very slight stain on the robe, tape stain on the

Hashiguchi Goyo, dated Taisho 9, 3rd month (March 1920), a half-length portrait of a beauty combing her hair, silver mica background, fine color and condition, dai oban tate-e, signed Goyo ga on the print, sealed Hashiguchi. $28,000.00

reverse, otherwise good condition **12,100.00**

Dai oban tate-e, $16\frac{1}{4}''$ x $11\frac{1}{8}''$, a half-length portrait of a maiko painting her lips, signed Goyo ga, sealed Hashiguchi and dated Taisho 9 (1920) 2nd month-fine impression, color and condition **11,000.00**

Dai-oban tate-e, $16\frac{1}{4}''$ x $10\frac{3}{4}''$, a portrait of a teahouse waitress seated and holding a round lacquer tray, signed Gogo ga and sealed, dated Taisho 9 (1920) very good impression and color, water spots and slight rubbing to the mica, ink stains to the right margin, otherwise good condition. **6,600.00**

Dai oban tate-e, $17\frac{3}{4}''$ x $11\frac{3}{8}''$, beauty kneeling before a mirror, signed Gogo ga, sealed Goyo and dated Taisho 9 (1920)-very good impression, color and condition. . . . **22,000.00**

Dai oban tate-e $17\frac{3}{4}''$ x $13\frac{5}{8}''$, girl combing her hair, signed Goyo ga, sealed Hashiguchi and dated Taisho 9 (1920), fine impression, color and condition **46,200.00**

Ko-kakemono, 33" x $11\frac{3}{4}''$, a portrait of a woman in the summer kimono holding a mica highlighted obi, signed Goyo ga and sealed Goyo, dated Taisho 9 (1920), good impression color and condition, possibly published posthumously **8,800.00**

Hashimoto Okiie (1899-), "Young Woman and Iris," $17\frac{1}{2}''$ x $24\frac{1}{2}''$, 1952, signed in pencil, the right margin stamped in kanji, Hashimoto Okiie saku, with red seal, Hashi. . . . **1,760.00**

Ishikawa Toraji "Stripper 1934," 19" x $14\frac{3}{4}''$, signed Ishikawa, artist's seal, publisher's seal Yamagishi Kazue, and early printing, very good condition, ... **2,090.00**

Ishiwata Koitsu

Oban yoko-e (15" x 10"), "Canal scene at sunset," 1932 . . . . **550.00**

Oban tate-e (15" x 10"), "Night scene with cherry trees and bridge," 1932. . . . . **250.00**

Oban tate-e (15" x 10"), "Nezu Shrine in light snow," c.1935. . . . **385.00**

Ito Shinsui

Dai oban tate-e, $16\frac{3}{4}''$ x $10\frac{1}{4}''$, Kotatsu, signed Shinsui ga, sealed Ito and dated Taisho 12 (1923), 1st month-good impression and color, laid down and margins soiled **880.00**

Dai oban tate-e, $16\frac{7}{8}''$ x $10\frac{7}{8}''$, a half length portrait of a beauty hanging up a lantern, signed Shinsui, sealed Ito, dated Showa 5 (1930), no. 136/250, published by Watanabe, good impression, color and condition **3,300.00**

Dai oban tate-e, $15\frac{3}{4}''$ x $10\frac{3}{4}''$, a half length portrait of a beauty holding a fan, signed Shinsui ga, sealed Ito and published by Watanabe-very good impression, color and condition **2,640.00**

Dai oban tate-e, $17\frac{1}{4}''$ x $11\frac{1}{4}''$, a beauty clipping her toenails, signed Shinsui ga, sealed Ito, dated 1929, no. 107/250, published by Watanabe-very good impression, color and condition **7,700.00**

"Artist's wife," $17\frac{3}{8}''$ x $11\frac{3}{8}''$, signed Shinsui, with artist's seal, dated Taisho 5 (1916), inscribed and signed on reverse in penciled English, 101/150, publisher's signature, S. Watanabe Tokio, publisher's red seal Watanabe, very good condition **16,500.00**

Jacoulet, Paul (1902-60)

Le chemin a l'eglise "Charmoros de Guam," $18\frac{1}{2}''$ x $14\frac{1}{8}''$, from the Treasure boat series, 47 x 36 cm., signed Paul Jacoulet, printer Uchikawa Matashiro, engraver Maeda Kentaro, stamped on the reverse 163/350, a good impression and color, tiny paper tape marks on top margin. **1,170.00**

A portrait of a Chamorro woman in blue, $18\frac{3}{8}''$ x $12\frac{1}{4}''$, from the Baren series, signed Paul Jacoulet, dated 1934, published by Kato Junji, stamped on the reverse 115/150 (in Japanese), good impression

Okuyama Gihachiro Cour de St. Michael, April 1940, a stark scene of wartime Paris in the courtyard of St. Michel, oban tate-e, published by Sekiguchi. $1,200.00

and color, very slightly soiled mainly at left margin **1,325.00**

Le Betel "Yap," $18\frac{1}{2}$" x $14\frac{1}{4}$", from the Treasure boat series, signed Paul Jacoulet, printer Uchikawa Matashiro, engraver Maeda Kentaro, stamped on the reverse 228/350, very good impression, very slightly faded, very slight foxing, minor fault on the reverse **1,000.00**

Une averse a Metalanim, Ponape-Est Carolines, $18\frac{3}{8}$" x $13\frac{7}{8}$", from the Mandarin duck series, signed Paul Jacoulet, printer Honda Tetsunosuke, engraver Maeda Kentaro, stamped on the reverse 244/350, fine impression, color and condition **1,650.00**

Kasamatsu Shiro

Oban yoko-e, (15" x 10") "Mount Fuji at sunset," 1937 . . . . **385.00**

Oban tate-e, (15" x 10") "The Inlet-Riverboat at Mooring," publisher Watanabe, 1938 . . . . **220.00**

Oban tate-e (15" x 10"), "A woman preparing tea" **140.00**

Kawanishi Hide

Three prints, including Botan, "Peony," signed in pencil, Hide Kawanishi, Sensou, "Porthole," and "Iris Season, 1955, signed in pencil twice, Hide Kawanishi, and in kana, Kawanishi Hide, each with black seal, Hide, and red circular seal, each with labels to reverse stating title and artist, the first two with hinges at corners **2,200.00**

Two prints, 19" x $24\frac{1}{2}$" and $26\frac{1}{8}$" x $19\frac{7}{8}$", including Shitsunai, Suisen, "Interior with Narcissus," 1947, signed in pencil, Hide Kawanishi; and Snow at Lakeside, 1942, with penciled title, signed in pencil twice, Hide Kawanishi and in kana, Kawanishi Hide, each with black seal Hide, red circular seal, and label to reverse, margins slightly toned, ... **3,025.00**

Kawase Hasui (1883-1957)

Chuban yoko-e, $7\frac{5}{8}$" x $10\frac{3}{8}$", Tsuki no Matsushima "Matsushima in moonlight," signed Hasui, dated Taisho 8 (1919), publisher Watanabe's small round seal, very good impression, color and condition **2,000.00**

Oban tate-e (15" x 10"), Izu, Yugashima, dated Showa 11 (1936), signed Hasui, rectangular seal of Wantanabe Shozaburo in the right margin, very good impression color and condition **700.00**

Kawase Hasui, Kawaguchiko, dated March 1935, Lake Kawaguchi, number 279 in Kawase Hasui, Mokuhangashu 1979 (number 278 is identical with the trees in foreground), fine impression, color, and condition, oban yoko-e, published by Watanabe, $1,200.00

Oban yoko-e ($10\frac{3}{8}$" x $15\frac{1}{4}$"), Aki no Koshiji "Road along the North western coast in autumn," from Tabi-miyage dai-isshu "Souvenirs of my travel-First edition," a crouching woman by bundles of rice straws on drying frames by Japan Sea, signed Hasui, dated autumn of Taisho 9 (1920), a small round seal of the publisher Watanabe, very good impression, color, and condition **2,850.00**

Oban tate-e ($15\frac{1}{2}$" x 10"), Yuki no Zozoji "Snow at Zozoji," signed Hasui, sealed Kawase, dated Taisho 11 (1922) 1st month, 18th day, published by Watanabe, very good impression, color and condition **4,400.00**

Munakata Shiko (1903-1975)

Sumizuri-e ($5\frac{3}{4}$" x $7\frac{1}{2}$"), depicting a reclining goddess, signed Shika Muna and with one artist's seal-good impression, slight staining lower right, otherwise good condition **2,200.00**

Sumizuri-e ($9\frac{5}{8}$" x $11\frac{7}{8}$"), depicting a reclining nude in an interior, signed Shiko Munakata in pencil, sealed Shiko and dated 1959, and on MS watermarked paper-good impression and condition **7,700.00**

Sumizuri-e ($15\frac{3}{8}$" x $11\frac{7}{8}$") depicting a seated goddess in a garden, one artist's seal-good impression, slightly foxed, otherwise good condition **6,600.00**

Sumizuri-e ($14\frac{1}{4}$" x $16\frac{1}{4}$"), depicting a woman opening a door, $14\frac{1}{4}$" x $16\frac{1}{4}$", signed Shiko Munakata in pencil, sealed Muno-good impression, lower margin with horizontal crease, otherwise good condtion **10,450.00**

Sumizuri-e ($15\frac{3}{8}''$ x $11\frac{1}{8}''$), with hand-applied color depicting a fox amonst flowers with the poem Ureshi sa no kitsune te o dase kumoribana "The fox likes dancing in clouds of flowers," signed Shiko Munakata in pencil, sealed Shiko-good impression and color, bottom edge with horizontal crease, otherwise good condition. **16,500.00**

Sumizuri-e, ($21\frac{1}{2}''$ x $15\frac{1}{2}''$), with hand-applied color depicting a bodhisattva among fishes in waves, signed Shiko Munakata in pencil, dated 1959, and sealed Shiko Muno, good impression and color, creased **33,000.00**

Sumizuri-e, ($16\frac{1}{8}''$ x $10\frac{7}{8}''$), with hand-applied color depicting an okubi-e portrait of a richly-jewelled goddess, signed Shiko Munakata in pencil, sealed Hogan Muna Shiko—good impression, color and condition **88,000.00**

Onchi Koshiro

$21\frac{5}{8}''$ x $17\frac{1}{4}''$, a half-length portrait of the poet Sakutaro Hagiwara, signed "Onzi" and sealed, the verso sealed "Portrait of an artist," artist Koshiro Onchi, printer Junichiro Sekino and Onchi Koshiro saku" very good impression upper margin slightly thinned and damaged, otherwise good condition **5,500.00**

"Object No. 3," $20\frac{7}{8}''$ x 15", 1954, stamped Onzi, upper corners thin, remains of mounting material to upper left corver, creasing throughout **16,500.00**

"Lyric No. 24," 1953, $37\frac{3}{8}''$ x $28\frac{7}{8}''$, the reverse inscribed in ink, "Lyrique No. 24, 3-4, '53," and with two labels each inscribed in ink "Lyric No. 24, 1953," upper right corner torn and reattached, small creases. **27,500.00**

"Study of a Human Body," No. 8, 8" x $5\frac{3}{8}''$, 1928, unsigned, inscribed in pencil at botton left corner "Jintai Kosatsu, No. 8," and dated in pencil at lower right corner, "23, Sep-28," very minor vertical folds **3,025.00**

Saito Kiyoshi

$23\frac{3}{4}''$ x $17\frac{3}{4}''$, "Maiko Kyoto G", 1961, numbered 14/300, dated 1961, signed in black ink, Kiyoshi Saito, with red seal, Kiyo, watermark, Kiyoshi Saito, and label to the reverse stamped, self carved self printed Kiyoshi Saito **1,760.00**

"Doll Awaji," $32\frac{5}{8}''$ x $19\frac{1}{4}''$, 1957, numbered 75/80, the lower margin with penciled title and date, signed in pencil, Kiyoshi Saito, with red seal, Kiyo, label to the reverse stamped, self carved self printed Kiyoshi Saito **2,200.00**

"Cat," $30\frac{1}{8}''$ x 17", signed "Kiyoshi Saito" with label attached to the reverse inscribed "Staring 1/10, 1950 II., self carved, self-printed, K. Saito," with seal-good impression, very slightly toned, mounted as a hanging scroll **5,500.00**

A child drinking a glass of milk, $18\frac{1}{8}''$ x $12\frac{3}{8}''$, signed Kiyoshi Saito, label attached to the reverse inscribed "Milk, September 1950, self-carved, self-printed K. Saito," with seal-good impression, mounted as a hanging scroll. **1,980.00**

A woman and conch shells, $16\frac{7}{8}''$ x $26\frac{1}{2}''$, label attached to the reverse inscribed "Fantasia, September 1950, self-carved, self-printed, K. Saito" and sealed, signed Kiyoshi Saito-good impression, mounted as a hanging scroll **4,400.00**

"Tenderness," $17\frac{3}{4}''$ x $23\frac{3}{8}''$, 1959, numbered 13/80, penciled title and date, signed in white ink, Kiyoshi Saito, with red seal, Kiyo, the reverse with label stamped, self carved self printed Kiyoshi Saito **1,650.00**

Takane Yasuhiro Bijinga 1930s, a beautiful woman adjusting her hair by the light of a lantern, directly inspired by the Utagawa tradition, fine impression and color, and good condition, oban tate-e. $1,500.00

"Garden Autumn," 23⅝" x 17¾", 1961, numbered 28/150, dated 1961, with penciled title, signed in black ink, Kiyoshi Saito, with red seal Kiyo, the reverse with label stamped, self carved self printed Kiyoshi Saito **1,210.00**

"Bunraku C.," 23⅞ x 17⅞", 1959, numbered 93/100, dated 1959, with penciled title, signed in white ink, Kiyoshi Saito, with red seal, Kiyo, watermark, label on reverse stamped, self carved self printed Kiyoshi Saito................ **1,760.00**

Seiho Takeuchi (1864-1942), "a bear in winter," 15½" x 20", signed Seiho and sealed Seiho-good impression, color and condition **1,870.00**

Sekino Jun'ichiro

Portrait of Koshiro Onchi, 25¾" x 19¾", signed in pencil, Junichiro Sekino, and with black stamp, J. Sekino, label to reverse with title in kanji, margins slightly soiled, tiny folds to corners **6,600.00**

"My Daughter," 21⅜" x 17", 1956, numbered 5/100, signed and dated in pencil, Jun. Sekino 1956, with red seal Jun **1,650.00**

"A Boy and His Rooster," 28⅛" x 20¾", 1956, inscribed in pencil "15/50 IIme etat 1956," signed in pencil , Junichiro Sekino, with red seal Jun, minor folds at upper corners....................... **2,200.00**

"Boy and Dog," 28" x 21⅛", 1957, numbered 3/100, signed in pencil, Junichiro Sekino, penciled title and inscribed in pencil, Japan 1957, with red seal, Jun, remains of mounting material at corners **2,750.00**

"Jade Beauty," 24⅞" x 17", 1959, numbered 17/100, dated 5, Feb.,1959, signed in white ink, Jun. Sekino, with red seal, Sekijun **880.00**

"Siamese Cats," 16⅞" x 21⅝", 1962, numbered 68/200, signed and dated in pencil, Jun. Sekino(?) 1962, with red seal Jun......... **1,760.00**

"Aquarium," 24⅞" x 19⅜", 1946, numbered 21/50, with penciled title, Suizoku-kan, signed and dated in pencil, Jun. Sekino, with red seal..................... **3,850.00**

Tadashi Nakayama (1927-) Heian, 26" x 33⅛", 1961, numbered 8/50, dated and signed in pencil at the bottom margin, 1961 T. Nakayama, the reverse with red seal, Nakayama, and typed label stating title and artist, minor creases to top margin **880.00**

Tokuriki Tomikichiro (1902-), "Sanjo Bridge," 15½" x 20¾", 1954, numbered 14, signed in pencil, T. Tokuriki, stamped Tomikichiro Tokuriki, with black stamp, Tomi **1,100.00**

Torii Kotondo

Dai oban tate-e, (18¼" x 11⅞"), "Yuki", signed Genjin ga, sealed Genjin, dated Showa 4 (1929), no. 71 and published by Sakai/Kawaguchi-good impression, color and condition **3,850.00**

Dai oban tate-e, (18⅝" x 11½"), a beauty making up before a mirror, signed Genjin ga, and sealed Genjin, no. 4/100-very good impression color and condition **4,620.00**

Dai oban tate-e, (18¼" x 11¾"), "Ame", signed Genjin ga, sealed Genjin, dated Showa 4 (1929), no. 65, published by Sakai/Kawaguchi-good impression, color and condition **2,640.00**

Yamamura Toyonari (1886-1942)

"Bijin," 15¾" x 11", signed Toyonari ga, with artist's seal Toyonari, date seal Taisho 4 (1914), on mica ground, very good condition **1,760.00**

"Shanghai Dancers," 16¼" x 11¼", unsigned, stamped with artist's brown seal Toyonari, dated 1924, with mica background, very good condition **4,675.00**

Oban tate-e, (15⅞" x 11"), okubi-e of a maiko, signed Toyonari ga, sealed Toyonari in the margin, dated Taisho kino-e (1924), silver mica background, very good impression and color, good condition....................... **900.00**

Yoshida Toshi (1911-), 2 prints, both 21¼" x 13⅜", one with a shrike perched on a maple branch and the other with a bird on a snow-covered nandin branch, both signed Toshi and again in pencil Yoshida Toshi in the bottom margin, both good impressions, color and condition..... **350.00**

Urushibara Mokuchu (1888-1953)

Pink cyclamen in a square black pot with faint gold design, 12⅝" x 8¼", signed Urushibara go-koku (designed and carved), sealed Urushibara, numbered "No. 78," signed again in pencil in the bottom margin, framed **500.00**

A view of Venice with a gondola in the foreground, 10⅜" x 14⅜", signed Urushibara in pencil in the margin, numbered "No. 86," good impression and color, a tiny stain **400.00**

Yamaguchi Gen, 23¾" x 18½", "' Ab-

Hiratsuka Un'ichi, Maple Trees along Potomac River, 23½" h. x 19¾" w., 1926, number 8 of 80, sealed in red, signed in pencil, Unichi Hiratsuka (the artist is most famous for his stylized depictions of trees in black and white; he is presently living in Washington, D.C.). $2,200.00

stract topography, signed Gen Yamaguchi and no. 5/50-good impression, color and condition **2,860.00**

Yamakawa Shuho (1894-1944)
  Oban tate-e, three prints, 15⅛" x 10⅜", 15" x 10¼", and 15¼" x 10⅜", the first, okubi-e of a young woman raising her sleeve to her face, titled Yuki moyoi "Threatening to snow," dated Showa 2 (1927); another Tasogare "Twilight," a bust portrait of a lady with uchiwa wearing a light blue kimono, dated Showa 3 (1928), and another, Aki "Autumn," a bust portrait of a young woman among falling leaves, all signed Shuho, generally good impressions, color and condition **1,400.00**
  Oban tate-e, (15⅛" x 10⅛"), Aki, "Autumn," signed Shuro with maple seal-good impression, color and condition **500.00**
  "Red Collar and Bijin with Fan," 15⅜" x 10⅜" two prints, both signed Shuho, with artist's seal, dated Showa 3 (1928), good condition **1,100.00**

Yoshida Hiroshi (1876-1950)
  Oban tate-e (16⅛" x 10⅜"), Seto-nai-kai shu, hikaru umi "Inland Sea series, Glittering sea", signed Yoshida, dated Taisho 15 (1926), Jizuri seal, good impression and color, one slight crease, otherwise good condition **2,000.00**
  Oban yoko-e, (10⅜" x 15½"), Hodakayama from the Nihon arupes junkei no uchi 'Twelve views of the Japan alps' signed Hiroshi Yo-

Yoshida Hiroshi, Hayase, dated Showa 8 (1933), from Kansai District series, good impression, color, and condition, oban yoko-e, has Jizuri seal, artist's signature and seal, and signed Hiroshi Yoshida in pencil. $1,100.00

shida in pencil, Yoshida in brush, Jizuri seal, no date (1926) **1,100.00**
  Oban yoko-e, (10⅞" x 16"), "Kuzukawa", the River Suzu in the foreground and Mt. Fuji in the distance, signed Yoshida in sumi and again in pencil in margin, jizuri seal, dated Showa 10 (1935), good impression and color, very slight creases **750.00**

YATATE

History: Long before today's ballpoint pens simplified the procedure, writing was a complicated and time-consuming matter in Japan and the Far East. An ink cake made of black pressed carbon and glue had to be wetted and rubbed on an inkstone to make a smooth mixture. The writer then stroked a brush on the stone to load it with ink. When traveling, this obviously became impractical. Portable brush and inkpot sets, called yatate, were devised to fill the need. The brush holder portion, called fudetsutsu, is generally a long thin cylinder; the ink container, called a sumitsubo, can be round, oval, or rectangular.

Most commonly, the two portions were united in a one-piece construction, called ittaigata yatate. When the two portions are separated (held together by a small chain, a silk cord, or a leather thong), the two-piece arrangement is called bunrigata yatate. To avoid leakage in either form, the sumitsubo was generally stuffed with fibrous wadding, resembling absorbent cotton. Furthermore, the closure on the inkpot was fairly tight. The yatate could then be suspended from the obi by a toggle (netsuke) or held behind the sash in the manner of a sashi netsuke.

Most yatate are made of metal, although a few are made of wood; they date from the late eighteenth or early nineteenth centuries. Yatate styles range from rustic, simple pieces without embellishment to quite ornate, elaborately decorated and shaped pieces used by wealthy merchants or nobility. Most pieces are in the 7'' to 8'' range, but there are some delightful miniatures about 3'' long. In the Japanese tradition of making functional items into works of art, the yatate makers used all the known techniques of metalwork from simple etching to complicated multimetal inlays, from unadorned bamboo to elaborate gold lacquer work.

Reference: Shoichi Tarawa, *The Yatate Handbook*, Hoyusha Co., Ltd., n.d.

Museum: Margaret W. Strong Museum, Rochester, New York.

Reproduction Alert: There seems to be no real reproduction or forgery problem. However, one may come across one-piece brass pieces that seem to be yatates but were made in Mideastern countries in the late nineteenth century. These can usually be distinguished by their heavy designs, sometimes featuring Arabic calligraphy or recognizable non-Japanese decoration.

Collecting Hints: Yatates are not among the most heavily collected antique Japanese objects. They fall into the low or moderate price category, although prices can be quite high for pieces with elaborate decoration or of unusual shape and design. It is common to find yatates without the original brush; this is to be expected in old pieces. Occasionally, the hinge pin in the inkpot cover will be broken or missing, but this is usually a simple repair.

Yatates are most likely to be found at antiques shows and at shops specializing in Japanese material. Most general dealers will probably not be familiar with yatates. Occasionally, yatates can be found in specialized auctions of Japanese art and antiques. Finding yatates can require a good deal of hunting to uncover interesting pieces, but their variety and ingenuity make the search a rewarding activity.

Advisors: Irene and Bernard Rosett

Bunrigata
4'' l., mid 19th century, brass, miniature with flat rectangular ink pot on cord	200.00
7½'' l., early 19th century, brass, ensemble with ink pot in inro form, two sections and ojime bead in bean pod form	250.00
7½'' l., mid 19th century, ink pot in inro form, single case, coral ojime bead	225.00
7½'' l., mid 19th century, brass inkwell, bamboo stem bone lid on ink pot	250.00

3'' h., late 19th century, miniature, in the form of netsuke, multimetal (bronze, copper, silver, and gold), formed as a suit of armor with face mask and helmet, the two sections snap together, very rare. $2,500.00

8'' l., early 19th century, bamboo stem, copper ink pot in inro form, three sections	550.00
8'' l., mid 19th century, brass ink pot, lacquered bark simulation on stem	400.00
8'' l., mid 19th century, brush holder with compartment for thin knife, ink pot round with small compass set in cover, signed Ruundo	550.00
11½'' l., late 19th century, brass, ink pot in biwa form, repoussé dragon in clouds, brass ojime bead	375.00

Ittaigata
3'' l., late 19th century, multimetal bronze, silver, gold copper, shakudo and shibuichi, representing a full suit of armor beautifully engraved in great detail; figure opens at the knee, to accept brush, ink pot in the lower portion, unique	2,500.00
4½'' l., late 19th century, bronze, dragon raised design on ink pot lid	200.00
6¼'' l., mid 19th century, copper, brush and small knife inside handle, raised calligraphy on brush holder	350.00
6½'' l., early 19th century, bronze, formed to resemble a rough barked log	225.00

7½'' l., 19th century, fan shape, rosewood with tortoise shell insert on top. $275.00

7" l., 19th century, bamboo brush section and inkpot with metal insert, small coral netsuke. $325.00

8" l., 19th century, shakudo metal with floral menukis (sword hilt ornaments), flat rectangular brush section, inner knife compartment. $575.00

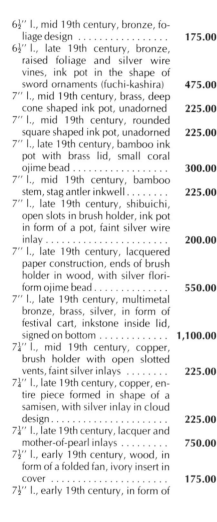

6½" l., mid 19th century, bronze, foliage design	175.00
6½" l., late 19th century, bronze, raised foliage and silver wire vines, ink pot in the shape of sword ornaments (fuchi-kashira)	475.00
7" l., mid 19th century, brass, deep cone shaped ink pot, unadorned	225.00
7" l., mid 19th century, rounded square shaped ink pot, unadorned	225.00
7" l., late 19th century, bamboo ink pot with brass lid, small coral ojime bead	300.00
7" l., mid 19th century, bamboo stem, stag antler inkwell	225.00
7" l., late 19th century, shibuichi, open slots in brush holder, ink pot in form of a pot, faint silver wire inlay	200.00
7" l., late 19th century, lacquered paper construction, ends of brush holder in wood, with silver floriform ojime bead	550.00
7" l., late 19th century, multimetal bronze, brass, silver, in form of festival cart, inkstone inside lid, signed on bottom	1,100.00
7¼" l., mid 19th century, copper, brush holder with open slotted vents, faint silver inlays	225.00
7¼" l., late 19th century, copper, entire piece formed in shape of a samisen, with silver inlay in cloud design	225.00
7¼" l., late 19th century, lacquer and mother-of-pearl inlays	750.00
7½" l., early 19th century, wood, in form of a folded fan, ivory insert in cover	175.00
7½" l., early 19th century, in form of folded fan, silver emblem on cover	300.00
7½" l., mid 19th century, copper, unadorned, round, flat ink pot	175.00
7½" l., late 19th century, bronze, round ink pot, all over inlaid silver wire inlay	275.00
7½" l., late 19th century, bronze, square shaped ink pot, overall inlaid silver wire	275.00
8" l., early 19th century, brass, shishi on ink pot lid, mythical animal head at the end of brush holder	300.00
8" l., mid nineteenth century, raised floral design	250.00
8" l., mid 19th century, bronze, engraved mandarin ducks on ink pot, signed in grass script	350.00
8" l., mid 19th century, wood, silver hinged lid on ink pot	550.00
8" l., late 19th century, shakudo, flowers and basket designs	475.00
8" l., late 19th century, brass, finely detailed wood grain effect	200.00
8½" l., mid 19th century, brass, brush holder designed to simulate woven strips with rats entering and leaving openings in the tube, touches of silver trim on ink pot and brush holder end, signed in silver reserve on bottom	600.00
8½" l., mid 19th century, brass, white metal scale on top of brush holder, containing brush and small knife, with stained ivory ojime bead	375.00
11½" l., late 19th century, brass, with measuring scale imprinted on top	300.00

KOREAN CERAMICS

History: Though Korean ceramics were coveted by Chinese connoisseurs as early as the twelfth century and have been an obsession of Japanese collectors since the sixteenth century, Westerners discovered Korean ceramics only in the last half of this century. The first English text on the subject was published in 1947. Today, however, Korean ceramics are among the most-sought after antiques in the world, increasing in value approximately 300 to 500 percent over the last five years. A deeper understanding of Korean wares has greatly contributed to their increasing popularity. Whereas the finest of Chinese ceramics were produced under strict standards and dictated by a cautious aristocracy; fine Korean wares were often crafted without these constants. The peasant potter and the fire god of the kiln were given much freedom in the creation of the finished product. In Korean ceramics, uniformity and perfection are subordinate to spontaneity and creative expression.

Two factors limit the availability of Korean ceramics. First, Korea never was a ceramic exporting country, so the actual number of pieces that were ever made is small compared with China and Japan. Second, because of its geographical location, Korea has had a tumultuous history. At various times it was overrun by the Tartars, the Mongols, the Manchus, the Chinese, and most recently the Japanese. It is amazing that any ceramics have survived.

There are four types of Korean ceramics available to today's collector: (1) natural ash glazed stoneware of the Silla Period (fourth to tenth centuries), (2) celadons and inlaid celadons of the Koryo Dynasty (tenth to fourteenth centuries), (3) Punch'ong slip decorated wares of the early Yi Dynasty (fifteenth to sixteenth centuries), and (4) white porcelains of the late Yi Dynasty (seventeenth to nineteenth centuries).

Silla Wares: Most surviving Silla stonewares come from the fifth and sixth centuries, just before the first unification of Korea. The Silla culture descended from the "horse-riding people" of the steppes and forests of northern Asia. The most distinguishing feature of Silla stoneware, a tall pedestal foot, was derived from the shamanistic belief that the universe is held up by a strong World Tree. The pedestals may be separate pieces or may be part of various sacrificial vessels. These wares are unassuming; they have grey clay bodies, incised designs, and natural ash glazes. The earthy quality of these wares was no doubt intentional, considering that more sophisticated glazes and methods of decorating had been used in Asian for more than 500 years. The free-hand incised designs of Silla wares began a tradition of spontaneity that has always symbolized Korean ceramics.

Koryo Celadons: At the turn of this century, the kingfisher green celadons of Korea's Koryo Dynasty (918–1392) were considered to be more myth than reality. Chinese classical references to these wares were considered an exaggeration, and the handful of these wares in existence were considered to be more of an aberration than a tradition. But railroad construction by the occupying Japanese in the early twentieth century unearthed one of the world's most important ceramic accomplishments—the Koryo celadon.

The Koryo Dynasty roughly coincided with the Chinese Sung and Yuan Dynasties. During this period Korea developed a celadon tradition quite distinct from the rest of the world. The unique kingfisher green color is the result of a thin translucent celadon glaze over the native, grey Korean clay. Early Koryo celadons are simple and unobtrusive, shallow incised and impressed decorations are visible only on close inspection. By the twelfth century, however, the Koreans began to fill these shallow decorations with white and black slip, creating the first inlaid celadons. This process became very sophisticated over the following two centuries. The two most common motifs are a stylized wild chrysanthemum and flying cranes. Inlaid celadons are strictly a Korean tradition.

Punch'ong Wares: The cultural changes associated with the establishment of the Yi Dynasty (1392) are reflected in the Korea's ceramic tradition. The excesses of a Buddist-dominated ruling class during the Koryo Dynasty gave way to a somewhat more benevolent Confucianist aristocracy under the Yi Dynasty. The wares used by the vast majority of Korean society during the fifteenth and sixteenth centuries were a ceramic known as Punch'ong. Though related to the Koryo inlaid wares, Punch'ong pieces are more freely decorated and much more thinly glazed. Designs are most often impressed and filled with white slip. Motifs are stylized and repetitive. In later pieces, decorating is abandoned altogether and pieces are simply dipped into the fluid white slip. It was Punch'ong wares, particularly bowls, that captured the hearts of the Japanese tea ceremony enthusiasts in the Japanese conquest of Korea in 1598, sometimes called the Ceramic War.

White Porcelain: While the commoners of the fifteenth century were eating off of Punch'ong wares, royalty used nothing but white porcelains. These were a sign of purity and reverence and represented a break with the celadon tradition of the Koryo kings. These early Yi porcelains will seldom be encountered outside of museums. White porcelains from the seventeenth to nineteenth centuries are available. These later porcelains are frequently bluish white in color, similar to Chinese Ying Ching wares of the Sung Dynasty. During this period many underglaze decorated porcelains were also produced, first using copper and iron and later cobalt blue. The red copper underglaze decoration was developed by the Koreans in the twelfth century. Blue and white porcelains were not common until the nineteenth century. Underglaze designs are often casually or even carelessly applied. However, as in the case in other Korean ceramics, this spontaneity of design is revered.

References: Edward B. Adams, *Korea's Pottery Heritage*, Vol. 1, Seoul International Publishing House, 1986; —, *Korea's Pottery Heritage*, Vol. 11, Seoul International Publishing House, 1990; Goro Akaboshi and Heiichiro Nakamura, *Five Centuries of Korean Ceramics*, Weatherhill/Tankosha, 1975; Sun-U Choi and Yang-mo Chung, *The Arts of Korean Ceramics*, Dong-wha Publishing Co., 1979; G. St. G. M. Gompertz, *Korean Celadon and Other Wares of the Koryo Period*, Thomas Yoseloff, 1964; —, *Korean Pottery and Porcelain of the Yi Period*, Faber and Faber, 1968; W. B. Honey, *Korean Pottery*, Pitman Publishing Corp., 1947; Robert J. Moes, *Korean Art from the Brooklyn Museum Collection*, Universe Books, 1987.

Museums: Los Angeles County Museum of Art, Los Angeles, California; Avery Brundage Collection, Asian Art Museum, M. H. de Young Museum, San Francisco, California; Mrs. Charles Cooke Collection, Academy of Art, Honolulu, Hawaii; Russel Tyson Collection, Chicago Art Institute, Chicago, Illinois; Charles B. Hoyt Collection, Museum of Fine Arts, Boston, Massachusetts; James Plumer Collection, University of Michigan Art Museum, Ann Arbor, Michigan; Cleveland Art Museum, Cleveland, Ohio; Newark Art Museum, Newark, New Jersey; Brooklyn Art Museum, Brooklyn, New York; Metropolitan Museum of Art, New York, New York; John D. Rockefeller III Collection, The Asia Society, New York, New York; John R. Fox Collection, Syracuse University Museum, Syracuse, New York; Charles Freer Collection/Horace Allen Collection, Freer Gallery of Art, Smithsonian Institute, Washington, D.C.

Reproduction Alert: Most reproductions were made after 1890 and production reached a peak in the 1930s during the Japanese occupation. Silla stonewares are quite easily reproduced so caution must be exercised. Authentic Silla wares

were fired at very high temperatures and should exhibit a resonant ring when struck. Most efforts at reproduction focused on Koryo celadons. However, the color and quality of the kingfisher green glaze is not easily imitated. Authentic pieces have a bubble-infused, crackled, translucent glaze. Reproductions often have a lack-luster olive green glaze, although very convincing reproductions are available. Authentic pieces of celadon will have sand particles fused to the base. One should never make a major investment in a Korean ceramic without the assistance of a knowledgeable dealer. Authenticating important pieces often requires inspection by several authorities.

Collecting Hints: The collecting of fine, undamaged inlaid celadons or other rare Korean ceramics must be left to the few collectors that can afford tens of thousands of dollars for a single piece. But many rewarding collections have been built with pieces in the $100 to $1,000 range. Many Silla ash glazed stoneware pieces can be obtained in this price range—stemmed cups, cup stands, and bowls, for example.

One can also obtain Koryo celadons, but a few compromises are necessary. First, purchases will generally be limited to small items (bowls or dishes), and in addition, one must be ready to accept either a less desirable celadon color (olive to brown) or some damage (chips or repairs). The fact that this level of compromise is necessary just to get pieces under $1,000 emphasizes the importance of these wares. The demand for punch'ong wares is only slightly less than that of Koryo celadons. In Korean ceramics, even nineteenth-century wares are considered rare. Undamaged white porcelain with underglaze decorations in either iron, copper, or cobalt blue will rarely be found for under $1,000.

A review of Korean ceramics resold at auction over the last five years indicates a continuing price spiral, fueled largely by the emergence of Korea as and affluent industrial economy. There are many examples of a tenfold increase in value for the same piece at auction over the last five years; the average is probably threefold to fivefold over five years.

SILLA NATURAL ASH GLAZED STONEWARE

Bowl, 5" dia., 5th/6th centuries, deep bowl on tall flaring foot, gray stoneware decorated with incised and vertical dotted lines, no glaze, no repairs **250.00**

Cup with lid, 8" h., 5th/6th centuries, pedestaled gray stoneware cup with lid, tall pedestal with two tiers of rectangular perforation, incised wavy pattern, round and flatten finial with two rectangular perforations,

**Pedestal Jar with Lid, Silla period, 14",
5th/6th century, grey stoneware, minor
chipping. $3,000.00**

**Vase, 8" h., 12th century, muskmelon
shaped. $8,000.00**

burnished black, small chips, no re-
pairs **600.00**

Jar

7" h., 5th/6th century, gray pottery
jar of ovoid shape with flaring
mouth and flaring pedestal of approximately equal size, whorled
handles, natural ash glaze on upper surfaces, small chip restored
on pedestal **1,000.00**

11" h., 5th/6th century, gray pottery, ovoid jar with tall pedestal,
one row of triangular perforations
in pedestal, whorled handles on
body, natural ash glaze on upper
surfaces, restored pedestal **1,200.00**

11" h., 5th/6th centuries, gray pottery, slightly compress ovoid tapering to flat base, faintly impressed overall with fine rope-like
textures, galleried-rim neck, restored rim chip, underside with
impressed mark **1,500.00**

Stand, 7" h., 5th/6th centuries, gray
pottery stand (to support a rounded
bottom jar) spreading conical foot,
combed with two bands of wavey
lines, three tiers of triangular apertures in foot, no glaze, chips to base **1,000.00**

KORYO CELADONS AND INLAID
CELADONS

Bowl

4" dia., 13th/14th century, small
bowl on short foot, inlaid, stylized
white chrysanthemum design on
interior and exterior, bubble
infused, crackled, gray-green celadon glaze, firing irregularity (pitting) repaired with gold lacquer. **200.00**

5" dia., 12th century, shallow bowl,
interior with inlaid white slip central flowerhead medallion, beneath crackled and bubble
suffused celadon glaze **1,500.00**

6" dia., 12th century, deep bowl tapering to short foot ring, no decoration, thick olive green, finely
crackled, celadon glaze, no deco-
ration, repaired chip on lip **350.00**

6" dia., 12th century, deep bowl on
flat base, exterior with four incised
flower sprays, beneath fine cela-
don glaze, lacquer restoration . . . **2,000.00**

6" dia., 12th century, deep bowl,
thinly potted and faintly molded
on interior with dragons, covered
with rich blue-green glaze, three
spurs on foot, repairs **2,500.00**

7" dia., 12th century, shallow bowl
tapering to short foot ring, impressed floral design on interior,
sculpted lotus petal design on exterior, crackled gray-green celadon glaze, two repaired chips on
lip **550.00**

7" dia., 12th century, shallow bowl
on short foot, faintly incised on
interior with two parrots, pale sea-
green glaze, crack with gilt lac-
quer repair, glaze gaps **600.00**

7" dia., 12th century, shallow bowl
on short foot, molded on the interior with a single leafy floral blossom below an incised line, cov-
ered in a gray-green glaze, repairs **600.00**

7" dia., 12th century, scrap bowl,
globular drum-shaped body with
sharply flaring mouth, body
deeply carved with scrolling and
flowering chrysanthemum, flaring
mouth with scrolling flowering

peony, thick celadon glaze, burial discoloration and restoration 8,000.00

8″ dia., 12th century, fine inlaid celadon bowl on raised foot ring, interior with black and white slip flower roundels and reverse inlaid scrolling, exterior four flower sprays, beneath fine crackled and bubble suffused celadon glaze . . .   8,000.00

8″ dia., 12th century, conical shaped bowl on low foot, interior with impressed leafy floral sprig, covered with crackled grayish-green glaze, large repaired rim chips, hairline cracks 1,500.00

8″ dia., 12th century, deep bowl with incised flower sprays below band of scrolling leaves, interior incised with cranes and clouds centering on recessed flowerhead, grayish green celadon glaze pooling above foot. 6,000.00

10″ dia., 14th century, deep bowl on raised foot ring and inturned rim, crackled celadon glaze 1,500.00

Box and cover, 3″ dia., 12th century, circular dish on recessed ring foot, cover decorated with central medallion in inlaid black and white slip of flower spray, incised clouds, finely crackled and bubble-suffused celadon glaze 15,000.00

Cup, 5″ dia., 12th/13th century, flared cup on short foot, incised with line above foot and in interior, light green dense crackle glaze, firing irregularity on rim. 6,000.00

Ewer, 8″ h., 12th century, melon-form ewer, twelve-lobed oviform body with looped handle, slender spout, finely crackled and bubble-suffused celadon glaze, chip to spout and replaced lid 20,000.00

Oil bottle

3″ h., 12th century, globular bottle on raised ring foot with short flared spout, decorated in inlaid black and white slip of cranes in clouds, crackled celadon glaze   6,000.00

4″ dia., 13th century, globular bottle on raised ring foot sloping to short narrow neck with cup shaped mouth, crackled and bubble-suffused celadon glaze pooling toward base, chip on foot 1,500.00

Stem Cup, 4″ dia., 13th century, interior with inlaid black and white slip with central flowerhead medallion surrounded by cranes and clouds, beneath crackled and bubble suffused celadon glaze. 2,000.00

Vase, 12″ h., 13th/14th century, inlaid, neck extensive restoration, realized price, including 10 percent buyer's premium at Christie's, New York, in 1991. $30,800.00

Vase, 12″ h., 13th/14th century, large vase, hexagonal neck, inlaid white and black slip with four peony medallions above stylized leaves, inlaid rings and tassels, pale and finely crackled glaze, extensive body crack and neck restoration. 50,000.00

Wine cup, 3″ h., 12th century, ten-lobed cup, short flared foot, barbed rim, incised central medallion of chrysanthemum flowerhead, lobes incised with flower sprays, exterior inlaid in white and black slip floral spray, finely crackled celadon glaze, haircracks and rim chip 15,000.00

PUNCH'ONG WARES

Bottle

9″ h., 15th century, flattened ovoid form on ring foot, decorated in white slip in sgraffito (line-incised) style revealing gray body, decorated with large lotus design on one side and different floral pattern on other, neck replaced in silver. .50,000.00

13″ h., globular bottle with flared neck and ring foot, decorated in brush-applied white slip beneath a finely crackled clear glaze pooling 2,500.00

13″ h., 15th century, elegantly potted pear-shaped bottle on ring foot and with flared rim, decorated with inlaid white slip with "rope-curtain" pattern, shoulder with stylized leave design, celadon glaze. 10,000.00

Bowl

5" dia., deep bowl supported by short ring foot, decorated by partial submergence in white slip, five spur marks on interior, thin transparent celadon glaze **500.00**

7" dia., 15th/16th century, deep sides supported on ring foot, inlaid on interior in white slip with central flowerhead encircled by radiating "rope-curtain" design, radiating design repeated on exterior, thin watery glaze, restoration to rim **1,200.00**

7" dia., 16th century, shallow splayed bowl tapering to recessed ring foot, interior decorated with brush-applied white slip under finely crackled clear glaze **2,000.00**

7" dia., 15th/16th centuries, finely potted shallow bowl on raised ring foot, decorated with white slip running over darker gray-green body, well decorated with incised circle, five spur marks on interior **3,000.00**

8" dia., 15th century, bowl on raised ring foot finely decorated in inlaid black and white slip with undecorated central medallion surrounded by band of scrolling lotus flowers, exterior with stylized flowerhead roundel and leaf pattern, beneath crackled and bubble-suffused celadon glaze **10,000.00**

8" dia., 15th century, deep bowl on raised foot ring, interior with inlaid white slip with central medallion of flowersheads, exterior with inlaid "rope-curtain" pattern, thin glaze, minor restoration **1,200.00**

Dish

4" dia., shallow dish on short ring foot, decorated with inlaid white slip with central stylized floret and "rope-curtain" pattern interior

Bowl, 7" dia., 15th/16th century, Rope Curtain design. $1,200.00

Bowl, 5" dia., 16th century, dipped in white slip. $500.00

and exterior, thin celadon glaze tending to brown, kiln cracks **150.00**

5" dia., shallow stoneware dish on ring foot, decorated in inlaid white slip, central medallion surrounded by band of "rope-curtain" pattern, exterior with four Chinese characters between bands of "rope curtain" pattern, clear glaze **1,000.00**

5" dia., shallow dish tapering to short ring foot, decorated in brush-applied white slip over impressed design with central roundel containing auspicious characters surrounded by flowerhead motif, gray-green crackled glaze flowing down, wooded box   **2,500.00**

7" dia., deep dish supported by short ring foot, decorated by partial submergence in white slip, five spurs on interior, thin crackled transparent celadon glaze **200.00**

Jar

5" h., 15th century, jar with squat globular body sharply tapering to raised foot and slightly everted rim, decorated in inlaid black and white slip with "rope-curtain" design, beneath clear finely cracked glaze **3,000.00**

6" h., 15th century, squat globular body on ring foot, decorated in brush-applied gray slip over darker gray and incised to reveal latter, stylized lappet design, clear glaze flowing down to partially cover foot **3,000.00**

Stem cup, 3" h., 15th century, stoneware cup set on high splayed foot and with slightly everted rim, decorated in inlaid white slip, interior with central medallion of stylized floral patterns surrounded by

"rope-curtain" pattern, exterior also with "rope curtain" pattern, clear crackled glaze **2,500.00**
Vase, 12" h., 15th/16th centuries, pear-shaped stoneware vase, globular shape supported on raised ring foot, decorated in white slip and incised sgraffiato style to reveal darker body below, freely executed floral leaves, thin glaze, restoration to lip, pinhole glaze gaps, hairline graze cracks **4,000.00**

WHITE PORCELAIN

Bowl, 7" dia., 19th century, deep bowl on raised ring foot with slightly flared rim, blue tinged white glaze   **1,500.00**
Bottle
   5" h., 17th/18th centuries, tall faceted milk bottle, everted rim, flat base, decorated with thick bubble suffused white glaze........... **2,500.00**
   5" h., 19th century, rectangular bottle with short and flaring neck, decorated in relief with floral sprays, thick, blue-tinged, and bubble-suffused glaze, crack on one side **10,000.00**
   7" h., 19th century, compressed globular form, tall cylindrical neck, rolled rim, decorated with two sprays of flowering orchids in underglaze blue, overall in blue-tinged white glaze **20,000.00**
   9" h., 19th century, pear shaped body tapering to flared spout, supported by short ring foot, blue tinged white glaze, reassembled and repaired in gold lacquer **600.00**
Brushpot, 5" h., 19th century, rectangular form carved with rib pattern and pierced with circular motif, carved foot................... **8,000.00**

Dish, 7" dia., 19th century, very fine shallow dish on raised ring foot, decorated in underglaze blue with central character roundel and sprays of chestnut **15,000.00**
Ewer, 7" h., 19th century, oviform body, recessed ring foot, loop handle, curved spout, decorated in underglaze copper-red with sprays of bamboo, chip on cover restored ... **10,000.00**
Jar
   13" h., 17th/18th century, ovoid storage jar on short ring foot, rolled rim, decorated with iron-brown stylized plant forms, gray glaze ending above unglazed foot, firing crack on base **70,000.00**
   16" h., 19th century, tall baluster vase, high-shouldered, tall cylindrical neck, bluish white glaze, chips and repairs **6,000.00**
   16" h., 19th century, high-shouldered and ovoid form with tall cylindrical neck, underglaze blue four-clawed dragon with clouds and flaming pearl **10,000.00**
Offering dish, 6" dia., 19th century, shallow dish on high splayed foot, green tinged white glaze, sand adhering to foot **250.00**
Oil lamp, 3" h., 19th century, cylindrical form with side handle and fitted wick holder, covered with white glaze, wick holder cracked **1,500.00**
Waterdropper
   3" h., late 19th century, modeled after peach, spray of leaves forming base, decorated in underglaze blue and copper-red........... **1,500.00**
   3" h., 19th century, flower spray and grasses in underglaze blue

Offering dish, 19th century, bluish white color. $350.00

Vase, 9" h., 19th century, bluish white color, broken and repaired with gold lacquer. $600.00

and copper-red under bluish-white glaze, spout chipped **1,500.00**

3″ h., rectangular form decorated in underglaze blue, top with Han river scenery, sides with abstract design, crack and glaze scratching **1,500.00**

3″ h., 19th century, rectangular dropper on flat base, decorated with underglaze blue of scholars admiring Han River scenery and sprays of flowers **25,000.00**

APPENDIXES

Appendix I   Chronological Table of Chinese Emperors

Wade-Giles		Pinyin
	Tang	
Kao-tzu	618–626	Gaozu
T'ai-tsung	627–649	Taizong
Kao-tsung	650–683	Gaozong
Chung-tsung	684–709	Zhongzong
Jui-tsung	710–712	Ruizong
Hsuan-tsung	713–755	Xuanzong
Su-tsung	756–762	Suzong
Tai-tsung	763–779	Daizong
Te-tsung	780–804	Dezong
Shun-tsung	805	Shunzong
Hsien-tsung	806–820	Xianzong
Mu-tsung	821–824	Muzong
Wen-tsung	827–840	Wenzong
Wu-tsung	841–846	Wuzong
Hsuan-tsung	847–859	Xuanzong
Yi-tsung	860–873	Yizong
Hsi-tsung	874–888	Xizong
Chao-tsung	889–903	Zhaozong
Chao-hsuan	904–907	Zhaoxuan
	Northern (Sung) Song	
T'ai-tsu	960–976	Taizu
T'ai-tsung	976–998	Taizong
Ch'en-tsung	998–1022	Chenzong
Jen-tsung	1023–1063	Renzong
Ying-tsung	1064–1067	Yingzong
Shen-tsung	1068–1085	Shenzong
Che-tsung	1086–1100	Zhezong
Hui-tsung	1101–1126	Huizong
Ch'in-tsung	1126	Qinzong
	Southern (Sung) Song	
Kao-tsung	1127–1162	Gaozong
Hsiao-tsung	1163–1189	Xiaozong
Kuang-tsung	1190–1194	Guanzong
Ning-tsung	1195–1224	Ningzong
Li-tsung	1225–1264	Lizong
Tu-tsung	1265–1275	Duzong

Kung-ti	1275	Gongdi
Tuan-tsung	1276–1278	Duanzong
Ti-ping	1278–1279	Dibing

Yuan

(Khubilai)		
Shih-tsu	1260–1294	Shizu
Ch'eng-tsaung	1295–1307	Chengzong
Wu-tsung	1308–1311	Wuzong
Jen-tsung	1312–1320	Renzong
Ying-tsung	1321–1323	Yingzong
Dai-ting-ti	1324–1328	Taidingdi
Yu-chou	1328	Youzhu
Ming-tsung	1329	Mingzong
Wen-tsung	1329–1332	Wenzong
Ning-tsung	1332	Ningzong
Shun-ti	1333–1368	Shundi

Ming

Hung-wu	1368–1398	Hongwu
Yung-lo	1403–1424	Yonglo
Hsuan-te	1426–1435	Xuante
Ching-tai	1450–1456	Jingtai
Ch'eng-hua	1465–1487	Chenghua
Hung-chih	1488–1505	Hongzhi
Cheng-te	1506–1521	Zhengde
Chia-ching	1522–1566	Jiajing
Lung-ch'ing	1567–1572	Longqing
Wan-li	1573–1619	Wanli

Transitional

| T'ien-ch'i | 1621–1627 | Tianqi |
| Ch'ung-cheng | 1628–1643 | Chongzheng |

Early (Ch'ing) Qing

Shun-chih	1644–1661	Shunzhi
K'ang-hsi	1662–1722	Kangxi
Yung-cheng	1723–1735	Yongzheng
Ch'ien-lung	1736–1795	Qianlong

Late (Ch'ing) Qing

Chia-ching	1796–1820	Jiaqing
Tao-kuang	1821–1850	Daoguang
Hsien-feng	1851–1861	Xianfeng
T'ung-chih	1862–1874	Tongzhi
Kuang-hsu	1875–1908	Guangxu
Hsuan-tung	1909–1911	Xuantong
Hung-hsien	1916	Hongxian

Appendix II   The Wade-Giles and Pinyin System

The Pinyin system of spelling Chinese words, which represents a more phonetic approach to pronunciation of Chinese sounds from the printed word, was adopted by the international community in the late 1970s. Although Pinyin is used currently in new publications and auction catalogs, much of the traditional literature was written in the old Wade-Giles system of spelling. It appears that researchers should be familiar with both systems to cover adequately the established reading matter on Chinese history and works of art. Since both systems are used interchangeably in various section of this book, we have provided some pronunciation keys that will help the reader translate from one system to another if necessary.

Beginning Letter(s)			Final Letter(s)		
Wade-Giles		Pinyin	Wade-Giles		Pinyin
ch	=	zh	en	=	an
ch	=	k	i	=	yi
ch'	=	ch	ieh	=	ie
ch'	=	q	ih	=	i
hs	=	x	o	=	e
j	=	r	o	=	ou
k	=	g	u	=	i
k'	=	k	ueh	=	ue
p	=	b	uei	=	ui
p'	=	p	ung	=	ong
t'	=	d	yu	=	you
ts, tz	=	z	yu	=	yu
ts, tz	=	c			

Some Common Ceramic-Related Terms
(Wade-Giles to Pinyin)

Wade Giles	Pinyin	Wade Giles	Pinyin
An-hua	Anhua	Kuan-yin	Guanyin
Chien	Jian	Ku Yueh Hsuan	Guyuexuan
Ch'ing Pai	Qingbai	Lohan	Lehan
Chi-chou	Jizhou	Lung Ch'uan	Longquan
Ching-te-chen	Jingdezhen	Nien hoa	Nianhoa
Chun Yao	Junyao	Peking	Beijing
Fa Hua	Fahua	San-ts'ai	Sancai
Fukien	Fujian	T'ao-t'ieh	Taotie
Hsing	Xing	Tê-hua	Dehua
Honan	Henan	Ting	Ding
I-hsing	Yixing	Tou-ts'ai	Doucai
Ju	Ru	T'zu-chow	Cizhou
Ju-i	Ruyi	Wu-ts'ai	Wucai
Ko	Ge	Yi-hsing	Yixing
Kuan	Guan	Ying-ch'ing	Yingqing
Kuan-tung	Guangdong	Yueh	Yue

Appendix III   Japanese Periods and Selected Glossary of Japanese Terms

Japanese Periods

Jomon Period	4500–200 B.C.	Muromachi Period	1333–1568
Yayoi Period	200 B.C.–250 A.D.	Momoyama Period	1568–1615
Kofun Period	250–552	Edo Period	1615–1868
Asuka Period	552–646	Meiji Period	1868–1912
Nara Period	646–794	Taisho Period	1912–1926
Heian Period	794–1185	Showa Period	1926–present
Kamakura Period	1185–1333		

Selected Glossary of Japanese Terms

Aburazara: Oil dish

Aka: The color red

Akaji-kinga: Red with gold designs painted on

Ao: The color green

Aubergine: Color popular in both Chinese and Japanese enamels, a dark purple shade likened to the color of the skin of the eggplant

Cha: Tea

Cha-ire: Tea caddy

Chajin: Master of the tea ceremony

Cha-no-yu: The Japanese tea ceremony

Cha-wan: Japanese name for tea bowl (dark glazed Chinese tea bowls used in Japanese ceremonies are called temmouku)

Daimyo: Lord

Da-wan: Teacup

E-: Painted

Edo: Old city name for Tokyo

Fuku: Japanese character translating as "good fortune"

Gosu: A blue color of varying hue used before 1872

Hana-ike: Vase for flowers

Hanakago-de: Pattern used to decorate porcelain, a filled flower basket with a large loop handle, used as a popular theme on Imari porcelain

Heian: Old city name for Kyoto

Iro: Word meaning "color" or "colored"

Jido: Porcelain clay

Kacho: Design of flowers and birds

Kaga: Old name for Ishikawa Prefecture, the place that Kaga ware was made

Kannon: God of mercy

Karako: Decoration of Chinese children on ceramics

Ki: The color yellow

Kinrande: Red and gold decoration adopted from the Chinese

Ko: Old

Kogo: Incense box

Kuro: The color black

Kushi-de: Typical comb decoration found on the bases of Nabeshima wares

Mingei: Folk art

Mizusashi: Tea ceremony water container

Mon: Family crest

Mukozuke: Tea ceremony small deep bowl used for a side dish in the tea ceremony

Nihon: Japanese term for Japan

Nippon: Japanese term for Japan

Nishikide: A term associated with Imari wares, referring to all over enamel brocade decoration

Seiji: Japanese name for celadon

Sencha: Tea leaves

Shiro: The color white

Sometsuke: Underglaze blue decoration on white porcelain

Tsubo: Jar

Yaki: Ware

Yakimono: Ware made of ceramic

Appendix IV   Glossary of Japanese Woodblock Print Terms

Aiban: Size of a print approximately 9″ x 12″, between chuban (medium) and oban (large)

Aizuri: A print primarily using indigo

Awase: A game or contest

Ayame: Siberian iris

Baren: A pad used by a printer when taking impressions from a woodblock

Beni-e: A black print on which pink (beni) is spread by hand—a term used to refer to the early two-color prints

Beni-girai: A particularly delicate pink

Benizuri-e: Paintings printed in two or three colors with pink

Bijin-ga: Paintings of beautiful women

Binzashi: Hairpins

Chuban: Medium-size vertical prints

Chubon: Book measuring 7″ x 4¾″

Chushingura: Kabuki play about the story of the Forty-seven Ronin

Diptych: A woodblock print in two sheets, usually side by side

Edo: The old name of Tokyo; period from 1603 to 1868

Egoyomi: Calendar prints, most commonly surimono

Ehon: Illustrated books

Gauffrage: Printing without color being applied; the print is laid on the block face up (not in the reverse as in color printing) and pressure gives it an embossed look

Genroku: Period from 1688 to 1704; a time of special elegance in Japanese life

Goh: Assumed or stage name

Hanshi-bon: Book measuring 9″ x 6¼″

Harimaze: Sheets printed with multiple designs to be pulled apart later

Hashira-e: A long narrow print made to hang on the pillars of a Japanese house (circa 30″ x 5″)

Higa: Erotic picture

Honmoto: Publisher

Hoso-ban Sanpuku-Tsui: A narrow triptych

Hoso-e or Hoso-ban: A small vertical, narrow print (circa 12″ x 6″), a common size for portraits of actors

Ichimai-e: A single sheet print

Kabuki: Popular classical theater

Kacho-ga: Prints of flowers or birds

Kakamono-e: Rectangular paintings (similar to a scroll) composed of vertically hung sheets (circa 30″ x 9″)

Kamuro: Apprentice courtesan

Kano school: Traditional Japanese painting of Chinese-style ink painting

Kento: Marks used in printing to ensure accurate register

Kimekomi: A method of creating a three-dimensional effect

Kirazuri: Application of mica powder to print paper yielding a silvery effect

Koban: A small vertical print (approximately 5″ x 3″)

Korin School: Edo period painting school with primary emphasis on decorative effects

Meiji: Period from 1868 to 1912

Mon: A family crest often seen on a robe

Nagasaki-e: Nagasaki prints depicting foreigners

Nishiki-e: Polychrome (formerly called brocade) prints

Noh: A drama, usually with religous content

Oban: A rectangular full-size vertical print (15″ x 10″); large oban (22¾″ x 12½″)

Obi: Kimono sash

Obon: Book measuring 10½″ x 7½″

Okube-e: Close-up portraits

Onna-e: Pictures of women

Onnagata: Male Kabuki actors taking female roles

Sansui-ga: Landscape painting

Sensu: Folding fan

Shijo school: Kyoto school of realistic painting in the late Edo period

Showa: Japanese historical period from 1926

(Courtesy of Whittman's Oriental Gallery)

Shunga: Erotic prints (literally, "spring pictures")

Sumi-e: Black or white print or painting

Sumizuri-e: Black ink prints, hand colored

Sumo: Japanese wrestling

Surimono: Small-size prints for greetings, and so forth (literally, "printed things")

Suzuri: Hollowed out slab for ink

Taisho: Japanese historical period from 1912 to 1926

Tan-e: Print in which brick red color predominates

Tanjaku: Narrow slips of paper on which verses are written; used by Hiroshige for brief descriptions of subject matter (15" x 5")

Tokaido: The highway between Edo and Kyoto, when Kyoto was the capital

Torii school: A group of print makers specializing in depiction of Kabuki scenes and actors

Tosa school: Painting school from which Ukiyo-es are derived

Triptych: A composition consisting of three separate sheets side by side

Uciwa-e: Fan painting

Uki-e: Perspective prints (literally "bird's eye view pictures")

Ukiyo-e: Pictures of the floating world (woodblocks)

Urushi-e: Lacquer prints decorated with metallic dust

Yakusha-e: Portraits of actors

Yamato-e: Classical narrative scroll painting

Yokobon: Book measuring $4\frac{1}{2}''$ x $6\frac{3}{4}''$

Yoko-e: Full-size horizontal print (approximately 15" x 10")

Yojo: Courtesans

Yoshiwara: The Edo brothel district

Appendix V   Chinese Pottery and Porcelain Marks
Ming Reign Marks

Hongwu (1368-1398)	Hongwu (1368-1398)	Yongle (1403-1424)	Yongle (1403-1424)
洪武 篆書	年製 洪武	年製 永樂	年製 永樂
Xuande (1426-1435)	Xuande (1426-1435)	Chenghua (1465-1487)	Chenghua (1465-1487)
篆書	德年製 大明宣	成化 篆書	年製 成化
Chenghua (1465-1487)	Hungzhi (1488-1505)	Zhengde (1506-1521)	Jiajing (1522-1566)
化年製 大明成	治年製 大明弘	德年製 大明正	靖年製 大明嘉
Lonqing (1567-1572)	Wanli (1573-1619)	Tiangi (1621-1627)	Chongzhen (1628-1644)
慶年製 大明隆	曆年製 大明萬	啟年製 大明天	年製 崇楨

Qing Reign Marks

Shunzhi (1644–1661)	Shunzhi (1644–1661)	Kangxi (1662–1722)	Kangxi (1662–1722)
Yongzheng (1723–1735)	Yongzheng (1723–1735)	Qianlong (1736–1795)	Qianlong (1736–1795)
Qianlong (1736–1795)	Qianlong (1736–1795)	Jiajing (1796–1820)	Jiajing (1796–1820)
Daoguang (1821–1850)	Daoguang (1821–1850)	Xianfeng (1851–1861)	Xianfeng (1851–1861)

Qing Reign Marks, *continued*

Tongzhi (1862–1874)	Tongzhi (1862–1874)	Guangxu (1875–1908)	Guangxu (1875–1908)
大清同治年製	大清同治年製	大清光緒年製	大清光緒年製

Xuantong (1909–1912)	Hongxian (1916)	Hongxian (1916)	Hongxian (1916)
大清宣統年製	洪憲御製	洪憲年製	洪憲御製

Republic of China (1911–1948)

中華民國

Various Song Marks

Made in the Xiande years of the Great Sung Dynasty	Da guan Nothern celadon ware	Zheng he Northern celadon ware
大宋顯德年製	大觀	政和
Premium Quality	Prolong	Imperial ware
甲	申	官
New Imperial ware	Supreme beauty	"in and up" gift to Imperial Personage
新官	奉華	進上
Happiness within	Northern Palace	Merciful Happiness
内府	北苑	慈福

Various Song Marks, *continued*

Royal retreat	gift to Imperial Personage	Beautifully Assembled
禁苑	供御	聚秀
offering to Imperial Personage	Beautiful as a Phoenix	Department of Medical Taxation
進琖	鳳華	尚藥局
Department of Food Taxation	1080 A.D.	Made by the Zhang family
尚食局	元豐三年	張家造
Palace of the Five Lords	Zhang family mark	978 A.D
五王府	張家枕	太平戊寅

Various Song Marks, *continued*

Flower garden	1108 A.D.	Fine sample from the water's edge
花園	大觀貳年	河濱遺範
Made in 1111 A.D.	1072 A.D.	Official ware
政和年製	熙寧四年	官
Residence of Benevolence and Harmony	Mark used only on Song imitation wares	
仁和館	豐年製 大宋元	

Various Ming Marks

Yongle (1403-1424)	Made by Wang Shouming	Potter's mark Hu Hun
Potter's mark Chui Gong	Potter's mark Wu Zhenxian	Potter's mark Zhong Mei
Potter's mark Dong Han	Potter's mark Ming Yuan	Wanli
Xuande Period	Artist Li Mao	Flower garden

Various Ming Marks, *continued*

Potter's mark Hu Yun dao Ren Yi-hsing teapots	Potter's mark Xu You Quan Yi-hsing ware	Potter's mark Shi Peng Yi-Hsing ware
壺隱道人	友泉	時鵬
Potter's mark Shi Peng Yi-Hsing ware	**Potter's mark Gong Chun Yi-Hsing ware**	**Potter's mark Yun Cong Yi-hsing ware**
時鵬	供春	雲逕
Potter's mark Gong Hsi Yi-Hsing ware	**Studio For Investigating Antiquity**	**Fine Vessel For The Jade Hall**
共之	博古齋	佳器 玉堂
The Daoist Hidden In The Pot	**May All Be Peaceful Under Heaven**	**For The Public Use Of The General's Hall**
道人壺隱	太平 天下	公用 師府

Various Ming Marks, *continued*

Potter's mark He Chao Chun Te-Hua ware	Potter's mark Yi-Hsing ware	Potter's mark Xu ling Ying Zhi Yi-Hsing ware
朝宗 恒記	強祖 足畦	徐令 喜製 盈金
Potter's mark Chen Han Wen Yi-Hsing ware	**First Year Reign Of Tiangi In Great Ming Dynasty**	**First year of Chenghua of the Great Ming Dynasty**
漢文	啟元年 大明天	元年乙酉 大明成化
May the wind and the rain joined, bring prosperity and great peace	**Made by Jin Shi in the Yichou year of Tiangi**	**Made by Chen Wenchuangin the Dingyu year of Wanli**
風調雨順 國泰民安	天啟乙丑 年金式製	陳文床塑 萬曆丁酉
A long ancestry keeps life forever like Spring	**Long life as south mountains, good fortune as eastern seas**	**Made by Shi Dabin Yi-Hsing ware**
萬古長春	壽比南山 福如東海	時大彬製

Various Kangxi Marks

Made by Imperial order	Rank/Position	By Imperial order
稇	祝	瓶
Massed Brocade	**Hall of Waving Reeds**	**Secret precious objects**
集錦	崇漪堂	深珍藏
Rare Jade Hall	**Made for the Hall of the Forests of Jade**	**Made for the Pleasant Jade Hall**
堂奇玉製	堂林製玉	堂怡製玉
Made for the Jade Sea Hall	**Made for the Studio of Quiet Stillness**	**Scholarship high as the mountain and the Great Bear**
堂玉製海	澹寧齋製	山文斗章

Various Kangxi Marks, *continued*

Made for the Hall of Kangxi	Neutrality	Made for the Hall where fame continues
堂乾 製惕	齋拙 製存	堂紹 製聞
Made in the Bingxu year	Made for the Hall of Profit and Honor	Made for the Hall of Friends and Scholars
年丙 製戌	堂益 製右	堂友 製于
Made by Gu Yue Xuan	Made for the Hall for the Cultivation of Virtue	Made for the Hall of Moss Green Jade Clouds
軒古 製月	博慎 古德 製堂	堂碧 製雲
Made for the Epidendrum Studio	Made for the Hall of Fragrant Virtue	Made for the Hall of Central Harmony
艸 芝蘭 製蘭	堂德 裘馨	堂中 製和

Various Yongzheng and Qianlong Marks

Remain beautiful	Made by Li Yu Yuan	The myriad rocks retreat
懈嵿宮懲耆	李裕元造	居品
Lichee Village	Eastern garden	Clear studio
荔莊	東園	坦齋
Small garden	Pavilion for moonlight recitation	Old moon pavilion (Qianlong Imperial ware)
略園	朗吟閣	古月軒
Made for the look lily boat	Made as a copy of an antique at the Jing Lian hall	Studio where I wish to hear my faults
觀蓮舫製	倣古景濂堂製	過唯聞齋

Various Yongzheng and Qianlong Marks, *continued*

Terrace of abstraction from mundane affairs	The study of remote tranquillity	The hall of quiet reflection
塵定軒製	寧遠齋製	靜鏡堂製
The Taoist Yao Hua	**The bright remote hall**	**Respecting elders**
瑤華道人	明遠堂製	敬畏堂製
The hall of self respect	**Rejoicing in the stream**	**The hall of classic lore**
敬慎堂製	在川知樂	經笥堂製
Made for the most beautiful hall	**The hall where harmony is nurtured**	**The great tree hall**
彩華堂製	養和堂製	大樹堂製

Various Yongzheng and Qianlong Marks, *continued*

Made for the hall of enriched by colorful favors	The one hundred and one studios	Library of true friendship
堂彩 製潤	齋百 製一	書正 屋誼
Straw hall on the river bank	The hall of the colorful and beautiful	Imperial script (Emperor's collection)
草斯 堂干	堂彩 製秀	御丙 題申
The hall of peaceful rain		
堂雅 製雨		

Various Jiaqing Marks

The hall of colorful flowers	Made by Wang Zuoting	The hall of rich colors
彩華堂製	王佐廷作	彩潤堂製
Made by Jiang Zhenlong	Made for the silent hall	Made by Wang Shenggao
	寧靜齋製	嘉慶三年四月既日 王陞高製
Pavilion for presentation of books	The study of virtuous honesty	Made for the hall of recluse
賜書閣	德誠齋製	寧遠齋製
The study of promotional advancement		
寧晉齋製		

Various Daoguang Marks

Made in the Reign of Daoguang1848	The ten inkstone studio	The hall for cultivation of virtue	The hall for remembering solitude
年戊道 製申光	齋十 製硯	堂慎 製德	堂惜 製陰
The lord of the Xie Bamboos	The study for supplementary thinking	The hall of consistency	Greatly enjoy the fine and precious object
主籫 人竹	齋思 製補	恆行 堂有	珍文 玩甫
The hall of complete virtue	The hall for hearing the rain	Hall for remembrance of the beginning	Pavillion in the air, wind is high
堂成 置德	堂聽 製雨	堂植 製本	髙縢 風閣
Made for the garden of pure contemplation	Made for the Emperor's garden	The hall of bright rising sun	Made by Wen Langshan
澄懷 園 製	園御 製花	堂旭 製華	文道 朗光 珊丁 製未

Various Tongzhi Marks

Made in the Guiyu year 1873	Made by Huang Ziliu Tongzhi period	Made by Jie Chen Tongzhi period
同治十二年癸酉	黃子同製六治	介臣製同治年

Various Seventeenth-Century Marks

Potter's mark Te hua ware	A wish for happiness as as vast as the heavens	Made by Li Zhong Fang
來觀	齊洪 天福	芳李 造仲
The hall where harmony is nourished	Made by Li Maolin	
堂聚 製順	林李 造茂	

Various Eighteenth-Century Marks

The Hall of the Purple Thorn	Culture, Stone Mountain retreat	Red Lichee Mountain retreat
堂製 貲剌	山房 文石	山房 紅荔
Made by Guang Yuanji	Made by Jiang Menxi	Made by Ge Yuan Xiang Kuang-tung ware
吉造 庙㷴	江鳴 皂造	祥製 葛源
Made by Ge Ming Xiang Kuang-tung ware	Made by Wang Shenggao Kuang-tung ware	Library of the friends of the wild plum and inkstone
祥製 葛明	王陞高製	書屋 浴硯 友棠
Hall of Green Ripples	Quiet studio	Appreciate Antiques
菜漪堂		尚古堂製

Various Eighteenth-Century Marks, *continued*

Made for the Hall of Respectful awe	Made for the Hall of Heaven Sent Prosperity	Made for the Hall of Heavenly Joy
堂敬 製畏	堂天 製昌	堂永 製樂
Made by Jiang Minggao	**Made by Chen Guozhi**	**Early spring by Jin Chen**
皐江 造鳴	治陳 造國	戌金 先春
Beautiful female by Xuyang	**Potter's mark Yang Lin of Yu Feng**	**The Kylin's foot brings great luck**
映旭 哇麗	楊丞 琳峯	呈麟 祥趾

Various Nineteenth-Century Marks*

Made for the hall of the great trees	Made by Xu Shunchang	Made by Cheng Yitai	Made by Wang Bingrong
大樹堂製	許順昌造	程義泰造	王炳榮
The hall of triple harmony	Made for the Xie bamboo	The hall of quiet distance	Made by Wang Shenshu
三和堂製	山解竹	靜遠堂製	王慎修
Made for the Lord of the Xie bamboos	Made by Zhou Shunxing	Made by Zhu Yishun	Secretly made by You Lan
解竹	周順造	朱義順造	尤蘭
Graceful and refined	Huang Yun company mark	Hall for the worship of ancestors	Li Da Lai potters mark
大雅齋	黃雲記	奉先堂	李大來

*Some marks may be enclosed within a box

Various Twentieth-Century Marks*

Lang Shining	The mountain of clear brilliance	The mountain of the clouds veiling the sunset
Mountain where the classics are stored	The hall where one dwells in benevolence	The hall where harmony is nurtured
The mountain of the red Artemesia	The hall of bright virtue	Made at Jingdezhen
Made at Jingdezhen	Commercial ware Jingdezhen	Made for the Chuxiu Palace

*Some marks may be enclosed within a box

Various Twentieth-Century Marks*, *continued*

The hall of the quiet distances	Made for the store of the Jui Palace	The hall where benevolence is cherished
The hall where one retires for thinking	Painted by Lang shining	The hall of great virtue
Cheng Xue Li Men painter	Made in the Dingwei year of Guangxu (1907)	

Single-Character Marks Found in Various Periods

A terrace	Prolong	Ancient Antique
軒	申	古
A dwelling	Holy Imperial	A hall
居	聖	堂
Workmanship	Flourishing	Perfect
工	興	全
Prosperity	Harmony	A gem
祿	順	珍

Single-Character Marks Found in Various Periods, *continued*

Wine	Studio	Issued
酒	寀	發

Jade	Great	Congratulations
玉	大	慶

National	A retreat	Cultured
國	房	文

Heaven	Longevity	Emolument
天	喬	祿

Various Two-Character Marks

Precious jade	inner office of department	Potter Yue Chang
珍玉	內府	悅昌
Merciful happiness	Genuine Jade	Western jade
慈福	真玉	西玉
Body of jade	Potter's mark Yao Shan	Central palace or mansion
胎玉	竹旱	樞府
Trinket jade	Five precious things	Gift to Imperial personage
玩玉	五珍	進上

Various Two-Character Marks, *continued*

Red olive	Wedding joy	Beautiful assembled
丹桂	囍	聚秀
Zhenghe Reign title	Presenting royal gift	Offering of supreme beauty
政和	進琖	奉華
Northern palace	For coming friends	Potter Hu Chang
北苑	友來	厚昌
Ever prosperous	Royal retreat	Of unique value
永盛	禁苑	宝勝

Various Two-Character Marks, *continued*

Offering of Imperial personage	To contain fragrance	Beautiful as a phoenix
供御	含馨	鳳華
Potter Yuan Ti	Town of Yixing	Precious trinket
原泰	宜興	珍玩
Great luck	Antique gem	Life garden
大吉	古珍	生苑
Essence of ginger	Elegant trinket	Daguan Reign title
薑湯	雅玩	大觀

Various Three-Character Marks

Studio of grand culture	Office of the medical dep't.	Happiness rank and lonegevity
大雅齋	尚藥局	福祿壽
Study where one examines one's thoughts	Pillow of the Zhang family	Made by the Zhang family
問心齋	張家枕	張家造
Essence of dates	Office of the food department	Potter Hui Meng Chen
棗湯	尚食局	惠孟臣
Palace of the five princes	Superintendent of the office	Made by Rong Jing
五王府	府理督	蓉鏡作

Various Four-Character Marks

Eternal joy and enduring Spring 永慶長春	The studio where modesty is protected 拙存齋製	Blue waves upon the green waters 滄浪綠水
For the elegant circle of revered friends 聖友雅集	As timeless as a mountain good luck as wide as the sea 寿山福海	Made for the study of the precious and miserly 寶嗇齋製
May you have long life and happiness as you wish 寿喜如意	The hall of happiness and good fortune 福慶堂製	Fine vessel for the rich and honorable 富貴佳器
Made for the colorful world hall 世錦堂製	The quiet and peaceful study 寧靜齋製	Vessel for use in the Palace 內用之器

Various Four-Character Marks, *continued*

A wish for life everlasting	May you attain the degree of Zhuang Yuan	Library of the jade cup
萬疆 無疆 壽	及狀 弟元	書玉 屋杯
The hall of honesty	Terrace where one is intoxicated by the moon	The dragon came thru the cloud to bring the emperor a birthday wish
堂敦 製厚	軒醉 製月	聖雲 壽龍
A trinket rare as jade	May infinite happiness embrace your affairs	May you have the happiness of 8 Buddhist emblems
如奇 玉玩	攸萬 同福	如吉 意祥
As rare and precious as jade	The hall for respecting elders	Made for the hall of jade belt ornaments
如奇 玉珍	堂奉 製先	堂佩 製玉

Various Four-Character Marks, *continued*

Secretly made by You Lan 秘友 製蘭	The study for the precious and virtuous 寶 齋善 製	The Bingshen year written by the Emperor 御丙 題申
Precious gift for the lover of the lotus 珍愛 賞蓮	The Jinyan Yu company 俞金 記元	A precious vessel of worked jade 文 寶玉 鼎
The pavillion where one hears the pine trees 盧聽 製松	The hall for everlasting and deep respect 堂乾 製愓	A jewelled trinket of antique art 珍博 玩古
A wish for universal goodwill and serenity 清乾 泰坤	A wish for happiness longevity and good health 福 康壽 寧	The well shaded hall 嘉 堂蔭 製

Various Four-Character Marks, *continued*

May the universe always remain tranquil	The hall where one rejoices in antiques	The hall of wide extensions
永保 乾坤	樂古 堂製	致遠 堂製
Benificent Ancients	Sand of Yixing	Third year of reign of Taiping
益古 堂製	宜興 紫砂	太平 戊寅
May the powers of heaven grant happiness	Bright hall where great luck is recorded	Made of beautiful and refined jade
天官 賜福	錦堂 福記	美玉 雅製
The jade vessels conseals	Fine sample from the water's edge	Riches honor and enduring spring
玉壺 買春	河濱遺範	富貴 長春

Various Four-Character Marks, *continued*

Embroidered jade of Nanchuan	Lingnon (Canton)	Made by Ma Chenzhi
錦南玉川	嶺南繪者 囘囘	馬臣之造
The studio of peace and tranquillity	The hermit Chen Wei	Long life riches and honor
齋製 澄冥	山人陳偉	長倍 富貴
	Made in the Government kiln	
	內官造窰	

Various Character Marks

Made for the Xu Hua Hall for presenttion 旭華堂製贈	Studio where I want to hear my faults 願聞吾過之齋	Made during the years of the republic 中華民國年製	Eternal preservation as 4 seas come to pay homage 永保長壽四海來朝
A gem among precious vessels of rare jade 奇玉宝鼎之珍	Liang Ji in the Wushen year 戊辰年良記土	Waterside Landscape 景濂堂倣古製	Precious trinket of green bamboo mountainlodge 綠竹山房珍藏
To be treasured like a gem of the boiling steam 濩溪若深珍蓺	A gem among precious vessels of rare stone 奇石寶鼎之珍	Made by Xu Shunchang of Jingde town 景鎮許順昌造	The beautiful Jade hall of Riches and success 聚順美玉堂製
5th year of the period Liang Tu Co. 戊辰年良圖記	For use at great sacrifices to the Jin Lu 金籙大醮壇用		

Archaic, Symbolic, and Seal Script Marks

Spring on heaven and earth - one family	Recorded by Xiu Longde	Harmonious Prosperity	Potter He Chou Zong
Potter mark He Chao Chun Zhi	Potter mark Li Zhi	Potter mark He Chao Zhi Yin	Potter mark Shang Su
Potter mark Yi Mo Zhi	Potter mark Hu Liuxing	Potter mark He Chao Chun	Zhong Tun Family
Potter mark Zhu Shisu	Made by Xu Shunchang	Made by Lin Chenfa	Made to order

Archaic, Symbolic, and Seal Script Marks, *continued*

Gao bin	Made for Shu Chang College	Precious	Made to order
Dawn	Happiness and lonegevity	Precious vessel for use	Great Qing
Potter mark Wen Rong	Stone building	Long life	Happiness and longevity
Good fortune and fulfillment of wishes	Made by Chen Mingde	Made on the borders of Fukien	Made at the studio of great elegance

Archaic, Symbolic, and Seal Script Marks, *continued*

Manifest happiness	A wish for everlasting life	The eighth month village	To be treasured like a gem from the deep
Xuande reign title	Beautiful vessel of the hall of Jade	Made for the terrace of azure clouds	Hall of the South office
Virtue extends to all, even fishermen	Jade sea	Made in Qing	The studio of the old pines
First rank at court	Fine vessel for the rich @ honorable	Fame, riches @ honor, vast happiness ='s heaven	Happiness rank and longevity

Symbols

Swastika Buddhist symbol and lucky sign	Swastika in a lozenge	Tripod vase
Incense burner	**Incense burner**	**Sacred Axe**
Symbols of Shou Longevity	**Long life**	**Flower**
unknown emblem	**Fungus, longevity and immortality**	**Stork longevity**

Symbols, *continued*

Lotus	Lotus	Lotus
Lotus	Artemisia leaf	Artemisia leaf
Moon	Flower	Fly
Mandarin mark of honor	Married happiness	Brush, ink, cake and septre

Symbols, *continued*

Plum blossom	Ruyi	Bat	Longevity
Mongolian banner	Banner Longevity	Flower	Fungus Longevity Immortality
Hare Longevity	Hare	Moon Hare	Stork Longevity
Knot Longevity	Buddhist emblems	Peach Longevity Happiness	Fungus Longevity Happiness

Appendix VI   Glass Interior-Painted Snuff Bottle Marks

Artist's Signatures

Ch'en Ch'uan	Kan Huan	Tseng T'ien-chih
陳　銓	甘　桓	增田之
early period	early period	early period
Chang Pao-tien	Chang Shao-yuan	Ch'en Chung-san
張葆田	張少元	陳仲三
middle period	middle period	middle period
Ch'en Shao-fu	Chiang Yuan-lin	Chou Lo-yuan
陳少甫	蔣元霖	周樂元
middle period	middle period	middle period
Chou-Shou-yuan	Chu-Chan-yuan	Hsueh Shao-fu
周少元	朱占元	薛少甫
middle period	middle period	middle period

Artist's Signatures, *continued*

Hsueh Hsi-hsing	Liu-Shou-pen	Pi Heng-yuan
雪西向	劉守本	畢恆遠
modern period	modern period	modern period
Pi Pao-San	Sun Chien-yu	Sun Chi-che
三羆畚	孫振宇	孫基磔
modern period	modern period	modern period
Ch'en Hsue-yen	Hai-Ling	Liu Ta-sheng
陳學燕	海　玲	劉大勝
contemporary	contemporary	contemporary
Wang Ssu-min	Wu-Su-yen	Yau Kuei-hsin
王嗣敏	吳苏岩	姚桂新
contemporary	contemporary	contemporary

Appendix VII   Japanese Pottery and Porcelain Marks

Banko and Bizen

Bizen ware Kichi	Bizen ware Yei-Zan	Bizen ware Teiichi	Bizen ware Hitasuke
吉	萬	高 真一	Ⓘ

Bizen ware Migakite	Banko ware Teki-zan	Banko ware GanTo,SanZin	Banko ware GanTo SanZin
❀	萬 摘山	鐵山	萬 鐵山

Banko ware GanTo SanZin Tsukuru	Banko ware Mori Uji	Banko ware Yusetsu	Banko ware Nippon Yusetsu
鐵山造	茂氏	萬 日本	萬 日本

Banko-Fuyeki	Banko-Yofu Ken Senshu Factory	Banko nippon	Banko
萬古 不易	陽桐軒萬古千秋	萬古 日本	古山

Hizen Pottery
(Saga and Nagasaki Prefectures)

Arita- made by Tikuba Shiomodo 竹芭袋 松茂堂	made by Hichozan Jiosen 如仙造 肥蝶山造	Hirado-made by Yedamats 枝葉造 平戸産	Hirado-made by Zoshuntei San Ho 蔵春亭造 三保造
Sometsuke made by Zohuntei SanHo 蔵春亭 三保造	Hizen Arita 有田 肥前田	Made by Hirabayashi Arita, Hizen 平林製 肥前有田	Arita - made by Gorota & Shozui 是祥瑞造 五良太申
by Atsusada at the Shinkai factory 深海真製	Yamaka Artist 山嘉造	Mori Chikara of Mikawachi 森力造 三川内	Hirado 制衣 平戸
Good fortune 福	Good fortune 福	Happiness 嘉力	Mark found on Hirado wares

Kaga and Kutani
(Ishikawa Prefecture)

Kutani	Iwazo Kutani, Japan	Kutani Iwazo Seisu	Made at Kinto factory, great Japan
Kutani Yu-zan	Dai Nippon Kutani Yu-zan-do, Great Japan	Kutani Yuzando	Made in Kutani Great Japan
Kutani Yu-zan	Made by Yu-zan in Kuta-ni, Japan	Kutani Fuku	Made in Kutani, Great Japan
Kutani Sei	Made in Kutani	Temple of Ikudama of Naniwa	Tozan Artist

Yamashiro (Kyoto Prefecture)
Japanese Pottery Makers' Marks (names)

Yei-Raku	Yei-Raku	Yei-Raku	Yei-Raku

Kin-Un-Ken	Ninsei	Kichizayemon	Kiomidzu (a quarter in Kyoto)

Kyoto	Makuzuhara (District in Kyoto)	Awata (District in Kyoto)	Kitei Artist

Makuzu Kozan Artist	Shuzan Artist	Seikozan Artist	Kanzan Denshichi Artist

Yamashiro (Kyoto Prefecture)
Japanese Pottery Makers' Marks (names), *continued*

Ses-Sen-Sai Shunichi	Hozan	Osinokozi	Nagano Karastu Pottery
Kiuraku	Ran-Tei Tsukuru	Ran (short for Ran-Tei)	Sahei
Sahei	Kinkozan	Kinkozan	Taizan
Taizan	Taizan	Yei-Raku	Yei-Raku

Satsuma Marks
(Kagoshima Prefecture)

Crest of the Prince of Satsuma	Shiozan Artist	Ide Artist	Ran-Zan Artist
Gioku-Zan Artist	Shioho Furo-kusai-Artist	Hoju Artist	Hohei Artist
Koku Artist	Siekozan Artist	Hoyei Artist	Kai Artist
Togan Artist	Kinkozan Artist	Kinkozan Artist	Satsuma place mark

Nippon Marks

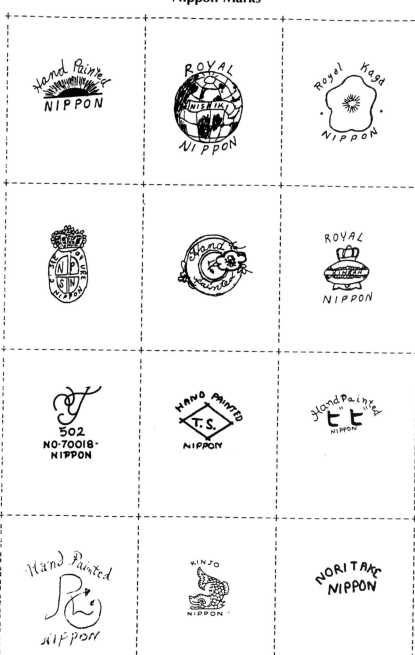

Nippon Marks, *continued*

Imperial

Nippon Marks, *continued*

Appendix VIII   Netsuke Artist's Signatures

Anraku Early 19th C. 安樂 Ivory: animals human figures	Anrakusai mid 19th C. 安樂齋 Ivory: human figures	Baigyoku mid-19th C. 梅玉 Ivory: masks
Bazan mid 19th C. 馬山 Wood: varied designs, animals	Beisai mid 19th C. 小川米齋 Horn carvings	Bokugyuken mid 19th C. 牧牛軒 Wood carvings
Bokusai mid 18th C. 穆齋 Wood: human figures	Bumpo mid 19th C. 文峰 Ivory: masks	Chikko 19th C. 竹光 Wood: masks
Chikko mid 19th C. 草川竹香 Ivory: figures	Chiku-unsai mid 18th C. 竹齋 Ivory: human figures	Deme Mitsuhisa 18th C. 出目滿久 Wood - Ivory: masks

Netsuke Artist's Signatures, *continued*

Deme Saman mid 18th C.	Deme Taiman Early 18th C.	Dohachi 18th/19th C.
出目左滿	出目泰滿	道八
Ivory, wood: masks	Wood: masks	Wood: masks, figures
Eijuken 18th/19th C.	Einen 19th C.	Garaku mid 19th C.
永壽軒	英年	雅樂
Wood: masks	Wood: masks, figures	Wood: masks, figures
Gyokkin 19th C.	Gyokusai 18th/19th C.	Gyokuso 19th C.
飯田玉琴	玉哉	玉藻
Wood, bamboo: masks, figures	Wood: human figures	Ivory: figures
Gyokuyosai 19th C.	Gyokuzan 19th/20th C.	Heishiro 18th C.
玉陽齋光雛	旭玉山	草花平四郎
Ivory: human, dragon figures	Ivory: snakes, sculls, crabs, frogs	Ivory: flowers, birds

Netsuke Artist's Signatures, *continued*

Hidariissan late 18th C. 左 一 山 Wood: snails, toroises	Hidekazu 18th C. 秀 一 Wood: shishi	Hidemasa mid 18th C. 秀 正 Wood, Ivory: animals, humans
Hisamasa 20th C. 壽 正 Ivory: figures	Hojitsu 19th C. 山 田 法 實 Ivory: figures	Ho-In mid 19th C. 豐 尹 Wood: masks
Hozan 18th/19th C. 高 橋 寶 山 Ivory: Buddhist figures	Hozan 19th C. 寶 山 Wood: figures, masks	Hozan mid 19th C. 田 中 法 山 Wood: birds, human figures
Ichiboku late 19th C. 田 島 一 木 Ivory, wood: figures	Ichiro 20th C. 一 呂 Ivory: colored human figures	Ichiyusai 19th C. 一 遊 齋 Ivory: human figures

Netsuke Artist's Signatures, *continued*

Ichu 19th C.	Ikkan mid 19th C.	Ikkei late 18th C.
惟中	一貫	一徑
Wood: masks	Wood: animals insects, figures	Ivory: animals human figures
Ikko 1 19th C.	Ikko 4 late 18th C.	Ikkosai early 19th C.
一孝	一行	齋藤一光齋
Ivory: human figures	Ivory: demons	Ivory: demons, animals human figures
Iotsu 19th C.	Joko 18th C.	Jubi 19th C.
爲乙	上幸	長谷川重美
Wood: snails	Ivory: human figures	Gold lacquer
Jugyoku early 19th C.	Kaigyokusai Masatsugu	Kajun Kumoura 18th C.
上田壽玉	懷玉齋正次	雲浦可順
Ivory, wood: animals, figures	Ivory, wood: animals, figures	Ivory: human figures

Netsuke Artist's Signatures, *continued*

Kigyoku early 19th C. 龜玉 Wood: masks human figures	Kohosai-Ueda late 19th C. 上田公鳳齋 Ivory: flowers	Kokie 1 mid 19th C. 光慶 Wood: masks
Komei 19th/20th C. 好明 Wood: masks	Kyusai Hirai 19th/20th C. 平井汲哉 Bamboo, Wood, ivory: figures, animals	Kyusan 19th C. 久山 Wood: human figures
Masakazu Sawaki 19th C. 澤木正一 Wood, ivory: insects, animals human figures	Masakazu 18th/19th C. 昌一 Wood: masks, figures	Masamitsu late 19th C. 正光 Ivory: animals
Masanao Suzuki late 19th C. 鈴木正直 Wood: animals	Masanobu early 19th C. 正信 Ivory: animals, figures	Masatami Moribe 19th/20th C. 森部正民 Wood, Ivory: animals

Netsuke Artist's Signatures, *continued*

Masatami mid 19th C.	Masatoshi 19th C.	Minko late 18th C.
正民	正壽	田中岷江
Ivory: masks, animals	Ivory: figures	Wood: animals human figures
Minko 20th C.	Minkoku late 18th C.	Mitsuhiro Ohara 19th C.
眠虎	民谷	大原光廣
Ivory: human figures	Wood, ivory: human figures	Wood, ivory: insects, animals masks, humans
Nobumasa 19th C.	Norishige 18th/19th C.	Okakoto 19th C.
信正	則重	岡言
Wood, ivory: animals, figures	Wood, ivory: original design	Ivory: animals
OkatomoYamaguchi 18th C.	Okatori 18th C.	Ryukosai early 19th C.
山口岡友	岡佳	龍光齋
Ivory: animals birds, flowers	Ivory: animals	Ivory: figures

Netsuke Artist's Signatures, *continued*

Ryukosai **3** early 19th C.	Ryumin early 19th C.	Ryuraku mid 18th C.
龍光齋	小野龍眠	龍樂
Ivory: figures	Ivory: masks human figures	Wood: masks
Ryusai 19th C.	Ryusen 18th C.	Sessai 19th C.
佐野立齋	立川	島雪齋
Ivory, wood: figures	Wood: animals, masks	Wood: serpents
Setsutei Sasaki 19th C.	Shibayama 18th C.	Shibusai 19th C.
佐々木雪亭	芝山	芝布齋
Ivory: animals	Wood and ivory inlays	Wood: human figures
Shigechika mid 19th C.	Shigemitsu 18th/19th C.	Shokasai 2 19th C.
重親	重勝	松可齋
Wood: animals	Wood: masks	Horn, wood ivory: animals

Netsuke Artist's Signatures, *continued*

Shugetsu I Hara mid 18th C. 原舟月 Ivory: masks, animals	Shu-ichi 19thC. 舟一 Wood: masks	Shumin Hara late 18th C. 原舟民 Wood: masks, figures
Shungetsu 19th C. 春月 Ivory, wood: human figures	Shuraku Kawamoto 19th C. 川本州樂 Ivory, wood: animals, figures	Taishin 19th C. 池田泰眞 Gold lacquer: Figures
Tameoto 18th C. 爲乙 Ivory: animals	Tokosai 19th C. 東光齋 Ivory: animals	Tokusei 18th C. 得哉 Wood: tigers
Tomochika mid 19th C. 山口友親 Ivory: animals human figures	Tomokazu Kano 18th/19th C. 加納友一 Wood: animals	Tomonobu late 18th C. 友信 Wood: animals, insects human figures

Netsuke Artist's Signatures, *continued*

Tomotada mid 18th C. 友忠 Wood, ivory: known for Oxen	Tomotane 18th C. 友胤 Ivory: animals, insects human figures	Tomotoshi 18th C. 友利 Ivory: animals
Toyo Iizuka 18th C. 飯塚桃葉 Gold lacquer: figures	Toyomasa Naito 18th/19th. C. 内藤豊昌 Wood, ivory: figures	Umboku 17th/18th C. 雲卜 Wood: masks
Umon late 19th C. 禹門 Wood: colored masks	Yoshihisa early 19th C. 義久 Wood: colored masks	Yoshimasa early 19th C. 吉正 Ivory: colored human figures
Yoshimoto 18th C. 宜元 Wood: figures	Yoshinori Kagei late 19th C. 景井美徳 Ivory and inlaid wood	Yoshitada early 19th C. 義忠 Wood: masks

Appendix IX   Woodblock Print Artist's Signatures

Ashihiro	Ashikuni	Ashimaro	Banki
Banri	Buncho	Bunro	Choki
Eiju	Eiri	Eisen	Eizan
Eisho	Enshi	Fusatane	Gakutei

Woodblock Print Artist's Signatures, *continued*

Gokyo	Harunobu	Hiroshige	Haruji
五郷	春信	廣重	春次

Hidemaro	Hirokage	Hokkei	Hokuba
秀麿	廣景	北溪	北鳥

Hokuga	Hoku-I	Hokuju	Hokusai
北雅	北為	北壽	北舟

Kako	Kiyomasu	Kiyomine	Kiyomitsu
可候	清倍	清峯	清滿

Woodblock Print Artist's Signatures, *continued*

Kiyonaga	Kiyonobu	Kiyotada	Koriusai
清長	清信	清忠	湖龍齋

Kuniaki	Kuni Haru	Kunimaru	Kunimasa
國明	國春	國九	國政

Kunimori	Kuninaga	Kuninao	Kunisada
國盛	國長	國直	國貞

Kunitomi	Kuniyasu	Sharaku	Shigemasa
國富	國安	寫樂	重政

Woodblock Print Artist's Signatures, *continued*

Shigenaga	Shigenobu (Yanagawa)	Shigenobu (Hiroshige II)	Shikimaro
重長	柳川 重信	重宜	弐麿
Shiko	**Shuncho (Katsukawa)**	**Shundo**	**Shunjo**
子興	勝川 春潮	春童	春常
Shunko	**Shunman**	**Shunsen (Katsukawa)**	**Shunsho**
春好	後滿	春泉	春章
Shuntei	**Shunei**	**Shuntei**	**Shunyei**
春亭	春英	春亭	春英

Woodblock Print Artist's Signatures, *continued*

Shunzan	Sori	Sugaku	Sugakudo
春山	宗理	髙岳	嵩岳堂

Taito	Toshinobu	Toyoharu	Toyohiro
廣斗	利信	豊春	豊廣

Toyonobu (Ishikawa)	Tsukimaro	Utamaro	Yeiri (Hosoda)
石川豊信	月麿	哥麿	栄里

Yeisen (Keisai)	Yoshichika	Yoshiharu	
渓齊英泉	芳幾	豊春	

Appendix X   Woodblock Print Publisher's Seals

Aeto of Yedo	Arita-ya	Daihei
相ト	艮	本大平

Enhiko	Fuji-Hiko	Fuji-Kei
遠彦	藤彦　松原堂	藤慶

Hoyeido (Takeuchi)	Ibakiu	Ibasen
保永堂	久伊場久	伊場仙

Isekane	Iseya Rihei (Ise-Iri)	Iwato-ya
伊勢彔	林	岩戸屋

Woodblock Print Publisher's Seals, *continued*

Jo-Shu-ya	Jzutsu-ya	Kawa-cho
Kawa-sho	Koshimura-ye (Heisuke)	Ko-yeido
Marujin	Maru-kyu	Marusei
Masugin	Mori-Ji (Jihei)	Omi-ya of Yedo

Woodblock Print Publisher's Seals, *continued*

Sen-Ichi	Soshu-ya	Takasu (Shiba)
Tsuru-ya	Tsuta-ya Juzaburo	Tsuta-ya Kichizo
Urokogata-ya	Uwo-yei (Heikichi)	Wakasa-ya
Yamamoto Heikichi	Yetatsu	Yeijudo

Appendix XI   Various Marks for Cloisonné, Ivory, and Metal

Japanese Cloisonné Artists

Kumeno Teitaro	Kawaguchi	Ota Tamesiro
Takahara Kohajiro	Miwa Tomisaburo	Adachi
Tamura	Ando	Hattori Kodenji
Hayashi Kodenji	Gonda Hirosuke	Inaba Nanaho

Japanese Ivory Artists

Toshitaka	Ryuho	Shijui
Gyokuju	Rinko	Masatami
Ryoen	Seigioku	Sakurai
Tanianaga	Shojusai	

Japanese Makers' Marks on Metalwork

Masatoshi Katsuyama, Fujiwara	Katsuyama Masa-Toshi	Fujiwara Tomoyoshi	Fujiwara Mitsushige
勝山藤原正歳	勝山正歳	藤原友吉	藤原光重
Ten-ka Ichi saku	**Fujiwara Mitsunaga**	**Masayasu Fujiwara**	**Fujiwara Tsukuru**
天下作	藤原光永	藤原正安作	藤原作
Ko-Shiu Hiko-ne Jiu	**Mo-Gara-shi nui-do SoTeng Seisu**	**Hide-Hisa**	**Nagaharu**
江州 彦根住	古宗柄子 遥宗典製	英久	永春

Komai of Kyoto	Matsuhita	Okada Zenzayemon	
京都住 駒井製		宣政作 善左衛門 長列村住園田	

Japanese Makers' Marks on Metalwork, *continued*

Shigehisa	Hiraishi Atsuchika	Kato Kyomasa
加列住　車久作	越中住人　平石篤親	先祖　咖藤清正　小手氏

Torajiro　Murakami

大日本　明治年製　村上虎治郎造

Index

Page numbers in boldface denote
main categories